Music and Musicians in Late Mughal India

Based on a vast, virtually unstudied archive of Indian writings alongside visual sources, this book presents the first history of music and musicians in late Mughal India c.1748–1858, and takes the lives of nine musicians as entry points into six prominent types of writing on music in Persian, Brajbhasha, Urdu and English, moving from Delhi to Lucknow, Hyderabad, Jaipur and among the British. It shows how a key Mughal cultural field responded to the political, economic and social upheaval of the transition to British rule, while addressing a central philosophical question: can we ever recapture the ephemeral experience of music once the performance is over? These rich, diverse sources shine new light on the wider historical processes of this pivotal transitional period, and provide a new history of music, musicians and their audiences during the precise period in which North Indian classical music coalesced in its modern form.

KATHERINE BUTLER SCHOFIELD is Fellow of the Royal Asiatic Society, and recipient of a European Research Council Grant and a British Academy Mid-Career Fellowship. She is co-editor of *Tellings and Texts: Music, Literature and Performance in North India* (2015) and *Monsoon Feelings: A History of Emotions in the Rain* (2018).

Music and Musicians in Late Mughal India

Histories of the Ephemeral, 1748–1858

KATHERINE BUTLER SCHOFIELD
King's College London

CAMBRIDGE
UNIVERSITY PRESS

CAMBRIDGE
UNIVERSITY PRESS

Shaftesbury Road, Cambridge CB2 8EA, United Kingdom

One Liberty Plaza, 20th Floor, New York, NY 10006, USA

477 Williamstown Road, Port Melbourne, VIC 3207, Australia

314–321, 3rd Floor, Plot 3, Splendor Forum, Jasola District Centre, New Delhi – 110025, India

103 Penang Road, #05–06/07, Visioncrest Commercial, Singapore 238467

Cambridge University Press is part of Cambridge University Press & Assessment, a department of the University of Cambridge.

We share the University's mission to contribute to society through the pursuit of education, learning and research at the highest international levels of excellence.

www.cambridge.org
Information on this title: www.cambridge.org/9781316517857

DOI: 10.1017/9781009047685

First published 2024

A catalogue record for this publication is available from the British Library.

Library of Congress Cataloging-in-Publication Data
Names: Schofield, Katherine Butler, author.
Title: Music and musicians in late Mughal India : histories of the ephemeral, 1748-1858 / Katherine Butler Schofield.
Description: [1.] | New York : Cambridge University Press, 2023. | Includes bibliographical references and index.
Identifiers: LCCN 2023018212 | ISBN 9781316517857 (hardback) | ISBN 9781009048521 (paperback) | ISBN 9781009047685 (ebook)
Subjects: LCSH: Hindustani music – India – 18th century – History and criticism. | Hindustani music – India – 19th century – History and criticism. | Hinustani music – Iranian influences. | Musicians – India. | Hindustani music – Social aspects – India – History – 18th century. | Hindustani music – Social aspects – India – History – 19th century. | Mogul Empire – Court and courtiers – History – 18th century. | Mogul Empire – Court and courtiers – History – 19th century. | East India Company – History – 18th century. | East India Company – History – 19th century.
Classification: LCC ML338.4 .S36 2023 | DDC 780.954–dc23/eng/20230510
LC record available at https://lccn.loc.gov/2023018212

ISBN 978-1-316-51785-7 Hardback

In memory of Bruce Wannell and Allison Busch.

To Mirwaiss Sidiqi, Waheedullah Saghar, Mohsen Saifi, Ferishta Farrukhi, Najeba Arian, Homira Sabawoon and all my other Afghan sisters and brothers in music: may you find your way home.

Contents

List of Figures [*page* viii]
List of Tables [xi]
List of Boxes [xii]
List of Examples [xiii]
Acknowledgements [xiv]
Notes on the Text [xviii]
Ruling Dynasties [xxii]
Genealogies of Principal Musicians and Music Treatises [xxv]

1 Chasing Eurydice: Writing on Music in the Late Mughal World [1]

2 The Mughal Orpheus: Remembering Khushhal Khan Gunasamudra in Eighteenth-Century Delhi [20]

3 The Rivals: Anjha Baras, Adarang and the Scattering of Shahjahanabad [49]

4 The Courtesan and the Memsahib: Khanum Jan and Sophia Plowden at the Court of Lucknow [79]

5 Eclipsed by the Moon: Mahlaqa Bai and Khushhal Khan Anup in Nizami Hyderabad [117]

6 Faithful to the Salt: Mayalee Dancing Girl versus the East India Company in Rajasthan [147]

7 Keeper of the Flame: Miyan Himmat Khan and the Last of the Mughal Emperors [180]

8 Orphans of the Uprising: Late Mughal Echoes and 1857 [219]

Glossary [248]
Bibliography [257]
Tazkira: List of Names [285]
Index [296]

Figures

Front cover: Portrait of a Delhi *qawwāl*. Illustration for James Skinner's *Tashrīh al-Aqwām*. Hansi, 1825. Add. 27,255, f. 457v. © **The British Library Board.**

1.1 Painting of the *pietra dura* inlay of Orpheus in the Hall of Public Audience, Shahjahanabad. 1845. 292D-1871. © **Victoria & Albert Museum, London.** [*page* 18]

2.1 Khushhal Khan Gunasamudra performing at Dara Shukoh's wedding (detail). c. 1700. RCIN1005068, f. 26v. **Royal Collection Trust © Her Majesty Queen Elizabeth II 2015.** [33]

2.2 Ragini Todi. c. 1755. Catherine and Ralph Benkaim Collection, 2013.340. **The Cleveland Museum of Art.** Public Domain. [34]

2.3 The connections between celestial bodies, musical notes, elements and effects. [43]

2.4 *Dhrupad* in Ragini Todi. 18 C. 1939.552, verso. **Yale University Art Gallery**. Public Domain. [47]

3.1 Anup's musical genealogy as a fantasy *majlis*. Anup, *Rāg Darshan*. 1800, illustrated by Haji Mir Ghulam Hasan 1804. Lawrence J Schoenberg Collection, LJS 63, f. 3v. **University of Pennsylvania Special Collections Library.** CC–BY. [52]

4.1 Probably Sir David Ochterlony, watching a *nāch*. c. 1820. Add. Or. 2. © **The British Library Board.** [80]

4.2 Mrs Sophia Elizabeth Plowden. John Russell, 1797. © **The Birla Museum, Pilani.** [90]

4.3 A and B. Persian *rubāᶜī*, '*Sāqī-ā! Fasl-i bahār ast!*' Plowden, *Album*, f. 8 and *Tunebook*, f. 14v. 1787–8. MS 380. © **Fitzwilliam Museum, University of Cambridge.** [93]

4.4 Courtesan performing for Colonel Antoine Polier in Lucknow. 1786–88. 2005.83. Bequest Balthasar Reinhart. **Museum Rietberg, Zürich © Rainer Wulfsberger.** [101]

4.5 A and B. Urdu k͟hayāl, '*Sunre maᶜshūqā be-wafā!*' Plowden, *Album*, f. 21 and *Tunebook*, f. 39v. MS 380. © **Fitzwilliam Museum, University of Cambridge.** [109]

4.6 ‘*Tāza ba tāza no ba no*’. Plowden, *Album*, f. 1. MS 380. © **Fitzwilliam Museum, University of Cambridge.** [111]

4.7 A and B. Persian *g͟hazal*, ‘*Surwi ruwān-i kīstī*’ by Khaqani (1122–90). Plowden, *Album*, f. 11 and *Tunebook*, f. 19v. MS 380. © **Fitzwilliam Museum, University of Cambridge.** [115]

5.1 Mahlaqa Bai Chanda singing for Raja Rao Ranbha, by Haji Mir Ghulam Hasan. Khushhal Khan Anup, *Rāg Darshan*. LJS 63, f. 2v. **University of Pennsylvania Special Collections Library.** CC–BY. [119]

5.2 *Hoṛī*, *k͟hayāl* and *ṭappa* compositions in Ragini Khamaj. Khushhal Khan Anup, *Rāg-Rāginī Roz o Shab*. 1833–6. Urdu Mus 2, f. 123v–4r. © **Salar Jung Museum Library, Hyderabad.** [122]

5.3 Ragini Khambhavati, Khushhal Khan Anup, *Rāg Darshan*. LJS 63, f. 9v. **University of Pennsylvania Special Collections Library.** CC–BY. [125]

5.4 Ragini Khambhavati. c. 1675. 2000.321. Gift of Doris Wiener, in honour of Stephen Kossak, 2000. **Metropolitan Museum of Art**. Public Domain. [128]

5.5 Ragini Khambhavati. Khushhal Khan Anup, *Rāg Darshan*. Late 18 C. © **Photo courtesy of Sotheby’s, 2019.** [129]

5.6 Detail, Raja Rao hunting, by Haji Mir Ghulam Hasan. Khushhal Khan Anup, *Rāg Darshan*. LJS 63, f. 18r. **University of Pennsylvania Special Collections Library.** CC–BY. [139]

5.7 Chand Bibi of Ahmadnagar hunting. c.1700. 1999.403. Louis E. and Theresa S. Seeley Purchase Fund for Islamic Art, 1999. **Metropolitan Museum of Art**. Public Domain. [140]

6.1 Measuring salt piles at Sambhar Lake, Jaipur State, 1870s. Photo 355/1(59). **The British Library**. Public Domain. [148]

6.2 Map of Sambhar Lake. [156]

6.3 *Bhagtan* performing the role of Krishna in Raslila, attr. Sahib Ram, c.1800. © **The Private Collection of the Royal Family of Jaipur**. [164]

6.4 Pensions paid from Sambhar Treasury on account of Jaipur State, 1 January to 30 June 1839, Section 2. **The British Library**. Public Domain. [168]

6.5 A steamboat ride on a lake. Mid 19 C. © **Christie’s Images Limited, 2022.** [176]

7.1 Portrait of Miyan Himmat Khan, from James Skinner, *Tashrīh al-Aqwām*. 1825. Add. 27,255, f. 134v. © **The British Library Board.** [181]

7.2 'A Nautch at Colonel Skinner's Given to Me By Himself 1838'. Add. Or. 2598. © **The British Library Board.** [189]
7.3 Illustration of the *bāzīgār* (conjuror) for Skinner's *Tashrīh al-Aqwām*. Add. 27,255, f. 120v (detail). **The British Library.** Public Domain. [190]
7.4 *Qawwāls* at the shrine of Hazrat Nizam-ud-din Chishti, after Mazhar ^{c}Ali Khan. 1836. IM.41–1923. © **Victoria & Albert Museum, London.** [192]
7.5 A and B. Khwaja Moin-ud-din Chishti and a gathering of mystics and musicians; and detail. c. 1650–55. IS.94–1965. © **Victoria & Albert Museum, London.** [193]
7.6 Performing communities in the Gentil Album. 1774. IS.25:26–1980. © **Victoria & Albert Museum, London.** [198]
7.7 North Indian *kanchanīs*. Tanjore, c.1828. Add. Or. 62. © **The British Library Board.** [200]
7.8 The Mughal *tawā'if* Malageer, by Lallji or Hulas Lal. 1815. © **Collection of Prince and Princess Sadruddin Aga Khan**. [202]
7.9 Shahamat Jang and Ikram-ud-daula giving an evening of musical entertainment (detail). 1748–50. © **National Museums of Scotland. Accepted in lieu of inheritance tax by H M Government and allocated to the National Museums of Scotland.** [203]
8.1 The Nawab of Awadh, Wajid ^{c}Ali Shah, accompanying courtesan Sarafraz Mahal on the *tabla*. Wajid ^{c}Ali Shah, *^{c}Ishqnāma*. 1849–50. RCIN 1005035, f. 242r. **Royal Collection Trust © Her Majesty Queen Elizabeth II 2015.** [222]

Tables

3.1 Comparison of musical *tazkiras* and genealogies that use Rasikh's *Risāla*. [*page* 60]

4.1 Correlation of Plowden's texts with their tunes. [86]

7.1 The Hanuman *mat* vs. Ghulam Raza's *rāga-rāginī* system. [210]

7.2 The *tāla* systems of Ras Baras Khan, Hakim Hasan Maududi Chishti and Ghulam Raza, cf. Ranj/Himmat. [212]

Boxes

2.1 The canonical Mughal Persian treatises on Hindustani music. [*page* 39]

3.1 List of key writings c. 1740–1850 that include musicians' *tazkiras* and/or genealogies. [59]

7.1 The ten 'vedic and shastric' texts cited in Skinner's entries on performers found in Tod's manuscript collection in the Royal Asiatic Society. [204]

Examples

4.1 'I. The Ghut' (*gat*) from William Hamilton Bird, *Oriental Miscellany* (Calcutta, 1789), p. 1. Public Domain. [*page* 82]

4.2 B and C melodies of '*Sāqī-ā!*' compared. Plowden, *Tunebook*, f. 13v, f. 20v. MS 380. © **Fitzwilliam Museum, University of Cambridge**. [95]

4.3 Notation of medium speed *jald tītāla*. 1788. Or. MS 585, f. 64v. **Edinburgh University Library**. [106]

4.4 Persian ghazal '*Tāza ba tāza no ba no*' by Hafiz. Bird No. IV with the first Persian line underlaid [112]

4.5 Persian *ghazal*, '*Tāza ba tāza no ba no*' by Hafiz. Sophia Plowden, *Tunebook*, f. 11r with the first line underlaid. Lucknow, 1787–8. MS 380. © **Fitzwilliam Museum, University of Cambridge** [113]

4.6 '*Tāza ba tāza no ba no*' set in Rag Bhairavi to a cycle of seven beats. [114]

7.1 Ghulam Raza's notation of the *sthyā'ī tān* of Ragini Bhairavi. [208]

7.2 *Dhīmā titāla kalāwantī*, the first *tāla* in the eleven *tāla* system of the *Asl al-Usūl*. [215]

Acknowledgements

Twenty-five years since I started a master's degree at SOAS, University of London that would lead to a life-long love affair with Hindustani music and Mughal history, I have finally finished my first single-authored book. Were I to thank everyone who has made an impact on my journey this past quarter of a century, I would have to write a second one, and would undoubtedly still forget to mention someone's name! With that in mind, I have decided to name in these acknowledgements only those individuals and institutions that have made a direct contribution to the writing of this book. But know this: if you find that your name is not here, and you have at any point interacted with me about my work or supported me with a cuppa or a chat – I did notice and appreciate it; you did make an impact; and I thank you for your immeasurable insights and acts of kindness over the years.

The research and writing of this book were generously funded by a five-year Starting Grant from the European Research Council (no. 263643 MUSTECIO, PI: Katherine Butler Schofield); a one-year British Academy Mid-Career Fellowship in conjunction with the British Library (no. MD160059); and a publication subvention from King's College London. I was fortunate to write much of the first draft at the Centre for South Asian Studies at the University of Cambridge, and the final draft was pulled into shape thanks to a visiting professorship at the Department of South Asia Studies, University of Pennsylvania; I am hugely grateful to everyone in both places. The following kindly invited me to share my research with audiences: Dr Ashok da Ranade Memorial Lecture, Mumbai; Australian Historical Association; Reinhard Strohm's Balzan Programme in Musicology; Chhatrapati Shivaji Maharaj Vastu Sanghralaya, Mumbai; ÉHÉSS Paris; Jaipur Literature Festival; Lahore Literary Festival; Max Planck Institute for the History of the Emotions, Berlin; Prof SAH Abidi Memorial Lecture, Delhi; Serbian Academy of Sciences and Arts, Belgrade; University of Cambridge; UC Berkeley; UC Davis; UCLA; and University of Oxford. Thank you.

The following generously provided access to their collections, and I hope that this book will give something back to them: Andhra Pradesh Government Oriental Manuscripts Library, Hyderabad; Andhra Pradesh

State Archives, Hyderabad; Asiatic Society of Bengal, Kolkata; Ashmolean Museum, Oxford; Bibliothèque Nationale de France, Paris; Birla Museum, Pilani; Bodleian Library, Oxford; British Library, London; Cambridge University Library; Christie's; Collection of Prince and Princess Sadruddin Aga Khan; Edinburgh University Library; Fitzwilliam Museum, Cambridge; Government Oriental Manuscripts Library, University of Madras; John Rylands Library, Manchester; Khuda Bakhsh Oriental Public Library, Patna; Maharaja Sawai Man Singh II Museum, Jaipur; Musee für Islamische Kunst und Asiatische Kunst, Berlin; National Archives of India; National Museums of Scotland; Rietberg Museum, Zürich; Norfolk Records Office; Royal Asiatic Society, London; Royal Collection, Windsor; Royal Green Jackets (Rifles) Museum, Winchester; Salar Jung Museum Library, Hyderabad; Sotheby's; University of Pennsylvania Rare Book and Manuscript Library; UK National Archives; Victoria & Albert Museum; Yale University Art Gallery; Royal Family of Jaipur, Geoffrey Plowden, Kathy and Malcolm Fraser, Nicolas Sursock and Ustad Irfan Muhammad Khan-sahib.

Thanks for scholarly assistance and friendship are due in alphabetical order to Daud Ali, Jon Barlow, Nick Barnard, Priyanka Basu, Amy Blier-Carruthers, Olivia Bloechl, Robin Bunce, Esther Cavett, T S Rana Chhina, Adil Rana Chhina, Nicholas Cook, Amlan Das Gupta, John Deathridge, Katie De La Matter, Chris Duckett, Arthur Dudney, Munis Faruqui, Darren Fergusson, Roy Fischel, Andy Fry, Elizabeth Gow, Bendor Grosvenor, Vivek Gupta, Emily Hannam, Matthew Head, Tom Hodgson, Liam Rees Hofmann, Ranjit Hoskoté, Danish Husain, Tom Hyde, ICFAMily, David RM Irving, Radha Kapuria, Max Katz, Pasha M Khan, Razak Khan, Ustad Wajahat Khan-sahib, Shailaja Khanna, Mana Kia, Tanuja Kothiyal, Daniel Leech-Wilkinson, Saif Mahmood, Yusuf Mahmoud, Nicolas Magriel, Peter Marshall, M Athar Masood, Nick McBurney, Phalguni Mitra, Mohsen Mohammedi, Anna Morcom, Daniel Neuman, Laudan Nooshin, Jenny Norton-Wright, Rosalind O'Hanlon, Roger Parker, Heidi Pauwels, Norbert Peabody, Cayenna Ponchione-Bailey, Regula Qureshi, Yael Rice, Malini Roy, Vikram Rooprai, Zahra Sabri, Rana Safvi, Kevin Schwartz, Sunil Sharma, Yuthika Sharma, Chander Shekhar, Ayesha Sheth, Gianni Sievers, Nur Sobers-Khan, Gabriel Solis, Martin Stokes, Mirwaiss Sidiqi, Sue Stronge, Lakshmi Subramanian, Jim Sykes, Nathan Tabor, Giles Tilletson, Mrinalini Venkateswaran, Guy Walters, Friederike Weiss, Richard Wolf, Pete Yelding, Zehra Zaidi, my amazing PhD students and all my beloved #Twitterstorians. Thank you particularly to Chris Brooke for lending me his nearby flat when I needed a quiet space to work in.

I have travelled on this journey for the past decade with the most wonderful companions on the Awadh Case Study of my ERC project: to Jim Kippen, Allyn Miner, Meg Walker and Richard David Williams, I owe you a debt of intellectual enrichment I can never repay. Thank you, too, to my paracolonial partners-in-crime, Julia Byl and especially David Lunn, who has not only been my main and wisest sounding board for as long as I can remember but who also did the index and map for this book. It was my enormous privilege to work with harpsichordist Jane Chapman and podcast producer Chris Elcombe in bringing some of this research to life through sound. Many thanks, too, to Ursula Sims-Williams for her shared enthusiasm over the decades for the extraordinary South Asian musical materials in the British Library. I am indebted for help with translations at various stages to Parmis Mozafari and the late Bruce Wannell especially, but also Kashshaf Ghani, Richard David Williams, David Lunn and Zahra Sabri.

Over the years of this book's gestation, I have been nourished by the deep friendship, kind mentorship, brilliant conversations and gentle critique of Molly Aitken, Michael Bywater, William Dalrymple, Emma Dillon, Francesca Orsini, Margrit Pernau, Davesh Soneji, Meg Walker and the late, much-missed Allison Busch and Bruce Wannell. Thank you, too, to all those who read the draft, especially my two anonymous reviewers, William Dalrymple, Aneesh Pradhan, my mother Ruth Butler and my husband Paul. I finally wish to pay tribute to the academic forebears upon whose shoulders I stand: Najma Perveen Ahmad, Shahab Sarmadee, Madhu Trivedi, Françoise 'Nalini' Delvoye and especially Richard Widdess, who many years ago now was my PhD supervisor. There is one final person I would like to thank in this vein: my aunt Elizabeth Wiedemann, local historian of the Inverell district in New South Wales and author of *World of Its Own: Inverell's Early Years, 1827–1920* and *Holding Its Own: The Inverell District Since 1919.* From the time I was a tiny child, it was her inspiring example that taught me that 'historian' was something you could be – and that small stories of ordinary striving matter to the bigger picture.

This book was written and completed painfully slowly during the years of the Covid-19 pandemic, and delayed further due to my involvement in the international effort to help Afghanistan's musicians get themselves to safety after the fall of Kabul to Taliban in August 2021; never has the 'scattering' of Shahjahanabad 260 years ago felt so close. I am forever grateful to have found such a patient and generous editor in Kate Brett and her team at Cambridge University Press (especially Abi Sears) to steer this very stately ship to shore. But their patience is nothing in comparison to that of my son Alex, who was seven when this book's journey began and is now a teenager. Every so often he asks me politely, 'How is your book going?' Finally I can tell him, 'It is finished! *tamām shod*!'

The best ideas in here were inspired by conversations with Paul Schofield, a broad intellectual and cultural enthusiast beyond compare. This book is for him, my own dear *rasika*.

Notes on the Text

On Transliteration

This book is based largely on sources in the Persian language that contain a great deal of Indic vocabulary, and more selectively from texts in early forms of Urdu (*rek͟hta*) and Hindi (*Brajbhāṣā*) written in the *nast^{c}alīq* script. I use a simplified system of transliteration which only marks long vowels (ā ī ū); retroflex consonants (ḍ ḍh ṇ ṛ ṣ ṭ ṭh) and nasalisation (ṅ) in words of Indic origin; *^{c}ain* (superscript ^{c}) and *hamza* ('); and distinguishes kh کھ from k͟h خ and gh گھ from g͟h غ. The glossary and titles of untranslated sources in the bibliography include full diacritical markings following F Steingass' *Comprehensive Persian–English Dictionary* and John T Platts' *Dictionary of Urdū, Classical Hindī and English.*[1] In accordance with Steingass I use *-i* for the *izafat* construction (e.g. *majlis-i samā^{c}*), and *al-* in titles of works (e.g. *Uṣūl al-Nag͟hmāt*).

Spellings (except for proper nouns) are per Steingass and Platts, deferring to Steingass for words of Persian and Arabic origins (e.g. z, not dh, for ذ). The key exception is the important term *meḥfil* (not *maḥfil*) as it is used today for private musical assemblies. Titles of published works in the bibliography are spelled in accordance with their publishers' preferences for romanisation.

In a text this complex, there will inevitably be mistakes and inconsistencies; when you find one, feel free to shout 'bingo'!

On Dates and Calendars

I have translated dates from the al-Hijri lunar calendar (AH) into Christian/Common Era (CE) dates throughout, using the useful tool available at www.muslimphilosophy.com/ip/hijri.htm. The AH lunar year and CE solar year are of different lengths, so there is no systematic date correspondence between them. Where the source gives the AH month

[1] F Steingass, *A Comprehensive Persian–English Dictionary* (London: Routledge and Kegan Paul, 1963 [orig. 1892]); John T Platts, *Dictionary of Urdū, Classical Hindī and English* (New Delhi: Munshiram Manoharlal, 1997 [orig. 1884]).

(and sometimes day) along with the year, I give the exact CE year (e.g. 1800); where just the AH year is provided, I give a forward-slashed year range (e.g. 1862/3). If only the regnal year is given, this is presented as a dashed year range (e.g. 1752–3).

The Vikram Samvat (VS) solar year of the Hindu calendar is the same length as CE, although the months are lunar. It has generally not been necessary to calculate the VS–CE conversion, as for the chapter on Rajasthan I am mainly using British documents. But for the record, the Vikram ritual year (*samvat*) in use in Jaipur and Jodhpur began on 1 Chaitra (March), the revenue year began on 2 Bhadrapada (August)[2] and the year conversion is generally calculated by taking fifty-seven years from the VS year to arrive at the CE year.

On Proper Nouns

For names of places I have generally used the Anglicised names prevalent during the period covered in this book (e.g. Calcutta, Tanjore rather than Kolkata, Thanjavur). With festivals, I have chosen to use common spellings without diacritical markings; for example, Diwali rather than Dīwālī, Eid not ^{c}Īd.

Many of the people in this book have long names, pseudonyms and/or multiple titles, some of them easily confused (there are two Khushhal Khans and two Ghulam Razas, for instance). I use the long form of individuals' names in the first instance, without any diacritical markings, spelled to reflect their usual pronunciation in Indian languages today (e.g. Moin-ud-din rather than Mu^{c}īn al-Dīn). Thereafter, I have used a variety of strategies:

- Where the person was a poet, author or musician, I refer to them when possible using their *takhallus* or *nom de plume*/stage name; so ^{c}Inayat Khan Rasikh and Ni^{c}mat Khan Sadarang become Rasikh and Sadarang. There are a few exceptions, such as where individuals are only ever referred to by one name (e.g. Tansen). To avoid confusion I refer to Khushhal Khan Gunasamudra of Chapter 2 as Khushhal, as his father was also Gunasamudra, and Khushhal Khan Anup of Chapter 5 as Anup.

[2] Monika Horstmann, *In Favour of Govinddevjī: Historical Documents Relating to a Deity of Vrindaban and Eastern Rajasthan* (New Delhi: Indira Gandhi National Centre for the Arts and Manohar, 1999), pp. 69–70.

- Where I use an individual's name rather than their *takhallus*, I use the shortest form that makes meaningful sense and won't easily be confused with another individual, for example Himmat for Miyan Himmat Khan, Raushan-ud-daula (not Raushan) for Raushan-ud-daula Zafar Khan Bahadur Rustam Jang. To avoid confusion with the Mughal Emperor Ahmad Shah (r. 1748–54), I refer to the Afghan warlord Ahmad Shah Abdali Durrani as Abdali. I call the *sitār* player Ghulam Raza of the 1840s–50s by his title, Razi-ud-daula, to distinguish him from the important treatise writer of the 1790s Ghulam Raza *qawwāl*.
- Emperors, queens, royal princes and independent rulers are referred to using their common ruling titles: so Muhammad Shah; Lal Kanvar; Muhammad A^{c}zam Shah; (Nawab) Asaf-ud-daula; (Maharaja) Ram Singh; and so on. Shah ^{c}Alam in this book always refers to Shah ^{c}Alam II (r. 1759–1806).
- I use the honorific titles Hazrat, Khwaja, Shaikh, Hakim, Miyan and so on where they are present in the original texts.

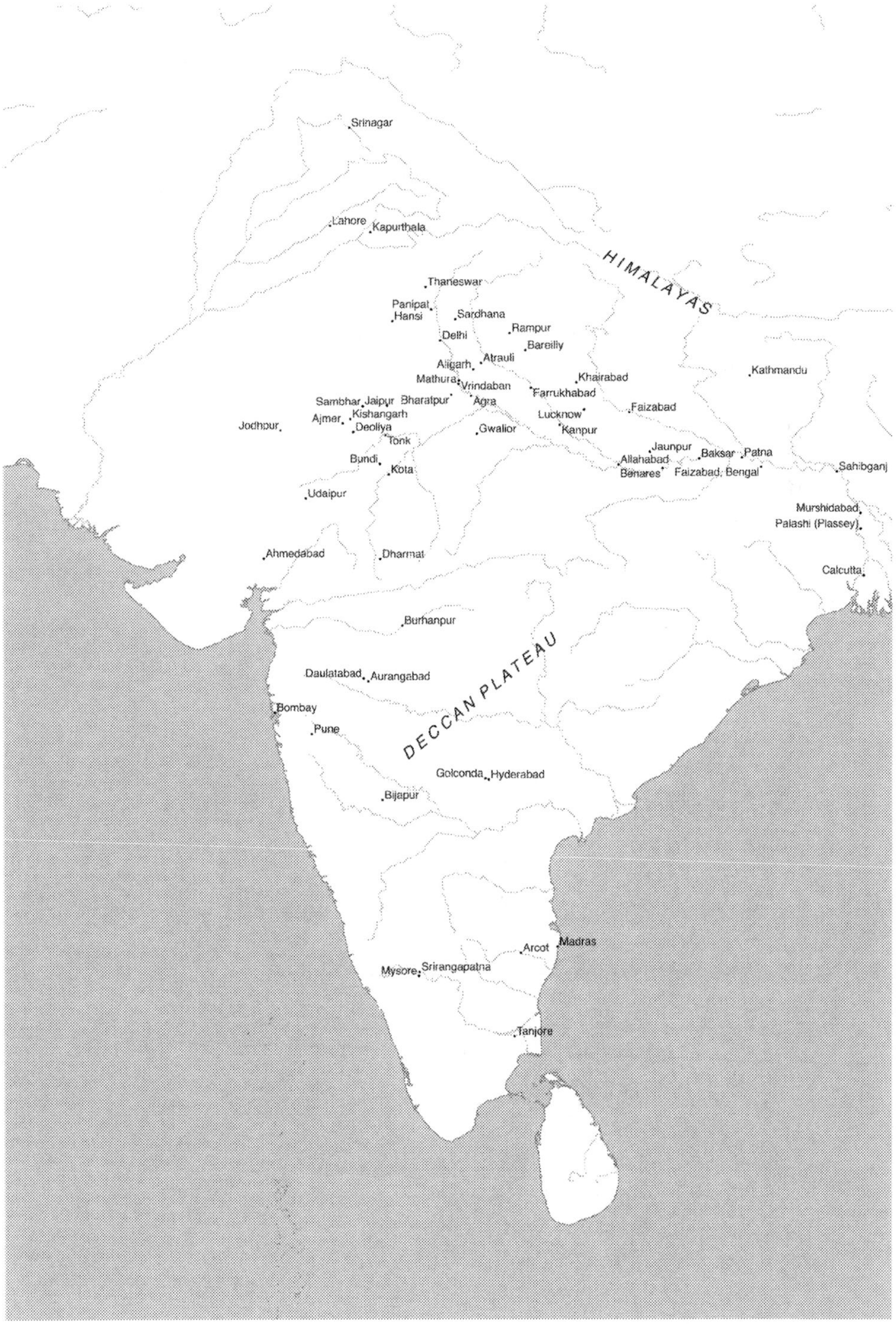
Srinagar
Lahore
Kapurthala
HIMALAYAS
Thaneswar
Panipat
Hansi
Sardhana
Rampur
Delhi
Bareilly
Aligarh
Atrauli
Mathura
Vrindaban
Khairabad
Farrukhabad
Kathmandu
Sambhar
Jaipur
Bharatpur
Agra
Faizabad
Ajmer
Kishangarh
Lucknow
Jodhpur
Deoliya
Kanpur
Gwalior
Tonk
Jaunpur
Bundi
Kota
Allahabad
Baksar
Patna
Benares
Faizabad, Bengal
Sahibganj
Udaipur
Murshidabad
Palashi (Plassey)
Ahmedabad
Dharmat
Calcutta
Burhanpur
DECCAN PLATEAU
Daulatabad
Aurangabad
Bombay
Pune
Golconda
Hyderabad
Bijapur
Arcot
Madras
Mysore
Srirangapatna
Tanjore

Ruling Dynasties*

* Only individuals with a tenure of a year or longer are listed

The Mughal Dynasty (Agra/Delhi)

Babur (1526–30)
Humayun (1530–40, 1555–6)
Akbar (1556–1605)
Jahangir (1605–27)
Shah Jahan (1628–58)
Aurangzeb ^{c}Alamgir I (1658–1707)
Shah ^{c}Alam I Bahadur Shah (1707–12)
Jahandar Shah (1712)
Farrukhsiyar (1713–19)
Muhammad Shah (1719–48)
Ahmad Shah (1748–54)
^{c}Alamgir II (1754–9)
Shah ^{c}Alam II (1759–1806)
Akbar Shah II (1806–37)
Bahadur Shah II Zafar (1837–58)

The Nawabs of Awadh (Lucknow)

Burhan ul-Mulk (1722–39)
Safdar Jang (1739–54)
Shuja^{c}-ud-daula (1754–75)
Asaf-ud-daula (1775–97)
Sa^{c}adat ^{c}Ali Khan (1798–1814)
Ghazi-ud-din Haider (1814–27)
Nasir-ud-din Haider (1827–37)
Muhammad ^{c}Ali Shah (1837–42)
Amjad ^{c}Ali Shah (1842–7)
Wajid ^{c}Ali Shah (1847–56)

The Asaf Jahi Nizams of Hyderabad

Nizam-ul-mulk (1720–48)
Nasir Jang (1748–52)
Salabat Jang (1752–62)
Nizam ^{c}Ali Khan (1762–1803)
Sikandar Jah (1803–29)
Farkhanda ^{c}Ali Khan (1829–57)

The Maharajas of Jaipur (Amber)

Jai Singh II (1699–1743)
Ishwari Singh (1743–50)
Madho Singh I (1750–68)
Prithvi Singh II (1768–78)
Pratap Singh (1778–1803)
Jagat Singh II (1803–18)
Jai Singh III (1819–35)
Ram Singh II (1835–80)

East India Company Governors-General (Calcutta)/Residents of Delhi

Warren Hastings (1773–85)	
John Macpherson (1785–6)	
Charles Cornwallis (1786–93)	
John Shore (1793–8)	
Richard Wellesley (1798–1805)	David Ochterlony (1803–06)
George Barlow (1805–07)	Archibald Seton (1806–11)
Lord Minto (1807–13)	
Francis Rawdon-Hastings (1813–23)	Charles Theophilus Metcalfe (1811–18)
	David Ochterlony (1818–20)
	Alexander Ross (1820–3)
Lord Amhurst (1823–8)	William Fraser (1823)
	Charles Elliott (1823–5)
	Charles Theophilus Metcalfe (1825–7)
	Edward Colebrooke (1827–8)

William Bentinck (1828–35)	William Fraser (1828–9)
	Francis James Hawkins (1829–30)
	W B Martin (1830–2)
	William Fraser (1832–5)
Charles Metcalfe (1835–6)	Thomas Theophilus Metcalfe (1835–53)
Lord Auckland (1836–42)	
Lord Ellenborough (1842–4)	
Henry Hardinge (1844–8)	
Lord Dalhousie (1848–56)	Simon Fraser (1853–7)
Viscount Canning (1856–62)	

Genealogies of Principal Musicians and Music Treatises

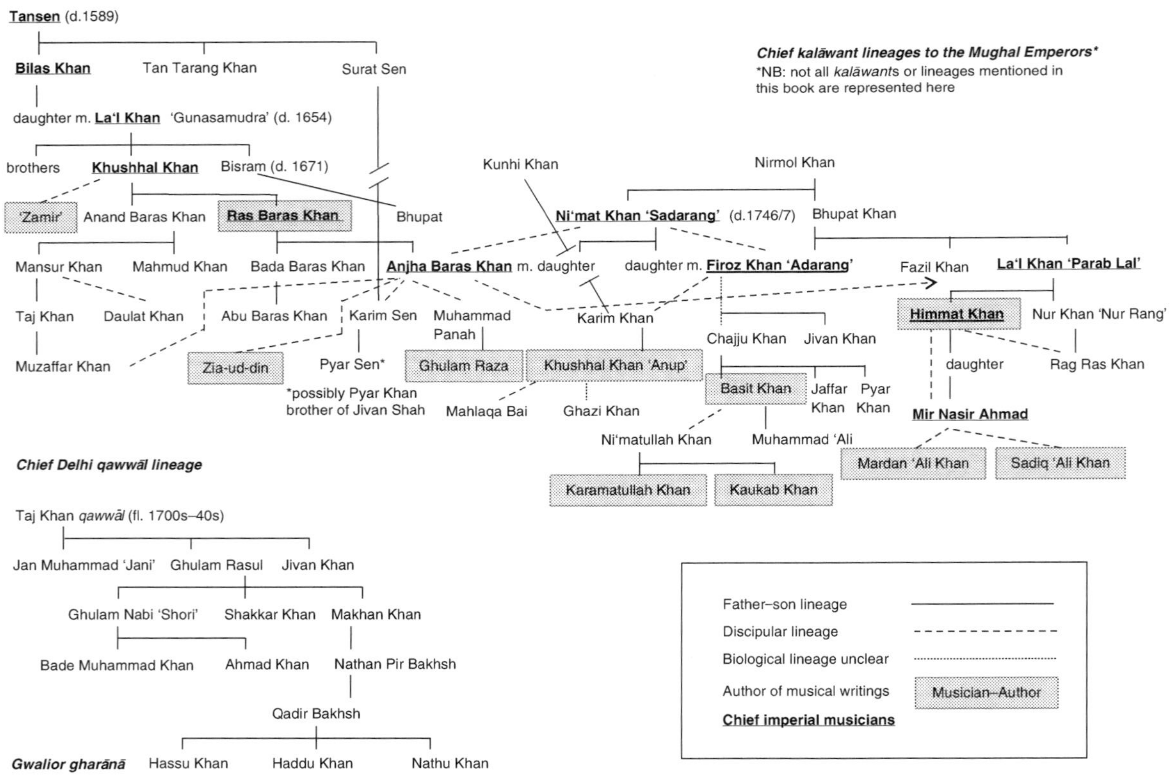
Chief kalāwant lineages to the Mughal Emperors*
*NB: not all kalāwants or lineages mentioned in this book are represented here
Tansen (d.1589)
Bilas Khan
Tan Tarang Khan
Surat Sen
daughter m. La'l Khan 'Gunasamudra' (d. 1654)
brothers
Khushhal Khan
Bisram (d. 1671)
'Zamir'
Anand Baras Khan
Ras Baras Khan
Bhupat
Kunhi Khan
Nirmol Khan
Ni'mat Khan 'Sadarang' (d.1746/7)
Bhupat Khan
Mansur Khan
Mahmud Khan
Bada Baras Khan
Anjha Baras Khan m. daughter
daughter m. Firoz Khan 'Adarang'
Fazil Khan
La'l Khan 'Parab Lal'
Taj Khan
Daulat Khan
Abu Baras Khan
Karim Sen
Muhammad Panah
Karim Khan
Chajju Khan
Jivan Khan
Himmat Khan
Nur Khan 'Nur Rang'
Muzaffar Khan
Zia-ud-din
Pyar Sen*
Ghulam Raza
Khushhal Khan 'Anup'
Basit Khan
Jaffar Khan
Pyar Khan
daughter
Rag Ras Khan
*possibly Pyar Khan brother of Jivan Shah
Mahlaqa Bai
Ghazi Khan
Mir Nasir Ahmad
Ni'matullah Khan
Muhammad 'Ali
Mardan 'Ali Khan
Sadiq 'Ali Khan
Karamatullah Khan
Kaukab Khan
Chief Delhi qawwāl lineage
Taj Khan qawwāl (fl. 1700s–40s)
Jan Muhammad 'Jani'
Ghulam Rasul
Jivan Khan
Ghulam Nabi 'Shori'
Shakkar Khan
Makhan Khan
Bade Muhammad Khan
Ahmad Khan
Nathan Pir Bakhsh
Qadir Bakhsh
Gwalior gharānā
Hassu Khan
Haddu Khan
Nathu Khan
Father–son lineage
Discipular lineage
Biological lineage unclear
Author of musical writings
Musician–Author
Chief imperial musicians

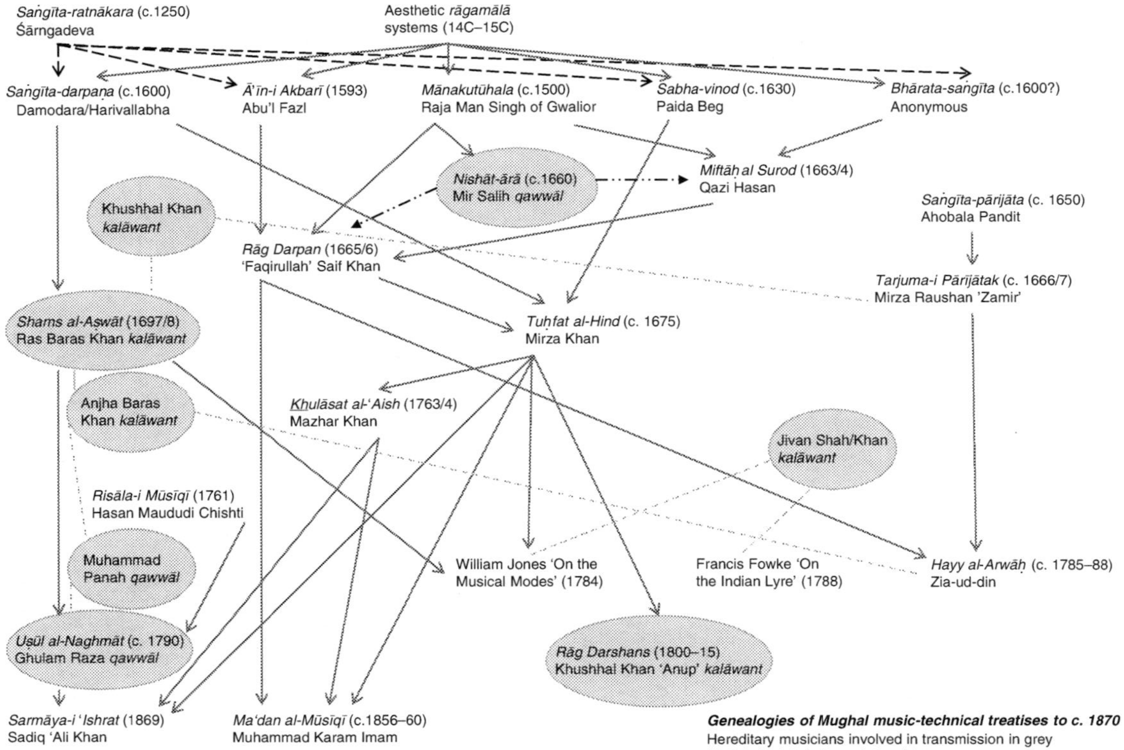

Genealogies of Mughal music-technical treatises to c. 1870
Hereditary musicians involved in transmission in grey
Ustād–disciple/writer relationships

Du aber, Göttlicher, du, bis zuletzt noch Ertöner,
da ihn der Schwarm der verschmähten Mänaden befiel,
hast ihr Geschrei übertönt mit Ordnung, du Schöner,
aus den Zerstörenden stieg dein erbauendes Spiel.

Keine war da, daß sie Haupt dir und Leier zerstör.
Wie sie auch rangen und rasten, und alle die scharfen
Steine, die sie nach deinem Herzen warfen,
wurden zu Sanftem an dir und begabt mit Gehör.

Schließlich zerschlugen sie dich, von der Rache gehetzt,
während dein Klang noch in Löwen und Felsen verweilte
und in den Bäumen und Vögeln. Dort singst du noch jetzt.

O du verlorener Gott! Du unendliche Spur!
Nur weil dich reißend zuletzt die Feindschaft verteilte,
sind wir die Hörenden jetzt und ein Mund der Natur.

But you, godlike one, you, resounding with song to the very last,
When seized by the swarm of the despised maenads,
Drowned out their shrieking with Order, yes
Beauteous one,—from the very midst of the ravagers
arose the edification of your playing.

There were none then who could destroy either your head or your lyre,
Even as those furious ones raved and tore;
And all the sharp stones which they threw at your heart
Turned to softness upon your breast and, behold, were
blessed with Hearing.

Finally they destroyed you, hunted down out of vengeance,
While your timbre abides in lions and cliffs
And in trees and birds. In these you sing still.

Oh you lost god! You unending trail!
Only because hatred at last tore asunder and dispersed you
Are we now the hearers and a mouth to Nature.

Rainer Maria Rilke, *Sonnets to Orpheus*, Book I Number XXVI.[3]

[3] Rainer Maria Rilke, *The Sonnets to Orpheus*, tr. Robert Temple (London: Eglantyne, 2022).

1 | Chasing Eurydice

Writing on Music in the Late Mughal World

Introduction

You should know, dear brother . . . that in every manual craft the matter dealt with consists of naturally occurring material, and that all its products are physical forms. The exception is music, for the 'matter' it deals with consists entirely of spiritual substances, namely, the souls of those who listen to it.

The Ikhwan us-Safa' (Brethren of Purity), c. 950–1000.[1]

It is impossible to capture the essence of music in pen and ink on the surface of a page.

Sher ᶜAli Khan Lodi, 1691.[2]

How do we write histories of the ephemeral: of emotional and sensory experiences, of ecstatic states and aesthetic journeys, of the live performance of music and dance, of the tangible yet transient texture of the experiential moment? More to the point, how do we write such histories when those moments have long passed into silence? Can experiential moments even have histories? Surely, the momentary is the very definition of something that lies beyond history, beyond historical method. Isn't that the essence of its bittersweet pleasures: that, once over, it forever lies beyond our reach? How far can ink and paint on the surface of a page transport us into the experience of those, long dead, who once tasted those intensities, and for whom those moments were the warp and weft of their deepest personal and collective selves?[3] Can reflections on the emotions,

[1] Ikhwan us-Safa', *On Music: An Arabic Critical Edition and English Translation of Epistle 5* [c. 950–1000], ed. and tr. Owen Wright (Oxford: Oxford University Press and the Institute of Ismaili Studies, 2010), p. 76.

[2] Sher ᶜAli Khan Lodi, *Tazkira-i Mir'āt al-Khayāl*, ed. Hamid Hasani and Bihruz Safarzadeh (Tehran: Rawzaneh, 1998), p. 141.

[3] Christopher A Bayly, *Empire and Information: Intelligence Gathering and Social Communication in India, 1780–1870* (Cambridge: Cambridge University Press, 1996), p. 55; Mana Kia, *Persianate Selves: Memories of Place and Origin Before Nationalism* (Stanford: Stanford University Press, 2020).

the senses and the performing arts tell us critical things about the harder-edged worlds of political, economic and social history that we could never otherwise access? What *was* the relationship between the aesthetic, the affective, the ethical, the political and the personal in South Asian history?[4] And what was at stake for North Indian men and women when their cherished musical worlds were turned upside down in the final century of upheaval that saw the Mughal empire give way to the British Raj?

In a series of six interlocking essays and a summative discussion, this book addresses these compelling but elusive questions through a focus on music, musicians and writing about them in late Mughal India (c. 1748–1858). The Mughals were a Central Asian Sunni Muslim dynasty who from 1526 ruled over large parts of the Indian subcontinent from the magnificent northern cities of Delhi and Agra, ostensibly until 1858. In reality, the Mughal empire began to disintegrate after the death of Emperor Aurangzeb ᶜAlamgir in 1707,[5] which created a power vacuum that was filled initially by a series of resurgent regional powers, most successfully the Maratha Confederacy,[6] and ultimately by their ruthless foreign competitors the British East India Company. Through an exploration of six different types of writing on music prominent in late Mughal India, this book retells the stories of nine mostly forgotten élite musicians – five men, four women – and the courtly worlds they inhabited during the consequential final century of transition from Mughal to British rule. My time frame begins with the death in 1748 of the last Mughal emperor to retain any real geopolitical power, Muhammad Shah. It ends with the British overthrow of the last emperor Bahadur Shah Zafar in 1858, as punishment for his role as

[4] On emotions history in South Asia: Margrit Pernau (ed.), *South Asia History and Culture* 12.2–3 (2021), 111–355, especially Margrit Pernau, 'Studying Emotions in South Asia', *South Asia History and Culture* 12.2–3 (2021), 111–28; and Dipti Khera, *The Place of Many Moods: Udaipur's Painted Lands and India's Eighteenth Century* (Princeton: Princeton University Press, 2020). This opening paragraph is based on my review of Kavita Panjabi (ed.), *Poetics and Politics of Sufism and Bhakti in South Asia: Love, Loss and Liberation* (Hyderabad: Orient Blackswan, 2011), in *The Indian Economic and Social History Review* 52.1 (2015), 116–19, p. 116.

[5] Aurangzeb ᶜAlamgir I (r. 1658–1707) should not be confused with his descendent ᶜAziz-ud-din ᶜAlamgir II (r. 1754–59).

[6] The powerful Maratha Confederacy (1674–1818) is only occasionally touched upon in this book, and remains a major lacuna in our understanding of Hindustani music history. I would encourage historians working in relevant languages and Modi script to take up this challenge; there are certainly sources, for example in the Bibliothèque Nationale de France. For general histories, see the work of Prachi Deshpande, Stewart Gordon, A R Kulkarni and Rosalind O'Hanlon; for music, Justin Scarimbolo, 'Brahmans Beyond Nationalism, Muslims Beyond Dominance: A Hidden History of North Indian Classical Music's Hinduization', Unpublished PhD Dissertation, University of California, Santa Barbara (2014).

figurehead of the cataclysmic 1857 Indian Uprising, the *Ghadar*.[7] For those more familiar with colonial perspectives, this was the century of the East India Company's conquest of India, from the Battle of Palashi (Plassey) in 1757 to the imposition of British Crown rule in 1858 after the Company nearly lost control of its Indian possessions entirely.[8]

The geographical heartlands of this book are the vast alluvial plains and rocky hills of northern India, known as Hindustan,[9] that stretch out beneath the Himalayan foothills for over 1,200 miles watered by the rich Yamuna and Ganges river systems, though the Deccan Plateau to the south also comes into frame from time to time (see Map, p. xxi). Because of the violent collapse of the Mughal centre (c. 1739–61), which Indian writers of the time called 'the scattering' (Chapter 3),[10] this book's time frame was one of unprecedented migration across India for Mughal service personnel of all kinds, including many of the court's greatest performing artists (alongside numerous others who claimed to be). Successive chapters follow élite musicians chronologically from the Mughal imperial capital, Delhi, with its grand new city and fortress of Shahjahanabad completed in 1648,[11] to major alternative centres of cultural patronage in Lucknow, Hyderabad, Jaipur and among the British (1748–1842). We then return to Delhi and Lucknow for final chapters on the late flowering and sudden death of the Mughal imperium (1803–58), after the East India Company finally took Delhi from Maratha control in 1803.

The transition from Mughal to British rule has been of critical interest to historians of South Asia for the past forty years.[12] The dominant historiographical debate concerns the nature and extent of colonialism's impact on

[7] Meaning 'rebellion, disturbance'; alternatively the First War of Independence, the Sepoy/Indian Mutiny, or simply 1857.

[8] See Jon Wilson, *India Conquered: Britain's Raj and the Chaos of Empire* (London: Simon and Schuster, 2016); Shashi Tharoor, *Inglorious Empire: What the British Did to India* (London: Hurst, 2017); and most comprehensively the four volumes of William Dalrymple's *Company Quartet* (London: Bloomsbury, 2021).

[9] Manan Ahmed Asif, *The Loss of Hindustan: The Invention of India* (Cambridge, MA: Harvard University Press, 2020).

[10] For example, Zia-ud-din, *Hayy al-Arwāh*, John Rylands Library, Manchester, Persian 346 (c. 1785–88), f. 43r.

[11] Shahjahanabad is now called 'Old Delhi', but then it was known as the 'new city', *shahr-i no*, as opposed to the older cities of Sultanate Delhi surrounding it, known as the 'old city', *shahr-i kohna*.

[12] Going back to Bernard S Cohn's work on eighteenth-century Benares, with early landmarks Christopher A Bayly, *Rulers, Townsmen and Bazaars: North Indian Society in the Age of British Expansion, 1770–1870* (Oxford: Oxford University Press, 1983); and Muzaffar Alam, *The Crisis of Empire in Mughal North India: Awadh and the Punjab, 1707–48* (New Delhi: Oxford University Press, 1986).

the knowledge systems of the colonised, from the very fundamentals of South Asian civilisation such as caste, religion and law to language politics and artistic production. Until the mid-2000s, opposing arguments contended that British authorities either made use of pre-existing Indian knowledge systems, gradually transforming them as they gained power and territory, or, alternatively, 'invented' them largely ex nihilo in the Orientalist exercise of power-knowledge over those they ruled.[13] Jon Wilson has noted that proponents of both sides were in fact largely arguing past each other: those perceiving continuity and incremental change were mostly eighteenth-century historians, while those insisting on dramatic rupture and invention of tradition generally did so from the perspective of late colonialism.[14] But the central flaw in the whole debate was articulated by Sheldon Pollock in 2004. He noted that the argument was largely raging in the absence of sufficient, sometimes any, knowledge of those pre-existing Indian systems: very few of the main contenders were working from the early modern Indian sources that embody such knowledge, other than those translated into English during the colonial era.[15] This was not due to a lack of pre- or paracolonial Indian sources, either.[16] 'South Asia', Pollock wrote, 'boasts a literary record far denser, in terms of sheer number of texts and centuries of unbroken multilingual literacy, than all of Greek and Latin and medieval European culture combined'.[17]

Music and Musicians in Late Mughal India thus stands on Pollock's foundational proposition, that while

> the impact of colonialism on culture and power has been the dominant arena of inquiry in the past two decades . . . colonial studies has often been skating on the thinnest ice, given how much it depends on a knowledge of the precolonial realities

[13] For example, Bayly, *Empire*; vs. Bernard S Cohn, *An Anthropologist Among the Historians* (New Delhi: Oxford University Press, 1987); Norbert Peabody, 'Cents, Sense, Census: Human Inventories in Late Precolonial and Early Colonial India', *Comparative Studies in Society and History* 43.4 (2001), 819–50; vs. Nicholas B Dirks, 'The 'Invention' of Caste', in *Castes of Mind: Colonialism and the Making of Modern India* (Princeton: Princeton University Press, 2002). See overviews in Rosalind O'Hanlon and David Washbrook, 'Histories in Transition: Approaches to the Study of Colonialism and Culture in India', *History Workshop Journal* 32.1 (1991), 110–27; Jon Wilson, 'Early Colonial India Beyond Empire', *The Historical Journal* 50.4 (2007), 951–70; and Ricardo Roque and Kim A Wagner, 'Introduction: Engaging Colonial Knowledge', in Roque and Wagner (eds.), *Engaging Colonial Knowledge: Reading European Archives in World History* (London: Palgrave Macmillan, 2012), pp. 1–32.

[14] Wilson, 'Early'.

[15] Sheldon Pollock, 'Forms of Knowledge in Early Modern South Asia: Introduction', *Comparative Studies of South Asia, Africa and the Middle East* 24.2 (2004), 19–21. Crucial exceptions included Peabody, 'Cents'.

[16] On the paracolonial, see p. 16 below. [17] Pollock, 'Forms', p. 19.

that colonialism encountered, and how little such knowledge we actually possess ... *we cannot know how colonialism changed South Asia if we do not know what was there to be changed.*[18]

In the two decades since, several scholars have enthusiastically taken up Pollock's challenge to examine 'what was there to be changed', notably in the fields of Mughal, Rajput and sectarian literary and cultural history during the long eighteenth century. By foregrounding South Asian visual and especially textual sources in Persian, Hindavi and other early modern languages that had mostly remained unstudied in modern times, this rich new scholarship has delivered groundbreaking insights into the wider social, economic and political dynamics of pre- and paracolonial North India.[19] Fewer scholars prioritising Mughal sources and perspectives, however, have moved past the 1750s,[20] or specifically engaged the thorny historiographical questions of how and why Pollock's 'precolonial realities' changed as a result of the Mughal–British transition (c. 1748–1858).[21]

Crucially, then, this book addresses both the 'what' and the 'how' parts of Pollock's challenge. Firstly, it extends the new scholarship on pre-existing Indian knowledge systems for the first time to the field of music (including dance[22]) through an extensive evaluation of Persian and to a lesser extent

18 ibid; my emphasis.

19 For example, works listed in the bibliography by Molly Emma Aitken, Allison Busch, Chanchal B Dadlani, William Dalrymple, Arthur Dudney, Walter Hakala, Radha Kapuria, Prashant Keshavmurthy, Dipti Khera, Mana Kia, David Lunn, Saif Mahmood, Anne Murphy, Naveena Naqvi, Heidi Pauwels, Stefano Pelló, Holly M Schaffer, Kevin L Schwartz, Yuthika Sharma, Nathan Tabor, Madhu Trivedi and Richard David Williams. Rather fewer new works of political history have been attempted, a stand-out being Abhishek Kaicker's *The King and the People: Sovereignty and Popular Politics in Mughal Delhi* (Oxford: Oxford University Press, 2020). The tremendous scholarly production of Rosalind O'Hanlon, Francesca Orsini and Margrit Pernau remains essential reading.

20 But see Yuthika Sharma, 'Art in Between Empires: Visual Culture and Artistic Knowledge in Late Mughal Delhi, 1748–1857', Unpublished PhD Dissertation, Columbia University (2013); Richard David Williams, 'Hindustani Music Between Awadh and Bengal, c. 1758–1905', Unpublished PhD Dissertation, King's College London (2015) and *The Scattered Court: Hindustani Music in Colonial Bengal* (Chicago: University of Chicago Press, 2023); Naveena Naqvi, 'Writing the Inter-Imperial World in Afghan North India ca. 1774–1857', Unpublished PhD Dissertation, UCLA (2018); and Arthur Dudney, *India in the Persian World of Letters: Ḳhān-i Ārzū among the Eighteenth-Century Philologists* (Oxford: Oxford University Press, 2022). Remarkably, there is still no modern history of the pivotal reign of Emperor Shah ᶜAlam II (r. 1759–1806), though see William Dalrymple, *The Anarchy: The Relentless Rise of the East India Company* (London: Bloomsbury, 2019).

21 But see the work of Margrit Pernau, Yunus Jaffery and Kumkum Chatterjee; also Robert Travers, *Empires of Complaints: Mughal Law and the Making of British India, 1765–1793* (Cambridge: Cambridge University Press, 2022).

22 The Sanskrit and Hindavi word *saṅgīt(a)* holistically incorporates music, dance and drama.

Brajbhasha and Urdu writings on Hindustani music and its reception between 1593 and 1869, most of which have not been examined before.[23] Secondly, by narrowing the focus to the decades of the Mughal–British political transition (1748–1858), and by placing Indian writings from this critical period into sustained dialogue with East India Company and other English-language texts, I am able to demonstrate how and why late Mughal fields of music and dance changed through this critical century of British colonisation, including via select European patronage of Indian performing arts.

Music and Musicians shows that the transitional world of late Mughal and early colonial India does look different when we prioritise the perspectives (plural) of Indian sources and triangulate them against European ones. And as we shall see, the many traces that remain on paper of the ephemeral arts of music and dance, their theory, practice and appreciation, do indeed tell us things we would not otherwise know about how very different types of people related to the arts and to each other in intense, intimate moments of both relief and tension; how those relationships and moments were experienced and understood; and what all this meant for politics, economics, society and culture in North India at this pivotal time.

The chapters in this book are thus of substantial relevance to all historians of the transition to British rule in South Asia, not simply those interested in the arts. But this time frame is also crucial to Indian music history because, as this book demonstrates, this was simultaneously the century during which the major pre-existing knowledge system known today as 'North Indian classical' or Hindustani music became fully established in its modern form. It is the discrete, socially élite field of Hindustani music, its performers and its audiences that is the specific focus of *Music and Musicians*, and thus a brief introduction to what this musical field then encompassed is essential.

The Field of Hindustani Music c. 1700

The Persian word Hindustani means 'of or from the geographical region of Hindustan'. It is most commonly used to denote the dominant colloquial language of late Mughal India that was divided into what we now call Hindi and Urdu in the later colonial period.[24] These days, literary historians tend

[23] Though see Williams, *Scattered Court*, which uses the same European Research Council-funded archive as this book.

[24] Introduction, Francesca Orsini (ed.), *Before the Divide: Hindi and Urdu Literary Culture* (Hyderabad: Orient Blackswan, 2010).

to use the umbrella term Hindavi for the related early modern dialects of Hindustan that include the two courtly ancestors of Hindi and Urdu, Brajbhasha and *rekhta*, in which many (but not all) song genres of Hindustani music were composed.[25] But the referents of 'Hindustani music' are more particular than simply geographical or linguistic, not least because this distinct musical system was patronised in courtly centres well beyond the borders of Hindustan proper, from Gujarat and Punjab in the west to Nepal in the north, Bengal in the east and as far south as Hyderabad, Arcot and Maratha Tanjore.[26]

The term 'Hindustani music' to describe a circumscribed field of music-technical features, theoretical and aesthetic discourse, song and instrumental repertoires, performing communities and performance and listening practices was established at the Mughal imperial court before the mid-seventeenth century. The earliest uses I have found of the term are in the *Pādishāhnāma* (c. 1636–48), the official chronicle of Emperor Shah Jahan's reign (r. 1628–58), to segregate a set of Indian song genres, key music-technical features and specialist performers from the Persian and Central Asian musical systems also patronised by the Mughals.[27] In 1663/4, the Mughal theorist Qazi Hasan further narrowed down the field to northern India specifically, distinguishing the *rāga*-based system of 'the province of Hindustan' – the subject of his treatise – from the *rāga*-based systems then current in the southern 'provinces of the Deccan, Telangana and Karnataka'.[28] But Hindustani music as a recognised, delimited field long predated its labelling: by 1593 the key Mughal ideologue Abu'l Fazl had

[25] See contributions to Sheldon Pollock (ed.), *Literary Culture in History: Reconstructions from South Asia* (Berkeley: University of California Press, 2003). On song lyrics, see Françoise 'Nalini' Delvoye, 'Collections of Lyrics in Hindustani Music: The Case of Dhrupad', in Joep Bor, Françoise 'Nalini' Delvoye, Jane Harvey and Emmie te Nijenhuis (eds.), *Hindustani Music: Thirteenth to Twentieth Centuries* (New Delhi: Manohar, 2010), 141–58; and Katherine Butler Schofield, '"Words Without Songs": The Social History of Hindustani Song Collections in India's Muslim Courts c.1770–1830', in Rachel Harris and Martin Stokes (eds.), *Theory and Practice in the Music of the Islamic World: Essays in Honour of Owen Wright* (London: Routledge, 2017), 171–96.

[26] Chapter 5; Davesh Soneji, *Unfinished Gestures: Devadāsīs, Memory, and Modernity in South India* (Chicago: University of Chicago Press, 2012), pp. 37–54.

[27] Both *naghma-i hindūstān* and *naghma-i hindūstānī* are used; Abd al-Hamid Lahawri, *The Badshah Nama*, ed. Kabir al-din Ahmad and Abd al-Rahim, *Bibliotheca Indica Series* (Calcutta: College Press, 1867–8), vol. i, p. 152; vol. ii, pp. 5–7; Abu'l Fazl, *The Ain i Akbari*, vol. i, tr. H. Blochmann, *Bibliotheca Indica Series* (Calcutta: Baptist Mission Press and Asiatic Society of Bengal, 1873), p. 612.

[28] Qazi Hasan, *Miftāh al-Surod*, Victoria and Albert Museum, IS-61:1–197 (Indur (Nizamabad), 1691; orig. 1663/4), p. 6; Katherine Butler Schofield, 'Music, Art and Power in 'Adil Shahi Bijapur, c. 1570–1630', in Kavita Singh (ed.), *Scent Upon a Southern Breeze: The Synaesthetic Arts of the Deccan* (Mumbai: Marg, 2018), 68–87.

already mapped what was clearly the same field as it was practised at the North Indian court of Emperor Akbar I (r. 1556–1605) – but instead called it by the proper Sanskrit term for *rāga*-based music and its connected arts, *saṅgīta*.[29]

As the term *rāga*-based indicates,[30] the core defining feature of Hindustani music, then as now, is the primacy placed on *rāga* as its fundamental melodic framework. *Rāga* refers to the unique South Asian system of highly aestheticised melodic modes that have been theoretically systematised in written treatises and performance practice for more than a millennium.[31] The Hindustani and Karnatak (South Indian) *rāga* systems began to diverge in their aesthetic conception around 1550.[32] For those unfamiliar with South Asian music, a *rāga* is not the same kind of entity as a European scale or mode, nor is it a fixed melody. In the Hindustani system, as David Lunn and I have explained, each *rāga* exists 'in both a sonic form, and an iconic form. . . . In their sonic form, *raga*s are melodic formulae – ascending and descending note patterns with special additional rules – that act as blueprints for composition [and improvisation], and produce a unique character or *soundmark* for each *raga*. The soundmark produced by specific melodic gestures in each *raga* is associated with a distinct emotional flavour . . . and with a particular time of day or season of the year. Sung correctly, every *raga* is supposed to have a specific effect on the listener's physical or psychological well-being or on the wider natural world. . . . In the *raga*s' iconic forms, these associations are assembled into painted icons and poetic imagery. Since the fourteenth century, Indian poets and musicologists have described the *raga*s as beautiful heroines, brave heroes, sages, *jogini*s and gods. . . . And since the sixteenth century, the *raga*s have been painted in suites of six male *raga*s, each with five wives called *ragini*s and known as a "garland of *raga*s" – the *ragamala*'

[29] Abu'l Fazl, 'Sangita', 'On the Classes of Singers', and 'The Akhārā', '*Ain-i-Ākbari*', vol. iii, tr. Col. HS Jarrett, rev. Jadunath Sarkar (Calcutta: Royal Asiatic Society of Bengal, 1948), pp. 254–73; *Áín i Akbarí*, ed. H Blochmann, *Bibliotheca India Series* (Calcutta: Baptist Mission Press, 1869), vol. ii, pp. 136–44.

[30] On using *rāga*-based instead of 'classical', see Davesh Soneji, 'Exploring Complex Histories of Islamic Musical Production in Colonial South India', unpublished lecture, British Library, 19/04/21.

[31] On the development of *rāga* c. 800–1300 CE, see D Richard Widdess, *The Ragas of Early Indian Music* (Oxford: Clarendon, 1995).

[32] Matt Rahaim, Srinivas Reddy and Lars Christensen, 'Authority, Critique, and Revision in the Sanskrit Tradition: Rereading the *Svara-mela-kalānidhi*', *Asian Music* 46.1 (2015), 39–77; Lakshmi Subramanian, 'The Reinvention of a Tradition: Nationalism, Carnatic Music and the Madras Music Academy, 1900–1957', *Indian Economic and Social History Review* 36.2 (1999), 131–63, pp. 134–6.

(e.g. Figures 2.2, 5.4).[33] By the late seventeenth century, music theorists had reached a consensus on the pre-eminence of one principal *rāgamālā* system (*mat*) in Hindustani music, the Hanuman *mat* (Table 7.1).

In other words, before the Mughals even arrived in India, the *rāga*s were already richly aestheticised objects of erudite connoisseurship associated with India's courtly arts and literature. The primacy of *rāga* to Hindustani music thus further marked this field out, explicitly, as élite – as the exclusive provenance of the courtly and literate social classes who together ran the institutions of government and civil society in late medieval and early modern North India. Indeed, as it metamorphosed over previous centuries, the whole field of *rāga*-based music had been repeatedly subject to deliberate processes of canonisation, standardisation and systematisation in writing – what I have called 'classicisation' processes[34] – most recently in the fifteenth century under the Rajput rulers of Mewar and Gwalior and the sultans of Jaunpur and Delhi.[35] But it was under the Mughals, between the reigns of Akbar I (r. 1556–1605) and Akbar II (r. 1806–37), that the full constellation of élite discourse, practices, performers and modes of listening that became known as 'classical' in the twentieth century was consolidated and codified.[36]

[33] David Lunn and Katherine Butler Schofield, 'Desire, Devotion, and the Music of the Monsoon at the Court of Emperor Shah 'Alam II', in Imke Rajamani, Margrit Pernau and Katherine Butler Schofield (eds.), *Monsoon Feelings: A History of Emotions in the Rain* (New Delhi: Niyogi, 2018), 220–54, pp. 229–30. See also Joep Bor, *The Raga Guide: A Survey of 74 Hindustani Ragas* (Monmouth: Nimbus, 1999).

[34] Katherine Butler Schofield, 'Reviving the Golden Age Again: "Classicization," Hindustani Music, and the Mughals', *Ethnomusicology* 54.3 (2010), 484–517.

[35] Major monuments were the *Saṅgītarāja* (Sanskrit), the *Saṅgītashiromaṇi* (Sanskrit), the *Mānakutūhala* (Hindavi), the *Mṛgāvatī* (Awadhi) and the *Lahjāt-i Sikandar-shāhī* (Persian); Emmie te Nijenhuis, *Musicological Literature*, A History of Indian Literature Series, vol. vi (Wiesbaden: Otto Harrassowitz, 1977), pp. 16–8; Shaikh Qutban Suhrawardi [1503], *Mṛgāvatī*, tr. Aditya Behl as *The Magic Doe*, ed. Wendy Doniger (Oxford: Oxford University Press, 2012); Allyn Miner, '*Raga* in the Early Sixteenth Century', in Francesca Orsini and Katherine Butler Schofield (eds.), *Tellings and Texts: Music, Literature, and Performance in North India* (Cambridge: Open Book, 2015), 385–406; Sama ᶜUmar ibn Yahya Kabuli [c. 1500], *Lehjāt-e-Sikāndershāhi* [sic], ed. Shahab Sarmadee (New Delhi: Indian Council of Historical Research, 1999); also William Rees Hofmann, 'Singing Sufis in Text: Music, and Sufi Poetics ca. 1250–1600', Unpublished PhD Dissertation, SOAS, University of London (2022).

[36] Schofield, 'Reviving'. For the wholesale 'reclassicisation' process Hindustani music underwent under the British dispensation, see Janaki Bakhle, *Two Men and Music: Nationalism and the Making of an Indian Classical Tradition* (New York: Oxford University Press, 2005); but see Katherine Butler Brown [Schofield], Review of *Two Men and Music*, *Journal of Asian Studies* 67.1 (2008), 335–7; also works listed in the bibliography by Davesh Soneji (also with Indira Peterson), Lakshmi Subramanian, Amanda Weidman, Gerry Farrell, James Kippen and Margaret E Walker.

Thanks to the pioneering research of Shahab Sarmadee, Françoise 'Nalini' Delvoye, Najma Perveen Ahmad, Madhu Trivedi and Prem Lata Sharma, it is now well established that in the seventeenth century, authors associated with the Mughal court started producing a plethora of new systematic writings on the *rāga*-based music of Hindustan.[37] As I discuss in Chapter 2, they translated older, especially Sanskrit, treatises and oral lore into the two new Mughal languages of courtly power and literature, Brajbhasha and Persian, intermingling the old with new material to remake élite musical discourse for a culturally mixed courtly regime that actively delighted in difference. From the sixteenth century onwards both the Mughals and their courtly Hindu counterparts the Rajputs prized a virtuosic aesthetic of borrowing and reuse from the Indic to the Persianate realms and vice versa. Artists and writers adopted ideas, literary topoi, visual and sonic symbols and complex imagery from one realm, and repurposed them across religions, languages, media and genres. This led over time to multiple depths and tangents of meaning speaking simultaneously in any one work of art or literature.[38] The new wave of seventeenth-century Mughal writings on music were steeped in this aesthetic. Their authors translated, mixed and remade written musical discourse afresh in order to 'reclassicise' Hindustani music for the ascendant Mughal dispensation with its cognate central ideology of *sulh-i kull*, 'universal civility', in which the emperor's role was to unify India's considerable religious, social and cultural diversity under his unitary harmonious benevolence.[39] But in making *rāga*-based music *theirs* by writing knowledgeably about it, Mughal courtiers also marked themselves out as true members of India's élite classes, firmly set apart from the uneducated masses who

[37] Françoise 'Nalini' Delvoye, 'Indo-Persian Literature on Art-Music: Some Historical and Technical Aspects', in Delvoye (ed.), *Confluence of Cultures* (New Delhi: Manohar, 1994), 93–130; Najma Perveen Ahmad, *Hindustani Music: A Study of Its Development in Seventeenth and Eighteenth Centuries* (New Delhi: Manohar, 1984); Madhu Trivedi, *The Emergence of the Hindustani Tradition: Music, Dance and Drama in North India, 13th to 19th Centuries* (Gurgaon: Three Essays Collective, 2012); Saif Khan Faqirullah, *Tarjuma-i-Mānakutūhala and Risāla-i-Rāg Darpan*, ed. and tr. Shahab Sarmadee (New Delhi: Indira Gandhi National Centre for the Performing Arts and Delhi: Motilal Banarsidass, 1996 [orig. 1665/6]); Nayak Bakhshu, *Sahasarasa: Nāyaka Bakhśu ke Dhrupadoṃ kā Saṅgraha*, ed. and tr. Prem Lata Sharma (New Delhi: Sangit Natak Akademi, 1972); see also my articles and Richard David Williams' work on the pre-1748 period.

[38] Molly Emma Aitken, 'Repetition and Response: The Case of Layla and Majnun', *The Intelligence of Tradition in Rajput Court Painting* (New Haven: Yale University Press, 2010), pp. 155–210; also Aitken, 'Parataxis and the Practice of Reuse, from Mughal Margins to Mīr Kalān Khān', *Archives of Asian Art* 59 (2009), 81–103.

[39] Rajeev Kinra, 'Revisiting the History and Historiography of Mughal Pluralism', *ReOrient* 5.2 (2020), 137–82.

did not listen to *rāga*, and nouveau riche upstarts who didn't properly know how to.[40]

By the end of Aurangzeb's reign (r. 1658–1707), then, Hindustani music was a long-established *rāga*-based art music identified culturally with the courts of northern India, Hindu and Muslim, but now overwhelmingly connected with Mughal imperial and provincial, especially Rajput, patronage. With the *rāgas* at its aesthetic heart, the Hindustani musical field encompassed, firstly, a flourishing corpus of music-technical and philosophical writings in Sanskrit, Brajbhasha and Persian (*saṅgīta-shāstra*; *ᶜilm-i mūsīqī*); and secondly, a performance repertoire of virtuosic song genres and instrumental forms that used *rāga* and *tāla* (the metrical cycles of the rhythmic system) as the basis of short fixed compositions and extended live improvisations. These song genres, all still in the repertoire, were composed in courtly registers of North Indian languages including Persian,[41] notably *dhrupad*, *hoṛī*, *k͟hayāl*, *ṭappa*, *tarānā* and *g͟hazal*; and the main instruments were the stringed *bīn* (*rudra vīṇā*), *rabāb*, *sārangī* and Persian *tambūr*, and the drums *pakhāwaj*, *ḍholak* and *daf/dā'ira* (see Glossary).[42] Thirdly, as is still the case today, except on grand occasions these forms were performed as chamber music by small professional ensembles comprised of one or two singers and accompanying instrumentalists; slightly larger troupes of women and transfeminine[43] performers also danced. By the early seventeenth century, these forms and their performance practices were the exclusive intellectual property of multigenerational hereditary guilds built around households of male professional musicians from the endogamous *kalāwant*, *qawwāl* and *ḍhāḍhī* communities, and the highest-status female

[40] Schofield, 'Reviving'; Katherine Butler Brown [Schofield], 'If Music Be the Food of Love: Masculinity and Eroticism in the Mughal *Mehfil*', in Francesca Orsini (ed.), *Love in South Asia: a Cultural History* (Cambridge: Cambridge University Press, 2006), 61–83; Katherine Butler Schofield, 'Musical Culture under Mughal Patronage: The Place of Pleasure', in Richard Eaton and Ramya Sreenivasan (eds.), *The Oxford Handbook to the Mughal Empire* (Oxford: Oxford University Press, forthcoming); also Chloë Alaghband-Zadeh, 'Listening to North Indian Classical Music: How Embodied Ways of Listening Perform Imagined Histories and Social Class', *Ethnomusicology* 61.2 (2017), 207–33.

[41] Persian was the official language even of the East India Company until 1837.

[42] e.g. Faqirullah, *Rāg Darpan*; and Ras Baras Khan [1697/8], *Shams al-Aṣvāt: The Sun of Songs by Ras Baras*, ed. and tr. Mehrdad Fallahzadeh and Mahmoud Hassanabadi (Uppsala: Acta Universitatis Upsalensis, 2012).

[43] During the eighteenth and nineteenth centuries, the role of women dancers at court was sometimes taken by young men dancing in the persona and dress of women; Brown [Schofield], 'If Music Be'. It is impossible to know how they construed their own gender, so I use transfeminine.

courtesan communities (Chapters 4, 5 and 6).[44] The great master-teachers in the male lineages, responsible for preserving and transmitting these forms, practices and their theory and aesthetics to future generations, were called *ustāds*.

Finally, this select repertoire was performed for discrete same-sex groups of élite friends in intimate (or semi-intimate) gatherings dedicated to the connoisseurship of the arts of pleasure called the *majlis* or *mehfil* ('assembly'); this book largely deals with men's assemblies.[45] *Mehfil* is the pervasive term today for the modern private gathering of musicians and expert listeners that is directly descended in form and etiquette from the late Mughal *majlis*. But like their Ottoman and Safavid counterparts, Mughal writers most often used *majlis* (pl. *majālis*) for this highly scripted élite socio-cultural institution practised throughout the Persianate world,[46] whose specific Mughal boundaries, values, transgressions and delights were so widely recorded in painting, poetry and the biographical writings called *tazkira*s we will spend time with in Chapters 2 and 3.[47] As we shall see, what took place in the late Mughal *majlis*, and what we can make of it from the faded, fragmented testimony of its long-dead participants, is key to answering the questions I posed in my opening paragraph.[48]

Writing on Music in the Late Mughal World

Eagle-eyed aficionados of Hindustani music will already have noted key absences in my outline of the field above. This is because several crucial developments in Hindustani music towards its modern state happened during the time frame of this book – the arrival of the now-ubiquitous *tabla* and *sitār* in the 1730–40s and the *sarod* a century later;[49] the rise of *ṭappa*

44 Katherine Butler Schofield 'The Courtesan Tale: Female Musicians and Dancers in Mughal Historical Chronicles', *Gender and History* 24.1 (2012), 150–71.

45 also *bazm, jalsa*. I have always studied male *majālis* in my work on Mughal listening cultures; but art historian Molly Emma Aitken has recently opened our eyes to just how many Mughal paintings depict female-only *majālis* (personal communication).

46 Walter G Andrews and Mehmet Kalpaklı, *The Age of Beloveds: Love and the Beloved in Early-Modern Ottoman and European Culture and Society* (Durham, NC: Duke University Press, 2005); Kathryn Babayan, *The City as Anthology: Eroticism and Urbanity in Early Modern Isfahan* (Stanford: Stanford University Press, 2021).

47 For my chief work on the Mughal *majlis* (c. 1593–1748), see Schofield, 'Musical Culture'; and Brown [Schofield], 'If Music Be'; also Kaicker, *King*, pp. 108–34.

48 Parts of this section are digested from Schofield, 'Musical Culture'.

49 James Kippen, 'Les battements du cœur de l'Inde', in Bor, Joep and Philippe Bruguiére (eds.), *Gloire des princes, louange des dieux: patrimoine musical de l'Hindoustan du xive au xxe siècle*

and *ṭhumrī* under the Nawabs of Lucknow c. 1780–1850;[50] and wholesale shifts that we know took place in the technical conceptualisation of both *rāga* and *tāla*, from aesthetic to melodic classification and from additive to divisive cycle measurement respectively (Chapters 4, 5 and 7). The period 1748–1858 was one of the most significant eras of change for Hindustani music, in which new musical concepts, genres, instruments, performers and patrons asserted themselves on a fiercely competitive pan-Indian stage. Yet despite some vital earlier work on music-technical developments, most importantly Allyn Miner's *Sitar and Sarod in 18th and 19th Centuries*,[51] what happened to Hindustani music and musicians during this pivotal transition has never been properly mapped.

This significant lacuna exists for a curious historiographical reason: a pervasive belief that the guilds of hereditary musicians now called *gharānās* ('house' like 'house of Dior') who exclusively possessed and passed on Hindustani music from the Mughal period down to the modern age were 'illiterate'.[52] Historians and music scholars have long highlighted the two-thousand-year-old tradition of writing *saṅgīta-shāstras* in Sanskrit. But for reasons that are still obscure, Sanskrit ceased to be a significant medium for new works of music theory in North India (though not elsewhere) from c. 1700 until it was revived in the late nineteenth century as the 'authoritative' language of Hindustani musicology by nationalist reformers, led by upper-class Western-educated Brahmins Vishnu Narayan Bhatkhande and Sourindro Mohun Tagore.[53] In the intervening years, so Bhatkhande asserted

(Paris: Musée de la Musique, 2003), 152–73; Allyn Miner, *Sitar and Sarod in the 18th and 19th Centuries* (Wilhelmshaven: Florian Noetzel Verlag, 1993); James Prinsep, *Benares Illustrated in A Series of Drawings* (Calcutta: Baptist Mission Press, 1831).

50 Peter Manuel, *Ṭhumrī in Historical and Stylistic Perspective* (Delhi: Motilal Banarsidass, 1989), pp. 34–5; but there is no evidence for *ṭhumrī* as a distinct song genre before the nineteenth century.

51 Miner, *Sitar*; also Madhu Trivedi, *The Making of the Awadh Culture* (New Delhi: Primus, 2010); Regula Burkhardt Qureshi, 'Other Musicologies: Exploring Issues and Confronting Practice in India', in Nicholas Cook and Mark Everist (eds.), *Rethinking Music* (Oxford: Oxford University Press, 1999), 311–35; contributions to Joep Bor, Françoise 'Nalini' Delvoye, Jane Harvey and Emmie te Nijenhuis (eds.), *Hindustani Music: Thirteenth to Twentieth Centuries* (New Delhi: Manohar, 2010); and Jon Barlow and Lakshmi Subramanian, 'Music and Society in North India: From the Mughals to the Mutiny', *Economic and Political Weekly* 42:19 (2007), 1779–87.

52 Bakhle, *Two Men*, p. 16; Dard Neuman, 'Pedagogy, Practice, and Embodied Creativity in Hindustani Music'. *Ethnomusicology* 56.3 (2012), 426–49, pp. 426–8, 447 fn. 10; Daniel M Neuman, 'Indian Music as a Cultural System', *Asian Music* 17.1 (1985), 98–113, pp. 100–4 and fn. 6; Walter Kaufmann, *The Ragas of North India* (Bloomington: Indiana University Press, 1968), p. 6.

53 Vishnu Narayan Bhatkhande, *A Comparative Study of Some of the Leading Music Systems of the 15th, 16th, 17th and 18th Centuries* (Delhi: Low Price, 1990); e.g. Sourindro Mohun Tagore, *Saṅgīta-sāra-sangraha* (Calcutta: I C Bose, 1875); also Bakhle, *Two Men*.

in his famous address to the First All India Music Conference in 1916, the hereditary *ustāds*' alleged ignorance of written theory – 'the real backbone of practice' – caused Hindustani music 'to drift away and run into disorder and confusion', and writing on music itself to cease. 'Our old Sanskrit Granthas', he averred, 'having thus become inapplicable to the current practice, we naturally have come to be thrown on the mercy of our *illiterate, ignorant, and narrow-minded* professionals'.[54]

Modern scholarship has been considerably kinder than Bhatkhande towards North India's hereditary professional musicians and particularly to non-written modes of transmitting traditional knowledge. Both South Asian and foreign musicologists have come to understand that while oral, aural and kinaesthetic systems of knowledge transmission from master to disciple may be configured differently to written systems, they demonstrate equivalent levels of discursive sophistication, cognitive complexity and long-term reliability.[55] But instead of treating what was so obviously an ideological topos with suspicion, modern scholars have overwhelmingly accepted as fact the basic thrust of Bhatkhande's assertion – that the hereditary musicians could not read or write, or if the occasional *ustād* did possess a measure of functional literacy, they did not use it in teaching, performing or musical discourse. This is despite Ashok Ranade's authoritative but overlooked evidence to the contrary, that hereditary musicians frequently used writing as an essential supplement to embodiment and memory.[56] Our widespread assumption of musicians' illiteracy (or a-literacy) in the late Mughal and colonial periods has sustained an entrenched belief that there were few, if any, writings on Hindustani music between c. 1700 and the post-1857 development of printed publications in modern Urdu, Hindi and Bengali.[57]

54 Vishnu Narayan Bhatkhande, *A Short Historical Survey of the Music of Upper India* (Baroda: Indian Musicological Society, 1985 [orig. 1916]), pp. 17, 40, in Dard Neuman, 'Pedagogy', pp. 427–8; my emphasis.

55 Daniel Neuman, 'Indian Music', pp. 100–4 and especially Daniel M Neuman, *Life of Music in North India: The Social Organization of an Artistic Tradition* (Chicago: Chicago University Press, 1990 [orig. 1980]); Ashok Da Ranade, *On Music and Musicians of Hindoostan* (New Delhi: Promilla, 1984), esp. p. 25; Dard Neuman, 'Pedagogy'.

56 Ranade, *On Music*, pp. 29–30, 38; e.g. marginalia in Basit Khan, Collection of Three Treatises: *Saṅgīt Sarāvartī [Sarāvalī], Shams al-Aswāt* and *Uṣūl al-Naghmāt al-Āsafī*, private collection of Ustad Irfan Muhammad Khan, Kolkata (1856). See also Francesca Orsini and Katherine Butler Schofield (eds.), *Tellings and Texts: Music, Literature, and Performance in North India* (Cambridge: Open Book, 2015).

57 Bakhle, *Two Men*, p. 16; Daniel Neuman, 'Indian Music', p. 100, though crucially he has since changed his position – Daniel M. Neuman, 'A Tale of Two Sensibilities: Hindustani Music and its Histories', in Jonathan McCollum and David G. Hebert (eds.), *Theory and Method in*

The long-standing consensus that the late Mughal was a 'silent' period has thus left a substantial hole in our understanding of Hindustani music's history that has been patched only partially with the oral histories, older repertoire and remembered genealogies of modern musicians.

If this book does nothing else, it demonstrates unequivocally that this consensus is not true. *Music and Musicians* showcases and evaluates a vast, rich corpus of writings on Hindustani music c. 1660–1860 that has mostly been overlooked to date. In a recent European Research Council project, we documented an enormous number of writings on Hindustani music for the late Mughal period in multiple North Indian languages, as well as visual records.[58] What is more, several of the most important and original late Mughal works turn out to have been written by the very hereditary musicians written off as 'illiterate'. Most of these writings on music have languished in the archive unnoticed, and the handful that are almost accidentally known to posterity have been misunderstood and very underutilised.[59]

This book explores the contents of these writings in depth to track how and why the field of Hindustani music changed over time. But in focussing on a different genre of writing on music in each chapter, I also foreground *how* to read such writings in the context of broader generic considerations and of wider historical events. For alongside fresh music-technical treatises in the canonical mould, several new genres of writing on Hindustani music arose during the period 1748–1858 whose advent in the field, not merely their content, demands explanation. Among élite Indian audiences, and those Europeans who for a time aspired to be like them,[60] this proliferation of Indian-language genres included *tazkira*s and genealogies, song collections, innovative musical notations, *rāgamālā* paintings and poetry, copies of old and the creation of new musical treatises, bureaucratic records and ethnographic writings and paintings.

Many of these late Mughal writings coincided in close proximity with colonial cultural interest and/or territorial encroachment. To help us understand late Mughal authors' varied and often surprising relationships

Historical Ethnomusicology (Lanham: Lexington, 2014), 279–308. For Hindi and Urdu print, see Miner, *Sitar*; for Bengali and Urdu, see Williams, 'Hindustani Music'.

58 Katherine Butler Schofield and David Lunn, 'The SHAMSA Database 1.0: Sources for the History and Analysis of Music/Dance in South Asia', Zenodo (2018), https://doi.org/10.5281/zenodo.1445775.

59 e.g. the *Usūl al-Naghmāt al-Āsafī* (c. 1790–3); see Chapters 7 and 8.

60 William Dalrymple, *White Mughals: Love and Betrayal in Eighteenth-Century India* (London: Bloomsbury, 2003).

with colonial presence without downplaying North Indian writers' considerable agency, I make gentle use throughout this book of a novel theoretical concept: the 'paracolonial'. This concept was first articulated by Stephanie Newell in her work on West African literary communities, and denotes 'alongside' and 'beyond' the colonial.[61] Paracoloniality has become increasingly key to our understanding of South and Southeast Asian written, visual and auditory sources during the time frame conventionally marked off as the 'colonial period'.[62] In relation to the performing arts, we have theorised the paracolonial to refer to systems of musical knowledge and practice – Hindustani music being a principal example – that operated alongside and beyond the British colonial state. These knowledge systems were often facilitated by colonial infrastructures and technologies, and constrained by colonial law and violence. But they were not necessarily, or indeed even often, in thrall to colonial systems of knowledge. Rather, they coexisted in many differing relations and tensions with colonial thought and action on music, 'noise' and their proper place in society.[63]

Listening to writings on music during the Mughal–British transition through the filter of the paracolonial opens up revolutionary historical soundscapes, and allows for the autonomous agency of a plurality of Indian voices within the conditions of possibility afforded to them during this time frame. But to understand these conditions, we must deal not just with the views of the Mughal and princely states, but with colonial perspectives on Hindustani music. While I prioritise Indian and mixed-race (Eurasian) voices in this book, the period c. 1770–1840 was also when leading British interest in the Indian arts was at its peak. Many European colonisers in this century collected and even commissioned Indian musical manuscripts and paintings; and their marginalia, private papers, musical transcriptions and treatises, published travels and the official records of the East India Company illuminate shadowy corners that the more brilliant lights of the Indian materials don't always reach. When these rich and diverse Indian and European writings are read in context and, crucially, in conversation with each other, this extraordinary

[61] Stephanie Newell, '"Paracolonial" Networks: Some Speculations on Local Readerships in Colonial West Africa', *Interventions* 3 (2001), 336–54.

[62] Katherine Butler Schofield, 'Musical Transitions to European Colonialism in the Eastern Indian Ocean: Final Summary Report', Project ID 263643; Principal Investigator Katherine Butler Schofield, European Research Council (2016) https://cordis.europa.eu/project/id/263643.

[63] David Lunn and Julia Byl, '"One Story Ends and Another Begins": Reading the *Syair Tabut* of Encik Ali', *Indonesia and the Malay World* 47.133 (2017), 391–420, pp. 416–17.

written and visual archive dramatically changes what is possible to write about the history of music, musicians and their audiences in late Mughal and early colonial India.

Chasing Eurydice

But this book is not just concerned with the content and historical emergence – the 'what' and 'how' – of these writings on Hindustani music. My deeper interest lies in the *act* of writing on music in late Mughal India. *Music and Musicians* seeks to answer the question *why* all these Indian, mixed-race and English intellectuals and musicians chose to write about Hindustani music so copiously in this particular century, when all of them believed – as Sher ^{c}Ali Khan Lodi put it so eloquently in 1691 – that the task was impossible. Before the advent of the sound recording, once music stops sounding all we are left with is what Persian writers called the scratchings of a 'broken pen', a common idiom expressing authorial inadequacy,[64] but one that I will take seriously in this book. What were writers on music in the late Mughal and early colonial world trying so desperately to hold onto? Why? And what can we learn from their attempts?

The underlying quest of this book takes its inspiration from the figure of Orpheus inlaid in *pietra dura* in solitary splendour above the throne in Shahjahanabad's Exalted Fortress (Qil^{c}a-i Mu^{c}alla) at the heart of the Mughal imperial city of Delhi (Figure 1.1) – a figure with whom the Mughal emperor personally identified as a sonic symbol of his divinely ordained power (Chapter 2). My fundamental philosophical question is this: if writers are akin to Orpheus, and if Eurydice is the music of late Mughal Hindustan in all its fullness – all its sensory, emotional, intellectual, ethical, social and political manifestations – is it ever possible for Orpheus to bring Eurydice back from the dead? To what extent, in other words, were writers on Hindustani music at the time able to pin music's experiences and meanings down on the page; and to what extent, centuries later, can we use what they wrote to understand what Mughal listeners heard and felt then, when we can no longer hear a single note of the music they were so desperately trying to capture on paper with broken pens?

The ultimate answer is no. For music is fundamentally an impossible object of historical enquiry. Music is only ever fully realised in the living

[64] Rajeev Kinra, *Writing Self, Writing Empire: Chandar Bhan Brahman and the Cultural World of the Indo-Persian State Secretary* (Oakland: University of California Press, 2015), pp. 174, 184.

Figure 1.1 Painting of the *pietra dura* inlay of the figure of Orpheus behind the throne in the Hall of Public Audience, Shahjahanabad. Delhi, 1845. 292D-1871. © **Victoria and Albert Museum, London**

moments of our experience of it; once its sounds have died away, those moments cannot be recaptured. In theory, the music-technical treatises I deal with in this book, especially those written by the hereditary Mughal *ustāds* who sang Hindustani music into being, should give us privileged access to its sounds. And indeed, as always, the devil does lie in the detail; there are whole worlds in these manuscripts that I am unable to explore here. But in my decades' experience of working with Mughal treatises, when it comes to the essence of what they truly believed music to be – 'the arousal of tender sympathy in the heart'[65] – Mughal music-technical writing can be as dry and unyielding as old bones.[66]

More than a thousand years ago, the Sufi Brethren of Purity knew that the matter of music did not lie in such things, in any case, but in the souls of

[65] Faqirullah, *Rāg Darpan*, p. 152.

[66] Katherine Butler Schofield, 'Emotions in Indian Music History: Anxiety in Late Mughal Hindustan', *South Asian History and Culture* 12.2–3 (2021), 182–205, pp. 184, 190–3.

those who listen to it. The performers and listeners whose souls once delighted in the refined emotions and sensory experiences of the late Mughal *majlis*, too, have long turned to clay. And yet, we still have their writings. Theirs are the very same voices that echo back to us through the pages of our extraordinary primary sources. And they did not just write technically; they wrote other things, in other places, other voices and other genres that enable us to breathe back into those skeletal remains some vestige of the spirit that once enlivened them. This is why I have chosen to focus, not so much on the 'music itself' in this book, as on the life stories of musicians and those who loved them. Because it is the collective experiences of all those human souls, living through an era of terrible disquiet, that are the true substance of Hindustani music in late Mughal India.

Writing on music can never bring Eurydice back. But *Music and Musicians* shows that it is the journey into the underworld of the written archive itself, where her many echoes still resound, that tells us more about those lived musical worlds than we ever imagined. Music in late Mughal India existed to move the emotions of men and women in collective experiences; music was a whirl of sound and emotional response and search for meaning. In the writings of long-dead musicians and their élite patrons, we hold in our hands the earwitness testimonies of historical listeners. Although we have lost the sounds of late Mughal India, their writings – their own histories of the ephemeral – not only give us qualified access to what music meant and felt like then to all those who loved it, but may also enable us to sense those things too.

2 | The Mughal Orpheus: Remembering Khushhal Khan Gunasamudra in Eighteenth-Century Delhi

Canonical Knowledge and Seventeenth-Century Music Treatises

Only he who does not place a foot outside of the carpet
Will earn the royal mandate of high distinction.

Verse attributed to Niᶜmat Khan Sadarang (d. 1746/7)[1]

The Tribulations of Mughal Delhi, 1739–61: Outer Frame

It was the fifth year of Ahmad Shah's reign (1752–53). Half a decade had passed since the last Mughal emperor to hold any real power, Muhammad Shah Rangile (r. 1719–48), had died. Sitting at home in Panipat, north of Delhi, ᶜInayat Khan Rasikh had just finished putting the final touches to his latest literary work: a set of musical biographies.[2] It was something entirely new in Hindustan. Given the enthusiastic reception of the first-ever biographies of Urdu poets that had just stormed through the Delhi salons,[3] he hoped it would prove popular. For times were uncertain in the Mughal capital. The urbane residents of this cosmopolitan city had shrugged off the 1739 invasion of the Persian Emperor Nadir Shah with sangfroid, his

1 ᶜInayat Khan Rasikh, *Risāla-i Zikr-i Mughanniyān-i Hindūstān*, ed. Syed Ali Haider (Patna: Arabic and Persian Research Institute, 1961 [orig. 1752/3]), p. 19. Rasikh wrote this work in the fifth year of Ahmad Shah's reign (4 May 1752–3 May 1753); D N Marshall, *Mughals in India: A Bibliographical Survey of Manuscripts* (London: Mansell, 1967), p. 205.

2 Rasikh, *Risāla*; Shakir Khan, *Tārīkh-i Shākir Khānī*, British Library, Add. 6568, f. 99v; Nawwab Samsam-ud-Daula Shah Nawaz Khan and ʻAbdul Hayy, *Maāthir-ul-Umara*, ed. and tr. H Beveridge, rev. ed. Baini Prashad, vol. i (Patna: Janaki Prakashan, 1971), p. 840; JCC Sutherland, *Reports of Cases Determined in the Court of Sudder Dewanny Adawlut*, vol. v (Calcutta: Sreenauth Banerjee, 1871), pp. 146–8.

3 The first four *tazkiras* of Urdu poets appeared in 1751/2 by Mir and ᶜAli Hussaini in Delhi, and in the Deccan 1752/3 by Azad Bilgrami and c. 1752 by Khwaja Khan Hamid Aurangabadi; Shamsur Rahman Faruqi, ʻA Long History of Urdu Literary Culture, Part Iʼ, 805–63, p. 845 and Frances W. Pritchett, ʻA Long History of Urdu Literary Culture, Part IIʼ, 864–911, pp. 865–6, both in Sheldon Pollock (ed.), *Literary Cultures in History: Reconstructions from South Asia* (Berkeley: University of California Press, 2003); also A. Sprenger, *A Catalogue of the Arabic, Persian and Hindustany Manuscripts of the Libraries of the King of Oudh* (Calcutta: Baptist Mission Press, 1854), pp. 175–8.

attempted massacre of Delhi's population notwithstanding.[4] The 1730s and 40s burst with new life on the cultural front, with waves of innovation in Urdu poetry, musical composition and painting enrapturing audiences on a daily basis in Delhi's select assemblies (*majlis*, pl. *majālis*). This was the age of the poets Mir Taqi Mir and Mirza Muhammad Rafi^{c} Sauda^{c}; of musicians Ni^{c}mat Khan Sadarang and Firoz Khan Adarang; of courtesan Nur Bai and of Taqi *bhagat*; of painters Kalyan Das and Mir Kalan Khan – a golden age looked back upon with bittersweet delight half a century later as the last embers of precolonial power sputtered and died.[5]

But Nadir Shah's brief incursion had exposed the threadbare nature of the Mughal emperor's new clothes for all to see. By the 1730s the resurgent Marathas had already diverted the rivers of revenue from central India that had once poured into Mughal coffers. Nadir Shah may have torn away the best of the Mughal treasures, but it was his stripping of Muhammad Shah's dignity that triggered the Mughals' own provincial viceroys in Hyderabad, Awadh and Bengal likewise to look to their own interests – from 1739 they no longer remitted taxes back to the centre.[6] The denizens of Delhi kept calm and largely carried on, at least until Muhammad Shah's death. But it wasn't long before the effects of this disappearing revenue made themselves felt keenly in the pockets, indeed the very bones, of Delhi's cultivated élites.

Rasikh was born in 1701/2[7] and came from a wealthy local family with a tradition of service to the Mughal throne: his father and he and his five brothers were all trusted favourites during Muhammad Shah's reign. His father, Shams-ud-daula Lutfullah Khan Sadiq, was director of the royal household and the city of Shahjahanabad, and Rasikh himself was paymaster of the trainees in the Mughal army.[8] Mughal favour continued for the family

4 William Dalrymple and Anita Anand, *Koh-i-noor: The History of the World's Most Infamous Diamond* (London: Bloomsbury, 2017), pp. 63–92; Kaicker, *King*, pp. 18–53; and Abhishek Kaicker, 'Unquiet City: Making and Unmaking Politics in Mughal Delhi, 1707–39', Unpublished PhD Dissertation, Columbia University (2014), pp. 475–577. Kaicker argues Delhi's citizens were far more resilient to Nadir Shah than historians have previously given credit; see Chapter 3.

5 Dargah Quli Khan, *Muraqqa^{c}-i Dehlī*, ed. Khaliq Anjum (New Delhi: Anjuman-i Taraqqī-i Urdu, 1993); also Nathan Lee Marsh Tabor, 'A Market for Speech: Poetry Recitation in Late Mughal India, 1690–1710', Unpublished PhD Dissertation, University of Texas, Austin (2014); Dudney, *India*; Miner, *Sitar*; William Dalrymple and Yuthika Sharma, *Princes and Painters in Mughal Delhi, 1707–1857* (New Haven: Yale University Press and Asia Society Museum, 2012); Terence McInerney, 'Chitarman II (Kalyan Das)' and 'Mir Kalan Khan', in Milo C. Beach, Eberhard Fischer and B N Goswamy (eds.), *Masters of Indian Painting, vol. II, 1650–1900* (New Delhi: Niyogi, 2016), pp. 547–62, 607–22.

6 Bayly, *Rulers*, pp. 77–84.

7 1114 AH; Herman Ethé and Edward Edwards, *Catalogue of Persian Manuscripts in the Library of the India Office*, vol. ii (Oxford: Clarendon Press, 1937), pp. 763–4.

8 Shakir Khan, *Tārīkh*, ff. 12v–14v, 57r–58r; Shahnawaz Khan, *Maāthir*, p. 840; Kaicker, 'Unquiet City', 483–502.

after 1748 under the new emperor, Ahmad Shah (r. 1748–54). But favours come at a price, and Ahmad Shah soon began calling them in to prop up his cratering finances. Rasikh's brother, the historian Shakir Khan, wrote that under the pressure of threats and vain promises from the emperor:

> All of us brothers and our sisters too, gathered together whatever remained to us after the plunder of Nadir Shah, sold most of our properties [in Delhi, Panipat and Patna], called in promissory bills ... borrowed what we could and altogether gathered a total sum of one *lākh* thirty thousand (130,000) rupees, which we paid into the royal treasury.[9]

They were never repaid, as things went from bad to worse.[10] 1752–3 saw a weak Ahmad Shah, under the control of his mother, the ex-courtesan Udham Bai and the chief eunuch Javed Khan, expel his capable prime minister, the Nawab of Awadh Safdar Jang (d. 1754),[11] and replace him with the violent, duplicitous Ghazi-ud-din Firoz Jang III ᶜImad-ul-mulk. Less than two years later ᶜImad-ul-mulk blinded and imprisoned Ahmad Shah, then formed an alliance with the Marathas and in 1759 murdered the elderly puppet ᶜAlamgir II (r. 1754–59) he had set up in Ahmad Shah's place; all the while laying Delhi wide open to the predations of the Afghan ruler Ahmad Shah Abdali Durrani.[12] These years saw Rasikh and his brothers personally rescue Emperor Ahmad Shah's women and children as he abandoned them trying to flee; cower within earshot in 1759 as future Emperor Shah ᶜAlam II (r. 1759–1806) fought his way out of the *havelī* (mansion) that once belonged to ᶜAli Mardan Khan,[13] miraculously escaping from Delhi as ᶜImad-ul-mulk hunted him down; watch helplessly as the Marathas commandeered and camped all over their family's beautiful orchards, fields and gardens before the 1761 battle of Panipat; and lose everything but the clothes they stood up in after the battle, as Abdali's victorious army swarmed through their lands like locusts.[14]

Yet, in 1752–3, ᶜInayat Khan Rasikh sat down amidst the shady orchards and fruitful gardens of his family estate and put the finishing touches to his

[9] Shakir Khan ff. 98v–99r, tr. Bruce Wannell. I am grateful to Bruce and to William Dalrymple for sharing this resource.

[10] ibid, f. 101r–104v.

[11] The catalyst was Safdar Jang's premeditated assassination of Javed Khan in September 1752.

[12] James Burgess, *The Chronology of Modern India* (Edinburgh: John Grant, 1913), pp. 197–216; on Abdali see Dalrymple and Anand, *Koh-i-noor*; and Richard David Williams, 'Krishna's Neglected Responsibilities: Religious Devotion and Social Critique in Eighteenth-Century North India', *Modern Asian Studies* 50:5 (2016), 1403–40.

[13] Now known as Dara Shukoh's Library.

[14] Shakir Khan ff. 70v–71r, 81v–2v, 87v–88r, 101r–02v, tr. Bruce Wannell.

latest literary work: the *Risāla-i Zikr-i Mug͟hanniyān-i Hindūstān-i Bihisht-nishīn* – the first ever *tazkira* (roughly, biographical collection)[15] of the lives of the 'late, blessed musicians of Hindustan'.

Why did he choose to write, in this moment, something genuinely new to Hindustani musical culture: the first stand-alone *tazkira* of revered Hindustani musicians of the past? He clearly captured something key to the mood of his times, because his *Risāla* was almost immediately circulated and much copied and emulated[16] (see Chapter 3). There are certain key things to note about Rasikh's *tazkira* as a whole. The first is that it came hard on the heels of the first *tazkira*s entirely dedicated to Urdu (*rek͟hta*) poets, no fewer than four of which appeared in c. 1752, two of them in Delhi. They included the *Nikāt al-Shuᶜarā* (*Sayings of Poets*) by one of the greatest Urdu poets, Mir Taqi Mir, who claimed that his work was 'the first book of its kind: a *tazkira* of Urdu poets compiled on the model of existing books on Persian poets'.[17] It is inconceivable, given Rasikh's interests and eminence in Delhi's courtly and literary circles, that he did not know these new poetical *tazkira*s. Indeed, he appears to address them; he wrote his *Risāla* to remedy what he saw as a similar lack for music: 'that while the lives of the poets and of masters in many other arts and sciences are recorded in the history books, those of the ancient singers of India,[18] unlike their counterparts in other countries, are not memorialised' in written histories.[19] It seems very likely that Rasikh's 'history books' on the 'lives of the poets' refer to the brand new *tazkira*s. Rasikh's *Risāla* was thus a novel twist on a current fashion for life-history writing that was both competitive, reflecting flourishing levels of activity in the high-vernacular arts of Urdu poetry and Hindustani music in the middle decades of the eighteenth century, and canonising in its intent (see Chapter 3).

For the second thing of note is that the musicians he memorialised had all passed away before the end of Muhammad Shah's reign in 1748; this is signified in his title by the compound *Bihisht-nishīn*, 'seated in paradise', which I have translated as 'late, blessed'. The last entry in Rasikh's *tazkira* is

[15] Kia, *Persianate Selves*, pp. 15–24; also Schofield, 'Emotions', and Chapter 3.

[16] e.g. Delhi Persian 1501, British Library (late 18C).

[17] Mir Taqi Mir, *Zikr-i Mir: The Autobiography of the Eighteenth-Century Mughal Poet Mir Muhammad Taqi Mir*, tr. CM Naim (New Delhi: Oxford University Press, 1999), pp. 6–8; also Dudney, *India*; Tabor, 'Market'; and fn. 3 above. Two more important *tazkira*s of Persian poets had also just been written: the 1750/1 *Majmaᶜ al-Nafā'is* by Sirajuddin ᶜAli Khan Arzu and Muhammad ᶜAli Hazin's 1751/2 *Tazkirāt al-Mu'āsirīn*. See Kia, *Persianate Selves*.

[18] *sarāyān-i qadīm-i Hind* [19] Rasikh, *Risāla*, p. 5.

the greatest musician of the eighteenth century, the hereditary *bīn*-player and revolutionary *dhrupad* and *khayāl* song composer Ni^c^mat Khan *kalāwant* Sadarang, who had come to manhood in the service of Emperor Aurangzeb's favoured son, prince Muhammad A^c^zam Shah (d. 1707), and died in 1746/7.[20] Rasikh's focus on the glorious dead does not reflect a scenario in which all remaining musicians had fled from Nadir Shah, as has often been assumed.[21] As we shall see in Chapter 3, most court musicians remained active in Delhi well into the 1750s. Take, for example, the joint chief musicians of Muhammad Shah's atelier, Anjha Baras Khan and Firoz Khan Adarang. We know that Anjha Baras, the grandson of Khushhal Khan Gunasamudra, sang at the third anniversary of Ahmad Shah's enthronement in May 1751; and that Adarang, Sadarang's nephew, composed a *dhrupad* song for ^c^Alamgir II (r. 1754–59) that is preserved in the collection of the second Khushhal Khan Anup[22] (Chapters 3 and 5). Instead, Rasikh's fantasy assembly of musicians, with occasional legendary forerunners from medieval times, are all those who flourished or came to maturity during the era of the so-called 'great' Mughal Emperors Akbar (r. 1556–1605), Jahangir (r. 1605–27), Shah Jahan (r. 1628–58, d. 1666) and Aurangzeb (r. 1658–1707), with a particular focus on the last two reigns.

Critically, the latest of these musicians belonged to the generation before Rasikh – those who were already men when Aurangzeb died. This canonising instinct to gather together and memorialise key artefacts and moments from the previous period of the 'great' Mughals permeates Rasikh's other literary works as well – a selection of the most exquisitely written letters of the emperors from Humayun to Aurangzeb and a set of their horoscopes.[23] His *Risāla* is similarly a monument to what he, a member of a generation who had been too young to know it, considered the golden age of the Mughal empire and of Hindustani music.

We thus come to the final curiosity of note. The reason why Rasikh wrote this work, at this moment, lies I suggest in the subject of Rasikh's longest entry.[24] It is not, as we might expect, the life of a legendary figure like Amir Khusrau or Tansen, or even the greatest musician of his own lifetime, Sadarang. Rather, it takes us back to the mid-seventeenth century

[20] Dargah Quli Khan, *Muraqqa^c^* (1993), pp. 90–1; Rasikh, *Risāla*, pp. 30–1; Katherine Butler Brown [Schofield], 'The Origins and Early Development of Khayal', in Joep Bor, et al. (eds.), *Hindustani Music*, 159–91; Tabor, 'Market', pp. 318, 388–407.

[21] Barlow and Subramanian, 'Music', p. 1784; Miner, *Sitar*, pp. 81, 90–92.

[22] Zia-ud-din, *Hayy*, ff. 45r–46r; Khushhal Khan Anup, *Rāg-Rāginī Roz o Shab*, Salar Jung Museum Library, Urdu Mus 2 (1833–6), f. 44r.

[23] Syed Ali Haider, 'Introduction' to Rasikh, *Risāla*, pp. vi–vii; Marshall, *Mughals*, p. 205.

[24] Rasikh, *Risāla*, pp. 14–19.

and tells a single anecdote from the life of Khushhal Khan Gunasamudra, the 'Ocean of Virtue', who died sometime after 1671.[25] He is now largely forgotten, but at the time could not have been more important – he was chief musician of the Mughal imperial atelier under the emperors Shah Jahan and Aurangzeb. In this story Khushhal is given the role of musical deus ex machina in the 1657–8 War of Succession between Aurangzeb and his elder brother Dara Shukoh for the Mughal throne.

This revealing anecdote concerns the entanglement of music with political and supernatural power and needs to be understood within three contexts, presented here as frame stories around a central core. The middle frame is the political crisis of the mid-seventeenth-century War of Succession in which the story – the inner frame – was set. The core is the consolidation in exactly the same period of a canon of Mughal knowledge about Hindustani music and its powerful role at court, embodied in a series of music treatises in Persian written for Aurangzeb. Finally, I shall return to the outer frame – the perspective of the 1750s – to consider how Rasikh's tale reveals hidden anxieties concerning the uncertain future of the Empire and of its musical life.[26]

The War of Succession, 1657–8: Middle Frame

The 1657–8 War of Succession between the sons of Shah Jahan for the Mughal throne is regarded as a major turning point in Mughal history. The Mughals did not practise primogeniture; that is to say, the throne did not automatically pass to the eldest son. This inevitably led to fratricidal wars of succession, but also, during an emperor's lifetime, constant tension between royal princes and outright rebellions against the emperor. Every emperor from Akbar onwards faced armed rebellion from one or more of his sons.[27] But only one of them was successful: Aurangzeb, who defeated his brothers and usurped his father, Shah Jahan, in 1658.

Shah Jahan, builder of the Taj Mahal and the magnificent new fort and walled city of Shahjahanabad,[28] had four sons. The most powerful of these were the eldest, Dara Shukoh, and the third, Aurangzeb. They were like

[25] Saqi Musta'idd Khan, *Ma'āsir-i ᶜĀlamgīrī*, tr. Jadunath Sarkar, Bibliotheca Indica Series (Calcutta: Baptist Mission Press, 1947), p. 68.

[26] See Schofield, 'Emotions'.

[27] Munis D Faruqui, *The Princes of the Mughal Empire, 1504–1719* (Cambridge: Cambridge University Press, 2012), especially Chapter 6 'Wars of Succession' and pp. 162–78; also John F Richards, *The Mughal Empire* (Cambridge: Cambridge University Press, 1993), pp. 151–64.

[28] The Taj Mahal in Agra was built 1632–53; Shahjahanabad was completed in 1648.

night and day. Dara was intellectually curious, artistic and religiously ecumenical – he had the Hindu scriptures the *Upaniṣads* translated into Persian. Aurangzeb was efficient, strategic, legalistic and pious – he stitched his own prayer caps and copied out the Qur'an. Unfortunately, Shah Jahan played favourites. While he kept Aurangzeb as far away as possible, administering the southernmost Mughal provinces of the Deccan and fighting Shah Jahan's wars for him, the emperor kept Dara at court in luxury and favoured him as successor.[29] This was not good for Dara. As Munis Faruqui has shown in his work on the Mughal princes, the lack of a predetermined succession meant that princely cultivation of friendships and alliances outside the royal household and the building of powerful courtly and military factions were crucial to princely success; he who commanded the greatest loyalty and the largest faction would likely become emperor.[30] Dara didn't think he needed a faction because he had his father's blessing; the disfavoured Aurangzeb was practised at building up and sustaining alliances. Dara didn't exercise his military accomplishments much; Aurangzeb repeatedly proved himself able at the vital skills of both sword and pen.[31] As a result, when the inevitable war of succession broke out, Aurangzeb was far better placed to succeed than Dara.[32]

When Shah Jahan fell grievously ill in 1657, Dara seized the opportunity to take over the reins of imperial administration. Aurangzeb and his two other brothers rose up to oppose what they saw as a power grab and a year-long war of succession ensued. In 1658, Aurangzeb emerged victorious, executed his brothers (they would have done the same to him),[33] imprisoned his father in Agra fort until his death in 1666 and ascended the throne as the Emperor ^{c}Alamgir, the 'world-seizer'.

And thus, so historians have often told us, the first seeds of Mughal decline were sown.[34]

29 Faruqui, *Princes*, pp. 162–78; also Audrey Truschke, *Aurangzeb: the Life and Legacy of India's Most Controversial King* (Stanford: Stanford University Press, 2017), pp. 19–24, 34, 66; and Supriya Gandhi, *The Emperor Who Never Was: Dara Shukoh in Mughal India* (Cambridge, MA: Harvard University Press, 2020).

30 Faruqui, *Princes*, pp. 135–80 especially pp. 162–78.

31 ibid, pp. 175–77 and 78–80, 152; also Kinra, *Writing Self*, pp. 68–9, 111–14.

32 Faruqui, *Princes*, p. 163. Rajeev Kinra notes that 'there was a significant, and important, constituency of Hindu and Muslim alike that disliked [Dara] for entirely non-sectarian reasons . . . that Dārā's narcissistic arrogance made him unfit for the throne'; Rajeev Kinra, 'Infantilizing Bābā Dārā: The Cultural Memory of Dārā Shekuh and the Mughal Public Sphere', *Journal of Persianate Studies* 2 (2009), 165–93, 168.

33 Dara and Murad; Shah Shuja^{c} was killed by the King of Arakan in 1661; Christopher Buyers, *The Royal Ark*: 'India: The Timurid Dynasty', www.royalark.net/India4/delhi6.htm.

34 e.g. Richards, *Mughal Empire*, p. 173.

The war between Dara and Aurangzeb has traditionally been seen as a struggle for the soul of the Mughal empire – between a liberal vision of the empire as open and tolerant of all religions and cultures, and a narrow vision of it as an Islamic military enterprise that doomed it to failure. Aurangzeb's piety led him to attempt to rule his extremely diverse and majority Hindu polity along more strictly Islamic lines from 1668, the year he turned fifty, including restrictions on a wide range of activities not considered 'positively approved' (*halāl*) under Islamic law.[35] The story that encapsulates better than any other the distress of more ecumenical Indian groups faced with this narrower regime is the so-called 'burial of music'. One of the things Aurangzeb renounced personally in 1668 was listening to music. A famous legend has it that his court musicians staged a public protest in the form of a funeral procession, carrying coffins through the streets of Delhi to the foot of Aurangzeb's palace shouting '*Rāga* is dead!' to which he famously responded: 'Then bury her so deep under the earth that no sound of her voice will ever be heard again.'[36]

Historically, it was Khushhal Khan *kalāwant* Gunasamudra, Aurangzeb's chief musician in 1668, who received the emperor's order that he, his brother Bisram Khan and the other court musicians 'might [still] come to the Court, but must not make music'.[37] If such a procession had happened, it would have been Khushhal who led it.[38]

But this is *not* the story Rasikh chose to tell about Khushhal – in fact, the burial story does not appear in any Indian writings on music until the 1845 *Naghma-i ᶜAndalīb* (*Melody of the Nightingale*), whose author was heavily influenced by colonial historiography.[39] Nor does the picture I have just presented resemble how the War of Succession or Aurangzeb's reign were seen by many at the time, or in the century that followed – as the story Rasikh *does* tell about Khushhal reveals.

35 The range of these is disputed; Truschke, *Aurangzeb*, pp. 70–9. Aurangzeb is on record pronouncing that music is *mubāh*, 'permissible'; Katherine Butler Brown [Schofield], 'Did Aurangzeb Ban Music? Questions for the Historiography of his Reign', *Modern Asian Studies* 41.1 (2007), 77–120, p. 101; Lois Ibsen al-Faruqi, 'Music, Musicians and Muslim Law', *Asian Music* 17.1 (1985), 3–36.

36 Brown [Schofield], 'Aurangzeb'. 37 Saqi Musta'idd Khan, *Ma'āsir*, p. 45.

38 There is no evidence that the burial of music story is anything other than a rumour circulated by Aurangzeb's enemies; see Brown [Schofield], 'Aurangzeb'. Aurangzeb was in fact a music lover and his renunciation was purely personal. At least some musicians of the imperial atelier remained on the payroll and the royal princes and *mansabdārs* took up the mantle of principal patrons; see Box 2.1.

39 Muhammad Riza Najm Tabataba'i, *Naghma-i ᶜAndalīb*, British Library, Or. 1811 (1845), ff. 210r–v. Najm was in extensive contact with British officials throughout his career, including historian Henry M. Elliott to whom Najm dedicated a copy of the *Naghma*; Charles Rieu, *Catalogue of the Persian Manuscripts in the British Museum*, vol. iii (London: British Museum, 1883), pp. 914–5, 978.

Shah Jahan's Chief Musicians

Khushhal Khan Gunasamudra (fl. 1630–75) was the head of the Mughal imperial atelier during the last part of Shah Jahan's and the first part of Aurangzeb's reign. We know quite a lot about him from sources of his own time – from Mughal historical chronicles, but also from two canonical works on music: the *Sahasras* or '1000 *dhrupad* songs of Nayak Bakhshu' compiled for Shah Jahan (1637–46); and the *Shams al-Aswāt* (*Sun of Songs*), written for Aurangzeb in 1697/8 by Khushhal's son Ras Baras Khan. In addition to this, the author of the greatest Mughal Persian treatise on Hindustani music of the seventeenth century Mirza Raushan Zamir was Khushhal's singing student.[40]

Khushhal was a *kalāwant*, the term for élite court musicians who specialised in singing *dhrupad* songs and playing the stringed instruments *bīn* and *rabāb* (Chapter 3). *Kalāwant* simply means 'artist'; but by the mid-seventeenth century the *kalāwants* of the Mughal court were organised into household guilds built on interrelated lineages of hereditary professional musicians.[41] The most prestigious *kalāwant* lineage was the senior branch of the greatest Mughal musician that ever lived, Akbar's chief musician Tansen (d. 1589). Khushhal Khan was Tansen's great-grandson in that branch and in turn inherited the position of chief musician that had belonged to his illustrious father Laʿl Khan. As a boy, Laʿl had been taken to sing for Tansen, who discerned such potential in him that he presented him to his own son Bilas Khan to train and set Laʿl even further along the path to greatness by marrying him to Bilas' daughter. Laʿl was renowned for his absolute mastery of Tansen's song compositions and musical style and was esteemed even by his rivals as unequalled. When Bilas died, Shah Jahan confirmed Laʿl in his position as chief musician and inheritor of Tansen's place at court and gave him a new Sanskrit title, Gunasamudra, the 'Ocean of Virtue'.

Bilas' daughter and Laʿl had four sons together, Khushhal and his three brothers, and they all learned the traditions of Tansen's lineage at their father's knee. From an early age, the boys sang at the court of Shah Jahan with their father and other leading musicians of the era, like the poet-singers Jagannath

[40] Lahawri, *Badshah Namah*; Nayak Bakhshu, *Sahasras*, or *Hāzār Dhurpad-i Nāyak Bakhshū*, comp. Islam Khan, British Library, I O Islamic 1116; Islam Khan, '*Dībācha-i Dhurpad-hā-i Nāyak*', in Iqtidar Hussain Siddiqi (ed.), *Majmūʿ al-Afkār* (Patna: Khuda Bakhsh Oriental Public Library, 1993); Ras Baras Khan, *Shams*; Mirza Raushan Zamir *Tarjuma-i Kitāb-i Pārījātak*, British Library, Egerton 793 (before 1666/7); Ziauddin, *Hayy*, ff. 9r, 57v.

[41] Lahawri, *Badshah Namah*, vol. ii, pp. 5–7; Faqirullah, *Rāg Darpan*, pp. 192 and passim; Mirza Khan ibn Fakhr-ud-din, *Tuhfat al-Hind*, ed. NH Ansari, vol. i (Tehran: Bunyād-i Farhang-i Īrān, 1968), pp. 356–61; Daniel Neuman, *Life*, p. 91.

Kabirai and Rang Khan, accompanied by the best *kalāwant bīn* and *rabāb* players like Saras Bin and Sughar Sen (Figure 2.1).[42] Khushhal and his brother Bisram would stand one on each side of their father on the carpet beneath Shah Jahan's throne and play the drone *tambūr*[43] to support La^{c}l while he sang the lengthy unaccompanied *ālāp* introduction. Then Khushhal and Bisram would join him to sing the *dhrupad* composition, their youthful voices increasing the strength and power of their father's. But as La^{c}l grew old and gradually gave over to his sons the honour of singing the *ālāp*, it became clear that of all his brothers, it was Khushhal who was the 'true singer'. In a gloriously ornamented voice arising from the clearest of throats, he articulated the most obscure melodic rules of the *rāgas*, systematically exploring all the intricate ways of ascending and descending in a virtuosic display of rigorous organisation that combined taste with grace.[44] It was to Khushhal that his father entrusted the full secrets of Tansen's style, repertoire and esoteric lore.

By the time he reached maturity, Khushhal had become the skilful master of his age, being especially noted for his rendition of the moderate-tempo *dhrupad* compositions of his ancestor Tansen. But Khushhal also embraced the intellectual and literary aspects of the musical arts – theoretical learning and the art of composing songs, even training notable music theorists like Zamir in the practical art of music making. Khushhal's own compositions were considered remarkable for their mastery of the full range of styles and tempos and became renowned in later centuries for their technical precision, subtlety of ideas and correctness of style. He wrote songs in the praise of Shah Jahan that delighted the emperor so much that yearly Khushhal was weighed against rupees and showered with them publicly in the audience hall. When La^{c}l died in 1654, it was only natural that his most accomplished son should take on the mantle of chief musician and Shah Jahan duly bestowed upon Khushhal his father's title, Gunasamudra, and gave to him Tansen's hereditary standing place in the royal court.[45]

[42] Faqirullah, *Rāg Darpan*, pp. 194–95, 198–99, 206–07.

[43] The Persian *tambūr* was used in two ways: as a drone instrument held upright and played with one hand, and as a melody instrument held across the body and played with both hands. The drone *tambūr* developed into the *tambūra* in the mid to late eighteenth century, with the replacement of its carved bowl with a gourd.

[44] Mirza Khan, *Tuhfat al-Hind*, pp. 338–43; Faqirullah, *Rāg Darpan*, pp. 160–71.

[45] Information in this section is from the following sources: Lahawri, *Badshah Namah*, vol ii, pp. 5–7; Islam Khan, '*Dībācha*', pp. 18–21, Faqirullah, *Rāg Darpan*, pp. 194–9, Zia-ud-din, *Hayy*, ff. 40r-v; Rasikh, *Risāla*, p. 14; Anon, Untitled Treatise on *Tāl*, University of Edinburgh, Or. MS 585 [ff. 37v–66r] (1788), ff. 58v–60r; Khafi Khan, *Muntakhāb al-Lubāb*, ed. and tr. Anees Jahan Syed as *Aurangzeb in Muntakhab-al-lubab* (Bombay: Somaiya, 1977), p. 175; Ritwik Sanyal and Richard Widdess, *Dhrupad: Tradition and Performance in Indian Music* (Aldershot: Ashgate, 2004), pp. 50–3, 58–9.

But although in talent he was a match for his ancestors, in virtue Khushhal was not his forefathers' equal. He was a great musician; but he had fallen more than a little in love with the adulation of the court and with the riches his talents commanded – and, according to Rasikh, he gave in to the temptation to intrigue in dangerous political waters.

Rasikh's Life of Khushhal Khan Gunasamudra: Inner Frame

Here begins Rasikh's intricate story, though in my own expanded and interpretive retelling.[46]

Sometime between 1654 and 1657, Shah Jahan's commander-in-chief (*amīr al-umarā'*) ᶜAli Mardan Khan (d. 1657) was at court. ᶜAli Mardan was an Iranian nobleman who, as Safavid commander of Qandahar when Shah Jahan besieged it in 1638, made the fateful decision to go over to the Mughals, ensuring their victory. In return, Shah Jahan gave him the highest *mansab* (rank)[47] of any Indian nobleman (7000/7000), command of the army and the trust and friendship of his new sovereign.[48]

On this particular occasion, the emperor asked his friend: 'In your opinion, which I trust, which one of the royal princes will seize the kettledrum ensemble (*naubat*) of the sultanate after me?'[49] – i.e. become the next emperor. Now the commander-in-chief was a canny operator. He knew that Shah Jahan blindly favoured his elder son Dara Shukoh as the next emperor, but also that speaking out against the favourite would violate both the rules of etiquette and his duty as the emperor's servant. So instead the commander prophesied this: 'He who is closest to Murshid Quli Khan son of Ahwal Khan will be successful.' Murshid Quli Khan Khurasani had come to India with the commander-in-chief as one of his most trusted subordinates and quickly made a name for himself as a superior revenue officer.[50]

[46] This is an explanatory paraphrase, not a direct translation of Rasikh; original text *Risāla*, pp. 14–9. Information external to Rasikh's account is footnoted.

[47] A *mansab* was an official numerical rank made up of a nominal hierarchical position (*zāt*) and the number of cavalry (*suwār*) under the *mansabdār*'s control.

[48] Shah Nawaz Khan, *Maāthir*, vol. i, pp. 186–94; Richards, *Mughal Empire*, pp. 132–34, 144.

[49] The emperor possessed the exclusive right of sounding the drums of the *naubat* ensemble, the great sonic signifier of Islamicate sovereignty throughout the Indian Ocean; Bonnie C. Wade, *Imaging Sound: An Ethnomusicological Study of Music, Art and Culture in Mughal India* (Chicago: University of Chicago Press, 1998), pp. 4-12.

[50] Shah Nawaz Khan, *Maāthir*, vol. ii, pp. 304–09. Not to be confused with the later founder of the autonomous state of Bengal and its capital Murshidabad.

The emperor placed complete faith in the commander-in-chief's judgement, so he assigned this revenue officer to Dara Shukoh's entourage and instructed the prince to spend time befriending him. But according to the author of our tale, Dara was immature and pampered, and far from respecting Shah Jahan's advice he gave excessively burdensome orders to Murshid Quli and treated him with disdain.[51] Very soon, the revenue officer began to avoid Dara altogether, seeking to return to the commander-in-chief.

Meanwhile, Shah Jahan's younger son Aurangzeb, who was viceroy of the Deccan, came to visit ᶜAli Mardan. Unlike Dara, who behaved towards the commander-in-chief and others in his father's circle with arrogance and suspicion, Aurangzeb made a point of cultivating respectful friendships with the emperor's chief confidantes, and the commander was already inclined to his cause.[52] Knowing Murshid Quli's renowned talents as a revenue officer as well as a warrior, Aurangzeb decided to enlist the commander-in-chief's assistance in getting the revenue officer transferred to his command in the Deccan. Aurangzeb knew that because of the poor relations he had with his father, Shah Jahan would not release the revenue officer if he asked him personally. So he asked the commander-in-chief to do it for him. The prince's request put ᶜAli Mardan in a dilemma – if he agreed to act on Aurangzeb's behalf as common sense suggested would be best, he would be seen to be manipulating his own prophecy and thus openly defying the reigning monarch. He accepted the task, but reluctantly, and try as he might he couldn't quite seem to light upon the right moment to present the petition at court.

One day, the commander-in-chief shared his quandary with a man who just happened to be Khushhal's neighbour. During an intimate drinking party the neighbour laid the whole issue before the emperor's chief musician, who instantly perceived an opportunity to enrich himself. After the party, Khushhal went straight to the commander-in-chief and said: 'Sir, if you give me 1 *lākh* (100,000) rupees, I can easily accomplish the formal release of this revenue officer. All you need to do is present the petition [to the emperor] when I give the signal.' So the commander left arrangements in the chief musician's capable hands.

[51] Kinra notes that many of the Mughal nobility at the time 'found Dārā's superiority complex to be off-putting, boorish, immature and downright unseemly for one with pretensions to the throne'; Kinra, 'Infantilizing', p. 168.

[52] Faruqui reminds us that Dara 'had an absolutely unrivaled propensity for making enemies among the highest echelons of the Mughal nobility . . . Alarmed, Shah Jahan reminded his son . . . to "not be ill-disposed or suspicious of royal grandees . . . [and] treat them with favor and kindness"'; Faruqui, *Princes*, p. 167.

At court, it was customary that Khushhal and Bisram, according to precedent established during Tansen's time, would sing standing at a distance of 10 forearms-length[53] from each other on two corners of the carpet beneath the emperor's throne. On the appointed day, just before Nauroz (Persian New Year, which falls at the spring equinox), Khushhal and Bisram took their hereditary places in the great Hall of Public Audience of Shah Jahan's Exalted Fortress and began to clear their throats in preparation for singing. The single human figure of Orpheus enchanting the animals with his *lira di braccio*, inlaid in stone high in the wall above Shah Jahan's throne (Figure 1.1), gazed intently down upon the chief musician[54] as he embarked on a slow, rocking *ālāp* in Tansen's version of the feminine *rāga*, Ragini Todi (then in its Bilaskhani scale[55] and known as Todi Darbari). As Khushhal sang through the mood of gentle love and adoration, Todi gradually took on her personified shape (Figure 2.2), until she stood before the assembly, a delicate white woman wearing a white blouse (*angiyā*) and *sārī*, with camphor flowers and saffron on her body, standing in a wilderness alone playing the *bīn* and enchanting the gazelles by her feet who listened with sheer joy and delight to her playing, eventually succumbing to ecstatic insensibility.[56] The emperor's attention was rapt by the extreme loveliness of this music. By the time Khushhal and Bisram finished, the effect on Shah Jahan was total; the whole universe seemed to slow down around him as he listened intently with the ear of his heart. Feeling its effects, all around him the great noblemen present also became silent and still.

Now was Khushhal's moment. Imperceptibly, he gave the signal to the commander-in-chief that he should present the petition for the revenue officer's release to the emperor. As Shah Jahan was still under the musician's spell, he was in no fit state to read anything – and stamped the petition without looking at it.

[53] 10 *zar*^{c}.

[54] My small piece of poetic license here assumes the court was at Shahjahanabad for the celebration of Nauroz that year; the figure of Orpheus takes pride of place in the top centre of the wall behind the throne in the Hall of Public Audience; Ebba Koch, 'The Mughal Emperor as Solomon, Majnun and Orpheus, or the Album as a Think Tank for Allegory', *Muqarnas* 27 (2010), 277–312.

[55] Zamir, *Tarjuma-i Kitāb-i Pārījātak*, f. 61v.

[56] The apparition of Todi as an embodied presence is not in the original, though her effect of rendering the audience insensible is and her appearance was theoretically what was *supposed* to happen; this is the description of Ragini Todi in Mirza Khan, *Tuhfat*, p. 370. The ability of a singer to conjure up a *rāga* like a spirit is Hakim Muhammad Karam Imam Khan, *Ma*^{c}*dan al-Mūsīqī*, ed. Sayyid Wajid ^{c}Ali (Lucknow: Hindustani Press, 1925 [orig. after 1858]), pp. 111–6.

Figure 2.1 Portrait of Khushhal (front and left of centre) performing with his father Laᶜl Khan, Jagannath Kabirai, Sughar Sen and others at Dara Shukoh's wedding in 1633. Mughal, c. 1700, probably a copy of a mid-seventeenth-century original. RCIN1005068, f. 26v (detail). **Royal Collection Trust © Her Majesty Queen Elizabeth II 2015**

The next day, Murshid Quli duly presented himself before the emperor to receive his robe of release (*khilᶜat*). Until this point, Shah Jahan was still oblivious to what had happened during the previous day's proceedings. Taken aback, he whispered to the commander-in-chief, 'I do not recall giving permission for Murshid Quli's release!' ᶜAli Mardan directed his attention to the petition and the place where he had stamped it. Horrified, the emperor realised he had done so without reading it – but that he could not take back his decision without admitting he had been so entranced by Khushhal's music that his attention had drifted. So in order to save face, and in full knowledge of the fateful consequences, the emperor authorised the release of the revenue officer into Aurangzeb's service.

In the Deccan the revenue officer became Aurangzeb's constant companion and the prince treated him with respect and kindness until, during the War of Succession, Murshid Quli was killed securing Aurangzeb's victory over Dara at the battle of Dharmat in April 1658.[57] Thus did the commander-in-chief ᶜAli Mardan Khan's prophecy come true.

But what of Khushhal and his reward for putting Aurangzeb on his throne through the power of music? When Shah Jahan realised the chief musician's pivotal role in cheating his favourite son of his future – and that too from

[57] The battle is referred to in Rasikh, but the date of death is Shah Nawaz Khan, *Maāthir*, vol. ii, pp. 304–9.

Figure 2.2 Ragini Todi. Murshidabad, c. 1755. Catherine and Ralph Benkaim Collection, 2013.340. **The Cleveland Museum of Art.** Public Domain

purely venal motives – he removed Khushhal and Bisram from their positions as chief *kalāwants*, banning them from ever again standing and singing in the place of Tansen at the foot of his throne. But Emperor Aurangzeb, a long-standing connoisseur of Hindustani music,[58] took no time in restoring them to their hereditary place and showering special attention on Khushhal, whom Faqirullah described in 1665/6 as being matchless among the *kalāwants* of his day.[59] When Aurangzeb reached his fiftieth solar birthday in 1668, officially becoming an old man in Mughal eyes,[60] he resolutely turned his face against

[58] Bakhtawar Khan, *Mir'āt-i ᶜĀlam*, in Sir H M Elliott and John Dowson (eds.), *The History of India as Told by its Own Historians*, vol.vii (London: Trübner, 1877), p. 177.

[59] Faqirullah, *Rāg Darpan*, pp. 198–9.

[60] The Mughals considered the fiftieth solar birthday to be the threshold of old age and thus time to begin preparing for the hereafter; Mir Taqi Mir, *Remembrances*, tr. C M Naim (Cambridge, MA: Harvard University Press, 2019a), pp. 252–3.

the pleasures and diversions of his youth and instructed Khushhal, Bisram, Ras Bin and other musicians to continue attending him at court but no longer to sing in his presence. Nonetheless, for many years after this he continued to bestow considerable largesse and honours on Khushhal and the other *kalāwants* on notable court occasions, including honouring Khushhal and his nephew, Bisram's son Bhupat, on the occasion of Bisram's death in 1671.[61]

Here ends the story of Khushhal Khan Gunasamudra. The moral Rasikh drew from it was directed at those who got too big for their slippers and strayed from their rightful place in the order of things – a saying he attributed to the greatest singer of his own times, Sadarang:[62]

Only he who does not place a foot outside of the carpet
Will earn the royal mandate of high distinction.[63]

But the story's underlying message concerns Rasikh's unshakeable belief in the powers of Hindustani music to alter the fundamentals of the universe, for good or for ill. Music could make, or break, kings. In the Mughal worldview, music's supernatural powers underpinned sovereign power.[64]

To understand where this belief was coming from, we need to turn to the canonical Mughal treatises on Hindustani music written from the peak of Khushhal's career until the end of Aurangzeb's reign.

Theorising the Supernatural Powers of Music: Central Core

As I noted in Chapter 1, hundreds of works on music were written in the time of the Mughals: in Sanskrit, Brajbhasha[65] and most extensively from the seventeenth century onwards in the Persian language. Particularly key to unravelling the story of Khushhal's deployment of Ragini Todi to enchant Shah Jahan is the wave of treatises written in Persian during Aurangzeb's reign that aimed to systematise a canon of Hindustani music suitable for élite listening.[66] Critically, what I call the canonical

[61] Saqi Musta'idd Khan, *Ma'āsir*, pp. 45, 68.

[62] Ironically, given Sadarang's own period of disgrace for doing exactly this in the reign of Jahandar Shah; [Brown] Schofield, 'If Music Be'; [Brown] Schofield, 'Origins', 189–91.

[63] Rasikh, *Risāla*, p. 19.

[64] Schofield, 'Music, Art'.

[65] Richard David Williams, 'Reflecting in the Vernacular: Translation and Transmission in Seventeenth- and Eighteenth-Century North India', *Comparative Studies of South Asia, Africa and the Middle East* 39.1 (2019), 96–110; also Allison Busch, *Poetry of Kings: The Classical Hindi Literature of Mughal India* (Oxford: Oxford University Press, 2011).

[66] Schofield, 'Reviving', esp. pp. 497–8; Schofield and Lunn, 'SHAMSA Database'.

Mughal treatises include a major work by Khushhal's aristocratic disciple Zamir and another by Khushhal's son and successor, Ras Baras.[67]

Theoretical writing on Indian music in Sanskrit, known as *saṅgīta-shāstra,* flourished from the very first centuries CE.[68] The earliest known writings in Persian on Indian music date from the thirteenth and fourteenth centuries[69] and in regional languages from c. 1500.[70] These new writings drew from and often directly translated Sanskrit theoretical texts. An especially authoritative model was Sharngadeva's *Saṅgīta-ratnākara* (*Ocean of Music*) written for Yadava king Singhana of Devagiri (r. 1210–47), now Daulatabad, in the Deccan. But Persian and regional-language authors added to their Sanskrit models in interesting ways. One especially important example is Shaikh ᶜAbd-ul-karim's *Jawāhir al-Mūsīqāt-i Muhammadī* (*Jewels/Elements of Muhammad's Music*), a Persian treatise compiled c. 1630 for the Sultan of Bijapur, Muhammad ᶜAdil Shah, at the core of which lie the material remains of a c. 1570 Dakani-language translation of the *Saṅgīta-ratnākara.*[71] It is an especially important codex for several reasons, but what is critical in relation to what follows is that the c. 1570 treatise abandoned the *Saṅgīta-ratnākara*'s obsolete way of discussing the *rāga*s and replaced it with a new-fangled *rāgamālā* of potent iconic depictions of the six male *rāga*s and each of their five wives or *rāginī*s.[72]

Sanskrit intellectuals continued to write musical texts for imperial and regional patrons in the great Mughal period.[73] But in the seventeenth century a substantial new effort to recodify and systematise – to canonise or classicise – Hindustani music and its theoretical writing specifically for the

67 The *Tarjuma-i Kitāb-i Pārījātak* and the *Shams al-Aswāt.*

68 See Nijenhuis, *Musicological Literature.*

69 Amir Khusrau (1250–1325), see Madhu Trivedi, *Emergence*, pp. 20–26; *Ghunyat al-Munya* manuscript: British Library, I O Islamic 1863 (1375); edition and translation: *Ghunyat al-Munya : The Earliest Known Persian Work on Indian Music*, ed. and tr. Shahab Sarmadee (Bombay: Asia, 1978).

70 e.g. Dakani: Shaikh ᶜAbd-ul-karim, *Jawāhir al-Mūsīqāt-i Muhammadī*, British Library, Or. 12,857 (c. 1570/c. 1630); Marathi: untitled, in Mark Zebrowski, *Deccani Painting* (London: Philip Wilson for Sotheby's, 1983), pp. 60–4; Awadhi: Qutban, *Mrgāvatī*, tr. Behl, pp. 131–33; Madhyadeshi: Raja Man Singh Gwaliyari, *Mānakutūhala.*

71 Dakani (alt. Dakhni) was the variety of Hindavi used in the Deccan; Richard M Eaton, 'The Rise of Written Vernaculars: The Deccan, 1450–1650', in Francesca Orsini and Samira Sheikh (eds.), *After Timur Left: Culture and Circulation in Fifteenth-Century North India* (New Delhi: Oxford University Press, 2014), 111–29.

72 ᶜAbd-ul-karim, *Jawāhir*; Schofield, *Music, Art*; and Katherine Butler Schofield, 'Indian Music in the Persian Collections: The Javahir al-Musiqat-i Muhammadi', Parts 1 and 2, *British Library Asian and African Studies Blog*, 7th and 13th October 2014. https://blogs.bl.uk/asian-and-african/index.html

73 Bhatkhande, *Comparative Study.*

new Mughal era was undertaken in more accessible languages. The first major piece of Mughal theoretical writing in Persian on Hindustani music could not be more canonical: the chapters on music and musicians written by Akbar's great ideologue Abu'l Fazl in his monumental gazetteer of Indian arts and sciences, the c. 1593 *Ā'īn-i Akbarī* (*Institutes of Akbar*).[74] But for the next half century or so, this Persian work was an outlier. What has recently emerged is that high-level Mughal ventures to recodify Hindustani music moved first into Brajbhasha under the emperors Jahangir and Shah Jahan.[75] Two texts were especially important and continued to circulate well into the nineteenth century. The first is the careful curation for Shah Jahan of 1000 authenticated *dhrupad* songs by the sixteenth-century master Nayak Bakhshu (fl. c. 1500–40), the *Sahasras* (*Thousand Sentiments*) (1637–46). Islam Khan's preface is in Persian, but the songs themselves are in courtly Brajbhasha.[76] The second is Harivallabha's c. 1653 translation into classical Hindi verse of a major Sanskrit music treatise of the early seventeenth century, Damodara's *Saṅgīta-darpaṇa* (*Mirror of Music*). Harivallabha's verses personifying the *rāgas* and *rāginīs* according to the Hanuman *mat* (system) instantly became *the* go-to texts for Mughal and Rajput artists wanting to create sets of *rāgamālā* paintings. A late eighteenth-century interlinear copy of Damodara and Harivallabha in the British Library shows its enduring influence into the colonial realm: it includes a gloss in modern Hindi by a living hereditary musician, Jivan Khan, written for East India Company official Richard Johnson (see Chapters 4 and 7).[77]

[74] Abu'l Fazl, '*Ain-i-Ākbari*, vol. iii, pp. 254–73.

[75] Thanks to the work of Richard David Williams. Ahmad has recently published a Persian facscimile of the *Tashrīh al-Mūsīqī*, which purports to be a translation of a treatise by Tansen called *Budh Prakash*. But the Persian recension is by Muhammad Akbar ᶜArzani, Aurangzeb's physician, who wrote prolifically on medicine c. 1700; [Muhammad Akbar ᶜArzani] Najma Perveen Ahmad (ed. and tr.), *Tashrīh-ul-Moosiqui: Persian Translation of Tansen's Original Work 'Budh Prakash'* (New Delhi: Manohar, 2012), p. 3 (Persian), p. 16 (English); Seema Alavi, 'Medical Culture in Transition: Mughal Gentleman Physician and the Native Doctor in Early Colonial India', *Modern Asian Studies* 42.5 (2008), 853–97, pp. 862–72. ᶜArzani's text may be related to the late 17C Brajbhasha *Buddhi-prakāsh-darpaṇa* composed by Diwan Lacchiram in Lahore; British Library, Or. 2765.

[76] *Sahasras*; Islam Khan, '*Dībācha*'; Françoise 'Nalini' Delvoye, 'The Verbal Content of Dhrupad Songs from the Earliest Collections, I: The *Hazar Dhurpad* or *Sahasras*', *Dhrupad Annual* (1990), 93–109 and elsewhere.

[77] Williams, 'Reflecting'. Sanskrit: Catura Damodara, *Saṅgīta-darpaṇa*, ed. K Vasudeva Sastri (Tanjore: Saraswathi Mahal, 1952); Brajbhasha: Harivallabha, *Saṅgīta-darpaṇa*, British Library, Add. 26,540 (1653); Interlinear: Damodara/Harivallabha/Jivan Khan, British Library, I O San 2399 (late 18C); Painting: Klaus Ebeling, *Ragamala Painting* (Basel: Ravi Kumar, 1973). Jivan Khan could be: 1) Jivan Khan *qawwāl* son of Taj Khan *qawwāl*, who brought *khayāl* from Delhi to Asaf-ud-daula's Lucknow; 2) Jivan Khan *kalāwant*, the *rabāb*-playing brother of Miyan Chajju Khan; or 3) Jivan Shah *kalāwant*, brother of Pyar Khan (or Sen) based in Benares, the

But it was in the Persian language in Aurangzeb's reign[78] that this recodifying impetus manifested itself in earnest, in a flurry of treatises written to satisfy the needs of high-ranking connoisseurs of Hindustani music who were more comfortable in the official language of the Mughal empire. At least fifteen unique, datable Mughal Persian texts on Hindustani music from the period 1660–1700 survive. But certain treatises – those that I have categorised as canonical in Box 2.1 – became the authoritative core of Mughal music theory (*ᶜilm-i mūsīqī*, musical science) until the empire's end in 1858.

Mughal music-technical writers used a palimpsestic technique in which they cumulatively built upon Sanskrit models,[79] Arabic and Persian ideas, discussions with hereditary musicians and each others' treatises in such a way that an established canon was maintained at the same time as accepted innovations were successively canonised. The canonical treatises were structured around extended citations (sometimes full translations) of earlier treatises, into which authors would then interleave original commentary and completely novel sections on matters of interest to contemporary audiences. These new music-technical writings were then *themselves* taken, often verbatim, as authoritative models for new palimpsests of citation, commentary and insertion. Take, for instance, Faqirullah's 1665/6 *Rāg Darpan* (*Mirror of Rāga*). It opens with his translation of an early sixteenth-century Hindavi *rāgamālā* text, but for much of the remainder he used Abu'l Fazl's chapters on *saṅgīta* as the base layer of his palimpsest. Faqirullah's section on vocal genres cites Abu'l Fazl word for word, but he interleaved more recent developments into Abu'l Fazl's sentences. Faqirullah's insertions in this case neatly give us the time frame and cultural context for the emergence of the most prominent Hindustani song genre today, *k͟hayāl*.[80]

The canonical treatises were then themselves copied, collected, circulated, commented upon and used as models for new music-technical treatises throughout the eighteenth and nineteenth centuries in Persian, Brajbhasha, modern Hindi, Bengali, Urdu and even English.[81] It is precisely because the

celebrated informant for Francis Fowke's 'On the Vina or Indian Lyre', in Sourindro Mohun Tagore (ed.), *Hindu Music from Various Authors*, 2nd ed. (Calcutta: I C Bose, Stanhope, 1882 [orig. 1788]), 193–7. Fowke's Jivan Shah may also have worked with Sir William Jones; Mirza Khan ibn Fakhr-ud-din, *Tuhfat al-Hind*, British Library, RSPA 78 (c. 1675, copy 1768), f. 181r marginalia.

78 Possibly very late in Shah Jahan's reign; Box 2.1.

79 Probably mediated through Brajbhasha translations and discussions with *paṇḍits*.

80 Brown [Schofield], 'Origins'.

81 Katherine Butler Brown [Schofield], 'Hindustani Music in the Time of Aurangzeb', Unpublished PhD Dissertation, SOAS, University of London (2003), pp. 27–81; Schofield, 'Reviving'; Williams, 'Reflecting'.

Box 2.1 The Core Canonical Mughal Persian Treatises on Hindustani Music Written during the Time of Aurangzeb

The *Miftāh al-Surod* (*Key to Music*): a translation of a lost Sanskrit work called *Bhārata-saṅgīta* (*Music of India/Bhārata's Music*), by Mughal official Qazi Hasan bin Khwaja Tahir, written for Aurangzeb in 1663/4 near Daulatabad; the 1662/3 draft also survives. It was probably designed to be illustrated: the earliest extant copy, made near Hyderabad in 1691, has paintings of the *rāgas* throughout, as does a nineteenth-century copy in the Bodleian.[82]

The *Rāg Darpan* (*Mirror of Rāga*): written in 1665/6 by high-ranking Mughal nobleman Saif Khan Faqirullah, completed when he was governor of Kashmir and dedicated to Aurangzeb. Faqirullah cites verbatim from several earlier sources, especially the *Mānakutūhala*, an early sixteenth-century Madhyadeshi work attributed to Raja Man Singh of Gwalior, but also Abu'l Fazl's *Ā'īn-i Akbarī* and Qazi Hasan's *Miftāh al-Surod*.[83]

The *Nishāt-ārā* (*Pleasure's Ornament*): by the hereditary *qawwāl* Mir Salih Qawwal Dehlavi ('of Delhi'). This text is most likely mid-seventeenth century, and certainly no later than 1725, the date of the Royal Asiatic Society copy.[84] The probable author was the *qawwāl* of the same name that Faqirullah memorialised as the 'greatest singer' of Delhi, who had passed away by the time he was writing. The later suggestion that it was written by Shah Jahan's librarian, renowned Iranian poet of Hindavi Mir Muhammad Salih Kashfi, is unlikely.[85]

The *Tarjuma-i Kitāb-i Pārījātak* (*Translation of the Book 'Pārījātak'*): the meticulous translation of Ahobala Pandit's Sanskrit masterpiece *Saṅgīta-pārijāta* (*Music of the Coral Tree*),[86] written no later than 1666/7 by high-ranking Mughal

canonical epistemology of Mughal music-technical writing was palimpsestic that we are able to trace the changes that occurred to Hindustani music in the

82 Qazi Hasan, *Miftāh al-Surod*; the draft is Qazi Hasan, *Surod al-Bahr*, Salar Jung Museum Library, Persian Mus 8 (1662/3), ff. 1v–14r; Bodleian Library, Ms.Pers.c.38.

83 Faqirullah, *Rāg Darpan*.

84 Mir Salih Qawwal Dehlavi, *Risāla-i Nishāt-ārā*, Royal Asiatic Society, RAS Persian 210 (5) (1725), ff. 78–89.

85 This suggestion is in the colophon of the copy of the *Nishāt-ārā* in the British Library, Delhi Persian 1502c. Mir Muhammad Salih Kashfi was 'said [by whom?] to have written a treatise on music, a fact that is not recorded by other sources'; Sunil Sharma, 'Reading the Acts and Lives of Performers in Mughal Persian Texts', in Francesca Orsini and Katherine Butler Schofield (eds.), *Tellings and Texts: Music, Literature and Performance in North India* (Cambridge: Open Book, 2015), 285–302, p. 301.

86 The *pārijāt* tree was one of the five trees of the Hindu paradise 'produced at the churning of the ocean'; Platts, *Dictionary*, p. 216.

Box 2.1 (cont.)

nobleman Mirza Raushan Zamir for Aurangzeb.[87] Zamir was a renowned poet in Brajbhasha under the *nom de plume* Nehi as well as being Khushhal's disciple. A particularly early copy, completed in the thirty-first year of Aurangzeb's reign (1688), was left to the India Office Library by Sir William Jones (1746–94).[88]

The fifth chapter of the *Tuhfat al-Hind* (*Gift from India*): Mirza Khan ibn Fakhruddin's famous work on Indian arts and sciences, written in c. 1675 for Aurangzeb's favoured son Muhammad A^c^zam Shah (1653–1707). A^c^zam himself wrote Hindustani songs, including *khayāls* dedicated to his beloved male companion Mirza Muzaffar, grandson of Shaista Khan (d. 1694, Aurangzeb's uncle and leading general). Importantly, A^c^zam was the first patron of a young Sadarang (see Chapter 3). Chapter V of the *Tuhfat* is a truly canonising work in that almost all of it is drawn from earlier treatises, particularly the *Saṅgīta-darpaṇa* and the *Rāg Darpan*; but it is exhaustive and was very influential in later centuries.[89]

The *Shams al-Aswāt* (*Sun of Songs/Sounds*): written in 1697/8 for Aurangzeb by the chief hereditary musician of his atelier, Ras Baras Khan, son of Khushhal Khan Gunasamudra. This work is ostensibly a Persian translation of the *Saṅgīta-darpaṇa*, but is full of invaluable insights from the orally transmitted knowledge of Ras Baras' esteemed lineage.[90] It became the model for the important c. 1790–3 Lucknow treatise, the *Usūl al-Naghmāt al-Āsafī* (*Fundamentals of Asaf[-ud-daula]'s Melodies*) (see Chapter 7).

late Mughal period, as new treatise writers successively wrote over the base layers of previous treatises (Chapters 5, 7 and 8).

The seventeenth-century Persian treatises on Hindustani music range over wide terrain in significant depth.[91] But if they have one urgent, central theme, it is their concern with the nature of the *rāga* and their need to explain the basis of its tremendous supernatural power, in order to harness it for the wellbeing of individual Mughal men and the polity as a whole. 'The authors

87 1666/7 is Zamir's death date; Lodi, *Tazkirah*, p. 130.

88 Mirza Raushan Zamir, *Tarjuma-i Kitāb-i Pārījātak*, British Library, RSPA 72 (1688); Ahobala Pandit, *Saṅgīta-pārijāta* (Hathras, U P: Sangit Karyalaya, 1971 [orig. mid 17C]); Lodi, *Tazkirah*, pp. 130–1; Zia-ud-din, *Hayy*, ff. 57v–8r.

89 Mirza Khan, *Tuhfat*; on A^c^zam Shah see Brown [Schofield], 'Aurangzeb', pp. 105–06; and 'Hindustani Music', p. 74; Zia-ud-din, *Hayy*, ff. 17v, 43r–44r, 51v, 52v, 54v; and 59r on the life-long mutual passion A^c^zam enjoyed with Mirza Muzaffar (*bā ham ta^c^ashshuq dāsht*).

90 Ras Baras, *Shams*.

91 The remaining paragraphs in this section are paraphrased from Schofield, 'Music, Art'; and Schofield, 'Musical Culture'.

were obsessed with the relationship between the sonic properties of the *rāga* as a framework for composing melodies, and its extramusical powers, embodied in visual and poetical imagery, to awaken specific emotional states in the listener or to transform the natural world, if sung at exactly the right, predetermined time.'[92] As theorist Kamilkhani wrote:

When I engaged my friends in informal conversation and they introduced the topic of *rāga* I . . . found myself utterly in the dark as to why the people of Hind have specified a time for every *rāga* at which its performance is most pleasing; for example, the fact that Rag Bhairav should be sung in the morning . . . I made searching inquiries of scholars, *ustāds* and performers alike . . . I have spent much time conversing with the singers of *rāga*, the players of instruments and friends who are connoisseurs of this art; and I have also to a small degree myself learned the practices of singing, composing and instrumental playing. I have thought in depth about . . . the sciences of astrology and of mathematics; and in this respect the endeavours of previous authors on the sciences of music and astrology . . . were gifts to this inquirer. The result is this guide, which I have written to explain *why the rāgas must be sung at their specified times.*[93]

The seventeenth-century theorists wished to understand each *rāga*'s 'potent effect on the listener' when performed properly at the right time – 'that is to say', wrote Zamir, 'why it is that the gentle singing of the beautiful voice causes dusk to fall, or vengeful snakes to be tamed by melancholy harmonies, or deer to faint dead away from listening to heart-stealing melodies'.[94] But they were also terrified of what would happen if they got it wrong. Qazi Hasan scolded:

The first *rāga* must be sung at [its prescribed] time, followed by its five wives, then its eight sons, then its [other] relations . . . [Unfortunately] although the *nāyaks* of previous ages . . . practised this science . . . [today's singers] don't know the [correct] times at all! For example, Sarang is a son of Rag Megh and its time is night. Departing from this time, they [now] sing it during the second *pahr* of the day. This is an error! . . . Many other *rāgas* are now sung 'out of time'[95] . . . For this reason, God's blessings have fled [their] households . . . If [a musician] first sings one *rāga*, then after it sings the wife of another *rāga*, they induce the two to commit adultery and lead the unmarried patrons of the *majlis* who are listening into fornication![96]

[92] Schofield, 'Music, Art', p. 69; Schofield, 'Reviving'; Katherine Butler Schofield, 'Learning to Taste the Emotions: the Mughal *Rasika*', in Orsini and Schofield (eds.), *Tellings*, 407–21.

[93] ᶜIwaz Muhammad Kamilkhani, *Risāla dar ᶜAmal-i Bīn*, Bodleian Library, Oxford, Ouseley 158 (1668/9), ff. 123r–32v, ff. 123r–25r; my emphasis.

[94] Zamir, *Tarjuma*, Egerton 793, f. 1v. [95] *bī-waqt.* [96] Qazi Hasan, *Miftāh*, pp. 18–19.

All of the Aurangzeb-era treatises were written to give patrons of Hindustani music the full, esoteric knowledge required to control and channel the powers of the *rāga* correctly so that 'in the musical assembly musicians and others who have the stamp of genius are not put to shame and the connoisseurs of music do not find fault'.[97]

So, what was the source of the *rāgas*' magical powers? How did Ragini Todi gently lead the listening beasts of the forest into a peaceful, ecstatic reverie, just as Orpheus pacified the guard dog of Hades and Khushhal hypnotised the emperor into acting against his will? Why did the timing need to be exact? And what was the connection between musical power and the emperor's sovereign power – why was there a picture of Orpheus above the Mughal throne?

It is in the two treatises written by Khushhal's disciples, the gentleman theorist Zamir and Khushhal's son Ras Baras, that we find the clearest answer.

The Mughal understanding of the source of the *rāgas*' power was rooted in ancient Greek ideas, filtered through Arabic and Persian writings into India, about how music affected the listening body: in ideas about the mind, with its struggle between the rational intellect and the powers of anger and desire;[98] about the body, with its four humours constituted of the four elements earth, air, wind and fire; and about astrology – and these last two knowledge systems were strongly paralleled in Sanskrit sciences as well. By the seventeenth century, Sanskrit as well as Persian theorists[99] were using mathematical proportions devised by Pythagoras to tune their stringed instruments, thus tying the powers of the *rāga* to the Pythagorean and Platonic theory of the music of the spheres. This theory states that the same mathematical proportions audible as musical harmony – seven principal notes of the scale, twelve acoustical positions for those notes in the octave – underpinned the inaudible but equally harmonious movement of the seven celestial bodies through the twelve houses of the zodiac. In this way music's powers over the listening body were tethered to astral power.[100] More importantly, because musical acoustics are based in pure mathematical ratios, Persianate theories of kingship presented music as a scientific proof

97 Qazi Hasan *Surod*, f. 3v; Schofield, 'Reviving', pp. 496–8.

98 The Aristotelian *ᶜaql-i ᶜamalī*, the practical intellect, and the *quwwat-i g͟hazabī* and *quwwat-i shahwī*, the irascible and concupiscible faculties; Schofield, 'Musical Culture'.

99 ᶜAbd-ul-karim, *Jawāhir*; Ahobala, *Saṅgītapārijāta*; Zamir, *Tarjuma*; Kamilkhani, *Risāla*; and Ras Baras, *Shams*.

100 Schofield, 'Music, Art', pp. 74–6; Schofield, 'Musical Culture'; Katherine Butler Brown [Schofield], 'The *Ṭhāṭ* System of Seventeenth-Century North Indian *Rāga*', *Asian Music* 35.1 (2003–4), 1–13; also Andrew Hicks, *Composing the World: Harmony in the Medieval Platonic Cosmos* (Oxford: Oxford University Press, 2017).

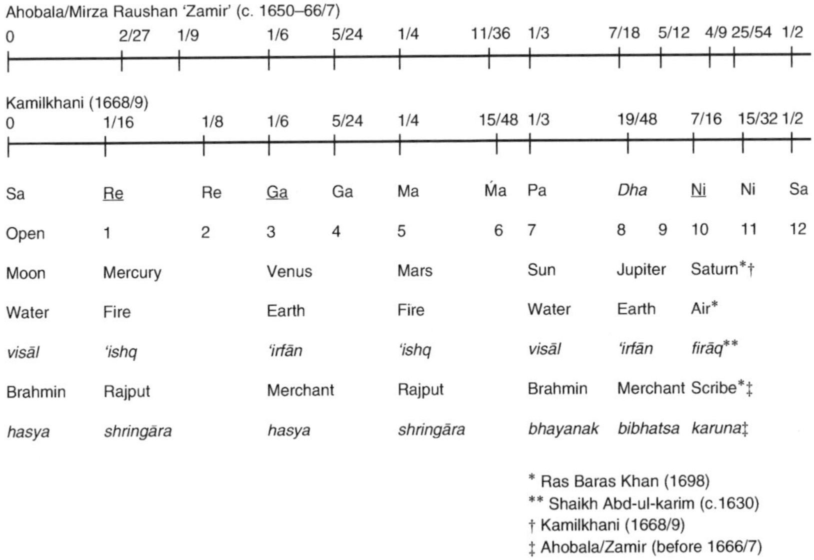

Figure 2.3 The connections between celestial bodies, musical notes, elements and effects

of *ᶜadālat*, justice or equity, produced when the rational intellect holds the powers of anger, desire and contemplation in perfect balance.[101] A person could thus harness music to control their own self or, if that self happened to be a ruler, the entire body of the kingdom.

Each of the seven celestial bodies – the Sun, the Moon, Mercury, Venus, Mars, Saturn and Jupiter – dictated which element ruled each of the seven notes of the Indian scale (Sa, Re, Ga, Ma, Pa, Dha, Ni). The two most emphasised notes in each *rāga*, called the *vādī* and *samvādī*, controlled whether it was dominated by fire, water, air or earth. This gave each *rāga* a unique emotional temperament that determined the effect that *rāga* would have on the listening world. Listening to a fiery *rāga* like Dipak inflamed the heart with passionate love;[102] whereas listening to watery *rāga*s, such as Khushhal's Ragini Todi, increased such bliss in the heart that the listener would be annihilated in ecstatic union[103] with Divine Truth. When choosing *rāga*s to be performed in the court, then, patrons and musicians needed to be sensitive to the time and atmosphere of the occasion and the temperament of their audience, deploying *rāga*s that would bring their humours back into equilibrium. It also explained why *rāga*s had to be played at particular times:

101 See for example Jalaluddin Dawwani, *Akhlāq-i Jalālī* (Lucknow: Nawal Kishore Press, 1879 [orig. c. 1453–78]), pp. 99–101; Schofield, 'Musical Culture'.

102 *ᶜishq*. 103 *wisāl*.

for instance, *rāgas* with dominant cold notes should be played at midday, in order to balance out the heat of the day with the cool element; while watery *rāgas*, like Rag Megh, should be sung at the end of the hot dry months in order to precipitate the monsoon rains.[104]

But the most telling connection is the one Khushhal's disciples Ras Baras and Zamir drew between music and the political order: between the seven notes and the social hierarchy of their day. It is virtually identical to the one Abu'l Fazl made between the different people of Akbar's empire – the rulers and nobility were fiery; the scholars and philosophers watery; the scribes and bureaucrats airy; and servants earthy.[105] In other words, the theory of harmony and balance dictating successful musical performance was identical to the theory underpinning Mughal political ideologies of *sulh-i kull* and the balanced kingdom.[106]

What is more, Ebba Koch reminds us that Shah Jahan saw Orpheus and his musical powers as supernaturally connected to his own divine powers as the King Solomon (Suleiman) of his age to bring all the fractious factions of the empire together in harmony and balance (Chapter 8).[107] This was no metaphor. Music was an essential technology in maintaining the whole structure of empire and proper governance. This is why musicians featured so prominently in Mughal historical accounts together with astrologers on major state occasions, such as regnal anniversaries and royal births, as generators of auspiciousness and guarantors of dynastic success.[108] Music's powers, rationally controlled, were absolutely necessary to Mughal sovereignty. Music made kings.

But it could also break them.

Musical Knowledge in Delhi, 1719–61: Outer Frame

What did Rasikh make of all this, looking back upon Khushhal's times from the much more politically troubled perspective of 1752–3?

104 Ras Baras, *Shams*, pp. 100–02, ʿAbd-ul-karim, *Jawāhir*, ff. 66v–8v; 105r–106v.

105 Ras Baras, *Shams*, pp. 100–02; Zamir, *Tarjuma*, Egerton 793, ff. 11v–12r (translation and commentary on Ahobala, *Saṅgītapārijāta*, pp. 31–2); Abu'l Fazl, *Ain-i-Akbari*, vol. i, pp. iv–vi.

106 On the Mughal use of various technologies of supernatural power more generally to underpin their sovereignty, see A Azfar Moin, *The Millennial Sovereign: Sacred Kingship and Sainthood in Islam* (New York: Columbia University Press, 2012).

107 Ebba Koch, 'Mughal Emperor'.

108 e.g. Abu'l Fazl, *Akbarnāma*, vol. i, tr. H Beveridge (Calcutta: Asiatic Society and Baptist Mission Press, 1897), pp. 50–68, 85–95; Khafi Khan, *Muntakhab*, pp. 106, 112, 131, 161–2, 175; Wade, *Imaging Sound*, pp. 63–7.

Widespread belief that the *rāgas* had decisive, even occult, power over human affairs continued in North India even after the British deposed the last Mughal emperor, well into the era of the British Raj.[109] And until the middle of the eighteenth century, the scientific explanation of the *rāgas*' powers seems to have remained current in musical circles. No new music treatises of major impact appear to have been produced in Persian in the first decades of the eighteenth century. What we see instead is increased copying and circulation of the core Aurangzeb-era treatises and widespread dissemination of their ideas, alongside further moves to consolidate them as canonical Mughal knowledge on Hindustani music.

The canonical treatises were already being copied and circulated far from their points of origin in the late seventeenth century, as we can see from the copies of the *Tarjuma-i Kitāb-i Pārījātak* and the *Miftāh al-Surod* produced in 1688 and 1691 respectively (Box 2.1). Individual connoisseurs also began compiling and passing down collections of music treatises. Two important collections, for example, are RAS Persian 2010 (5), now held in the Royal Asiatic Society, London, which Dinanath son of Basudeo compiled in 1725;[110] and Or. 2361 in the British Library, which largely concerns the works on Arabic and Persian music that Shah Qubad Diyanat Khan (d. 1672) collected in the 1660s and which his grandson, historian Mirza Muhammad Khan (1687–c.1776), inherited in 1708.[111] We know little about Dinanath, other than that he was a Hindu and thus, given his high literacy in Persian, probably a *kāyasth* or *khatrī* in service as a professional bureaucrat (*munshī*).[112] Mirza Muhammad's grandfather, father and he himself as a young man all served Aurangzeb as *mansabdārs*. Diyanat Khan and his son Mut^camid were clearly major patrons and connoisseurs of music in Shah Jahan's and Aurangzeb's time; they also had several important individual works on Hindustani music copied or created for them (1666–69) that are

109 Imam Khan, *Ma*^{c}*dan*, pp. 111–6.

110 Dinanath son of Basudeo, collection of treatises on music, Royal Asiatic Society, London, RAS 2010 (5) (1725).

111 Shah Qubad Diyanat Khan, collection of treatises on music, British Library, Or. 2361 (1660s); Jenny Norton-Wright, 'A Mughal Miscellany: The Journey of Or. 2361', *British Library Asian and African Studies Blog*, 31 July 2020, https://blogs.bl.uk/asian-and-african/2020/07/a-mughal-musical-miscellany-the-journey-of-or-2361-1.html; Hermann Ethé, *Catalogue of Persian Manuscripts in the Library of the India Office* (Oxford: India Office, 1903), vol. i, col. 146; Charles Rieu, *Catalogue of the Persian Manuscripts in the British Museum* (London: British Museum, 1883), vol. iii, p. 895.

112 Muzaffar Alam and Sanjay Subrahmanyam, 'The Making of a Munshi', *Comparative Studies of South Asia, Africa and the Middle East* 24.2 (2004), 61–72, pp. 61–2.

now in the Bodleian, including a copy of the *Sahasras* and Kamilkhani's important original works on the Hindustani *rāgas*.[113]

That Aurangzeb's reign was understood in the first half of the eighteenth century as the heyday of the 'classical' in the musical arts, and the reference point for musical discussion and practice, is supported by the evidence of other eighteenth-century artistic productions. An exquisite *rāgamālā* once belonging to the Maharaja of Kishangarh and made in Delhi in Muhammad Shah's period – probably commercially to cash in on the era's nostalgia for the imagined Mughal golden age[114] – includes a *dhrupad* song in praise of Aurangzeb on the back of every *rāga* painting in the set (Figure 2.4).

Clearly, Aurangzeb retained a reputation as a connoisseur of music well into Muhammad Shah's reign. More importantly, this *rāgamālā* brings to the fore the still-intact connection between music well-ordered and eighteenth-century perceptions that Aurangzeb successfully maintained imperial control. Aurangzeb does not seem to have had the wholly bad reputation in the decades after his death that he has now, either when it came to music or to politics.[115] Rasikh's brother, Shakir Khan, wrote that their father had instituted 'the custom now widespread in India' of 'reciting prayers to the memory of *the just Emperor* ᶜAlamgir Aurangzeb with a food-offering of roast chick-peas and dark cane-sugar'.[116] In collecting and consolidating the music theory, songs, musical models and stories of Aurangzeb's era, patrons, writers and musicians were also remembering the ruler they saw in hindsight as the last Mughal emperor (however austere) to maintain the scales of power in balance.

In the 1750s, subjects of the erstwhile Mughal territories across Hindustan still genuinely believed in the power of the *rāgas*, performed at exactly the right time, to strengthen or subvert the natural and political orders. In his history of the reign of Muhammad Shah and the anarchy that followed,[117] Rasikh's brother retold their father's first-hand account of a neighbour in Panipat who deployed music supernaturally to bring on

113 All of these were acquired by Sir Gore Ouseley and/or Sir William Ouseley; see entries 1844, 1845, 1846, 1848 and 1849, in Sachau and Hermann Ethé, *Catalogue of the Persian, Turkish, Hindûstânî and Pushtû Manuscripts in the Bodleian Library, Part I* and 2346 and 2813 in *Part II* (Oxford: Clarendon Press, 1889). In my 2003–4 article, I stated erroneously that the Diyanat Khan in question was Abdul Qadir Diyanat Khan (d. 1713), when it was in fact Shah Qubad (d. 1672).

114 Molly Aitken and Debra Diamond (personal communication, 2014); provenance details 'Ragini Todi, from a Garland of Musical Modes (Ragamala) Manuscript', online catalogue entry, Yale University Art Gallery Collections, https://artgallery.yale.edu/collections/objects/38733.

115 But see Heidi Pauwels and Anne Murphy (eds.), *From Outside the Persianate Centre: Vernacular Views on ᶜAlamgir*, special issue of the *Journal of the Royal Asiatic Society* 28.3 (2018).

116 Shakir, *Tārīkh*, ff. 57r–v; tr. Bruce Wannell, my emphasis. See also Kaicker, *King*, pp. 148–53.

117 Dalrymple, *Anarchy*.

Figure 2.4 *Dhrupad* Ragini Todi. Mughal, 18C. 1939.552, verso. **Yale University Art Gallery**. Public Domain

the monsoon rains. In a period of severe drought, Raushan-ud-daula (d. 1737), a major nobleman, Sufi and musical patron (see Chapter 3), promised the emperor that if he donated one *lākh* (100,000) rupees to the shrine of Sufi saint Shah Bhikha of Thaneswar, the rains would come. Raushan-ud-daula gathered together the *qawwāl*s at his house in Panipat to sing the clouds into bursting and presided over a spiritual musical *majlis* in which he and Rasikh's father went deep into ecstasy:[118]

When my father left and rode on towards my uncle's house, clouds appeared and rain started falling! Still uplifted by the spiritual music, Raushan-ud-daula [also] mounted his horse and went to greet the Emperor and collect his wager. A memorable miracle in the annals of the time![119]

[118] *majlis-i samāʿ*; *wajd o hāl*. [119] Shakir, *Tārīkh*, ff. 73v–75r; tr. Bruce Wannell.

Rasikh's ground-breaking musical text the *Risāla-i Zikr-i Mug̱han-niyān-i Hindūstān* could never reproduce *this*: the potent, world-changing force of music itself. So why, then, *did* he write about music in the form of a *tazkira*? In doing so – in memorialising the master musicians of a period in the near past in which Mughal power was still real, in underlining within it his unshakeable belief in music's ongoing power to change things – I think he was trying to hold the fragile world together with little more than a broken pen.[120]

Listen more closely to Rasikh's longest story. Khushhal knew exactly what state his singing of Ragini Todi would put Shah Jahan in. He over-stepped the simple but profoundly important boundaries of his mandated position – to maintain the empire's stability through the power of his song – by abusing his knowledge and his considerable powers to subvert the political destiny of the Mughal dynasty. More than that: he usurped the powers of Orpheus and turned them against the Orpheus sitting upon the throne. I think Rasikh's story held a prophetic warning – not for musicians, but for the young Emperor Ahmad Shah and for the powerful plotters seeking to control him: his mother Udham Bai and the recently assassin-ated chief eunuch Javed Khan who together had run the empire; but also the emperor's hastily regretted choice for new prime minister, ᶜImad-ul-mulk. Less than two years after Rasikh put down his pen, Ahmad Shah became the first emperor since Shah Jahan to be dethroned and imprisoned alive by a power-hungry usurper stepping way outside the borders of his ordained place on the carpet for his own political gain.

And, as prophesied, in the end it was his imprisoner ᶜImad-ul-mulk who reaped the whirlwind, when Abdali came and swept it all away.

120 Lodi, *Tazkirah*, p. 141.

3 The Rivals: Anjha Baras, Adarang and the Scattering of Shahjahanabad

Tazkiras and Genealogies

Jamshed, who invented the wineglass – what happened to him?
Where did those gatherings go? Where, that music and drinking?

Except in the bowl of the tulip, there is no trace of his glass;
the poppy now carries the wine flask in his place.

Where young men once tossed back wine, the willows sway;
The host's head, long turned to clay, now forms the brick that stops the wine cask.

Mir Muhammad Taqi Mir (1720–1810)[1]

The Ocean of Names

Ten years after Rasikh put down his pen, his *tazkira* resurfaced as an unmarked section of a music treatise written for the new Mughal emperor in exile, Shah ᶜAlam II (r. 1759–1806): the *Khulāsat al-ᶜAish-i ᶜĀlam-Shāhī* (*The Quintessence of Pleasure of the King of the World*). Its authorship and manuscript history are a little hazy. The likely author's father was a man we briefly met orchestrating the rains in Chapter 2: Raushan-ud-daula Zafar Khan Bahadur Rustam Jang, *bakhshī ul-mulk* (d. 1737). In the 1720s and 30s, Raushan-ud-daula, a music aficionado and Sufi adept, was paymaster-general and favourite of Emperor Muhammad Shah.[2] It was his son, Nawab Mazhar Khan, who first wrote the *Khulāsat al-ᶜAish* in 1763/4: a 'comprehensive work on all that is connected with sexual intercourse', apparently including music.[3] But the version I am interested in was written

[1] Translation based on Frances W Pritchett, *A Garden of Kashmir: The Ghazals of Mir*, *ghazal* 239 verses 7–11, www.columbia.edu/itc/mealac/pritchett/00garden/index.html; also Mir Muhammad Taqi Mir, *Selected Ghazals and Other Poems*, ed. and tr. Shamsur Rahman Faruqi, Murty Classical Library of India (Cambridge MA: Harvard University Press, 2019b), p. 12.

[2] Shakir Khan, *Tārīkh*, ff. 18r-v, 73v-75r, Khan and Hayy, *Maāthir*, vol. ii, pp. 605–8.

[3] Nawab Mazhar Khan, *Khulāsat al-ᶜAish-i ᶜĀlam-Shāhī*, Bodleian Library, Oxford, Elliott 182 (1763/4), ff. 1–288; British Library, I O Islamic 3623. From the *Ā'īn-i Akbarī* until at least the post-1858 *Maᶜdan al-Mūsīqī*, the association of music with the erotic arts in treatises on Indian sciences was widespread; Faqirullah, *Rāg Darpan*, pp. 132–49; Abu'l-Fazl, *'Ā'īn* (tr.), 'Sahitya'

in 1798, in Lucknow.[4] Mazhar is again credited as its author, though this copy was written for famous Orientalist Sir Gore Ouseley (1770–1884),[5] then working for the Nawab of Awadh Saᶜadat ᶜAli Khan (r. 1798–1814). But this version is entirely on Hindustani music alone and is a prominent example of a new wave of Persian and vernacular music treatises produced after 1760 that built and reflected on the changes to the canonical Mughal tradition of Chapter 2 (see also Chapter 7).

Did Mazhar recraft his 1798 *Khulāsat* around the musical chapter of his earlier text? The original work on sex was intended to include 'the knowledge and wisdom of the famous [music] books of India like the *Sangīt-darpan* ... concerning the qualities of the *rāgas* and *rāginis*', though neither copy I have been able to access includes this section.[6] But the 'humble narrator' of the 1798 version then says he substantially 'contributed to the writing of this book, adding fine things that were approved by [my] respected uncle'.[7] Was it, then, reworked by someone other than Mazhar? Only five years later in 1803/4, a major notable of Shah ᶜAlam's court instead named the famed hereditary musician and scholar Khushhal Khan Anup[8] (c. 1750s–c. 1834) as its author[9] (Chapter 5). Anup was a child in 1763/4 and firmly fixed at the court of Hyderabad before 1790, but this confusion is understandable. For Anup did write a Persian treatise in Hyderabad in 1808/9 that is very similar to the 1798 *Khulāsat al-ᶜAish*, the *Rāg Darshan* (*Vision of Rāga*).[10]

(immediately before 'Sangita'), vol. iii, pp. 254–60; Imam Khan, *Maᶜdan*; manuscript: final chapter on *nāyikā-bheda* pp. 246–65.

4 Mazhar Khan, *Khulāsat al-ᶜAish-i ᶜĀlam-Shāhī*, Bodleian Library, Oxford, Ouseley Add. 123 (1798); Sachau and Ethé, *Catalogue Bodleian*, pp. 977, 1069, cf. Ethé and Edwards, *Catalogue of the India Office*, vol. ii, p. 26.

5 Mumtaz ul-Mulk Imtiaz-ud-daula Gore Ouseley Sahib Bahadur Zafar Jang; Mazhar, *Khulāsat* (1798), f. 2r; Peter Avery, 'Ouseley, Gore', *Encyclopaedia Iranica* (Online Edition, 2004) www.iranicaonline.org/articles/ouseley-sir-gore.

6 Thanks to Covid-19; Mazhar, *Khulāsat*, Elliott, f. 8v; the last chapter on *ᶜilm-i sangīt* is missing from this copy. The *Sangīt-darpan* is Damodara's *Saṅgītadarpaṇa*, but likely refers to its reception through the *Tuhfat al-Hind*.

7 Mazhar, *Khulāsat* (1798), ff. 3r, 5r–v. It is not clear here whether Mazhar is the uncle or the nephew. Raushan-ud-daula had six sons and two brothers, Mukhtar-ud-daula Munawwar ᶜAli Khan and Fakhr-ud-daula Shujaᶜat Jang; Mazhar's brothers included Qa'im Khan and Muzaffar-ud-daula; Shakir Khan, *Tārīkh*, ff. 12v, 18r–v; Khan, *Maāthir*, vol. ii, pp. 607–8.

8 Not to be confused with Khushhal Khan Gunasamudra.

9 Abd-ur-rahman Shahnavaz Khan (d. 1809 as prime minister to Emperor Akbar Shah), *Mir'āt-i Āftāb-numā*, British Library, Add. 16,697 (1803/4), ff. 269r-v; this copy belonged to Sir David Ochterlony, the first British Resident to Shah ᶜAlam (1803–06).

10 Khushhal Khan Anup, *Rāg Darshan*, Government Oriental Manuscripts Library, University of Madras, Persian MS D515 (1808/9); *Rāg Darshan and Risala-i-Mosiqi-e Mast Mohammadshahi* ed. and tr. Chander Shekhar (New Delhi: National Mission for Manuscripts, 2014), pp. 151–213. The date of the treatise is 1223 AH = 1808/9 CE, f. 80r; 11/4/1229 AH (1814 CE) is the date of the GOML copy.

This similarity is because, apart from their unrelated introductions, the 1798 *Khulāsat* and 1808/9 *Rāg Darshan* are both modelled closely on Chapter V of Mirza Khan's c. 1675 *Tuhfat al-Hind*.[11] Indeed, the main point of diversion between the two is the insertion into the *Khulāsat* of Rasikh's *tazkira*. As we saw in Chapter 2, Mazhar's and Rasikh's families were friends and neighbours in Panipat, so it is not surprising that Mazhar would know and admire Rasikh's monument to the late great musicians of Hindustan. Nor was Mazhar the only later writer on music to draw heavily from Rasikh's *Risāla* in compiling his own new work of musical scholarship, as we will see. The question is *why*. Why had life histories become so necessary to writing authoritatively on music in late Mughal India that the monumental *Tuhfat al-Hind*, of all things, had to be expanded with a new section?

The introductions of the 1798 *Khulāsat* and the *Rāg Darshan* share one particularly striking thing: an obsession with names, and with connecting them; with distinguished individuals, with genealogies, with memorialising the names of the dead and the great in the generally somewhat biased and selective views of the authors. And both were particularly concerned to somehow connect the separated Delhi, Lucknow and Hyderabad courts of the present diminished age c. 1800 quantifiably back to the intact court of Muhammad Shah, a time remembered in these introductions with profound nostalgia.

Take for example the introductory section to Anup's first version of his *Rāg Darshan*, written in Brajbhasha in 1800 and illustrated in 1804 (Chapter 5).[12] Here he not only wrote down his genealogy, connecting the musical inheritance of his own lineage and those of other branches of the Mughal *kalāwant* brotherhood[13] back to the great Tansen; he had it illustrated with the fabulous fantasy *majlis* in Figure 3.1, uniting the dead and the living in one supernaturally charged musical assembly.

Tansen is there of course. But he is joined by the two most famous musicians of Muhammad Shah's court, Sadarang and Adarang. Beneath Adarang is Anup's father, Karim Khan, and right in the bottom corner, in

[11] In the introduction to the *Khulāsat* (1763/4), Mazhar explicitly noted he was drawing from the *Tuhfat al-Hind*; ff. 2v–3r.

[12] Khushhal Khan Anup, *Rāg Darshan*, University of Pennsylvania Rare Book and Manuscript Library, Lawrence J Schoenberg Collection, LJS 63 (Brajbhasha, 1800); see Chapter 5.

[13] Katherine Butler Schofield, 'Chief Musicians to the Mughal Emperors: The Delhi *Kalawant Biradari*, 17th to 19th Centuries', in ITC Sangeet Natak Academy (Kolkata) (ed.), *Dhrupad, Its Future: Proceedings of the 2013 ITC-SRA (West) Seminar* (ITC-SRA: Mumbai, 2013).

Figure 3.1 Anup's musical genealogy as a fantasy *majlis*. Top to bottom, left to right: 'Miyan Tansen, Shah Adarang Sahib i.e. Miyan Firoz Khan, Shah Sadarang Sahib i.e. Miyan Ni^{c}mat Khan, Miyan Karim Khan', and the author Khushhal Khan Anup; *Rāg Darshan*, Hyderabad 1800, illustrated by Haji Mir Ghulam Hasan 1804. Lawrence J Schoenberg Collection, LJS 63, f. 3v. **University of Pennsylvania Special Collections Library**. CC-BY

the junior-most spot, Anup himself. According to his 1808 Persian introduction, his father:

was the special disciple[14] of Miyan Adarang, who was himself the special disciple of the reigning prince of music Miyan Ni^{c}mat Khan Sadarang, whose status in the science of music is brighter than the sun and goes without saying. Because of their eminence in this unique science, they were honoured attendants upon the late

[14] *shāgird-i k͟hāss.*

Emperor Muhammad Shah;[15] but due to the changing fortunes[16] of the time and the collapse of the sultanate, Khushhal Khan with the late Karim Khan came to Hyderabad.[17]

Forty years separated the death of Muhammad Shah and the approximate arrival of Karim Khan and his sons in Hyderabad. Why foreground Muhammad Shah's court here, but nothing of the intervening years?

The introduction to the 1798 *Khulāsat* wallows even more deeply in the sea of nostalgia for Muhammad Shah's reign. The author's grand/father Raushan-ud-daula was responsible as *bakhshī ul-mulk* for introducing all musicians to Muhammad Shah's court, and for paying them. According to the *Khulāsat*, Raushan-ud-daula disbursed twenty *lākh* (two million) rupees creating musical pleasure at court, thus personally bringing into being 'the entire realm of music lovers and beloved musicians, all of them unsurpassed in their time':[18]

All of the *kalāwants* perfect in this art, and the most accomplished of the time, entered Muhammad Shah's service and earned thousands for *tarānā* and *tān* [song and vocal improvisation]. The masters (*ustāds*) of the *kalāwants*, Miyan Anjha Baras Khan and Firoz Khan [Adarang] came frequently to the blessed court, received purses of gold for their steadfast friendship,[19] brought everyone together in the conviviality and sincerity of their gatherings[20] and enjoyed themselves in that place. Miyan Niᶜmat Khan [Sadarang] often honoured the gathering with his presence and increased its splendour, as did the late Taj Khan *kalāwant*, who was unique in Hindustan . . . Then there were the *kobids* (learned men) and *paṇḍits* of the time, those gentlemen incomparable in theoretical understanding, such as Mishra Surat Singh Pandit and Kripa Ram Pandit . . . Most of the magical-voiced courtesans like Khamiya Bai, Lalita Bai, Nur Bai, Chapala Sarup, Saras Rup, and so forth, were there. In that delightful, flourishing *mehfil*, that assembly without sorrow, there gathered the exceptional ones of the time, the beautiful people of the world and the flirtatious beloveds. With heart-warming songs and dances and lively melodies, life-enhancing music-making and heart-stealing flirtations, fire was lit from afar in the winecups of the eager ones, earth and time were brought together to dance, and Mars and Venus danced in the heavens.

[15] 'The Shadow of God Muhammad Shah *Firdaus Ārāmgāh*' (Emperor Muhammad Shah's death title).

[16] *inqilāb*, revolution. [17] Anup ed. Shekhar, *Rāg Darshan* (Persian 1808/9), p. 156.

[18] Mazhar, *Khulāsat* (1798), ff. 3r; William Irvine, 'The Army of the Indian Moghuls: Its Organization and Administration', *Journal of the Royal Asiatic Society* July (1896), 509–70, pp. 539–44.

[19] i.e. loyalty.

[20] *ikhlās-i suhbat*. *Suhbat* means conversation, companionship, association, but it can also be used as a synonym for *majlis* or *mehfil*.

These were the great individuals in the *majālis* most of the time: esteemed *kalāwants* like Miyan Udit Sen and Rahim Sen, and blessed *qawwāls* like Miyan Taj Khan,[21] Jani and Ghulam Rasul, Lallu, Ghulami, Fazlu, Burhani, Burhan Khan, Jivan Khan, Kallu, Giyan Khan, Kanhri Khan, Miyan Fazil Khan, and other *ustāds* like Miyan Tan Parbin, Udit Khan, Chau Baras Khan and their sons; and *bīn* players such as Miyan La^{c}l Khan, who along with his sons Nur Khan and Himmat Khan are unique in the world in this art; *qānūn* players such as Miyan Nur Muhammad *qānūn-nawāz*; magical *rabāb* players; *mṛdang* (*pakhāwaj*) players like Bhavanidas, Tanka, Subhan, Dinanath and Premanand; *ḍholak* players like Miyan Baqa and Tahna – all of them unparalleled in their time. They came together, tuned their instruments, assembled with other experts in enchantment, and stole the hearts of their lovers with burning melodies.[22]

Who were all these people? We readers and listeners are supposed to know exactly who they were, just by their names; and their names are supposed to unleash a torrent of memories in us of *majālis* we once attended (or maybe our fathers attended) – where, perhaps, Bhavanidas accompanied Sadarang on the *pakhāwaj* in that fabled all-night performance of Tansen's famous *dhrupad* 'Music is like the ocean, and from this endless entity I could only ever drink one drop'.[23] 250 years later we have no idea who these people were. And there are hundreds more such unremembered names in the *tazkiras*, genealogies, introductions, and colophons of late Mughal writings on music. We drown in an ocean of musicians' names, all of whom are centuries dead, and nearly all long forgotten. What are we supposed to do with all these names?

They were important once, and the proliferation of miniature stories telling their lives in the eighteenth and early nineteenth centuries has much to tell us – not least because musicians' genealogies and anecdotes about great masters remain central to Hindustani music to this very day.[24] And so in this chapter, I am going to remember these names by looking at the written genre in which their lives rise to the surface in the voices of their own disciples and patrons, and sometimes in their own voices: the Persian-language *tazkira* – the commemorative text *par excellence* of Persian

[21] Not to be confused with Taj Khan *kalāwant*. Taj Khan *qawwāl* is second only to Sadarang in Dargah Quli's biographies of musicians: *Muraqqa^{c}* (1993), pp. 91–2.

[22] Mazhar, *Khulāsat* (1798), ff. 3r-5v.

[23] For Bhavanidas see Zia-ud-din, *Hayy*, f. 43r; for this Tansen *dhrupad*, Anup ed. Shekhar, *Rāg Darshan*, pp. 160–1. For Rahim Sen's famous all-night *majālis* see Dargah Quli, *Muraqqa^{c}* (1993) p. 93.

[24] Daniel Neuman, *Life*, pp. 59–84 and 145–67; James Kippen, *The Tabla of Lucknow: A Cultural Analysis of a Musical Tradition* (Cambridge: Cambridge University Press, 1988), pp. 63–85; Dard Neuman, 'Pedagogy'.

literature, often simplistically defined as a biographical collection – and in other places, like introductions, in which musicians' names and their genealogies were recorded.

In particular, I will explore the question of what the musical *tazkira* did for Hindustani music and musicians in the second half of the eighteenth century through the story selected *tazkira*s and genealogies tell of rivalry between the two main dynasties of imperial *kalāwant*s: the families of the joint chief musicians of the Mughal atelier during the time of Muhammad Shah, Miyan Firoz Khan Adarang and Anjha Baras Khan, the grandson of Khushhal Khan Gunasamudra. Both were pivotal musical figures at Muhammad Shah's court; both left Mughal service during what Zia-ud-din called the 'turmoil', the 'disturbance', and the 'scattering of the people of Shahjahanabad';[25] and both died in the 1760s. But Adarang is still remembered and revered today, while Anjha Baras is almost entirely forgotten. A study of musical biographies and genealogies enables us to reflect on who gets remembered, who gets forgotten, and why.[26]

I will begin with a summary of what a *tazkira* is in general terms, and a brief discussion of *tazkira*s of Hindustani musicians as they developed after Rasikh's *Risāla*. I will then return to the life stories of Adarang and Anjha Baras, and what they and the writings they are embedded in have to tell us about the scattering of Shahjahanabad c. 1740s–80s.

The *Tazkira* of Musicians

The *tazkira*, meaning 'remembrance, memory', is a major and very old genre of Persian literature (and later Urdu) that is understood as factual in nature. At root, each *tazkira* is a collection of short biographies that commemorate the life stories of a discrete set of people, chosen by the author according to a specific, personal or communal, logic as to who was worthy of remembrance. *Tazkira*s are usually concerned with a particular category of people, most commonly and importantly poets or Sufis, but there are *tazkira*s of noblemen, artists or the noteworthy inhabitants of a particular city. The connection of *tazkira*s with urban life has frequently been noted, and two key sources for musicians in Delhi between 1740 and 1847, Dargah Quli Khan's *Muraqqa*ᶜ*-i Dehlī* (*Delhi Album*) and the first edition of Sir Sayyid Ahmad Khan's *Āsār*

[25] *hangāma*, *āshob*, *tafriqa*, etc. Zia-ud-din, *Hayy*, e.g. ff. 43r, 44v, 47v, 55r, 57r.

[26] Kippen, *Tabla*, pp. 85–5.

al-Sanādīd (*Monuments of the Great*), fall into this 'cityscape' category.[27] *Tazkiras* may be organised along different lines: alphabetically, chronologically, regionally, by gender, by religious order or occupational category, etc. And they are frequently our major sources of information on historical individuals: not merely concerning the facts of their lives, their lineages, origins, dates of birth and death, itineraries, patrons, friends, personal anecdotes, and so on, but more importantly about the conceptual universe, social habitus and values of the *community* made up of the individuals being remembered, *and* of those remembering them. A great deal of sophisticated work has been done on this complex and capacious genre in the fields of literature and religious studies, and in what follows I am especially indebted to the insights of recent scholarship on poetical *tazkiras* as 'commemorative texts',[28] as well as older ethnographic scholarship on the functioning of *gharānā* genealogies in Hindustani musical life.[29] But very little has been done on written *tazkiras* of Hindustani musicians, and in this chapter I am merely opening the gates onto vast terrain.

Specialist musicianship in North India seems to have been a hereditary occupation before the Mughals arrived in Hindustan, but from at least the 1630s, Mughal writers, too, were drawing exclusionary genealogies for Hindustani music in terms of biological and musical inheritance. By the 1660s and 70s, theorists regularly used the terms *qaum* (community) and

[27] Dargah Quli, *Muraqqa*^{c} (1993); Sayyid Ahmad Khan, *Āsār al-Sanādīd*, 1st ed. (Shahjahanabad: Matba^{c} Sayyid al-Akhbār, 1847). English translations: Dargah Quli Khan, *Muraqqa*^{c}*-e Dehli: The Mughal Capital in Muhammad Shah's Time*, tr. Chander Shekhar and Sharma Mitra Chenoy (Delhi: Deputy, 1989); Sayyid Ahmad Khan, *Asār-us-Sanadīd*, tr. and ed. Rana Safvi (New Delhi: Tulika, 2018).

[28] The most important study of the Persian poetical *tazkira* in India is Kia, *Persianate Selves*. On the musicians' *tazkira*, see Schofield, 'Emotions'. Classic studies include Marcia K. Hermansen and Bruce B. Lawrence, 'Indo-Persian Tazkiras as Memorative Communications', in David Gilmartin and Bruce B. Lawrence (eds.), *Beyond Turk and Hindu: Rethinking Religious Identities in Islamicate South Asia* (Gainsville: University Press of Florida, 2000), 149–75; Faruqi, 'Long History, Part I'; Pritchett, 'Long History, Part II'; Paul Losensky, *Welcoming Fighani: Imitation, Influence, and Literary Change in the Persian Ghazal, 1480–1680* (Costa Mesa, CA: Mazda, 1993); Tabor, 'Market'; Dudney, 'Desire' and *India*; Mana Kia, 'Contours of Persianate Community, 1722–1835', Unpublished PhD Dissertation, (Harvard University,2011), esp. pp. 259–309; Kinra, *Writing Self*, pp. 258–95; Stefano Pelló, 'Persian as a Passe-Partout: The Case of Mīrzā 'Abd al-Qādir Bīdil and his Hindu Disciples', in Thomas de Bruijn and Allison Busch (eds.), *Culture and Circulation: Literature in Motion in Early Modern India* (Leiden: Brill, 2014), 21–46; Stefano Pelló, 'Persian Poets on the Streets: The Lore of Indo-Persian Poetic Circles in Late Mughal India', in Orsini and Schofield (eds.), *Tellings*, 303–26; Kevin L. Schwartz, 'A Transregional Persianate Library: The Production and Circulation of Tadhkiras of Persian Poets in the 18th and 19th Centuries', *International Journal of Middle East Studies* 52.1 (2020), 109–35; Sunil Sharma, 'Reading'.

[29] Daniel Neuman, *Life*; Kippen, *Tabla*.

asāmī (people group) to group Indian musicians, and to detach all professional musician *qaums* from what Mirza Khan called the *zāt-i sharīf*, the 'respectable classes' (see also Chapter 7).[30] Élite musicians at the Mughal court thereby formed a highly unusual social category: despite their comparatively low social status, their much-admired skills meant they mingled closely with the upper classes during musical *majālis*. Their occupational liminality – the licence their skills gave them to cross ordinarily rigid social boundaries during the execution of their musical duties – meant that their names and exploits were widely remembered across a range of Mughal writings[31] from the time of the first Emperor Babur (r. 1526–30).[32]

But it was the act of remembering individuals through writing about them in a concerted way from the mid-seventeenth century – through short genealogies and, later, *tazkiras* – that completed the process of 'establish[ing] those individuals as a "class"'[33] – in this case, the select communities of musicians considered worthy of Mughal élite and imperial patronage. A variety of performing communities were employed at court in different capacities or enjoyed elsewhere in the city. But seventeenth-century Mughal writers singled out four communities they considered worthy to admit into the exclusive intimate gathering for male musical patrons, the *majlis*. These were: 1) *kalāwants* ('artists'), who sang and composed the *dhrupad* genre and played the *bīn* (*rudra vīṇā*) and *rabāb* (Figure 7.9); 2) *qawwāls* ('singers of *qaul*'), hereditary Sufi-shrine singers who in courtly *majālis* sang the virtuosic genres *k͟hayāl* and *ṭappa* (Front Cover); 3) their instrumental accompanists, especially *ḍhāḍhīs*, 'players of the *ḍhāḍha*' or *ḍholak* drum who also played the bowed *sārangī*, and *pakhāwaj* drum specialists;[34] and 4) élite female courtesans of various hereditary communities (see Chapter 6). Young transfeminine dancers belonging to the *naqqāl*, *bhāṅḍ*, *bhagat* and *bāhurūpiya* communities, like the famous Taqi *bhagat*, were also (more controversially) patronised in a similar role to courtesans.[35]

30 Lahawri, *Badshah Namah*, vol. ii, pp. 5–6; Faqirullah, *Rāg Darpan*, pp. 192 and passim; Mirza Khan *Tuhfat*, vol. i, pp. 356–61; also Kaicker, *King*, pp. 35–6.

31 Katherine Butler Brown [Schofield], 'The Social Liminality of Musicians and Performers: Case Studies from Mughal India and Beyond', *Twentieth-Century Music* 3.1 (2007), 13–49.

32 Babur, Emperor of Hindustan, *The Bābur-nāma in English (Memoirs of Bābur)*, tr. Annette Susannah Beveridge (London: Luzac, 1922), vol i, pp. 271–2.

33 Schwartz, 'Transregional', p. 110.

34 Unlike most hereditary musicians memorialised at this time, *pakhāwaj* players were largely Hindu; see Mazhar's list.

35 Brown [Schofield], 'If Music Be'. Their presence in the courtly *majlis* was controversial because of their low class status, not because of their homoeroticism or their gender status, which were accepted.

In the first volume of the *Ā'īn-i Akbarī*, Abu'l Fazl presented a cursory list of the musicians in Akbar's atelier, including brief information about their community (e.g. Muhammad Khan *ḍhāḍhī*), city of origin (e.g. Tansen of Gwalior), and biological relationships (e.g. Tan Tarang Khan son of Miyan Tansen).[36] Writing in the 1630s and 40s, the official chronicler of Shah Jahan's reign, ᶜAbd-ul-Hamid Lahori, went further and included longer descriptions of some of the key *kalāwant*s and *qawwāl*s of Delhi at that time and the genres exclusive to each community.[37] Then, in 1665/6, Faqirullah included an original *tazkira*, mainly of musicians he had personally heard, as the last chapter of the *Rāg Darpan*.[38] But it was largely ignored by his successors: despite the huge influence of his treatise in later centuries, Faqirullah's unique list of musicians does not appear in another source again, to my knowledge, until after the Uprising.[39] Although Mirza Khan quoted vast swathes of the *Rāg Darpan* verbatim in the *Tuhfat*, he dropped Faqirullah's biographies of living and recent musicians in favour of a simple set of revered older names, ending with those on Abu'l Fazl's now canonical list.[40]

It wasn't until 1752–3, as we saw in Chapter 2, that Rasikh composed the first stand-alone *tazkira* on Hindustani musicians, which included both ancient and more recent subjects. His *Risāla* was qualitatively different from what had come before. It openly cited sources like Lahori's *Pādishāhnāma*, and acted as what Hermansen and Lawrence have called a 'memorative communication', connecting past with present generations – as Anup's fantasy *majlis* likewise did in visual form (Figure 3.1).[41] At the same time it gave the contemporary music lovers who were Rasikh's desired audience a sense of community with each other.[42] His *Risāla* commemorated the great musicians and assemblies of the past in order to console present generations who were worried that the Mughal culture these musicians had helped build, still basically intact in 1753, was endangered by the instability of the times (which it was).[43] From that point onwards a comparative rush of musical *tazkira*s and extended genealogies were written, with more than ten that I know of written between 1750 and 1850, generally as sections of larger works, with several but not all of them building on Rasikh's *tazkira* (Box 3.1).

36 Abu'l Fazl, *Ā'īn-i Akbarī* (tr.), vol. i, pp. 612–13; Chapter 7.
37 Lahawri, *Badshah Nama [Pādishāhnāma]*, vol. ii, pp. 2–6.
38 Faqirullah, *Rāg Darpan*, pp. 186–211. 39 Imam Khan, *Maᶜdan*, pp. 25–30.
40 Mirza Khan, *Tuhfat*, pp. 359–61. 41 See Tabor, 'Market', pp. 20–46.
42 Hermansen and Lawrence, 'Indo-Persian Tazkiras'; Rasikh, *Risāla*, pp. 1–2.
43 Schofield, 'Emotions'.

Box 3.1 List of key writings c.1740–1850 that include musicians' *tazkiras* and/or significant genealogies. Unless otherwise stated, these are in the Persian language. See bibliography for full details

Drawing on the *Risāla-i Zikr-i Mughanniyān-i Hindūstān* (1753), by ᶜInayat Khan 'Rasikh':

Risāla dar ᶜIlm-i Mūsīqī (1770–1)	Anon
Hayy al-Arwāh (c. 1785–88)	Zia-ud-din (although greatly independent)
Khulāsat al-ᶜAish (1798)	Mazhar Khan/nephew?
Mir'āt-i Āftāb-numā (1803/4)	Abd-ur-rahman Shahnawaz Khan
Naghma-i ᶜAndalīb (1845)	Muhammad Riza Najm Tabataba'i

Independent:

Muraqqaᶜ-i Dehlī (1739–41)	Dargah Quli Khan
Edinburgh MS 585(4) (1788)	Anon (Ras Baras lineage)
Rāg Darshan (Brajbhasha; 1800)	Khushhal Khan Anup
Rāg Darshan (Persian; 1808/9)	Khushhal Khan Anup
Asl al-Usūl (c. 1815)	Mir Nasir Muhammadi Ranj/ Miyan Himmat Khan
Yādgār-i Bahādurī (1834)	Bahadur Singh
Āsār al-Sanādīd (Urdu; 1847)	Sayyid Ahmad Khan

In the following section I will use these *tazkiras* and significant genealogies to trace the rivalry between the musician who is still remembered, Adarang, and the musician who has been forgotten, Anjha Baras, focussing on those written between 1739 and 1809, especially the *Muraqqaᶜ-i Dehlī*; the 1798 *Khulāsat al-ᶜAish*; the Persian and Brajbhasha *Rāg Darshans*; Oriental Manuscript 585 no. 4 in the Edinburgh University Library (henceforward Edinburgh MS 585(4)) and particularly Zia-ud-din's revelatory *Hayy al-Arwāh* (*Everliving Spirits*). But before doing so, I shall provide a brief analysis of how these musical *tazkiras* worked as a genre and individually, using the diagram in Table 3.1 to help guide us. In Table 3.1 I have compared the *tazkiras* in Box 3.1 that use Rasikh as a source; I will also cross-reference information found in these texts with that in the 'independent' *tazkiras* and genealogies.

The list of names on the far left of Table 3.1, from Nayak Baiju at the top down to Niᶜmat Khan Sadarang, the 'Nayak of his age',[44] represents the entire contents of Rasikh's *tazkira*. Rasikh organised it loosely chronologically, with

[44] Zia-ud-din, *Hayy*, f. 44r. Nayak was an honorific title bestowed on the great male *dhrupadiyas* of the pre-Mughal period; using it of a living musician was like saying he was a 'legend'.

Table 3.1 Comparison of musical *tazkiras* and genealogies that use Rasikh's *Risāla* as a key source

Rasikh (1753)	Anon *Risāla* (1770)	Mazhar (1798)	Abd-ur-rahman (1803)	Najm (1845)	Zia-ud-din (1785–88)
		Nayak list from *Tuhfat*	Nayak list from *Tuhfat*		***legendary ancients***
Nayak Baiju					Nayak Baiju
Nayak Gopal		Nayak Gopal	Nayak Gopal	Nayak Gopal	Nayak Gopal
Amir Khusrau		Amir Khusrau	Amir Khusrau	Amir Khusrau	Nayak Bakhshu
Nayak Bakhshu			Nayak Bakhshu	Nayak Bakhshu	
			Baba Ram Das & Nayak Dhondhu		***kalāwants***
Tansen	Tansen		Tansen	Tansen	Tansen
				Baba Ram Das & Nayak Dhondhu	
La^{c}l Khan Gunasamudra	La^{c}l Khan Gunasamudra		La^{c}l Khan Gunasamudra	La^{c}l Khan Gunasamudra	La^{c}l Khan Gunasamudra
Khushhal & Bisram	Khushhal & Bisram	Khushhal & Bisram	Khushhal & Bisram	Khushhal & Bisram	Khushhal
					[. . . incl. Muzaffar]
Baba Ram Das & Nayak Dhondhu					**Ni^{c}mat Khan Sadarang**
Sultan Husain Shah Sharqi				Sultan Husain Shah Sharqi	Anjha Baras Khan
Baz Bahadur and Rupmati					Fazil Khan son of Bhupat
Shaikh Sher Muhammad & Kabir				Shaikh Sher Muhammad & Kabir	[. . .]
Shaikh Moin-ud-din					

Zulqarnain Firangi				Zulqarnain Firangi	***qawwāls***
Budh Singh			Budh Singh	Budh Singh	Amir Khusrau
			Zulqarnain Firangi		Samit
			Sultan Husain Shah Sharqi		Shaikh Sher Muhammad & Kabir
			Baz Bahadur and Rupmati		
			Shaikh Sher Muhammad & Kabir		Shaikh Moin-ud-din
			Shaikh Moin-ud-din		[. . .]
					Taj Khan Q and sons Jani, Ghulam Rasul, Jivan
Ni^{c}mat Khan Sadarang	**Ni^{c}mat Khan Sadarang**	**Ni^{c}mat Khan Sadarang**	**Ni^{c}mat Khan Sadarang**	**Ni^{c}mat Khan Sadarang**	[. . .]
	Anjha Baras Khan			Anjha Baras Khan	
	Firuz Khan Adarang	Firuz Khan Adarang	Firuz Khan Adarang	Firuz Khan Adarang	***gentlemen amateurs***
	Fazil Khan son of Bhupat				Mirza Raushan Zamir [2 x 18C entries]
		La^{c}l Khan (Adarang's brother)		La^{c}l Khan (Adarang's brother)	
				Muzaffar Khan	Zulqarnain Firangi
				Nur Bai	[. . .]
	Jani & Ghulam Rasul			Jani & Ghulam Rasul	Sultan Husain Shah Sharqi
		Himmat & Nur Khan sons of La^{c}l		Himmat & Nur Khan sons of La^{c}l	[. . .]
				Chajju son of Adarang	
				Rahim & Karim Sen	

legendary musicians of the pre-Mughal past before Tansen; Tansen and musicians roughly of his time; then musicians of Shah Jahan's and Aurangzeb's time in living memory of the present generation's grandparents; finishing with early eighteenth-century musicians who passed away before the end of Muhammad Shah's reign. As later authors drew upon or directly cited Rasikh's work (the next four lists, left to right), they added entries after Sadarang to update the biographies to the present, especially taking notice of his principal successor Adarang. But they also took entries away. As the eighteenth wore into the nineteenth century, increasingly those erased were the vaguely remembered legends from before the mid-seventeenth century, such as Nayak Baiju and Baz Bahadur. Prominent exceptions were 'founder fathers' Nayak Gopal and Amir Khusrau and the main lineage of Mughal chief musicians descending from Tansen, which of course extended into the present day of all current authors in an unbroken line.[45] Clearly, these later authors were not especially interested in legends of the distant past. What mattered to them was recording the names of the present and immediate past for posterity, and connecting those names back to the glorious heritage of the Mughal era in its late sixteenth- and seventeenth-century heyday.

This earnest attempt to immortalise the immediate past and present in the light of a very uncertain future is particularly obvious in the case of the final chapter of Zia-ud-din's c.1785–88 music treatise the *Hayy al-Arwāh* (far right-hand list),[46] with its constant litany 'It is some time since we saw or heard of X' and 'we don't know if Y is alive or dead'. I have greatly redacted Zia-ud-din's list of names for the purpose of this exercise: his *tazkira* – which takes up almost half his text – has sixty-nine formal entries and mentions dozens of additional names. Miyan Zia-ud-din 'Zia' was a native of Shahjahanabad, born early enough (c. 1725–30) to remember the opulence of Muhammad Shah's city before Nadir Shah's invasion. He was a well-connected minor Mughal official and, like many other gentlemen-amateurs of the time, a poet, keen Sufi and, crucially for what is coming next, a devoted disciple of chief musician Anjha Baras.[47] He was writing from Patna in the late 1780s, where he had settled about twenty years previously having become part of what he repeatedly called the 'scattering of Shahjahanabad'. He had escaped Delhi with his then-employer Iftikhar-ud-daula Mirza ᶜAli Khan in 1754, shortly after ᶜImad-ul-mulk deposed Ahmad Shah. Before coming to Patna around 1765,

[45] Schofield, 'Chief Musicians'. [46] On the dating c.1785–88, see Schofield, 'Emotions', p. 189.
[47] See Mir Taqi Mir, *Nikāt al-Shuᶜarā*, Urdu tr. Hamida Khatoon (New Delhi: Dihli Urdu Akademi, 1994), p. 130; also Schofield, 'Emotions', pp. 189–91.

Zia-ud-din moved around various places in the eastern regions, including Lucknow in Awadh, Sahibganj in Bihar, and Faizabad in Bengal.[48] Once settled in British-run Patna, he actively sought musical news from travellers arriving in this bustling commercial city from places between Bengal and Lahore.[49] While Zia-ud-din didn't much cite Rasikh directly, he did use his name order – and he did something interesting with it. Rather than organising chronologically, he explicitly broke up Rasikh's list and arranged the entries into four social categories: legends of the ancient past treated in a very brief manner; *kalāwants*; *qawwāls*; and finally gentlemen-amateurs.[50] Into those last three categories he added dozens of entries on musicians who were active in Muhammad Shah's Delhi, or were their sons and grandsons, most of whom had scattered to the four winds during the 'turmoil' of the 50s and 60s.

Musicians' *tazkiras* and genealogies of this period thus have distinctively different flavours, depending on the concerns of their authors. Rasikh's *tazkira*, written from Delhi just before everything went horribly wrong, has the feel of a man surveying an ocean crossed from the vantage point of the journey's end. Zia-ud-din's *Hayy al-Arwāh*, written in permanent exile from his beloved Delhi, feels more like a man trying desperately to contain a torrent of rushing floodwater in a sieve. Finally, the genealogies of the Baras Khan and Sadarang lineages found in Edinburgh MS 585(4), the introductions to Anup's *Rāg Darshans* (Chapter 5), and the early nineteenth-century *Asl al-Usūl* (Chapter 7) – all written by members or disciples of those lineages – are more concerned with mapping a particular water course belonging to the author's family to ensure it continues to flow despite fate's and rivals' attempts to divert or disperse it.

The Rivals: The Remembered and the Forgotten

In considering the rivals, I will start with the one who is remembered, Firoz Khan Adarang. His footprints in the *tazkiras* are curiously light – indeed, absent altogether from Zia-ud-din's otherwise most painstaking recollections. Adarang was the nephew and chief disciple of Sadarang (d. 1746/7), the 'Zulqarnain [Alexander the Great] of his time and the Tansen of his age'.[51]

[48] Not to be confused with Faizabad in Awadh.

[49] Zia-ud-din, *Hayy*, ff. 1r, 56v, 57v, 44r–45v, 52v, 47r–v, 46r, 49v, 62v; Schofield, 'Emotions'.

[50] *nujabā'*; see Schofield, 'Emotions', pp. 194, 200 fn.116.

[51] Anon, *Risāla dar ʿIlm-i Mūsīqī*. Salar Jung Museum Library, P Kash 38, ff. 369v–387r (1770–1), f. 387r; Anup ed. Shekhar, *Rāg Darshan*, p. 155; Mazhar, *Khulāsat* (1798), f. 2v.

Sadarang is still hailed today as the greatest musician of the eighteenth century. He was memorialised in the last entry of Rasikh's *tazkira*, and in the first and longest entry of Dargah Quli's chapter on Delhi's finest contemporary musicians, dancers and seductive beauties, male and female, in his salacious c. 1740 *Muraqqa^c*.[52] There are all sorts of legends about Sadarang,[53] but I will restrict my account to stories told of him in his own century. In a nutshell, due to falling out of political favour in the 1710s, Sadarang was forced to reinvent himself, which he did to eternal acclaim at the court of Muhammad Shah. Born in Aurangzeb's reign, he came from one of the prestigious Delhi *kalāwant* lineages that served the Mughal court. In the late seventeenth century he got his start under the patronage of renowned music-lover and songwriter Prince Muhammad A^{c}zam Shah (d. 1707), Aurangzeb's favoured son.

Fate, however, played an unkind trick on Sadarang when one of Aurangzeb's less satisfactory grandsons, Jahandar Shah, fell in love with Sadarang's cousin, the famous courtesan Lal Kanvar. When Jahandar Shah became emperor in 1712 he made the 'low-born' Lal Kanvar his queen, to the horror of the Mughal establishment, and at her insistence sought to put her relatives into high positions, including Sadarang. The upending of the social order that followed was so egregious that within a year Jahandar Shah was strangled to death by his own courtiers, and Lal Kanvar imprisoned for the rest of her life.[54] At this point, Sadarang disappeared from the record, only to reappear in Delhi several years later in the time of Muhammad Shah, in a slightly different guise.[55]

As a *kalāwant* he had been trained in traditions exclusive to his lineage: composing and singing the *dhrupad* genre and playing the *bīn*, for which he was most famous. On hearing him play, Dargah Quli sighed:

Just as the singers of this gathering steal hearts
When his hand strikes his instrument his fingernail scratches my heart.[56]

[52] Rasikh, *Risāla*, pp. 30–31; Dargah Quli, *Muraqqa^c* (1993), pp. 90–111 (Sadarang, pp. 90–1); also Brown [Schofield], 'If Music Be'.

[53] e.g. Susheela Misra, *Some Immortals of Hindustani Music* (New Delhi: Harman, 1990), pp. 33–41; and Manu Katyal, *Nemat Khāṅ-Fīroz Khāṅ evam Samkālīn Saṅgītjña* (New Delhi: Chaukhamba Surbharati Prakashan, 2014).

[54] Muhammad Hadi Kamwar Khan, *Tazkirāt al-Salātīn Chaghta*. ed. and tr. Muzaffar Alam (Mumbai: Asia Publishing House, 1980), pp. 159–67; and especially Kaicker, *King*, pp. 176–211; also William Irvine, *Later Mughals*, ed. Jadunath Sarkar (Delhi: Oriental Books Preprint Corporation, 1971), pp. 192–200.

[55] Brown [Schofield], 'Origins', pp. 163, 189–91 and 'If Music Be', pp. 79–81; Zia-ud-din, ff. 17v, 43v–44r, 51v, 57v; Tabor, 'Market', pp. 392–6.

[56] Dargah Quli, *Muraqqa^c* (1993), p. 90; tr. adapted from Tabor, 'Market', p. 393.

But now Sadarang reappeared in Muhammad Shah's Delhi as a fêted composer and singer of the *khayāl* genre,[57] which had until then been the exclusive property of the *qawwāls* of Delhi.[58] Sadarang was a devout Sufi himself, and learned *khayāl* as a child from one Tatar Khan *qawwāl*,[59] who was also in A^{c}zam Shah's service. *Khayāl* was a courtly genre with mingled *bhakti*-Sufi origins,[60] and Sufism was centrally important to Sadarang and his lineage, the Khandari branch of the Delhi *kalāwants* – they were disciples of the Tariqa-i Muhammadiyya branch of the Naqshbandi Mujaddidi order headed by the mystical poet Khwaja Mir Dard (d. 1785) (see Chapter 7).[61] *Khayāl* had been popular at court since at least the 1660s, but Sadarang's compositions and new style[62] were so ingenious and widely applauded that he has been credited in modern times with *khayāl*'s invention.[63] He was the greatest virtuoso and innovator of Hindustani music of the late Mughal age, and many of his *khayāls* are still sung today. I could go on, but Sadarang is not the direct subject of my story – except that lineage is everything in Hindustani music, and musicians are nothing without it.[64]

Adarang[65] was the son of Sadarang's brother, the singer and *bīn* player Bhupat Khan.[66] The young Adarang was so talented that Sadarang took him on personally as his special disciple, married him to one of his daughters, and trained him in *bīn*-playing and song composition to the full extent of his extraordinary abilities. Adarang first appears nameless in Dargah Quli's *Muraqqa*^{c} as another, critically important, innovator – the first musician known for certain to have adapted courtly *rāga* music to the *sitār*, an

[57] It is widely claimed today that Sadarang never sang *kh ayāl*, but Rasikh specifically states he was renowned as a *khayāl* singer.

[58] Brown [Schofield], 'Origins'.

[59] Possibly either Tatari or Nasr Khan. Rasikh has 'Tatari Qawwal', *Risāla*, p. 30; Zia-ud-din has 'Tatar Khan A^{c}zam Shahi', *Hayy*, f. 17v; and 'Nasr' نثر rather than 'Tatar' تتر Khan, f. 53r. Nasr, 'effusive with words', is more likely, but Tatar, 'Tartar', is better attested.

[60] Brown [Schofield], 'Origins'.

[61] Homayra Ziad, 'I Transcend Myself Like a Melody: Khwaja Mir Dard and Music in Eighteenth-Century Delhi', *The Muslim World* 97.4 (2007), 548–70; and 'Poetry, Music and the Muhammadi Path: How Khvājah Mīr Dard Brought Three Worlds Together in Eighteenth-Century Delhi', *Journal of Islamic Studies* 21.3 (2010), 345–76.

[62] *tāzagī-i tarz*. [63] Rasikh, *Risāla*, p. 30; Brown [Schofield], 'Origins'; Miner, *Sitar*, pp. 83–7.

[64] Daniel Neuman, *Life*, pp. 165–7.

[65] The best study of Adarang remains Miner, *Sitar*, pp. 87–95, 205–20.

[66] The most reliable genealogy of Sadarang's lineage is in the *Asl al-Usūl* [c. 1815], by Mir Muhammad Nasir Muhammadi Ranj written in conjunction with Adarang's nephew, Miyan Himmat Khan; British Library, I O Islamic 3162 (c. 1815), ff. 1r–2v (see Chapter 7). Miner argued that a figure known today as Khusrau Khan was Adarang's father and Sadarang's brother; Miner, *Sitar*, 21–4. The c.1740–1850 sources repeatedly state that Bhupat was Adarang's father; but it is possible Bhupat may have been Khusrau Khan's *takhallus*.

instrument that only emerged in the early eighteenth century.[67] He was also famed in several later *tazkiras* as a *bīn* player, a major composer of *dhrupads*, *khayāls* and *tarānās*, and as 'unique, special, matchless; virtuous and kind; spending his life in poverty and the garb of a mystic'.[68] Dargah Quli attended a number of Adarang's famous all-night musical assemblies in Delhi and breathlessly recalled his 'incomparable' musical talents. But Adarang was also important institutionally: together with Anjha Baras, Adarang was the head of the imperial musicians' atelier at Muhammad Shah's court.

And that is all the Persian tazkiras tell us about him. In one, his entry is less than a line long: 'Among the singers, Miyan Firoz Khan has attained consummate fame in this art.'[69] Everything else we know about his remaining life story comes instead from later legends and his music: from the longevity of his famous Firozkhani *sitār* style, which is still played; and those of his *khayāl* and *dhrupad* compositions that were written down at the time or still remain in the repertoire. From his compositions, we know Adarang retained his position as chief musician in Delhi right through the reign of ^{c}Alamgir II. But when the emperor's successor Shah ^{c}Alam II was forced into exile in 1759, Adarang fled east to the country of the Rohillas, where he found refuge first with Sa^{c}dullah Khan (d. 1764), son of Nawab ^{c}Ali Muhammad, and died sometime in the late 1760s.[70] Revered at the time, Adarang is still remembered today. His voice and his name live on in the performances of modern *sitār*, *sarod* and *khayāl* performers.

Posterity has not been so kind to Muhammad Shah's other chief musician, Miyan Anjha Baras Khan Muhammad Shahi.[71] Today he is forgotten by all except a handful of dedicated collectors of classical Hindustani song lyrics.[72] Even as early as 1845, the author of the *Naghma-i ^{c}Andalīb*, an

[67] Dargah Quli, *Muraqqa^{c}* (1993), p. 91; Miner, *Sitar*, pp. 24, 88. Miner's meticulously documented account of the eighteenth-century origins of the *sitār* is authoritative.

[68] Mazhar, *Khulāsat* (1798), ff. 3v, 37r; Dargah Quli, *Muraqqa^{c}* (1993), p. 91; Shahnawaz Khan [1803/4], *Mir'āt-i Āftāb-numā*, f. 270v; Anon (1770–1), *Risāla dar ^{c}Ilm-i Mūsīqī*, Salar Jung Museum Library, P Kash 38, ff. 369v–387r, f. 387r; Najm, *Naghma*, ff. 211r–v; Bahadur Singh, *Yādgār-i Bahādurī*, British Library, Or. 1652 (1834), p. 719.

[69] Bahadur Singh, *Yādgār*, p. 719.

[70] *Khayāl* and *dhrupad* compositions that Adarang wrote for ^{c}Alamgir II and Sa^{c}dullah Khan are preserved in Anup, *Rāg-Rāginī*, e.g. ff. 44r, 21v; also Miner, *Sitar*, pp. 87–8, 205–20. Adarang died before the twelfth year of Shah ^{c}Alam's reign, 1770–1, as he is recorded as having passed away in Anon, *Risāla* (1770–1), f. 387r.

[71] Anjhā, 'postponement', possibly should be *an-ichhā*, 'absence of desire'; Persian manuscripts of this period usually do not differentiate between ج jim and چ che. Either would be an appropriate epithet for this retiring character, but given the second half of his title, Baras, 'rain', it is most likely Anjha.

[72] I am grateful to Phalguni Mitra and Amlan Das Gupta for this information.

encyclopedia written for Lucknow prince Wajid ᶜAli Shah,[73] could barely remember his basic biographical details. 'It is not clear', Najm wrote, 'which family Anjha Baras belonged to, but he was related to the *kalāwant*s, the *dhrupad* singers'.

Ironically, he was the leading representative at Muhammad Shah's court of *the* most prestigious lineage of Mughal imperial *kalāwant*s: the direct father-to-son lineage of Tansen and the chief musicians to the Mughal emperors. The star of Chapter 2, Tansen's great-grandson Khushhal, was Anjha Baras's paternal grandfather, and Anjha Baras inherited Tansen's hereditary place on the Mughal carpet from his father, Ras Baras, the author of the *Shams al-Aswāt*. Muhammad Shah gave Anjha Baras the titles 'Sarāpāras' and 'Chūnpāras', the 'complete' and 'choicest touchstone' of music.[74] 'He was so beautiful inside and out that everyone, men and women, became enamoured of him . . . in his proficiency in the art of music there was noone like this dear person in his time', recalled Zia-ud-din.[75] 'Whoever heard [his] *dhrupad*s were convinced that it was magical, the way he combined the purest essence of the *rāga* with perfect lyrics and elegant vocal improvisations[76] . . . to produce a beneficial effect on the mind.'[77] He was, wrote an unnamed member of his *silsila* in 1788:

> the Sultan of the realms of singing, the skilled master of the ways of Tansen, god bless him. Truly, his compositions have a great richness; some of them are superior to the [classical Hindi] poetry of both ancient and contemporary authors . . . He was the Tansen of his time.[78]

Was he? The simple fact is that, as accomplished, well-trained and well-placed as he was, Anjha Baras was unfortunate to be eclipsed in virtuosity, innovation and fame in his own lifetime, first by his older rival Sadarang and then by his contemporary Adarang. We don't need this snide remark from our 1845 commentator to know that in Muhammad Shah's time, all was not entirely breezy in the house of Tansen:

> Anjha Baras aspired to be given the title of 'Second Tansen' by Muhammad Shah. But since Niᶜmat Khan was more accomplished than he was, the king's approval went to Niᶜmat Khan and Anjha Baras remained unacknowledged.[79]

The last statement is not strictly true; Anjha Baras and his cousins Mahmud Khan and Mansur Khan were all official retainers in the emperor's atelier,

[73] Later Nawab of Awadh, r. 1847–56; see Chapter 8.
[74] Anon, Edinburgh 585(4), f. 59v, tr. Richard David Williams. [75] Zia-ud-din, *Hayy*, ff. 44r-v.
[76] *tān*. [77] Najm, *Naghma*, f. 211v. [78] Anon, Edinburgh MS 585(4), ff. 59v–60r.
[79] Najm, *Naghma*, f. 211v.

permitted to use the title Muhammad Shahi.[80] But there can only be one Tansen at a time. And once you start looking at the *tazkiras* and genealogies written by junior members of Anjha Baras' own lineage, especially Zia-ud-din's *Hayy al-Arwah*, anxiety, envy and defensiveness begin to seep out everywhere.

For one thing, it must have been both an honour and somewhat galling for Anjha Baras, the head of Tansen's house, to be married off to Sadarang's daughter – the two major lineages were joined together in a dynastic marriage sometime in Muhammad Shah's reign in order to shore up both families' survival.[81] We know he did feel it was an honour to be brought into Sadarang's family and thus become privy to its innovative musical secrets, because his devoted disciple Zia-ud-din said so. But by becoming Sadarang's disciple, Anjha Baras was subordinating his far older traditions to the trendy innovations of Sadarang's family, and was also forced into a slightly lower status *within* the family to Adarang, also son-in-law and special disciple, and Anjha Baras' main contemporary rival. Concern for his teacher's injured pride almost certainly explains why Zia-ud-din refused to include even the name of the greatest musician of his day in his *tazkira*, rendering Adarang 'unacknowledged' instead of Anjha Baras.

He also included an amusing little anecdote that betrayed Anjha Baras' hurt over being superseded. Having been married into the Sadarang family, he took on one of Sadarang's other nephews, Fazil Khan, as a student. When he started out, Fazil played in the style peculiar to the Khandari branch of *kalāwants*, i.e. the branch represented by Sadarang's line. But when he went to learn with Anjha Baras, the master made Fazil write a formal note of agreement[82] stating that Fazil's forefathers had no musical integrity, and were servants of Anjha Baras's lineage. He sweetened this demand a little by reassuring his new student: 'He who makes himself a servant shall in turn become master', which Fazil took on the chin, as a loyal disciple must. In due course, Fazil did indeed become a senior performer, basing himself in Benares, and possibly attending the court of Kathmandu, dying a few years after 1780.[83]

[80] Anon, Edinburgh MS 585(4), f. 59v.

[81] Schofield, 'Chief Musicians'; Anon, *Risāla* (1770–1), f. 386v; Zia-ud-din, *Hayy*, ff. 44r-v.

[82] *muchalka*.

[83] Zia-ud-din, *Hayy*, ff. 43v, 46r–v; Schofield, 'Chief Musicians'. Zia-ud-din states Fazil died about five years before he was writing; and he is most likely to be the Maha-Ustad Miyan Fazil Khan Tan Baras who accompanied Anjha Baras' disciple Karim Sen Nad Baras to Kathmandu in the late eighteenth century; Richard Widdess, personal communication.

Rivalry between musicians is standard fodder in Hindustani musical anecdotes,[84] and in happier times this level of competition would not have mattered. But at a point in time after Nadir Shah had looted the Mughal treasury, when the Mughal emperor could sustain only so many musicians, competition was rather closer to a matter of life and death. And there is indeed evidence that the instability at court after this point knocked Anjha Baras off course – as it eventually did his great rival too. Dargah Quli and Zia-ud-din, who were both eyewitnesses to Nadir Shah's invasion, noted that afterwards Muhammad Shah released a number of his best musicians from his service, whether out of grief, lack of funds or both.[85] In Anjha Baras' case, the nobleman and noted music connoisseur Amir Khan *ᶜumdat al-mulk* (d. 1746), who had taken a distinct shine to the musician, requested the emperor's permission to put Anjha Baras on his staff at a salary of 300 rupees, and take him and a number of other musicians to Allahabad where he was being sent as governor. When Amir Khan returned to Delhi in 1744, Anjha Baras came back with him. Shortly afterwards, Anjha Baras apparently went into retirement, remaining in Delhi throughout the forthcoming invasions, massacres, looting and wars until his death about 1764, five years into the reign in exile of Shah ᶜAlam.[86]

In another telling story of the supposed decline of contemporary morals, Zia-ud-din pitted a particularly unworthy rival against his hero to justify his so-called retirement from performing in Delhi. The musician in question was Shujaᶜat Khan, another court *kalāwant* but a rather fruity character; Dargah Quli was especially contemptuous of Shujaᶜat's vanity and presumption (and, the implication is, lack of talent).[87] Here is Zia-ud-din's account of the fateful event:

When Anjha Baras was summoned to return from Allahabad to the Emperor's presence in Shahjahanabad, a musical *majlis* was held at the [erstwhile] mansion of Mahabat Khan, which is at Darya-i Khun [just outside the city walls].[88] Permission was granted to the musicians of Delhi that each of the groups from the [different]

[84] Max Katz, 'Rival Tales and Tales of Rivalry', *Lineage of Loss: Counternarratives of North Indian Music* (Middletown: Wesleyan University Press, 2017), pp. 68–99.

[85] e.g. Sadarang's female disciple Kamal Bai; Dargah Quli, *Muraqqaᶜ* (1993), p. 109.

[86] Zia-ud-din, *Hayy*, ff. 44r–46r; Shah Nawaz Khan, *Maāthir*, vol. i, p. 138; vol. ii, 1064. On Amir Khan see Dargah Quli, *Muraqqaᶜ* (1993), p. 94.

[87] Dargah Quli, *Muraqqaᶜ* (1993), p. 95; Brown [Schofield], 'If Music Be', pp. 63–4, 79–80.

[88] Reti Mahabat Khan, a mansion on the banks of the Yamuna river in the area now known as Daryaganj, was a popular site for holding *majālis*; Dargah Quli, *Muraqqaᶜ* (1993), pp. 77–8. It was probably located where the police station by ITO now stands; I am grateful to Rana Safvi for this information.

branches of the *kalāwants* should perform the salutation (*mujrā*) in turn.[89] When it was Shuja^{c}at Khan's turn (who was known [ironically] as Shuja^{c}ati Beg (Lord Shuja^{c}at)), he asked Miyan Anjha Baras' permission to sing, insisting 'Miyan Sahib, as you are the chief of our community, you should perform *mujrā* first'. Anjha Baras declined, saying, 'It's of no consequence, Miyan Shuja^{c}at, you perform first'. Since anger is human nature, Shuja^{c}at Khan replied sarcastically: 'Miyan Sahib, I don't know any performing. If you ask me [to go first], I will just give a couple of seductive winks[90] and then get up'. [The governor] Amir Khan smirked at what Shuja^{c}at had said. Because Miyan Anjha Baras was a wise and serious person and was recognised as such by men of knowledge, and was of a most honourable and independent bent, he left the gathering at once; and not only ceased his friendship with Amir Khan, but left behind all worldly things ... He spent time with the poor, and [enjoyed] the rewards of poverty. And he never again went to the houses of rich people to perform music.

When Emperor Ahmad Shah celebrated the third anniversary of his enthronement [1751] he was asked, once more, to come before the emperor. The emperor asked him, 'Are you Anjha Baras Khan, whom my late father Muhammad Shah described to me'? He replied, 'That Anjha Baras has passed away, and this Anjha Baras is another person who has come into your presence' ... The king ordered him to sing and improvise something. Then they say that the king said to him 'I will give you anything you want'. Anjha Baras replied: 'It is my greatest wish not to be asked to come into your presence again'. This was genuinely because he had become a companion of the dervishes and embraced their ideas.[91]

Anjha Baras clearly was a devoted Sufi – from the beginning both he and Sadarang had found a place at the feet of mystical poet Shah Sa^{c}dullah Gulshan (d. 1728), the head of the Naqshbandi order in Delhi. Anjha Baras was also a regular attendee of the poetry gatherings held at the house of the great Delhi intellectual Siraj-ud-din ^{c}Ali Khan Arzu (d. 1756).[92] This is where he first met Zia-ud-din and agreed to take him on as a disciple, as long as Zia-ud-din presented him with a copy of Jalal-ud-din Rumi's *Masnawī* (Chapter 7).[93] And Sufi shrines and hospices in the capital do seem to have been places of long-term refuge for musicians who remained in Delhi throughout the turmoil and scattering of the 1750s and 60s, as several other of Zia-ud-din's biographies attest.

But Anjha Baras seems also to have found the overwhelming rise to dominance of the *khayāl* genre of the *qawwāls* and of Sadarang, at the expense of the ancient *dhrupad* traditions of Tansen, disheartening. In

89 Either generically 'perform ritual respects' or specifically 'a salutation piece of music/dance'.
90 Term unclear. 91 Zia-ud-din, *Hayy*, ff. 44r–45r. 92 Arthur Dudney, *India*.
93 Zia-ud-din, *Hayy*, ff. 45r–v.

particular, he thought they were polluting the purity of Hindustani music's melodic framework, the *rāga*. In this final anecdote, Zia-ud-din, with clear discomfort, reflected his *ustād*'s disdain for one of the greatest *khayāl* singers of the day, the *qawwāl* Shaikh Moin-ud-din, whose grandfather Shaikh Sher Muhammad had introduced *khayāl* to Shah Jahan's court.[94] Dargah Quli Khan remembered Moin-ud-din as 'the master of the age, unique in the arts belonging to the *qawwāls*. The proliferation of his melodies is beyond reckoning like the flowers of the gardens of Kashmir ... with the colour of Bihzad's brush, he paints pictures with his melodies on the surface of the wind.'[95]

Anjha Baras' view of the man was not so flattering.

> People with a good understanding of music said that Shaikh Moin-ud-din was so powerful in his singing, that when he started a musical performance he would sing one *khayāl* in several *rāgas* without any strain. One day I asked Anjha Baras his opinion about composing and performing *khayāl* in several *rāgas*. He answered: 'Composing in several *ragas* is *raschandī* [mixing your moods], and it would be better just to perform correctly in one *rāga*. Some *kalāwants* perform in a specific way, where a *dhrupad* is sung continuously in a single session in several *rāgas* and *rāginīs*, a practice that is called *rāg-sāgar*. But it is unpleasant to listen to'. Nonetheless, Shaikh Moin-ud-din performed in this style and handled *raschandī* well. I don't know enough about music to evaluate the Shaikh on the basis of Miyan Anjha Baras's statement, but it is sufficient to know that in performing *khayāl*, no *qawwāl* has attained his status.[96]

While Adarang retained his place in the firmament of Hindustani musical stars because of his virtuosity as a performer and the ongoing appeal of his musical compositions, Anjha Baras clearly found his real place in the development of Hindustani music during the twenty years of his retirement, as a sought-after teacher and noted authority on the traditions of both the Baras Khan and Sadarang branches of the Delhi *kalāwants*. Zia-ud-din names at least eight students who were not related to his *ustād*, including *kalāwants*, *qawwāls* and gentlemen-amateurs, though his principal disciples were from within his own lineage: his cousin's grandson Muzaffar Khan, and the celebrated Karim Sen.[97] It was one of Anjha Baras' gentleman students, Zia-ud-din, who ensured that one day, centuries down the line, I would pick up what he wrote about his *ustād* and recall his name.

[94] Brown [Schofield], 'Origins', pp. 172–4.

[95] Dargah Quli, *Muraqqa*ᶜ (1993), p. 94. Bihzad of Herat (d. 1535) was one of the greatest medieval Muslim painters, and his illustrations were prized by Mughal collectors. On *khayāl* belonging to the *qawwāls*, see Brown [Schofield], 'Origins'.

[96] Zia-ud-din, *Hayy*, f. 52v.

[97] Zia-ud-din, *Hayy*, f. 43v. Anon, Edinburgh MS 585(4), ff. 59v–60r.

Mapping the Scattering, Mitigating Anxiety, Memorialising Names

In conclusion I wish to zoom out from the details of this microhistory of two rival musicians of the mid-eighteenth century – both important, if in different ways – and suggest on a more macro level what we can make of the rivalries Zia-ud-din tried so hard to construe in his *ustād*'s favour, but also of the sheer detail attached to all those names. The two things I want to draw attention to are encapsulated in the two halves of the quotation I cited at the beginning of this chapter from Anup's 1808/9 *Rāg Darshan*, which I have reversed here:

> Because of their eminence in this unique science, they were honoured attendants upon [Emperor] Muhammad Shah . . . but due to the changing fortunes of the time and the collapse of the sultanate, Khushhal Khan with the late Karim Khan came to Hyderabad;

and:

> Karim Khan was the special disciple of Miyan Adarang, who was himself the special disciple of the reigning prince of music Miyan Ni^{c}mat Khan Sadarang, whose status in the science of music is brighter than the sun and goes without saying.[98]

Firstly, the phenomenon I have highlighted of a big expansion in the writing of Hindustani musicians' biographies after 1750 was paralleled by a large upsurge of poetical *tazkira* production in Mughal India around the same time, the second and third quarters of the eighteenth century.[99] The answer to the why question – why did the recording of all these names and life histories become so important to writing on music in late Mughal India – concerns the need to preserve intact the memory of historical traditions and to keep track of contemporary artistic developments in a situation of considerable geo-political upheaval, when performers and patrons were on the move in unprecedented numbers.[100] Unlike the poetical *tazkira* tradition, which is full of the memories of oral performance and aural enjoyment via the preservation of poetry within biographies,[101] the musical *tazkiras* almost never preserve any of the songs that were composed or sung by their protagonists. Instead, these were hived off into a separate genre, which newly proliferated in the same time period as the musicians' *tazkira* – the song collection (Chapter 5).[102] But what

98 Anup ed. Shekhar, *Rāg Darshan*, p. 156. 99 Schwartz, 'Transregional'.
100 I have also made this argument for the art-song collection; Schofield, ' Words'.
101 Tabor, 'Market'. 102 Schofield, 'Words'.

tazkiras do preserve is traces of musicians' and patrons' movements, and the reasons why they moved: they actively remember how musicians, and the music they carried with them, survived in the face of existential threat to their world.

From the perspective of musical and poetical life in the Mughal capital, as reflected in the key commemorative texts of Zia-ud-din, Dargah Quli and Mir, Nadir Shah's 1739 invasion appears to have been inconsequential.[103] The real threat arose later, from the time the Nawab of Awadh Safdar Jang fell out with Emperor Ahmad Shah, worsened through ^{c}Alamgir II's reign and reached a peak of intolerability with Abdali's devastating 1757–61 invasions, which Zia-ud-din repeatedly invoked in his *tazkira* as the '*hangāma*', the turmoil, 'of Abdali'. It was these events that led to the 'scattering of Shahjahanabad', and played no small role in facilitating the rise of the East India Company at this exact time. Emperor Shah ^{c}Alam was himself forced into exile for thirteen years between 1759 and 72, taking a tiny nucleus of his favourite musicians with him to Patna then Allahabad, including the famous *qānun* player Nur Muhammad, as well as Adarang's brother La^{c}l Khan and his sons, Nur and Himmat Khan (Chapter 7).[104] Meanwhile, 1757 famously saw Robert Clive emerge victorious over the Nawab Nazim of Bengal, Siraj-ud-daula, at the Battle of Palashi (Plassey).[105] When Shah ^{c}Alam lost the Battle of Baksar (Buxar) against the Company in 1764 and signed the 1765 Treaty of Allahabad that ceded Bengal's revenues and administration to the British, he effectively signed his empire's death warrant.[106]

But it seems to have been the emperor's enforced absence from Delhi 1759–72 that really knocked the stuffing out of the capital as the established musical epicentre of the Mughal world. The 'scattering' was an exaggeration – not everyone left Delhi, even after the 1761 Battle of Panipat.[107] But those with significant talent or prospects elsewhere do mostly seem to have departed in a hurry, even if they returned to Delhi later. Take just Anjha

[103] There is one reference to Nadir Shah's '*hangāma*' in Zia-ud-din, *Hayy*, f. 57r; Dargah Quli's three oblique references to it show that Zia-ud-din was not alone in thinking it immaterial, *Muraqqa^{c}* (1993), pp. 71, 91, 109; also Mir, *Remembrances*, 2019a.

[104] Zia-ud-din, *Hayy*, f. 57r; Najm, *Naghma*, f. 211r. Sayyid Ahmad, *Āsār*, pp. 229–7.

[105] The material significance of Palashi/Plassey in the transition to Company rule in India has rightly been contested, though it was important symbolically; e.g. Philip J Stern, *The Company-State: Corporate Sovereignty and the Early Modern Foundations of the British Empire in India* (New York: Oxford, 2012), pp. 205–12.

[106] Wilson, *India Conquered*; Dalrymple, *Anarchy*.

[107] This was also true of poets, despite Mir's famous lamentations; see e.g. Schofield, 'Emotions'; Tabor, 'Market'; Ziad, 'Transcend', and 'Poetry', esp. p. 555; and Chapter 7.

Baras' students as an example. One of his special disciples, his cousin's grandson Muzaffar Khan, ended up working for the rulers of Awadh, Shuja^{c}-ud-daula (r. 1754–75) and Asaf-ud-daula (r. 1775–97), in Faizabad and Lucknow. His other special disciple Karim Sen went to the court of Kathmandu, while Sadarang's nephew Fazil became a star fixture in British-run Benares. Talented *qawwāl* Muhammad Panah went to work for Asaf-ud-daula's estranged brother Sa^{c}adat ^{c}Ali Khan when he was in the entourage of Shah ^{c}Alam's commander-in-chief, Mirza Najaf Khan (d. 1782), while Muhammad Panah's son Ghulam Raza went to Faizabad (Chapter 7) and his grandson took up residence in Patna.[108] Zia-ud-din himself tried Lucknow, Faizabad in Bengal, Sahibganj and then, when it became clear he could not return to Delhi, settled in Patna. And while Anjha Baras stayed in Delhi during his final twenty years,[109] Adarang and Moin-ud-din both went east to Rohilkhand around 1759, while Adarang's special disciple Karim Khan went south to Hyderabad (Chapter 5).[110] For many Delhi musicians such as the famous *qawwāl* brothers and *khayāl* singers Jan Muhammad Khan Jani, Ghulam Rasul and Jivan Khan, the flourishing and sophisticated court of the Nawabs of Awadh was a particular draw (Chapters 4 and 8). But plenty also went to Benares and Patna, further east to Murshidabad, and smaller places that supported musicians for religious reasons, like the Vaishnavite centre of Mathura.[111]

The chief reason Zia-ud-din mapped these movements in such meticulous detail and urgency becomes clear in his many small asides about people he knew who could no longer be traced. For example, when the *pakhāwaj* player Chabbar Khan left Delhi he first went to Patna. Zia-ud-din wrote plaintively, 'It is nearly twenty years ago that he came to my house for the music and poetry gatherings that were held every month . . . He went to the court of Murshidabad some years since, but nothing has been heard of him or the other *kalāwant*s there for some time now' (see Chapter 6). The poignancy of Zia-ud-din's failed attempt to keep track of another musician, the gentleman-amateur Mirza Tali^{c} Yar, is palpable: 'After the calamities unleashed upon Shahjahanabad . . . he fled to Sa^{c}dullah Khan Rohilla, after his death came to Lucknow, and then went to Farrukhabad . . . Wherever

[108] Zia-ud-din, *Hayy*, ff. 43v, 45r–46r; Anon, Edinburgh MS 585(4), ff. 59v–60r; Najm, *Naghma*, f. 211r.

[109] Najm suggested that Anjha Baras moved to Awadh with Muzaffar Khan to serve Shuja^{c}-ud-daula, but I consider this to be spurious; it conflicts with Zia-ud-din's much earlier and more reliable testimony of his own teacher, and Najm admitted his haziness about the details of Anjha Baras' life; Zia-ud-din, *Hayy*, ff. 43v–45r; Najm *Naghma*, f. 211v.

[110] Zia-ud-din, *Hayy*, ff. 51v–52v; Anup ed. Shekhar, *Rāg Darshan*, p. 156.

[111] e.g. Zia-ud-din, *Hayy*, ff. 47v–48r.

he is now, may God Almighty bless him with health and safety, by the prayers of the Prophet and his followers – for he was my beloved friend.'[112] Zia-ud-din's *tazkira* conveniently sketches out for us an invaluable map of all the major late Mughal centres of musical culture. Above all, however, it is a monument to the anxieties of this most uncertain age.[113] His determination to track down all those names also illuminates the specific quality of the anxiety bubbling beneath the surface of Zia-ud-din's remembrances of his own master.

There was still plenty of money in Hindustan and plenty of patrons who wanted to hear the best music the Mughal court could offer. As many historians have argued, and as we shall see in the next three chapters, the eighteenth century saw many regional powers rise and flourish, albeit at the expense of the centre. That money, that prestige, that authority, all those names had once been concentrated at Muhammad Shah's court. But within a relatively short period of time, they were suddenly all on the move accompanied by significant risks to life and limb. This meant great uncertainty and upheaval for musicians – they not only had to move, but be able and willing to adapt to new fashions and tastes in the patrons they moved to, or find another way to survive than performing.[114] While Anjha Baras seems to have been willing to learn the new, more *dhrupad*-like *k͟hayāl* style of Sadarang (who at least was a *kalāwant*), he was unwilling to compromise his lineage's traditions by singing *rāga*s like a *qawwāl*, even one as universally acclaimed as Moin-ud-din. What Anjha Baras uniquely offered to posterity instead was his mastery as a *teacher* with a distinctive product – the authentic traditions of the Mughal golden age, which would still have delighted a number of potential patrons with more refined (or more conservative) tastes.

For the second thing *tazkira*s, and even more so genealogies, underline is the increasing importance in this period of verifiable lineage – through the name of your father or *ustād*, and your possession of musical materials unique to your inheritance – as employment credentials for musicians on the move. Pedigree was essential to survival in this new world.[115] Plenty of talented migrating musicians seem to have used the eighteenth-century chaos across Hindustan as a means to reinvent themselves as being of higher (or different) musical heritage than they originally were[116]

[112] Ibid., ff. 49v–r, 60v. [113] Schofield, 'Emotions'.

[114] See Schofield, 'Words'; also Daniel Neuman, *Life*, pp. 168–201.

[115] Daniel Neuman, *Life*, pp. 168–201.

[116] e.g. Umrao Khan, a fine hereditary *bīn* player who according to Imam Khan migrated to Awadh c. 1800. In post-Uprising Lucknow, Imam recognised Umrao and his sons as the only

(Chapters 4 and 5), thus increasing competition for established lineages. I don't think it is a coincidence that most of the post-Rasikh *tazkiras* and genealogies were written by members and disciples of the two authenticated Delhi *kalāwant* lineages embodied in the celebrated figures of Anjha Baras and Adarang. *Tazkiras* and genealogies were the ultimate proof to new patrons that you were indeed connected by blood or discipleship with Mughal court performers, and thus genuinely worthy of patronage;[117] this was often true of the highest-status female courtesans such as Panna Bai[118] as well as male hereditary musicians.

But as Edinburgh MS 585(4) shows, remembering names and how they were connected was also important knowledge *within* lineages, because names acted as triggers to remember musical materials transmitted via oral and aural methods of training. Without a detailed written notation system, such materials are subject to loss at the best of times. But in the absence of the proximate embodied knowledge of extended families living together in the one place, much of it was now potentially threatened with extinction. What do you do if you are working thousands of miles from your ancestral community, and can no longer go next door and ask, 'Grandfather, what are the words to the second verse?' or 'Exactly how we are related to Sadarang?' Large-scale migration is why genealogies, biographies and song compositions had to be written down in this period, as well as new technical works on *rāga* and *tāla* – to remember.[119]

Rivalry between lineages rose to the surface when the survival of a particular musical tradition was seriously at stake. This was why Zia-ud-din took such pains to memorialise the life of his beloved *ustād*, who was at real risk of being forgotten while his rivals' names rose ever higher. But rivalry was only part of the story. Most of the time, biographical writers simultaneously rendered lineages *distinct*, through differentiating their musical styles and personnel, and embraced those distinct lineages as *equally valuable*. Thus Zia-ud-din, the gentleman student of a *kalāwant*,

'true' descendents of the original Khandari lineage, but so far I have not found any references in the c. 1750–1850 sources to an Umrao Khan connected with the Sadarang family. In contrast Imam gave Mir Nasir Ahmad – verifiably the leading contemporary blood member of the Khandari lineage in Delhi (Chapter 7) – short shrift; *Ma^{c}dan*, pp. 24, 43.

117 Schofield, 'Chief musicians'; Schofield, 'Words'.

118 Dargah Quli, *Muraqqa^{c}* (1993), pp. 108–9. Panna Bai was clearly a major courtesan. There is a portrait of her in one of Antoine Polier's albums (Museum für Islamische Kunst, Berlin, I 4593, f. 10); and she is also known from Kishangarh paintings to have performed by invitation in Rupnagar c. 1760 with her father Miyan Khidar on *tabla*; Heidi Rika Maria Pauwels, *Cultural Exchange in Eighteenth-Century India: Poetry and Paintings from Kishangarh* (Berlin: E B Verlag, 2015), pp. 69–73.

119 Also Kia, *Persianate Selves*.

went out of his way to describe the life histories of *qawwāls* – in a separate section but with equal enthusiasm and respect. He also drew attention to the clear difference between the styles of two separate *kalāwant* lineages in his wry story about Fazil's apprenticeship to Anjha Baras. Indeed, it was from the 1780s, in the texts written by members and disciples of these two entangled *kalāwant* families – Zia-ud-din, Anup, the author of Edinburgh MS 585(4), Ranj and Miyan Himmat Khan (Chapter 7) – that the four distinctive *kalāwant* family styles of *dhrupad* known as *bānīs* started being named and described in melodic and rhythmic detail as distinctive but equal: the Khandari style (in these texts unequivocally Sadarang's family lineage) the Gorari (also Gorhari/Gobahari), the Nohari and the Dagari.[120]

In concluding this chapter, it is worth underlining the multiple correspondences of the social and pedagogical formations being described in late Mughal writings with Daniel Neuman's classic definition of contemporary *gharānās* in Hindustani music. We have long accepted the premise that today's *gharānās* are a modern phenomenon, born in the searing aftermath of the 1857 Uprising, another violent political watershed in which musicians and patrons were killed, forced into exile and scattered all over India (Chapter 8).[121] This is James Kippen's summary of Neuman's analysis of what a Hindustani musical lineage must possess to qualify as a *gharānā*:

> The *gharānā* must have, at its core, a family (*khāndān*) of musicians passing on a musical tradition from generation to generation through their disciples and students ... a founder member with a charismatic personality ... [it] must be represented by a living member of the original *khāndān* ... have a famous personality who is living ... at least three generations of distinguished musicians representing the musical tradition ... [and] a distinct and unique musical style.[122]

[120] Zia-ud-din, *Hayy*, ff. 13r (all four), 43r (Dagari), 46r-v (Khandari=Sadarang, vs. Anjha Baras style); Anup, *Rāg Darshan* (Brajbhasha 1800), ff. 3r–4r; Anon, Edinburgh MS 585(4), ff. 51r, 58v–60r; Ranj/Himmat, *Asl al-Usūl*, f. 1r; Sanyal and Widdess, *Dhrupad*, pp. 61–94. In 'Chief Musicians' I was wrong that 'it was not until Karam Imam [Khan] ... that the different *dhrupad* families were referred to as "*bānīs*"'. Zia-ud-din stated c. 1785–88 that '[the way of performing *rāga*] is divided into four *bānīs* ... They are 1) Dagari, 2) Gobarhari, 3) Nohari, 4) Khandari, and the types of *kalāwants* and their classes [*zāts* → *jātis*] are divided into these *bānīs*'; Zia-ud-din, *Hayy*, f. 13r. A century earlier, in the glossary at the back of the *Tuhfat al-Hind*, Mirza Khan stated (without naming the four) that '*bānī* means a style, school, and mode of embellishment of speech/singing (*goftan*)'; RSPA 78, f. 329r.

[121] Daniel Neuman, *Life*, p. 146.

[122] Kippen, *Tabla*, p. 63; summarising Daniel Neuman, *Life*, pp. 145–67.

All of these elements must also be backed up by oral histories of the family's genealogy, and anecdotes about élite patrons, famous ancestors, and – of course – infamous rivalries.[123]

The musical *tazkiras* and genealogies of late Mughal writers demonstrate that every one of these ingredients was already present and prized in the social configurations of hereditary musicians in the eighteenth century and even earlier, and in the way they preserved and passed on the élite musical traditions of the Mughal court to future generations. These particular writings on music show us that guild-like formations in Hindustani musical culture have a much longer continuous history than we have hitherto imagined – even though they were not, yet, called *gharānās*.[124]

And that bewilderment of names in the introduction to the 1798 *Khulāsat al-ᶜAish*? Who were all those people? Of the forty unremembered names I listed at the beginning of this chapter, brief lives of twenty-five of them are found in the writings of the biographers and genealogists we have been keeping company with here. They were important once. Thanks to the foresight of those who loved and cared about them, they have been remembered in these pages once again.

[123] Daniel Neuman, *Life*, pp. 59–84; also Dard Neuman, 'Pedagogy'.

[124] The earliest use of *gharānā* in a written source, to my knowledge, is in connection with dancers in Lucknow; Mardan ᶜAli Khan, *Ghuncha-i Rāg* (Lucknow: Naval Kishore, 1862/3), pp. 123–5; Williams, 'Hindustani', p. 22, fn. 41.

4 | The Courtesan and the Memsahib: Khanum Jan and Sophia Plowden at the Court of Lucknow

European Private Papers and Musical Notations

Tanana	*tanana*	*tananana*	*tana*	*tanana*	*tanana*	*tanana*
Flūṭ	*harp*	*vayūlīn*	*fayf*	*ārgīn*	*harpsī-*	*kārḍ*

Chronogram, 1788 CE. Untitled Persian treatise on Hindustani *tāla*s (Edinburgh 585(4)).[1]

Two Worlds Colliding

We don't know who wrote the treatise on the Hindustani rhythmic system now designated Oriental Manuscript 585 no. 4 in the Edinburgh University Library. Nor do we know precisely where he was working, or for whom.[2] But in 1788, in Lucknow or Benares, or maybe Patna or Allahabad, one member of Anjha Baras' *kalāwant* lineage was engaging musically on apparently convivial terms with Europeans. 'They *write* in books of music', he enthused. 'They have another instrument of the string family that is extremely fine and noble named *the harpsichord*.'[3] So inspired was he after playing this marvellous instrument that he gave the date of his treatise as the above chronogram[4] according, unusually, to the Christian calendar, along with the customary *al-hijrī* date. Recite it out loud: it resounds joyfully. The first line, '*Tanana tanana* . . . ' set

[1] Anon, Edinburgh MS 585(4), f. 50r. I am grateful to harpsichordist Jane Chapman and dance historian Margaret E. Walker for their extensive practice-based input on this chapter. You can hear all the pieces discussed in this chapter on Chapman's 2015 recording, Jane Chapman, harpsichord, with Yu-Wei Hu, flute, *The Oriental Miscellany: Airs of Hindustan, William Hamilton Bird*, Signum Classics, 2015, SIGCD415.

[2] Edinburgh MS 585(4); ff. 58v–60r. 'He' is an educated assumption. To my knowledge only one music treatise was written by a woman in the Mughal era: Jana Begum (daughter of Abd-ur-rahim Khan-i Khanan), *Risāla-i Mūsīqī* [early 17C], Bodleian Library, Ouseley 225; personal communication, Richard David Williams, 2019.

[3] My emphasis; ibid., ff. 45v–46r.

[4] Dates in Persian manuscripts are frequently given as a chronogram, a line of poetry in which all the letters are allocated a number according to the traditional *abjad* system that, when added up, give the year of composition; Kaicker, *King*, pp. 110–11. The chronogram for the *hijrī* date is 1202 AH, ibid., f. 50v; this narrows the timeframe to January–September 1788, exactly when Plowden was in Lucknow.

Figure 4.1 Probably Sir David Ochterlony, first British Resident to the Mughal court (1803–06, 1818–25), watching a *nāch* in his house in Delhi, c. 1820. Add. Or. 2. **© The British Library Board**

the metrical groove using the new notation our musician had just borrowed from Perso-Arabic music theory to overhaul how he wished Hindustani *tālas* to be understood and written down in the modern era.[5] For his second line, he set the names of six European instruments to his effervescent metre, revelling in the unorthodox feel of the English sounds in his mouth that he carefully preserved in diacritical markings in the *nast*ᶜ*alīq* script. But most cleverly, when each was given its traditional numerical value, the Persian letters he used to transcribe these delightful *firangī* words neatly added up to the English date of his manuscript: 1788.[6]

[5] James Kippen, 'Mapping a Rhythmic Revolution Through Eighteenth- and Nineteenth-Century Sources of Rhythm and Drumming in North India', in Richard K. Wolf, Stephen Blum and Christopher Hasty (eds.), *Thought and Play in Musical Rhythm: Asian, African, and Euro-American Perspectives* (Oxford: Oxford University Press, 2019), 253–72; also Chapter 7 of this book.

[6] In exactly this period, 1786–8, we know that one *kalāwant bīn*-player, Jivan Shah, worked closely with the Resident to Benares, Francis Fowke, in a set of musical experiments comparing the *bīn* to the harpsichord; see below. It is possible Jivan Shah wrote Edinburgh MS 585(4); if Jivan's brother Pyar Khan (Peer Cawn) was the same as the Pyar Sen the author celebrated as the greatest living *dhrupad* singer, then it is likely: Pyar Sen was the son of Karim Sen, Anjha Baras' most feted disciple (ff. 59r, 60r). Francis Fowke, 'On the Vina'; Joep Bor, 'The Rise of Ethnomusicology: Sources on Indian Music c. 1780–1890', *Yearbook for Traditional Music* 20 (1988), 51–73, pp. 55–6.

Just one year later, in Calcutta in 1789, William Hamilton Bird published his *Oriental Miscellany*: the first-ever publication of Hindustani music in European staff notation, arranged for that same 'fine and noble' instrument, the harpsichord.[7] Bird's pieces were based on what he called 'Hindustani Airs' taken from the performances of North Indian court music and dance that Europeans knew as the *nautch* (*nāch*)[8] – intimate musical assemblies at which troupes of North Indian courtesans,[9] with their professional male accompanists, would sing, dance, recite Persian and Hindustani poetry and match wits with the assembled company. 'The diversions in India are but few', wrote Mrs Jemima Kindersley from Allahabad in October 1767:

> But the favorite and most constant amusement of the great, both Mahomedans and *Hindoos* ... is called a *notch*; which is the performance of the dancing girls ... It is difficult to give you any proper idea of this entertainment, which is so very delightful ... A large room is lighted up; at one end sit the great people who are to be entertained; at the other are the dancers and their attendants; one of the girls who are to dance comes forward, for there is seldom more than one of them dance at a time; the performance consists chiefly in a continual removing the shawl, first over the head, then off again; extending first one hand, then the other; the feet are likewise moved, though a yard of ground would be sufficient for the whole performance. But it is their languishing glances, wanton smiles, and attitudes not quite consistent with decency, which are so much admired; and whoever excels most in these is the finest dancer. The girl sings, while she is dancing, some Persian or Hindostan[i] song; some of them are really pleasing to the ear.[10]

Bird's opening piece 'The Ghut' (Example 4.1)[11] is a faint echo of just such a performance, of the kind executed 235 years ago by the courtesan Khanum Jan in the city of Lucknow for its ruler the Nawab of Awadh, Asaf-ud-daula (r. 1775–97), and mixed *majālis* of Muslim notables, wealthy Hindus, European adventurers, East India Company officials – and

[7] William Hamilton Bird, *The Oriental Miscellany; Being a Collection of the Most Favourite Airs of Hindoostan, Compiled and Adapted for the Harpsichord, andc.* (Calcutta: Joseph Cooper, 1789); also (Edinburgh: Gow and Shepherd, 1805).

[8] Nautch is a corruption of the Hindi/Urdu word *nāch*, 'dance', but song performance was always a central component; see Margaret E Walker, *India's Kathak Dance in Historical Perspective* (Aldershot: Ashgate, 2014). In line with Walker, I shall be rehabilitating the term *nāch* as the best term to describe these performances.

[9] Now known generically as *tawā'if*, but this term does not seem to have been in customary use as an umbrella for the plethora of Indian courtesan communities before about 1800; Schofield, 'Courtesan Tale', pp. 152–8, 167 fn. 24. Plowden's *Album* uses *lūlī*, ff. 14, 39.

[10] Jemima Kindersley, *Letters from the Island of Teneriffe, Brazil, the Cape of Good Hope, and the East Indies* (London: J Nourse, 1777), pp. 229–32.

[11] It is spelled 'Ghut' in the table of contents, 'Gut' on the page.

Example 4.1 'I. The Ghut' (*gat*), from William Hamilton Bird, *Oriental Miscellany* (Calcutta, 1789), p. 1. Public Domain

a handful of Englishwomen, including the redoubtable Mrs Plowden. The term *gat*, combined with the many surviving European descriptions of *nāch* like Kindersley's,[12] gives away what Bird was trying to depict in this opener: a choreographed sequence known in *kathak* dance today as *gat nikās*, characterised by a gliding walk called a *chāl*.[13] Famous Delhi resident James Skinner (Chapter 7) described the dance in 1832 thus: 'After coming forward a little distance, their arms moving gracefully in concord with their feet in a species of 'glissade', for all their steps are sliding, they sink suddenly and make the prettiest pirouêtte imaginable.'[14]

[12] Walker, *Kathak*, pp. 52–66.

[13] ibid, pp. 3, 64; also Margaret E. Walker, 'The "Nautch" Reclaimed: Women's Performance Practice in Nineteenth-Century North India', *South Asia: Journal of South Asian Studies* 37.4 (2014), 551–67.

[14] James Skinner, 1832, quoted in Walker, *Kathak*, p. 63.

Stylistically, Bird's 'Ghut' sounds nothing but quintessentially European, with its simple common-practice-period harmonies.[15] But there is still a trace of the original Hindustani *gat* here: not in the main piece, nor in the mind's eye, but in the 'curtain raiser' with its distinctive quaver-quaver-rest-quaver rhythm (Da dā – da | Da dā – da) and tempo marking, *andante*, 'at a walking pace'. According to *kathak* historian Margaret Walker, this rhythm does indeed describe the movements of the dancer's feet as she performs the *chāl* in *gat nikās*. This is not something apparent from the visual evidence of the score alone. Walker's embodied knowledge as a dancer of Hindustani repertoire was required to realise that calling this piece 'The Ghut' wasn't entirely Mr Bird's fantasy. Something of the Indian dancers' original performances are still buried within Bird's notation.

Glimpsing Eurydice

This chapter gets to the heart of the philosophical question I raised in my introduction to this book: whether it is ever possible for Orpheus to bring Eurydice back from the dead – specifically, in this case, whether it is possible to rehear, and more speculatively to re-experience, the sounds of the past *as they were then*, from those of their material remains that have survived into the present day. My story here concerns two remarkable women musicians, the courtesan and the memsahib of my title: the celebrity Kashmiri courtesan Khanum Jan and Mrs Sophia Elizabeth Plowden, wife of a British East India Company official.[16] It was their extraordinary personal interactions through music at the Lucknow court of Asaf-ud-daula in 1788 that lay behind Bird's *Oriental Miscellany* and later publications of what came to be known as 'Hindustani Airs'.

The European side of this story has been told before, most expansively by Ian Woodfield, Gerry Farrell and Nicholas Cook. To summarise, the Hindustani Air was a European-style keyboard piece that enjoyed a flurry of popularity in British colonial society in North India and Bengal in the 1780s and 90s. Hindustani Airs were short salon pieces based on original

[15] Track 2 of Chapman's studio recording.

[16] Plowden just called her Khanum; she is Khanum Jan in Sayyid Muhammad Hasan Shah tr. Sajjad Hussain Kasmandavi, *Nashtar*, ed. ᶜIshrat Rahmani (Lahore: Majlis-i Tarqi-i Adab, 1963); see also Shweta Sachdeva Jha, 'Eurasian Women as *Tawa'if* Singers and Recording Artists: Entertainment and Identity-Making in Colonial India', *African and Asian Studies* 8 (2009), 268–87.

Indian melodies, with tunes taken down in European staff notation from live performances by female and male court musicians, either at *nāch* performances or at specially arranged private sessions in European homes. Their melodies were transcribed and then harmonised in arrangements for solo keyboard, or keyboard and voice with English words that owed nothing to the original Hindustani or Persian lyrics. Bird's *Oriental Miscellany*, published by popular subscription in 1789, was the epitome of the vogue for European arrangements of *nāch* songs in the soirees of British Calcutta at the time.[17] It was the forerunner of many European publications and performances of Hindustani Airs from the 1780s until at least the 1850s, enjoyed from the firesides of rural Invernesshire to the cantonment balls of Singapore.[18]

The Hindustani Airs episode was a musical cul-de-sac at the time, and is little more than a musicological footnote now. But it still reveals a great deal about face-to-face emotional engagements between Europeans and Indians during the rise of British colonial power. And it also turns out to be critically important to unlocking what Hindustani music may have sounded like in the late Mughal period, long before the era of recorded sound. The key lies in Sophia Plowden's exquisite manuscript collection of Hindustani Airs from the court of Lucknow, now in the Fitzwilliam Museum, Cambridge,[19] which she and Goan musician John Braganza

[17] Ursula Sims-Williams, 'British Interest in Indian Music in the Late 18th and Early 19th Century', *India Office Library and Records Newsletter*, No. 22 (March 1981); Bor, 'Rise'; Ian Woodfield, 'The "Hindostannie Air": English Attempts to Understand Indian Music in the Eighteenth Century', *Journal of the Royal Musical Association* 119.2 (1994), 189–211; Ian Woodfield, 'Collecting Indian Songs in Late 18th-Century Lucknow: Problems of Transcription', *British Journal of Ethnomusicology* 3.1 (1994), 73–88; Gerry Farrell, *Indian Music and the West* (Oxford: Oxford University Press, 1997), pp. 15–44; Ian Woodfield, *Music of the Raj: A Social and Economic History of Music in Late Eighteenth-Century Anglo-Indian Society* (Cambridge: Cambridge University Press, 2000), pp. 149–80; Nicholas Cook, 'Encountering the Other, Redefining the Self: Hindostannie Airs, Haydn's Folksong Settings and the "Common Practice" Style', in Martin Clayton and Bennett Zon (eds.), *Music and Orientalism in the British Empire, 1780s–1940s* (Aldershot: Ashgate, 2007), 13–37; Shweta Sachdeva [Jha], 'In Search of the *Tawa'if* in History: Courtesans, *Nautch* Girls and Celebrity Enterainers in India (1720s–1920s)', Unpublished PhD Dissertation, SOAS, University of London (2008), pp. 120–6; Schofield, 'Words'.

[18] See Sims-Williams, 'British Interest'; the latest I have found is Osmond George Phipps, *Taza ba Taza, Nao ba Nao: The Famous Song of the Persian Poet Hafiz*, British Library, H.1771.o.(39) (1857). For Invernesshire: William Fraser, letter, Fraser of Reelig Archives, 'William Fraser: Correspondence'; I was unable to check the date of this reference due to Covid-19. For Singapore: *Singapore Free Press and Mercantile Advertiser*, 7 April 1842, p. 2, and 26 August 1841, p. 2.

[19] Sophia Plowden, *Album* and *Tunebook*, Fitzwilliam Museum, University of Cambridge, MS380 (1788). The coversheet states the collection was made in Lucknow in 1786, but Plowden's *Diary*

took down from Khanum Jan and her fellow court musicians in 1788.[20] The melodies that Plowden compiled into her *Tunebook* have already come under substantial scrutiny.[21] What has remained largely in the shadows is the *Album* of illustrated loose-leaf folios that goes with the *Tunebook.*[22]

The *Album* has previously been passed over as a set of miniature paintings of likely but unclear relevance to the *Tunebook.*[23] Instead, unusually among her contemporaries, Plowden simultaneously collected the lyrics that went with the melodies she transcribed, in Persian, Urdu, Brajbhasha, Punjabi and other languages of North Indian courtly song. Bird used snippets of Indian phrases to entitle his thirty Hindustani Airs – 'Sakia! fusul beharust', 'Mutru be khoosh nuwa bego', etc.[24] – whose significance and often sense have baffled previous scholars. Many of these turn out to be partial first lines or refrains of songs from Plowden's *Album*. This confirms previous arguments that Bird took much of his published collection from her manuscript. But more importantly, Bird's titles, supplemented with songs reproduced by William Crotch and John Gilchrist,[25] have enabled me to reunite, for the first time in well over two centuries, about a quarter of Plowden's tunes with their original Indian lyrics (Table 4.1).[26] This makes it possible – potentially – to rehear some of these compositions as they might have been sung at the court of Lucknow in the 1780s.

But what does this reuniting of melody and lyric really tell us? Even if we could recreate these songs in the here and now to some extent, does that reveal anything about what was it like to hear them there and then: for

establishes that she did not arrive until 19th December 1787, and that her collection was produced largely in August–September 1788; Sophia Plowden, *Diary*, British Library, MSS Eur F127/94 (January 1787–January 1789).

20 Plowden, *Album* coversheet. Woodfield has Braganza as Portuguese, *Music*, p. 152; but he was most likely Goan. The Braganzas were a well-known Goan family in Lucknow, and two Braganzas served the Nawabs as piano tuners between 1834 and 1855; Rosie Llewellyn-Jones, *A Fatal Friendship: The Nawabs, the British, and the City of Lucknow* (New Delhi: Oxford University Press, 1985), pp. 21–2, 27.

21 Woodfield, 'Hindostannie Air', and *Music*, pp. 189–211; Farrell, *Indian Music*, pp. 15–44; Cook, 'Encountering'.

22 But see Schofield, 'Words'.

23 Farrell and Woodfield briefly note the presence of texts that may be 'the words to the songs' (Woodfield, 'Collecting', p. 85) but both missed their significance; Farrell, *Indian Music*, p. 36; Woodfield, *Music*, p. 152.

24 Bird, *Oriental*, no.s 2 and 4.

25 William Crotch, 'National Tunes', Norfolk Records Office, 11097, pp. 60–1; handwritten musical examples to accompany his 'Lecture on National Music' (1798–1829), Norfolk Records Office, 11229; and *Specimens of Various Styles of Music*, vol. i, 1st ed. (London: Robert Birchall, 1807), pp. 156–62; John Gilchrist, *The Oriental Linguist* (Calcutta: Ferris, 1798), pp. 152–62.

26 Schofield, 'Words', especially pp. 180–5.

Table 4.1 Correlation of Plowden's texts with their tunes. *Album* and *Tunebook*. Lucknow, 1788. MS 380. Fitzwilliam Museum, University of Cambridge

Plowden *Tunebook*	Plowden *Album*	Text, genre, author (if known)	Correlation
no. 5	32 a	'Sun re sujan ke tumse', *rekhta*, Wali	Tune-book title, only *rekhta* by Wali in album folios
no. 7,36,49	21	'Sun re mashuqa! be-wafa!', *khayāl* of the 'snake-men'	Bird no. 6, Crotch no. 336, album folio illustration
no. 8	6 a	'Ai yad lutfi kon be-ru dar', Persian *ghazal*, Amir Khusrau	Tune-book title, same page & folio as Plowden no. 9
no. 9	6 b	'Komani rana', *ṭappa*	Crotch no. 327
no. 10	1 a	'Har shab manam', Persian *ghazal*, Amir Khusrau	same page & folio as Plowden no. 11
no. 11	1 b	'Mutrib-i khush/taza ba taza', Persian *ghazal*, Hafiz	Bird no. 4, Gilchrist text & tune, Nashtar
no. 14,20	8	'Saqi-a! Fasl-i bahar ast', Persian *rubā'ī*	Bird no. 2
no. 15	9 b	'Awwal ke ma-ra be-'ishq', Persian *rubā'ī*	Bird no. 5, Johnson
no. 16	9 a	'Ki bashad o ki bashad', Persian *rubā'ī*	Bird no. 7
no. 18	11 b	'Saiya saqf-i bar-in ta', Persian *ghazal*	preceding page & same folio as Plowden no. 19
no. 19	11 a	'Surwi ruwani kisti', Persian *ghazal*, Khaqani	Bird no. 30, Gilchrist text & tune, Crotch no. 331, Nashtar
no. 21	12	'Kya kam kya dil', *rekhta*, Sauda[c]	Bird no. 3, Gilchrist text & tune, Crotch no. 332
no. 43	25 a	'Awa akala mera yekta', *ṭappa*	same page and folio as Plowden no. 44
no. 44	25 b	'Ai bina ai bina ai bina', *ṭappa*	Crotch no. 337
no. 69	38	'Ran hain zohra nahin', Urdu *marsiya*	Crotch no. 338, album folio illustration
	3 a	'Dadar va ki bundi', *ṭappa*	Bird no. 13
	7 b	'Ati se bol band ho jati se', *khayāl*	Bird no. 9
	15 a	'Mera bala sinhi. . .machari ke bind yali', *ṭappa*	Bird no. 21 'Mera Mutchelli'
	27 b	'Ai pari chehrah be-yek naz', Persian *rubā'ī*	Bird no. 8
	29 a	'Ai bibi mon karela', *khayāl*	Bird no. 23

a courtesan, for a Lucknow Nawab, for an English gentlewoman? Music and dance, and our experience of them, are only ever fully real in the moment of their embodiment and sounding; once the performance is over, they are lost beyond recall. And neither transcriptions of sound into pen strokes, nor writing about musical experience, can ever bring them back.

This is true even of the kind of detailed European musical notations that we pretend allow the sounds of the past to be reproduced in the present.[27] How much more true is this of Khanum Jan's great song and dance performances, the only remains of which today lie skeletal on the page, swathed in European dress?

I shall anticipate my conclusion here: the task is fundamentally impossible. But the effort of imaginative recreation is worth it, because the revelation lies in the journey, not its end. Plowden's collection, with its Indian-language song texts side-by-side with its European musical notations, creates a crucial link in the chain between Hindustani music and these harpsichord pieces produced for the British leisured classes. The Occidental distortions of Plowden's harpsichord transcriptions and Bird's arrangements, which make the Indian originals impossible to recover, have lent themselves to the interpretation that they were instances of colonial epistemic violence to Indian culture.[28] But if we reconsider them from the point of view of the song texts Plowden collected, as well as paracolonial Indian sources for similar musical engagements, the story of this music-induced intimacy between others emerges as more complicated.

It is critically important to keep in mind when exploring this moment of musical harmonisation that this was *not* why Plowden and her compatriots were in Lucknow; localised instances of cultural rapprochement or personal sympathy do not mitigate the systemic colonial will to domination.[29] The East India Company was in India to pursue a colonial project designed entirely to benefit themselves. Less than seventy years later in 1856, the Company used the last Nawab of Lucknow's love of exactly the same forms of music and dance as their excuse to depose him and annex his kingdom – a major grievance that fed directly into the all-too-real violence of the 1857 Uprising (Chapter 8).[30] The wider ramifications of this mutually pleasurable, liminal moment of cross-cultural engagement are thus ambiguous and troubling.

Nevertheless, viewing Plowden's efforts from the perspective of the Hindustani musicians who engaged with her and others like her reveals it to have been a two-way affair of mutual curiosity and delight in musical

[27] Daniel Leech-Wilkinson, 'The Emotional Power of Musical Performance', in Tom Cochrane, et al. (eds.), *The Emotional Power of Music: Multidisciplinary Perspectives on Musical Arousal, Expression, and Social Control* (Oxford: Oxford University Press, 2013), 41–54, pp. 41–3.

[28] Farrell, *Indian Music*, pp. 32–44, esp. 42; Woodfield, 'Hindostannie Airs', pp. 199–200, 206–8.

[29] See Anand Yang, 'Bandits and Kings: Moral Authority and Resistance in Early Colonial India', *Journal of Asian Studies*, 66.4 (2007), 881–96, esp. pp. 885, 892–3.

[30] Lieut. Col. W H Sleeman, *Diary of a Tour Through Oude*, vol. ii. (Lucknow: n.pub., 1852), p. 188; Williams, 'Wajid ᶜAli Shah and Nawabi Decadence', in 'Hindustani Music', pp. 82–126.

minutiae – an exploration of affinities and possibilities through trained bodily proficiencies, rather than a closing of ears to objectionable differences. And by taking Indian and European sources together, we can also reverse engineer some of Khanum Jan's songs to get closer to the conditions under which Plowden produced her *Album* and *Tunebook*, as well as to how these songs might have been sung and experienced at the time.

The Memsahib: Sophia Plowden in Lucknow

Sophia Elizabeth Plowden (née Prosser, 1751–1834) was the wife of a well-connected East India Company official, Richard Chicheley Plowden.[31] Richard and Sophia arrived in British Calcutta, their main base, in 1777, but by their return to London in 1790 they had spent two lengthy stints in Lucknow, the capital of the autonomous princely state of Awadh: c.1780–82, when Richard was employed in the personal bodyguard of the ruler, Asaf-ud-daula; and 1787–8, when they returned to collect money owed to them there.[32] Independent Lucknow, situated between the old Mughal capital, Delhi, and the new centre of political power, Calcutta, was a space of immense possibility for adventurous and ambitious men and women from all over India, as well as from Europe.[33] As we saw in Chapter 3, it became a particular magnet for Mughal noblemen and élite literary and artistic figures seeking new patronage in the face of Delhi's upheaval and decline. Both of the eighteenth century's leading Urdu poets, Sauda[c] and Mir, moved to Lucknow.[34] Delhi musicians who made new homes in Awadh in the 1750s–80s included the great *kalāwant* Rahim Sen and his young relative Musahib Khan; Taj Khan *qawwāl*'s sons, the important *k͟hayāl* singers Jan Muhammad Khan Jani, Ghulam Rasul and Jivan Khan; Ghulam Rasul's even more famous son Ghulam Nabi Miyan Shori, who transformed the *ṭappa* vocal genre; several of Anjha Baras' disciples

[31] Walter FC Chicheley Plowden, *Records of the Chicheley Plowdens, A.D. 1590–1913* (London: Heath, Cranton and Ouseley, 1914), esp. pp. 151–75; Maya Jasanoff, *Edge of Empire: Conquest and Collecting in the East, 1750–1850* (London: Harper, 2006), pp. 60–9; Tillman W Nechtman, *Nabobs: Empire and Identity in Eighteenth-Century Britain* (Cambridge: Cambridge University Press, 2010), pp. 185, 199–203. I am especially grateful to Geoffrey Plowden for sharing his family history in person.

[32] Plowden, *Records*, pp. 154–9.

[33] Stephen Markel and Tushara Bindu Gude (eds.), *India's Fabled City: The Art of Courtly Lucknow* (Munich and New York: Prestel, 2010); on music under Asaf-ud-daula see Madhu Trivedi, *Making*, and Miner, *Sitar*.

[34] Saif Mahmood, *Beloved Delhi: A Mughal City and Her Greatest Poets* (New Delhi: Speaking Tiger, 2018), pp. 55–88, 117–56.

including his cousin's grandson Muzaffar Khan; Adarang's key disciple in Lucknow Chajju Khan, who was reputed to be his son; the descendants of fêted Delhi *qawwāls* Shaikh Moin-ud-din, Shaikh Kabir, Allah Banda, and many others; and a large number of élite courtesans including, apparently, the greatest of all eighteenth-century imperial prima donnas Nur Bai (though better sources place her in Murshidabad in the 1750s).[35]

The Treaty of Allahabad in 1765 between the triumphant East India Company and the defeated Mughal Emperor Shah ᶜAlam saw the British take effective sovereign control of Awadh's immediate geographical neighbours, Bihar and Bengal, as well as confiscate parts of Awadh itself, notably the important Ganges river city of Allahabad where the Mughal emperor was himself based under British protection until 1772. From this time forward, the Awadh court became increasingly entangled in British interests. Asaf-ud-daula succeeded his father Shujaᶜ-ud-daula as Nawab in 1775, hard on the heels of the appointment of the first British Resident to Awadh in 1773. Under Asaf-ud-daula, Awadh's capital Lucknow became a hub of cultural activity that drew inspiration from both Indian and European inputs.[36] We know from Sophia's *Diary* that the Plowdens kept up a giddy social life of élite parties and engagements throughout their 1787–8 residency in Lucknow. Those most noteworthy to Sophia involved music, but she also attended unmissable events like Colonel Mordaunt's cock matches, made legendary through Johan Zoffany's famously noisy painting now in Tate Britain.[37] She and her husband were intimate with all the important Indian and European figures in Lucknow, including the Nawab himself, high-ranking Awadhi ministers like Hasan Raza and Haider Beg and notable long-term European residents Antoine Polier and Claude Martin, the last of whom lent Sophia an all-important harpsichord as soon as she arrived.[38] Sophia had known the famous Hindustani music aficionado and fellow song collector Richard Johnson when he was

[35] Kaicker, *King*, pp. 132–3.

[36] Jasanoff, *Edge*, 45–80; Rosie Llewellyn-Jones, *Fatal*; Claude Martin, *A Man of the Enlightenment in Eighteenth-Century India: The Letters of Claude Martin, 1766–1800*, ed. Rosie Llewellyn Jones (New Delhi: Permanent Black, 2003); Antoine Polier, *A European Experience of the Mughal Orient: The* Ijaz-i Arsalani *(Persian Letters, 1773–1779) of Antoine-Louis-Henri Polier*, ed. Seema Alavi and Muzaffar Alam (New Delhi: Oxford University Press, 2007).

[37] Plowden, *Diary*, 8 and 15 June 1788; Johan Zoffany, *Colonel Mordaunt's Cock Match*, Lucknow c. 1784–6, Tate Britain, T06856, www.tate.org.uk/art/artworks/zoffany-colonel-mordaunts-cock-match-t06856.

[38] e.g. Plowden, *Diary*, 17 July and 27 December 1787; 10 and 18 February, 20 April, 4 May, 19 August, 18 September, 8 October. On Colonel Martin's harpsichord, see *Diary* 5 January 1788.

Figure 4.2 Mrs Sophia Elizabeth Plowden and her children in Lucknow dress. John Russell. London, 1797. © **The Birla Museum, Pilani**

deputy British Resident in Lucknow in 1780–82;[39] and William Bird was also in Lucknow in March 1788, where he accompanied Sophia as she sang her Hindustani Airs.[40] Sophia mixed with all these men frequently, and they indulged her insatiable hunger for Indian songs for her collection.[41]

The portrait in Figure 4.2 with three of her ten children shows Sophia in the adventurous, almost tigress-like guise of her Lucknow self revealed in

[39] On Johnson as perhaps the most prolific collector of Hindustani musical writings, including songs, see Schofield, 'Words', 177–80.

[40] Plowden, *Diary*, 7–8 March 1788.

[41] Jasanoff, *Edge*, 59–62. Asaf-ud-daula and Polier: Plowden, *Album*, flyleaf; Asaf-ud-daula, Bellas, Bird, Polier: Plowden, *Diary*, in Woodfield, 'Hindostannie', pp. 198, 209–11. She also corresponded with other lovers of Indian music among the *Who's Who* of British society in India, including Sir Warren Hastings, Sir William Jones and Richard Johnson.

her *Diary* and letters. Sophia's present-day reputation as an avid consumer of what I call India's 'auditory picturesque' obscures the fact that at the time her main concern was keeping her children alive – she gave birth to seven of them in the twelve years she and her husband were in India and must have been constantly pregnant or nursing.[42] Her *Diary* is consumed throughout February and March 1787 with her account of one child after another contracting measles immediately followed by smallpox, then in September, en route to Lucknow, their river boat nearly capsized.[43] Amazingly, given the very high child mortality rate in early colonial India, all of them survived.

Sophia appears to have developed a taste very early on for the songs performed by the women of the *nāch* sets employed by all the best people in Calcutta and Lucknow. She had already started collecting Hindustani songs during her first Lucknow residency and was singing them herself by 1783; back in Calcutta, her friend and fellow collector Margaret Fowke recalled Sophia singing 'her little collection very frequently and always with applause – two of these airs I think tender and delicate in a very high degree'.[44] Sophia's performances were quite elaborate; she sang the songs in their original languages, often in full Lucknow dress (Figure 4.2). She wrote to her sister Lucy in 1783:

> I had long had it in idea that a set of Cashmerian singers would make an excellent Groupe at a Masquerade . . . I was lucky enough to have a sufficient number of my Lucknow acquaintance in Calcutta to assist . . . Mr Taylor was the head of the band. He is very musical and easily learnt to play on the Sirindah or fiddle of this country all my Persian and Indostani songs. A Mr Turvey [?] played the Sittar . . . and young Playdell play'd the Tabla . . . Mine was a very elegant dress . . . which gives me a compleat Indostani appearance. The songs I sang were very pretty ones, and . . . many people insisted on our being really Indostanis . . . after wearing my Mask about 2 hours I was glad to take it off and speak in my own language.[45]

Both Sophia in Lucknow and Margaret in Benares, where Margaret's brother Francis was the Resident, transcribed the songs they heard into European notation with the aid of the harpsichord, sitting with Indian musicians; and Braganza and others helped Sophia add bass lines. From

42 Plowden, *Records*, pp. 159–60; Maya Jasanoff, 'The Unknown Women of India', *New York Review of Books*, 18 December 2008.

43 Plowden, *Diary*, February–March and 28 September 1787.

44 Margaret Fowke to her brother Francis Fowke, Letter, 5 August 1783, quoted in Woodfield, 'Hindostannie', pp. 190–1.

45 Plowden to her sister Lucy, Letter, 4 April 1783, British Library, Eur MSS B187; Woodfield, 'Hindostannie', pp. 204–5.

Plowden's, Bird's and Gilchrist's collections of 'airs' or 'odes', we can see that certain Hindustani vocal genres lent themselves better to European settings as songs with harpsichord: those with clear lyrics, regular metres and repeated tunes.[46] Chief among them was the most widely popular genre in the repertoire of courtesans and male court singers: the *g̲hazal* and its related forms, such as the four-line *rubāʿī* (quatrain), the five-line *muk̲hammas* and the *tarānā*, in which a single *g̲hazal* couplet was embedded at the heart of a set of *bol*s, non-lexical syllables used by dancers and drummers to memorise and reproduce rhythmic patterns.[47] Another Lucknow genre well-represented in Plowden's collection was the virtuosic *ṭappa*, undoubtedly because it was at the height of Hindustani fashion. But it was the more straightforward *g̲hazal* and its related forms that Plowden definitely preferred: after a wedding party she famously complained that the courtesans 'only sung Tappas a sort of Wild harsh Music without any air'. She 'was not much pleas'd'.[48]

G̲hazal-related Song Forms: *Sāqī-ā! fasl-i bahār ast!*

The *g̲hazal* is the major form of élite Persian and Urdu poetry, and is based on rhyming metrical couplets.[49] Hindustani musicians of the time set both Persian and Urdu *g̲hazal*s to the North Indian *rāga*s and *tāla*s.[50] Bird misunderstood the constellation of *g̲hazal*-related forms to be a single song genre called *rek̲hta* (*rek̲hta* was the current name for the Urdu language and could only ever be used, as in Plowden, to designate the Urdu *g̲hazal*).[51] He wrote:

46 Schofield, 'Words', pp. 177–80, 183–4; Richard Johnson, untitled collection of songs [c. 1780–85], British Library, I O Islamic 1906; Gilchrist, *Oriental*, pp. 152–62.

47 For an example of Plowden's *tarānā*s, see Schofield, 'Words', p. 176.

48 Plowden, *Diary*, 18 February 1788. Of her 68 song texts, 39 are Persian and Urdu *g̲hazal*s and related forms including 11 *tarānā*s (also spelled *tillānā*), 20 are, ironically, *ṭappa*s and there are 5 *k̲hayāl*s, 2 *holī*s, 1 *sargam* and 1 *marsīya*. See Schofield, 'Words'.

49 Scott Kugle, '*Qawwālī* Between Written Poem and Sung Lyric, Or . . . How a *Ghazal* Lives', *Muslim World* 97 (2007), 571–610; also Wheeler M. Thackston, *A Millennium of Classical Persian Poetry* (Bethesda: IBEX, 2000), ix–xxvi.

50 Schofield, 'Words', p. 177; see Plowden, *Album*, f. 36 for a Persian *ghazal* with a section of *sargam*, the oral notation similar to *sol-fa* used to notate Hindustani *rāga*s.

51 In the Plowden *Album*, *g̲hazal* is used as the genre designation for Persian *g̲hazal*s, while *rek̲hta* is used for Urdu *ghazals*. Gilchrist did not make Bird's error either; he thought Bird in general a complete idiot; *Oriental*, pp. 275–6.

The Rekhtahs are most admired, because they are comprehensible, and exceed all others in form and regularity . . . [in contrast] The Raagnies [probably indicating *khayāl*] are so void of meaning, and any degree of regularity, that it is impossible to bring them into a form for performance, by any fingers but those of their country (Hindostan).[52]

Figure 4.3 provides an excellent example of how the *ghazal* and its related forms were set to music. Bird called this piece 'Sakia! fusul behar-ust', a 'Rekhtah' sung by 'Chanam' (Khanum). Both lyrics and melody

(a)

(b)

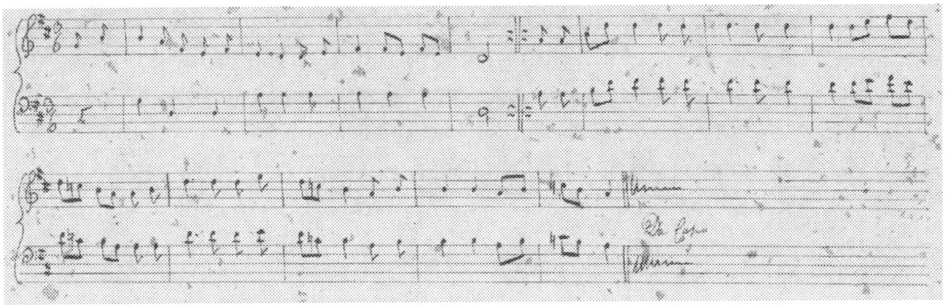

Figure 4.3 A and B. Anonymous Persian *rubā*^{c}*ī*, '*Sāqī-ā! Fasl-i bahār ast!*' Sophia Plowden, Album, f. 8 and Tunebook, f. 20r. Lucknow, 1787–8. MS 380. © **Fitzwilliam Museum, University of Cambridge**

[52] Bird, *Oriental*, pp. iv–v; Schofield, 'Words', pp. 183–4.

appear in Plowden's collection, where the song is not an Urdu *ghazal*, but a Persian *rubāᶜī*, '*Sāqī-ā! fasl-i bahār ast!*' (Oh cupbearer! it is the season of spring!). It is on the perennial theme of the *sāqī*, the beautiful young male cupbearer who pours the wine at the intimate *majlis*, and who is the stereotypical beloved of the Persian poetical imagination:[53]

sāqī-ā! fasl-i bahār ast mubārak bāshad!
bāda pesh ārad ke kār-i to mubārak bāshad!

shīsha paimāna ba-lab gīr o surāhī ba-kinār:
tāba mai būsa-kinār-i to mubārak bāshad!

Oh cupbearer! it is the season of spring – let's celebrate!
The wine is brought before us, so pour it out – let's celebrate!

Bring the cup to the lip and the flask to the breast:
Your kisses and embraces are as heady as wine – let's celebrate![54]

Bird's wordless keyboard arrangement gives away little of how this *rubāᶜī* would have sounded in its Indian context. We are thus fortunate that, as well as transcribing two alternative versions of the tune, Plowden collected the words, which are appropriately decorated in her *Album* with a painting of a cupbearer. Lyrics and illustration together give us a much better sense of the emotions and images this song once conveyed to its Indian listeners. But crucially, the structure of the poem also tells us why European musicians felt such affinity with this form, and why it was so easily adaptable to the keyboard. In essence, European art songs and North Indian *ghazal*s had a similar melodic structure.

The standard form of the late eighteenth-century European air, or aria, was in simplified terms an A–A–B–A form: an A melody, usually repeated; followed by a different melody, B; with a return to the A melody to end with, signified on the page by the words *da capo* (see Figure 4.3B).[55] Without reference to Hindustani musical structures, Woodfield analysed Plowden's two variant melodies for this song (f. 13v, f. 20r) alongside three more produced by her contemporaries. He concluded that European

[53] Paul Losensky, 'Vintages of the *Saqi-nama*: Fermenting and Blending the Cupbearer's Song in the Sixteenth Century', *Iranian Studies* 47 (2014), 131–57; and Sunil Sharma, *Mughal Arcadia: Persian Literature in an Indian Court* (Cambridge, MA: Harvard University Press, 2017), pp. 170–1.

[54] Plowden, *Album*, f. 8, and *Tunebook*, f. 20r. The Plowden MS calls this piece a *rubāᶜī*; strictly speaking, however, Sunil Sharma notes that this is not *rubāᶜī* metre; personal communication 2019.

[55] Marita P McClymonds, 'Aria (It.: 'Air'): 4. 18th Century,' *Oxford Music Online* (Oxford University Press, 2001) https://doi.org/10.1093/gmo/9781561592630.article.43315.

Example 4.2 B and C melodies of '*Sāqī-ā! Fasl-i bahār ast!*' compared. Plowden, *Tunebook*, f. 13v, f. 20v. Lucknow, 1787–8. MS 380. **Fitzwilliam Museum, University of Cambridge**

listeners perceived '*Sāqī-ā!*' as a rondo: that is, an (A–)A–B–A–C–A form, where A is a melody that returns like a refrain between melodies that are new each time (B, C; Example 4.2). He noted that the A section in Plowden's two versions, repeated in both cases, was fundamentally the same;[56] whereas version 1 had a B and a C melody, while version 2 (f. 20r) included only the C melody (which is not identical to version 1C, but an embellished variation). Woodfield concluded that the varying transcriptions of B and C melodies might indicate that the non-A sections were improvised melodies that differed from performance to performance.[57]

His analysis was insightful. This is indeed the structure of sung Urdu *ghazal*s today: a cyclical A–A–B–A form in which the precomposed melody of the initial line, called the *sthāyī*, is also used for the second line of every couplet (with slight variations characteristic of the style), creating a highly

[56] Taking into account a probable transcription error in f. 20r.

[57] Woodfield, 'Collecting', pp. 78–86.

identifiable melodic refrain or anchor for the performance; while the first lines of subsequent couplets 'are sung to a florid, more melismatic melody', called the *antarā*, 'which may be loosely improvised . . . through extended and varied melodic elaboration'.[58] The melodic structure of the sung *ghazal* and associated forms like the *rubāʿī* follows its end-rhyme scheme (*radīf*); here *mubārak bāshad*, 'let's celebrate!' The first two lines, comprising the first couplet (called the *matlaʿ*), are each sung to a lower A melody (*sthāyī*); the third, non-rhyming line (the first line of the second couplet) is sung to a higher B melody (*antarā*), which is often altered substantially through improvisation; and finally the fourth line, which rhymes with the *matlaʿ*, reprises the *sthāyī*.

A/*sthāyī* *sāqī-ā! fasl-i bahār ast* ***mubārak bāshad!***
A/*sthāyī* *bāda pesh ārad ke kār-i to* ***mubārak bāshad!***

B/*antarā* *shīsha paimāna ba-lab gīr o surāhī ba-kinār:*
A/*sthāyī* *tāba mai būsa-kinār-i to* ***mubārak bāshad!***

Plowden's B/C melodies identified by Woodfield should therefore all represent plausible improvisations on the *antarā*, '*shīsha paimāna ba-lab gīr o surāhī ba-kinār*'. It's worth noting, firstly, that none of these transcriptions can be entirely accurate. The poetical metre of all lines of a *rubāʿī* is identical in length, and the phrase lengths of Plowden's *sthāyī* and *antarā* should, correspondingly, be the same. But they are not: the *sthāyī*/A melody is four or six bars long, and the *antarā*/B and C melodies are eight bars (there is also an extra bar at the beginning of the version 1 B melody, which seems to be a duplication error). What is clear though is that, in contrast to the *sthāyī*/A melody, which focusses on the lower half of the octave between G/A (Ma/Pa) and the lower tonic, D (Sa) (Figure 4.3B), all three B/C melodies (Example 4.2) explore the upper tetrachord of the octave, gravitating between A (Pa) and upper D (Ṡa) in the first half of the section and centring on B (Dha) in the second half. This in turn anticipates the return to the *sthāyī*/*da capo*, whose opening likewise rests on B (Dha) before descending to the lower tonic (Sa).

This is *exactly* what we would expect of the *antarā* in terms of tessitura, contrast with the *sthāyī*, its end leading back towards the *sthāyī*'s opening, and wide flexibility and variation in its performance.[59]

[58] Peter Manuel, 'The Popularization and Transformation of the Light-Classical Urdu *Ghazal*-Song', in Arjun Appadurai, et al. (eds.), *Gender, Genre and Power in South Asian Expressive Traditions* (Philadelphia: University of Pennsylvania Press, 1991), 347–60, p. 349.
[59] Sanyal and Widdess, *Dhrupad*, pp. 223–7.

The A–A–B–A structure of the European air thus serendipitously resembles the quintessential *sthāyī-sthāyī-antarā-sthāyī* form of the sung *ghazal*. Khanum's renditions of this joyful, romantic *rubāᶜī*, especially in the *antarā*/B sections, would indeed have been full of improvised variations and ornaments, not notated in transcription, to show off her mastery of the emotional nuances of the lyrics and the melodic structure of the *rāga* on which Plowden's tune is based, which is reminiscent of Rag Desh.[60] It is worth remembering that at the time, vocal improvisation in repeated sections was as normal in the European aria as it still is today in Hindustani music. Sophia and her fellow song collectors would have taken Khanum's many variations of the *antarā* in their stride.

The Courtesan: Khanum Jan

Plowden's *Diary* suggests that her chief aim for her second visit to Lucknow in 1787–8 was to collect more songs and complete her compilation: she wrote to Colonel Polier's *nāch* set months in advance to announce these intentions.[61] When she finally did arrive in late December 1787, all her expectations were wildly exceeded. For there was new prima donna in town: 'Had a Notch[.] Morade Bux and Khanam's sett[.] Think the latter superior to any thing I have seen in the Country. She sing [sic] the Cashmerian airs and dances these dances in the best stile.'[62]

Khanum Jan was the star of an élite troupe of courtesans that traversed the major North Indian courts and British cantonments. Her Kashmiri ethnicity is debatable; many fair-skinned courtesans from the north west, especially from Punjab, miraculously turned into 'Kashmiris' when they arrived on the plains of Hindustan, because Kashmiri courtesans were esteemed as great beauties and thus commanded more prestige and higher fees.[63] Whatever the case, as an élite courtesan Khanum was highly trained in Hindustani music, singing, Persian and Urdu poetry, courtly etiquette, wit and of course the arts of seduction; courtesans generally did not marry, but had sexual relationships on their own terms with their most ardent patrons. This was not considered

[60] Based on observations by Hindustani musicians Surgeet Singh Aulak and Amardep Singh Sari, and Afghan classical singer Yusuf Mahmoud, as they prepared to perform this piece with Jane Chapman as part of her Leverhulme-funded Artist in Residency at King's College London (2011).

[61] Plowden, *Diary*, 17 July 1787. [62] ibid., 23 December 1787.

[63] George Forster, *A Journey from Bengal to England, Through the Northern Part of India, Kashmire, Afghanistan, and Persia* (Calcutta: Cooper and Upjohn, 1790), vol. i, p. 185.

remotely extraordinary in late Mughal India.[64] Contemporary traveller George Forster, who travelled through North India in 1782–3, noted that:

Dancing girls, whose occupations are avowedly devoted to the public pleasures, are, on the contrary [to wives], taught the use of letters, and are minutely instructed in the knowledge of every attraction and blandishment, which can operate in communicating the sensual pleasure of love. These women are not obliged to seek shelter in private haunts, nor are they on account of their professional conduct, marked with opprobrious stigma. They compose a particular class of society, and enjoy the avowed protection of government . . . They usually attend on a certain day of the week, at the court of the prince or governor of the district, either to make an obeisance, or exhibit a professional entertainment; and in some of the provinces they are endowed with grants of the public lands [see Chapter 6].[65]

We first hear of Khanum in c. 1786 working in the British military cantonment at Kanpur (Cawnpore), sixty miles from Lucknow, where she enjoyed great celebrity among Europeans stationed there.[66] Woodfield documented what we know of her life from British sources;[67] but we also have what I suggest is a fictionalised Urdu biography of Khanum's life: the 1893 novel *Nashtar* (*Lancet*). Based on a Persian original completed in 1788/9,[68] *Nashtar* has multiple uncanny resemblances to the details of Khanum's biography known from contemporaneous European sources.[69] The story is autobiographical and concerns the doomed love of the author, a *munshī* (multilingual secretary) named Hasan Shah, for Khanum Jan. They met when both he and her *nāch* troupe were working for a colonial official in Kanpur called 'Manning'. Khanum's fate as a budding courtesan was to sell her virginity to the highest bidder, so for love Hasan Shah married her in secret to subvert her destiny. Sadly there could be no happy ending according to the conventions of the Mughal courtesan tale.[70] In about 1786 Khanum's set left Manning's employ and relocated

64 Schofield, 'Courtesan Tale'. 65 Forster, *Journey*, vol i, p. 45.

66 e.g. Charles Doyley and Thomas Williamson, *The European in India: From a Collection of Drawings* (London: Edward Orme, 1813), p. xv.

67 Woodfield, *Music*, pp. 155–8.

68 The colophon states the author's story is relayed up to 1203 AH, 1788/9 CE, and the copy made in 1205 = 1790/1, contra Qurratulain Hyder; Hasan Shah, *The Nautch Girl*, tr. Qurratulain Hyder (New Delhi: Stirling, 1993), p. 93.

69 Hasan Shah, *Nashtar*; Shah, *Nautch Girl*, tr. Hyder. Christina Oesterheld has argued that the 1893 translator, Kasmandavi, was really the author, but she was unaware of the historical Khanum Jan; 'Entertainment and Reform: Urdu Narrative Genres in the Nineteenth Century', in Stuart H. Blackburn and Vasudha Dalmia (eds.), *India's Literary History: Essays on the Nineteenth Century* (New Delhi: Permanent Black, 2004), 167–212. Sentences in this paragraph are taken from my longer discussion in Schofield, 'Words'.

70 Schofield, 'Courtesan Tale'.

to Lucknow – a real event lamented in English verse by Company officers in Kanpur.[71] In the novel, Khanum tragically fell sick on the journey and died when she reached Lucknow. Of course we know that in real life she didn't die, but went on to even greater success at the court of Asaf-ud-daula. Her death in the novel was required as a technicality of the genre: the courtesan tale always has to end in tragedy.[72]

By the time Khanum arrived in Lucknow, in other words, she was already famous in European circles. Her British admirers were especially enamoured of her singing, and her song repertoire in *Nashtar*, which is extensively detailed, is remarkably similar in kind to the songs that Sophia collected – including versions of two songs that actually ended up in Plowden's *Album*, Figures 4.6 and 4.8.[73] Sophia seems to have viewed Khanum much as she would a celebrity opera singer back in London; someone with whom men might enjoy more intimate liaisons, but whose charismatic presence as a star performer nevertheless bestowed cachet on any socialite's gatherings, and was thus equally pursued by women.[74] In her *Diary*, Sophia enthusiastically documented all of Khanum's performances at court and in European residences, Khanum's visits to her home, and the extensive lengths to which she went to secure her songs. Sophia also commissioned the society artist Zoffany, another of her Lucknow acquaintances, to paint Khanum's portrait in April 1788.[75]

We have no idea if he did, or if it survived; but Sophia recorded that Zoffany made portraits of Khanum for others, and that local copies were also being made of his portraits of other Lucknow celebrities, including Claude Martin and Antoine Polier.[76] Zoffany made his famous painting of 'Colonel Polier with his friends' Claude Martin, John Wombwell and Zoffany himself

[71] See Woodfield, *Music*, p. 157. [72] Schofield, 'Courtesan Tale'.

[73] Shah, *Nashtar*, pp. 75, 35.

[74] e.g. the great prima donna of the London operatic stage Angelica Catalani, with whom many early nineteenth-century Indian courtesans were compared; Rachel Cowgill, '"Attitudes with a Shawl": Performance, Femininity, and Spectatorship at the Italian Opera in Early Nineteenth-Century London', in Rachel Cowgill and Hilary Poriss (eds.), *The Arts of the Prima Donna in the Long Nineteenth Century* (Oxford: Oxford University Press, 2012), 217–51; also Jennifer Hall-Witt, *Fashionable Acts: Opera and Élite Culture in London, 1780–1880* (Hanover and London: University of New Hampshire Press, 2007), pp. 40–4, 65, 89–95; and Felicity Nussbaum, *Rival Queens: Actresses, Performance, and the Eighteenth-Century British Theater* (Philadelphia: University of Pennsylvania Press, 2013), pp. 46–57, 107–12, 146–50.

[75] Woodfield, *Music*, p. 156; Plowden, *Diary*, esp. 21, 26, 29 April 1788. Zoffany was a regular visitor to Lucknow 1784–88, and was in Lucknow when the Plowdens were in 1787–8; Mary Webster, *Johan Zoffany, 1733–1810* (New Haven and London: Yale University Press, 2011), pp. 483–532.

[76] Of Claude Martin: Plowden, *Diary*, 23 January 1788; of Polier, Figure 4.4. A second copy of this painting is reproduced in Webster, *Johan Zoffany*, p. 512.

in Lucknow in the winter of 1786 or 87.[77] Polier's face and angle in this painting, and the mustard colour of his dress, are strikingly similar to the portrait of Polier in Figure 4.4, 'Colonel Polier watching a nautch', a copy of another painting attributed to Zoffany made by an Indian artist in Lucknow c. 1786–88.[78] The dominant figure in this painting, however, is not the reclining Colonel Polier. It is the courtesan in the centre foreground, with her highly distinctive face that seems to be the portrait of a real person. This exact time frame was also the high-water mark of Khanum's success in Lucknow. Polier was keenly interested in the music and dance of courtesans. He was a prominent patron of the best Lucknow courtesans and had his own troupe, his albums now in Berlin hold many portraits of courtesans in costumes indistinguishable to Zoffany's, and he was painted as a patron of *nāch* more than once.[79] Critically, Polier himself supplied Sophia with Hindustani songs for her collection. I think it is very likely that the distinctive courtesan in Figure 4.4 is Khanum Jan.

And so, Khanum's eyes met Sophia's over a crowded dance floor. What might Sophia's first impressions been? This suggestion comes from *Nashtar*:

> [She was a] ravishing beauty [with] a magnolia face and narcissus eyes. She must have ruined the piety of a thousand men. Dressed in fineries, she ambled in, and struck a pose which was utterly devastating. Our eyes met and I was struck by the arrow of love. I became still like a picture and was petrified like a statue. Then I felt a surge of blood in my veins and my heart fluttered helplessly . . . Khanum Jan began the song of felicitation [*mujrā*]. She knew many *ghazal*s of Hafiz and rendered them well. [Mr Manning] kept asking me their meaning and relayed my explanations to his English friends. They were all spellbound and they, too, waved their hands and stamped their feet, like the possessed.[80]

When Emily Eden accompanied her brother, Governor-General Lord Auckland, to Delhi in 1839, her impressions of a real *nāch* at Colonel

[77] Victoria Memorial Hall, Calcutta; reproduced in Webster, *Johan Zoffany*, pp. 518–21. Webster suggests two different dates for 'Colonel Polier and his friends': mid 1786 on p. 518; but winter 1787 on p. 521. Winter is most likely from the costumes.

[78] Again, the dates art historians have suggested differ slightly, as does the artist attributed as the painter of the original. This is the details for the Rietberg copy in Markel and Gude, *India's Fabled City*, p. 257, which is most likely; but Gude also suggests 1782–88, p. 69. Webster suggests 1780, but this is aligned with her implausible suggestion that the painting is after Tilly Kettle, *Johan Zoffany*, p. 512. Another candidate is Arthur William Devis (1762–1822), who worked in India 1783–95, and whose attention to the details of faces, costumes and occupations is similar. I'm grateful to Bendor Grosvenor for this suggestion.

[79] Mihr Chand, Faizabad, 1773–4, reproduced in Merkel and Gude, *India's Fabled City*, pp. 180–1; and a very different Indian interpretation of Figure 4.4, sold by Christies 10 October 2006. www.christies.com/lot/lot-4791423.

[80] Hasan, *Nautch Girl*, pp. 15–16, 31.

Figure 4.4 Hindustani courtesan, possibly Khanum Jan, performing for Colonel Antoine Polier in Lucknow. Indian artist after Johann Zoffany. Awadh, 1786–88. 2005.83. Bequest Balthasar Reinhart, **Museum Rietberg, Zürich © Rainer Wulfsberger**

James Skinner's (Chapters 6 and 7) were remarkably similar, although the music was not exactly to her taste:

He had all the best singers and dancers in Delhi, and they acted passages out of Vishnu and Brahma's lives and sang Persian songs, which I thought made a very ugly noise, but Mr. B., who speaks Persian as fluently as English, kept saying 'Well this is really delightful – this I think is equal to any European singing – in fact, there is nothing like it'. There *is* nothing like it that I ever heard before, but certainly the words, as he translated them, were very pretty. One little fat nautch girl sang a sort of passionate song to [the governor-general] with little meaning smiles, which I think rather attracted his lordship, and I thought it might be too much for him if I forwarded to him Mr. B.'s translation. 'I am the body, you are the soul: we may be parted here, but let no one say we shall be separated hereafter'.[81]

[81] Emily Eden, *Up the Country: Letters Written to her Sister from the Upper Provinces of India*, 2 vols. (London: Richard Bentley, 1866), vol. i, pp. 143–4.

These lyrics are remarkably close to a famous couplet, still sung in South Asia today, by the greatest Persian poet of India, Amir Khusrau (1253–1325):

man to shodam, to man shodī, man tan shodam, to jān shodī
tā kas nagoyad baᶜd az īn man dīgaram to dīgarī

I have become you, and you me; I have become the body, you the soul
So that none hereafter may say that 'I am someone and you someone else'.[82]

The Courtesan (and Her Brethren) Encounters the Memsahib (and Hers)

Unlike Emily Eden, Sophia patently loved the music of these songs as much as their poetry; the proof is in her *Album* and *Tunebook* and enduring reputation as an amateur singer of Hindustani songs. But what of Khanum, and other professional musicians whose songs Plowden, Fowke, Polier and Bird took and made their own? What did they think of European music, and the European musicians they engaged with?

In Benares, Margaret Fowke worked with male musicians in the service of Governor-General Sir Warren Hastings to take down some 'Indostaun Airs' she sent her father Joseph in 1785; in this case four *hoṛīs* in Hindi. She believed they enjoyed the experience:

You may be assured [the song transcriptions] are exact, and to me they are pretty. Notwithstanding this I cannot be quite clear that they will please you; for notes cannot express Style, and that of these airs is very peculiar and new. I have often made the Musicians tune their instruments to the harpsichord that I might join their little band. [In doing so she was following in her brother Francis' footsteps, who in 1784 had got the *kalāwant bīn* players, brothers Jivan Shah and Pyar Khan, to tune their instruments to his harpsichord so that he could compare their tuning and scale systems scientifically.[83]] They always seemed delighted with the accompaniment of the harpsichord and sung with uncommon animation, and a pleasure to themselves, which was expressed in their faces.[84]

To postcolonial ears her views sound patronising and naïve. But Indian records from the same time and place indicate Margaret's impression of reciprocated interest was not unfounded.

[82] Tr. Yusuf Saeed. [83] Francis Fowke, 'On the Vina'.
[84] Margaret Fowke, letter to Joseph Fowke, 11 January 1785, quoted in Woodfield, *Music*, pp. 160–1.

European keyboards – organs, harpsichords and later pianos – were found in India from at least the early sixteenth century, mainly in European settlements, but they were also given to Indian rulers and notables as technological novelties and diplomatic gifts; Polier, for instance, went to great trouble to import an organ from Calcutta for Asaf-ud-daula.[85] The British Library houses an imperial Mughal copy of Nizami Ganjavi's *K͟hamsa* that includes a famous 1593–5 Mughal painting of 'Plato playing the organ' modelled on a Portuguese diplomatic gift to the Emperor Akbar.[86] And the first written description in an Indian musical text of what sounds very like a harpsichord – a 'strange/foreign' (*g͟harīb*) instrument of large and unwieldy size shaped like a penbox (*qalamdān*) that opened to reveal a series of strings' – dates to 1655/6.[87] By the late eighteenth century, in the midst of the craze for transcribing Hindustani songs, Indian poets and musicians were also writing down their impressions of keyboards and their players. How might Khanum have viewed Sophia? There is every possibility she found her sexually alluring. Oldenburg noted that, historically, Lucknow courtesans' most intimate relationships were with each other.[88] The following couplet is an example of *rek͟htī* (as opposed to *rek͟hta*), an often explicit style of Urdu poetry in the feminine voice especially prized in Nawabi Lucknow, which reflected the language of courtesans and secluded women.[89] In this verse by male poet Sa^cadat Yar Khan Rangin (1755–1835), a woman upbraids her lesbian lover (*zanak͟hī*):

Oh Zanakhi, ever since you heard the keyboard play,
You have become obsessed with a foreign woman.[90]

[85] Polier, *European Experience*, pp. 110, 122–4, 161, 325–6. On keyboards in India, see Ian Woodfield, 'The Keyboard Recital in Oriental Diplomacy, 1520–1620', *Journal of the Royal Musical Association* 115.1 (1990), 33–62; and Ian Woodfield, 'The Calcutta Piano Trade in the Late Eighteenth Century', in Christina Bashford and Leanne Langley (eds.), *Music and British Culture, 1785–1914: Essays in Honour of Cyril Ehrlich* (Oxford: Oxford University Press, 2000), 1–22.

[86] Nizami Ganjavi, *K͟hamsa*, Or. 12,208, British Library, f. 298; Mika Natif, *Mughal Occidentalism: Artistic Encounters between Europe and Asia at the Courts of India, 1580–1630* (Leiden: Brill, 2018), pp. 135–51.

[87] Brown [Schofield], 'Origins', p. 176; Faqirullah, *Rāg Darpan*, p. 190; Shaikh Ala-ud-din Muhammad Chishti of Barnawa, *Chishtiyya-i Bihishtiyya*, Asiatic Society of Bengal, Curzon Coll. 78 (1655/6).

[88] Veena Talwar Oldenburg, 'Lifestyle as Resistance: The Case of the Courtesans of Lucknow,' in Violette Graff (ed.), *Lucknow: Memories of a City* (New Delhi: Oxford University Press, 1997), 136–54.

[89] Contrary to Woodfield and Farrell, there are no *rek͟htī*s in Plowden's *Album* or *Tunebook*; all the Urdu *g͟hazals* are masculine-voice *rek͟hta*s.

[90] Slightly modified from 'Rekhti Poetry: Love Between Women (Urdu)', in Saleem Kidwai and Ruth Vanita (eds.), *Same-Sex Love in India: Readings From Literature and History* (London: Palgrave, 2001), p. 226; also Ruth Vanita, *Gender, Sex, and the City: Urdu Rekhti Poetry in India, 1780–1870* (New York: Palgrave Macmillan, 2012).

But Indian familiarity with keyboards was not just restricted to gazing and listening: Indian musicians repaired and played pianos and harpsichords in the late eighteenth century. One early piano for instance was repaired in India in 1789 by Daulat Ram, an instrument repairer from the Indian firm Mistry Instrument Makers in Lalbarga, Calcutta, according to a contemporaneous note pasted inside the instrument.[91] Polier similarly instructed one of his Lucknow employees, Gora Mistri, to learn how to play and maintain the Nawab's organ so that there would be a reliable person keeping this 'precious and rare gift' in good order.[92] And the remarkable passage from Edinburgh MS 585(4) I cited at the beginning of this chapter also confirms that in 1788, hereditary musicians from the Mughal tradition – the very people working at exactly this time with amateur musicologists like the Fowkes, Jones, Johnson and Plowden – had hands-on experience of playing the harpsichord:

The Europeans . . . have another instrument of the string family that is extremely fine and noble named the harpsichord.[93] It has thirty-five fundamental strings [i.e. a five-octave range measured using the natural notes of a keyboard instrument].[94] The melody is split into high and low melodies, which those knowledgeable in this science write in books of music. Between the two [main] melodies other distributions are also made. [This I suggest is an attempt at describing the use of treble and bass lines in right and left hands, and chordal harmony][95] . . . This instrument developed from the *qānūn* (the plucked dulcimer). Every string has a plectrum[96] that is placed parallel to each string. [I], the humble drafter of this treatise, composed [music] in every particular using nineteen fundamental strings: seven for the lower octave, that is, the *khūr saptak*; seven for the main (middle) octave (*sur saptak*);[97] and the remaining five for the upper gamut up to Pa (the perfect fifth of the upper octave). One can create the *sargam* (*sol-fa*) for every *rāga* very well from this. When I play the accidentals (*shrutis*) from the lower Sa to upper Pa strings [in one hand] and also play the sixty-one other strings [in the other], greater subtleties are possible.[98] The phrases of *dhrupad* can [thus] be created on this

91 Personal communication, Jean Maurer via Jane Chapman, 2013.

92 Polier, *European Experience*, pp. 122, 325.

93 *harp-sīkārḍ.*

94 The 'natural' notes (*surs* in Edinburgh MS 585(4)) are the equivalent to the white keys on the modern piano, and the 'accidentals' (five semitonal variants here called *shrutis*) to the black keys.

95 The two preceding sentences, which continue into a marginal note, are very difficult to translate.

96 *mizrāb.*

97 *sur* (*swara*) refers to the 7 principal/natural notes of the scale (Sa Re Ga Ma Pa Dha Ni); generally the middle octave is called *madhya saptak*.

98 35 fundamental strings refers to the 7 natural notes over 5 octaves (*saptaks*). 19 fundamental strings pertains to the two-and-a-half octaves (7 + 7 + 5) between lower Sa and upper Pa that constitutes the standard vocal range required of a Hindustani singer. 61 strings are all 12 chromatic notes (7 principal notes, 5 accidentals) over the same 5 octaves, plus a sixth tonic.

[instrument]! This is possible because in some *rāgas* the fundamental *surs* (natural notes) are not used; instead their *shrutis* (accidental notes) are used, requiring [the deployment of] upper *shrutis* and lower *shrutis*.[99]

This accurate description of a five-octave harpsichord, with the author's perceptive comparison of the instrument to the local *qānūn* and his use of Hindustani terminology to describe its various aspects, shows the author had the opportunity to scrutinise its operation closely. But it also reveals his unexpected affinity for the harpsichord, despite its strangeness: his ability to translate its technical features accurately into his own musical terms, and the thrill of his recognition that this quintessentially European instrument could be turned to the service of even the most revered Hindustani musical structures. It is worth remembering that Hindustani musicians had used scale temperaments derived ultimately from Pythagoras to tune Indian stringed instruments since at least the seventeenth century (Chapter 2).[100] This would have been another point of affinity with European harpsichord practice that made translation between worlds possible. In many ways, our anonymous *kalāwant*'s description is a fitting counterpart to Francis Fowke's 1784 tract 'On the Vina or Indian Lyre', which highlighted similar compatibilities between Jivan Shah's *bīn* and the harpsichord, and detailed the *bīn*'s physical construction, its range of over two octaves and the scale fixed by its nineteen frets (see Box 7.1). Fowke likewise notated the scale of the *bīn* as being identical to the twelve semitones of the harpsichord: 'it is very observable', he wrote, 'that the semitones change their names on the same semitone as in the *European* scale'.[101]

There is also circumstantial evidence that the European custom of writing music down using a uniquely detailed, linear graphical notation system may have inspired new Indian music-theoretical writings in the 1780s and 90s. Although the new-style[102] notation system the author of Edinburgh MS 585(4) devised to overhaul the Hindustani *tāla* system was based on West Asian models of measuring rhythmic cycles verbally, using the syllables *ta na* and *da ka*, he clearly found the European system of *writing* music on paper stimulating. He devised a novel system of showing each *tāla* in current practice graphically as a red horizontal line with counts

[99] Anon, Edinburgh MS 585(4), ff. 45v–46r. This colloquial use of *shruti* for the 5 variant notes (accidentals) of the Hindustani scale (the scale degrees flat 2nd (Re), 3rd (Ga), 6th (Dha) and 7th (Ni) and sharp 4th (Ma)) was common at the time.

[100] Brown [Schofield], '*Ṭhāṭ* System'; Katherine Butler Brown [Schofield], 'Evidence of Indo-Persian Musical Synthesis? The *Tanbur* and *Rudra Vina* in Seventeenth-Century Indo-Persian Treatises', *Journal of the Indian Musicological Society* 36–7 (2006), 89–103.

[101] Fowke, 'Vina', pp. 195–6. [102] *tarh-i tāza.*

represented as red or black dots above the line, all within a red box. The stressed or clapped beats (*tāli*s) are represented as black dots, and the *k̲h̲ālī*s – the 'empty' segments (*vibhāg*s) marked in performance as a wave of the hand – as vertical black lines above the dots. The *mātra*s (counts) are also numbered right to left below the line in red, with *k̲h̲ālī*s in black. Zia-ud-din independently used a similar conception c. 1785–88 that envisaged *tāla*s as a horizontal line with the stressed beats represented as unevenly spaced vertical lines.[103]

These linear representations were *not* related to the Middle Eastern system of notating rhythmic cycles (*usūl*s), well known to Hindustani musicians, which represented them as circles (*dā'īra*s) drawn with a compass.[104] Nor did they resemble the non-graphical Sanskrit notations in which letter-like symbols stood in for different numbers of counts, even when authors used the Sanskrit symbols for extra detail as Zia-ud-din did. For the first time, Edinburgh MS 585(4)'s new linear graphical notation system made it possible to see at a single glance that, for example, the sixteen-beat medium-speed *tīntāl* (Example 4.3) was structured the way it is today, but beginning on what he considered count 5. This is, in fact, how traditional ('non-college-educated') musicians still count the *tīntāl* cycle[105] (see Chapter 7).

The author of Edinburgh MS 585(4) was not the only Indian writer on music at this time who seems to have been taken with the precision and reproducibility of European staff notation. Staff notation can represent rhythms, melodies and words simultaneously – features previously rendered separately in Indian notation systems. As we shall see in Chapter 7, the Lucknow-based *qawwāl* Ghulam Raza, who worked for the music-obsessed Richard Johnson c. 1790, began to render whole tunes with

Example 4.3 Notation of *jald tītāla-i madhya lay* (medium speed *jald tīntāl*) with red ink represented in grey. North India, 1788. Or. MS 585(4), f. 64v. **Edinburgh University Library**

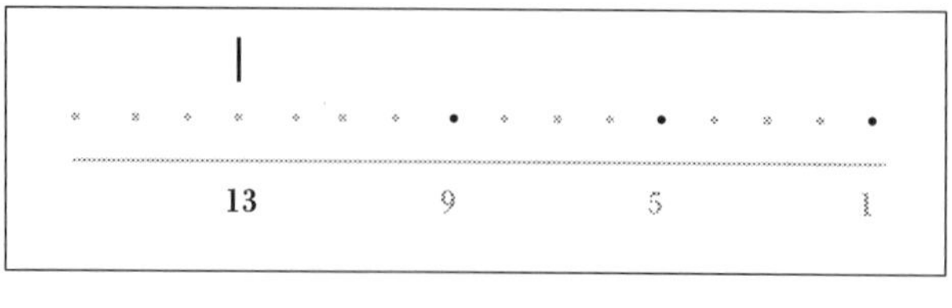

[103] Ziauddin, *Hayy*, ff. 36v–38r.

[104] e.g. Mirza Muhammad Khan, Collection (1708/9); Basit Khan, Collection (Chapter 8).

[105] Kippen, 'Mapping p. 257'.

simultaneous rhythmic, melodic and lyrical information in unprecedentedly reproducible – but still unmistakably Indic – notations that give us a good idea of what several *rāgas* sounded like.[106] But we also have outstanding evidence of how the élite Indian patrons of music Plowden mixed with viewed her own considerable efforts to notate and sing Hindustani songs herself. They did not take offense; rather, they honoured her. For her 'exceptional devotedness, and rare fidelity, high titles, and honourable address', the Nawab Asaf-ud-daula obtained a *farmān* (order) from the Mughal Emperor Shah ᶜAlam II giving Sophia Plowden the formal Mughal title of Begum ('Lady').[107]

Khanum Jan's Performances via Sophia Plowden's Pen

In this closing section, I will enter more deeply into three more of Khanum's and Plowden's songs, to see if we can dispel some of the confusion created by successive European arrangements and get a little closer to how they may have been sung and experienced in 1780s Lucknow.

The first is '*Sunre maᶜshūqā be-wafā*' – 'Listen, oh faithless beloved', another wrongly named '*rekhta*' arranged by Bird. This example shows how lyrics and ideas imposed on a melody cast adrift from its original words can alter how a song is performed and understood. In around 1805, Edward Biggs rearranged Bird's Air no. VI, 'Soonre mashukan! Be wufa!' with new English lyrics by popular poet Amelia Opie (1769–1853). Her idea for the song, which features Delia as a 'faithless beloved', may have been inspired by the fragment of Urdu that now stands in as the song's title:

Oh why are my accents so broken and weak,
What means this emotion that flushes my cheek,
Whenever with Delia I rove?
Ah! Whence is this change, whence symptoms so strange?
Spring they from Love? . . .
Tis Love prompts the anguish which forces the tear,
When praise of another from Delia I hear,

[106] Ghulam Raza, *Usūl al-Naghmāt al Āsafī*, Salar Jung Museum Library, Persian Mus 2 (1793/4), ff. 80r–85v; and Johnson's partial copy, British Library, I O Islamic 2083 (c. 1790). See Chapter 7.

[107] British Library, I O 4439; tr. Plowden, *Records*, pp. 173–5; photograph Katherine Butler Schofield, 'Sophia Plowden, Khanum Jan, and Hindustani Airs,' *British Library Asian and African Studies Blog*, 28 June 2018, https://blogs.bl.uk/asian-and-african/2018/06/sophia-plowden-khanum-jan-and-hindustani-airs.html.

And dare not his merit disprove,
Yes fond, jealous fears, sighs, blushes and tears
Yes I love.[108]

Opie's lyrics bear no relation to the original words. The pioneering musicologist Dr William Crotch (1775–1847), who first published his global collection of *Specimens of Various Styles of Music* in 1807 based on his lecture series on 'National Music', got rather closer. His understanding of how to interpret the tune came from Plowden herself. In his introduction to the first edition, Crotch noted that '[Specimen No.s 326 through 339] are from a most valuable manuscript collection in the possession of Mrs Plowden . . . No. 336 is the song with which the natives charm the snakes'.[109]

Snake charming was regularly exhibited alongside public *nāch* performances, though conducted by a different group of hereditary specialists, *bāzīgār*s or conjurors (Chapter 7).[110] Maria Graham, writing from Bombay in 1809, noted that:

The evening closed, as usual, with music, dancing, and exhibitions of tumblers, jugglers, and tame snakes . . . The tame snakes are mostly cobra-capellas; at the sound of a small pipe they rise on their tails, and spread their hoods, advance, retreat, hiss, and pretend to bite, at the word of command.[111]

In earlier versions of his lectures, Crotch stuck to the letter of what Plowden had told him about this tune. But by 1829 the 'snake charming' idea had radically altered how he interpreted the melody during his lecture-demonstrations:

The following appears to be one of the Airs used in charming the snakes. At the Arpeggio passage performed with a crescendo the snakes rear their heads and appear angry. At the diminuendo they all sink down again into their accustomed torpor, and the tune quietly proceeds unnoticed.[112]

[108] Edward Smith Biggs, *A Second Set of Hindoo Airs with English Words Adapted to Them by Mrs Opie* (London: Robert Birchall, c. 1805), pp. 13–4.

[109] William Crotch, *Specimens of Various Styles of Music Referred to in a Course of Lectures Read at Oxford and London and Adapted to Keyed Instruments* (London: Robert Birchall, 1807), vol. i, p. 12.

[110] James Skinner, *Tashrīh al-Aqwām*, British Library, Add. 27,255 (1825), ff. 120–23, 323–7; also John Zubrzycki, *Empire of Enchantment: The Story of Indian Magic* (London: Hurst, 2018).

[111] Maria Graham Lady Callcott, *Journal of a Residence in India* (Edinburgh: Constable, 1812), pp. 35–6.

[112] William Crotch, 'Lecture I: On the Music of the Ancients and National Music', Royal Institution London, 12/05/1829, Norfolk Records Office, 11066, f. 5r.

(a)

(b)

Figure 4.5 A and B Anonymous Urdu *khayāl* 'sung by the snake charmers', '*Sunre ma*^{c}*shūqā be-wafā!*' Sophia Plowden, *Album*, f. 21, and *Tunebook*, f. 39v. Lucknow, 1787–8. MS 380. © **Fitzwilliam Museum, University of Cambridge**

The passage he was referring to is the two bars in Figure 4.5B marked *ad lib*[*itum*], which are to be improvised 'at the liberty' of the performer. These have no crescendo or diminuendo markings in either Plowden's *Tunebook*,

Crotch's manuscript or the first edition of his *Specimens.*[113] The idea that this tune in its original form mimetically traced the movements of snakes rearing and lowering their heads was a later product of Crotch's imagination. There is nothing in Plowden's notated melody that suggests any such interpretation.

In fact, the only way Crotch could have known that this was a 'snake charmers' song' was by the picture in Plowden's *Album* that illustrates the lyrics of '*Sunre ma*ᶜ*shūqā be-wafā!*' (Figure 4.5A). Note the cobra swaying to the snake charmer's pipe (*pungī*), but also the tethered mongoose and the pigeon in the covered wicker basket; together these had constituted the classic Mughal visual topos for depicting *bāzīgārs* since the seventeenth century (Chapter 7). As the Persian title says, this is, again, not a *re*k͟h*ta*, but a k͟h*ayāl*, a fantasia 'sung by the snake charmers' (*mār-wār*).

But, again, its sophisticated Urdu lyrics say nothing about snakes:

Listen, oh faithless beloved! What are you scheming?
I bestow honours upon you, and pallid greys burst into colour.
Worn out, I cry out, weeping and weeping: your golden locks tied up my heart.
The Beloved called out, entrancing and charming: you bewitched me with your ploys!
I brought my confusion into the garden, the judge opened the books:
I should follow this path – I might deceive someone else the same way.
The Beloved's house is far away; the Lover is as slippery as a thief.[114]

The link between the song and snake charming here is frankly somewhat opaque. But there are some delightfully ambiguous connections here between the arts of seduction that courtesans and their audiences played out in the Lucknow musical *majlis* and the musical enchanting of snakes, if we consider the lyrics metaphorically: if we imagine that the snake is the woman speaking, and the pipe and its song are her bewitching, tantalising and ultimately deceptive beloved. Such levels of subtlety and ambiguity of meaning, especially when the subjects are seduction and longing, have long been relished by lovers of Indian poetry and music.

With the second example, I am going to reverse our direction of travel, and demonstrate how we might use technical knowledge of lyrical metre and musical setting to reverse-engineer the most popular *nāch* song of them all, to get back to the way both Sophia and Khanum might have sung it. '*Mutrib-i* k͟h*wush-navā bego/Tāza ba tāza no ba no*' or 'Sing, sweet-voiced musician, ever fresh and ever new' is one of many Plowden songs with a clear refrain. Sophia wrote to Margaret, 'Have you ever met with an Indostani Song the

[113] Plowden, *Tunebook*, f. 39v; Crotch, 'National Tunes', p. 60; Crotch, *Specimens*, no. 336.
[114] Plowden, *Album*, f. 21, tr. Richard David Williams.

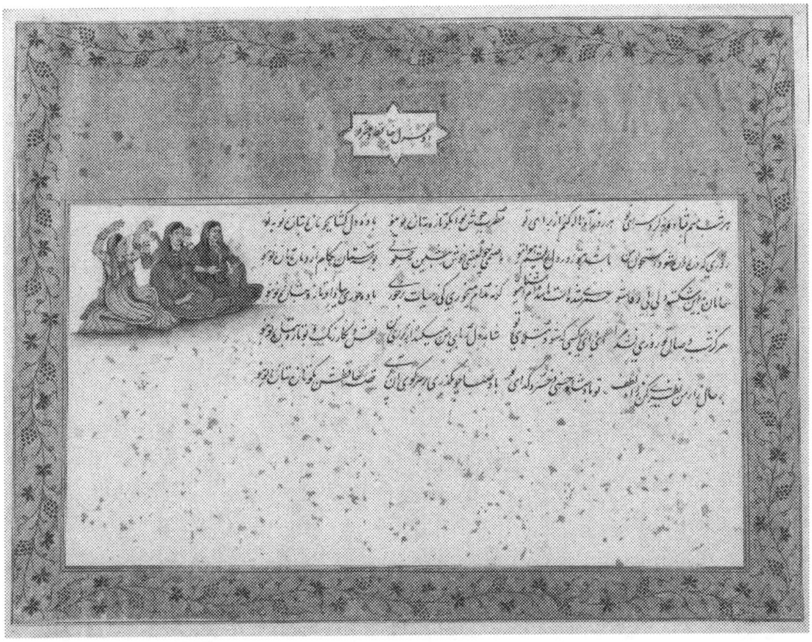

Figure 4.6 Persian ghazal, '*Mutrib-i khwush-navā bego/Tāza ba tāza no ba no*' by Khwaja Shams-ud-din Muhammad 'Hafiz' Shirazi (1315–90). Sophia Plowden, Album, f. 1. Lucknow, 1787–8. MS 380. © **Fitzwilliam Museum, University of Cambridge**

Chorus of which is "Tazzy bat Tazzy No bat No"? It is a very common one . . . all the Notch Girls know it.'[115] This song is a classic *ghazal* by one of the greatest Persian poets, Khwaja Shams-ud-din Muhammad 'Hafiz' Shirazi (1315–90). Its catchy *radīf*, '*tāza ba tāza no ba no*' or 'ever fresh and ever new', is an entire half-line long, and very clearly gives away how the lyrics fit the melody and create a 'refrain', here in Bird's version:

sthāyī *mutrib-i khwush-navā bego* ***tāza ba tāza no ba no***
sthāyī *bāda-i dilkushā bejo* ***tāza ba tāza no ba no***

antarā *bā sanamī cho lu^cbatī khwush benishīn ba khalwatī*
sthāyī *būsa sutān ba kām az ū* ***tāza ba tāza no ba no***

Sing, sweet-voiced musician, ever fresh and ever new!
Pour the exhilarating wine, ever fresh and ever new!

While you play, sit cosily in a secluded place with a lover,
And snatch kisses from him as you desire, ever fresh and ever new!

[115] Letter, Plowden to Margaret Fowke, March 1785, quoted in Woodfield, 'Hindostannie,' p. 197.

Example 4.4 Persian *ghazal 'Tāza ba tāza no ba no'* by Hafiz. Bird No. IV with the first Persian line underlaid

To European ears, Hafiz' lyrics fit Bird's 6/8 time signature nicely, and it is easy to imagine Plowden singing them just like this to appreciative British audiences. But to aficionados of Hindustani music, the text of this *ghazal* sounds rushed and awkward when set to a six-beat musical metre.[116] Persian and Urdu poetical forms use a sophisticated system of lyrical metres (*bahr*s) based on different patterns of long and short syllables. '*Tāza ba tāza*' is in the metre called *rajaz musamman matwī makhbūn*, which has a built-in caesura at the end of the half-line and naturally fits into a seven-beat musical cycle, not six:[117]

L	S	S	L	S	L		S	L	caesura
muf	ta	ʿi	lun	Ma	fā		ʿi	lun	||
1	2		3	4		5		6	7
L	S	S	L	S	L		S	L	
muf	ta	ʿi	lun	Ma	fā		ʿi	lun	

Plowden/Braganza's transcription of the melody (Example 4.5) preserves a hint that the original was indeed performed using a seven-count *tāla* cycle such as *rupak*, but that most Europeans at the time couldn't comprehend metres that were more complicated than equal multiples of two or three. Plowden (or Braganza) couldn't decide whether to notate the metre in triple or duple time, and the transcription shifts from one to the other. More tellingly: notice the strange offsetting of the refrain by one beat in bar 3:

116 I am grateful to singer Yusuf Mahmoud and to James Kippen for these observations.

117 Frances W Pritchett and Khaliq Ahmad Khaliq, *Urdu Meter: A Practical Handbook* (New York: private printing, 1987), www.columbia.edu/itc/mealac/pritchett/00ghalib/meterbk/00_intro .html.

Example 4.5 Persian ghazal, '*Tāza ba tāza no ba no*' by Hafiz. Sophia Plowden, *Tunebook*, f. 11r with the first line underlaid. Lucknow, 1787–8. MS 380. © **Fitzwilliam Museum, University of Cambridge**

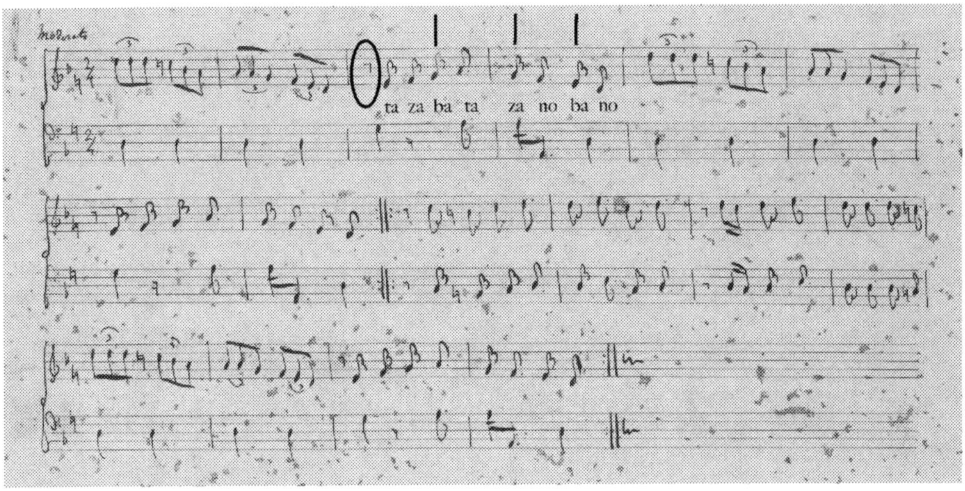

The lyrics don't match this setting either, as the emphasis has shifted onto the wrong syllables, '*tāza* ***ba*** *tāza no* ***ba*** *no*', which sounds terribly ugly. This song is most natural in a cycle of seven counts (or multiples thereof), which gives the singer plenty of room to breathe and improvise.

In Example 4.6 I have made a suggestion of how this *ghazal* might have been rendered in its basic, unornamented form by Khanum Jan, and notated it using both staff notation and *sargam*. Certain features of Plowden's transcription suggest Rag Bhairavi, one of the most popular *rāgas* for setting *ghazals*, then as now, as a suitable home for its melody. I have thus slightly modified the tune to fit Bhairavi's contours.

This is a lovely *ghazal* by a great Persian master, in which the voice of the singer, music, wine, the garden, kisses, embraces and love all stand in for one another as metaphors for intoxication with life, with a lover or with God himself. In his 1898 translation, Walter Leaf faithfully reproduced the metre as well as the end and internal rhymes[118] of Hafiz's original:

Minstrel, awake the sound of glee, joyous and eager, fresh and free;
Fill me a bumper bounteously, joyous and eager, fresh and free.

O for a bower and one beside, delicate, dainty, there to hide;
Kisses at will to seize and be joyous and eager, fresh and free.

[118] *radif*, end rhyme, and *qāfiya*, internal rhyme, here the last syllable of the first half of the second line.

Example 4.6 ‘*Tāza ba tāza no ba no*’ as it may have been sung by Khanum Jan, set in Rag Bhairavi to a cycle of seven beats

How shall the fruit of life be thine, if thou refuse the fruitful vine?
Drink of the vine and pledge with me, joyous and eager, fresh and free.

Sweet is my dear, a thief of hearts; bravery, beauty, saucy arts,
Odours and unguents, all for me, joyous and eager, fresh and free.

Wind of the West, if e’er thou roam, pass on the way my fairy’s home;
Whisper of HAFIZ am’rously, joyous and eager, fresh and free.[119]

We have come on a long, meandering journey with Sophia Plowden and Khanum Jan, as they and others like them engaged each other sincerely and joyfully across what should have been an impassable cultural and political river. Sadly, they and the cosmopolitan world of princely Lucknow they inhabited are long gone, and we cannot bring them back. There is too much distance between us and Plowden’s transcriptions, and too much darkness between those material remains and the performances they so poorly reflect. Rather, it is what we learn in the attempt, in the journey to the underworld to draw that shade back towards the light, that makes Khanum’s and Sophia’s story so much richer and more fascinating than we knew, and draws out the unexpected complexities of this moment in India’s and Britain’s entangled histories.

119 Walter Leaf, *Versions from Hafiz: An Assay in Persian Metre* (London: Grant Richards, 1898), p. 23. To fit Plowden’s version, I have reversed Leaf’s third and fourth couplets and omitted the fifth.

(a)

(b)

Figure 4.7 A and B. Persian *ghazal*, '*Surwi ruwān-i kīstī*' by Afzal-ud-din Badil Khaqani Sherwani (1122–90). Sophia Plowden, *Album*, f. 11, and *Tunebook*, f. 19v. Lucknow, 1787–8. MS 380. © **Fitzwilliam Museum, University of Cambridge**

And something of their musical and social interests in each other, and of the emotional spaces they explored together, does live on in what remains of their songs. My last example, '*Surwi ruwān(-i) kīstī*', is found along with '*Tāza ba tāza*' in Plowden, Bird, Gilchrist and the novel *Nashtar*. This was clearly another very popular *ghazal*, attributed to the medieval Persian poet Afzal-ud-din Badil 'Khaqani' Sherwani (1122–90),[120] and it is in the same

[120] It is not found in Khaqani's *dīwān*; Sunil Sharma, personal communication.

poetical metre as '*Tāza ba tāza*'. It may be that *ghazal*s in this metre were considered especially suited to song setting in late Mughal India.

lāla rukhā suman berā surwi ruwān(-i) kīstī?
sang-dilā sitamgarā āfat-i jān(-i) kīstī?

Oh, you with cyprus-like elegance, tulip cheeks and breasts like jasmine;
hard-hearted, cruel oppressor, bane of my life – who are you?

The concluding translation is by Plowden's contemporary, the Edinburgh-trained surgeon, famous linguist and lover of Indian poetry John Gilchrist. It is a fitting counterpart to our snake-charmer's song, with its fatally attractive but utterly implacable beloved, and a lover shot through with the pains of unrequited love. In an eloquent final twist, like Walter Leaf, and like our nameless Hindustani harpsichord enthusiast of 1788, Gilchrist set his English words to the *ghazal*'s Persian metre. Eurydice's echo still lingers here, when you know how and where to listen.

Say, blooming maid! with bosom fair as snow,
High o'er our heads like some majestic pine;
Whence camest thou, and whither dost thou go?
To kill unfeeling with thy form divine.

In flowery meadows if thou heedless roam,
Each fond Narcissus lifts its eyes to view;
Thy mouth, more luscious than the honey comb,
Or virgin rose buds set with pearly dew.

Like some keen fowler, here, you plant a snare,
And wanton there, with kisses raise a flame;
Then with portentious glance thy bows prepare;
Hold anchor! say – what means this cruel aim?

Thy jetty eye-brows lunar crescents seem,
In beauteous arches o'er bright stars to bend;
Whence rays like fatal arrows swiftly gleam,
Ah! spare me now, and to my prayer attend!

Khaqanee, angel! is thy captive slave,
A prostrate victim of thy matchless charms;
Say, who art thou? and snatch him from the grave,
To clasp thee, grateful in his longing arms.[121]

[121] Gilchrist, *Oriental*, pp. 158–9.

5 Eclipsed by the Moon: Mahlaqa Bai and Khushhal Khan Anup in Nizami Hyderabad

The Collected Writings of a Hereditary Musician

To decorate the lofty shrine, with pure intent and sincerity
He built a mosque, an ashur-khana and grand archway
What a good fate that Khush-hal Khan has built
On this noble hill with good planning and sacrificial soul.

Inscription on the arch built by Khushhal Khan Anup at
Maula ᶜAli *dargāh* in Hyderabad, 1822/3.[1]

The Eclipsed *Ustād* and His Celestial Disciple

In October 1799, twelve years after Khanum Jan first dazzled Sophia Plowden on a Lucknow winter's night, an ambitious, high-ranking Shiᶜa nobleman at the court of the Nizam of Hyderabad put on a *nāch*.[2] This wasn't just any old evening's *majlis*. Mir ᶜAlam's assembly was a massive song, dance and fireworks extravaganza to celebrate the recent victory of the combined British and Hyderabad forces over the powerful ruler of Mysore, Tipu Sultan (r. 1782–99).[3]

Into the midst of this party stepped a woman – elegant and beautiful, dark hair plaited to beneath her waist, dressed in the airiest of coloured muslins weighted down with exquisite jewels.[4] She was the fabled Chanda Bibi Mahlaqa Bai Chanda (1768–1824), the Moon of Hyderabad, and her presence was as political and ritually auspicious as her role was to give all eyes and ears there pleasure. Intimate companion in her lifetime to three prime ministers and two Nizams – never married and independently wealthy, a patron of the arts in her own right, the best-known female Urdu poet of the age and a famously talented performer – she danced and sang her way into British history that night, by pirouêtting up to the

[1] Scott Kugle, *When Sun Meets Moon: Gender, Eros, and Ecstasy in Urdu Poetry* (Chapel Hill: University of North Carolina Press, 2016), p. 151; Syed Ali Asgar Bilgrami Asafjahi, *Landmarks of the Deccan: A Comprehensive Guide to the Archaeological Remains of the City and Suburbs of Hyderabad* (New Delhi: Asian Educational Services Reprint, 1992 [orig. 1927]), pp. 12, 16.

[2] For general histories, see John Zubrzycki, *The Last Nizam: The Rise and Fall of India's Greatest Princely State* (New Delhi: Picador India, 2007); Dalrymple, *White Mughals*.

[3] Kate Brittlebank, *Tiger: The Life of Tipu Sultan* (New Delhi: Juggernaut, 2016).

[4] Portrait in Kugle, *Sun*, p. 144.

Deputy British Resident of Hyderabad, Captain John Malcolm, and presenting him with a sought-after collection of her *ghazal*s, the *dīwān* of Chanda, the 'Moon', her *takhallus* or *nom-de-plume*.[5] It eventually made its way out of Malcolm's breast pocket, and lies where he left it, in the India Office collections now at the British Library in London, where this breathtaking moment in which two rival cultures brushed hands is pinned down ever so fleetingly in a note on the flyleaf.[6]

Obscured by Mahlaqa's luminescence today is a man who was equally central to the musical life and prestige of the Hyderabad court, if not quite so exposed to the limelight or so fascinating to British correspondents. More importantly, he was crucial to Mahlaqa. He was her *ustād*, the master-musician who trained her, teaching her everything he knew about singing and composing songs in Hindustani *rāgas* – but also seems to have been the closest thing she had to a father figure. He was the same Delhi-lineage *kalāwant* we met briefly in Chapter 3, Khushhal Khan Anup, whose *takhallus* meant 'beyond compare'.[7] He may have slipped quietly into the edge of the picture in Figure 5.1 of Mahlaqa singing to their earliest great patron, Raja Rao Ranbha; you can see Anup there at the bottom, the calmly seated man in white and green. But he wrote the book in which this illustration is housed, his Brajbhasha *Rāg Darshan* of 1800,[8] thus immortalising both their lives and their connection with each other.

As we saw in Chapter 3, Anup belonged to what had become by the mid-eighteenth century the most prestigious lineage of hereditary musicians attached to the imperial Mughal court in Delhi – his father, Karim Khan, had been the special disciple of Adarang during the reign of Emperor Muhammad Shah. But sometime in the middle decades of the eighteenth century, Karim moved his family southwards, ending up in the independent princely state of Hyderabad. His son Anup was prominent in the court circles of successive Nizams, especially Nizam ᶜAli Khan (r. 1762–1803) and Sikandar Jah (r. 1803–29), as a vocalist, teacher, song composer and treatise writer in Persian and Brajbhasha

5 Kugle's *Sun* provides an outstanding literary biography of Mahlaqa; also Shweta Sachdeva [Jha], 'In Search', pp. 126–39. For Mir ᶜAlam and John Malcolm, see Dalrymple, *White Mughals*, index entries pp. 567, 575.

6 Kugle, *Sun*, pp. 175–6, 222; Dalrymple, *White Mughals*, pp. 124, 172–3, 199–200; Mahlaqa Bai Chanda, *Dīwān-i Chandā*, British Library, I O Islamic 2768 (1799).

7 The later nineteenth-century note on the flyleaf of the *Rāg-Rāginī* calls him a *qawwāl*, but Anup called himself a *kalāwant*; Anup, *Rāg Darshan* (Brajbhasha, 1800), ff. 3v–4r.

8 Anup himself called it 'the language of Braj' ('*ba zabān-i Hindī yaᶜnī zabān-i Braj*'); Anup, *Rāg Darshan* (Persian 1808 and 1815), p. 157.

Figure 5.1 Mahlaqa Bai Chanda singing for Raja Rao Ranbha, by Haji Mir Ghulam Hasan. Khushhal Khan Anup, *Rāg Darshan*. Hyderabad, text 1800 paintings 1804. Lawrence J Schoenberg Collection, LJS 63, f. 2v. **University of Pennsylvania Special Collections Library**.

from before 1791 until his death around 1836.[9] Anup was clearly a brilliant figure, revered in his time as a singer of Mughal court music in the most exclusive private *majālis*, whose patrons included many of the major notables of the city; and if his endowments at the hilltop shrine of Maula ᶜAli are anything to go by, he departed this earth a wealthy man.

[9] Kugle states that Anup died two years before Mahlaqa, in 1822; *Sun*, pp. 138, 282 fn. 5 and 6. But this date doesn't add up with the dozens of songs in Anup's *Rāg-Rāginī* giving his name as author and a year of composition much later than 1822/3; e.g. ff. 80v (1826), 86v (1828), 81r (1829), 28v (1834/5). The latest of Anup's dated songs are October 1836 (13th Rajab 1252 AH).

But he is largely remembered today – when he is remembered at all – only as the man behind the illustrious Moon of Hyderabad.[10]

We have become used to thinking of celebrated Indian courtesans like Khanum and Mahlaqa as powerful, refined and highly literate: thanks in large part to Hindi cinema, the Mughal-era image of what a courtesan was and meant to wider society before the British Raj has never quite faded away.[11] But musicians like Anup explode enduring preconceptions of the hereditary male masters of Hindustani music, the Muslim *ustāds*. Today's music histories still tell us that the *ustāds* of North India were illiterate – or, more generously, did not use writing or theory in teaching and performance – thus rendering their historical performances and lives unrecoverable, and their music passed down to the present only by oral/aural transmission.[12]

A major aim of this book is to demonstrate that this wasn't true. We have already seen that top hereditary musicians such as Ras Baras Khan *kalāwant* and Mir Salih *qawwāl* Dehlavi were writing highly technical music treatises in Persian as early as the seventeenth century (Chapter 2). A hundred years later, Anup was one of at least three members of the conjoined Delhi *kalāwant* lineages just in his own lifetime who left behind erudite, innovative, sometimes even moving and witty writings on music theory and history (the others being the author of Edinburgh MS 585(4) and Miyan Himmat Khan).[13] These prove beyond doubt such musicians' command of Persian, Hindavi and even Sanskrit; and their extraordinary personal knowledge of the depths and delights of Hindustani music.

In this chapter I am going to retell the lives of Anup, Mahlaqa, their main patrons and Hindustani musical life in Nizami Hyderabad through the collected writings of a single literate musician. In doing so, I will also show how we can use what might appear to be marginal and unpromising source material to shed unexpected light on the political, social and ritual life of

[10] Kugle, *Sun*, p. 157, 282 fn. 6.

[11] For a selected bibliography see Schofield, 'Courtesan Tale', p. 166 fn. 4; Ruth Vanita, *Dancing with the Nation: Courtesans in Bombay Cinema* (London: Bloomsbury, 2018); Richard David Williams, 'Songs Between Cities: Listening to Courtesans in Colonial North India', *Journal of the Royal Asiatic Society, Series 3*, 27.4 (2017), 591–610; and on Hyderabad's courtesans especially, Karen B. Leonard, 'Political Players: Courtesans of Hyderabad', *Indian Economic and Social History Review* 50.4 (2013), 423–48.

[12] Dard Neuman, 'Pedagogy', esp. pp. 427–8. Janaki Bakhle accepts as factual Bhatkhande's assertions that hereditary musicians could not write; Bakhle, pp. 4–8, 12, 16–17; but see Katz, *Lineage*, pp. 129–58, esp. 136–8.

[13] Also Zia-ud-din, who was a non-hereditary disciple.

this important Mughal successor state. I am coaxing my stories almost entirely from Anup's two major works of musical writing: his music treatise the *Rāg Darshan* (*Vision of Rāga*), which went through at least three versions in Brajbhasha and Persian 1800–15; and his massive song collection, nearly 2000 strong, the *Rāg-Rāginī Roz o Shab* (*Rāga*s *and Rāginī*s, *Day and Night*), completed 1833–36.[14]

Although we know a great deal more about her than him, thanks especially to Scott Kugle's landmark biography of Mahlaqa, their life stories were utterly entangled with each other's. They worked for the same series of patrons at the same times; later in life they lived in the same house; and both are buried at the foot of the holy mountain of Maula ᶜAli in Hyderabad, to whose shrine they were devoted. While Mahlaqa did not write *on* music to our knowledge, she did compose accomplished song lyrics – notably, the exquisite *ghazal*s for which she became famous throughout the land[15] – and some of the occasion pieces she wrote in Hindavi under Anup's musical instruction are included in his *Rāg-Rāginī*. And it was for Mahlaqa's use that Anup wrote the last, bilingual version of the *Rāg Darshan* in 1815.[16] The question I particularly want to explore in this chapter, then, is this: what did a late Mughal master of the quintessentially ephemeral and unwritable act of performing and passing on Hindustani music write when he wrote about music, and why?

Anup's Song Collection: The *Rāg-Rāginī Roz o Shab*

I will begin with a brief examination of the two works I will be drawing upon. Figure 5.2 is a folio from Anup's song collection, the *Rāg-Rāginī Roz o Shab*, now in the Salar Jung Museum in Hyderabad, showing a page of compositions set in the feminine *rāga*, or *rāginī*, Khamaj.

The main collection was completed on 3 March 1833 and is an exhaustive set of the élite courtly songs in the repertoire of Anup's *kalāwant* lineage stemming from the Mughal court in Delhi.[17] It is a cornucopia of compositions by great names of the Mughal past, like Surdas, Tansen, Baz Bahadur,

[14] Anup, *Rāg Darshans*; Persian 1808, Government Oriental Manuscripts Library, University of Madras, Persian MS D515 (modern copy D1024); Persian 1815, ed. Chander Shekhar (New Delhi: National Mission for Manuscripts, 2014); *Rāg-Rāginī Roz o Shab*: mixed languages, Salar Jung Museum Library, Urdu Mus 2 (1833–36).

[15] Williams, 'Songs Between Cities', pp. 601–2; Sachdeva [Jha], 'In Search', pp. 210–11.

[16] Shekhar, 'Introduction', *Rāg Darshan*, p. xx. The date of this MS is 1230 AH = 14 Dec 1814–12 Dec 1815 ÇE, so 1815 is most likely.

[17] Anup, *Rāg-Rāginī*, f. 130v; Schofield, 'Words', esp. pp. 174–6, 180, 185–8.

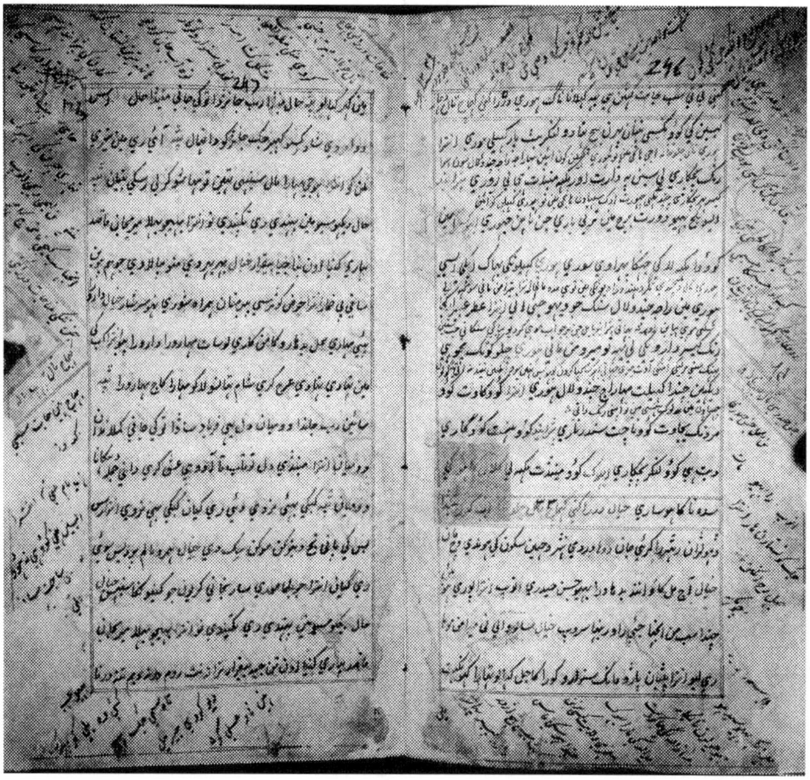

Figure 5.2 *Hoṛī*, *khayāl* and *ṭappa* compositions in Ragini Khamaj. Khushhal Khan Anup, *Rāg-Rāginī Roz o Shab*. Hyderabad, 1833–6. Urdu Mus 2, f. 123v–4r. © **Salar Jung Museum Library, Hyderabad**

Jagannath Kabirai, Sadarang and Adarang especially, and many more besides.[18] This collection represents a much earlier stage of the transmission of élite Hindustani songs than the earliest sound recordings or even the earliest printed compendia,[19] and the *Rāg-Rāginī* is thus one of the most valuable remaining documents of its kind. It also includes several songs written in the style and genres of the Mughal tradition that Anup himself, and occasionally Mahlaqa, wrote as professional singers in Hyderabad in honour of a number of patrons.

The songs are in multiple languages: alongside their main language, Brajbhasha, like the Plowden and Johnson collections they are in *rekhta*,

[18] Anup, *Rāg-Rāginī*, e.g. ff. 40r (Surdas), 37r (Tansen), 22v (Baz Bahadur), 22v (Jagannath Kabirai), 24v (Sadarang), 50v (Adarang).

[19] To my knowledge the earliest is Krishnananda Vyasadeva and Basu [1842–9], *Saṅgīta-rāga-kalpadruma* (Calcutta: Bangiya Sahitya Parishad, 1914).

Persian and Punjabi; and they serve to demonstrate the enormous range of Anup's and his lineage's literacy, linguistic ability and astonishing powers of recall. In terms of genre, they are representative of the discrete set of pan-regional genres that at this time marked out the élite repertoire of Hindustani music from other rural, devotional or local repertoires, while making room for new compositions in art music styles designed specifically for local devotional events.[20] In addition to the main collection, a substantial number of devotional or praise songs were added to the margins that are frequently dated, the latest of them to October 1836. These mostly have Shiᶜa themes and were written and performed by Anup and/or Mahlaqa to mark the various festivals on the hill of Maula ᶜAli. For example, Anup wrote the *jashn-i ᶜīd-i g͟hadīr* in the top right of Figure 5.2 for the anniversary celebration on 28 April 1834 of the Prophet Muhammad naming his nephew Hazrat ᶜAli as his successor.[21]

The *Rāg-Rāginī* was patently designed for the practical use of singers who needed to find and recall an appropriate song quickly. The book is very easy to navigate with its paginated table of contents and is set out according to a wholly musical logic. It is organised at the top level by *rāgas* appropriate to the daytime versus those that should be sung at night. Within that, all the songs in a particular *rāga/rāginī* are grouped together. The order of *rāgas* is interesting, in that all those sung in particular seasons of the year – the springtime *rāga/rāginīs* Hindol, Basant and Bahar, or the monsoon *rāga/rāginīs* Megh, Gaund, Malhar and Sur Malhar – are clustered together, as are *rāgas* with multiple famous varieties, such as the Sarang family. Not only are the *rāgas* *not* ordered according to the aesthetic *rāgamālā* system of six male *rāgas* each with five wives that Anup used in his *Rāg Darshans*, but several of the *rāginīs* he described in his music treatises don't appear at all in his song collection. The *Rāg-Rāginī* was clearly representative of the *rāgas* in the current practice and categorisation of singers (see Chapter 7). Finally, Anup divided the songs in each *rāga/rāginī* into genre sections: *dhrupads*, historically the birthright of the *kalāwants* of Delhi; *hoṛīs*, which are specific to the Holi festival in spring celebrating Lord Krishna; and *k͟hayāls* and *ṭappas*, which traditionally belonged to the *qawwāl* lineages, but which were also now established repertoire within Anup's own Khandari lineage of *kalāwants* (Chapter 3).

We can use the songs in the *Rāg-Rāginī* to tell us various stories; but a study of this enormous collection is well beyond my scope – it could easily fill a book in its own right. In this chapter I will mainly use Anup's collection in its capacity as a trove of information about the history of his

[20] Schofield, 'Words', pp. 172–6. [21] Anup, *Rāg-Rāginī*, f. 123v.

lineage, the state of Hindustani music at this point in time, the courtly musical life of Hyderabad and especially the annual cycle of ritual events there – principally at the Maula ᶜAli *dargāh*, but also the spring festivals of Basant, Holi and Nauroz (Persian New Year), which feature heavily in the collection.

Anup's Music Treatises: The *Rāg Darshans*

Most of the paintings in this chapter are illustrated folios from Anup's earliest version of the *Rāg Darshan* in Brajbhasha.[22] This version of his music treatise was dedicated to Anup and Mahlaqa's early patron the Maratha general Raja Rao Ranbha Nimbalkar Jayawant Bahadur, and written in Brajbhasha verse, the classical Hindi register of the Delhi-Agra region widely used throughout India at this time as a pan-regional language of courtly poetry and song. Figure 5.3 shows the illustration for the *rāginī* Khambhavati that accompanies Anup's compact verse description (*dohā*) of her iconic form.

Anup's first *Rāg Darshan* is a fascinating landmark, not because of its very canonical contents, but because of what it is, and what Anup did with it subsequently. It is a translation into Brajbhasha verse of the key Mughal Persian treatise on music, Chapter V of Mirza Khan's *Tuhfat al-Hind* (c.1675) (see Chapters 2 and 3). The *Tuhfat* was a comprehensive manual of Indian aesthetic sciences: everything a Persian-reading aspiring aficionado would need to know in order to appreciate, and perhaps to compose and perform, poetry and song in Brajbhasha: the 'language of Braj', Lord Krishna's playground in the region of Vrindaban and Mathura, but also the Mughal courtly register of Hindavi since the late sixteenth century.[23]

The *Tuhfat* was a masterpiece of erudite scholarship, with a royal provenance dating from the reign of the last genuinely powerful Mughal emperor, Aurangzeb. It was inevitable that it would rapidly become a major canonical reference work for later writers and aspirants to connoisseurship; there are at least eight full or partial copies in the British Library alone. This included Europeans interested in music such as Richard Johnson and Sir William Jones, the latter of whose heavily annotated copy of the whole *Tuhfat* in the British Library is a major source for

[22] https://dla.library.upenn.edu/dla/medren/detail.html?id=MEDREN_9949529953503681.

[23] Busch, *Poetry of Kings*; Françoise 'Nalini' Delvoye, *Tânsen et la tradition des chants dhrupad en langue braj, du XVIe siècle à nos jours* (Paris: Université de la Sorbonne Nouvelle Paris III, 1990).

Figure 5.3 Ragini Khambhavati, by Haji Mir Ghulam Hasan. Khushhal Khan Anup, *Rāg Darshan*. Hyderabad, text 1800 paintings 1804. Lawrence J Schoenberg Collection, LJS 63, f. 9v (detail). **University of Pennsylvania Special Collections Library.** CC–BY

understanding his own pioneering 1784 English-language treatise 'On the Musical Modes of the Hindoos' (Chapter 8).[24]

Consciously conservative even in its own time, Chapter V of the *Tuhfat* is almost entirely a digest of earlier seventeenth-century writings on music in Sanskrit, Persian and Brajbhasha.[25] Often cited verbatim, Mirza Khan's sources were Damodara's Sanskrit *Saṅgīta-darpaṇa* (c.1600–25), probably via Harivallabha's mid-century Brajbhasha translation (earliest manuscript 1653) and/or Paida Beg's *Sabha-vinoda* (c. 1628–49);[26] and Faqirullah's Persian *Rāg Darpan* (1665/6) (Chapter 2). The *Tuhfat*'s appeal to élite lovers of Hindustani music lay in its comprehensive coverage and systematic reconciliation of all the information fit to know at the Mughal court at its peak, drawn from the most authoritative works of the age in Sanskrit,

[24] Mirza Khan, *Tuḥfat*, RSPA 78; Sir William Jones, 'On the Musical Modes of the Hindoos: Written in 1784 and Since Much Enlarged', in Lady Anna Maria Jones (ed.), *The Works of Sir William Jones, in Six Volumes; Vol. I* (London: G G and J Robinson, 1789), 413–43.

[25] Brown [Schofield], 'Hindustani', pp. 35–6, 50, 67, 73–6.

[26] Williams, 'Reflecting'; I am grateful to the author for additional information on the *Sabha-vinoda*.

Brajbhasha and Persian – in other words, its analytical and symbolically ecumenical synthesis of Indic and Persianate streams of Hindustani musical knowledge. Its appeal also lay in its royal pedigree – it was written for Mughal prince Muhammad A^{c}zam Shah (d. 1707) – which led to its early acceptance as a work of unimpeachable authority.

But it also lay in its inclusion of a Persian prose translation of the *Saṅgīta-darpaṇa*'s popular set of verse descriptions (*dhyānas*) of the six male *rāgas* and thirty female *rāginīs* as heroes, heroines, *joginis* and deities in the Hanuman *mat* scheme of the *rāgamālā* tradition. Damodara's translated *dhyānas*, in both Persian and Brajbhasha versions, were quickly dislodged from their surrounding treatises and used to inspire and caption new sets of *rāgamālā* paintings which then proliferated wildly in the eighteenth century; Richard Johnson for instance commissioned a full set of new *rāgamālā* paintings in Lucknow inscribed with the *Tuhfat*'s descriptions.[27] Finally, the *Tuhfat* is written in a straightforward and accessible style, with full diacritical markings for all Brajbhasha and Sanskrit terminology, making it a very easy manual to use.

Very early on, music lovers detached Chapter V from its parent volume, and it began circulating in its own right as a stand-alone music treatise, to be studied, copied and built upon. From the eighteenth century, Chapter V of the *Tuhfat* began to be reused widely in the writing of new music treatises, as both a structural model and an authoritative source of canonical information; not just in Persian (Chapters 3 and 7), but in Hindavi and later Bengali (e.g. Radhamohan Sen Das' 1818 *Saṅgīta-Taraṅga* or *Ocean of Music*), Urdu (e.g. Imam Khan's post-Uprising *Ma^{c}dan al-Mūsīqī* or *Mine of Music*) and even English (e.g. Augustus Willard's 1834 *Treatise on the Music of Hindustan*).[28]

What Anup did with the *Tuhfat*, however, was unique. He clearly owned a copy, and in his successive *Rāg Darshans* he reworked Chapter V of the *Tuhfat* at least three times to suit the abilities, needs, tastes and agendas of different patrons. Firstly, he translated it into Brajbhasha verse and had it copiously illustrated with paintings for Raja Rao Ranbha c. 1800. Then, in 1808/9, Anup reworked his Brajbhasha version into simplified Persian prose for Nizam Sikandar Jah at the request of Nawab Mir ^{c}Alam, the prime minister at the time. Finally, in 1815, he produced a bilingual version

27 Text: British Library, I O Islamic 1861; Paintings: British Library, Johnson Album 34.

28 Schofield, 'Reviving', pp. 508–9. For Bengali, see Richard David Williams, 'Music, Lyrics, and the Bengali Book: Hindustani Musicology in Calcutta, 1818–1905', *Music and Letters* 97.3 (2016), 465–95, esp. pp. 468–70.

for Mahlaqa that interleaved his Brajbhasha verse translation with yet another slightly different rewriting in Persian. In what follows, I will concentrate largely on the first and most remarkable *Rāg Darshan* in Brajbhasha, though I will refer to the other versions as they unfold more of the story of Anup's and Mahlaqa's relationships with their later patrons after 1800: successive prime ministers of Hyderabad, Mir ᶜAlam and Maharaja Chandu Lal.

I have worked primarily with the intact copy of Anup's Brajbhasha *Rāg Darshan* at the University of Pennsylvania, produced for Rao Ranbha in April 1800, with charming but slightly inexpert illustrations made in 1804 by a forgotten minor painter, Haji Mir Ghulam Hasan.[29] It has long been apparent that many of his illustrations were copies of paintings by major Hyderabad artists such as Rai Venkatchallam and Tajalli ᶜAli Shah.[30] But it has recently become clear that Anup prepared an earlier copy of the entire treatise, written in a very similar hand, but with much more beautiful illustrations.[31] Several detached folios from Anup's treatise, complete with the correct *dohā*s of Anup's Brajbhasha text, came up for sale at Sotheby's in 2013. It is likely to be the original from which Ghulam Hasan was copying.

Figure 5.3 above depicts the night *rāginī* Khambhavati in the University of Pennsylvania copy of the *Rāg Darshan*. In the classic *rāgamālā* iconography, Khambhavati is usually shown as the god Brahma being worshipped and served by a female attendant, as in Figure 5.4.[32]

But the image in Figure 5.3 was instead created to match the more worldly, courtly scenario presented in the *Tuhfat al-Hind*. Here Brahma is replaced by 'a beautiful lady enjoying the company of her friends who sing beautifully; night and day she is joyful and busy experiencing the full richness of the sights and sounds of music and dance'. This is simplified in Anup's 1808/9 Persian translation as 'a very beautiful lady in a red sari and green *angiyā* . . . sitting in the seat of honour, face to face with her dancing *tawā'ifs* (courtesans)'.[33] Figure 5.5 is an icon of Khambavati from what is patently an earlier copy of Anup's *Rāg Darshan* for Rao Ranbha – not only

29 Artist's signature, f. 24v.

30 e.g. compare Anup, *Rāg Darshan* (Brajbhasha, 1800; paintings 1804), f 2r, with Rai Venkatchellam, Hyderabad, late 18C, Edward Binney 3rd Collection, San Diego Museum of Art, 1990.56, https://collection.sdmart.org/objects-1/info/5201.

31 There was also a third copy produced in 1800 with paintings that also appear to be by Haji Mir Ghulam Hasan; five folios are in the Metropolitan Museum of Art (acc. no. 2007.32).

32 cf. Khambhavati, Manley Ragamala, British Museum (c. 1610), www.britishmuseum.org/collection/object/A_1973-0917-0-24.

33 Mirza Khan, *Tuhfat*, vol. i, p. 381; Anup, *Rāg Darshan* (Persian 1808/9), p. 178.

Figure 5.4 Ragini Khambhavati. Bikaner, c. 1675. 2000.321. Gift of Doris Wiener, in honour of Stephen Kossak, 2000. **Metropolitan Museum of Art**. Public Domain

are the visual similarities with Figure 5.3 obvious, it is captioned with Anup's *dohā*s describing Khambhavati exactly as in the University of Pennsylvania copy.

There is no section for *rāginī* Khambhavati in Anup's song collection, the *Rāg-Rāginī*; but there is for Khambhavati's close melodic relative, Khamaj (Figure 5.2), in which Anup wrote the following *khayāl* composition[34]:

KHAYĀL: Today bliss spreads through the abstinent heart, meeting the one whose love for ᶜAli is 'beyond compare' [i.e. Anup].

ANTARĀ: By the full 'moon' [i.e. Chanda], all hearts pause before beautiful Rao Ranbha.[35]

[34] Joep Bor, Suvarnalata Rao, Wim van der Meer and Jane Harvey, *The Raga Guide: A Survey of 74 Hindustani Ragas* (Monmouth: Nimbus, 1999), p. 100.

[35] Anup, *Rāg-Rāginī*, f. 124v; tr. Richard David Williams.

Figure 5.5 Ragini Khambhavati. Khushhal Khan Anup, *Rāg Darshan*. Hyderabad, late 18C. © **Photo courtesy of Southeby's, 2019**

If we combine the iconic with the sonic – as is the whole point of the *rāga* – the paintings in Figures 5.3 and 5.5 take on a whole new resonance.[36] Look at that moon! Rao Ranbha was one of Mahlaqa Bai's earliest patrons, he is remembered today for his devoted love for her,[37] and named pictures of Mahlaqa are everywhere in Anup's treatise for Rao Ranbha. This strongly suggests that Khambhavati is, in fact, a painting of Mahlaqa, perhaps seated in the garden of her house with her atelier of trainee courtesans dancing before her.[38] But this rendition is much more than mere narrative record. A whole world meets in Kambhavati–Khamaj: the saintly presence of Hazrat ᶜAli to whom Mahlaqa and Anup were devoted,

36 Schofield, 'Music, Art', pp. 68–87; Laura Leante, 'The Lotus and the King: Imagery, Gesture and Meaning in a Hindustani Rāg', *Ethnomusicology Forum* 18.2 (2009), 185–206.

37 Kugle, *Sun*, p. 177. 38 ibid., pp. 189, 206.

the worldly blessing of Rao Ranbha, Mahlaqa's luminescence and Anup's knowledge as the man behind the Moon, the Mughal heritage of the author and the canonical treatise he was translating, the Maratha heritage of its new patron, the Nizami heritage of the painters, the long journeys they had all taken to end up in this single space of Hyderabad – all wrapped up in a musical mode, a page in a music treatise, watched over by Hazrat ᶜAli and the auspicious light of the illustrious moon.

The whole world of Nizami Hyderabad, and the tiny world of Anup, Mahlaqa and Rao Ranbha within it, is here in the treatise Anup first composed for Rao Ranbha.[39] I will now turn to their lives as they unfold within his various acts of writing, beginning with what we can piece together of Anup's life before sketching Mahlaqa's rather better-known story. And then I will turn again to Anup's works, to consider what they tell us about the life of music among Hyderabad's most prominent players at the turn of the nineteenth century: Mughals, Marathas, musicians – and, obliquely, the British.

The Earlier Lives of Anup and Mahlaqa

While their names are now inseparable from our image of Nizami Hyderabad, both Khushhal Khan Anup and Mahlaqa Bai Chanda were second-generation migrants to the Deccan from Mughal North India. Their presence at the court of Hyderabad in the late eighteenth century was due to what Anup referred to broadly as 'the changing fortunes of the time and the collapse of the sultanate' but which Zia-ud-din had called the 'scattering'[40] – the demographic upheaval in the Mughal heartlands caused by the series of invasions and pitched battles between the Mughals, Marathas, Afghans, Rohillas, British and other smaller players that marred the middle decades of the eighteenth century.[41] As we saw in previous chapters, this led to a major shift of talented and able people out of their original homelands in search of (comparatively) more settled and prosperous places to live and work. Many moved eastwards along the Ganges river, or to Rohilla country or the great Mughal successor state of Lucknow; but others went west to Rajasthan and Punjab, north to Nepal, or

[39] Michael Bywater, *Lost Worlds: What Have We Lost and Where Did It Go?* (London: Granta, 2004), p. 264.

[40] Anup, ed. Shekhar, *Rāg Darshan*, p. 156; P MS D1024 (Persian 1808), p. 3; Zia-ud-din, *Hayy*, e.g. ff. 43r, 44v, 47v, 55r, 57r.

[41] Schofield, 'Emotions'.

south to the Maratha courts or to Hyderabad in the eastern Deccan.[42] Among latter migrants were a privileged and well-connected Delhi hereditary musician from the central imperial lineage, named Karim Khan – Anup's father – and an abandoned-daughter-turned-courtesan from Ahmedabad in Gujarat, whose name was Raj Kanvar Bai – Mahlaqa's mother.

Anup was born in Delhi probably sometime in the early 1750s, and died in Hyderabad, where he was apparently still composing songs as late as 1836.[43] The carefully curated snippets of autobiography Anup presented in his three *Rāg Darshan*s root the court music of Nizami Hyderabad c. 1800 firmly back in the soil of Mughal Delhi at its cultural peak. His genealogical imagination and his placement of himself within it was highly Delhi-centric, even while overtly honouring his later Hyderabad location – as if he saw his life's work to be recreating through music, insofar as was possible, Mughal imperial court culture at the break-away court of the Nizam. As we saw in Chapter 3, Anup traced his blood and musical descent from the two most important, intermarried lineages of Mughal imperial *kalāwants*: those of Tansen of Akbar's court in the sixteenth century and Sadarang of Muhammad Shah's (see Figure 3.1 for Ghulam Hasan's visualisation of Anup's dual lineage as a fantasy *majlis*).

Alongside Zia-ud-din and the author of Edinburgh MS 585(4), Anup was among the earliest theorists to draw attention to the fact that the four main branches of the Delhi *kalāwant* brotherhood by the end of the eighteenth century practised different stylistic schools that we now call *bānīs*. He wrote:

> The term for each of these is *got* [class, family, lineage], which means *aqwām* [sg. *qaum* (community); it is *jāti* (caste, lineage) in the Brajbhasha version]: that is to say, there are numerous branches and sub-branches [of *kalāwants*]. Each of these has an originator who had a fresh style, and who was the progenitor of a large stylistic school.[44] Premier among them is [the line of] Miyan Tansen [the founder of the Gorari branch and school].[45]

[42] Munis D Faruqui, 'At Empire's End: The Nizam, Hyderabad and Eighteenth-Century India', *Modern Asian Studies*, 43.1 (2009), 5–43. For Maratha patronage of *kalāwants*, *tawā'ifs*, *kathaks*, and other Hindustani performers see Thomas D Broughton, *The Costume, Character, Manners, Domestic Habits and Religious Ceremonies of the Mahrattas* (London: John Murray, 1813), pp. 94–5, 236, 304–5; also Scarimbolo, 'Brahmans'.

[43] e.g. Anup, *Rāg-Rāginī*, f. 123v.

[44] *tarz-i tāza*; *ravish*.

[45] Anup ed. Shekhar, *Rāg Darshan* (Persian 1815), p. 11; (Brajbhasha 1800), ff. 3r–4r; Zia-ud-din, *Hayy*, ff. 13r; Anon, Edinburgh 585(4), ff. 51r, 58v–60r.

Anup's treatises leave precisely how he was descended from Tansen ambiguous.[46] What is clearer is that, properly, he belonged to the Khandari branch of the Delhi *kalāwant*s, whose most important eighteenth-century representatives had been Sadarang and Adarang (Chapters 3 and 7). According to Anup, the founder of his family line, his great-great-grandfather Miyan Kunhi Khan, was originally of Rajput heritage and belonged to the Khandari branch.[47] Anup's grandfather, Kunhi's daughter's son Nanhe Khan, who was 'a perfect master of the art' of music, married one of the daughters of Anand Khan, and had eleven sons including Karim.[48] If Anand were Anand Baras Khan, second son of Khushhal Khan Gunasamudra (also Ras Baras Khan's brother and Anjha Baras Khan's paternal uncle), this would explain Anup's lineal connection with Tansen.[49]

Sadarang was still alive when Anup's father, Karim, started learning the family trade in Delhi. But it was Sadarang's nephew Adarang who trained Karim up as his 'special student'.[50] Of the three *kalāwant* specialisms – *dhrupad*-singing, playing the *bīn* and playing the *rabāb* – Karim became a singer, and in his prime he was known by the epithet 'Ghogā-āwāz', the 'full-bloomed voice'[51]. Two key features of the eighteenth-century Khandari school were that, after Sadarang, its masters composed as many *k͟hayāl*s and related forms as they did *dhrupad*s; and they were devoted Sufi adepts with strong discipular connections to the Tariqa-i Muhammadiyya branch of the Naqshbandi Mujaddidiyya (see Chapter 7).[52] Both of these characteristics are amply demonstrated in Anup's song repertoire.

It is not clear when Karim left Delhi for good, taking his family with him. Anup's 1808 autobiographical note leaps over several decades from Karim's service under Muhammad Shah directly to father and son coming to Hyderabad, finding there a patron in Raja Rao Ranbha.[53] Élite musicians and courtesans were almost certainly among the first large group of Mughal migrants who returned south with the first Asaf Jahi Nizam, Chin Qilich

46 The rather poor copy we have of the 1815 *Rāg Darshan* suggests Anup's grandfather Nanhe Khan was one of Tansen's 'sons'; (Persian 1815), pp. 11–12. For that to be true we would have to collapse an entire century, and it is also contradicted by Anup's 1800 Brajbhasha version, where 'Nanhe' is the maternal grandson of Miyan Kunhi Khan; f. 3v.

47 Anup, *Rāg Darshan* (Brajbhasha 1800), f. 3v.

48 Anup ed. Shekhar, *Rāg Darshan* (Persian 1815), pp. 11–12.

49 Anon, Edinburgh MS 585(4), ff. 58v–60r.

50 Anup, *Rāg Darshan* (Brajbhasha 1800), f. 4r; Anup ed. Shekhar (Persian 1808/9), p. 156.

51 Anup, *Rāg-Rāginī*, note on front flyleaf.

52 Brown [Schofield], 'Origins', pp. 163, 189–91; and 'If Music Be', pp. 79–81; Ziad, 'Transcend'; and 'Poetry, Music'.

53 Anup ed. Shekhar, *Rāg Darshan* (Persian 1808/9), p. 156.

Khan Nizam-ul-mulk (r. 1720–48), after Nadir Shah humiliated the Mughal armies defending Delhi in 1739. As noted previously, Muhammad Shah released a number of musicians from the imperial atelier immediately after this financially ruinous event. And the Nizam held a particular allure for servants of the Mughal empire who wanted to maintain their loyalties, culture and way of life. Although Nizam-ul-mulk essentially held power in the Deccan outright from the 1720s, he and his successors continued to consider and even call themselves Mughals well into the nineteenth century; indeed, 'Mughal authority continued to be the source of [the Nizams] symbolic legitimacy' throughout this period.[54] Faruqui notes that Hyderabad was especially attractive to Northern migrants:

> Hyderabad's success in attracting the talented and the adventurous can be seen in the arrival of large numbers of often highly skilled and educated Punjabi Khatris, north Indian Kayasths, Shaikhzadas and Awadhis, and ethnic Iranians and Central Asians. Others who joined this influx included trading, cultivating and warrior groups.[55]

As a result, when Nizam-ul-mulk 'marched back to the Deccan after a two-year stint in Delhi between 1738 and 1740, he returned with thousands of administrators, religious scholars, intellectuals, military men and master craftsmen in tow'.[56]

It is very unlikely that Karim and Anup were among this early group of Mughal migrants, not least because it is improbable that Anup was born as early as 1740.[57] It was only when the second Nizam, Nizam ᶜAli Khan, shifted his capital from Aurangabad to Hyderabad in 1763 that the city was restored to anywhere near the glory it had enjoyed a century previously under the Qutb Shahi rulers of Golconda.[58] More to the point, the latest of Adarang's songs in Anup's *Rāg-Rāginī* were composed for Mughal Emperor ᶜAlamgir II (r.1754–59) and Saᶜdullah Khan Rohilla (d. 1764).[59] These are occasion pieces of limited mobility that would have been transmitted to Karim orally, indicating that he and his family were still resident in the Delhi region c. 1754–64. As Mahlaqa Bai's *ustād*, Anup must have been at least ten to fifteen years older than her; she was born in 1768. I am

[54] Karen B. Leonard, 'The Hyderabad Political System and Its Participants', *Journal of Asian Studies* 30.3 (1971), 569–82, p. 570.
[55] Faruqui, 'At Empire's End', p. 36. [56] ibid.
[57] Given his death date of c. 1836, but also his appearance in the *Rāg Darshan* where he is painted as a mature but not elderly man.
[58] Kugle, *Sun*, p. 137. [59] Anup, *Rāg-Rāginī*, e.g. ff. 44r, 21v; also Miner, pp. 87–8, 205–20.

going to suggest in the absence of firmer evidence that Anup was probably born in the mid-1750s, and that his family left Delhi for the south around 1760 during the time of greatest chaos and threat to life in the Mughal capital.[60]

Anup's 1815 account suggests that Karim Khan and his family, including his brothers and his sons Anup and Raza Khan, left Delhi for the Deccan and eventually found their way to Hyderabad sometime before 1791, the year Karim died. Karim and his family found Hyderabad particularly hospitable and full of appreciative, well-educated and financially generous patrons.[61] The first to take Karim and Anup under his wing seems to have been Rao Ranbha – the man who was also probably Mahlaqa's first patron.[62] Karim and Anup's passport into élite Hyderabadi circles – the authoritative proof that they were who they said they were – was the exclusive musical property they carried with them in their bodies from Delhi: their ability to remember and reproduce multiple *rāgas* and thousands of songs composed by their ancestors at the Mughal court, especially by practitioners of their own Khandari style. Precisely because it was proof of status, family song repertoire was and still is fiercely guarded intellectual property within musical lineages.[63] Anup's enormous song collection thus adds significant empirical weight to his claims that he and his father were indeed members of the prestigious Khandari lineage come down from Mughal Delhi.

In contrast, the details of Mahlaqa Bai's ancestry are somewhat less verifiable, even though she dictated her authorised family history herself to Ghulam Husain Jawhar, whose 1814 history of Hyderabad the *Tarīkh-i Dil-Afroz* is better known by its nickname the *Māh-nāma* or 'Chronicle of the Moon'.[64] Unlike Anup, Mahlaqa was born in Hyderabad in 1768, as Chanda Bibi, to a *sayyida*-turned-courtesan married late in life to a Hyderabadi nobleman. Mahlaqa claimed her maternal grandparents were *sayyids*, direct descendants of the Prophet, and therefore of high social status. According to Ghulam Husain, her grandfather was posted as a Mughal administrator in Ahmedabad in Gujarat during the reign of Muhammad Shah. Having fallen on hard times, he abandoned his family, leaving his wife and three daughters in poverty to fend for themselves.[65]

[60] Schofield, 'Emotions', and Chapter 3.

[61] Anup ed. Shekhar, *Rāg Darshan* (Persian 1815), pp. 11–12.

[62] Anup ed. Shekhar, *Rāg Darshan* (Persian 1808), p. 156; Kugle, *Sun*, p. 177.

[63] Daniel Neuman, *Life*, pp. 48–53, 165–7. [64] Kugle, *Sun*, p. 190. [65] ibid., pp. 204, 191.

Resourcefully, and somewhat unusually, Mahlaqa's chaste grandmother and her daughters joined a troupe of *bhagats*, performing artists who served the minor Rajput court of Deoliya near Ajmer. Kugle argues this was the community of travelling male performers otherwise called *bhāṅḍs* or *naqqāls*, of controversial status at the Mughal court and renowned for mimicry and satire as well as the attractive singing, dancing and seductive wiles of their transfeminine dancing boys, who were often, as courtesans were, taken as lovers by élite men.[66] However, I would argue the description he translates from Ghulam Husain indicates these *bhagats* were, instead, the much higher-status, ritually auspicious *female* courtesans called *bhagtans* I discuss in Chapter 6. Often Muslims, *bhagtans* were employed at Rajput courts to perform for religious and state ceremonies and to train women of the *zanāna* in music and dance; this identification seems considerably more likely.[67]

Either way, this particular troupe undertook to train Mahlaqa's mother, Mida Bai, and aunts in singing and dancing, and took them with them from Rajasthan to the northern Deccan. Eventually at Burhanpur, the three sisters met up with the army of Nizam-ul-mulk and became camp followers in the capacity of entertainers. Mida Bai especially became famous among the Nizam's courtiers for her singing, dancing and beauty, and 'by the time they reached Awrangabad', according to Kugle, 'the whole family of females changed their names, adopting stage names befitting royal courtesans'. Late in life, having had two daughters already and settled in Hyderabad, Mida Bai, now entitled Raj Kanvar Bai, married a nobleman and gave birth to the girl who became Mahlaqa Bai Chanda.[68]

Mahlaqa was raised and trained in the household of her eldest half-sister, Mahtab Kanvar Bai, also a courtesan, who had become the second wife of Nizam ᶜAli Khan's prime minister of the day, Rukn-ud-daula.[69] Although traditionally élite courtesans did not marry – and Mahlaqa did not – being a successful courtesan in Hyderabad clearly was not a barrier to marriage into the nobility, and perhaps even acted as a passport into it. This reinforces previous studies that suggest women played unusually

[66] ibid., p. 153, 191–9; Brown [Schofield], 'If Music Be', pp. 76–83; Christopher Shackle, 'Persian Poetry and Qadiri Sufism in Late Mughal India: Ghanimat Khanjai and his Mathnawi Nayrang-i ᶜIshq', in Leonard Lewisohn, ed., *The Heritage of Sufism: III. Late Classical Persianate Sufism (1501–1750)* (Oxford: Oneworld, 1999), 435–63; Dargah Quli, *Muraqqaᶜ* (1993), p. 97.

[67] Kugle *Sun*, pp. 195–9; Skinner, *Tashrīh al-Aqwām*, ff. 139r–v; Giles Tillotson and Mrinalini Venkateswaran, *Painting and Photography at the Jaipur Court* (New Delhi: Niyogi, 2016), p. 48.

[68] Kugle, *Sun*, pp. 191–3, 204. [69] ibid., pp. 154–6, 203–4.

important and even autonomous political roles in early Nizami Hyderabad.[70] After marriage, Mahlaqa's mother continued close ties of an undisclosed nature with several of Hyderabad's most powerful and notable people. These men – some of whose portraits also appear in Anup's first *Rāg Darshan* – seem to have taken a close interest in Mahlaqa's upbringing: the poet and painter Tajalli ᶜAli Shah (1731–1800); Aristu Jah (d.1804), Hyderabad's most powerful man and the next prime minister; and his protégé and rival Nawab Mir ᶜAlam, the prime minister after that (d.1808).[71] Mir ᶜAlam claimed he first fell in love with Mahlaqa as a young man when he was her Persian teacher; and she learnt Urdu poetry with Tajalli ᶜAli and his senior disciple Muhammad Sher Khan Iman (d. 1806). Given the matrilineal nature of courtesan training, she almost certainly learned to dance from her sister, or possibly her mother, but she also had some training with a *naqqāl* known as Panna.[72]

Crucially for our story, however, it was also in this setting that Mahlaqa first entered into her life-long connection with Anup. He trained her in the Khandari lineage of Mughal court music, including the arts of singing and composing élite song forms in the North Indian *rāgas*. It was from Anup that Mahlaqa learned to set her famous *g͟hazal*s to the most suitable *rāga*s and *tāla*s; how to compose *k͟hayāl*s, *ṭappa*s, *hoṛī*s and occasion pieces (*jashns*) in *dhrupad* form to celebrate various events; and how to sing all of them tastefully and well with her accompanying musicians.[73] I am going to suggest that it was, in fact, with Anup that Mahlaqa enjoyed her most enduring and significant relationship. We can't know its exact nature because we don't have enough information. But right from this early formative moment until her death in 1824/5, Anup and Mahlaqa worked for the same patrons at the same points in time, and lived together in her mansion at Nampally, where he continued to advise her and train her many female protégés.[74] Perhaps, as an *ustād* should be, he was a trusted and beloved father figure to a woman for whom all other men were ultimately only available to be manipulated for wealth and preferment.[75]

[70] Dalrymple, *White Mughals*; Kugle, *Sun*, pp. 17–19, 201–04; Leonard, 'Political Players'.

[71] Kugle, *Sun*, pp. 154, 157–8, 171–3; paintings Anup, *Rāg Darshan* (Brajbhasha, 1800), ff. 2r (Aristu Jah and Nizam Ali Khan), f. 4v (Iman). Raja Rao Ranbha is depicted throughout.

[72] ibid., pp. 171–2, 179; Sachdeva [Jha], 'In Search', p. 136; not to be confused with the early eighteenth-century courtesan Panna Bai.

[73] e.g. Anup, *Rāg-Rāginī*, *munājāt* f. 11r, *dhrupad* f. 28v, *khayāl* and *ṭappa* f. 33v, *hoṛī* f.88r.

[74] Kugle, *Sun*, pp. 157, 189, 226; Sachdeva [Jha], 'In Search', p. 136.

[75] Kugle, *Sun*, pp. 166–9.

Early Patrons: A Mughal Nizam and a Maratha General

Between the 1780s and 1820s, Mahlaqa and Anup worked within the rarified circles of Hyderabad's top nobility for several overlapping patrons – two Sunni Nizams, two Shi^{c}a prime ministers of Iranian extraction, a Maratha Hindu general, and a North Indian Hindu finance minister. Neither musician appears to have been on an exclusive retainer with a single patron at any point. The list of their principal shared patrons indicates the extent to which élite members of the main competing factions in southern India at this time – the Marathas, the Mughal successor states and the British – had come to a level of cultural and political accommodation at the Nizam's court. Present-day identity politics do not map well onto this historical situation. While a Hindu Maratha like Rao Ranbha could serve the Nizam with loyalty and love to the extent of celebrating Muslim festivals with personal fervour, the two patrons who hated each other the most – Aristu Jah and Mir ^{c}Alam – were both aristocratic Iranians by heritage and Shi^{c}a by religion.[76] Nor did friendships or tensions between patrons appear to dictate for whom Mahlaqa and Anup were able to work. This suggests that their esteem as performers and literary figures was so high that patrons were forced to compete for their attentions, not the other way around.

Kugle has suggested that Aristu Jah 'groomed' Mahlaqa from childhood to get her into Nizam ^{c}Ali Khan's permanent household, as part of a 'political strategy . . . to influence [him] through female companions'. We know Aristu Jah deployed related tactics to devastating effect in the tragic saga, narrated by William Dalrymple, of noblewoman Khairunnissa's romantic relationship with the British Resident James Kirkpatrick between 1799 and 1805.[77] Aristu Jah was probably a pivotal patron for Mahlaqa in that, as prime minister from the time she was seven years old, he was a powerful advocate for her at the Nizam's court. Nizam ^{c}Ali Khan did indeed take her up as an intimate companion in the mid-1780s, when she was about fifteen, and she remained a favourite until he died in 1803. Mahlaqa accompanied the Nizam hunting and on military campaigns, and sang and danced as the star performer in his private parties and at public occasions, which were as much political as they were entertainment. After her particularly stunning performance at Nauroz in 1802, aged thirty-four and in her prime, she was given the formal court title Mahlaqa Bai,

[76] ibid., pp. 176–7, 169–71; Dalrymple, *White Mughals*, pp. 134, 196–8, 202–12.

[77] Kugle, *Sun*, p. 157; Dalrymple, *White Mughals*, esp. pp. 184–5, 202–12.

Lady Moon Cheek; the Nizam ennobled her and endowed her with sufficient lands to make her wealthy for life.[78]

But the entire time she was working for Nizam ᶜAli Khan and Aristu Jah, she and her beloved music teacher were also being patronised by the Maratha general Raja Rao Ranbha. Indeed, Mahlaqa's biography and Anup's first two *Rāg Darshan*s indicate that Rao Ranbha was for both of them their first highly-ranked patron.[79]

Rao Ranbha belonged to the Maratha Nimbalkar dynasty, who were relatives of the ruling Bhonsle family in Pune. According to family legend, Rao Ranbha's grandfather had a history of distinguished service to the Mughal empire, and his father had already gone over to Nizam-ul-mulk in Delhi before he left for the Deccan. Rao Ranbha was widely admired, even by the British, for his military skills, astonishing bravery, and loyalty to the Nizam's (and the Company's) interests; and especially for his conspicuous valour fighting with the forces of the Nizam and the British against Tipu Sultan in the 1790s.[80] Rao Ranbha was famously in love with Mahlaqa; and taken as a whole, I would argue Anup's production of his first *Rāg Darshan* is designed to celebrate the union of patron and musician in a very specific historical context, down to the unusual choice to compose it in Brajbhasha verse, the high vernacular of the Mughal court *and* of devotion to the Hindu god Krishna.

Many of the paintings in Anup's *Rāg Darshan* celebrate Mahlaqa's intimacy with Rao Ranbha, her Maratha Hindu patron, but also her prowess in the context of his mastery of the Mughal courtly arts of both pen and sword.[81] In a sequence of paintings, Rao Ranbha studies poetry with Iman, who was also Mahlaqa's teacher, at the same time as his animal keeper feeds his pet tigers; he selects a choice pair of captive birds; he flies pigeons with his bird keeper; he examines a beautiful new stallion; and he goes hawking on horseback (Figure 5.6).[82] This last painting of Rao Ranbha is, I think, particularly important. Firstly, Rao Ranbha was famous for his love of horses, and Mahlaqa is known to have brought horses back from her

[78] Kugle, pp. 157–63, 170–1; see also a painting by Venkatchallam of Mahlaqa hunting with the Nizam, in the Salar Jung Museum https://artsandculture.google.com/asset/nizam-ii-on-a-hunting-expedition/1QFepflHb-vrqQ and detail https://artsandculture.google.com/exhibit/5gKSeXib WxmrJg.

[79] Anup, *Rāg Darshan* (Brajbhasha, 1800); Anup tr. Shekhar, *Rāg Darshan* (Persian, 1808), pp. 106–7; Kugle, *Sun*, p. 177. Raja Rao was one of the ten most powerful men in the Nizam's service; Leonard, 'Hyderabad Political', p. 579 fn. 44, 45.

[80] Kugle, *Sun*, pp. 176–8; IOR/H/563 (1784–98), p. 505.

[81] Kinra, *Writing Self*, pp. 68–9, 111–14; Eaton, *India*.

[82] Anup, *Rāg Darshan* (Brajbhasha 1800), ff. 4v, 5v, 8r, 18v, 19r, 18r.

Figure 5.6 Raja Rao Ranbha hunting, by Haji Mir Ghulam Hasan. Khushhal Khan Anup, *Rāg Darshan*. Hyderabad, text 1800 paintings 1804. Lawrence J Schoenberg Collection, LJS 63, f 18 r **University of Pennsylvania Library CC-BY**.

expeditions with the Nizam as a present especially for Rao Ranbha, including one instance around this very time.[83]

It is also, quite obviously, a homage to the iconic paintings of Mahlaqa Bai Chanda Bibi's illustrious historical namesake Chand Bibi, the famous warrior queen of the sixteenth-century Deccan, hunting with hawks (Figure 5.7).[84] And it incorporates a subtle element taken from Venkatchallam's paintings of Mahlaqa herself going hunting with the Nizam – the bullock cart carrying hunting cheetahs.[85] Through this rich intermediality, the two of them, patron and courtesan, are joined together here in a heavily symbol-laden image.

But all three of them, Anup, Mahlaqa and Rao Ranbha, are also made intimate through the gentler courtly arts as well. In the opening of the *Rāg Darshan* we see Mahlaqa singing to Rao Ranbha, and Anup presenting his

[83] Kugle, *Sun*, p. 177.

[84] Roy S. Fischel, 'Deccan Sultanates'. in John Mackenzie (ed.), *Encyclopedia of Empire* (Oxford: Wiley-Blackwell, 2016). https://search.credoreference.com/content/entry/wileyempire/deccan_sultanates/

[85] See detail (top centre) of Venkatchallam's painting of Mahlaqa hunting in the Salar Jung Museum.

Figure 5.7 Chand Bibi of Ahmadnagar hunting. c.1700. 1999.403. Louis E. and Theresa S. Seeley Purchase Fund for Islamic Art, 1999. **Metropolitan Museum of Art**. Public Domain

book to his patron. The paintings towards the end show Rao Ranbha in a private *majlis* with Anup singing to the *tambūra* accompaniment of his disciple (and son?) Ghazi Khan, playing Holi in a riot of pink and orange colours with Mahlaqa and Anup, and finally, just before the colophon that concludes the book, watching Mahlaqa dance for him by candlelight, the Moon lighting up the starry sky.[86]

Later Patrons: An Iranian Vizier and a Khatri Diwan

Both Mahlaqa and Anup long outlived these early patrons: Nizam ᶜAli Khan died in 1803, Aristu Jah shortly afterwards in 1804, and Rao Ranbha likewise. The deaths of these powerful old men marked the definitive end of an era, and the beginning of a more British-leaning dispensation in Hyderabad. The Nizam had already signed a permanent treaty of alliance with the East India Company in 1798 that placed Hyderabad under British

[86] Anup, *Rāg Darshan* (Brajbhasha 1800), ff. 20r, 23v, 24r.

protection. And the new prime minister in 1804, Aristu Jah's old enemy Nawab Mir ᶜAlam, was an Anglophile who had risen to power in Hyderabad as an agent of the Company.[87] Nonetheless, Mahlaqa and Anup segued seamlessly over to the patronage of the new Nizam, Sikandar Jah, and especially to Mir ᶜAlam, with whom Mahlaqa almost certainly had a sexual relationship (though the Persian sources are characteristically coy).[88] In fact, we know Mir ᶜAlam was already commissioning her to perform several years before Aristu Jah died, because it was at Mir ᶜAlam's *majlis* in 1799 that she danced for John Malcolm.

In 1808, at the request of Mir ᶜAlam acting on a suggestion by Mahlaqa, Anup retranslated the Brajbhasha verse *Rāg Darshan* he had made for Rao Ranbha back into Persian prose for Nizam Sikandar Jah. As he wrote, 'I put it back into Persian again, dressing the newly wedded bride of the Hindi language in Persian clothing.' Anup neatly rounded off this statement with a Persian couplet whose end rhyme, *tuhfat*, paid subtle homage to the original Mughal prose masterpiece that inspired this whole chain of clever translations.[89] The Persian of the 1808 translation backs up Anup's narrative of this process. Apart from the introduction, which is written in the highly rhetorical style of literary Persian suitable for these most courtly of readers,[90] like Anup's compact Brajbhasha verses the remainder of this rendering is quite simple and curtailed in comparison with Mirza Khan's – it really does seem like a retranslation directly from Anup's Brajbhasha version.

That same year, though, Mir ᶜAlam died suddenly, and power in Hyderabad – and our two protagonists with it – shifted decisively to Sikandar Jah's brilliant *dīwān* or finance minister Maharaja Chandu Lal: the high-placed and even more pro-British North Indian *khatrī* who was the most powerful nobleman in Hyderabad from this time until his death in 1845. Chandu Lal, who became prime minister *de jure* in 1833, was well known for his cultural pursuits. As a talented Persian and Urdu poet himself under the *takhallus* 'Shaida', Chandu Lal would have found Mahlaqa particularly compelling, because above even her singing and dancing, she was renowned across the land as India's best female poet. But from a more political point of view, in this new era she was also a prize asset, because she had a history of sharing her manifest talents, and those of the girls she was now training, with British lovers of courtesans. Chandu

[87] Dalrymple, *White Mughals*, pp. 145, 355–62; Kugle, *Sun*, pp. 171, 175; M K Chancey, 'The Making of the Anglo-Hyderabad Alliance, 1788–1823', *South Asia: Journal of South Asian Studies* 29.2 (2006), 181–214, pp. 207–10.

[88] Kugle, *Sun*, pp. 172–5. [89] Anup ed. Shekhar, *Rāg Darshan* (Persian 1808), pp. 156–7.

[90] On *inshā'*, or exemplary stylized prose, see Kinra, *Writing Self*.

Lal thus became famed for putting on lavish assemblies featuring Mahlaqa as star performer in a special pavilion he had built specifically to impress political, and especially British, guests.[91]

The final copy of the *Rāg Darshan* Anup wrote for Mahlaqa in 1815 was written in Chandu Lal's orbit; and it was bilingual. Anup quoted his original Brajbhasha verses line by line against a new and improved version of his Persian translation, as if he were creating a study manual for Mahlaqa in her journey towards mastery of both Brajbhasha lyrics and Mughal music theory. And in this version, out of subservience to Chandu Lal 'Maharaja Ocean of Gifts' and 'Maharaja Pearl of Good Manners', Anup erased the memory of all of his and Mahlaqa's previous patrons, including the late Mir ᶜAlam and Rao Ranbha, replacing references to them with encomiums to Chandu Lal.[92]

Reading Hyderabad's History through Their Songs

The *Rāg-Rāginī* was completed during the period of Maharaja Chandu Lal's political supremacy, and reveals him to have been Anup's and Mahlaqa's principal nineteenth-century patron (a bias that is perhaps an artefact of the fact that he outlived them both). Anup's song collection, in turn, also helps us identify key moments in the ritual year of Hyderabad for members of all communities. In particular, it reveals that spring festivals in the Persian and Indian solar calendars – Basant, Holi and Nauroz – were key ecumenical occasions for the Nizami court in this period. Interestingly, a large proportion of the songs written specifically for Chandu Lal were set in spring *rāgas* and *rāginīs* – *dhrupads* in Hindol and *k͟hayāls* and *ṭappas* in Bahar, with lyrics celebrating the spring festival Basant, clearly an important festival for Hindus in Hyderabad.[93] One of the last songs composed by Anup was a *kabit* for the spring wedding in 1834 of Chandu Lal's grandson, the son of Raja Bala Pershad.[94] There are also, of course, a large number of *hoṛīs* in numerous *rāgas* scattered throughout the collection, to be sung during the Holi spring festival to celebrate the love play of the god Krishna.

Anup's and Mahlaqa's songs show us a yearly cycle punctuated by ritual events and public affairs like weddings, all celebrated with music and dance.

[91] Kugle, *Sun*, pp. 178–84; Dalrymple, *White Mughals*, p. 483; Karen Leonard, 'Palmer and Company: An Indian Banking Firm in Hyderabad State', *Modern Asian Studies* 47.4 (2013), 1157–84, pp. 1160, 1174; Leonard, 'Hyderabad Political', p. 579 fn. 44, 45.

[92] Anup ed. Shekhar, *Rāg Darshan* (Persian 1815), pp. 9–12.

[93] Anup, *Rāg-Rāginī*, ff. 28v-34v. [94] ibid., f. 28v.

The main insight their lyrics give us into the annual life of Hyderabad, however, concerns the Shi^{c}a ritual year. For those interested in Mahlaqa as a poet, her *dīwān* has recently been the subject of Scott Kugle's definitive biography, and will not be discussed here. But apart from the usual concerns of the Urdu *ghazal* (see Chapter 4), one feature of her *dīwān* is especially noteworthy: her *ghazals* show her to have been a committed Shi^{c}a, devoted to the family of Hazrat ^{c}Ali, the cousin and son-in-law of the Prophet, and his son Husain, who was martyred at the battle of Karbala in 680 CE. Although the Nizams themselves were Sunni Muslims, since the time of the Qutb Shahi rulers of Golconda, Hyderabad had been an important Shi^{c}a centre. Hazrat ^{c}Ali is also venerated in Sufi traditions; ^{c}Alid devotion substantially crosses sectarian lines in South Asia.[95] Nizam ^{c}Ali Khan revived state patronage of Hyderabad's important Shi^{c}a shrine (*dargāh*) enclosing the relic of Hazrat ^{c}Ali's handprint, located on top of the holy mountain of Maula ^{c}Ali, an important site of Shi^{c}a but also Sufi and Hindu pilgrimage.[96] And Mahlaqa and Anup were both major donors to Maula ^{c}Ali *dargāh*, patronising and performing at the many annual Shi^{c}a and shrine-specific festivals there.

A few of the songs Mahlaqa composed for these occasions are preserved in Anup's *Rāg-Rāginī*,[97] as well as many more composed by him that she would very likely have performed. The mostly Shi^{c}a songs in the margins (many of them dated) and also in the 'occasion piece' sections of Anup's song collection help us to reconstruct the rhythms of the Islamic ritual year at Maula ^{c}Ali, for which musicians like Anup and Mahlaqa wrote and performed new songs annually. Except for the all-important ten days of Muharram for which no songs were composed,[98] these were, in chronological order: the birth of the Prophet of Islam (17th Rabi ul-Awwal),[99] the *^{c}urs* or death anniversary of the Sufi master ^{c}Abdul Qadir Jilani (11th Rabi us-Sani), the birth of Hazrat ^{c}Ali (13th Rajab),[100] the *^{c}urs* of the Maula ^{c}Ali *dargāh* (17th Rajab),[101] and *^{c}īd-i ghadīr*,[102] the day when the Prophet declared that 'whoever calls me master, ^{c}Ali is also their master [Maula

[95] Syed Akbar Hyder, *Reliving Karbala: Martyrdom in South Asian Memory* (New York: Oxford University Press, 2006); Richard Wolf, 'Embodiment and Ambivalence: Emotion in South Asian Muharram Drumming', *Yearbook for Traditional Music* 32 (2000), 81–116.

[96] Kugle, *Sun*, pp. 133–45.

[97] Those with her *chhāp* Chanda include e.g. a *jashn-i ^{c}īd-i ghadīr* in Asavari, and another in Kedara written in 1817; Anup, *Rāg-Rāginī*, ff. 49r, 86v.

[98] Other than *marsiyas*, of which there are no examples in the *Rāg-Rāginī*.

[99] Here *jashn-i nabī*. I am grateful to the current Maulana of Moula-Ali *dargāh* via Rana Safvi for confirming the correct date.

[100] Here *jashn-i haidarī*.

[101] The date of 17th Rajab for the *^{c}urs* is given in Asafjahi, *Landmarks*, p. 15; Kugle *Sun*, pp. 133–5.

[102] Also *^{c}īd al-ghadīr*.

ᶜAli]' (18th Zu'l Hijja). For example, Mahlaqa and/or Anup wrote this *munājāt* in *dhrupad* style[103] and set it in the versatile *rāga* Bhairavi:

Thus give me aid from the unseen, for I am weak and in need of your generosity, O king of men ᶜAli, the ruler of all land and sea! I may be just a dancing girl [*shād-khwār*] but let me remain joyful (*khushhāl*) in this, Anup's garden – this much please give me for the sake of Hasan and Hussain![104]

It is not clear whether or not Anup also became a Shiᶜa; other contemporary members of his lineage remained Sufis devoted to the Tariqa-i Muhammadiyya (Chapter 7). Anup did compose a number of songs on Shiᶜa themes, mostly for particular festivals but also in generic courtly styles.[105] But it is worth remembering that composing pieces for special occasions *was his job*. In this period in India, the personal beliefs of the composer or performer of songs were irrelevant; professional musicians like Anup were commissioned to compose and sing songs to their patrons and their patrons' deities and saints as a matter of course, regardless of whether or not they shared their beliefs. Even if some of Anup's Shiᶜa-themed songs in *Rāg-Rāginī* do appear to reflect his personal inclinations, devotion to Hazrat ᶜAli was embraced by Sufis as well. This courtly *khayāl* song, for instance, was composed by the head of Anup's lineage, Sadarang (Chapters 3 and 7), and venerates both Hazrat ᶜAli and the Sunni founder of the Chishti Sufi order in India, Khwaja Moin-ud-din:

Preserve the life, honorable Mawla ᶜAli, of those who call out for safety and security – make all their troubles easy. I find that, by your grace, Hasan and Husain rule over more than both worlds. Let me be sacrifice sacrifice sacrifice sacrifice for the sake of Mawla ᶜAli Mawla ᶜAli! [*Vār vār vār vār jaun Maula ᶜAli kī Maula ᶜAli kī!*] Give me faith and righteousness, let me achieve this goal. Look upon me with kindness, Khwaja Muin, and aid this humblest follower of faith. Please accept this small request of Sada-rang and protect us poor beggars.[106]

It would not have been necessary for Anup to convert in order to express his devotion to Hazrat ᶜAli to the extent that he did.

Without Mahlaqa's and Anup's personal patronage – and that of several of their patrons – the hill of Maula ᶜAli would look very different today. The *dargāh* itself was much older; but according to epigraphs on other monuments

103 It is set in the *dhrupad tāla chautāl*.

104 Anup, *Rāg-Rāginī*, ff. 11r–v, second half only; tr. Scott Kugle, *Sun*, pp. 287–8 fn. 49. In this example, although 'dancing girl' is in first person, the *chhāp* is Anup/Khushhal.

105 Anup, *Rāg–Rāginī*, e.g. ff. 8r, 25r (*jashn-i haidarī*, 1819, 1836), 8v (*astut* for the 12 Imams), 23r (*dhrupad astut* for Hazrat ᶜAli's footprint), 10r (*khayāl* in praise of Hazrat ᶜAli), etc.

106 Anup, *Rāg-Rāginī*, ff. 11r–v, tr. Scott Kugle, *Sun*, p. 288 fn. 49.

on the hill, most of the important buildings were endowed by members of Mahlaqa and Anup's circle. Raja Rao Ranbha built a summer pavilion (*bārahdārī*) there, and Maharaja Chandu Lal the great entrance gate housing the drum house (*naqqāra-k̲h̲āna*). On her mother's death in 1792, Mahlaqa built a magnificent tomb complex at the base of Maula ᶜAli hill, complete with a Muharram assembly hall (*ᶜashūr-k̲h̲āna*), set in a beautiful formal garden. Mahlaqa was herself laid to rest there in 1824/5. But it was Anup who expended his considerable wealth to build many of the principal buildings on the hill itself. The inscription on the great *ᶜashūr-k̲h̲āna* he erected reads:

> By good fortune Khushhal Khan with true and sincere intention, to seek the pleasure of God, erected the Arch (*kamān*), the Mosque (*masjid*) and the grand *ᶜashūr-k̲h̲āna*, the inn (*sarāy*) and the fakir's stand (*takya*) on the venerable hill (*koh-i sharīf*).[107]

Inscriptions elsewhere tell us that he also built a drinking-water basin 'on the route via which the sandal is carried', as well as a small garden just beneath the skirts of the hill.[108]

An ambiguous note on the flyleaf of his *Rāg-Rāginī* suggests the possibility that Anup may himself have been the one who built Mahlaqa's grave within her mother's tomb complex; a most appropriate duty for an adoptive father. Like his illustrious disciple, he too is buried in the garden that he planted at Maula ᶜAli.[109]

The Boundless Ocean of Musical Knowledge

A remarkable thing about the Brajbhasha lyrics Anup included in his song collection is that there is no literal overlap that I have yet been able to find with the Brajbhasha verses that constitute his first *Rāg Darshan*. Instead his two major works – his song collection and his music treatise in its various versions – complement, amplify and enrich each other, just as Mahlaqa Bai Chanda and Khushhal Khan Anup complemented and completed each other in their life's work together. Anup's two written works clearly embody different facets of the complex and comprehensive vision of a single master musician–scholar that saw no conflict, but a seamless continuity, between theoretical and practical, written and oral knowledge.[110] In one crucial

107 Asafjahi, *Landmarks*, pp. 12–16; quotation p. 12; Kugle, *Sun*, pp. 151–6. The inscription on Anup's arch, quoted at the head of this chapter, is different from the inscription on the *ᶜashūr-khāna*.

108 ibid., p. 16 and fn. 1; Anup, *Rāg-Rāginī*, flyleaf.

109 ibid.

110 Orsini and Schofield, 'Introduction', pp. 1–30.

self-referential image in his Brajbhasha *Rāg Darshan*, Anup sits opposite his patron, Rao Ranbha, and presents his written music treatise to him. Here, Anup is not merely a master of the practical arts of music making, but of its literature and theory as well, making him fit to sit face-to-face with the Nizami nobility. Anup's choice to write songs and a treatise in Brajbhasha verse, and to write in both rhetorical and practical registers of Persian prose, show off his mastery – despite his location in far-off Hyderabad – of the Mughal official language, and of the classical register of Hindavi local to the Delhi-Agra region used in its heyday at the Mughal court to write élite poetry, song lyrics and music treatises.

Anup's 1800 *Rāg Darshan* turns out to be many things. It is a celebration of the rich and fluid court culture of Hyderabad, as easily embraced by a Maratha Hindu warrior as a Shi^ca courtesan, during the time of Nizam ^cAli Khan, who was responsible for truly consolidating Hyderabad state as an independent entity. It is also a monument to the ultimately transient but consuming love between Rao Ranbha and Mahlaqa, as well as memorialising forever the Raja's patronage of the arts and gentlemanly pursuits, and Mahlaqa's public power, beauty and artistic mastery. But Anup's treatise also shows the enduring power of the Mughals, and the court culture and knowledge they developed, as a continuing source of symbolic authority throughout India, even as its power bled away in its northern heartlands. For those wanting to become the new Mughals in states like Hyderabad, Lucknow or Jaipur – where we are heading next – what could give a nobleman greater cultural legitimacy than patronising the music of the Mughal court, authenticated in the physical presence of a musician of the greatest imperial lineage, but made local in the extraordinary brilliance of that musician's Hyderabad-born protégé Mahlaqa Bai Chanda?

Finally, it is crucial testimony to the sheer intellectual virtuosity of this particular representative of the lineages of hereditary *ustād*s that had made their way all over India from the faltering Mughal court in Delhi. Ultimately, Anup wrote to prove his credentials as an authority, to preserve his heritage from the losses of the scattering, and to praise his new patrons and the joys he found in his new home. Fluent in the highest forms of Brajbhasha verse and able to deploy with great subtlety several registers of the Persian language – and a master performer and beloved teacher into the bargain – Khushhal Khan Anup was the very opposite of the stereotype of the 'illiterate *ustād*' bequeathed to us by posterity.

6 | Faithful to the Salt: Mayalee Dancing Girl versus the East India Company in Rajasthan

Official Records of the East India Company

Meyalee dancing girl . . . 25 [maunds of salt] . . . The Jodhpoor Govt having all saved a payment of Salt to this Pensioner, an equal portion has been granted in lieu of Cash by Jyepoor.[1]

Sambhar salt lake accounts, 1 July–31 December 1842.[2]

A Dancing Girl in the Salt Revenue Accounts

I was sitting in the reading room of the National Archives of India, methodically going through the Index of the East India Company's Foreign Department Proceedings, volume 1840–49 K–Z, when I first came across her: 'Pension to Meyalee, dancing-girl, from Jeypore share of Sambhur lake funds'. It was my first foray into the official records of British colonial rule in India to see if I could find any traces of Indian performers like Khanum Jan and Mahlaqa Bai that we know filled the long nights, dreams and often beds of many a Company officer in the early decades of the nineteenth century. And there she was: Mayalee dancing girl. But she wasn't alone. There was a whole set of entries for individual musicians, dancers and other performers named as so-called 'pensioners' of the revenues of Sambhar salt lake in Rajasthan between the years 1835 and 1842.

Out of the archives came detailed half-yearly financial accounts for the brief period when the East India Company sequestered the revenue and salt works of Sambhar Lake that belonged to the independent Rajput states of Jaipur and Jodhpur.[3] In 1818, faced with the Company's overwhelming military might, the Rajput states signed a treaty in which the British offered them political and military 'protection' in exchange for heavy cash tribute. By the 1830s, Jaipur and Jodhpur were swimming in debt and refusing to cooperate with the British. So, in 1835, the Company seized Sambhar Lake,

[1] Her name is spelled different ways in these accounts. [2] NAI FDC 25/11/1843, no. 59ii.

[3] NAI FDC 28/09/1835, no. 35; FDC 14/09/1840, no. 19; FDC 13/09/1841, no. 22, FDC 14/03/1842, no. 40, FDC 21/09/1842, no. 6, FDC 25/11/1843, no. 59ii. IOR F/4/1898/80683, 07/06/1840, no. 43.

Figure 6.1 Measuring salt piles on the new British leases at Sambhar Lake, Jaipur state, 1870s. Photo 355/1(59). **The British Library**. Public Domain

which remains one of India's largest sources of that most essential of commodities: salt. The British only returned the lake to Jaipur and Jodhpur in 1842 when, having been brought to the brink of ruin by the Company, their arrears were written off by the government in Calcutta.[4]

The 1835–42 Sambhar Lake accounts in the National Archives, some of which are replicated in full in the India Office collections, included long lists of local institutions and individuals who had historical rights in the salt revenues of Sambhar, and meticulous details of how much they were paid, when and for what reason, in what kind, and from which fund. At least some of the English accounts were translations of vernacular financial records, some of which still survive.[5] And among the individual recipients, whom the Company translators called 'pensioners', were several named performing artists who appeared grouped together, including six named 'dancing girls': courtesans. Four of these always performed together at all the religious festivals, accompanied by two female instrumentalists[6] and

[4] Vijay Kumar Vashishtha, *Rajputana Agency, 1832–1858* (Jaipur: Aalekh, 1978), see index, 'Sambhar', p. 315; Robert W. Stern, *The Cat and the Lion: Jaipur State in the British Raj* (Leiden: Brill, 1988), pp. 77–84; Anju Suri, 'British Relations with Jaipur State under the Company and the Crown: A Critical Appraisal', Professor G. N. Sharma Memorial Lecture, *Proceedings of the Rajasthan History Congress* 30 (2014–15), 35–48, pp. 40–1; and Jadunath Sarkar, *A History of Jaipur, c.1503–1938*, rev. ed. Raghubir Sinh (Hyderabad: Orient Longman, 1984), pp. 344–8.

[5] e.g. NAI FDC 14/09/1840 no. 19.

[6] Wafati *daf-wālī* (Wufatee Dufwalee) and Mamola *dāi'ra-wālī* (Mumolah Daer Walee), female players of the *daf* and *dā'ira* frame drums.

possibly two male musicians.[7] Two women were clearly more important, senior, and/or talented than all the others, going on their stipends: Oomda, a Muslim name or stage title; and Mayalee, a Hindu name.[8]

What particularly drew my eye to Mayalee was a set of exculpatory notes beside her name in the margins of the half-yearly accounts for 1842, the last Company accounts for Sambhar before the Company returned the lake to its rightful owners. These suggest that Mayalee put up a successful fight against the third and last British superintendent of Sambhar Lake, Lieutenant Robert Morrieson, for her historical right to receive payment in salt, rather than cash, from the lake. The 1835 'Statement of endowments of Temples, stipends and daily rations together with grants of Salt as sanctioned by Jeypoor' describes the status quo of Jaipur's charitable disbursements from Sambhar salt revenues at the point at which the British took over.[9] It shows that Jaipur paid Mayalee in several ways. She, along with her fellow courtesans Oomda, Kesur and Gangalee, were each paid 2 rupees and 6 annas[10] in cash from salt revenues every six months specifically for performing at festivals of the ritual calendar. But Oomda and Mayalee were also entitled to annual salt stipends, with Mayalee allocated 25 maunds of salt every year.[11]

How much was a salt maund? In cash terms, at Sambhar in 1835 Mayalee's salt was worth, wholesale, 6 rupees and 4 annas, at 4 annas per maund – a significant but not enormous part of her annual income.[12] What about in quantity? It's very difficult to work out how much a Sambhar salt maund weighed.[13] The maund differed greatly across South Asia; but if the Sambhar salt maund corresponded with the Company maund used in neighbouring Ajmer, the headquarters of the Company's Agency to Rajputana, one maund would have weighed about 40 British pounds – approximately the annual salt requirement of a small family.[14] In

[7] Munshiram Mishra (Munsaram Mifra), a common caste name for Hindu *sārangī* and *tabla* accompanists and *kathak* dancers; and Jivan Ram (Jeewan Ram).

[8] NAI FDC 28/09/1835 no. 35.

[9] NAI FDC 28/09/1835 no. 35. Jodhpur expenditures were accounted separately.

[10] 16 annas to the rupee.

[11] NAI FDC 28/09/1835 no. 35; IOR F/4/1898/80683, 07/06/1840, no. 43, Section 9.

[12] NAI FDC 28/09/1835 no. 35, p. 6.

[13] cf. Monika Horstmann, *In Favour of Govinddevjī: Historical Documents Relating to a Deity of Vrindaban and Eastern Rajasthan*, (New Delhi: Indira Gandhi National Centre for the Arts and Manohar, 1999), p. 294.

[14] The Ajmer maund weighed about half that of the Bengal Presidency, 82 lbs or 37.3 kg; James Prinsep, *Useful Tables, Forming an Appendix to the Journal of the Asiatic Society: Part 1, Coins, Weights, and Measures of British India* (Calcutta: Bishop's College Press, 1840), pp. 76, 81. Roy Moxham estimates the annual salt requirements of a small Indian family was 41 pounds

quantity, then, Mayalee's annual salt stipend of 25 maunds exceeded her personal requirements dozens of times over.

But throughout 1842, Morrieson tried to force Mayalee and all other recipients of salt grants to take payment instead in cash, at a much-reduced rate of exchange. In September 1841, Morrieson received a letter[15] from the secretary to the governor-general in Calcutta sanctioning 'a computation of four Rs per . . . 25 maunds . . . in lieu of the salt hitherto bestowed upon the petitioners in [Section 3]'. That was more than a third lower than the Sambhar wholesale price in 1835. Some pensioners, including some performers, did accept cash in lieu of salt; but Mayalee refused. Morrieson noted blandly in the margins of the 1842 half-yearly accounts to June that Mayalee was 'paid for [the] 1897 Samvat [year][16] in salt previous to the receipt of the Govt orders sanctioning a compensation in money'. But he wrote that a year after receiving the governor-general's letter, and it seems to have been a post hoc excuse for his failure to make her accept cash payment, because six months later she was again paid in salt: 'The Jodhpoor Govt having all saved a payment of Salt to this Pensioner, an equal portion [of salt] has been granted in lieu of cash by Jyepoor.'[17]

That is all we currently know for sure about Mayalee herself as a historical figure. But there is a great deal more behind her story. Why was Mayalee's salt stipend so important to her? Was her intransigence simply mercenary, a refusal to accept the reduced cash rates she was being offered, or to let go of a profitable sideline selling salt? But then, why was paying Mayalee in salt so important to Jodhpur and Jaipur that they went out of their way to fulfil her demand, in defiance of Lieutenant Morrieson? Was her resistance, and theirs, based on long-standing Mughal and Rajput notions of *namak-halālī* or 'faithfulness to the salt (*namak*)' and therefore in some way political? Or was there some larger ritual or cultural significance to the salt of Sambhar Lake that we need to consider? For Mayalee herself was ritually auspicious, a powerful hereditary courtesan dedicated to the service of Hindu and state ceremonies. Come to that, why did Lieutenant Morrieson draw up such minutely detailed accounts? Why do we have a record of Mayalee's existence at all?

(aka 1 Ajmer maund); *The Great Hedge of India: The Search for the Living Barrier that Divided a People* (London: HarperCollins, 2001), p. 46.

15 6th September; NAI FDC 14/03/1842 no. 40, p. 5.

16 1897 probably refers to the Kachchwaha revenue year 1840–1, which ended in August 1841; Horstmann, *In Favour*, 69–70.

17 NAI FDC 21/09/1842 no. 6; FDC 25/11/1843 no. 59ii.

In this chapter, I examine the writing of performers into the official records of the East India Company, and consider what their occasional appearance tells us about interactions between the British colonial state and the Indian peoples whose lives and cultures they were increasingly encroaching upon during the 1830s and 40s. My sources for this chapter are largely taken from the India Office Collections and the National Archives of India, but also from the Persian daily newsletters, or *akhbārāt*, of the British Resident in Delhi for 1810–30.[18]

These types of writing are unlike any of the others I draw upon in this book, and the resulting chapter reflects this change in tone. But official Company records are critically important to my overall story because, when read against and alongside paracolonial writings in Indian languages, they give a completely different perspective on the history of the transitions of Indian music and dance to British rule.

Situating Performers in the East India Company Records

Every archive has a distinctive texture that reveals the concerns of its makers.[19] It turns out that Indian performers appear in official colonial records only infrequently, and what they tell us tends not to be about music *per se*. Instead, their appearances in the British official records open up unusual windows onto wider ethnographic, economic and political terrain. CA Bayly wrote that, by the mid nineteenth century:

> The British were able ... to penetrate and control the upper level of networks of runners and newsletter writers with relative ease ... yet they excluded themselves from affective and patrimonial knowledges: the deep knowledge acquired by magnates with roots in the villages and the political sympathy which comes from ties of belief, of marriage and from a sense of inhabiting the same moral realm ... Loving sympathy which had ideally animated even the worst Indian ruler was largely alien to them ... British understanding, revealingly, was weakest in regard to music and dance, the popular poetry of sacred erotics, dress and food, though such concerns are near the heart of any civilization.[20]

[18] British Library Add. 24038, Add. 23149 and Add. 22624, translated by Margrit Pernau and Yunus Jaffery as *Information and the Public Sphere: Persian Newsletters from Mughal Delhi* (New Delhi and Oxford: Oxford University Press, 2009).

[19] Ann Laura Stoler, 'Colonial Archives and the Arts of Governance', *Archival Science* 2 (2002), 87–109, pp. 99–101.

[20] Bayly, *Empire*, p. 55.

Bayly's statement was not necessarily true of *individuals* in the colonial apparatus; in their private capacity, some remained sympathetic to Indian music, poetry and even religion right through the era of colonial rule.[21] But a lack of interest in 'affective knowledges' does seem to have been true of the *colonial state* when we read performing artists' appearances along the grain of its official records.[22]

In the 1830s and 40s, the cultural heartlands of North India's élite musical traditions remained the Mughal court in Delhi and the autonomous princely states – though there was thriving demand for these arts in the bustling colonial cities of Calcutta and Bombay too.[23] A survey of the c. 1830–58 Indexes to the NAI Foreign Department records of the Company's dealings with the autonomous states is telling. It indicates that in the last three decades of Company rule, the colonial state was interested in performing artists only when they were: perpetrators or victims of crime or disorder, or otherwise involved in court cases; scandalously mixed up in state politics; included as a budget or expenditure line in the household accounts of deposed rulers who were now Company pensioners; or beneficiaries of wills, pensions, land grants or other forms of disbursements, such as salt in the case of Sambhar.

Criminal and civil cases in which performers faced Company judicial proceedings seem largely to have concerned courtesans.[24] This suggests just how wealthy and important courtesans like Mayalee were in the early nineteenth century, but also highlights their vulnerability, as well as the distrust with which they were viewed for their apparently mercenary motives. The British Library's incomplete set of Delhi Persian akhbārāt c.1810–30 tell us for example that, on 11 May 1830, the Resident of Delhi Francis Hawkins:

> Went to [the Mughal Emperor's palace] and held the session of the appeal court. He heard the case of the Raja of Kishangarh[25] and Rasiya the *tawai'f.* [The Raja

[21] e.g. Nalini Ghuman, *Resonances of the Raj: India in the English Musical Imagination, 1897–1947* (New York: Oxford University Press, 2014); and Radha Kapuria, 'Music in Colonial Punjab: A Social History', Unpublished PhD Dissertation, King's College London (2018).

[22] Stoler, 'Colonial'.

[23] For Calcutta see e.g. Williams, *Scattered Court*; and Sumanta Banerjee, *Dangerous Outcast: The Prostitute in Nineteenth Century Bengal* (Kolkata: Seagull Books, 1998); for Bombay, see Aneesh Pradhan, *Hindustani music in Colonial Bombay* (New Delhi: Three Essays, 2014), pp. 16–26; and in general Walker, *India's Kathak Dance*, pp. 52–73.

[24] Sachdeva [Jha], 'In Search', pp. 147–52; and William R. Pinch, 'Prostituting the Mutiny: Sex-Slavery and Crime in the Making of 1857', in Crispin Bates (ed.), *Mutiny at the Margins: New Perspectives on the Indian Uprising of* 1857, vol. i (New Delhi: Sage, 2013), 61–79.

[25] The Rajas of Kishangarh had substantial interests in Sambhar Lake; Heidi Rika Maria Pauwels, *Mobilizing Krishna's World: The Writings of Prince Sāvant Singh of Kishangarh* (Seattle: University of Washington Press, 2017), pp. 79–82, 219 fn. 29.

claimed Rs 18,000 from the *tawa'if* and she refused to pay] [The Raja] said that he had given her Rs 1,000 and a shawl in advance and that she had no claim to further payment.[26]

These were huge sums of money for the time. Multiple reports of highway robbery, kidnap and murder indicate how defenceless *tawā'ifs* were on the bandit-infested roads of Upper India. As itinerant professionals carrying plentiful jewels and cash, they were clearly at risk of attack even when they travelled together in large troupes.[27]

Certain communities as well as individual musicians also became targets of Company suppression for supposedly malignant interference in the political affairs of autonomous states. The Company's most famous intervention began in Lucknow in 1848, when the Resident, Colonel Richmond, forced the last Nawab of Awadh, Wajid ᶜAli Shah (r. 1847–56), to stop appointing 'Singers and other improper persons' to government positions (Chapter 8).[28] But of particular relevance to Jodhpur and Jaipur in the 1830s–40s was the Company's attempt to destroy the power of the Rajputs' customary bards, the *bhāṭṭs* and *chārans*.[29] These were discrete communities, but both performed critical ritual roles in the legitimisation of Rajput rule.

According to Skinner writing in Persian in 1825, *bhāṭṭs* were scholars of the *vedas*, *shāstras* and *purāṇas*, and maintained in their impressive memories the elaborate genealogies of their patrons, all of which they recited at court on ceremonial occasions. *Chārans* were instead employed to sing the praise genres of *chhand* and *kabit* 'in the *rājās*' courts, on battlefields and at the weddings of *rājās*'.[30] Skinner also connected the *chārans* with the *banjārā* merchant community: indeed, the two worked together as traders and transporters in the salt trade at Sambhar.[31]

[26] Pernau and Jaffery, *Information*, pp. 69, 165, 231, quotation 253–4.

[27] ibid., pp. 69, 165, 172, 202, 215, 237; Pinch, 'Prostituting', pp. 67–70.

[28] NAI Foreign Political 08/07/1848, 'Agreement of the King for Preventing Eunuchs Holding Office'.

[29] Also Bhopal and Agra, NAI Foreign Political 13/08/1832 no. s 44–5, p. 37; for Rajputana generally e.g. NAI India Political Despatch from Court of Directors no. 9, 1848.

[30] Skinner, *Tashrīh*: *bhāṭṭs* ff. 131r–34v; *chārans* ff. 141r–v; Daniel M Neuman, Shubha Chaudhuri and Komal Kothari, *Bards, Ballads and Boundaries: An Ethnographic Atlas of Music Traditions in West Rajasthan* (Calcutta: Seagull, 2006), p. 225. On Tod's 'bards', a category he does not usually disaggregate, see Lieutenant-Colonel James Tod, *Annals and Antiquities of Rajast'han*, 2 vols (London: Smith, Elder and Co, 1829), vol. i, pp. xi–xiii.

[31] *Chārans* both acted as guides for *banjārā* caravans and traded salt, grain, sugar and cattle on their own account; Skinner, *Tashrīh*, f. 142v; Tanuja Kothiyal, *Nomadic Narratives: A History of Mobility and Identity in the Great Indian Desert* (Cambridge: Cambridge University Press,

The British, however, saw *bhāṭṭs* and *chārans* as rapacious extortionists who had too much sway over Rajput politics – worse, the British held them responsible for female infanticide.[32] Both groups were ritually indispensable to Rajput families on ceremonial occasions, and they charged eye-wateringly high prices for the weddings of daughters, such that poorer families would kill their girl babies rather than face ruin. In 1839, Captain John Ludlow, whom we shall meet again, was made agent of Jodhpur.[33] He was morally affronted by Rajput acceptance of female infanticide, and to end it persuaded Jodhpur to fix meagre 'maximum payments by Rajpoots to Bhats and Charans on nuptial occasions'.[34] It is impossible to regret any reduction in infanticide that may have eventuated. But it is also unquestionable that Ludlow's interference threatened the livelihoods and status of *bhāṭṭ* and *chāran* communities across the Rajput territories.[35]

What happened to the Nawab Nazim of Murshidabad's Department of Entertainment in 1773 is equally salutary. Music departments existed as bureaucratic units of most princely states long before the British, e.g. the *gunijān-k͟hāna*, 'Department of Virtuosos', in Jaipur, the *taᶜlīm-k͟hāna* in Jodhpur and the *arbāb-i nishāt*, 'Department of Entertainment', in Delhi, Murshidabad and Hyderabad.[36] In 1772 the British decided to cut the expenditure of the Nazim of Murshidabad, whom they had recently deposed. In January 1773, the young British official placed in charge reduced all department budgets slightly – except

2016), pp. 160–216, esp. pp. 178, 196, 205–9; also Aditya Behl, 'Poet of the Bazaars: Naẓīr Akbarābādī, 1735–1830', in Kathryn Hansen and David Lelyveld (eds.), *A Wilderness of Possibilities: Urdu Studies in Transnational Perspective* (New Delhi: Oxford University Press, 2005), 192–222, pp. 217–22.

32 NAI FP 30/11/1844, quoted in Kothiyal, *Nomadic Narratives*, pp. 211–4; Tod, *Annals*, vol. 1, pp. 637–8.

33 Vashishtha, *Rajputana Agency*, pp. 124–32; IOR F/4/1957/85429, 26/30/1840, pp. 260–6.

34 Maj-Gen John Ludlow (1801–82), letters and papers 1773–1880, British Library, MSS Eur D814; on suppresing *sātī*, ibid., *Town and Country Newspaper*, 30 June 1855, p. 10; also Tanuja Sarkar, *History*, pp. 349–52.

35 See Kothiyal, *Nomadic Narratives*, pp. 160–216.

36 Jaipur: Joan L. Erdman, *Patrons and Performers in Rajasthan: The Subtle Tradition* (Delhi: Chanakya Publications, 1985), pp. 74–115; Jodhpur: Neuman, Chaudhuri and Kothari, *Bards*, pp. 283–4; Delhi: Pernau and Jaffery, *Information*, pp. 44–5, 51; Hyderabad: Leonard, 'Political Players'; Murshidabad, see below. Jaipur: Rajasthan State Archives, Bikaner; Jaipur Kapat Dwara Collection, Jaipur; for details Erdman, *Patrons*, pp. 255–9; Sumbul Halim Khan, *Art and Craft Workshops under the Mughals: A Study of Jaipur Karkhanas* (New Delhi: Primus, 2015), pp. 1–16. Hyderabad: *Daftar-e Arbāb-e Nishāṭ* records, 1870–1885, Andhra Pradesh State Archives.

the budget of the 'Arbab Neshat Musicians', which he slashed from 1393 rupees per annum to just 16.[37] With one pen stroke, a culturally illiterate accountant might have destroyed Murshidabad as an important late Mughal musical centre (e.g. Figures 2.2, 7.9). Worse, he deprived the Nazim of a ritually important source of sovereignty and prosperity.[38]

Musicians' livelihoods were thus directly, and often harshly, affected by the Company's interference in older Indian modes of compensation for cultural labour. So what then of charitable grants and pensions: in cash, land or commodities like salt? Company officials were clearly not averse to meddling in the customary and economic practices of autonomous states, especially where revenue was at stake. And as Roy Moxham observes in his book on the Great Customs Hedge of India – planted around this very time to protect the Bengal presidency's 'monstrous' salt tax from Rajasthani smugglers – where salt revenues were concerned, the Company was insatiably greedy.[39]

But Mayalee's ineradicable name in the margins of the Sambhar Lake accounts suggests the Company never had things entirely their own way.

Sambhar Salt Lake

The lake at Sambhar is India's biggest inland salt lake, and one of its largest sources of commercial salt, producing about 196,000 tonnes a year. It is also a wetland of international importance for migrating waterbirds, such as the flamingo, who spend the winter there. The lake is located on a flat plain about seventy kilometres by car west of Jaipur and a slightly further distance north-east of Ajmer. Historically the border of the states of Amber-Jaipur and Marwar-Jodhpur ran through the lake (Figure 6.3), and the two states held the main interests in its salt production. In 1835, when the Company first took over the Jaipur portion of the lake, commercial salt production was undertaken at the town of Sambhar in the Jaipur portion, where a superior quality of salt was produced; and at less intensity and of a lower quality at the salt marts of Nawa and Gudha in the Jodhpur portion. All was watched over benevolently by the goddess of the lake,

37 NAI FS 25/01/1773 no.s 1 and 1A.

38 Zia-ud-din, *Hayy*, ff. 49v–r. e.g. two Murshidabad paintings: Figure 7.9, and 'Birth in a Palace', 1760–70, The David Collection, Copenhagen D28/1994.

39 The Inland Customs Line was established in 1823, and the Hedge in the 1840s; Moxham, *Great Hedge*, pp. 33, 65–73, 134. The verdict 'monstrous' was ICS Officer Sir John Strachey's, p. 3.

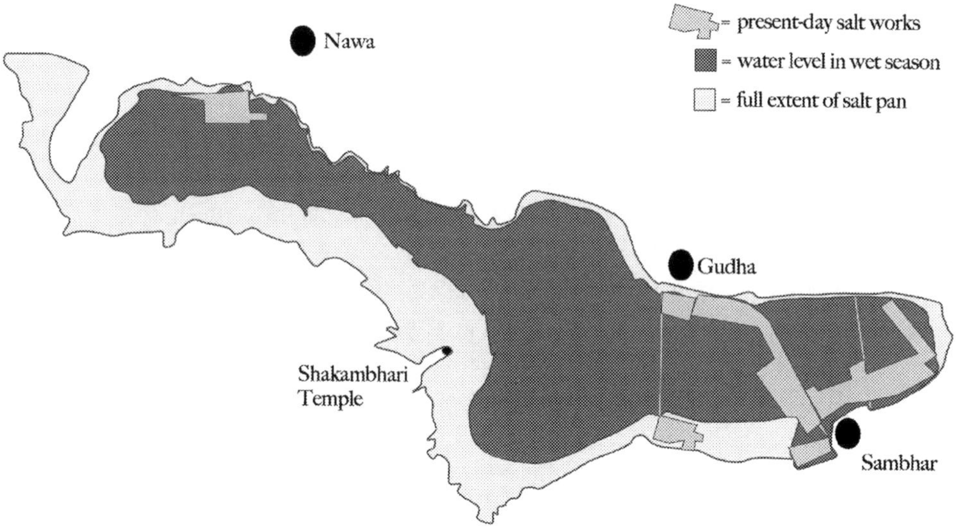

Figure 6.2 Map of Sambhar Lake

Shakambhari Mata, the *avatār* of Parvati concerned with earth's fertility, whose shrine projects out into the lake beneath a striking rocky outcrop that houses the Shakambhari Mata Mandir.[40]

The lake covers an area of approximately 225 square kilometres, but is shallow, and has no natural outlet other than evaporation. The water levels are replenished annually during the monsoon, and the evaporation of the water between monsoon seasons naturally leaves behind salt deposits.[41] When the Company took over the lake, they asked the chief Indian officer or *sarishtadār* of the Delhi Customs House to brief them on salt production at Sambhar. In a letter, translated by H Torrens on 17 October 1838, he noted that:

[The] Lake [is] in length 12 cofs (*kos*), and in breadth, in some places 3 and in others 4, the water of which is clear but brackish averaging a man's depth. The aforesaid Salt

[40] Sudhanshu Sanadhya, Ramesh Nagarajappa, Archana Jagat Sharda et al., 'The Oral Health Status and the Treatment Needs of Salt Workers at Sambhar Lake, Jaipur, India', *Journal of Clinical and Diagnostic Research* 7.8 (2013), 1782–6; Archana Gaur, 'Halophiles of Sambhar Salt Lake', in Joginder Singh and Praveen Gehlot (eds.) *Microbes in Action* (Jodhpur: Agrobios, 2015), 355–68; Seema Kulshreshtha, B K Sharma and Shailaja Sharma, 'The Ramsar Sites of Rajasthan: Ecology and Conservation of Sambhar Salt Lake, Jaipur and Keoladeo National Park, Bharatpur', in B K Sharma, Seema Kulshreshtha and Asad R Rahmani (eds.), *Faunal Heritage of Rajasthan, India: Conservation and Management of Vertebrates*, vol. ii (Heidelberg: Springer, 2013), 173–219; also F Ashton, 'The Salt Industry of Rajputana', *Journal of Indian Art and Industry* 9 (1902), 23–32, 48–64.

[41] Kulshreshtha, Sharma and Sharma, 'Ramsar Sites'; Sanadhya et al., 'Oral Health'.

is produced by the accumulation of Rain Water in that Lake, throughout the Summer and Cold Seasons ... When the wind agitates the surface of the Water and thereby extends the dimensions of the Lake, the additional space thus immersed, after water subsides, is found encrusted with the Saline matter ... One man in the course of a day can draw 50 maunds of Salt from the Lake ... by this method heaps of Salt to the amount of several Lakhs of maunds are collected ... Salt is produced by means of beds or pits, it is here adjacent to the Lake manufactured, the Pits being so extensive as to hold 1 or 2 lacs (*lākhs*) of maunds each.[42]

Over the centuries, highly skilled hereditary communities of salt workers, whom the British at Sambhar called 'Burs', have used their intimate knowledge of the lake's seasonal cycles to maximise the commercial production of salt through active water management and the building of dams, salt evaporation pans and earthwork enclosures called *kyārs*.[43] 'Bur' seems likely to have been a corruption of *bā'orī*, highly skilled workers with earth, stone and water who we know worked as engineering labourers in the salt and marble industries in nineteenth-century Rajasthan.[44] Writing in 1839, the aforementioned Captain Ludlow, the second British superintendent at Sambhar, described the Burs as:

a hardy race, inured to labor and acquainted with the mode of taking advantages of circumstances to produce the greatest amount of salt after an abundant season of rain – and of obtaining a supply from the Paees [*payas*? liquid] and dams in the bed of the Lake. It is the custom, when the waters are out, to form large beds along the shallows; and the Burs are on the watch night and day to take advantage of gusts of west wind, which, by raising the water at the East of the Lake, enables them to open channels of communication to fill the salt beds and again close them ere, on the wind abating, the water has time to recede. Such opportunities are anxiously looked for, and much of the success of ordinary seasons depends upon the manner in which this duty is performed.[45]

For centuries before the Company arrived, Sambhar Lake had been worked as one of India's finest sources of salt. From the sixteenth through early nineteenth centuries it was exported throughout India, where it was known variously as *sāmbhar*, *shākambharī*, *raum-lavaṇ*, *gaṛ-lavaṇ*, *vasuk*

[42] IOL F/4/1898/80683, Political Department 17/08/1838 'Abuses at Sambur', p. 11.

[43] Richard M Dane, 'The Manufacture of Salt in India', *Journal of the Royal Society of Arts* 72.3729 (1924), 402–18, pp. 408–9; Ashton, 'Salt Industry', pp. 24–6.

[44] Kothiyal, *Nomadic Narratives*, pp. 207–11; R Thomas Rosin, 'Quarry and Field: Sources of Continuity and Change in a Rajasthani Village', in Paul Hockings (ed.), *Dimensions of Social Life: Essays in Honor of David G Mandelbaum* (Berlin: De Gruyter Mouton, 1987), 419–38, pp. 423–7.

[45] IOR F/4/1898/80683 Political Department 31/081839 no. 43 no. 15. Letter from Ludlow to the Agent of Rajputana Colonel James Sutherland; cf. Sanadhya et al., pp. 1782–3.

and, in its darker varieties, *Kṛṣṇa* salt.[46] The Mughal government held a salt monopoly until Aurangzeb died in 1707, and the salt works at Sambhar were managed by the Mughal *jāgīrdār* and salt-pan *dīwān*. The Mughals considered the lake a crucial 'source of revenue, and its management, an important assignment'.[47] Various seventeenth-century Europeans estimated that the Mughal treasury obtained six to seventeen *lākh* rupees (600,000–1.7 million) annually from Sambhar salt revenues. The later Jaipur revenue records support such tallies: in 1726 CE, for instance, 25,000 bullock-loads of salt were transported from Sambhar,[48] and the Delhi Customs *sarishtadār* estimated the lake's annual revenue in the 1830s at fifteen to sixteen *lākh* rupees.[49]

But in 1708, the joint armies of Amber and Marwar (Jodhpur) rose alongside Mewar (Udaipur) in rebellion against the new Emperor Bahadur Shah I.[50] The Rajputs defeated the Mughal army at Sambhar, and Amber and Marwar joyously took the lake and its major salt-manufacturing towns back into their joint control. It was at Sambhar in 1708 that Sawai Jai Singh, the founder of the city of Jaipur in 1727, was proclaimed Maharaja of Amber. But it was also at Sambhar in 1791 that the Marathas forced his descendent Maharaja Sawai Pratap Singh (r. 1778–1803) to sign a tributary treaty after his humiliating military defeat by Mahadaji Shinde's French general Benoît de Boigne.[51]

Sambhar salt was fundamental to Jaipur's and Jodhpur's prosperity as their only major industrial source of revenue. But Sambhar Lake and its salt were also clearly central to their ideas of sovereignty. It is perhaps little wonder, then, that the Company's seizure of Sambhar in 1835 was followed by various acts of resistance: an attempt to assassinate the agent to Rajputana, corruption, labour strikes, and Mayalee's individual act of defiance. But courtesans like Mayalee were *themselves* believed to safeguard Jaipur's prosperity and sovereignty. We need to step outside the Company records for a moment, to consider how these two concepts – prosperity and sovereignty – were bound up in Jaipur and Jodhpur with

[46] Ruquiya K. Husain, 'Mirza Zulqarnain – An Armenian Noble' *Proceedings of the Indian History Congress* 59 (1998), 260–6, p. 261, citing the *Khulāsat al-Tawārīkh*; Kothiyal, *Nomadic Narratives*; salt names from Platts, *Dictionary*.

[47] Husain, 'Zulqarnain', p. 261.

[48] ibid.; Abdul Salam, 'Foundation and Early History of Jaipur City', Unpublished PhD Dissertation, Aligarh Muslim University (2011), p. 151 fn. 79.

[49] IOL F/4/1898/80683, Political Department 17/08/1838 'Abuses at Sambur', p. 12.

[50] Also entitled Shah ᶜAlam I.

[51] Salam, 'Foundation', pp. 25, 32; Giles Tillotson, *Jaipur Nama: Tales from the Pink City* (New Delhi: Penguin, 2006), pp. 42–52.

their courtesans, and with the cultural meanings of salt as *commons*, not as a commodity.

The Courtesans of Jaipur

Jaipur has long been a byword for the courtly music and dance traditions known today as Hindustani music and *kathak* dance. Court paintings show the importance of performers to court and religious ceremonial in all the Rajput states. While Pratap Singh was politically unsuccessful in keeping the Marathas at bay, he was famous for his cultural patronage, including overseeing the creation of a landmark Hindavi music treatise in 1799, the *Saṅgīt-sār* (*Essence of Music*).[52] After the 1857 Uprising, in which Jaipur sided with the British, several musicians took shelter there including (from 1866) the fabled Gorari-lineage *sitār*-player Amrit Sen (1814–93), son of Rahim Sen.[53] In modern times Jaipur is synonymous with its distinguished *gharānā* of *k͟hayāl* singers founded by Ustad Alladiya Khan (1855–1946), who spent his formative years in the modernising Jaipur of Maharaja Sawai Ram Singh II (r. 1835–80). It was also the Jaipur *gunijān-k͟hāna* that sheltered the founder of the modern Dagar lineage of *dhrupad*, Ustad Behram Khan (c. 1800–1878), and great colonial-era *tawā'if*s like Gauhar Jan (fl. 1930s–40s).[54]

But courtly musical life in Jaipur in the first half of the nineteenth century is rather mistier. Before 1882 only a small number of *gunijān-k͟hāna* records apparently survive; a fuller account awaits further research.[55] Jaipur politics between the accession of Maharaja Sawai Jagat Singh II in 1803 and 1835 were also rather messy, dominated by a series of powerful women. The first was a Muslim courtesan, Ras Kaphur. This was not uncommon in Rajasthan. An earlier crown prince of Kishangarh, Savant Singh, better known as Brajbhasha poet Nagaridas (1694–1764), was fabled for his relationship with the Muslim courtesan Bani Thani Rasik Bihari, a connection immortalised in Kishangarh painting and poetry as

[52] Maharaja Sawai Pratap Singh, *Saṅgīt-sār*, ed. B T Sahasrabuddhe, 7 vols. (Poona: Poona Gayan Samaj and Arya Bhushana, 1910–12).

[53] Sadiq ᶜAli Khan, *Sarmāya-i ᶜIshrat, Maᶜrūf Qānūn-i Mūsīqī* (Delhi: Faiz-i ᶜAm, 1869), pp. 11–12; also Miner, *Sitar*, pp. 106–8, 131.

[54] Alladiya Khan, *My Life: As Told to His Grandson Azizuddin Khan*, tr. Amlan Das Gupta and Urmila Bhirdikar (Calcutta: Thema, 2000); Sanyal and Widdess, *Dhrupad*, pp. 101–12; Erdman, *Patrons*, pp. 98–9, 106–10; not to be confused with Gauhar Jan of Calcutta; Vikram Sampath, *My Name is Gauhar Jaan! The Life and Times of a Musician* (New Delhi: Rupa, 2010).

[55] SH Khan, *Art*, pp. 12–4.

a Radha-Krishna homology.[56] But Jagat Singh II made Ras Kaphur his political consort. Again, a courtesan's rise to significant political power was not unknown. Begum Samru, who started out as an itinerant dancing girl, died in 1836 as an admired ruler in her own right, and a staunch line of defence for the Mughal emperors from her *jāgīr* at Sardhana, near Meerut.[57]

James Tod was considerably less enamoured of Jagat Singh and Ras Kaphur:

> We shall not disgrace these annals with the history of a life which discloses not one redeeming virtue amidst a cluster of effeminate vices . . . The pranks he played with the 'Essence of Camphor' (*ras-caphoor*) at one time led to serious thoughts of deposing him . . . In the height of his passion for this Islamite concubine, he formally installed her as queen of half his dominions . . . struck coin in her name, and not only rode with her on the same elephant, but demanded . . . forms of reverence towards her which were paid only to his legitimate queens.[58]

Worst of all, Jagat Singh's affair with Ras Kaphur meant that he died without a legitimate heir in 1818, just after signing the treaty with the East India Company that made Jaipur a British tributary at the heavy price of one-fifth of Jaipur's annual revenue. Fortuitously, it transpired that one of his legitimate queens, the Bhatiani Rani, was pregnant, and her infant son was installed in 1819 as Jai Singh III under her regency. The Bhatiani Rani firmly resisted the interference of the Company in her rule, installing an anti-British prime minister, Jhuta Ram, and trying various ruses to avoid paying tribute. The young maharaja, meanwhile, was kept an 'imbecile', according to Victor Jacquemont in 1832;[59] and was poisoned, probably by Jhuta Ram, in 1835 after his mother died. He was succeeded by his infant son Ram Singh II, then just two years old.[60]

The upshot of this instability is that there are fewer accessible sources for Jaipur court culture specific to these decades. European sources help, but such observers generally misunderstood North Indian courtesans as mere

[56] Pauwels, *Mobilizing*, pp.2–8, 77–8; and especially *Cultural Exchange*, pp. 80–107, 160–71.

[57] Julia Keay, *Farzana: The Tumultous Life and Times of Begum Samru* (New Delhi: Harper Collins, 2013).

[58] Tod, *Annals*, vol. ii, pp. 375–6; cf. Kaicker, *King*, pp. 188–209; and Brown [Schofield], 'If Music Be', pp. 80–1.

[59] Victor Jacquemont, *Voyage dans l'Inde*, 4 vols. (Paris, 1841), in Tillotson, *Jaipur Nama*, pp. 90–104, 93–4.

[60] Tod, *Annals*, vol. ii, pp. 375–86; Vashishtha, *Rajputana Agency*, pp. 20–45, 148–54; Tillotson, *Jaipur Nama*, pp. 71–116.

entertainment, a spectacle to be enjoyed (or not).[61] As we saw in Chapters 4 and 5, Europeans were avid patrons of the *nāch*. Jacquemont's description of a Jaipur *nāch* in 1832 shows that some high-flying Jaipur courtesans were indistinguishable from their sisters further east:

> One of the two girls . . . was dancing admirably well. Her performance represented someone flying a kite. She mimed lifting it up in a timid, uncertain manner; then tugged at its string and watched it rise proudly, glorious in success; and . . . followed its twists and turns with intense interest and concern. Her facial expressions and her gestures formed a beautiful poetic language to describe the fluctuating fortunes of this imaginary object.[62]

The courtesans' kite dance was famous right across North India, notably in the fabled heartland of *tawā'if* culture, Lucknow.[63] Likewise, Tod commented on the Maharana of Udaipur's preference for the now pan-regional *ṭappa* in the 1820s.[64] Alladiya Khan's memoirs of his Jaipur youth in the mid-1800s indicate that Rajput court musicians, many of whom were Muslim *ustāds*, formed a network that intersected with other circuits right across North India. While some were on retainer in state departments of entertainment, most also travelled regularly to perform in a large circuit of centres including Jaipur, Jodhpur, Udaipur, Bundi, Tonk, Agra, Atrauli-Aligarh, Delhi and Rampur.[65] All this suggests Jaipur and Jodhpur in the period of the Sambhar Lake affair were fully integrated into the pan-regional networks of late-Mughal art-music culture.

Conversely, musicians employed in the Jaipur *gunijān-k͟hāna* had a number of rights and obligations that were specific to the state.[66] Most particularly, courtesans had year-round ritual-auspicious functions to underpin Jaipur's prosperity and sovereignty through dancing and singing at court ceremonies and religious events: they were called *maṅgalā-mukhī*,

61 Walker, *India's Kathak Dance*, pp. 60–4.

62 Jacquemont in Tillotson, *Jaipur Nama*, pp. 102–3.

63 Illustration in Plowden, *Album*, reproduced in Katherine Butler Schofield, 'Musicians and Dancers in the Indian Office Records', *British Library Asian and African Studies Blog*, 26 March 2019 https://blogs.bl.uk/asian-and-african/2019/03/musicians-and-dancers-in-the-india-office-records.html.

64 Tod, *Annals*, vol. 1, pp. 648–9.

65 Khan, *My Life*. For Rampur as a major nineteenth-century musical hub, see Mir Yar Ali Jan Sahib, *The Incomparable Festival* [1865], ed. and tr. Shad Naved and Razak Khan (New Delhi: Penguin Classics, 2021); and *Musaddas-e Tahniyat-e Jashn-e Benazīr*, ed. W H Siddiqi and Imtiaz Ali Khandera (Rampur: Rampur Raza Library, 1999).

66 Jaipur: Erdman, *Patrons*, pp. 74–115; Jodhpur: D B Kshirsagar, *Jodhpur Riyasaat ke Darbari Sangeetagyo ka Itihas* (Jodhpur: Maharaja Mansingh Pustak Prakash, 1992) paraphrased in Neuman, Chaudhuri and Kothari, *Bards*. pp. 283–8.

auspicious faces.[67] Joan Erdman's in-depth study of the Jaipur *gunijān-k͟hāna* records for 1882–1933 shows that most courtesans in state employ were in fact Muslim. But they were designated in the records under the Jaipur-specific category *bhagtaniyā* or *bhagtan*, from the word *bhagat*, devotee[68] (Chapter 5), and they were initially delegated to dance in the state temples. This further underlines their special ritual-auspicious role in Jaipur state ceremonial.

Bhagtans appear as a distinctive group in James Skinner's 1825 entry on types of courtesan, or '*besyā*', in his *Tashrīh al-Aqwām* (Chapter 7). His entry suggests that the rights and obligations of the *bhagtans* in the Rajput areas close to Delhi were very similar to those of *bhagtans* attached to the Jaipur *gunijān-k͟hāna* later in the nineteenth century:

> Ogling, coquetting, heart-stealing and delivering perfection, [courtesans and their musical relatives] entered the presence of *rājās* and manifested their arts. For all the patrons of the *mehfil*, they drew attentions and favour to themselves by performing with the beautiful voice;[69] the singing of melody and of the *g͟hazal*; the gesture of hand and foot; and the bestowing of blandishments, languishing glances and eye-movements.[70] From witnessing dance and hearing music, the *rājās* were rendered blissfully content. They wrote the artists[71] [various] types of *in*ᶜ*āms* [grants], and in this way those [artists] who attended were assigned power and property . . . Their *svabhāv*, i.e. their defining personal characteristics, are imposture, self-interest, cunning/deception, and fornication . . . After some time, [some] original *besyā* became Muslim, and were named *musalmān-besyā*. *Besyā* belonging to the Hindu community were known in regional language[72] as *rāmjanī*, *bhagtan*, and *gaṇikā* . . . Muslim *besyā* are called *kanchanī*, *tawā'if*, *wārisan* and *kanchan* . . . Both sects [Hindus and Muslims] perform *nartakī* (here possibly drama), dance, and music . . . and *bhagtan* perform service for the *ṭhākurs* (lords). Because they are in possession of the gold of the *kanchanī*, are perennially ornamented with golden jewellery[73] and the clothing and dress of the *apsarā*, and [come] with prayers of happiness and rejoicing, all the people of the world call them *mangalā-mukhī* . . . In the palaces of *rājās* at the request of the authority they teach the servants of the *mahal* (the palace women's quarters) the arts of dance, instrumental playing, elegance and coquetry. Those [who work] in the interior parts of the *mahal* dance in the *mehfils* of women and do not come outside *parda*,[74] and, excepting the *rājā*, do not become bedfellows with anyone . . . .[Conversely] the communities

67 Skinner, *Tashrīh*, f. 139r (see below); Neuman, Chaudhuri and Kothari, *Bards*, p. 262. Platts gives 'musician, minstrel, singer, bard, dancing-girl' for *maṅgalā-mukhī*, p. 1080.

68 Erdman, *Patrons*, pp. 95, 115 fn. 16.

69 The 'beautiful voice', *k͟hwush-alhānī*, is an aesthetic concept of exceptional importance in Muslim cultures.

70 A reference to *abhinaya*, in which expressive eye and facial gestures and pantomime illustrate the lyrics of a song; Walker, *India's Kathak Dance*, pp. 2, 71.

71 ᶜ*atā'ī*. 72 *desh-bhākhā*. 73 or yellow gems, *zard-zewar*. 74 *andarūn* . . . *bīrūn*.

of *besyā* [that] belong to the *bazār* [the *pāturs*] . . . are not allowed to go into the interior parts of the *mahal*. Nonetheless, noblemen and princes who are pleasure-loving[75] in nature have established these troupes in their *mahals*.[76]

The *bhagtans* Skinner described turn out to be the very type of courtesan employed in the Jaipur court at the time he was writing. The Maharaja Sawai Man Singh II Museum in Jaipur retains a number of portraits of named court figures for this period, including one c. 1800–30 by painter Ramji Das of an important *bhagtan* named Ratni.[77] Figure 6.3 is a huge canvas painted in 1793 attributed to Jaipur court artist Sahib Ram covering the wall of one of the private rooms in the palace. It depicts two unnamed *bhagtans* dancing the roles of Radha and Krishna, accompanied by multiple female musicians and singers. Underlining the *bhagtans*' ritual-auspicious functions, Tillotson and Venkateswaran suggest it is 'based on an [historical] enactment of the Raas-lila at court where only women performed, even for the role of Krishna . . . they are real women even as they perform their parts in a divine play'.[78]

The 1882–1933 *gunijān-k͟hāna* records resonate with both Skinner's description and the Sambhar pension records. Jaipur state employed male *kalāwants*, instrumental accompanists, and a large cohort of *bhagtans*, as well as *bhāṅḍs* (buffoons, mimics and transfeminine dancers).[79] Joan Erdman notes that '*Bhagtans* were delegated . . . to dance for temple deities [and] brought into the courts before men and guests in the *Mardānā*,' and, 'in instructing the *bais* of the *zenana*, in the women's quarters as well'.[80] They were also required for all festivals, including those that involved public processions like Gangaur, and those like Raslila where dance-dramas were enacted.[81]

But their obligation to serve both state and deities also came with a number of rights. *Bhagtan* posts were frequently hereditary and could be passed from mother to daughter or adopted daughter-disciple – in fact heredity seems to have trumped merit in hiring. They had rights to request leave, exemption from certain services, permission to give private performances and free transport. And *bhagtans* were paid well in cash, both as regular stipends and on special occasions. They were also given

[75] *tafrīh*. [76] Skinner, *Tashrīh*, ff. 137r–40r.

[77] AG631.76, Maharaja Sawai Man Singh II Museum, Jaipur, reproduced in Tillotson and Venkateswaran, *Painting*, p. 48.

[78] ibid., pp. 100–1.

[79] Erdman, *Patrons*, pp. 76–82. On *bhāṅḍs*, see Brown [Schofield], 'If Music Be', pp. 75–82; Walker, *India's Kathak Dance*, pp. 66–72, 82–8.

[80] Erdman, *Patrons*, pp. 95, 112; also 107.

[81] On Gangaur, see the analyses of the painting 'Maharana Sangram Singh II at the Gangaur Boat Procession' that run throughout Dipti Khera's *The Place of Many Moods: Udaipur's Painted Lands and India's Eighteenth Century* (Princeton: Princeton University Press, 2020).

Figure 6.3 *Bhagtan* performing the role of Krishna in Raslila. Painting in the Banqueting Hall of Jaipur City Palace, attr. Sahib Ram. Jaipur, 1793. © **The Private Collection of the Royal Family of Jaipur**

grants of food, land, houses and income from villages. Their importance as ritual-auspicious specialists is reflected in the fact that in 1905-6, six individual *bhagtans* were each paid more than the chief musician of the *gunijān-khāna*.[82]

The Salt Commons of Sambhar Lake

Crucially, *gunijān-khāna* employees also called themselves salt-eaters. In 1931, a Jaipur musician asked to be promoted to a higher-salaried post, not because of merit, but because 'I am an old employee ... your old salt-eater' – someone who had eaten Jaipur's salt, figuratively and literally, and to whom, having been faithful to the salt, Jaipur owed a permanent

[82] Erdman, *Patrons*, pp. 78–9, 85–8, 92–100, 106; Tillotson and Venkateswaran, *Painting*; Vibhuti Sachdev, *Festivals at the Jaipur Court*, (New Delhi: Niyogi, 2015); for Jodhpur: Neuman, Chaudhuri and Kothari, *Bards*, pp. 283–8.

obligation of care and protection.[83] Without salt, we die; and the notion of 'faithfulness to the salt' – *namak-halālī* – is thousands of years old in Eurasian cultures.[84] It was central to notions of loyalty and honour throughout the Mughal and Rajput domains, enduring well into the colonial period.[85] The idea is very simple: eating the salt of a superior created a commitment of rights and obligations, on both sides, of loyalty, honour, protection and reciprocity; a sense that you were bound by the act of eating salt to share in each other's fortunes and misfortunes. The gift of salt from a ruler to a subject was literal as well as being symbolically charged; from at least the time of Akbar the Mughals distributed regular amounts of salt to their office holders, and also to horses, camels, mules and other animals, who all need salt for survival. Before the East India Company took control, the Mughals and subsidiary rulers did make revenue from salt sales, but salt taxes were low in recognition that salt was necessary for life.[86] The breaking of a salt bond – *namak-harāmī* – on either side was a very serious matter.[87]

The consumption of salt could also have significant religious resonances. According to myth, Shakambhari Devi, the goddess of Sambhar Lake and the tutelary (ruling) deity of the local Chauhan Rajputs, turned what was originally a forest into a plain of silver and then a salt lake at the request of her devotees, thus creating a salt bond between the goddess and the people and wildlife who relied on the lake's provisions.[88] In the eighteenth century, the maharajas of Jodhpur and Jaipur also gave large amounts of salt from Sambhar to the temple in Jaipur of Govinddevji, the incarnation of Krishna who is the tutelary deity of the ruling Kachchwaha Rajputs of Jaipur – in fact, Govinddevji is the ultimate ruler of the state. In 1751, Maharaja Madho Singh I of Jaipur ordered that 700 maunds of Sambhar

83 Erdman, *Patrons*, pp. 83–4.

84 Stewart Gordon, 'Babur: Salt, Social Closeness and Friendship', *Studies in History* 33.1 (2017), 82–97, pp. 82–4.

85 ibid., and throughout Abu'l Fazl's *Akbarnāma*; Kaicker, *King*, p. 29; Tod, *Annals*, vol. i, pp. 227, 621, 757; Masood Ashraf Raja, 'The Indian Rebellion of 1857 and Mirza Ghalib's Narrative of Survival', *Prose Studies: History, Theory, Criticism* 31.1 (2009), 40–54, pp. 46–9; Richard M Eaton, *A Social History of the Deccan, 1300–1761: Eight Indian Lives* (Cambridge: Cambridge University Press, 2005), pp. 113–8.

86 Abu'l Fazl, *Ā'īn-i Akbarī*, vol. i, pp. 135, 148, 152; vol. ii duties tables; Moxham, *Great Hedge*, pp. 34–5, 123–6; and Indrani Chatterjee, 'Women, Monastic Commerce, and Coverture in Eastern India circa 1600–1800 CE', *Modern Asian Studies* 50.1 (2016), 175–216, pp. 200–2, 207–10.

87 I Chatterjee, 'Women,' p. 200. On a Mughal prince's view of Ghulam Qadir, the warlord who blinded Shah ᶜAlam II, as a 'black-faced *namak-harām*', see Muzaffar Alam and Sanjay Subrahmanyam, 'Envisioning Power: The Political Thought of a Late Eighteenth-Century Mughal Prince', *Indian Economic and Social History Review* 43.2 (2006), 131–61, p. 139.

88 Gaur, 'Halophiles', p. 356; Ashton, 'Salt Industry', pp. 23–4.

salt be sent to the Govinddevji temple every year in perpetuity; and in the 1770s the maharaja of Jodhpur followed suit, annually sending 750 maunds from the lake to Jaipur.[89] This gift of Sambhar revenues and of salt itself to Govinddevji continued under British control. In the first half of 1837, for instance, Superintendent Lieutenant Morrieson allocated varying sums per month out of the main lake account to Govinddevji on behalf of Jaipur, with three quarters realised in cash and one quarter set aside as salt to be used in the temple.[90] In other words, salt for Govinddevji was raked off the very top of the pile in tribute to the deity.

The January–June 1837 accounts don't explain why the amounts varied so much monthly, but the contributions to Govinddevji are concentrated in March and April, which contain several big annual religious festivals in Jaipur including Holi, Navratri and Gangaur.[91] This highlights again the connection between Sambhar salt and religious obligations that becomes even clearer when we look at charitable payments the Company made on Jaipur's and Jodhpur's behalf from the Sambhar Lake accounts 1835–42.[92] All recipients seem to be local to the lake, including the musicians, dancers and other performers. It's a large number, and it is noteworthy that Jaipur and Jodhpur had so much care for the people, animals and institutions of the lake – a clear demonstration of Bayly's 'affective and patrimonial knowledges' and 'sympathy which comes from . . . a sense of inhabiting the same moral realm'.[93]

Section 1 of the accounts is dominated by salt revenues allocated in cash to a long list of Hindu temples and other religious institutions – about 50 in total – both monthly and for festivals, but also to pay for attar, dhal, ghee and oil for regular use in *pūjā*.[94] Some of the recipients are rather vague (which Hanuman temple?), but most are clearly identifiable as local to the lake; for example the Shakambhari temple, the Sambhar Jain temple and

[89] Horstmann, *In Favour*, Calendar of Documents and pp. 288–9, 295–6, 305–7; Tillotson, *Jaipur Nama*, pp. 20–1.

[90] IOL F/4/1807/74261A 11/11/1837 no. 9, accounts of Sambhar Lake salt disbursed on account of Jaipur, January–June 1837, 29/09/1837, pp. 90–5.

[91] ibid.; Sachdev, *Festivals*, pp. 1–18.

[92] Nawa and Gudha (Jodhpur) January–June 1839, Sambhar (Jaipur) January–June 1839 – IOL F/4/1898/80683; Sambhar (Jaipur) 1835, January–June 1840, 1841–1842 – NAI FDC 28/09/1835 no. 35, 14/09/1840 no.19, 13/09/1841 no. 22, 14/03/1842 no. 40, 21/09/1842 no. 6, 25 Nov 1843 no. 59ii.

[93] Bayly, *Empire*, p. 55.

[94] IOL F/4/1898/80683 12 July 1839 pp. 63–4 (Jodhpur), 81–2 (Jaipur). There is a slight lack of clarity here in the Jodhpur accounts as to whether they pertain to January–June 1839 as per Morrieson's covering letter p. 21, or whether they in fact pertain to the status quo at January–June 1836, see confusing statement on p. 63; also IOL E/4/745 India Political 16/09/35 no. 40. It may simply be both.

the *dargāh* of Sufi saint Husam-ud-din Chishti in Sambhar town (though most of the institutions in receipt of donations were Hindu). Section 2 documents people and institutions paid in cash, largely for festivals. This section intimately connects the 'dancing girls' Mayalee, Oomda, Gangalee and Kesur, who appear together in this list, with the festivals at which they performed.[95] All of the festivals listed in 1839 are still celebrated in Jaipur state: Navratri and especially the women's Gangaur procession; Jal Jhulani, the worship of water and lakes during the monsoon; Vijay Dashami; Sharad Purnima with its performances of Raslila; Diwali; Govardhan *pūjā* dedicated to Krishna; Chitragupta *pūjā*; Makar Sankranti, the kite festival; Holi; Mahashivratri; and the Muslim festival of Muharram, with cash designated for *ta^{c}ziyas* (tomb effigies).[96] Cash was also set aside separately for oil, with extra oil for Diwali; *ras* powder for Holi; *jaldhārās* (holy water containers) for Shiva; and for cows in the hot season. Cash and grain were set aside for the Jain temple to feed ants, fish, pigeons and dogs.[97]

A number of other performers also appear in these accounts, paid largely for festivals, but some of them paid annually or monthly as well: two clearly important male participants likely to be instrumentalists, Munshiram Mishra and Jivan Ram; two female drummers, the *daf* player Wafati and *dā'ira* player Mamola; three more 'dancing girls', Malzadi, Nagi and Chandu (who performed with Kesur and may have been her disciple or daughter); Lakshman *bhāṅḍ*; Surjoon Rao *bhāṭṭ*; a troupe of *bāhurūpiyas* (male tricksters, magicians and dancers); an unnamed trumpeter; and four people who I think are reciters or vocalists: Himmat Farosh, Panna Farosh, Niyamat Farosh and Naba Farosh.[98] There are dozens of other named individuals in these accounts; those who can be identified tend to be religious specialists or mendicants, or civil employees – cash for *gobarī*[99] and eight Brahmans, 25 maunds of annual salt for the *pūjārī* of Seetaram temple, several *nāths*, *jogīs*, *bairāgīs* and *faqīrs* (all mendicants); a number of *qāzīs*, *wakīls*, *muftīs* and *qānūngos* (all civil offices; see Glossary) – but also estates workers: sweepers, runners, washermen; and the repair of the courthouse for a festival.[100]

[95] NAI FDC 28/09/1835, no. 35 (Jaipur) annual, probably VS revenue year August 1834–August 1835; IOL F/4/1898/80683 12 July 1839 pp. 65–7 (January–June, Jodhpur), 83–4 (January–June, Jaipur).

[96] IOL F/4/1898/80683 12 July 1839 pp. 83–4 (Jaipur). [97] ibid., pp. 83–93 (Jaipur).

[98] *Farosh* means 'seller', and panegyrists including *bhāṭṭs*, *chārans*, *ḍoms*, *ḍhāḍhīs* and *ḍholīs* were called '*bād-farosh*', sellers of the breeze. Skinner, *Tashrīh*, ff. 142v–45v.

[99] Something (usually plaster) 'made out of cowdung', cowdung being ritually pure.

[100] NAI FDC 28/09/1835, no. 35; IOL pp. 65–78, 83–98.

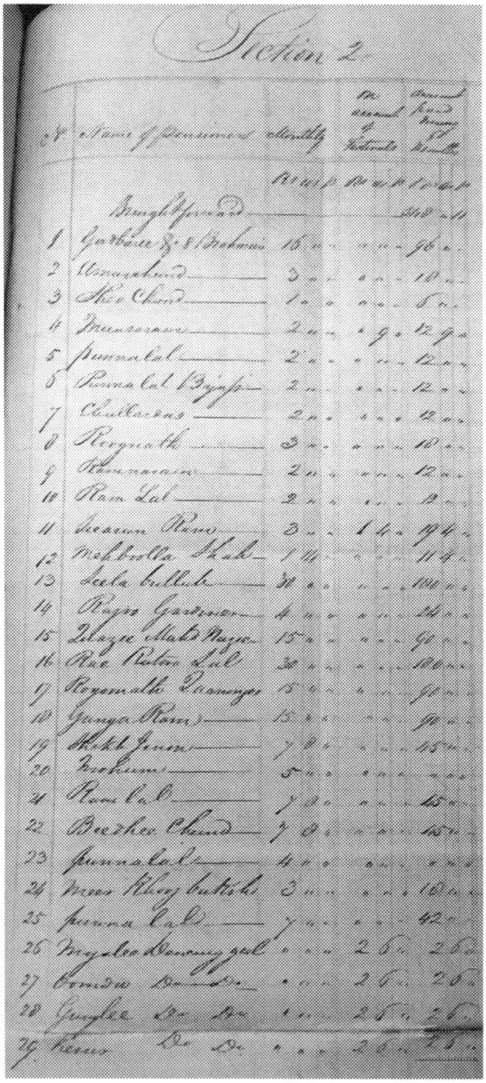

Section 2

No.	Name of pensioners	Monthly	On account of festivals	Amount for 6 months
	Brought forward			[illegible]
1	[illegible]	16		96
2	[illegible]	3		18
3	[illegible] Chund	1		6
4	[illegible]	2	9	12 9
5	Punna Lal	2		12
6	Punna Lal [illegible]	2		12
7	[illegible]	2		12
8	Roghunath	3		18
9	[illegible]	2		12
10	Ram Lal	2		12
11	[illegible] Ram	3	1 4	19 4
12	[illegible] Shah	1 14		11 4
13	[illegible]	30		180
14	Rugoo Gardener	4		24
15	[illegible]	15		90
16	Rao Rutun Lal	30		180
17	Roghunath [illegible]	15		90
18	Gunga Ram	15		90
19	[illegible]	7 8		45
20	[illegible]	5		[illegible]
21	Ram Lal	7 8		45
22	[illegible] Chund	7 8		45
23	Punna Lal	4		[illegible]
24	[illegible]	3		18
25	Punna Lal	7		42
26	Mayalee [illegible]		2 6	2 6
27	Oomda Do. Do.		2 6	2 6
28	[illegible] Do. Do.		2 6	2 6
29	[illegible] Do. Do.		2 6	2 6

Figure 6.4 'Detailed statement of pensions and endowments paid from the Sambhur Treasury on account of the Jeypur State from 1 January to 30 June 1839'. Section 2: cash payments monthly on account of festivals. **The British Library**. Public Domain

There are two things I think are worthy of note here. The first is the symbiotic connection of the salt of Sambhar Lake with its religious festivals and institutions – Hindu, Muslim and Jain – and with those performing artists who made ritual events auspicious: the *bhagtans* and other performers, chief among whom were Mayalee and Oomda. The salt, the ritual calendar, the performers – all were bound up together in ensuring the prosperity of the inhabitants of Sambhar and the states of Jodhpur and Jaipur. And Jodhpur and Jaipur were reciprocally bound to support the fullness of life at Sambhar from the salt revenues that accumulated to their state treasuries. The second thing to note is that this is a really wide cross-section of people and animals living at Sambhar. From *bhāṅḍs* to *brāhmaṇs*, *qāzīs* to sweepers, cows to ants: everyone seems to have had rights in the salt. None of these worked directly with the salt as labourers, overseers, merchants or transporters; and yet they all lived off and benefitted from the salt of the lake. Everyone seems to have had rights to share in Shakambhari Devi's bounty.

That everyone local to the lake had rights to benefit from its salt gets to the heart of the perverse reason Lieutenant Morrieson documented musicians and dancers in such minute detail in the Sambhar Lake accounts. Like the East India Company, we are used to thinking of salt as a commodity, to be sold at a profit and taxed. But in fact, as Gandhi realised, salt is a natural commons.[101] Like air or water, salt is abundantly available in nature, and humans and animals need it to survive. I suggest that the conflict reflected in the records of the Company's fraught management of the lake reveals the previous existence of a salt commons at Sambhar between the states and inhabitants of Jaipur and Jodhpur, where the British mistakenly saw a state revenue monopoly. To be a commons – 'a particular category of property rights based on collective rather than state or private ownership' – something does not have to be free of charge or indeed even unowned; it simply needs to be accessible on a reasonable and agreed basis to all who hold it in common.[102] This, I will argue, was the case with salt at Sambhar before 1835; indeed Wall and Egan note that 'legal theorists and historians have become increasingly aware that prior to the period of European colonialism, commons were the rule rather than the exception'.[103] The Company's failure to recognise the existence of a salt commons at Sambhar is a key reason, I will suggest, why the British met such resistance to their management of the lake.

[101] Thomas Weber, *On the Salt March: The Historiography of Mahatma Gandhi's March to Dandi* (New Delhi: Rupa, 2009), pp. 90–102; Dennis Dalton, *Mahatma Gandhi: Nonviolent Power in Action* (New York: Columbia University Press, 2012), pp. 99–101; Ramachandra Guha, *Gandhi 1914–1948: The Years that Changed the World* (New Delhi: Penguin, 2019), pp. 330–2. On the idea of the commons, see Elinor Ostrom, *Governing the Commons: The Evolution of Institutions for Collective Action* (Cambridge: Cambridge University Press, 1990).

[102] Derek Wall and Michael Egan, *The Commons in History: Culture, Conflict, and Ecology* (Boston: MIT Press, 2014), quotation p. 6, pp. 6–9.

[103] ibid., p. 9.

The Seizure of Sambhar and the Assassination of Martin Blake

The Company sequestered the revenue and salt works of Sambhar Lake in 1835 primarily because Jaipur and Jodhpur had got into large arrears with their punitive tributes, and could not (or would not) pay them. To oversimplify, the Company operated, effectively, as a protection racket: invading or threatening independent states with their overwhelming military might and then imposing asymmetrical treaties in exchange for states paying huge sums for Company regiments and civil agencies to be housed on their land to quell disorder and help the states manage their affairs to British advantage. In addition to not paying their tribute and having a virulently anti-British prime minister, Jhuta Ram, who since 1833 was also the regent, Jaipur had its portion of Sambhar Lake sequestered for failing to cooperate with the British in their paranoid crusade against *ṭhagī* ('thuggee', violent banditry) in Rajput territories.[104]

The seizure of Sambhar happened hard on the heels of the suspicious death of Jaipur's young maharaja in February 1835, and the coincidence of these two serious threats to Jaipur's sovereignty led to an assassination attempt on the British agent. Jhuta Ram was suspected of poisoning Jai Singh III in a power grab, and the British moved to support the new queen regent, the mother of Ram Singh II, in exiling a man they opposed in any case.[105] On 4 June 1835, the agent to Rajputana, Major Alves, was leaving a meeting with the queen regent when an assassin in Jhuta Ram's pay made a dramatic attempt on Alves' life on the steps of the palace:[106]

> A man sprung out from the armed crowd assembled near them and inflicted three sword wounds upon the Resident . . . [Captain] Ludlow . . . with much promptitude threw himself upon the assassin, and bore him to the ground . . . [Alves] immediately turned, and saw Ludlow on the prostrate assassin, keeping him down with all his strength, when he himself knelt, and held the villain's extended

[104] Barbara Ramusack, *The Indian Princes and Their States* (Cambridge: Cambridge University Press, 2004), pp. 48–87; Vashishtha, *Rajputana Agency*, pp. 126–31, 153, 218–25; IOR F/4/1807/74261A: 19/10/1837 Letter Hamilton to Alves, pp. 63–5; India Political 16/09/1835; E/4/745: India Political no. 40 and 42 16/09/1835; also Stern, *Cat*, pp. 77–82.

[105] Vashishtha, *Rajputana Agency*, pp. 21–9.

[106] [East India Company], *Abstract of State Trials Held, Under Special Commission, at Jyepoor, for the Trial of the Ex-Minister Sunghee Jotha Ram, His Brother and Son, and Other Persons Implicated in a Plot to Subvert the Local Government, Resulting in an Assault upon the Person of Major N Alves, Agent to the Governor General, and the Murder of Mr Martin Blake* (Calcutta: G H Huttman, Military Orphan Press, 1837); Vashishtha, *Rajputana Agency*, pp. 151–4, Sarkar, *History of Jaipur*, pp. 334–7.

arm and sword to the ground until satisfied that he was secured by the Residency chuprasses ... getting into a palankeen, he passed unmolested out of the Tripolea ... attend[ed] by Ludlow, who, fearing that he might faint from loss of blood ... got on a horse and galloped to the Residency to prepare Doctor Mottley for his patient.[107]

While Alves and Ludlow were safe, several other Company officers were still at the palace, and an angry crowd gathered, inflamed by a rumour that the British had murdered someone inside. But the conspirators also used the occupation of Sambhar as a grievance to whip the crowd up further against the remaining British officers.[108] Dodging missiles, Lieutenant Macnaghten (then Alves' secretary) made it through the crowd unscathed, but Alves' assistant Martin Blake was chased down, cornered in a temple and hacked to death.[109]

This inauspicious start to the Company's tenure at Sambhar heralded many more subtle acts of resistance and sabotage to come. But it also neatly introduces us to the three successive Company superintendents of the lake: Lieutenant John Dunkin Macnaghten (1810–61), 5th Cavalry;[110] Captain John Ludlow (1801–82), 36th Bengal Native Infantry;[111] and Lieutenant Robert Morrieson (1810–85), 51st Bengal Native Infantry.[112] Of the three it was the older Welshman, Ludlow, who had the most distinguished career in India. It was he who, as agent to Jodhpur (1839–44) then Jaipur (1844–47), convinced the Rajput states to take measures against female infanticide and *satī*, though he is best known as the man

[107] EIC, *Abstract*, p. ii.

[108] Alves to Macnaghten, NAI File no. 23–Jaipur 21/07/1835, cited in Vashishtha, *Rajputana Agency*, p. 153.

[109] EIC, *Abstract*, pp. ii–v. Shamsur Rahman Faruqi presented a fictionalised version of the assassination of Martin Blake (called Marston Blake) in his novel *The Mirror of Beauty* (New Delhi: Penguin, 2013), pp. 3–11, 203–54. Blake was supposedly the first husband of Faruqi's key protagonist, Wazir Khanum, the mother of late Mughal poet Dagh. According to Faruqi, after Blake was killed in Jaipur, Wazir returned to Delhi and married Shams-ud-din, the Nawab of Firozpur, before he too was executed for ordering the 1835 assassination of the Delhi Resident, William Fraser. But in real life Fraser (d. 22 March 1835) was killed over two months *before* Blake (d. 4 June 1835). At minimum Wazir and Blake must have been separated for five years before Blake's death, as Dagh was four when his father Shams-ud-din was executed. William Dalrymple, *City of Djinns: A Year in Delhi* (London: Penguin, 2003), pp. 236–41; Sir Thomas Metcalfe, *Reminiscences of Imperial Delhi*, British Library, Add. Or. 5475 (1843), pp. 28–9.

[110] Also spelled MacNaghten.

[111] Not to be confused with Lieutenant-Colonel James Ludlow (d. 1821) of the 6th Bengal Native Infantry.

[112] Major V C P Hodson, *List of the Officers of the Bengal Army, 1758–1834*, Part III (London: Phillimore, 1946 [orig. Constable, 1927–8]).

responsible for the hybrid traditional–modern education of Maharaja Ram Singh II.[113] But he largely intervenes in the middle of the Sambhar story as a safe pair of hands to handle a scandal.

For two men with such similar backgrounds, Macnaghten and Morrieson had remarkably different personalities.[114] Both were born in India within a month of each other; went from school in Britain to the Company training college at Addiscombe; and were fluent in Persian and Hindustani. Both of their fathers were judges in India, both had multiple brothers in Company service and highly distinguished older relatives.[115] But Macnaghten's feet were secure somewhat higher up the social ladder, while Morrieson's mother, Sophia, was illegitimate and half Indian, the daughter of Morrieson's grandfather and his Indian *bībī* (common-law wife).[116] This clearly caused Morrieson trouble when he signed up as a cadet; there is an additional handwritten sheet in his cadet papers that quotes the Standing Order of the Court of Directors of 19th April 1791: 'No person the son of a Native Indian shall henceforward be appointed by this court to employment in the Civil, Military or Marine Service of the Company.'[117] Fortunately, his mother had retired invisibly to Edinburgh and he passed muster. But his insecurity on this matter may have contributed to what his peers and superiors reported as the 'harshness' and 'severity' of Morrieson's dealings with Indians under his authority.[118]

113 Henry Jeffreys Bushby, *Widow Burning: A Narrative* (London: Longman, Brown, Green, and Longmans, 1855), pp. 21–40; John Ludlow, 'Statement of the Services of Colonel John Ludlow, Bengal Army, Retired List', British Library, MSS Eur D814; Sarkar, *History*, pp. 349–55; Tillotson, *Jaipurnama*, pp. 118–22.

114 Morrieson: Hodson, *List*, pp. 332–5 and Duke of Argyll [George John Douglas Campbell], 'Opening Address, Session 1864–5', *Proceedings of the Royal Society of Edinburgh* 5 (1866), 263–320, pp. 300–01. Macnaghten: Hodson, *List*, pp. 188–9, and Geo. Hill, 'Gleanings in Family History from the Antrim Coast: The MacNaghtens and MacNeills', *Ulster Journal of Archaeology* 8 (1860), 127–44.

115 Sir William Hay Macnaghten, Lietuenant Macnaghten's brother: William Dalrymple, *Return of a King: The Battle for Afghanistan* (London: Bloomsbury, 2013); and Sir James Brooke, Lieutenant Morrieson's eccentric but powerful uncle; Nigel Barley, *White Rajah: A Biography of Sir James Brooke* (London: Little, Brown, 2002).

116 Durba Ghosh, *Sex and the Family in Colonial India: The Making of Empire* (Cambridge: Cambridge University Press, 2006); and Dalrymple, *White Mughals*.

117 IOR L/MIL/10/28/147 no. 165 14/02/1827, pp. 367–72; Dalrymple, *White Mughals*, pp. 49–54.

118 IOR E/4/853 India Political, 971, no. 48, 11/08/1858, p. 919. Sir Henry Lawrence finally sacked Morrieson as agent to Bharatpur in May 1857 for his 'perverse disobedience', 'unwillingness and inability to conciliate the Native Ministers', and 'arbitrary power assumed . . . with harshness and injustice', which rendered him 'by petty and uncalled for interferences, by chilly observances and by harsh execution of necessary retrenchments, universally unpopular', pp. 912–28.

The Corruption Trial of Ganga Ram

Macnaghten was appointed superintendent in charge of Sambhar when the British took over in 1835, and he brought with him a trusted deputy from Delhi, Pandit Ganga Ram, whom he appointed as *sarishtadār* (head Indian overseer) of the salt works at Sambhar town.[119] It was Macnaghten who returned the first lists of pensioners in 1835 including Mayalee, using local accounting practice: these disbursements were not accounted for regularly in the main accounts, but less frequently as a set of contingent bills.[120]

At the beginning of 1837 Macnaghten was promoted and moved to superintendent at Ajmer.[121] Almost instantaneously on Ludlow's arrival at Sambhar to replace Macnaghten, he removed Ganga Ram, put him under house arrest, and investigated him for bribery and corruption.[122] Immediately Ludlow took command, he had received a complaint from Asa Ram, the *paṭwārī* or foreman of the Burs, that Ganga Ram was systematically 'extorting money from him on salt contracts'.[123] The investigation turned up a number of other complainants, which seemed to show that 'bribery and corruption' at Sambhar under Ganga Ram were much more widespread.[124] According to a statement[125] by a salt-works clerk Madhu Singh, 'The Pandit . . . took bribes in every department whether in gift Salt, payment of pensioners[,] Jageerdars (*jagīrdār*)[126] accounts in sales of salt to Beoparees (*be'opārīs*, dealers, traders), or in Bhoom payments (*bhūm*, land, i.e. land rents) . . . The tyranny which he practised is as notorious as the sun of noon.'[127]

119 IOR F/4/1711/69095 21/03/1837 Letter, Macnaghten to Alves, pp. 10–11.

120 NAI FDC 28/09/1835, no. 35; IOR F/4/1807/74261A: 25/11/1837 Alves to R N C Hamilton, Officiating Secretary to the Lieutenant Governor of the North-Western Provinces, Agra, pp. 120–1; 28/02/1838 Alves to H T Prinsep, Officiating Secretary to the Government in the Political Department, Fort William, pp. 143–4.

121 IOR F/4/1711/69095: 05/04/1837 Letter Alves to C G Mansell, Officiating Secretary to the Lieutenant Governor of the North West Provinces, Agra, p. 19; 20/04/1837 Letter Macnaghten to Alves, pp. 20–1; F/4/1807/74261A: 11/11/1837 no. 9 Joudpore Accounts, pp. 100–1; F/4/1711/69095: 29/04/1839 Letter Ludlow to Sutherland, pp. 134–5.

122 IOR F/4/1807/74261A 17/10/1838 no. 58 Letter to the Governor General on 'Abuses at Sambhar', pp. 21–6; F/4/1711/69095 ; F/4/1898/806183 29/04/1839 Ludlow to Suthlerland, pp. 134–5.

123 IOR F/4/1711/69095: 31/03/1837 Letter Alves to Mansell, pp. 6–7; 30/03/1837 Ludlow to Alves, quotation p. 33. Full depositions begin on p. 35. Asa Ram is elsewhere transcribed Asa Pura or Asa Putwaree (*paṭwārī*).

124 F/4/1807/74261A: Political Department 17/10/1838 no. 58 'Abuses at Sambhar', p. 23.

125 *ᶜarzī*.

126 Holder of a *jagīr*, crown land allocated to courtiers for their revenue and maintenance.

127 IOR F/4/1711/69095: 28/03/[1837] 'Arzee from Madhoo Singh', p. 107.

The investigation and trial of Ganga Ram generated reams of paper that made it all the way to the Court of Directors in London, not least because Macnaghten leapt hotly to his defence in such sympathetic terms he was later reprimanded: 'Pundit Gunga Ram . . . [is] a man conspicuous for his integrity, Zeal and general good conduct . . . I consider Gunga Ram the victim of grofs injustice and wanton opprefsion, and it is my request that I be arraigned at the same bar with him!'[128] But the Company had to tread very delicately at Sambhar because Ganga Ram was the Company's man. They were acutely conscious that their tenure was temporary, and that they were responsible to Jaipur and Jodhpur for its proper management.[129]

What seems to have happened is that the Burs and other locals in the Sambhar salt establishment were personally disadvantaged by the imposition of a different way of doing business under Ganga Ram. Crucially, the trial evidence suggests complainants were primarily outraged by the removal of long-standing customary common rights in the salt – an affront that was simply exacerbated by having to pay the foreign *sarishtadār* cash for access, when in accordance with Sambhar practice he should instead have helped himself to his own entitlements. Both Asa Ram and Madhu Singh had been pushed aside by the new regime. Macnaghten had sacked both of them: Madhu Singh, he said, for bad character; and Asa Ram, 'a disreputable fellow . . . for gross and repeated misconduct'. Ganga Ram's accusers cannily used Macnaghten's move to get rid of the hated outsider who had ridden roughshod over the traditional customs and practices at Sambhar.[130]

Reading the trial transcripts, which Ludlow translated himself from Hindi/Urdu and Persian, one gets the sense that payers of so-called 'bribes' – and crucially it is not clear what word is being translated as 'bribes' here – were not affronted by the *idea* that everyone all the way along the chain would take a bit on the side. Ludlow asked the plaintiff Jogul Kishore Mahajan, a merchant/banker from Naraina, why, 'as you were entitled to the Bhoom collections what induced you to give a portion of the amount to [Pundit Ganga Ram via] Madhoo Singh?' He testified: 'As the British authority had recently been established at Sambhur I was unacquainted with the[ir] custom of proceeding

[128] IOR F/4/1711/69095: 21/03/1837 Letter Macnaghten to Alves, pp. 10–11.

[129] IOR F/4/1711/69095: 31/03/1837 Letter Alves to Mansell, p. 7; IOR F/4/1711/69095; F/4/1807/74261A: 08–09/1837 Letters concerning Ganga Ram. pp. 29–50; E/4/782: 19/03/1845 no. 9 India Political, pp. 531–2.

[130] IOR F/4/1711/69095: 21/03/1837 Letter Macnaghten to Alves, p. 11; 05/04/1837 Letter Alves to Mansell, pp. 19–20; 20/04/1837 Letter Macnaghten to Alves, pp.21–2; 25/04/1837 Letter Ludlow to Alves, p. 104; 28/03/[1837] 'Arzee from Madhoo Singh', pp. 107–8.

in such affairs.'[131] Jogul Kishore, in other words, simply assumed cash on the side was the Company's customary way of doing business. Indeed, the trial evidence shows that everybody involved in the salt industry at Sambhar, from the Burs who manufactured the salt to the *banjārās* who took it away, traditionally had an open right literally to rake a bit off the top, in salt or cash. Salt was a perquisite of those who worked in the industry, and before the British sequestration it wasn't usually accounted for in pen and ink.

According to Shivlal Mahajan's evidence, before the arrival of Ganga Ram 'it was the custom . . . that a remission of 5 or 10 weighed seers (*ser*, weight measure) per borah (*borā*, sack, load) should be allowed to purchasers';[132] i.e. to the *banjārās* who bought the salt and transported and traded it to other parts of India. Under Rajput rule, the permitted remission had been variable, but considerably greater than ten *sers*: one to two *maunds*.[133] And it was Ganga Ram permitting the *banjārās* to take precisely this latter amount off the pile before the *borās* were weighed that saw the *panchāyat* of local worthies the British set up to try him convict him of corruption.[134]

The Paranoid Regime of Robert Morrieson

What the Ganga Ram affair made abundantly clear was the incompleteness, to British eyes, of the traditional way salt accounts were drawn up at Sambhar, and the necessity of creating comprehensive accounts that included all gifts of salt if they were to avoid a Ganga Ram situation happening again.[135] In October 1837, Ludlow was promoted to agent at Kota, and the British replaced him at Sambhar with a stickler for exact accounting and upstanding British values: Lieutenant Robert Morrieson.[136]

131 IOR F/4/1711/69095: 28/03/[1837] 'Deposition from Jogul Kishore', pp. 105–6.

132 IOR F/4/1711/69095: 25/04/1837, 'Arzee (*ᶜarzī*) of Sheolal Mahajun', pp. 125–6; see fn. 15 above; also Horstmann, *In Favour*, pp. 82–3, 294.

133 We know from the deposition of Boora weighman that there were 42 *sers* to the Sambhar maund and in Mughal times 24 maunds to the *borā*, pp. 126–7; but Morrieson noted that in 1838 the Sambhar *borā* was 42 maunds; F/4/1807/74261A 11/07/1838 Letter Morrieson to Alves, p. 173. At 42 maunds to the *borā*, the 10 *sers* remitted to purchasers under the British would be 0.5%.

134 IOR F/4/1711/69095: 25/04/1837, Ludlow to Alves and 'C[:] Second Series of the Sambhur examinations', pp. 125–31.

135 IOR F/4/1807/74261A: 25/11/1837 Alves to Hamilton, pp. 120–1.

136 IOR E/4/767: India Political 13/07/1841 no. 20, pp.229–32; Hodson, *List*, p. 89; F/4/1807/74261A, 'Receipts and Disbursements and Balances of the District of Sambhur on Account of Jyepore', pp. 160–1, 166.

Figure 6.5 A steamboat ride on a lake. Jaipur, mid-nineteenth century. © **Christie's Images Limited, 2022**

The sheer extent of the local inhabitants' common rights in the salt is revealed in the records of the Company's 1838 sequestration of the salt-manufacturing towns of Nawa and Gudha, which belonged to Jodhpur.[137] On 11th July, Morrieson described the scene that met him on his arrival:

I was no way surprised to find that a large portion of the salt in store was claimed by Beoparies (*be'opārīs*) and Pensioners as private property, which however I was no ways disposed to allow to be removed as such. Some part of this was never even weighed out by the Government servants, the claimants as they allege having been permitted to extract for themselves, while another part came into their hands by purchase from the [Jodhpur] Troops stationed at the place to whom . . . assignments of salt in lieu of pay had been made . . . The receipts which these different parties show in confirmation of their claims are quite unworthy of credit, they may be forged, they may be interpolated, they may be receipts for former applications, they may be bought for a trifle from a former Hakim (*hākim*, judge, local authority), or they may be attested on Oath by the Kyals (*kaiyāl*, weighman) and Estimators, whose occupations are notoriously and proverbially valuable only for their dishonest profits.[138]

[137] IOR F/4/1802/73994 Draft 135–1840 India Political Department, 'Affairs of Joudpore Vol. 1', 01/10/1838 Lord Auckland to Court of Directors, p. 10; F/4/1807/74261A 11/07/1838 Letter Morrieson to Alves, pp. 168–82.

[138] IOR F/4/1807/74261A 11/07/1838 Letter Morrieson to Alves, pp. 174–5.

These claims and payments clearly represented long-standing customary rights. The evidence given the same day by Purtab Qanungo (*qānūngo*)[139] and Dhun Raj and Bal Kishen *kaiyāls* shows the salt works and markets at Nawa were, to the contrary, well run under Rajput rule.[140]

But Morrieson refused to acknowledge these rights – he saw all claims to salt as little short of thievery. Morrieson's reports consistently demonstrate his overt suspicion of nearly all Indians as incorrigibly dishonest and deceitful. As Alves' secretary from 1836, he had been privy to the entire Ganga Ram affair, and viewed the Sambhar establishments as hotbeds of corruption that needed to learn 'motives of fear' inspired by 'dread of discovery' under his personal 'frequent enquiry' and 'watchful control'. He saw his job as the maximisation of revenue extraction for the British, and the minimisation of as many claims on the salt as he could get away with.[141] He began to find himself regularly reprimanded for going too far, suggesting radical reforms that the Company rejected as entirely inappropriate given the temporary, caretaker nature of their superintendence of the lake. Morrieson kept having to be reminded that it wasn't the Company's permanent possession but belonged to Jaipur and Jodhpur, and that any hint that permanent sequestration might be in their thinking was politically deeply unhelpful.[142] Nevertheless, he persisted.

Mayalee Dances from the Margins to Centre Stage

Morrieson's paranoia is the reason why we have such meticulous accounts of Mayalee's salt stipend – because Morrieson treated every single Sambhar

[139] The *qānūngo* was the very valuable hereditary official in each district whose job it was to know the local families, customs duties, land tenures, etc. Even Morrieson trusted the Sambhar *qānūngo*; IOR F/4/1807/74261A: 23/01/1838 Letter Morrieson to Alves, p. 137.

[140] IOR F/4/1807/74261A 11/07/1838 'Translation of part of the evidence of Purtab Qanungo' and 'Translation of the evidence of Dhun Raj and Bal Kishen Kyals', tr. Morrieson, pp. 182–91.

[141] Hodson, *List*, p. 334; IOR F/4/1807/74261A: 11/07/1838 Letter Morrieson to Alves, pp. 168–82; quotation pp. 179–80.

[142] IOR F/4/1807/74261A: 21/09/1839 no. 71 Letter CG Robertson and WW Bird to Court of Directors, beginning p. 11D; 26/01/1839 Letter Alves to GG, pp. 319–20; 11/07/1838 Letter Morrieson to Alves, pp. 172–3, 180; 16/07/1838 Letter Alves to Morrieson, pp. 191–6; on English weights and measures 12/11/1838 Letter Morrieson to Alves, pp. 274–7; 12/06/1839 GG to Court of Directors, para. 37; E/4/767: 27/08/1841 India Political no. 31, pp. 890–3; F/4/1985/87505: 24/05/1841 Letter Officiating Secretary to the Governor General TH Maddock to Sutherland, p. 9; F/4/1898/80683: 16/08/1839 Letter Sutherland to Morrieson, pp. 108–9.

pension as suspect.[143] In order to regularise and reduce charitable disbursements from Sambhar Lake revenues, he sought 'sanction . . . to make such amendments of the ancient forms' to serve 'the greater integrity of the sales'.[144] At minimum this meant requiring claimants to furnish him with 'satisfactory proof' that the salt was, by right, theirs; and the only proof he would accept was a signed and verified statement on paper[145] from the Jaipur or Jodhpur *darbār*. These frequently didn't exist because they had not before been required. At Morrieson's request, therefore, Alves sent to Jodhpur and Jaipur for 'authenticated list[s] of such existing Pensioners as the Darbar may desire to have continued'. Without such proof, Morrieson refused to pay out.[146]

The new agent to Rajputana, James Sutherland, was increasingly alarmed at Morrieson's unwelcome interventions.[147] Things came to a head when Morrieson entirely withheld the Burs' historic perquisites to the tune of 3000 rupees in one year, and proposed they be abolished altogether. He completely misunderstood the role of the Burs in the extraction of salt; he viewed them as a 'class of people . . . whose existence is not only useless but has been found to be expensive and injurious to the interests of the mart'. The situation became so bad by August 1839 that the Burs went on strike over their unpaid perquisites, and Morrieson engaged in breaking it by bringing in unskilled labour.[148]

Morrieson's bullish determination to violate the traditional customs and practices of Sambhar salt extraction deeply concerned Sutherland:

> I think that we should be slow even in our own territory, to deprive any class of persons like those denominated 'Burs' of perquisites which they have enjoyed from long antiquity . . . In a situation like Sambhur, where our interests in the concern are of a temporary character . . . [and would besides leave] 150 individuals and families destitute . . . the sum held in deposit on account of these Burs should be

143 Ludlow confidentially denounced Morrieson's suspicious attitude as improper and damaging to his authority; F/4/1898/80683: 31/08/1839 'Note on Sambhur Affairs', Ludlow to Sutherland, p. 122.

144 IOR F/4/1807/74261A: 11/07/1838 Letter Morrieson to Alves, pp. 174–5, 180–1, quotation pp.172–3.

145 *mukhtārnāma*.

146 IOR F/4/1807/74261A: 11/07/1838 Letter Morrieson to Alves, pp. 180–1; Letter Alves to Morrieson, quotation p. 196; 26/07/1838 Letter Morrieson to Alves, pp. 208–10, quotation p. 209; F/4/1898/80683 ; 31/07/1839 'Statement of Pensions . . . on account of Jodhpore State from 1st January to 30 June 1839', p. 79.

147 IOR F/4/1898/80683: 31/08/1839 full correspondence Sutherland to Maddock, beginning p. 101.

148 IOR F/4/1898/80683: 06/08/1939 Letter, Morrieson to Sutherland, pp. 101–8; quotation p. 101.

altogether distributed to them ... [I will not] give any sanction to these changes which must be considered a departure from ancient practice.[149]

Morrieson responded with a long, intransigent rebuttal. So Sutherland asked Ludlow to weigh in with the knowledge gained by his own superintendence of the lake and his investigations into the Ganga Ram affair.

Ludlow pointed out that the Burs possessed irreplaceable traditional skills and knowledge, without which commercial quantities of salt could never be extracted at Sambhar. The Burs could never be replaced with 'the services of inexperienced persons' because their services were 'imperative', exactly as the skilled iron workers of his native Wales were. Ludlow understood that the Burs' inherited artisanal knowledge was the reason why:

the Burs are largely invested with rights, privileges, and perquisites in which others including Brahmins and Mendicants shared, from a desire which has always been manifested by the Proprietors of the Lake to dispense something in charity in all concerns connected with a spot where nature has strewn her bounty with lavish and inexhaustible profusion.[150]

This was why Mayalee's salt stipend was so important to her: her salt was hers by the right of commons, as one of many hereditary artisans who served Sambhar Lake. But why was paying Mayalee in salt so important that Jaipur and Jodhpur went out of their way to fulfil her demand, in defiance of Lieutenant Morrieson? I suspect they all rather relished the opportunity to thwart him. But the columns and lists and figures of the Sambhar Lake accounts also fail to ink over the fact that Mayalee's salt was a *gift* to her, and to Jaipur and Jodhpur, from the goddess Shakambhari Devi. Sambhar's salt likewise sealed a reciprocal bond of loyalty and protection between Mayalee, the state she served, and her ultimate ruler, the god Govinddevji. These salt bonds could not be broken without great dishonour and misfortune. Salt, state, the gods and the courtesans of Jaipur and Jodhpur were

[149] F/4/1898/80683: 16/08/1839 Letter Sutherland to Morrieson, pp. 108–9.
[150] F/4/1898/80683: 31/08/1839 'Note on Sambhur Affairs', Ludlow to Sutherland, pp. 120–1.

tightly bound together at Sambhar Lake – until the Company reduced its salt to a commodity to be extracted, loaded up and sold.

7 | Keeper of the Flame: Miyan Himmat Khan and the Last of the Mughal Emperors

Ethnography and New Music Treatises

The Last of the Mughal *Bīnkārs*

In April 1806, the assistant British Resident to the Mughal emperor in Delhi, William Fraser, wrote a letter home to his father in the highlands of Scotland:

> On one of the late Mussulman festivals, I accompanied the king to the Mosque; and was much struck with the dignity and humility, with which the whole court offered their prayers to the Almighty. At this time, I was constantly at the side of the King; and could not but admire the extreme of nobility in his gait, aspect and mien. The loss of his eyes does not at all disfigure his countenance; but the history of their loss and of his misfortunes exalts to the highest our pity and our veneration. On his death, and not till then, we may say, that the Line of Timour is extinct as a Dynasty; beginning with the lame, and ending with the blind.[1]

Fraser wrote this about the diminished but still noble figure of the Mughal Emperor Shah ᶜAlam II, whom we first met right at the beginning of his long reign in 1759, fighting his way out of ᶜAli Mardan Khan's *havelī* to escape assassination (Chapter 2). After returning in 1772 under Maratha protection to his beloved Shahjahanabad after thirteen years' exile, in 1788 this most unfortunate of emperors was blinded in his own throne room by the Afghan marauder Ghulam Qadir. He died in 1806 a puppet of the East India Company, who finally took Delhi from Maratha ruler Daulat Rao Shinde (Scindia) in 1803.[2]

But Fraser could as easily have been describing the man in Figure 7.1: Shah ᶜAlam's chief hereditary musician Miyan Himmat Khan *kalāwant* – also blind, but unlike Shah ᶜAlam indeed destined to be the last of his direct line. Himmat was a *kalāwant*, esteemed as a singer of *dhrupad* and *k͟hayāl*, but especially as a *bīn* player, his great instrument here inscribed with his

[1] William Fraser, letter, 01 Apr 1806, Fraser of Reelig Archives, Vol. 29, 'William Fraser: Correspondence'.

[2] Dalrymple, *The Anarchy*, pp. 293–305; 359–89.

Figure 7.1 Portrait inscribed 'Miyan Himmat Khan'. Illustration for James Skinner's entry on the *bandijān* or *kalāwant* community. *Tashrīh al-Aqwām*, Hansi, 1825. Add. 27,255. © **The British Library Board**

name.[3] At the time of this painting, 1825, he was about 65–70 years of age, and the head of the '*qaum-i kalāwant-i Khanḍār*',[4] the hereditary lineage and stylistic school, or *bānī*, first made famous by his illustrious great-uncle Sadarang and uncle Adarang (Chapter 3). He was also a contemporary of that other noteworthy Khandari disciple Anup (Chapter 5).

Himmat was the son of Adarang's brother, Laᶜl Khan Parab Lal.[5] Laᶜl and his sons seem to have gone into exile with Shah ᶜAlam, returning to Delhi with the emperor in 1772, where Himmat stayed for the remainder of his life. In writings on music, we first meet him late in the reign of Shah ᶜAlam, performing the *bīn* with his father, but clearly already established with his brother Nur Khan Nur Rang as 'unique in the world in this

[3] Bahadur Singh, *Yādgār*, p. 819; Sir Sayyid Ahmad Khan, *Āsār* (1847), p. 226.
[4] Ranj/Himmat, *Asl al-Usūl*, British Library, I O Islamic 3162, f. 1v.
[5] ibid., ff. 1v–2r. Not to be confused with Laᶜl Khan Gunasamudra of Chapter 2.

art'.[6] By the late 1810s in the reign of Akbar Shah (r. 1806–37), Delhi courtiers like Bahadur Singh had elevated the brothers to the status of 'Nayaks of the age', with Himmat now legendary for his *bīn* playing and Nur his singing of *khayāl*, *tarānā* and *dhrupad*. Historian Muhammad Riza Najm Tabataba'i had the pleasure of hearing the brothers regularly when he served as Akbar Shah's treasurer 1812–20 – 'they were famous for their deeds', he said.[7] The veneration that Himmat received in his senior years is reflected in this portrait (Figure 7.1) James Skinner commissioned for his 1825 *Tashrīh al-Aqwām* (*Inventory of Communities*), which gives him the honorific title 'Miyan'. Himmat probably died early in the reign of the last Mughal emperor, Bahadur Shah Zafar (r. 1837–58); Sayyid Ahmad Khan (1817–98) wrote that he passed away a 'few years' before 1847, the date of Sayyid Ahmad's landmark publication on Delhi, the *Āsār al-Sanādīd* (*Monuments of the Great*).

And it is from the pen of a thirty-year-old Sayyid Ahmad that our most intimate portrait of this great musician comes.[8] Sayyid Ahmad's father was a follower of the Tariqa-i Muhammadiyya order of eighteenth-century Sufi, poet and theologian Khwaja Mir Dard (d. 1785). Dard had been a great supporter and theorist of music as a means of approaching the Divine beloved; and as a youth, Sayyid Ahmad regularly accompanied his mother's uncle, the music lover and poet Khwaja Zain-ul-ᶜabidin, to the musical assemblies held twice monthly at Dard's grave–shrine. These assemblies were, specifically, *majālis-i bīn-nawāzī* – concerts of *bīn* playing – and it was in this spiritual space that Sayyid Ahmad regularly heard Himmat and other members of the Khandari lineage play and sing.[9]

What captivated Sayyid Ahmad was not Himmat's *bīn*, but his voice:

> Himmat Khan [was the] best among the musicians of his time . . . His Dhrupad singing was incomparable; so much so that if Tansen were alive, he too would have become Himmat Khan's disciple, and if Baiju Bawra were alive, he would have become his slave for life. Kings, noblemen and notables from all over the world sent letters and offers in an attempt to employ the maestro, but he was quite content with what he had. He did not consider a single offer, however lucrative, and . . . never set a foot out of Delhi. Whoever came to Shahjahanabad to hear him would become oblivious to the world upon hearing just one note, and would make the

[6] Mazhar, *Khulāsat*, f. 5v.

[7] ibid.; Singh, *Yādgār*, p. 819; Najm, *Naghma*, f. 211v; S A Khan, *Āsār* (1847), p. 226.

[8] S A Khan, *Āsār* (1847), pp. 226–7.

[9] Ziad, 'Transcend'; Gulfishan Khan, 'Sayyid Ahmad Khan's Representations of Sufi Life of Shahjahanabad (Delhi)', *Indian Historical Review* 36:1 (2009), 81–108, pp. 85, 96–7; S A Khan, *Asār* (2018), p. 215.

dust of his feet the kohl in their eyes. On the second and twenty-fourth of every month, Himmat Khan would [perform for the] musical assembly [before] the late Hazrat Barbakat Shah Muhammad Nasir [Ranj], the [grandson and] successor of Hazrat Khwaja Mir Dard . . . The entire atmosphere would be intoxicated by his voice; it was as if Daood [the prophet David] himself were singing. His voice had the pain of the world, the spirituality of a mendicant [*faqīr*], the sweetness of piety, and it transported the listener to another world altogether. His music had reached a new level, as in this saying of the Maulvi of Rum, God's mercy be upon him:

Listen to the reed flute, how it laments! It tells the story of separations:
Since they cut me from the reed bed, every man and woman has wept as I weep.[10]

The power of Himmat's voice, accompanying himself on the *bīn* in the *majālis* held at Dard's grave–shrine, perhaps even singing these very verses, struck the assembled devotees with their own intense yearnings for their Creator, from whom they would remain ever separated until the reunion of death.[11]

This spiritual and musical connection between Himmat's Khandari lineage and the lineage of Khwaja Mir Dard was profoundly important to Himmat's life story. At least four generations of the Sadarang and Dard lineages enjoyed close reciprocal relationships, with the heads of the Sufi lineage becoming *pīrs* (spiritual masters) to the court's leading musicians, while the Khandari *ustāds* took their spiritual guides on as musical disciples, as well as serving in their gatherings as performers. Dard's father, ᶜAndalib, and both Sadarang and Anjha Baras (Chapter 3) were disciples together of the Naqshbandi Sufi, poet and musician Saᶜdullah Gulshan (d. 1728). For many years after Gulshan's death, Sadarang organised regular musical assemblies at his grave to commemorate him; and ᶜAndalib took over as host of Gulshan's monthly poetical and musical *majlis*.[12] But it is the relationship between the towering mid-century figures of Adarang and Dard that is critical. It is well known that Dard was widely read in Indian music theory; but he also intently studied the practical art of music under Adarang, performing with him and learning how to compose in a variety of song styles. Dard then wove his deep knowledge of music and of aesthetic and spiritual listening into the first major theological works of his order, the Tariqa-i Muhammadiyya. It is tempting to speculate

[10] Urdu paragraph to second-last sentence: Rana Safvi's translation, S A Khan, *Asār* (2018), p. 256; last Urdu sentence and the first line of Rumi's Persian *Masnawī*: my translation of S A Khan, *Āsār* (1847), p. 227; Maulana Jalaluddin Rumi, *Masnawī Maulawī Maᶜnawī* (Lucknow: Naval Kishore, 1865/6), p. 4; also Annemarie Schimmel, *Pain and Grace: A Study of Two Mystical Writers of Eighteenth-century Muslim India* (Leiden: Brill, 1976), pp. 55–7.

[11] Carl Ernst and Bruce B Lawrence, *Sufi Martyrs of Love: Chishti Sufism in South Asia and Beyond* (New York: Palgrave Macmillan, 2002), pp. 14–16.

[12] Tabor, 'Market', pp. 320–27, 392–3; Schimmel, *Pain*, 53–6; Dargah Quli, *Muraqqaᶜ*, pp. 90–1.

about Adarang's spiritual discipleship, given his intimate connection with Dard; he certainly performed in his assemblies with unstinting dedication. We also know that his nephew, Himmat's brother Nur Khan Nur Rang, became Dard's formal disciple.[13]

It was Dard who instituted the tradition of holding musical *majālis* on the second and twenty-fourth days of the month at his father's grave, centred on *bīn*-playing and singing, and showcasing Sadarang's nephews and great-nephews. These assemblies brought together all the best *kalāwants* and *qawwāls* with Sufis, members of the public and the nobility; even Shah ᶜAlam made his appearance once he returned to Delhi. Mushafi spoke in 1794/5 of '*bin* players lost in their instruments ... playing the *qanun* and singing'.[14] This tradition thrived well into the nineteenth century, long after Dard himself was buried beside his father. The Emperor Akbar Shah, following his father, participated in ceremonies and death-anniversary assemblies (*ᶜurs*) at the shrine and at the family house in Kucha Chelan, where he 'presented the customary *nazr* [offering] ... and participated in the gathering in the *majlis khana* [music hall], where he met the shaikhs. He then had the *tabarruk* [offering] distributed, enjoyed the songs recited by the *qawwals* and gave them eleven rupees'.[15]

The intimate relationship between the two lineages continued under the headship of Dard's grandson Mir Muhammad Nasir Muhammadi Ranj. At least three members of the Khandari lineage performed in Ranj's assemblies throughout the first half of the nineteenth century: Himmat, his nephew Rag Ras Khan and Himmat's grandson Mir Nasir Ahmad, who took Himmat's place in the *majlis* when his grandfather died, and continued to serve Ranj's successor Yusuf ᶜAli after Ranj too passed away in 1845.[16]

Like his grandfather Dard, Ranj was considered an expert in music, and also in mathematics. These came together in a consuming interest in the rhythmic theory of the *tāla* system of Hindustani music.[17] His mastery bore scholarly fruit in about 1815, in an incredibly important work on the Hindustani *tāla*s that he wrote in close consultation with Himmat: the

[13] Ziad, 'Transcend', pp. 554, 567 fn. 64–75; on Nur Rang, fn. 75; Ranj/Himmat, *Aṣl*, f. 1r; Schimmel, *Pain*, pp. 53–5; G Khan, 'Sayyid Ahmad', p. 96.

[14] Ziad, 'Transcend', pp. 554–5 and fn; Ghulam Hamadani Mushafi, *Tazkīra-i Hindī*, ed. Maulvi Abdul Haqq (Aurangabad: Anjuman-i Taraqqi-i Urdu, 1933), p. 93.

[15] Pernau and Jaffrey, *Information*, *ak͟hbārāt* for 31/05–01/06/1830, pp. 268–9. For the house in Kucha Chelan, see Mahmood, *Beloved Delhi*, p. 35; it is not clear whether this particular event took place at the shrine or the house. Eleven and seven are ritually auspicious numbers of rupees. *Tabbaruk* usually indicates material gifts, including food; *nazr* is usually a monetary offering.

[16] S A Khan, *Āṣār* (1847), pp. 226–8.

[17] S A Khan, *Asār* (2018), p. 215.

Asl al-Usūl (*Foundations of Rhythm*).[18] In explaining the genesis of this work, Ranj put his dual pedigree – the basis of his claim to speak with authority – up front: first Himmat's musical genealogy, the *qaum-i kalāwant-i Khanḍār*; and then his own intellectual and spiritual lineage, the Tariqa-i Muhammadiyya.[19]

Ranj said it was Himmat's and his whole Khandari lineage's 'heartfelt devotion to and faith in' successive heads of his spiritual lineage that was why the *Asl al-Usūl* came to be written:

> It was the praiseworthy Miyan Himmat Khan who urged this worthless author to put pen to paper, when he said: 'That which you sometimes explain to us regarding the true times and rules of the *tāla*s: if you put those things down in writing, other people in the future will benefit from knowing their fundamentals; they will gain pleasure by reading what you have written; and it will also act as a memorial to you on the face of the earth'. In accordance with his request, therefore, I began writing this short treatise, and called it the *Asl al-Usūl*.[20]

It is a remarkable, indeed overtly modern, work of rhythmic theory, which I will return to towards the end. Given the extent of the trade secrets Ranj laid out with such clarity, and the specific focus on preserving the *tāla*s of the Delhi *kalāwant*s and *qawwāl*s, it was undoubtedly a joint enterprise between the two masters – one made all the more necessary because Himmat was blind, elderly and had no worthy sons to succeed him.

Himmat Khan *Kalāwant* as Caste Type

There is of course one other crucial record of Himmat's life that has literally been staring us in the face: his portrait, commissioned by Delhi's famous mixed-race (Eurasian) resident Colonel James Skinner (1778–1841) to illustrate the entry on *kalāwant*s in the 1825 copy of his *Tashrīh al-Aqwām* now in the British Library. Skinner was born to a British father and a Rajput mother from a Benares lineage. Unlike Robert Morrieson, Skinner fell foul of the ban on mixed-race sons entering East India Company service, and instead joined the Maratha army under Benoît de Boigne (Chapter 6). He gained extraordinary renown as a cavalryman, and is best known for the irregular cavalry regiments, known as Skinner's Horse

[18] Andhra Pradesh Government Oriental Manuscripts Library, Falsafa 326.
[19] Ranj/Himmat, *Aṣl* (BL), ff. 1v–2r. [20] ibid., ff. 2r–v.

or 'Yellow Boys', that he raised at Hansi, near Delhi, in the service of the Company after the British defeated the Marathas in 1803.

As an accomplished man of mixed race, he bestrode two social and cultural worlds, frequently bringing them together in his fabled Delhi *majālis*: that of the Mughals and Rajputs, and that of the more intrepid sort of European who thrived in the old Mughal capital before the Uprising. On one hand, Skinner built St James' Church in Delhi, was inseparable from William Fraser until the latter's assassination in 1835, and deputed his Yellow Boys regularly as James Tod's military escort as political agent to Rajputana. On the other, Skinner was an acclaimed expert in Persian and Urdu literature, a patron of late Mughal painting of the highest quality, and a renowned connoisseur of Hindustani music from the most elevated to the most tantalising (Chapter 4).[21]

The *Tashrīh al-Aqwām* was one of several original Persian manuscripts that Skinner wrote and had illustrated by Delhi painters. In 1825, he presented what is now the British Library copy to the governor of Bombay, John Malcolm, twenty-six years after a much younger Malcolm had reverently taken hold of Mahlaqa Bai's little book of *g͟hazal*s mid-pirouêtte (Chapter 5). The *Tashrīh* is a descriptive catalogue of Hindu and Muslim castes, occupational groups and religious mendicants local to the regions around Delhi, with pen sketches of the typical habits, occupations, religious beliefs and customs of 104 named communities accompanied by representative illustrations by late Mughal master artists such as Ghulam ᶜAli Khan.[22]

This is what Skinner had to say about Himmat as an iconic representative of his community. A *kalāwant* or '*bandījān*', he wrote:

> is born from the union of a man from the *bhāṭṭ qaum* (community)[23] with a woman from the gardener community. When the son becomes an adult he does not wear the thread but is publicly differentiated [from his natal community] and busies himself acquiring . . . the science of music. Thus he emerges as an expert in the theoretical fundamentals of that subject – such as the knowledge of *kharaj* etc, *swara*, *brahma-tāla* etc, *tāla*, *uttam* etc, the three *grāmas* – and becomes powerfully skilled in singing Bhairav and the other *rāgas*; in playing the different

[21] Eden, *Up the Country*, vol. i, p. 143; Pernau and Jaffrey, *Information*, pp. 219, 241; David Ochterlony Dyce Sombre, 'Exhibit, No. 46: Mr. Dyce Sombre's Journal or Diary [1833–38]', in Prerogative Court of Canterbury, *Dyce Sombre Against Troup, Solaroli, and Prinsep, and the Hon. East India Company*, vol. i (London: Henry Hansard, n.d.) 220–415, e.g. 27–29/12/1835.

[22] N. G. McBurney, *The 1836 Tazkirat al-Umara of Colonel James Skinner: A Catalogue* (London: Bernard Quaritch, 2014); also Yuthika Sharma, 'Art', pp. 219–25; J. P. Losty, *Delhi: Red Fort to Raisina* (New Delhi: Roli, 2012), fig. 63, p. 121; also Sharma, 'Art', pp. 153–94.

[23] A *bhāṭṭ* being himself the product of a mixed marriage between a *kṣatriya* man and a *brāhmaṇ* woman; Skinner, *Tashrīh*, ff. 130r–34r.

types of instrument including the *bīn*, *qānūn*, *mridang* [*pakhāwaj*], *jaltarang* and so forth; and in teaching dancing, *sangīt* and *nriti*, i.e. dance. Through practice he arrives at perfection. He publicly devotes his own arts and skills to the service of the Suryavanshi and Somavanshi *rājās*,[24] who [in return] strew across the heavens gifts of ritual robes, cash and caps of honour ... His *dharma* [religious duty] is to worship Shri Devi and to serve *brāhmaṇs* and cows, and his *karma* [preordained action] is to sing in the presence of notables at all times [set aside for] performance. His *svabhāv* [innate personal qualities] are smooth speech and flattering utterance. The *kalāwants*' custom is to hold instruments in their hands as they play and sing in the *mehfils* of the ruling classes. They wear expensive and delicate clothing, and marry within their own community.[25]

This description is jarringly discordant. Skinner's account of the *kalāwants*' kinship and religious affiliations bears zero resemblance to what we know about Himmat's lineage and spiritual allegiances from every other source, as well as of all other *kalāwants* of the region including those actually in service to the Suryavanshi *rājās* of Udaipur, Jodhpur and Jaipur, all of whom were Muslim *ustāds* like Himmat.[26] It is frankly incompatible with the information we have from people in Delhi who knew the Khandari lineage well. The relationship of Islam to caste is complicated,[27] and south of Hindustan the word *kalāwant* could have different sociological connotations.[28] But the Hindustani and especially the Delhi *kalāwants* – the most sought-after lineages of élite musicians due to their Mughal service – had been Muslim for at least 250 years. What is more, we know that Himmat's particular lineage had been followers of the Tariqa-i Muhammadiyya branch of the Naqshbandi Mujaddidis for a century, and played a central role in its devotional practices.

24 The *kṣatriya* (Rajput) dynasties that drew their lineages from the sun (*sūrya*) and moon (*soma*).

25 Skinner, *Tashrīh*, ff. 135r–6r.

26 Udaipur: Tod, *Annals*, vol. i, p. 647; and Andrew Topsfield, 'The Kalavants on Their Durrie: Portraits of Udaipur Court Musicians, 1680–1730', in Rosemary Crill, Susan Stronge, and Andrew Topsfield (eds.), *Arts of Mughal India: Studies in Honour of Robert Skelton* (London: Victoria and Albert Museum, 2004), 248–63; Jodhpur: Munshi Hardyal Singh, *Report on the Census of 1891. Volume II: The Castes of Marwar* (Jodhpur: Marwar Darbar, 1894), p. 124; Jaipur: Alladiya Khan, *My Life* and Erdman, *Patrons*.

27 Julian Levesque, 'Debates on Muslim Caste in North India and Pakistan: From Colonial Ethnography to Pasmanda Mobilization', *CSH-IFP Working Papers* 15 (2020), hal-02697381.

28 Davesh Soneji, 'Memory and Recovery of Identity: Living Histories and the Kalavantulu of Coastal Andhra Pradesh', in Indira Peterson and Davesh Soneji (eds.), *Performing Pasts: Reinventing the Arts in Modern South India* (New Delhi: Oxford University Press, 2008), 283–312; Bakhle, *Two Men*, pp. 23–35; Anjali Arondekar, 'In the Absence of Reliable Ghosts: Sexuality, Historiography, South Asia', *Differences: A Journal of Feminist Cultural Studies* 25.3 (2015), 98–122.

Skinner would have known this, too. To illustrate his entry, he commissioned a portrait from life of a named musician who, in 1825, was a celebrity, chief *kalāwant* to the Mughal emperors and head of the renowned Khandari lineage. Skinner, indeed, employed his own *kalāwant*s. Captain Mundy of the 2nd Regiment of Foot, who was resident in India 1825–30, came to profoundly appreciate the quality of Skinner's 'Khalâmuts':

> These musicians who were the private servants of the Colonel, and the best of their *ját*, accompanied the Commander-in-Chief [Lord Combermere] for several weeks on his journey . . . Before the musicians left us, I had become quite a fanatico for Indian minstrelsy, and gave my 'wah! Wah!' of applause to a favourite gazzul (*g͟hazal*) of Hafiz, or a sprightly kuhirwa (*kahārwa*) air.[29]

Emily Eden was similarly charmed by Skinner 's own celebrated courtesan troupe (Chapter 4). Skinner was famed for his *majālis*, where he enjoyed performers of all kinds, but especially courtesans, in the company of his beloved William Fraser[30] and the full range of his British, Rajput and Mughal friends.[31] Several paintings of the *mise-en-scène* in Figure 7.2 exist; Dalrymple and Sharma suggest Skinner gave them to guests as souvenirs of their visit to his home, like very expensive postcards.[32] What is equally telling as to what Skinner knew about the *kalāwant*s is that his descriptions of their musical practices and roles are accurate, as are the same kinds of details in his entries on courtesans and mendicants (Chapter 6).[33] But the rest of his entry is a farrago of nonsense – for the Delhi *kalāwant*s collectively, and for Himmat personally.

This presents us with a knotty problem. Skinner's entry on the *kalāwant*s includes information that is wholly unreconcilable with Himmat's own intellectual output and biography. All of the texts I have dealt with so far in this chapter are in Persian and Urdu, and were written in the same place, at the same time, in closely overlapping social circles. If we want to understand Skinner's major work of ethnography better as a whole, we have to untie this musical tangle.

29 Captain Godfrey Mundy, *Pen and Pencil Sketches Being the Journal of a Tour in India*, vol. i (London: John Murray, 1832), pp. 348–9.

30 Fraser Papers, Bundle 35, James Baillie Fraser to his mother, Calcutta, 22/10/1813; Bundle 181, James Skinner to James Baillie Fraser, Delhi, 29/11/1836; Fraser, *Military Memoir*, pp. 239–41.

31 Y Sharma, 'Art', p. 227.

32 Dalrymple and Sharma, *Princes*, cat. 55, p. 140; 'A Group of Dancing Girls and Musicians', Delhi, c. 1815, Victoria and Albert Museum, IS.70–1977.

33 James Mallinson, 'Yoga in Mughal India', in Debra Diamond (ed.), *Yoga: The Art of Transformation* (Washington DC: Smithsonian Institution, 2013), 69–83, pp. 73–5, 82–3 fn. 37.

Figure 7.2 'A Nautch at Colonel Skinner's Given to Me By Himself 1838'. Delhi. Add. Or. 2598. © **The British Library Board**

Ethnographic Descriptions of Occupational and Ethnic Groups

In this chapter, I will consider this clash between biography and ethnography – the individual versus the 'type' – in the context of late Mughal and Company-style paintings and written descriptions of Indian performers as representative of their communities and occupations. Here, I am interested in all communities that used music and dance in their acts, not just élite performers (Figure 7.3). All performers were entertainers and purveyors of enchantment, and thus simultaneously slightly dubious in social status and highly desired for their spectacular skills – and therefore frequent subjects of description long before Europeans took an interest.[34] But c.1770–1830, multiple modes of describing communities – old and new, visual and written, Indian and European – converged in new and telling ways. This chapter considers what 'ethnographic' writings and paintings of musicians in late Mughal India tell us – crucially when considered alongside texts musicians wrote themselves – about lives stretched between Mughal and British rule in the run-up to the 1857 Uprising, especially in Delhi.

Throughout this book, I use the word 'community' to refer to hereditary occupational groups, instead of 'caste'. This is because my sources use

[34] Brown [Schofield], 'Social Liminality'.

Figure 7.3 Illustration for James Skinner's entry on the *bāzīgār* (conjuror) community. *Tashrīh al-Aqwām*, 1825. Add. 27,255, f. 120v (detail). **The British Library**. Public Domain.

qaum (community), *tā'ifa* (troupe or tribe), *zāt*/*jāt* (genus or tribe),[35] *got* (genus or lineage), or *firqa* (sect), none of which mean quite the same thing. But it is also because caste came to mean something subtly different when caste boundaries and intercaste hierarchies became hardened (and were also resisted and subverted) later in the colonial period.[36] As has been well documented, this hardening was in major part a result of the arrival of the official colonial census from the late 1860s, and of 'empirical' modes of colonial ethnography – of measuring and describing ethnic and social differences – that went hand in glove with the caste-wise surveys of the census and with the colonial governmentality they enabled.[37]

[35] Sources in Brajbhasha in *nastᶜalīq* script use *jāt*, which could be either Perso-Arabic *z̤āt* or Sanskrit *jāti*, whose meanings are in any case similar.

[36] Genetic evidence demonstrates that social organisation by endogamy has been endemic in the Indian subcontinent since 300–500 CE; Analabha Basu, Neeta Sarkar-Roy and Partha P Majumder, 'Genomic Reconstruction of the History of Extant Populations of India Reveals Five Distinct Ancestral Components and a Complex Structure', Proceedings of the National Academy of Sciences 113.6 (2016), 1594–99. The best recent history is Sumit Guha, *Beyond Caste: Identity and Power in South Asia, Past and Present* (Leiden: Brill, 2013), esp. on colonial 'caste' vs. *qaum, zāt, jāti* pp. 25–35; also Walker, *India's Kathak Dance*, pp. 75–88; and Joel Lee, *Deceptive Majority: Dalits, Hinduism, and Underground Religion* (Cambridge: Cambridge University Press, 2021).

[37] Susan Bayly, *Caste, Society and Politics in India from the Eighteenth Century to the Modern Age* (Cambridge: Cambridge University Press, 2001), pp. 97–143; Guha, *Beyond Caste*, pp. 164–77; Crispin Bates, 'Race, Caste and Tribe in Central India: the Early Origins of Indian

It is likewise somewhat anachronistic to call the type of description represented by Skinner's *Tashrīh* 'ethnographic'. My sources all predate and, as paracolonial texts, transcend the Raj-era hardening of caste boundaries. And yet, in company with other Mughal cultural historians, I am going to use the term. Descriptions of distinctive, demarcated people groups go back many hundreds of years in South Asian languages and visual sources.[38] I take Rebecca Brown's point that descriptions of North Indian people types apparently 'from life' in the late Mughal and Company period tended to be of people *doing things*, arrested mid-action, not really 'ethnic' types.[39] Similarly, very often visual and written catalogues in this period portrayed people not in sterile isolation, but in the context of topographical settings or distinctive events – buildings, festivals, gardens, wielding typical accoutrements – so that they collectively added up to a holistic city- or villagescape.[40] Works like Dargah Quli's *Muraqqa^c-i Dehlī* and Sayyid Ahmad's *Āsār al-Sanādīd*, though written more than a century apart, lovingly described the buildings and social spaces of Delhi as well as the city's important personages, grouped together under capacious occupational umbrellas (religious figures, poets, *hakīms*, musicians). Such texts were a heady mix of descriptive modes: topography, biography, ethnography, even signs and wonders, that were meant to be taken as truthful – 'not fiction'. Meanwhile, British observers of the eighteenth and early nineteenth centuries tended to be excited largely by differences in costume and manners[41] – by the 'picturesque' – rather than nuances of ethnicity.[42]

But fine-grained social hierarchies based on kinship patterns, occupation, skin colour and language difference – what hardened into modern

Anthropometry', in Peter Robb (ed.), *The Concept of Race in South Asia* (New Delhi: Oxford University Press, 1995), 219–59; and C J Fuller, 'Ethnographic Inquiry in Colonial India: Herbert Risley, William Crooke, and the Study of Tribes and Castes', *Journal of the Royal Anthropological Institute* 23 (2017), 603–21.

38 Sunil Sharma, 'Representation of Social Groups in Mughal Art and Literature: Ethnography or Trope?' in Alka Patel and Karen Leonard (eds.), *Indo-Muslim Culture in Transition* (Leiden: Brill, 2012).

39 Rebecca M Brown, 'Colonial Polyrhythm: Imaging Action in the Early 19th Century', *Visual Anthropology* 26.4 (2013), 269–97, pp. 272–82; also Y Sharma, 'Art', pp. 211–2, 221–3.

40 J P Losty, 'Depicting Delhi: Mazhar Ali Khan, Thomas Metcalfe, and the Topographical School of Delhi Artists', in Dalrymple and Sharma, *Princes*, 52–9; Sharma, 'Art', pp. 166–7; Yuthika Sharma, 'Village Portraits in William Fraser's Portfolio of Native Drawings', in Crispin Branfoot (ed.), *Portraiture in South Asia Since the Mughals: Art, Representation and History* (London: I B Tauris, 2018), 199–220.

41 e.g. Plowden, Letter, 4 Apr 1783; James Baillie Fraser, Fraser Papers, vol. 23, p. 139, in Mildred Archer and Toby Falk, *India Revealed: The Life and Adventures of James and William Fraser* (London: Weidenfeld Nicolson, 1989), p. 59.

42 Y Sharma, 'Art', pp. 166–7 and 221–2; also Woodfield, 'Hindostannie Air', pp. 199–200, 206–8.

Figure 7.4 *Qawwāls* at the shrine of Hazrat Nizam-ud-din Chishti, after Mazhar ᶜAli Khan. Delhi, 1836. IM.41-1923. © **Victoria and Albert Museum, London**

caste – were not 'invented' by the British.[43] Hierarchical catalogues and 'type' paintings of different communities, produced by and for Hindu and Muslim ruling classes and used for a variety of reasons, including classification, taxation and dividing to rule, long predated British colonialism. We can see this easily by comparing Figures 7.3 and 7.5, painted nearly two centuries apart.[44] What is more, the kinds of biographical writings I discussed at the beginning of this chapter and in Chapter 3[45] firmly underline what Skinner noted of every community in his inventory. Firstly, many occupations and roles – from *brāhmaṇ* to *bāzīgār* to bangle-maker – were hereditary;[46] and secondly, the multigenerational lineages or household guilds thus created were often endogamous: members only married within the community, or married out only for certain purposes. As we saw in Chapter 3, *kalāwants* did teach selected non-related disciples, but they were obsessed with maintaining the patrimonial integrity of their familial traditions. Imam Khan wrote as

[43] Norbert Peabody, 'Cents; *pace* Nicholas B Dirks, 'The "Invention" of Caste', op cit. in Chapter 1, fn 11; also John D. Rogers, 'Introduction: Caste, Power and Region in Colonial South Asia', *Indian Economic and Social History Review* 41.1 (2004), 1–6.

[44] Peabody, 'Cents'; S Sharma, 'Representation'; Guha, *Beyond Caste*, pp. 150–164.

[45] Indrani Chatterjee, 'Monastic Governmentality, Colonial Misogyny, and Postcolonial Amnesia in South Asia', *History of the Present* 3.1 (2013), 57–98; also Guha, *Beyond Caste*, Ch. 4.

[46] Skinner, *Tashrīh*, entries for *brahmaṇ* ff. 22v–30v, *bāzīgār*, ff. 121r–22v, *niyārī(ā)* or *chūṛī-sāz* (bangle-maker) ff. 314v–16r.

(a) (b)

Figure 7.5 A and B Khwaja Moin-ud-din Chishti and a gathering of mystics and musicians, and background detail. Mughal, c. 1650–55, IS.94-1965. © **Victoria and Albert Museum, London**

late as the post-Uprising period that *kalāwants* wouldn't even teach their daughters' sons the *bīn*, lest their trade secrets become dispersed and corrupted.[47]

In other words, when we come to consider written and visual descriptions of 'types' in late Mughal India, occupation and custom – 'doing things' – cannot be separated from inherited community identity in most cases. Whether or not we call such configurations caste, they predate colonialism but also the 'empirical-realist' mode of modern ethnography. Modes of ethnography themselves have histories. And older Mughal and Rajput ethnographic and biographical modes were still operational as paracolonial knowledge throughout this period (in chronological order: Figures 7.5, 7.6, 4.5A and 7.3),[48] and interacted with colonial imperatives for description in interesting ways. Critically, Mughal and Rajput modes of describing people did *not* have to be based in currently observed, empirical

47 Imam Khan, *Ma*^{c}*dan* (1925), p.44.

48 S Sharma, 'Representation', pp. 31–4; Peabody, 'Cents', pp. 829–37.

reality for them to qualify as ethnographic (though they often were) – there is a problematic conflation in the secondary literature of 'ethnographic' in the late Mughal/Rajput context to mean observably true, taken from life, realistic. Skinner's description of the *kalāwant*s as a 'type' itself demonstrates this was not necessarily the case. Sometimes the ideal, the obsolete or the supernatural took precedence over the real, the present or the natural.[49]

In this chapter, then, I use 'ethnographic' for all systematic descriptions of people as *representative types* rather than as individuals, regardless of imputed realism. Skinner's *Tashrīh* is definitively ethnographic in this sense. It is hugely valuable, because alongside other, more narrative descriptions in English and Persian, it confirms in detail that Delhi's musical life did not dissipate in the early nineteenth century, as posterity would have us believe. Performers like Himmat kept its flame burning brightly, sustained by the cosmopolitan, intimate patronage of Mughal *mīrzā*s and officials, merchants like Hindu Rao and *jagīrdār*s like Begum Samru, various *rājā*s, the entire Company establishment (Ochterlony, Malcolm, Tod, Metcalfe, the Frasers, Trevelyan, Hawkins, all of them patronised Hindustani musicians), and notable mixed-race figures like Dyce Sombre and James Skinner.[50] The imperial atelier had contracted to its core due to diminishing funds, but the emperors Akbar Shah and Bahadur Shah Zafar still had the best court musicians on staff, brought the best courtesans into their *majālis* at Shahjahanabad and Mehrauli,[51] went out to the *dargāh*s of the city to be spiritually transported by the *qawwāl*s, and sat on top of the Zafar Mahal to watch the *bhāṅḍ*s and *bāhurūpiya*s in the Mehrauli *bazār*. The British Resident, too, mirrored the

[49] e.g. on the obsolete, see the mixed-race author N Augustus Willard's 'Treatise on the Music of Hindostan [1834]', in Sourindro Mohun Tagore (ed.), *Hindu Music from Various Authors*, 2nd ed., (Calcutta: Bose and Co, 1882), pp. 1–122. In 1988 Joep Bor claimed Willard as the first 'ethnomusicological' 'field worker' of Indian music; but Bor did not then know that much of his treatise was verbatim translation of the *Tuhfat*; Bor, 'Rise', pp. 58–9; Schofield, 'Reviving', pp. 508–9.

[50] See various entries in Singh, *Yādgār*; Najm, *Naghma*; Pernau and Jaffrey, *Information*; Dyce Sombre, 'Journal'; the Fraser Papers; SA Khan, *Asar*; Mirza Sangin Beg, *Delhi in Transition, 1821 and Beyond: Mirza Sangin Beg's Sair-ul Manazil*, ed. and tr. Shama Mitra Chenoy (New Delhi: Oxford University Press, 2018); Metcalfe, *Reminiscences*; Mirza Asadullah Khan Ghalib, *Ghalib 1797–1869: Life and Letters*, ed. and tr. Khurshidul Islam and Ralph Russell (New Delhi: Oxford University Press, 1994); Mahmood Farooqui, tr. [The Mutiny Papers] *Besieged: Voices from Delhi 1857* (New Delhi: Penguin, 2010); and Mirza Farhatullah Baig (1883–1947), *The Last Mushaᶜirah of Dehli*, tr. Akhtar Qamber (New Delhi: Orient Blackswan, 2010).

[51] Lunn and Schofield, 'Desire'; Margrit Pernau, 'Celebrating Monsoon Feelings: The Flower-Sellers' Festival of Delhi', in Rajamani, Pernau and Schofield, *Monsoon Feelings*, 379–407.

emperor by employing *kalāwants* and courtesans for festive events and private entertainments.[52]

But Skinner's *Tashrīh* also takes a distinct leap in the direction of later colonial constructions of caste. Skinner's written text is no longer multi-modal: it only inventories people groups and neglects the broader settings they inhabited. What is more, the communities are listed in a distinctly British-style table of contents under their Indian *qaum* names in caste-hierarchical order.[53] Skinner's Persian text seems deliberately aimed at a British audience: as well as giving the British Library copy to Malcolm, he presented a second 1825 copy to Captain Charles Thoresby (68th Native Infantry and agent to Jaipur 1839–44),[54] and the c. 1836 copy now in the Library of Congress to Captain James Watkins (62nd Native Infantry).[55] All three copies bear strong traces of the influences of Skinner's closest British friends: William Fraser, whose Mughal artists were responsible for the *Tashrīh*'s best illustrations;[56] and James Tod, the famous Orientalist and historian of Rajput culture (see below).[57]

At the same time, some of the illustrations Skinner commissioned still involved an intrusion of the biographical and topographical into a work meant to be ethnographic. They betray the fact that, like its mixed-race author and its illustration of the *bāzīgār*, the *Tashrīh* still contains within it multiple older modes of describing communities in India.

Paracolonial Confluences of Ethnographic Streams in the *Tashrīh*

The streams of ethnographic knowledge that fed into Skinner's grand production need to be separated to better understand what this work represents. In his introduction Skinner claimed he:

> translated in summary from the Sanskrit books of the *vedas* and *shāstras*, into a clear and simple Persian style devoid of rhetoric, the reality of the origins of the

52 Entries in Pernau and Jaffrey, *Information*; also Y Sharma, 'Art', pp. 93–241; William Dalrymple, *The Last Mughal: The Fall of a Dynasty, Delhi 1857* (London: Bloomsbury, 2006); Dalrymple and Y Sharma, *Princes*; Dalrymple, (ed.) *Forgotten Masters*; and Pernau, *Delhi College* and *Ashraf*.

53 The Library of Congress copy may be viewed at www.loc.gov/resource/rbc0001.2015rosen2076/.

54 Vashishtha, *Rajputana Agency*, pp. 165–6. 55 McBurney, *1836 Tazkirat*, pp. 7–9.

56 J P Losty and Malini Roy, *Mughal India: Art, Culture and Empire* (London: British Library, 2013), pp. 221–8; Y Sharma, 'Art', pp. 195–241; also Archer and Falk, *India Revealed*, and Darlymple, (ed.) *Forgotten Masters*.

57 Tod, *Annals*; see below and vol. i, pp. 567, 654–5; vol. ii, pp. 673–4.

peoples, along with the condition of every community's [mode of] worship, ways, peculiarities, food, clothing and occupations, etc, alongside providing illustrations of each group with their situation, clothing and occupation.[58]

The first thing to note is that he claimed he drew some caste knowledge (largely the statements on mixed-*jāti* marriages, *dharma*, *karma* and *svabhāv*) from canonical Sanskrit *dharma-shāstra* literature, which carried huge weight with the British legal authorities.[59] Secondly, 'clear, simple and devoid of rhetoric' announced an intention to add faithful observations to those classifications. Finally, the paintings *are* supposed to illustrate what is said in the text.

For a start we know that Figure 7.1 does precisely the opposite – Skinner's use of Himmat as his iconic *kalāwant* clashes with his textual description. As for the *vedas* and *shāstras*, Skinner stated in the subheading to his *kalāwant* entry that he based it on the *Brahma-vaivarta-purāṇa*, the *Mahābhārata* and the *Qissa-i Prithī Rāj* (the *Pṛithvīrāj Rāso*, a Rajasthani epic poem).[60] But not one word of Skinner's peculiar information on the *kalāwants*' caste, kinship or religious adherence comes from those texts.

That leaves us with the portions that appear to be his own 'insider' observations. These are original, and as we have seen they do resonate with what we know from other sources about the musical training, performance practices and patronage of Mughal *kalāwants*. But this portion of his information seems to be drawn more from nearby Rajasthan than Mughal Delhi. The references to the *kalāwants*' profession being to serve the Suryavanshi and Somavanshi *rājās* are followed by descriptions of *Rajput* performance contexts and subcategories of *kalāwants*, and the separate but (supposedly) related *bhāṭṭ* community, who we know from Chapter 6 were bards to the Rajput states.[61]

But these 'truer-to-life' passages also have extensive precedent in earlier Persian literature. Long before the colonial era, the Mughals and other South Asian polities that used the Persian language had their own ways of cataloguing,

[58] Skinner, *Tashrīh*, f. 6r.

[59] On normative understandings of *jāti* and their *svabhāva* (inborn propensities), *svakarman* (occupation) and *svadharma* (duty), see Mikael Aktor, 'Social Classes: Varṇa', in Patrick Olivelle and Donald R. Davis (eds.), *The Oxford History of Hinduism. Hindu Law: A New History of Dharmaśāstra* (Oxford: Oxford University Press, 2017), 60–77. On *dhārma-shāstra* and the British 'invention' of Hindu law, see Rosane Rocher, 'The Creation of Anglo-Hindu Law', in Timothy Lubin, Donald R. Davis, and Jayanth K. Krishnan (eds.), *Hinduism and Law: An Introduction* (Cambridge: Cambridge University Press 2010), 78–88.

[60] Cynthia Talbot, *The Last Hindu Emperor: Prithviraj Chauhan and the Indian Past, 1200–2000* (Cambridge: Cambridge University Press, 2015).

[61] Skinner, *Tashrīh*, *kalāwant* ff. 134v–6v; *bhāṭṭ* ff. 129v–33v.

describing and enjoying cultural difference between the people groups of Hindustan. A cursory list might include Amin Ahmad Razi's geographically organised encyclopedia of 1594, the *Haft Iqlīm* (*Seven Climes*).[62] Razi's scheme gave rise to a host of Mughal encyclopedic writings that frequently included music and musicians.[63] Another key representative is Zulfiqar al-Hussaini's mid-seventeenth-century *Dabistān-i Mazāhib* (*School of Sects*), which documents the many different religious communities in India[64] – an obvious forerunner of Skinner's beautiful illustrations of mendicants and *faqīrs*.

Most evocative, though, is the prolific *shahr-āshob* or 'city-disturber' topos, in which the city was anatomised poetically through a 'catalogue' of representative beauties, usually male, from each of the city's religious communities, professions, trades and crafts. The aim of the Mughal Persian mode of ethnography, according to Sunil Sharma, was to document and celebrate religious and social diversity united under the harmonious benevolence of the emperor (*sulh-i kull*), in accordance with the Mughals' utopian vision of the cosmopolitan Islamicate society.[65] The *shahr-āshob* mode deeply affected the 'holistic cityscape' genre in North Indian painting and prose, with Dargah Quli's and Sayyid Ahmad's potted biographies of musicians nestling in among the monuments and festivals of late Mughal Delhi.

Performing communities featured prominently in many of these inventories. The most influential on later ethnographic depictions was Abu'l Fazl's *Ā'īn-i Akbarī* (Chapter 2). This work included for the first time a whole catalogue of the communities of Hindustani musicians, dancers, acrobats, actors and other performing artists.[66] '*Kalāwants*', he wrote:

> sing *dhrupad*. The *ḍhāḍhīs* … play the instruments *ḍhaḍha* and *kingara*,[67] and commonly sing the praises of brave men on the battlefield … The *qawwāls* … sing mostly in the style of Delhi and Jaunpur, and perform Persian poetry in the [same] manner.[68]

62 Kia, 'Persianate', pp. 76–81.

63 G Khan, *Sayyid Ahmad*, pp.84–5; Sunil Sharma, 'If There Is a Paradise on Earth, It Is Here: Urban Ethnography in Indo-Persian Poetic and Historical Texts', in Sheldon Pollock (ed.), *Forms of Knowledge in Early Modern Asia: Explorations in the Intellectual History of India and Tibet, 1500–1800* (Durham, NC: Duke University Press, 2011), 240–56.

64 Aditya Behl, 'Pages from the Book of Religions: Encountering Difference in Mughal India', in Pollock, *Forms*, 210–39; Sudev Sheth, 'Manuscript Variations of Dabistān-i Maẕāhib and Writing Histories of Religion in Mughal India', *Manuscript Studies* 4.1 (2019), 19–41.

65 S Sharma, 'If There is a Paradise', 'Representations' and *Mughal Arcadia*, pp. 89–124; also Schofield, 'Emotions', pp. 9–11.

66 Abu'l Fazl, *Ā'īn-i Akbarī* (1948), pp. 271–3.

67 A small double-headed drum related to the *dhol*, and a small *vīṇā* respectively.

68 Abu'l Fazl, *Áín i Akbarí*, vol. ii, p. 142.

Of the fifteen communities of performer Abu'l Fazl described, ten appear in Skinner's *Tashrīh*, where they are written about at much greater length but in a similar observational style.[69]

Abu'l Fazl's entries on musicians became canonical information in later writings on music. His ethnographic mode also directly influenced the new, culturally mixed style of ethnographic painting that emerged in the late eighteenth century in collaboration between Mughal artists and both European and Indian patrons.

Chanchal Dadlani demonstrates that the Gentil Album, now in the Victoria and Albert Museum and painted in Awadh in 1774 for French officer Jean-Baptiste Gentil, is a close, systematic visualisation of the *Ā'īn*.[70] The folio in Figure 7.6 is the one that best corresponds to Abu'l Fazl's catalogue of performing communities – from left to right across the top, mirror images to Skinner's illustrations: a *bhānmatī*, or female sleight-of-hand trickster; a string of *bāhurūpiya*s, *bhagat*s and *bhāṅḍ*s, drummers, jugglers, dancers, satirists, actors and mimics who dressed in all sorts of costumes; a *maimūnwāla* or animal handler – and there, again, our *bāzīgār*.

Figure 7.6 Performing communities in the Gentil Album. Faizabad, 1774. IS.25: 26-1980. © **Victoria and Albert Museum, London**

[69] *kalāwants, qawwāls, ḍhāḍhīs/ḍoms, bhāṅḍs/bhagats/bhavāiyas, kanjarīs, nāṭs, bāhurūpiyas, bāzīgārs*; ibid., pp. 142–3; cf. Skinner, *Tashrīh*, ff. 1r–4v.

[70] Chanchal B. Dadlani, 'Transporting India: The *Gentil Album* and Mughal Manuscript Culture', *Art History* 38.4 (2015), 748–61, pp. 749–54.

Stretched across the bottom two-thirds of the folio is a panoply of *nāṭ*s or acrobats.

Crucially, Dadlani emphasises the equal mixing of Mughal and French modes of ethnography in this album. 'The folio', she writes:

> might easily be interpreted as a product of European Enlightenment practices, and connected to an eighteenth-century French preoccupation with encyclopaedism. However ... this album was the product of several minds and hands collaborating in a transcultural context ... the legacies of Mughal classificatory and descriptive practices, in particular those exemplified by the *A'in-i Akbari* ... are equally significant.[71]

I would argue this extends to the visual depiction of people types as well. Paintings showcasing performing artists that carefully portrayed stereotypical differences between such communities through minutely observed detail – *bīn*s, *rabāb*s and court dress for *kalāwant*s; coiled cobras, tethered mongooses and wicker baskets for *bāzīgār*s, etc. – were not remotely new in Indian art. Since the sixteenth century, Indian painters had depicted people performing solo as *nāyika*s or *rāginī*s, *jogī*s or courtiers; or grouped them together in more-or-less realistic court scenes of dazzling variety (e.g. Figures 2.1 and 2.4).[72] But in this period, a new mixed Mughal–colonial set of artistic conventions evolved for painting musicians and other performers in North India, especially in Delhi, though copious examples may be found throughout India.

These mixed conventions reflected the intermingling of British and Indian lineages of ethnographic knowledge and styles of description. The classificatory impulses of the new British rulers were coupled with a late eighteenth-century artistic fashion for the 'picturesque' that affected depictions of the Scottish Highlands as much as the Himalayan foothills.[73] This led to an upsurge in the production by Indian artists of ethnographic portraiture and scenic tableaux of various castes, occupations and religious figures (e.g. Figure 7.7), which were conjointly influenced by both older

[71] Ibid., p. 751.

[72] Jim Masselos, Jackie Menzies, and Pratapaditya Pal, (eds.), *Dancing to the Flute: Music and Dance in Indian Art* (Sydney: Art Gallery of New South Wales, 1997); Wade, *Imaging Sound*; and Joep Bor and Philippe Bruguiére, eds. *Gloire des princes, louange des dieux: patrimoine musical de l'Hindoustan du xive au xxe siècle* (Paris: Musée de la Musique, 2003).

[73] GHR Tillotson, 'Indian Architecture and the English Vision', *South Asian Studies* 7 (1991), 59–74; Dorota Kamińska-Jones, 'Aesthetics in the Services of Colonialism: The Picturesque in the Indian Context', *The Polish Journal of the Arts and Culture* 14.2 (2015), 63–82; Yuthika Sharma, 'Ghulam Ali Khan and the Delhi School of Painting', and J P Losty, 'Sita Ram', both in Dalrymple (ed.), *Forgotten Masters*, 140–70 and 172–81.

Figure 7.7 North Indian *kanchanī* or 'dancing girls'. Tanjore, c.1828. Add. Or. 62. **© The British Library Board**

Indian modes and European renderings like Balthazar Solvyns' depictions of musicians in his 1799 *Catalogue of 250 Etchings Descriptive of the Manners, Customs, Character, Dress, and Religious Ceremonies of the Hindoos.*[74] Ethnographic illustrations by Indian artists proliferated in the context of a burgeoning souvenir market among Europeans. According to Yuthika Sharma, 'by the first quarter of the nineteenth century, ethnographic portrayals of castes and occupations would have been part of most albums collected by British and European officers in India, and in wide circulation', both in India and back at home.[75]

In Mughal Delhi, where some of the best of these paintings were created, the artists were usually from hereditary lineages of Mughal master painters, and they initially created these new works in close collaboration with Company patrons like the Frasers. But the fashion was also taken up extremely widely by notable Indian patrons as well, to the point that it is

[74] Balt. Solvyns, *A Catalogue of 250 Coloured Etchings* (Calcutta: 1799); Robert L Hardgrave and Stephen M Slawek, 'Instruments and Music Culture in Eighteenth Century India: The Solvyns Portraits', *Asian Music* 20.1 (1988–9), 1–92.

[75] Y Sharma, 'Art', pp. 112–22, 196–7; Dalrymple and Sharma, *Princes*, no. 55; Yuthika Sharma, 'Mughal Delhi on My Lapel: The Charmed Life of the Painted Ivory Minature in Delhi, 1827–1880', in Supriya Chaudhuri, Josephine McDonagh, Brian H. Murray, and Rajeswari Sunder Rajan (eds.), *Commodities and Culture in the Colonial World* (London: Routledge, 2017), 15–31; Sachdeva [Jha], 'In Search', pp. 121–3, 238–58.

generally impossible to tell just by looking whether the patron was European or Indian.[76] In this new ethnographic style, the full-profile portrait of the late eighteenth-century Mughal world gave way to a new taste for front-facing portraiture and naturalistic detail (e.g. Figure 4.1 cf. Figure 7.2). In portrait mode, stereotypically dressed figures look straight at the viewer against a simple, even white background, and in several cases they are named in tiny inscriptions;[77] in scenic tableaux, equally stereotypically dressed figures are shown going about their daily business or celebrating festivals against the backdrop of important monuments or rural landscapes.

Certain subject matter was swayed by European tastes: notably, portraits of named courtesans and scenes of male audiences enjoying the *nāch* only began to proliferate furiously after c. 1750, with several such paintings depicting European patrons.[78] Some of the most beautiful paintings of Delhi courtesans were made for the Fraser brothers and Skinner, including Lallji or Hulas Lal's extraordinarily vivid 1815 portrait of the great artist Malageer (Figure 7.8).[79] Many other communities, such as Skinner's *bāzīgārs* (Figure 7.3), were depicted with exactly the same accoutrements they always had been, but in the new style.

The illustrations Skinner commissioned of performers for the *Tashrīh*, many of them painted by Mughal-lineage Fraser artists including Ghulam ᶜAli Khan,[80] are in line with all these trends. Himmat's portrait is a model of late Mughal–Company style ethnographic painting. Compare him with the mid-eighteenth-century painting of *kalāwant* ancestors at the court of Murshidabad in Figure 7.9. Both parties are dressed in exquisite Mughal robes, kneeling to play their iconic hereditary instruments, with furnishings iconic of the *majlis* beside their knees – a dazzling candelabra, a *pān* spittoon – hinting at the intoxicating effect of their enchanting voices on the assembled company. But Himmat faces us straight on, his long years of musical experience etched into every wrinkle of his lined face, his blind eyes gazing upon inner mysteries, the plectrums on the fingers of his right hand rendered with naturalistic care by a Mughal artist creating an ethnographic type for a mixed-race mercenary keen on serving the information needs of his British friends in power.

76 Y Sharma, 'Ghulam Ali Khan'. 77 e.g. IS.03525 in the Victoria and Albert Museum.

78 Walker, *India's Kathak Dance*, pp. 51–74; Joep Bor, 'The Voice of the Sarangi: An Illustrated History of Bowing in India', *Quarterly Journal of the National Centre for the Performing Arts* 15.3–4 and 16.1 (1986–7), 1–183; Pran Nevile, *Nautch Girls of India: Dancers, Singers, Playmates* (New Delhi: Ravi Kumar, 1996); Shweta Sachdeva [Jha], 'In search', pp. 112–21.

79 Alternatively spelled Malaguire. 80 Y Sharma, 'Ghulam Ali Khan', pp. 146–7.

Figure 7.8 The Mughal *tawā'if* Malageer, by Lallji or Hulas Lal. Delhi, 1815. © **Collection of Prince and Princess Sadruddin Aga Khan**

This brings me to the final stream of ethnographic knowledge that we need to consider, one that explains something of the discrepancies between Himmat's portrait and Skinner's textual description: the classical Indic stream embodied in Sanskrit and Rajasthani sources.[81] Skinner cites quite a number of 'vedic and shastric' sources in the subheadings to his entries, but one stands out: the *Qissa-i Prithī Rāj*, better known as the Rajasthani epic the *Pṛithvīrāj Rāso* (*Epic of Prithviraj*). It was Skinner's contemporary James Tod who was largely responsible for the enormous weight placed until today on the *Pṛithvīrāj Rāso* in histories of Rajasthan.[82]

Tod's own monumental *Annals and Antiquities of Rajast'han* – which is cited copiously in James Fraser's memoir of Skinner[83] – was based not just on Tod's deep experience of living in the Rajput courts as the first political

[81] Molly Emma Aitken, 'The Laud Rāgamālā Album, Bikaner, and the Sociability of Subimperial Painting', *Archives of Asian Art* 63.1 (2013), 27–58.

[82] Talbot, *Last Hindu Emperor*, pp. 13–16, 183–5.

[83] Fraser, *Military Memoir*.

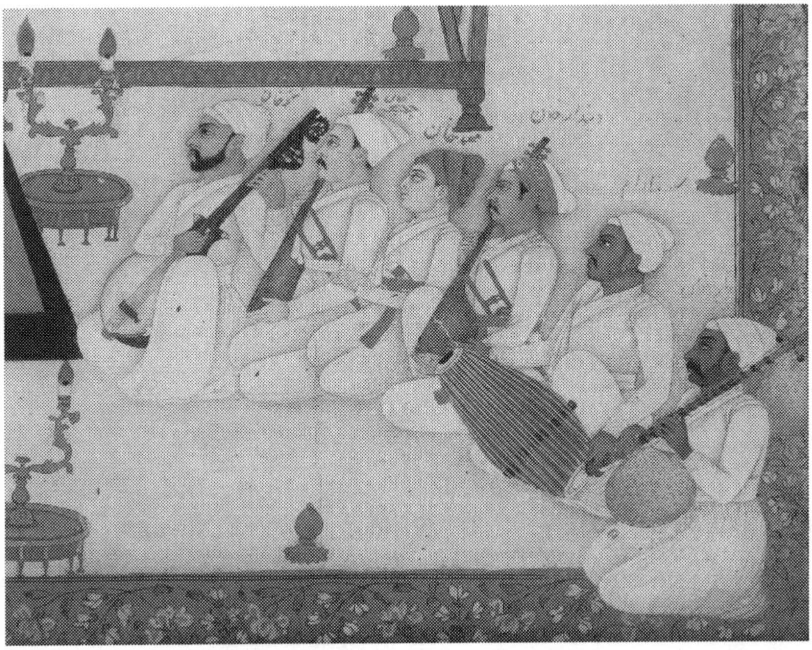

Figure 7.9 Detail of Shahamat Jang and Ikram-ud-daula giving an evening of musical entertainment; *kalāwants* L–R: Nathu Khan, Chajju Khan, Muhammad Khan, Dindar Khan, Sita Ram, Taj Khan. Murshidabad, 1748–50. **© National Museums of Scotland. Accepted in lieu of inheritance tax by H M Government and allocated to the National Museums of Scotland**

agent to Rajputana 1818–23, but on extensive reading of Sanskrit and Rajasthani manuscripts, which he gathered in the region and were interpreted for him by his principal teacher, the Jain intellectual Yati Gyanchandra.[84] Tod left most of his collection to the Royal Asiatic Society in London.[85] We already know Rajputs made detailed caste-wise surveys as early as the seventeenth century.[86] Rima Hooja's 2002 bibliographical examination confirms that caste-based genealogies, complete with material on mixed-*jāti* unions creating new castes, appear among Tod's Rajasthani manuscripts,[87] as do drawings of caste 'types' in Rajput

[84] ibid., pp. 186, 190–4.

[85] Rima Hooja, 'Tod Manuscript Collection', Unpublished Handlist (London: Royal Asiatic Society, 2002); also Florence D'Souza, *Knowledge, Mediation, and Empire: James Tod's Journeys among the Rajputs* (Manchester: Manchester University Press, 2015), pp. 195–7.

[86] Peabody, 'Cents'.

[87] Paraphrase translation of '5). Unnumbered Manuscript Containing Genealogies, etc.', in Hooja, 'Tod', pp. 76–87.

Box 7.1 The ten 'vedic and shastric' texts cited in Skinner's entries on performers that are found in Tod's collection in the Royal Asiatic Society

Mahābhārat Pūrān (Skt. Tod MS 77)
Brahma Baivart Pūrān (Skt. Tod MS 12)
Qissa-i Prithī Rāj (Hin. Tod MS 60, 82, 120, 153–4, 157, 159, 160, 1, 2, 171)
Bhavī Shūtar Pūrān (Skt. Tod MS 2)
Agnī Pūrān (Skt. Tod, MS 40)
Bhūjap Praband[h] (Skt. Tod MS 97, 135.)
Iskand Pūrān (Skt. Tod MS 25, 26)
Madam Pūrān [Padma] (MS 6)
Amarkosh (Skt. Tod MS 92)
Kurmā Pūrān (Skt. Tod MS 39)

style c. 1820. One of these depicts a mature *kalāwant bīn*-player resplendent in courtly dress.[88]

Skinner's connections with Rajasthan and Tod were multiple. Skinner took great pride in his mother's Rajput heritage, especially as a warrior. He and Tod were close friends, military associates and fellow historians and ethnographers of Mughal and Rajput localities. Skinner's Yellow Boys were Tod's frequent military escort throughout his time in the Rajput states.[89] And of the twelve 'vedic and shastric' texts Skinner cited for his entries on performing artists, ten of them remain in Tod's collection (Box 7.1). I think it is likely that Skinner got his discrepant information about the *kalāwant*s from written or oral sources collected in Rajasthan, possibly by Tod. Perhaps the information Skinner presented that can't be reconciled with the histories of Mughal imperial *kalāwant*s is to be found instead in Rajput ethnographic writings yet to be located.

In short, the paradoxical figure of Miyan Himmat Khan as *kalāwant* 'type' in Skinner's great ethnographic work acts as a divining rod, separating and bringing to the surface the multiple streams of knowledge mingling in the *Tashrīh* – Mughal, Rajput, British; Persian, Sanskrit, Rajasthani, English. I originally imagined Skinner was simply in thrall to British Orientalist attempts to use ancient Sanskrit *dharma* texts to encapsulate and control the proliferation of Hindu communities encountered in reality.[90] That the *Tashrīh* was in Persian would have made it no less of an exercise in colonial reinvention, considering Skinner's British audience. But the Persian, Rajasthani, painterly and 'from life' epistemological streams that surface in

[88] Engraving by Edward Finden after an Indian original, reproduced in D'Souza, *Knowledge*, p. 42.
[89] Tod, *Annals*, e.g. vol. 1 pp. 492, 567, 654–5. [90] Rocher, 'Creation'.

this text, thanks to Himmat's peculiar inclusion, suggest the *Tashrīh* is a great deal more than that. They betray the more complex, liminal and paracolonial position of James Skinner and of his manuscript – the synthesis of a mixed-race, multi-cultured man trying to straddle two political worlds that were pulling ever further apart as the nineteenth century wore on.

Paracolonial Musicological Modes: Modern Music Treatises, 1788–1857

What Skinner's description of the *kalāwant*s does not do, however, is tell us anything about Himmat himself; all we get are a portrait and a name. By focussing on representative types, Skinner presented much of ethnographic interest about different performing communities. But he erased the individual agents behind all that brilliant music making. Late Mughal–Company-style 'type' descriptions flatten court musicians into anonymous 'tradition bearers': picturesque servants with no voices other than the ones they sang with, whose words were largely not even understood by British audiences (Chapter 4). Such descriptions tell us nothing about individual musicians' gifts and intellectual contributions, nor about the incredible innovation in *rāga* and *tāla* underway in late Mughal musical *majālis* and theoretical writings.

For that, we need to turn to the sources Himmat and his fellow *kalāwant*s and *qawwāl*s composed themselves.

The 1780s through 1850s in North India saw the floraison of new theoretical treatises in Persian on Hindustani music, many written by Delhi *kalāwant*s and their disciples now scattered across India (see Chapter 5). These new works recognised the authority of the canonical treatises written at the seventeenth-century Mughal court, but regarded many of their technical features as outdated or obsolete. Together, these new treatises unequivocally demonstrate the emergence c. 1800 of what can only be called an incipient paracolonial modernity in Hindustani music: one that owed little debt to colonial thought, but rather grew out of an independent sense that so much had changed that the old ways of describing melody and rhythm were no longer useful, and that new modes needed to be devised.

In the field of *rāga*, three major courtly works written in the 1790s – Ghulam Raza's *Usūl al-Nag̲h̲māt* (*al-Āsafī*) (*Fundamentals of (Asaf[-ud-daula]'s) Melodies*) (c. 1790–93)[91] written for Lucknow Nawab Asaf-ud

[91] *Āsafī* is a play on the name of the dedicatee, Nawab Asaf-ud-daula; Asaf being the name of King Solomon's *wazīr*, and the Nawab of Awadh historically being the *wazīr* (*nawāb*) of the Mughal emperor. The earliest partial copy was made for Richard Johnson, who left India forever in

-Daula; Maharaja Sawai Pratap Singh of Jaipur's *Saṅgīt-sār* (*Essence of Music*) (1799);[92] and the *Nādirāt-i Shāhī* (*Choicest Pieces of the King*) (1797) composed by Mughal Emperor Shah ᶜAlam himself – show that the *rāgas* were converging on what we recognise today as their modern conception: that is to say, no longer organised on the basis of aesthetic convention, but as families grouped together purely on melodic grounds.[93]

The author of the *Usūl al-Naghmāt*, Ghulam Raza, was a hereditary *qawwāl* and a *bīn* player. His father, Delhi *qawwāl* Muhammad Panah, was a *bīn* disciple of Anjha Baras Khan (Chapter 3), and worked for Asaf-ud-daula's brother and successor Saᶜadat ᶜAli Khan, for whom the 1793/4 Salar Jung copy of the *Usūl* was made.[94] Ghulam Raza also used the 1697/8 *Shams al-Aswāt*, written by Anjha Baras' father, as the template for his palimpsest.[95] Thus the *Usūl* distilled the technical knowledge of both the *kalāwant* and *qawwāl* traditions of Mughal Delhi. At the same time, this work was distinctly modern.

Several parallel systems of describing *rāga* relationships had operated in North India since the sixteenth century.[96] Without going far into this technical subject, the *rāgas* could be grouped according to 1) motivic affinities; 2) basic scales; or 3) 'hierarchical schemes whose rationale is rarely if ever apparent'.[97] The third approach was hegemonic in the Mughal and Rajput world – the all-important aesthetic *rāgamālā* system (Chapters 2 and 5), in which the *rāginīs* were divided up between six male *rāgas* with no discernable sonic rationale. The shift to the modern conception of how *rāgas* relate to one another required the deprioritisation of the 'irrational' *rāgamālā* system in favour of grouping *rāgas* by their sonic characteristics, in tandem with developing a sufficiently detailed musical notation system. This shift is usually thought to have taken place at the turn of the twentieth century through the reformist musicology of VN Bhatkhande (Chapters 1 and 8), who proposed

February 1790. The earliest known full copies use the full title (Khuda Bakhsh, 1207 AH [1792/3 CE]; Salar Jung, 1208 [1793/4]). I am grateful to M Athar Masood for confirming these dates with me.

92 This is Miner's date, *Sitar*, p. 233; other suggestions are 1798 or 1800.

93 Lunn and Schofield, 'Desire'; Ghulam Raza, *Usūl* (1793/4); Shah ᶜAlam II, *Nādirāt-i Shāhī*, ed. I ᶜA Arshi (Rampur: Raza Library, 1944 [orig. 1797]); Pratap Singh, *Saṅgīt-sār*; also Alam and Subrahmanyam, *Writing*, pp. 418–20.

94 Zia-ud-din, *Hayy*, ff. 45r, 46r–v; Raza, *Usūl* (1793/4), f. 113v. There are at least two earlier copies; see bibliography.

95 The whole of the *Usūl* is structured closely on the *Shams*, but for explicit citations see e.g. *Usūl* (1793/4), f. 41v.

96 Harold Powers, 'Sargam Notations and *Rāg-Rāgiṇī* Theory', in Joep Bor, et al. (eds.), *Hindustani Music*, 579–671; Miner, '*Raga*'.

97 Powers, 'Sargam', pp. 584–605; also Brown [Schofield], 'Hindustani Music', pp. 177–225, and 'Ṭhāṭ System'.

a comprehensive notation system and ten *ṭhāṭh*s (scales) to use as a classificatory system for *rāgas*.[98]

It is critical to note that Bhatkhande made an extensive study of Ghulam Raza's work as a pivotal early theorist of *ṭhāṭh*.[99] Indeed, it was not Bhatkhande, but Ghulam Raza who devised the earliest known fully descriptive notation for Hindustani *rāga* examples c. 1790–3, one that uniquely brought together older Indic notations for register, pitch, duration and lyrics (Example 7.1). He then dropped the old Hanuman *mat rāga-rāginī* scheme of the *Tuhfat al-Hind* for a *rāgamālā* of his own creation, in which he placed *rāga*s and *rāginī*s in families based on clear melodic affiliations, not obscure aesthetic criteria. Crucially, Ghulam Raza did not just use *ṭhāṭh* to group his *rāgas*. It is well documented that modern musicians do *not* use shared scales to conceptualise *rāga* relationships, but common melodic motifs or *aṅga*s that build into characteristic phrases or *pakaḍ*s distinctive to each *rāga* – what Lunn and I have called soundmarks (Chapter 1).[100] Ghulam Raza's new scheme grouped *rāgas* and *rāginīs* by soundmark as well as *ṭhāṭh*. In many ways his system has more care towards modern principles of *rāga* relationships than Bhatkhande's.

On 'the writing of *tān*s', Ghulam Raza noted:

> This method is very uncommon and rare – few people know it . . . it is called *tān prastār*, that is, the rules for *writing* the *tān*s of *rāga*s and every *rāginī*, and the rules for the fixing of their *swara*s and their signs and symbols, so that the [melodic] contour of the *rāgas*, *tān*s and *swara*s may easily be understood thereby.[101]

It is possible he was inspired to devise his notation on encountering European models in Lucknow. We know the author of Edinburgh MS 585(4) found the Western method of 'writing music in books' fascinating; more importantly, Ghulam Raza wrote the earliest known partial copy of the *Usūl* for Company official Richard Johnson no later than 1790.[102] It is especially provocative that Plowden's staff notations in Chapter 4 were made in the same place as the *Usūl* only a year or two earlier.

[98] Bakhle, *Two Men*, pp. 20–49; Charles Capwell, 'Marginality and Musicology in Nineteenth-Century Calcutta: The Case of Sourindro Mohun Tagore', in Philip V Bohlman and Bruno Nettl (eds.), *Comparative Musicology and Anthropology of Music: Essays on the History of Ethnomusicology* (Chicago: University of Chicago Press, 1991), 228–43.

[99] Bhatkhande's *Hindustānī Saṅgīt Paddhati*, vol. III, cited in Powers, 'Sargam', pp. 622–3 and following.

[100] Lunn and Schofield, 'Desire', pp. 229–33; Widdess, *Rāgas*, pp. 31–5.

[101] Ghulam Raza, *Usūl* (1793/4), f. 76r.

[102] Schofield, 'Reviving', pp. 506–7; Schofield, 'Words', pp. 177–80; Richard Johnson is named in the body of the text of the British Library copy of the *Usūl* (IO Islamic 2083) as the patron; he left India in February 1790.

Example 7.1 Ghulam Raza's notation of the *sthyā'ī tān* of *rāginī* Bhairavi, and its realisation (C = Sa). *Usūl al-Naghmāt al-Āsafī*. Benares, 1793/4. Persian Mus. 2, f. 82v. **Salar Jung Museum, Hyderabad**

(a)

Pitch symbols:

- a short diagonal line above (*fatha*) the note for the high or sharpened position (*tīvra*) of the alterable *swaras* Re, Ga, Ma, Dha and Ni
- a short diagonal line below (*zīr*) the note for the low or flattened position (*komal*)
- a dot (*noqta*) for unaltered (*shuddh*) pitches — it is also apparent that *tīvra* and *shuddh* were becoming interchangeable terms for the heightened positions of Re, Ga, Dha, and Ni; and
- a longer horizontal line (*madda*) to indicate register: the three registers are indicated by one, two, or three lines above the note.

(b)

But Ghulam Raza based his new notation system entirely on earlier Indic symbols, while combining them in an unprecedented way not indebted to staff notation.

It is important to note that he adapted his register and pitch notation symbols from Ras Baras Khan's pioneering 1697/8 *Shams al-Aswāt*, the canonical work on which Ghulam Raza modelled the *Usūl*. But he added Sanskrit durational notations beneath each pitch, and then above each pitch the vocal syllables to be sung.[103] This created a complete yet wholly Indic notation for *rāga* for the first time in Hindustani music history that allows short melodies to be fully reconstructed.

[103] Ras Baras, *Shams*, pp. 105, 124–5; cf. Raza, *Usūl* (1793/4), ff. 76r–81v. Unfortunately we lack a critical edition of the *Usūl*, so it is difficult to make definitive determinations of the pitch contours of the twelve *rāgas* for which we have notations. For Example 7.1 I drew additionally on the accurate notation for Bhairav, f. 80r in the Salar Jung copy (*komal* Re, *komal* Dha, and both *komal* and *shuddh* Ni), alongside Ghulam Raza's statement f. 70r that the main scalar difference between Bhairav and Bhairavi was that Bhairavi used *komal* Ga, but it could sometimes borrow Bhairav's *shuddh* Ga.

Ghulam Raza duly reproduced the canonical descriptions of the *rāgas* and *rāginīs* of the Hanuman *mat*, which he paraphrased from the *Tuhfat*.[104] But, now armed with a precise way of writing down the melodic contours of the *rāgas*, he offered a wholly new *rāgamālā* system that grouped the six main *rāgas* with subsidiaries based only on sonic criteria (Table 7.1).[105] Again, Ghulam Raza derived the impetus behind some of his groupings from Ras Baras' own, original *rāga-rāginī* scheme, which suggests a much longer history for these melodic affinities in the practice of hereditary musicians. Several *rāginī* names appear in clusters that imply the same sonic rationale Ghulam Raza explicitly detailed a century later in his technical descriptions of each mode. But crucially, Ghulam Raza's families are also consonant with today's *rāga* families.[106]

Using Ragini Gaund as our focus (Ghulam Raza's Megh group), Lunn and I showed that Shah ᶜAlam's 1797 *Nādirāt-i Shāhī* also used the *rāgas*' soundmark relationships as its organising principle for the first time in a song collection. 'That the musical logic of these groupings strikes us as obvious from the point of view of modern, embodied and practised *raga* theory', we noted, 'attests to the modernity of Shah ᶜAlam's vision'. What is more, Harold Powers conducted an extensive technical examination of the *rāgas* in Ghulam Raza's Hindol group in comparison with Pratap Singh's 1799 *Saṅgīt-sār* and modern practice. Powers concurred that Ghulam Raza's groupings were consistent with today's conceptions, and also modernising in intent.[107]

The *Usūl* thus thoroughly reinforces the sense that the modernisation of *rāga* classification was a widespread preoccupation across North India at this time. Ghulam Raza in Awadh, the emperor in Delhi, the maharaja of Jaipur and slightly later Anup in Hyderabad were all, around the same time, independently theorising *rāga* groupings on melodic grounds. The closeness of their descriptions of the *rāgas* with today's forms demonstrates that by c. 1800 the *rāgas* were both converging on their modern sonic structures and, crucially, had attained their modern conceptual organisation by melodic, not aesthetic, criteria.

What was happening to *tāla* in the same period was even more radical: according to James Kippen 'nothing less than a rhythmic revolution that

[104] Raza, *Usūl* (1793/4), ff 40v, 42r.

[105] ibid., ff. 69v–91r; also Powers, 'Sargam', pp. 622–9. Raza, *Usūl* (1793/4), Chapter 2 Subchapter 3 and Subchapter 4 (ff. 69v–76r).

[106] e.g. his Nat family; Raza, *Usūl* (1793/4), ff. 75r–v; cf. Walter Kaufmann's Kalyan *ṭhāṭh*; Kaufmann, *Ragas*, pp. 63–116, 132–41.

[107] Lunn and Schofield, 'Desire', pp. 231–2; Powers, 'Sargam', pp. 616–38, quotation p. 638.

Table 7.1 Ghulam Raza's system cf. the Hanuman *mat*. Stars indicate the *rāgas* Ghulam Raza took from Ras Baras Khan's system

Hanuman *mat* according to the *Tuhfat al-Hind*

Bhairav	Madhamadh	Bhairavi	Bangala	Bairati	Sindhavi
Malkauns	Todi	Khambhavati	Gauri	Gunakri	Kakubha
Hindol	Bilavali	Ramkali	Desakhya	Patmanjari	Lalit
Dipak	Kedar	Karnata	Desi	Kamod	Nat
Shri Rag	Basant	Malva	Malshri	Dhanashri	Asavari
Megh	Mallar	Deskar	Bhupali	Gujri	Takka

Ghulam Raza's system in the *Usūl al-Naghmāt al-Āsafī*

Bhairav	Bhairavi*	Ramkali*	Gujri*	Khat	Gandhar*	Asavari
Malkauns	Bageshri	Todi	Desi Todi	Suha	Sughrai	Multani
Hindol	Puriya	Basant	Lalit	Pancham	Dhanashri	Marva
Shri Rag	Gauri*	Purbi*	Gaura	Triveni*	Malshri*	Jaitshri*
Megh	Madhamadh*	Gaund*	Sarang*	Badhans	Savanat	Sorath*
Nat	Chayanat*	Hamir*	Kalyan*	Kedar*	Bihagra	Aiman / Bhupali*

overturned many centuries of theory and practice'.[108] By the middle of the eighteenth century, a clear sense had emerged that the old prosody-based notations of Sanskrit treatises did not adequately reflect the cyclical divisions into weights and absences of the new and fashionable *tāla*s of the day. These were closely tied to the dances of new waves of courtesans coming through from the north-west – the very same who became wildly popular from Mughal Delhi to British Calcutta as 'Kashmiri' *nāch* girls (Chapter 4).[109] In this case, though, the written restructuring of *tāla* was more closely tied to Delhi and to Sufi circles of musical intellectuals. Ghulam Raza did play a small role, but only by publicising the new descriptive mode and categories created in 1761/2 in Delhi by his Sufi mentor, Hakim Hasan Maududi Chishti.[110]

By the Mughal period, the canonical number of *tāla*s was ninety-two.[111] In 1697/8, Ras Baras unceremoniously dispensed with these on the grounds that most were obsolete. Instead, he presented in brief, epigrammatic form what he considered to be the eleven principal *tāla*s in regular practice.[112] Six decades later, Hakim Hasan selected a somewhat different set of sixteen *tāla*s as the most important in current use. For the first time, he ordered them according to a practical logic based on the number of principal struck beats (*zarb* or *tāli*) in the cycle. Ghulam Raza reduced this set to thirteen, but in all other respects his chapter retained Hakim Hasan's organisational principles and descriptions (Table 7.2).[113]

But Hakim Hasan and Ghulam Raza were still using the Sanskrit symbols to notate these *tāla*s. The real shift towards a modern, graphical notation based on dividing the number of underlying counts (*mātra*s) in a cycle into sections (*vibhāg*s) marked by claps (*tālī*) and waves (*k͟hālī*) took place in the work of the Delhi *kalāwant*s and their disciples. It was here that Himmat and his Sufi interlocutor Ranj most powerfully asserted their original intellectual presence.

In Chapter 4 I described the new linear graphical schemes for notating *tāla* cycles that two theorists associated with Delhi *kalāwant* lineages, Zia-ud-din and our anonymous harpsichord enthusiast, independently put forward around 1788 (Example 4.3). Together they show that Ranj/Himmat were not working in a vacuum, but drawing on notations for

108 Kippen, 'Mapping', p. 254.

109 James Kippen, 'Mapping', and 'Les battements', in Bor and Bruguiére (eds.), *Gloire des princes,* 152–73.

110 Hakim Hasan Maududi Chishti, *Risāla-i Mūsīqī*, Salar Jung Museum Library, Persian Mus 7 (1761/2); Wajid ᶜAli Shah, Nawab of Lucknow, *Saut al-Mubārak* (Lucknow: private publication, 1852/3), British Library 14835.e.1, pp. 59–76;

111 Mirza Khan, *Tuhfat* (RSPA 78), ff. 242r–52r. 112 Ras Baras, *Shams*, pp. 124–6.

113 Raza, *Usūl* (1793/4), ff. 102r–10r; cf. Hakim Hasan, *Risāla.*

Table 7.2 The *tāla* systems of Ras Baras Khan, Hakim Hasan Maududi Chishti, and Ghulam Raza, cf. Ranj/Himmat

Ras Baras Khan	Hakim Hasan	Ghulam Raza	Ranj/Himmat
(not in order)	*1 zarb*	*1 zarb*	*Tā'ifa* 1: 11 *tālas*
	paṭṭa tāl		dhīmā titāla kalāwantī & dhīmā titāla qawwālī*
yektālī	ektāl*	ektāl	mārv (māja) in Arabic, Khairabadi/ādha* i.e. half dhīmā titāla
prasiddh yektālī	horī*	horī	jald titāla*/ tiwāra
	jhumra*		dhamālī
			chāchar
	2 zarb	*2 zarb*	qawwālī
rupak tāl	rupak*	rupak	laḍḍī
			tīvra*
	3 zarb	*3 zarb*	thumrī
tivrā tāl	tivra*	jald titāl/tritāl	kaharwa
	jald titāl/tritāl*	medium titāl/ brahmatāla	
	medium titāl/brahmatāla*	dhīma titāl	*Tā'ifa* 2: 7 *tālas*
	dhīma titāl*	tivra	savārī kalāwantī & savārī qawwālī*
jhaptāl/farodast (1)	jhaptāl*	surfākhta	farodast*
turangalīla/surfākhta	surfākhta*	jhaptāl	biram/das tāla
			tāla horī*
	4 zarb	*4 zarb*	jhumra*
	chautāl*	chautāl	āṛa chautāla*
	ād–chautāl*	ād–chautāl	rupak/ do-tāla*
chatlagan/savārī	savārī*	savārī	

			Tā'ifa 3: 4 *tālas*
	5 *zarb*	5 *zarb*	chautāla*
jhaptāl/farodast (2)	farodast*	farodast	ektāla kalāwantī & ektāla qawwālī*
	dobahr		bilambhitā/qaid
			bhaṇḍī
	6 *zarb*		
	sālvanaṭh (unique to Khandari family)		*Tā'ifa* 4: 5 *tālas*
			jhaptāla*
ādtāl			turangalīla*
samtāl			shish tāla
alhatālī			sūrfākhta*
prasiddh alhatālī			pashto

rhythmic cycles that were *already in use* by Delhi's *kalāwants*. But in writing the *Asl al-Usūl* they went much further and more systematically than previous writers. And their detailed notation system shows us that, like the *rāgas*, by the 1820s at the latest the *tālas* were also converging on their modern forms and were being described in recognisably modern ways.

Although it was Ranj who wrote down the *Asl*, he did so as Himmat's life-long disciple and in intimate communication with him.[114] He presented a brand new scheme for notating twenty-seven *tālas* in the living contemporary practice of Delhi's *kalāwants* and *qawwāls*, carefully differentiating how the same *tālas* were performed differently by each community. This is why Ranj devised his new scheme:

> Because the theorists of *sangīt* have not written anything in the chapters on *tāla* (*tāla-adhyāy*) regarding . . . its true realities . . . their writings on this subject are not well understood, and everyone remains uninformed. Consequently, the subject pleases nobody. [This is] because they appoint these seven words for measuring each *tāla*: a) *anudrut*; b) *drut* . . . *lagh[u]* [etc . . .] When I pondered this deeply, I realised that by *anudrut* they meant a quarter [measure]; by *drut* a half . . . by *lagh[u]* a whole [etc . . .] But the measurements indicated by these terms are not cognisable from the words themselves, nor from any other explanations. So, because I did not find the writings of previous [authors] on this subject within reach of understanding, I created some rules from my own poor intellect for understanding the truths of *tāla*. I wrote them down in a clean and tidy manner in accordance with the fashion of writing current in this age, and wholly abandoned the manner of writing espoused by previous [authors]. *I founded a new approach to explaining the truths of tāla that, to date, noone has heard of before or originated, nor anyone seen in a book. From my own poor mind alone I created and wrote down these rules*, and inaugurated this new method for the lords of good taste and intellectual discernment.[115]

Recognising the redundancy and inadequacy of an old descriptive mode, and devising something new and more fit for purpose based on empirical observation and systematic thought is the fundamental definition of modernity in Hindustani music as it has come to be understood.[116]

The *Asl*'s new scheme uses a graphical system of dots, lines, superscripts and subscripts, and is indeed simple to understand. Example 7.2 is Ranj's diagram of the first cycle in his system, *dhīmā* (slow) *titāla kalāwantī*.[117] *Tīntāl*, the sixteen-beat cycle meaning 'three claps', is still the most

[114] Ranj/Himmat, *Asl*, ff. 2r–v. [115] ibid., ff. 3r–4r; italics mine.
[116] Katz, *Lineage*, pp. 21–2, 155–8. [117] Ranj/Himmat, *Asl*, ff. 7r–8v.

Example 7.2 *Dhīmā titāla kalāwantī*, the first *tāla* in the eleven *tāla* system of the *Asl al-Usūl*, with red ink represented in grey, cf. Example 4.3

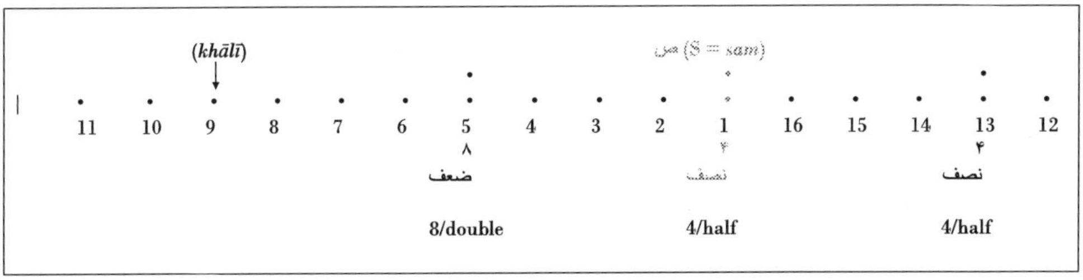

common *tāla* in Hindustani music. Although Ranj does not start his notation on the *sam*, it is identical in its basic structure to *tīntāl* today:

Using this practical and readable notation abstracted from the practice of Himmat and other Mughal *kalāwants* and *qawwāls*, Ranj went on to describe, entirely systematically, the twenty-seven *tālas* current in Hindustan, carefully differentiating the *qaum*, genre and occasion specific to each:

> The **First *Tā'ifa*** comprises eleven *tālas*: a) *dhīmā titāla kalāwantī* and *dhīmā titāla qawwālī*; b) *mārv*, which is called *māja* in Arabic, and which the accompanists of the battle standards (*ᶜalam*) during Muharram perform; c) Khairabadi, which is called *ādha*, i.e. half *dhīmā titāla*; d) *jald titāla*, which the professors call *tiwāra*; e) *dhamālī*, which the accompanists of *kalāwantī*-style *hoḷīs* play; f) *chāchar*, which the accompanists of *qawwālī*-style *hoḷīs* play; g) *qawwālī*, which is played in the *mehfil* where the *faqīrs* go into *hāl* (ecstasy); h) *laḍḍī*, which the accompanists of the *faqīrs* perform at the graves in the *dargāhs*; i) *tīvra*; j) *ṭhumrī*, which is the perfume of this age; and k) *kahārwa*, which is the *tāla* of the beautiful ones. The **Second *Tā'ifa*** comprises seven *tālas*: a) *savārī kalāwantī* and *savārī qawwālī*; b) *farodast*, which is exclusive to the *qawwāls*; c) *biram*, which is called *das tāla*; d)*tāla hoṛī* in *k͟hayāl* and *dhrupad*; e) *jhumra*, which is exclusive to the *qawwāls*; f) *āṛa chautāla*; and g) *rupak*, which is called *do-tāla*. The **Third *Tā'ifa*** comprises four *tālas*: a) *chautāla*, which is exclusive to *dhrupad*; b) *ektāla kalāwantī* and *ektāla qawwālī*; c) *balambhiyā* [*vilambit*?], which is called *qaid*; and d) *bhaṅḍī*, which is exclusive to the *naqqāls*. The **Fourth *Tā'ifa*** comprises five *tālas*: a) *jhaptāla*; b) *turangalīla*; c) *shish tāla*; d) *sūrfāk͟hta*; and e) *pashto*, which is exclusive to the Afghans.[118]

It is from a deeply practice-based and thoroughly systematic treatise like the *Asl al-Usūl* that we truly get a sense of the modern innovations and intellectual contributions of *kalāwants* and their disciples to the musical life of Delhi during the reigns of the last Mughal emperors. Note, for

[118] ibid., ff. 6r–7r; *naqqāls* = *bhaṅḍs*.

example, Ranj/Himmat's description of *ṭhumrī* as 'the perfume of this age'.[119] To my knowledge this is the first reference in the literature to *ṭhumrī* as a song genre. It became famous at the court of the last king of Lucknow, Wajid ᶜAli Shah (r. 1847–56) (Chapter 8). But here is evidence *ṭhumrī* was fashionable much earlier in Delhi, which was still clearly a major locus of musical innovation.

The evidence here, in the work of Ghulam Raza *qawwāl*, Miyan Himmat Khan *kalāwant*, and their Sufi mentors Hakim Hasan Maududi Chishti and Mir Muhammad Nasir Muhammadi Ranj, is of a clear, incipient modern vision being brought to bear on the key building blocks of Hindustani music, one that was established by the beginning of the nineteenth century. This modernity was a paracolonial one: it was not remotely dependent upon European discourse and was effected outside areas under direct British rule, though it was inevitably bound up in the changes wrought by the various modes of colonial interaction with Hindustani music that I have described throughout this book.

Who Lives? Who Dies? Who Tells Your Story?[120]

Given all this, why have we forgotten who Himmat was, or even that he existed, let alone played a key role in modernising how the Hindustani *tāla*s are conceptualised? The violent watershed of the Uprising of 1857 looms large here (Chapter 8). But so does the fact that Himmat had no sons to pass his traditions onto; he was the last of the direct Khandari line.

Himmat set about trying to preserve his musical contributions for posterity in three ways – two of them innovations. The first was conventional: to make his deceased brother's son Rag Ras Khan his disciple, and teach him everything he knew. And he achieved his ambition: Rag Ras became a brilliant *bīn* player. But he died young.[121] His second move was co-creating the *Asl al-Usūl*: passing all the secrets of his family's rhythmic traditions to the man he trusted more than any other, himself a music scholar: the *sajjāda-nishīn* of Khwaja Mir Dard's shrine. But in the aftermath of the Uprising, when writers on music were desperately trying to recover the tattered shreds of an endangered tradition and put them into the hands of the masses through Urdu print publishing – to save them that

[119] ibid., f. 6v.

[120] Lin Manuel Miranda and Jeremy McCarter, *Hamilton: The Revolution* (New York: Little, Brown, 2016).

[121] SA Khan, *Āsār* (1847), p. 227; Najm, *Naghma*, f. 211v.

way – they missed the *Asl* entirely, going back to the Sanskrit notations for rhythm that were in the canonical texts they could more easily get their hands on, and then reinventing the wheel, devising new notations for a radically altered musical economy.[122]

Finally, breaking with his community's traditions,[123] Himmat took on his daughter's son, Mir Nasir Ahmad, as his last *bīn* disciple. Sayyid Ahmad wrote of him:

> He was famous for his singing as well as for playing the veena [*bīn*], and he took both the arts to a zenith. Those who preceded him possessed not even one-tenth of his vocal and instrumental skills. After his grandfather's death, he also sang and played the instrument in assemblies in front of Khwaja Muhammad Nasir, on the second and twenty-fourth of every month.[124]

It was Mir Nasir Ahmad who was the very last *bīnkār* to the very last Mughal emperor, Bahadur Shah Zafar. And it was only by sheer luck that he survived the Uprising. Nasir's father was a *sayyid* and a highly ranked Delhi nobleman. In the chaotic violence after the British retook Shahjahanabad (Chapter 8), Nasir was rounded up as a rebel, one of the emperor's personal cohort. It was only because the brother of the Raja of Kapurthala, Bikramjit Singh, recognised him and assured the British that Nasir was 'just' a musician that he was not summarily executed. He entered Bikramjit Singh's service and died in Kapurthala sometime in the 1860s, where his tomb (*mazār*) still stands, slowly being consumed by foliage.[125]

It was there, in Kapurthala, that the two earliest and most important of the new wave of writers on Hindustani music, publishing in Urdu print for a mass audience, found the last *bīn* player to the last Mughal emperor, still keeping the flame of Mughal musical traditions alight. Nasir taught the first of these, Mardan ᶜAli Khan, himself; and he entrusted his secrets to the second, Sadiq ᶜAli Khan, because he was already a disciple of Nasir's lineage.[126] What is left of Nasir's *taᶜlīm* (instruction) thus still remains to us in two published works of the 1860s – Mardan ᶜAli Khan's <u>*Gh*</u>*uncha-i Rāg* (*Rosebud of Rāg*) (1862/3), and Sadiq ᶜAli's *Sarmāya-i ᶜIshrat* (*Treasury of Pleasure*) (1869).

[122] See e.g. Mardan ᶜAli, <u>*Gh*</u>*uncha* (1862/3); Sadiq ᶜAli, *Sarmāya* (1869).

[123] Imam Khan, *Maᶜdan* (1925), p.44. [124] SA Khan, *Asār* (2018), p. 257.

[125] Kirit Singh's PhD dissertation takes up the story of Mir Nasir Ahmad's biological and discipular lineages down to Rajkumari Lalita Khanna (1932–2021); 'Sikh Patronage of Hindustani music and Śabad Kīrtan in Colonial Punjab, 1857–1947', Unpublished PhD Dissertation (SOAS, University of London, 2022), pp. 43–63; see also Kapuria, 'Music', pp. 263–4; Mardan ᶜAli, <u>*Gh*</u>*uncha*, pp. 135–6; Sadiq ᶜAli, *Sarmāya*, pp. 11–12, 105.

[126] Mardan ᶜAli, <u>*Gh*</u>*uncha*, pp. 135–6; Sadiq ᶜAli, *Sarmāya*, pp. 11–12, 105.

Ironically, then, it was less in the bodies of Himmat's sons and grandsons that his traditions lived on, than in the written word. But while his traditions may have survived, memory of him did not. If Himmat is remembered at all these days, it is merely as the venerable blind *kalāwant*, transported to the inner spiritual realm of pure musical sound, who graces the pages of the *Tashrīh al-Aqwām* James Skinner gave to John Malcolm in 1825. Even then, Himmat is remembered only as a voiceless ethnographic 'type', rather than as an individual with his own truly remarkable biography and ground-breaking intellectual contribution.

In the way of the unworldly Sufi, reunited in death with his reed bed, perhaps he would not have minded.

8 | Orphans of the Uprising: Late Mughal Echoes and 1857

Discussion and Conclusions

Know this, oh heart: even a song of grief is a piece of luck,
For this instrument of existence will become voiceless one day.
Mirza Asadullah Khan Ghalib (1797–1869)[1]

The Departure of the Last King's Palanquin

It was autumn 1856 when the precious packet of manuscripts finally arrived at Basit Khan's temporary residence by the Ganges in Sahibganj, smelling of ink and mildew and coal smoke, but miraculously dry and undamaged from its 600-mile river journey south and eastwards to Bihar. He opened it with trembling hands: yes, they were all there – the *Sangīt Sarāvartī*,[2] the *Shams al-Aswāt* and the *Usūl al-Naghmāt*, scrawled in an untidy, hurried hand on cheap paper – but he had asked the scribe for his fastest service, and Mir Muhammad ᶜAli had done his best.[3] The elderly *kalāwant*, musician to the last king of Lucknow and one of the greatest *dhrupad rabāb* players of his day,[4] clasped the fresh manuscripts to his breast with profound thankfulness. They were all that was left to him of his forefathers' musical knowledge: they, and the great storehouse of musical treasure that he carried with him in his own, ageing body.

It had all happened so suddenly in the end. It had been clear for years that the British loathed the last king of Lucknow's love of music, dance and extravagantly expensive theatricals of his own devising – and especially his countless affairs with low-born musicians and dancers, dozens of whom

[1] Translation based on Frances W Pritchett, *A Desertful of Roses: The Urdu Ghazals of Mirza Asadullah Khan Ghalib*, *ghazal* 90 verse 4 www.columbia.edu/itc/mealac/pritchett/00ghalib/index.html#index.

[2] Alternatively spelled *Sangīt Sarāvatī* (attr. Rashik Kalyan, Khuda Bakhsh Oriental Public Library, hl. 2782) or *Sarāvālī* (attr. Inayat Khan ᶜAli, British Library, Delhi Persian, 1502d).

[3] Basit Khan, Collection; colophon, *Sangīt Sarāvartī*, Khairabad, 12 July 1856 (p. 30); colophon, *Usūl*, 28 August 1856 (p. 102); Katz, *Lineage*, pp. 50–2.

[4] Imam Khan, *Maᶜdan* (1925), p. 33; Miner, *Sitar*, pp. 60–7.

he married.[5] The last Nawab of Awadh, Wajid ʿAli Shah (r. 1847–56, d. 1887), was a prolific poet and song-writer, a highly trained musical performer and an intensely involved impresario of music, dance and drama. He is still known today for his pioneering innovations in the art-song *ṭhumrī*, the Shiʿa lament known as *marsiya*, *kathak* choreography and modern theatre.[6] He was also a serious intellectual: among other things, he wrote the last known Persian treatise on Hindustani music, the *Saut al-Mubārak* (*Blessed Sound*), which he published at his private lithographic printing press in 1852/3.[7] The king informed his readers that, having read the canonical works on music such as the *Usūl al-Naghmāt*, the *Khulāsat al-ʿAish*, the *Saṅgīta-darpaṇa* and so on, he found that these writings were largely in tune with what he had learnt through his lifetime of observation, listening and practice. So he set these old works aside and wrote something new, 'based on my own past experiments'. His treatise includes, for the first time, a chapter on dance *gat*s (Chapter 4), which has acted ever since as the founding text for modern *kathak*.[8]

The extraordinary amount of time and money the king spent on music and dance made sense to Basit Khan. For it was all that was left to Wajid ʿAli Shah of his sovereignty. The Nawab firmly believed that music's potency – its power to make kings – was present in the *rāga* still: in his *dhrupad* studies with Basit's brother Pyar Khan and *sitār* lessons with Qutub ʿAli Khan; and in his devotion to song and dance extravaganzas retelling the story of Lord Krishna and his human consort Radha in which all spectators, as well as his bevy of women performers and *kalāwant* and *mirāsī* musicians, had parts to play.[9] The king repeatedly used music's esoteric powers to control and synchronise the emotions of those he ruled over. 'I began to intone my own finely-balanced *ghazal* in Jhinjhoti *rāg*', he wrote in the 1849 memoir of his romantic exploits, the *ʿIshqnāma*. 'Ecstasy from my music took my mocking mistress by surprise, and she lost her grasp of her mind and senses. At last she clasped my hand and began to declare her love, *but I did not exploit her burning.*'[10] In fact, he argued,

5 Wajid ʿAli Shah, Nawab of Lucknow, *ʿIshqnāma*, Royal Collection, RCIN 1005035 (1849/50); translated into modern Urdu as the *Parīkhāna*, ed. Tehseen Sarwari (Karachi: n.p., 1958).

6 Williams, 'Hindustani Music'; Rosie Llewellyn-Jones, *The Last King in India: Wajid Ali Shah* (London: Hurst, 2014), pp. 50–61.

7 ʿAli Shah, *Saut*. 8 ibid., pp. 2, 6, 83–91; Walker, '"Nautch" Reclaimed'.

9 Imam Khan, *Maʿdan* [1925], pp. 33, 46; Williams, 'Hindustani Music', pp. 98, 118–19, 164–6.

10 ʿAli Shah, *Parīkhāna*, pp. 114–5; tr. Williams, 'Hindustani Music', p. 101.

in order to properly channel the powers of the *rāga*, a singer had to have complete control over his erotic self:

The result of my diligent labour was that [master musicians, performers, and music lovers] flocked to my side. From a surfeit of savouring and listening to me, most of them lowered their heads and shed copious pearly tears. Those who put their heads out of their houses and shops became silent like paintings ... Many suddenly entered the world of spiritual surrender ... Often when I sang *kharaj* [the note Sa] when I was in solitude, a light like the moon fell upon the door and wall. When I stopped singing *kharaj*, there was no light; and then when I started up again the light returned. [The reason for my powers is that] when I have sexual intercourse, I hold back my semen, so that I am able to enjoy being with women but the *swara* does not dissipate ... From the time the joy of the sevenfold *swaras* entered my heart, I had very little intercourse, and began the practice of holding back my ejaculations, until at last I brought my passions under my control. The desired result of all this is the music of the *swaras*.[11]

Believing he had mastered his passions, the king did, in fact, turn his attentions and considerable intelligence to more serious matters of worldly administration. In 1850 he wrote a manual for government, the *Dastūr-i Wājidī* (*Regulations of Wajid*), for the use of his chief minister that shows he knew exactly what was going on in his kingdom, and how it needed to be governed.[12] But by this time, the East India Company effectively ran everything of importance in Awadh. Music, dance and drama were the last remaining domains in which Wajid ᶜAli Shah was able to exercise his sovereign powers as king to control the daily movements and, most importantly, the hearts of his people.[13]

But the Company wilfully refused to understand the serious place of pleasure in his sovereignty, and despised him for it with vehemence. The Resident of Lucknow William Sleeman denounced him thus in 1852:

The king has done nothing to improve his administration – abstained from no personal indulgence – given no attention whatever to public affairs ... and the sufferings of the many millions subject to his rule. His time and attention are devoted entirely to the pursuit of personal gratifications – he associates with none but such as those who contribute to such gratifications – women, singers, and eunuchs; and he never, I believe, reads or hears read any petition from his suffering subjects.[14]

[11] ᶜAli Shah, *Saut*, pp. 6–7. [12] Llewellyn-Jones, *Last King*, pp. 99–100.
[13] Schofield, 'Musical Culture'. [14] Sleeman, *Diary*, p. 188.

Figure 8.1 The Nawab of Awadh Wajid ᶜAli Shah leaves his throne empty to accompany one of his dancers and mistresses Sarafraz Mahal on the lowly *tabla*; immediately behind him stands his favourite *sitār* player Ghulam Raza Razi-ud-daula. Wajid ᶜAli Shah, *ᶜIshqnāma*. Lucknow, 1849/50. RCIN 1005035, f. 242r. **Royal Collection Trust © Her Majesty Queen Elizabeth II 2015**

Already in 1848, the previous Resident Colonel Richmond had 'removed and banished' Basit's chief rival for the king's pleasure, the *sitār* player Ghulam Raza Razi-ud-daula (Figure 8.1),[15] along with a number of other musicians, for their 'improper' influence over Wajid ᶜAli Shah, who had elevated several unqualified favourites to government office.[16] Basit may have felt a secret thrill of Schadenfreude over this development. As clever and original a *sitār* player as he was, socially Razi-ud-daula was nothing but an overweeningly ambitious *ḍom* – the lowest class of musician communities.[17] It would have offended Basit's *kalāwant* sensibilities that one so unworthy had been promoted so highly in the Nawab's court.[18]

But in 1856 the Company finally stopped procrastinating on the Awadh question, and used the king's supposed 'pursuit of personal gratifications' as their excuse to strip him of all his remaining powers through imposing

[15] Not to be confused with the author of the *Usūl al-Naghmāt*.

[16] NAI Foreign Political 08/07/1848 nos. 64 and 65.

[17] Williams, 'Hindustani Music', pp. 102–12; Allyn Miner, 'The Scandalous Ghulam Raza', unpublished paper, Annual Conference on South Asia (Madison, 2013); Imam Khan, *Maᶜdan* [1925], pp. 49–50; Skinner, entry on *ḍoms*, *Tashrīh*, ff. 144v–46r.

[18] 'The *ustāds* disavow his style, and the best connoisseurs are ashamed of it'; Imam Khan, *Maᶜdan* [1925], pp. 44–5; see also Llewellyn-Jones, *Last King*, pp. 107–8.

a new treaty. When the king refused to sign away the last shreds of his dignity, the new Resident James Outram deposed him forthwith and annexed his kingdom. Five weeks later, a shocked Wajid ᶜAli Shah set off in a train of bullock carts, weeping, intent on travelling all the way to England to plead his case in person to his new sovereign, Victoria Regina.[19]

They say that Basit Khan was there that unforgettable day; indeed, that he followed in his king's entourage, himself weeping, strumming his *rabāb* gently, accompanying the last Nawab out of Lucknow as he sang his great Rag Bhairavi *ṭhumrī*, 'Babul Mora', the lament of the newly-wed bride leaving her natal home forever:

babul morā naihar chhūṭo jāye
chār kahār mil morī ḍoliyā uṭhāye
morā apnā-begāna chhūṭo jāye

Father, my maternal home is left behind.
Four water-carriers together lift up my palanquin;
what's mine, what's not, it's all being left behind.[20]

Wajid ᶜAli Shah never made it to England, only as far as Calcutta, where – when the whole of Awadh rose up in revolt in 1857 and joined the great Uprising against what the British had done – he was imprisoned for a time in Fort William, and never again permitted to return home. Like the last Mughal emperor, Bahadur Shah Zafar, exiled to Rangoon for his role as figurehead of the Uprising and buried there in 1862 in an unmarked grave, Wajid ᶜAli Shah died in exile in 1887, having recreated a musical paradise at Garden Reach that had a profound impact on the burgeoning modern music scene among élite Westernised Bengalis in the capital of the British Indian empire, Calcutta.

But that story is someone else's to tell.[21]

Writing on Music in Late Mughal India

The music treatises copied for Basit Khan in such haste as he departed Lucknow demonstrate once and for all the centrality that writing on music had assumed by 1856 in Hindustan and the Deccan, even – perhaps especially – for hereditary *ustāds* in the Mughal *kalāwant* lineages. Basit and his brothers Pyar and Jaffar, all of them *kalāwant dhrupad* singers and

[19] Llewellyn-Jones, *Last King*, pp. 16–17. [20] Katz, *Lineage*, pp. 30–32.
[21] See Richard David Williams, *Scattered Court*.

players of the *rabāb* and *sursingār*, were sons of Miyan Chajju Khan, who together with his brother Jivan had come to Lucknow during the reign of Asaf-ud-daula (r. 1775–97). It is a little difficult to be sure of their *bānī*. Both the *Sarmāya-i ᶜIshrat* (1869) and the *Maᶜdan al-Mūsīqī* (completed sometime shortly after the Uprising)[22] agree that Chajju belonged to the Gorari *bānī* of Tansen.[23] But the earlier 1845 *Naghma-i ᶜAndalīb* states that Chajju was Adarang's son, which would place him in the Khandari *bānī*.[24] Either way, it doesn't matter much: as we have seen, the two lineages of Tansen and Sadarang had been intermarrying and intermingling their family secrets for over a century by this point.

More importantly, the two canonical treatises Basit received in Sahibganj, the *Shams al-Aswāt* and the *Usūl al-Naghmāt*, together encapsulate two of the overarching umbrella stories I have unfurled in the course of this book. Firstly, they illuminate the crucial role played by the Delhi *kalāwant* and *qawwāl* lineages in preserving and innovating Hindustani music theory in writing, as well as in embodied form, throughout the late Mughal period. Secondly, they show the shifting weight of cultural power from imperial Delhi to other flourishing centres of Hindustani musical culture c. 1748–1858, while at the same time demonstrating that Delhi's musical traditions and its attested *ustāds* retained their role as the ultimate arbiters of élite musical authority.

Ras Baras Khan, the son of our Mughal Orpheus Khushhal Khan Gunasamudra, was the hereditary head of Tansen's Gorari *bānī* when he wrote the *Shams al-Aswāt* in 1697/8 for the last 'great' Mughal Emperor Aurangzeb. His treatise is simultaneously a translation of canonical Sanskrit *saṅgīta-shāstra* into Persian, and a distillation of the Gorari *bānī*'s own unique embodied inheritance. Ras Baras' son, Anjha Baras, physically carried that inheritance faithfully into the 1760s, and beyond that, too, in the bodies of his sons. But he also married into the Khandari *bānī* of Sadarang, and thus taught both Gorari and Khandari *bānī*s to his many disciples – some of whom, including the Delhi *qawwāl* Muhammad Panah, were drawn inexorably to the newer, brighter lights of Awadh.

It was Muhammad Panah's son, Ghulam Raza *qawwāl*, who wrote the *Usūl al-Naghmāt* for the Nawab of Awadh, in the same era that Chajju and

[22] The date on MSS Urdu 143 is 1855/6 CE, but several portions mention the Uprising in past tense, e.g. Imam Khan, *Maᶜdan* (1925), p. 63; Regula Burkhardt Qureshi, 'Other Musicologies: Exploring Issues and Confronting Practice in India', in Nicholas Cook and Mark Everist (eds.), *Rethinking Music* (Oxford: Oxford University Press, 1999), 311–35, pp. 324–6, 333.

[23] Sadiq ᶜAli *Sarmāya*, p. 105; Imam Khan, *Maᶜdan* [1925], pp. 32–4.

[24] Najm, *Naghma*, f. 211v.

Jivan Khan came to Lucknow, that another Delhi-lineage *qawwāl* Miyan Ghulam Nabi Shori was transforming *ṭappa* into a genre Lucknow could call its own, and that celebrity courtesan Khanum Jan was illuminating all the best *majālis* with her *ghazal*-singing and elegant *gat*s. In composing the *Usūl*, a Delhi-lineage *qawwāl* took the century-old authoritative writings of a Delhi *kalāwant* and added to it his own considerable original modern spin, based on his practice-informed assessment that music had changed and needed theorising anew. His work was not entirely unaffected by the Company's gradual encroachment on Indian terrain, with those *firangīs*' fascinatingly exotic way of writing the sounds of music into books, and their penchant for spending their ill-gotten gains on Indian musical collectibles.[25] But overwhelmingly it was for and in Nawabi Lucknow that Ghulam Raza reconceptualised the Mughal *rāga* system for its musically accomplished ruler Asaf-ud-daula, as a monument to him and his innovative courtly culture. Thus did Ghulam Raza ensure that the lamp lit in Delhi continued to burn brightly and truer than ever in its fashionable new home.

Crucially, though, he did so in ways that paralleled other reconceptualisation efforts independently underway in multiple locations across the old empire, in Jaipur, Hyderabad, Delhi and elsewhere. Together these efforts demonstrate the extraordinary innovation, intellectual creativity and considerable adaptability to change of Indian musical intellectuals, patrons and literate performers in the decades around 1800. As I have shown in these pages, Hindustani music's modernity dates back to the very late eighteenth century, not the turn of the twentieth. The way we conceptualise *rāga*s and *tāla*s today, the full range of the repertoire of what is now called North Indian classical music and the social organisation of musicians into household-based stylistic guilds, were all fully in place by the reign of Akbar Shah (r. 1806–37). And while the East India Company was *not* epiphenomenal to the changes both underpinning and being described in all this new writing on music, the modernisation of Hindustani music was a paracolonial, not a colonial, one – a modernisation that Indians developed alongside, beyond and independently of the colonial state, mostly outside the Company's directly ruled territories, in fact; and, crucially, not indebted to colonial epistemologies, though individual writers sometimes took inspiration from discrete European practices. The classic Indic–Persianate aesthetic dating back to the early Mughal and Rajput world, of borrowing and reusing the ideas of others to make things afresh, remains

[25] Schofield, 'Words', pp. 171–96.

fully on display in these late writings and paintings, repurposed once again to serve the needs of a changed musical world now under relentless British encroachment and occupation.

Collecting and Control: The Early Colonial Perspective

Over the course of this book, I have traced the sustained upsurge in various modes of describing Hindustani music and musicians on paper – in words, notations, diagrams and paintings – from the musical golden age of the reign of Muhammad Shah Rangile until the British Crown finally took control after the catastrophe of the Uprising, removing the Company and the last Mughal emperor in one clean sweep. In this final chapter I answer the 'why' question' of Chapter 1: why did Indian authors (primarily, but also Europeans and people of mixed race) write so prolifically about music and musicians in so many new and renewed ways during this tumultuous century of political change – especially when they considered it to be impossible?

The answers differ depending on whether we look at the question from the late Mughal or the early colonial point of view. I will bring the colonial perspective to the surface first, because I have deliberately left it submerged for much of this book in order to foreground Indian and mixed-race voices and their considerable independence. It is significant that a large number of the manuscripts and especially paintings I have drawn upon are held in European – and for the manuscripts, predominantly British – libraries and museums. All of them were collected in India during the period covered in this book by Company representatives and other Europeans who brought them home from India as souvenirs, and eventually donated them to public collections. Sometimes Europeans straightforwardly bought manuscripts and paintings from local dealers who generally served wealthy Indian buyers, especially as the contents of imperial and courtly libraries began to flood onto Indian book markets through the course of the eighteenth century.[26] By the same mechanism that Asaf-ud-daula acquired the magnificent imperial copy of Shah Jahan's *Pādishāhnāma* with its intensely sovereign aura,[27] so Richard Johnson picked up his gorgeously illuminated

[26] John Seyller, 'The Inspection and Vaulation of Manuscripts in the Imperial Mughal Library', *Artibus Asiae* 57.3–4 (1997), 243–349, p. 243.

[27] Acquired c. 1780–90; ᶜAbd al-Hamid Lahori, *Padishāhnāma*, Royal Collection Trust, RCIN 1005025 (1656–7).

Shah Jahan-era *Sahasras* that he sold to the India Office with his entire collection in 1807 to pay off his debts.[28]

In other cases, Indians presented manuscripts and paintings to Europeans as gifts: Asaf-ud-daula's successor as Nawab, Sa^{c}adat ^{c}Ali Khan, sent the *Pādishāhnāma* to King George III in 1799, the same year Mahlaqa Bai gave John Malcolm her *dīwān*; and it was also to Malcolm that James Skinner presented the deluxe British Library copy of his *Tashrīh al-Aqwām* in 1825. Others were unquestionably loot: all of the unique treatises documenting Tipu Sultan's musical innovations, for example, were plundered by British troops after they killed him at the siege of Srirangapatanam in 1799;[29] and the rump of the Mughal library, looted after the siege of Delhi in 1857 – its musical holdings already attenuated after a century of repeated pillaging and selling off – was purchased, mixed in with other pilfered manuscripts and entire libraries sequestered as prize by the government of India in 1859.[30]

But many other writings on music and paintings of musical content were freshly commissioned by Europeans explicitly for their collections, to be made for them by Indian intellectuals, scribes and artisans and then extracted from India: the Bodleian Library copy of the *Khulāsat al-^{c}Aish* with its unique introduction made for Sir Gore Ouseley; Sophia Plowden's spectacular illustrated *Album* of song texts; the veritable library of Persian, Sanskrit and Brajbhasha writings on music that Richard Johnson ordered alongside the hundreds of *rāgamālā* paintings he collected and commissioned; etc.[31]

As I have suggested, interest among Europeans who took to Indian music and dance during this transitional century was genuine, and for some individuals constituted a sustained intellectual fascination and emotional solace. For most collectors, accumulating manuscripts and paintings largely fed a project of self-reinvention from poor relations and black sheep to wealthy and sophisticated connoisseurs, with the primary aim of impressing the élites of Europe when they returned home as (hopefully) rich nabobs.[32] But those whose Indian interests ran deeper such as Richard

[28] Dated 1656; British Library, I O Islamic 1808.

[29] Ethé, *India Office Catalogue*, Columns 1123–6.

[30] Shaheen Islamuddin, 'Legalising the Plunder in the Aftermath of the Uprising of 1857: The City of Delhi and "Prize Agents"', *Proceedings of the Indian History Congress* 72.1 (2011), 670–82; Nur Sobers-Khan, 'Muslim Scribal Culture in India Around 1800: Towards a Disentangling of the Mughal Library and the Delhi Collection', in Christopher D Bahl and Stefan Hanß (eds.), *Scribal Practice and the Global Cultures of Colophons, 1400–1800* (London: Palgrave Macmillan, 2022), 197–218.

[31] Schofield, 'Words', pp. 177–80.

[32] Jasanoff, *Edge*, p. 111.

Johnson, I have argued, desired at least as much to impress Indian élites more immediately at hand with their 'near-native' fluency in late Mughal codes of social etiquette and connoisseurship.[33] As noted especially in Chapter 4, such interest was frequently reciprocated in this transitional century by *nawābs*, *rājas* and wealthy Indian merchants.[34]

But there are aspects running beneath the surface of this rash of European acquisition of Indian musical collectibles that are distinctly troubling. In the first instance, the only reason East India Company men and women could behave like wealthy Indian connoisseurs at all, bespeaking and purchasing all these manuscripts and paintings, was because they had made the huge amounts of excess capital needed to do so by trading in India on grossly exploitative terms in non-musical goods such as textiles and opium – not to mention the Company's imposition with menaces of eye-watering taxes on the Indian population, which they then expropriated to China to pay for tea.[35] As Dalrymple notes, Robert Clive's victory over Siraj-ud-daula at Palashi (Plassey) in 1757 initiated:

> a period of unbounded looting and asset-stripping by the Company which the British themselves described as the 'shaking of the pagoda tree'. From this point, the nature of British trade changed: £6 million had been sent out in the first half of the century, but very little silver bullion was sent out after 1757. Bengal, the sink into which foreign bullion disappeared before 1757, became, after Plassey, the treasure trove from which vast amounts of wealth were drained without any prospect of return.[36]

Secondly, this commissioning and collecting of musical manuscripts and paintings was *itself* extractive – an assuaging of an insatiable European hunger for what I have called India's 'auditory picturesque', with no thought of benefit to the Hindustani musical field because these items were *intended* to be removed from the country. Sir William Jones detailed the intensity of labour required to accrete the information that went into his 1784 'On the Musical Modes of the Hindoos', the first English-language publication on Hindustani music. He noted that Indian musicians frequented concerts of European music; that Europeans had plentiful opportunity to study Indian instruments from master musicians; and that they all had 'easy access to approved *Asiatic* treatises on musical

[33] Schofield, 'Words', p. 178.

[34] Takako Inoue, 'The Reception of Western Music in South India Around 1800', Summer International Symposium, *Orient on Orient: Images of Asia in Eurasian Countries* (Hokkaido University, July 2010), 69–96.

[35] Dalrymple, *Anarchy*, pp. 64, 143, 209. [36] ibid., p. 134, also xxviii.

composition'. Jones conversed frequently with Sanskrit *paṇḍits* on music theory, unquestioningly accepting their statements as authoritative; acquired several manuscripts in Indian languages on music; extensively consulted Richard Johnson's massive *rāgamālā* collection; borrowed several manuscripts from Colonel Polier and had them copied; and got a German violinist to play along with a '*Hindoo* lutanist' to conduct practical experiments.[37] He then published his findings exclusively for the benefit of the European 'we'; and for English-reading eyes only.

There are distinct resonances here with Dylan Robinson's idea of 'hungry listening' in settler orientations to Canada's indigenous soundworlds. While British and other European individuals may have felt strong, even overpowering, emotional affinities with what they heard in Hindustani music, they did so from a 'colonial listening positionality' – a profoundly asymmetrical mode of perception with an extractive approach to nature, ideas, culture, knowledge, etc. at its heart, which heard even the ephemeral phenomenon of music as a resource to be extracted, like Sambhar's salt.[38] Several rare treatises now lie only in European or American collections – the extraordinarily important Edinburgh MS 585(4) and the *Hayy al-Arwāh*, for instance – as do tens of thousands of unique paintings taken out of India into private and public collections abroad.

It needs to be noted, however, that considerably more copies of most of the writings on music I have discussed in this book were made for Indian patrons and performers, and many, including unique works, remain in South Asian libraries. It should also be clear that European patronising, commissioning, and collecting activities did not have noticeable negative impacts on the Indian musical field during this transitional century; though I will suggest below that they did have *unintended* effects. Crucially, 'colonial discourse' was wholly irrelevant to the epistemologies of writing about Hindustani music in Persian and regional languages c. 1748–1858; writers in these languages manifestly did not care what Europeans were saying about their music. If anything, Mughal epistemologies remained hegemonic even in English – Augustus Willard's 1834 'Treatise on the Music of Hindoostan' retained the Mughal palimpsestic structure of being modelled, citing verbatim without acknowledgement, on the *Tuhfat al-Hind*.[39]

37 William Jones, 'On the Musical Modes of the Hindoos: Written in 1784 and Since Much Enlarged', in Sourindro Mohun Tagore (ed.), *Hindu Music from Various Authors*, 2nd. ed., (Calcutta: Bose, 1882), pp. 133–42.

38 Dylan Robinson, *Hungry Listening: Resonant Theory for Indigenous Sound Studies* (Minneapolis: University of Minnesota Press, 2020), pp. 10–14.

39 Schofield, 'Reviving', pp. 507–9; Willard, 'Treatise'.

Rather, what did have profound impacts on the musical field were material and superstructural changes that gained traction across India in this century: British notions of the proper uses of space, time and resources; ways of doing business; employment of musical labour; interference in older economic modes; civic regulations and jurisprudence; new technologies and foreign goods; and significant acts of actual (not epistemic) violence. It was concrete acts of interference, like the Company's swingeing cut to the Nazim of Murshidabad's budget for musicians, Ludlow's curtailment of payments to *bhāṭṭ*s and *chārans*, and the forced exile of Wajid ᶜAli Shah that led to consequential damage and change to North India's musical life. It was *not* theoretical arcana like Jones' antiquarian tract on the minutiae of 'Musical Modes', widely unknown to Indian readers before its republication in 1875 by Bengali music reformer Sourindro Mohun Tagore.[40]

It is here that representative descriptions of *types* of musicians reveal another reason why Europeans wrote about music or consumed musical collectibles as the eighteenth century gave way to the nineteenth (Chapters 6 and 7). That reason was control: the gathering of knowledge about the people the Company ruled over in order to guide efficient governance of their Indian possessions. This is an old story in the historiography of colonial India, and does not need revisiting here.[41] But it is worth noting that sources for music history that are more deliberately oriented towards British eyes and ears, including in Indian languages – official Company records, published travel writings, ethnographic descriptions – do support the idea that information even about performers was increasingly grist to the mill of the colonial knowledge projects that fed Company governmentality. That Lucknow Residents Richmond, Sleeman and Outram 'knew' *sitār* player Razi-ud-daula to be a *ḍom* and therefore of 'despicable' caste,[42] as opposed to a respectable *kalāwant*, I suggest played a strong part in the Residents' removal of musicians from Wajid ᶜAli Shah's inner circle, and eventually their ousting of the Nawab altogether. *Ḍoms* in pre-existing Indian writings *were* of lower social status than *kalāwants*. But Sleeman was a key propagator of the new 'scientific' knowledge of

[40] Jones, 'Musical Modes' (1882); Tagore's first edition was 1875. Jones' treatise was republished in London in 1799 in his Collected Works and was known in Europe and Anglophone India; Bor, 'Rise', pp. 57–8; Fraser of Reelig Papers, Vol. 58, James Fraser to various, pp. 143–59. But there is no evidence that Indian writers on music knew of Jones' treatise before 1875.

[41] Wilson, 'Early'; and Roque and Wagner, 'Introduction'.

[42] Sleeman, *Diary*, p. 129.

'congenitally criminal' and 'degenerate' castes and tribes, into which delinquent category he and later colonial ethnographers placed *ḍoms*.[43]

There are two crucial complexities to note, however. Firstly, the colonial impetus to collect in relation to music needs to be delinked from the colonial impetus to control: they overlapped, but the first did not necessarily imply the second. Especially in the eighteenth century, there is scant evidence of a desire to control Indian music or musicians in the commissioning and collecting of music treatises and most paintings; rather, the impetus was a greedy curiosity, a European hunger to consume and know the auditory picturesque. The second is that while the impetus to control did follow on from the impetus to collect chronologically, and increasing in intensity, the two modes coexisted throughout the period and can be hard to disentangle, except via a case-by-case close reading. Even ethnographic paintings, for which the chain of transmission through to colonial knowledge projects is clear, were still overwhelmingly collected as trinkets, souvenirs and memorabilia of 'people and costumes' in the nineteenth century.[44] Few were, at this stage, placed in the service of sweeping 'scientific' classifications of caste.

Change and Crisis Mitigation: The Late Mughal Perspective

For late Mughal writers on music – my main focus throughout this book – the reasons they wrote were at times connected to colonial interactions with Indian musical worlds, but always epistemically disjunct. As we have seen, a large number of Indian artists, musicians and intellectuals in this transitional century – some of them of the highest calibre – were involved in creating musical collectibles for European as well as a huge diversity of Indian patrons. A straightforward reason Indian works on musical subjects flourished in this period was financial: service professionals always follow the money, whatever the myth of the romantic genius tells us. And there was now eager competition for their services across India. When it came to illustrated and canonical works especially, an influx into the musical economy of many newly wealthy and frequently naïve tourists hungry for the auditory picturesque provided a substantial new source of income for

[43] Bates, 'Race, Caste', pp. 13–18; Sleeman, *Diary*, pp. 129, 112; also William Crooke, *The Tribes and Castes of the North-Western Provinces and Oudh* (Calcutta: Government of India, 1896), vol. ii, pp. 316–9 and vol. iii, pp. 496–7.

[44] Y Sharma, 'Mughal Delhi', pp. 20–3; Fraser of Reelig Papers, vol. 58, James Baillie to his father, Jan 1818, pp. 23–4.

even the most mediocre of North India's scattered and job-hunting artisans and writers,[45] as well as, of course, for performers themselves.

But when we consider the flurry of new music-technical treatises in Persian and Hindavi that emerged in the later eighteenth century, most of these were not written with European audiences in mind, but for Indian connoisseurs and musicians who knew intimately the canonical literature these writings were knowingly departing from. The corpus of new treatises reveals a substantially more important impetus for Indians writing on music in the decades either side of 1800 – their conscious realisation that their musical world had changed since the seventeenth century, and that the canonical texts on which they continued to build music theory did not adequately describe the musical system as it was now. I would suggest that colonial collecting and commissioning projects played an inadvertent part in stimulating this fresh impulse to describe on paper what had changed, *without* notably influencing the content or structure of these new writings.

We know from both Indian and English sources that European song collectors and *rāga* enthusiasts personally sat with Indian musicians, music theorists, *munshī*s and painters, and even played along in order to collate their musical knowledge. We also know who several of the Indian experts were that worked for Europeans or within their orbit, including Khanum Jan, the author of Edinburgh MS 585(4), Jivan Khan/Shah and Ghulam Raza *qawwāl*. Most of William Jones' 'Musical Modes' was not, in fact, based on his in-person interactions, but instead a face-value reading of the c.1675 *Tuhfat al-Hind* and the mid-seventeenth-century Sanskrit *Saṅgīta-nārāyaṇa*, which he failed to realise described Orissa, not Hindustan.[46] But he noted two important truths about the relationship between the written theory he had chosen to prioritise and the music's late eighteenth-century practice. Firstly, he acknowledged along with William Bird[47] that any written notation of a *rāga* he could possibly devise would be 'scarce intelligible without the assistance of a masterly performer on the *Indian* lyre [*bīn*]', because so much of the music was improvised in the moment of performance. Secondly, and more significantly, he realised with bemusement that the seventeenth-century theory he was working with departed

[45] e.g. two in the British Library: Add. Or. 2796–2860, an exquisitely bound album of poor-quality paintings from Jaipur c. 1850; and Or. 14,328, Kalimatullah's crudely illustrated pornographic *rāgamālā*, the *Rāgsandhav* (Kashmir, 1812).

[46] Jonathan Katz, 'The Musicological Portions of the Saṅgītanarāyāyaṇa: A Critical Edition and Commentary', Unpublished PhD Dissertation (University of Oxford, 1987), part 1 pp. v–vi; Williams, 'Hindustani Music', p. 56.

[47] Bird, *Oriental Miscellany*, p. v.

substantially from the living practice of *rāga*-based music as he understood it in 1784 quite intimately. (His prejudiced speculations on the reasons were groundless.)[48]

The new Persian and regional-language treatises show unequivocally that late Mughal writers equally recognised the fissure that had opened up between canonical theory c. 1680 and contemporary practice c. 1780, notably authors who were working in proximity with confused foreigners who repeatedly asked them to explain it. Indeed, they explicitly stated they were writing, in part or in full, to present the authoritative up-to-date knowledge that would close the gap. 'The aforementioned *mat*s correspond with bygone writings [the *Tuhfat al-Hind* and the *Shams al-Aswāt*]',[49] wrote Ghulam Raza. 'But now [I] the compiler of these dazzling pearls will write that which accords with my own humble understanding and intellect and which is in alignment with what pleases the mind of [the current] Nawab Asaf-ud-daula, the most authoritative listeners, and established and verified master musicians.'[50] Ranj stated even more boldly, 'Because I did not find the writings of previous [authors] on this subject within reach of understanding, I created some rules from my own poor intellect [and] wrote them down . . . in accordance with the fashion of writing current in this age, and wholly abandoned the previous manner of writing.'[51] Indeed, the reason we know what changes happened to music in this century is precisely *because* Indian authors writing in Persian and regional languages documented it: because they were perennially interested in the fashionable and the new, and because the classical Mughal epistemology actively made space for updating conventional with new material (Chapter 2).

The large-scale shifts that occurred in Hindustani music itself have not been the primary focus of this book. But along the way I have documented some of the main changes to its *rāga* and *tāla* systems, repertoire of genres and instrumentarium that took place after Mughal canonisation efforts reached their apogee in the *Tuhfat al-Hind*. Crucially, the key changes largely predated European intellectual interest in this musical world. As we saw in Chapter 7, shifts in how literate musicians conceptualised the *rāga*s were already beginning to surface in the *Shams al-Aswāt*. As the eighteenth century wore on, the critical move towards prioritising melodic affinity over aesthetic criteria seems to have led to an attenuation of the technical knowledge of the medical and astrological underpinnings of

48 Jones, 'Musical Modes' (1882), pp. 151, 155–6. 49 Ghulam Raza, *Usūl* (1793/4), f. 42r.
50 ibid., f. 69v. 51 Ranj/Himmat, *Asl*, ff. 3v–4r.

the *rāgas*' supernatural powers documented in Chapter 2. By the nineteenth century, musical writers still fully believed in the *rāgas*' supernatural and sovereign powers, but generally had only a hazy and imprecise memory of their scientific underpinnings.[52] As I have argued elsewhere, the unmooring of the *rāgas* from their sources of power is most visible in the history of *rāgamālā* paintings: in the increasing displacement through the late seventeenth and eighteenth centuries of earlier *rāgamālā* icons' tangible tantric potency by worldly class power, manifested in multiple diverging notions of taste, beauty and meaning (cf. Figures 5.4 and 5.5). No wonder painters began to mix and match *rāginī* icons so frequently, and scribes to mistake their names one for another;[53] no wonder Jones and Willard found the relationship of the sonic to the iconic forms of the *rāgas* beyond comprehension. The knowledge that mapped their connections had been diluted long since.[54]

In the arena of rhythm, as discussed in Chapters 4 and 7, the revolution in *tāla* conception was likewise already being systematised on paper by 1761/2. The extensive connected research of Miner, Kippen and Walker on the eighteenth- and nineteenth-century sources for instruments and dance shows that the acceleration of post-*Shams* changes to the rhythmic system were tied to the arrival, sometime in the reign of Muhammad Shah, of *sitār* and *tabla* at the Mughal court.[55] These now-iconic instruments probably came to Hindustan with itinerant performers from Kashmir and Punjab respectively.[56] Attractive, charismatic and commercially savvy courtesan troupes were ideally placed to take advantage of the 'changing fortunes of the time;'[57] and *sitār* and *tabla* were universally played together to accompany the *nāch* of 'Kashmiri' courtesans and male *bhāṅḍs*.[58] The performance practices of *sitār*, *tabla* and *nāch* were based on a fundamental new technical structure: the *gat* of Chapter 4 – a fixed *sthāyī-antarā-sthāyī* composition in *rāga*, a *tāla* conceived as a beat-based cyclical groove, and a choreographed *nāch* set-piece.[59] *Sitār*, *tabla*, *nāch* and the *gat* structure rose to dominance in the late eighteenth century on the lithe shoulders of

52 ᶜAli Shah, *Saut*, pp. 6–7, 10-4; Imam Khan, *Maᶜdan*, pp. 111–4.

53 Lunn and Schofield, 'Delight, Devotion', p. 231.

54 Schofield, 'Music, Art', pp. 83–5.

55 The first evidence for the *sitār* is Dargah Quli Khan's description of Adarang in the *Muraqqaᶜ-i Dehlī*, and for the *tabla* in paintings by Pahari master Nainsukh from the 1740s.

56 Miner, *Sitar*, pp. 32–4; Kippen, 'Les battements', pp. 152–3.

57 Anup, *Rāg Darshan*, (Persian 1808), p. 156.

58 Walker, *India's Kathak Dance*, p. 61; Miner, *Sitar*, Figs. 16, 22, 23.

59 Walker, '"Nautch" reclaimed'.

dancing girls. But the first reference I know to specific drum *gats* is from Muhammad Shah's reign, and the *gat* structure was already affecting how the entire Hindustani *tāla* system was organised, even for *dhrupad* and *khayāl*, by the time Hakim Hasan chose to start reconceptualising *tāla* on a fresh page the same year Abdali took Delhi (Chapter 2).[60]

The 'rapidly changing political and entrepreneurial dynamics of ... North India' thereafter that so dramatically affected the lives of professional musicians likewise spurred shifts in the popularity of song genres, because the scattering 'opened up Hindustan's musical economy to unprecedented competition [for and] between an array of newly wealthy patrons'[61] with different tastes and interests. Although it has today been sidelined as a 'light-classical' form, the sung Persian and Urdu *ghazal* set to the entire panoply of Hindustani *rāgas* was undoubtedly the dominant prestige genre of this transitional century, at least in part because foreigners as well as Indians could appreciate it. It was sung for every type of patron by all professional musicians, from the best courtesans of Lucknow, Delhi, Hyderabad and the British settlements (Chapters 4 and 5) to the most revered élite *kalāwants* (Chapters 2, 5 and 7). Likewise, the greatest of India's contemporary poets, from Hazin and Sauda[c] to Mahlaqa Bai and Ghalib, had their *ghazals* set to *rāga* and sung in the *majlis*.[62] The period after 1770 also saw musicians based in Lucknow take minor but established Hindustani song forms, and transform them into 'Lucknow inventions' that are still in the 'light-classical' repertoire. In 1660, *ṭappa* was a Punjabi species of *khayāl* in the repertoire of Delhi *qawwāls*,[63] but by the late eighteenth century Miyan Shori had 'invented'[64] it as a genre in its own right belonging to Lucknow through 'magical' stylistic innovation and by composing new lyrics in 'Kashmiri, *rekhta*, Hindi and Persian'.[65] The other key example is *ṭhumrī*, which is now virtually synonymous with Wajid [c]Ali Shah, but which thirty years before was already regarded in Delhi as 'the perfume of the age', and which the king only learned in the 1840s from Aman and Amaman, two courtesans from Rampur.[66]

I wish to amplify this regular celebration and appropriation of the fresh, new, current and modern[67] in the writings of the late Mughal

[60] Dargah Quli, *Muraqqa*[c] (1993) p. 96; Hakim Hasan, *Risāla*.

[61] Schofield, 'Words', pp. 173–4. [62] Plowden, *Album*, ff. 17, 36; Ghalib, *Ghalib*, p. 319.

[63] Najm, *Naghma*, f. 212r. [64] *ikhtirā*[c]. [65] Najm, *Naghma*, f. 212r.

[66] Ranj/Himmat, *Aṣl*, f. 6v; Williams, 'Hindustani Music', p. 102; Manuel, *Ṭhumrī*.

[67] *tāza*, *no*, *jadīd*, *murawwaj*, *muta'akhkhir*, frequently contrasted with words for bygone, past, old, etc.

period – '*tāza ba tāza no ba no*' – because it is clear that Mughal writers routinely admired and theorised the new alongside the old.[68] For example, in 1666 Faqirullah endorsed, and was thus the first to bring into the Mughal canon, the stylistic innovations[69] of the earliest known court *khayāl* singer, Shaikh Sher Muhammad (d. c. 1660). 'None of his innovations were in accordance with [the established canons of] *sangīt*', he wrote, 'but they were so beautiful that they lie beyond description'.[70] Anup's insistence in the 1815 *Rāg Darshan* that each of the sixteenth-century progenitors of the four *dhrupad bānīs* originated a 'fresh style'[71] may have been a back-projection to explain their present-day descendants' unique distinctions.[72] But Dargah Quli's repeated references c.1740 to the 'current fashion'[73] in Delhi for Sadarang's *khayāl* compositions, and Rasikh's celebration of their 'freshness of style'[74] in 1753,[75] were contemporary (or nearly) with the great musician. The historian Najm likewise made a great deal of Shori's 'invention' of *ṭappa* on the grounds of Shori's unique vocal charisma: he was the 'perfect master and a devastating enchanter . . . noone who listened to his innovations could keep control of themselves'.[76] And of course the author of Edinburgh MS 585(4) and Ranj/Himmat explicitly swept aside the old system of writing down *tālas* in favour of their own 'fresh' and 'new' methods of notation.[77]

But change is never easy, especially for guardians of venerable traditions. It is harder still when change is rapid, widespread and propelled by chaotic and horrific events beyond individuals' control. Such was the 'scattering of Shahjahanabad' inaugurated by the invasion of Nadir Shah in 1739 and the greater predations of Abdali that followed. As well as endorsing the new, writing about change – intellectually assimilating the new into ongoing traditions, and organising and reconciling irreversible changes to align with older values – is, crucially, the principal way humans make order out of chaos and thereby alleviate our most profound anxieties.[78]

This was the main reason North Indian authors wrote about music so prolifically in the late Mughal period: to control and mitigate the existential threat posed to their entire musical world by the crumbling of the imperial centre. As I put it at the end of Chapter 2, particularly when it came to

[68] Mirza Khan, *Tuhfat* (1968), pp. 358–9; Schofield, 'Reviving', pp. 494, 500. [69] *ikhtirāᶜ*.
[70] Faqirullah, *Rāg Darpan*, p. 192; Brown [Schofield], 'Origins', pp. 172–3. [71] *tarz-i tāza*.
[72] Anup ed. Shekhar, *Rāg Darshan* (Persian 1815), p. 11; (Brajbhasha 1800), ff. 3r–4r.
[73] *murawwaj*. [74] *tāzagī-i tarz*.
[75] Dargah Quli, *Muraqqaᶜ* (1993), p. 102; Rasikh, *Risāla*, p. 30. [76] Najm, *Naghma*, f. 212r.
[77] *tarah-i tāza*, Edinburgh MS 585(4), f. 50r; *nabā-i no* and *tarīq-i jadīd*, Ranj/Himmat *Asl*, f. 4r.
[78] Schofield, 'Emotions', pp. 185, 192–6.

assembling musicians' lives and songs into books, I think late Mughal writers on music were trying to hold their fragile world together with little more than broken pens. The musicians' *tazkira* and the courtly song collection were genres new to Hindustani musical life that arose during the scattering, as a result of and in response to it.[79] Why did musicians and their disciples and patrons feel an overpowering need at this juncture to write down musicians' biographies; to trace their genealogies backwards and their onward journeys forwards as they scattered across India; to compile the texts of thousands of songs in their repertoires that they had for long centuries passed on orally, aurally and bodily to their sons and disciples, and did so still where they could?

Because faced with the wars, massacres, displacements, plagues, famines and violent regime changes of the eighteenth century, they were justifiably afraid that the human chains supporting Hindustani music's existence would all break at once[80] – that the unwritten music of the Mughal world would, once and for all, fade to black.

On Music and Mortality

In living with Mughal writings on music for many years, I have become convinced that to the Mughals music was about nothing less than life in the face of death: that its experience in the *majlis* was, most profoundly, a meditation upon mortality – a great, exuberant raging at the dying of the light. In other work I have pointed out that the aesthetic Mughal patrons treasured more than anything else in the intimate musical gathering was what I have called the 'poignancy of transience – the double-edged sword of delight in love found and grief in its inevitable loss'.[81] This sentiment lingers like a sweet, sad penumbra behind all Mughal descriptions of the joys of the *majlis*, whether expressed in prose, painting, poetry or song. The objects of delight that Mughal connoisseurs desired above all others – and most profoundly music – were all things that die: things whose ephemeral beauties can never be collected or controlled, for like a single note plucked from a *rabāb* they are perishable, and they pass into silence.

Hafiz's *ghazal* '*tāza ba tāza*', so very popular in this period (Chapter 4), perfectly encapsulates these ephemeral things and the exquisite intensity of their transitory existence. Note the objects of desire Khanum Jan sang into

79 For the musicians' *tazkira* see Schofield, 'Emotions'; for the song collection, Schofield, 'Words'.
80 Schofield, 'Emotions'. 81 Schofield, 'Musical Culture'.

being in the moment of performance: the acute joys of sweet music, overflowing wine, delicious scents, a fresh garden bower, breeze on the skin, the kisses of the beloved. None of these things can be held onto for more than the brief instant of their enjoyment. As the greatest late Mughal poet of them all, Mirza Ghalib, put it:

The span of your existence is not more than a single glance, heedless one!
The warmth of the gathering endures only as long as the single dance of a spark.[82]

Music's principal beauty, in other words – the source of its most profound affective powers – lay in its ephemerality, its mortality: in its fleeting presence in the world and the certain knowledge of its imminent death.[83]

That the potency of musical experience, especially in intimate company, was about mortality – a living emotional intensity sharpened to the point of pain[84] by the anticipated death of music and, in time, the human beloved – is repeatedly reinforced in *ghazal*s written on the subject of the *majlis*. This is no more powerfully so than in Mir's reflections on Jamshed in the opening of Chapter 3; and in these Urdu couplets, again, by Ghalib:

At night we imagined that every corner of the carpet [was so abundant with flowers that it]
Might be the apron of a gardener or the fist of a flower seller.

The gracefulness of the cupbearer's walk and the pleasure of the sound of the harp
made this a heaven for the eye, that a paradise for the ear.

But if you come into the gathering come the break of dawn, see:
There is no more joy or burning, hubbub or excitement.

The wound of separation from that night's companionship burns:
Only one candle remains, and it too is extinguished.[85]

Here, it is the night that is vital, bright; the morning that is grey, silent – come the dawn, Eurydice fades once more into the shadows. This is, of course, a deliberately cultivated Mughal aesthetic of centuries' standing that Ghalib was using to kindle the precious poignancy of transience in his listeners. This sentiment catches fire in the heart only when the music is largely extemporised as Hindustani music is, and thus intrinsically unrepeatable; but the sense of mortality it engenders is metaphorical, not real, and thus infinitely repeatable – when, in fact, it *has* been repeated many

[82] Translation based on Pritchett, *Desertful*, *ghazal* 78 verse 6. [83] Schofield, 'Musical Culture'.
[84] *dard*. [85] Translation based on Pritchett, *Desertful*, *ghazal* 169 verses 9–12.

times over.[86] In peaceful times, when talent and gatherings were plentiful, all it took to draw Eurydice back towards the light again, and to lose her again, and again, was to hold another *majlis*, and another the next night.

But the scattering of Shahjahanabad threatened the literal silencing of the Mughal *majlis* – the physical destruction of its spaces and the dispersal or death of its people – and the very real extinction of the poetry, music and listening that were its blazing heart (Chapter 3).[87] As the Mughal *majlis* was dispersed across India, the human chains of transmission and appreciation fundamental to music's survival became stretched dangerously thin over huge geographical distances and memory of their histories disrupted by the ravages of time and far too many untimely deaths. In this emergency situation, what the inhabitants of the *majlis* had to do was preserve in some other way those aspects of their musical and listening practices they believed were most crucial to remember, or most likely to be forgotten.

Writing on music enabled them to do this in a form that could travel through space and time without having to rely on living human chains. Music-technical treatises preserved the canonical Mughal heritage of Hindustani music theory, and endorsed approved modern changes. *Tazkiras* and genealogies traced who had passed on their knowledge to whom and tracked where they had all gone, so that the vital lineages of transmission and appreciation might be preserved intact in an everlasting form. Song collectors made sure the precious repertoire of the late, great masters of the Mughal court was poured out of singers' memories onto the page so that distance would never mean forgetting the words. And, in a situation of intense competition for patronage, *tazkiras* and song collections operated as hard proof that musicians who claimed to belong to Mughal court lineages really were who they said they were, and thus worthy of employing as true representatives of the authentic imperial traditions.

But all this writing on music, especially after 1780, is also abundant testimony that the worst fears of the mid-eighteenth century did *not* come to pass. Hindustani music and the Mughal *majlis* did not die. They metamorphosed. Even in the 1760s and 70s some musicians continued to sustain themselves in Delhi (Chapter 3). Many more participants of Delhi's *majālis* rescued the metaphorical lamps of their gatherings and carried them 'unextinguished', as Zia-ud-din put it, to their new homes in more lively places.[88] Of necessity musicians had to reshape their performance practices and repertoire to suit the varied new circumstances in which they

86 Schofield, 'Musical Culture'; and Andrews and Kalpaklı, *Age of Beloveds*, pp. 59–84.
87 Schofield, 'Emotions', pp. 191–2.
88 Zia-ud-din, *Hayy*, f. 55v; Schofield, 'Emotions', p. 195.

found themselves, or starve. But in doing so, they and their audiences more than merely survived the turmoil and the scattering. The evidence of the *majālis* and public festivals of Hyderabad, Jaipur, Lucknow and Delhi after 1780 is that Hindustani music and musicians, and their many communities of listeners, unquestionably thrived in the years before 1857. Galvanised with pen and paintbrush, the living chains linking Hindustani music's illustrious past and innovative present in the final reckoning proved supple and resilient in the tumultuous century between the death of Muhammad Shah and the imposition of Queen Victoria on the Mughal throne.

Above all else, musicians and music lovers wrote for posterity: for the generations yet to come. They strove valiantly to capture their ephemeral, fugitive beloved on paper with broken pens because they wanted us to remember her – and them.[89] When Basit Khan died in c. 1887, thirty years into the British Raj, he passed down his precious Awadh-made copies of the *Shams* and the *Usūl* to his chief disciple in Calcutta: one of the earliest *sarod* virtuosos, the Afghan musician Ni^{c}matullah Khan. Ni^{c}matullah in turn bequeathed them to his sons Karamatullah and Asadullah Kaukab, both of whom wrote their own original treatises in Urdu in 1908 and 1915 that drew on Basit's collection, but also on other sources in Sanskrit, Persian, Hindi, Urdu, Bengali and English.[90] And Basit's manuscripts survive today – well-thumbed, annotated by later hands with song texts and circular *tāla* diagrams (*dā'ira*), carefully rebound and wrapped against dust and silverfish. They lie tucked away in an almirah beside Karamatullah's and Kaukab's writings in the home of the last living performer of that lineage, the *sarod* player and teacher Ustad Irfan Muhammad Khan, himself both a hereditary musician and a highly literate *ustād* fluent in multiple languages, one of which is Persian.[91]

When Writing Fails: Orphans of the Uprising

It may seem an obvious point to make: but all the texts and paintings I have used in writing this book have survived into the present day – otherwise we could not access the world of late Mughal music at all. Most of these sources

[89] Ranj/Himmat, *Asl* (BL), ff. 2r–v.

[90] Karamatullah Khan, *Isrār-i Karāmat ^{c}Urf Naghmāt-i Ni^{c}mat* (Allahabad: Janaki, 1908); Asadullah Khan Kaukab, *Jauhar-i Mūsīqī* (1915), private collection, Ustad Irfan Muhammad Khan; Katz, *Lineage*, pp. 129–58.

[91] I am grateful to Ustad Irfan Muhammad Khan-sahib for allowing me access to his precious collection.

are easily found, too, their bibliographical data methodically entered by archivists, librarians and curators into the publicly available catalogues and handlists of major collections around the world. Given that this is so, why have nearly all my sources and most of the tales I have told in these pages been forgotten since 1858 – or remembered, at best, only in tiny warped fragments like the smashed and blackened pieces of a burnt-out lantern?

The stories I have unfolded in these chapters are bookended by not one, but two world-changing upheavals in North Indian history. The reason we have forgotten lies in the second: the terrible cataclysm of the Indian Uprising or *Ghadar* of 1857–8, known to the British as the Mutiny. The quashing and aftermath of the Uprising in the two principal cities of late Mughal musical life, Delhi and Lucknow, were horrifically violent. When the British broke the siege of Delhi, no man over sixteen was spared a brutal death, no woman rape, no household plunder.[92] Particular savagery awaited the musicians, poets, artists and intellectuals of Kucha Chelan (Chapter 7) – the 'men who were the pride of Delhi ... we will never see their like again' – where approximately 1400 civilians were dragged out of their houses and massacred.[93] Those deemed 'rebels' who escaped the initial atrocities were rounded up and executed without due process in bulk hangings. The remaining citizens of Delhi fled en masse into exile once more, most of them into destitution and many to death by starvation. Their enforced banishment lasted for years: it was only in 1860 that Delhi's Muslims successfully petitioned Queen Victoria to be allowed to return home.[94] Meanwhile, in retribution the Company systematically razed several Shahjahanabad neighbourhoods to the ground, while its prize agents went house to house throughout the city, methodically seizing all treasures that had not already been looted, including thousands of manuscripts and paintings (see above).

But the British reserved their greatest vengeance for Shah Jahan's architectural masterpiece and the epicentre of Mughal sovereignty, the Exalted Fortress (Qil^{c}a-i Mu^{c}alla) – now just the 'Red Fort'.[95] After the Company's soldiers had ransacked the entire place, eighty per cent of its priceless interior buildings were ruthlessly torn down by order of the viceroy, Lord Canning.[96]

[92] Mirza Asadullah Khan Ghalib, *Dastanbuy*, tr. Khwaja Ahmad Faruqi (Bombay: Asia Publishing House, 1970), p. 40; Dalrymple, *Last Mughal*, p. 335.

[93] Zahir Dehlavi, *Dastān-i Ghadir: Yā Tarāz-i Zahīrī* (Lahore, 1955), p. 128; Dalrymple, *Last Mughal*, pp. 357–8.

[94] Dalrymple, *Last Mughal*, p. 426.

[95] Lal Qil^{c}a.

[96] James Fergusson, *The History of Indian and Eastern Architecture*, vol. ii (London: J Murray, 1876), p. 312; Dalrymple, *Last Mughal*, pp. 353–5, 423–4.

It was during the first furious ravaging of the palace that a young captain of the King's Royal Rifles, John Jones, swarmed the unguarded *jharokā* (baldachin) of the emperor's throne in the great Hall of Public Audience (*dīwān-i khwāss o ᶜām*). Two hundred years earlier, it was here that an audacious imperial *kalāwant* had magically lulled Emperor Shah Jahan into a fateful trance with the gentle seductions of Ragini Todi. Now her soft tones were drowned out by the sharp crack of bullets and the shriek of steel-spurred boots on stone.[97] The captain, whose pitiless actions in the fierce battle for Delhi had earned him the epithet 'Jones the Avenger',[98] began tearing the marble throne canopy asunder, prising out its precious stones and inlay. At the very last, he hunted down and tore the still-resounding figure of Orpheus intact from the wall, and dragged everything away in dusty sacking. Like so many of Delhi's dispersed remains, Orpheus was shipped back to England, where Jones had him set into a table top. Only in 1911 was a now nearly faceless, silent Orpheus reinstated to his place behind Shah Jahan's empty throne, when the viceroy Lord Curzon disinterred him from the basement of the South Kensington Museum for the Red Fort's restoration on the occasion of King-Emperor George V's Coronation Durbar.[99]

The consequences for music of this second violent disruption were much greater than the scattering. Again, Hindustani music and dance did not die. Again, to survive this much further-reaching crisis, the field underwent yet another metamorphosis. The stories of the competing strategies that emerged to meet the challenge of the implacable colonial-modern dispensation of the British Raj are now well known – the simultaneous and competitive establishment of, on the one hand, new guild formations on the wreckage of the old called *gharānās*, and on the other, top-down Western-influenced Brahmin-led reform movements. Again, that tale is not mine to tell.[100] The end of *my* story concerns the orphans of the Uprising: the memory and legacies of the late Mughal musicians foregrounded in this book; and the Mughal traditions of writing on Hindustani music in Persian and Brajbhasha. Both of these chains were irrevocably broken by the Uprising.

[97] FC Maisey, 'The Capture of the Delhi Palace', National Army Museum, London, pp. 6309–26, 4–7; Dalrymple, *Last Mughal*, pp. 354–5.

[98] 'Portrait of Colonel Sir John Jones KRRC', The Royal Green Jackets (Rifles) Museum, Winchester, https://rgjmuseum.co.uk/object-archive-item/sir-john-jones/.

[99] Fergusson, *History*, p. 311; Herbert C Fanshawe, *A Handbook for Travellers in India, Burma and Ceylon*, 8th ed. (London: John Murray, 1911), p. 197. For the full horrors, read Dalrymple, *Last Mughal*, pp. 331–429. The Red Fort remains barren and desolate to this day.

[100] Chapter 1, fn. 36.

The major difference between the scattering and the Uprising for musical life concerned the value of connections with the Mughal court. After the scattering of 1739–61, verifiable links to the imperial atelier in Delhi were enormously prestigious and a tremendous advantage to musicians in exile: such associations made them highly desirable to Hindu, Muslim and Sikh patrons alike. But in the immediate wake of 1857, clear associations with the sophisticated Indic-Persianate culture of the late Mughal world, and especially with the Mughal and other rebel courts, were undeniably a disadvantage. For some years, known links could even mean execution, as we saw with Mir Nasir Ahmad's narrow escape. Rather than foregrounding their Mughal courtly connections, then, post-Uprising musicians had to downplay them, except in the private *majālis* of sympathetic patrons like the rulers of Kapurthala, Rampur and Jaipur. In 1858, in other words, the 'late Mughal' in Hindustan's musical culture went underground.

This makes it incredibly difficult to trace what happened to the descendants of the musicians documented in late Mughal writings. If we compare the *tazkira*s and genealogies written between 1635 and 1858 with, for instance, the seminal 1993 work of Amal Das Sharma, who rigorously compiled late nineteenth- and twentieth-century *gharānā* oral histories, the discrepancies are enormous – in most cases, an unbridgeable gulf. Take, for instance, the conjoined Gorari–Khandari lineages of the chief *kalāwant*s to the Mughal emperors who have been central to my narrative. In the oral histories Sharma compiled, the direct Tansen line is entirely missing after La^{c}l Khan Gunasamudra; Sadarang's father and therefore his ancestral lineage are incorrect; and the Khandari *bānī* line of chief musicians is missing after Adarang: La^{c}l Khan Parab Lal, Himmat Khan and Mir Nasir Ahmad are nowhere to be seen.[101] The lineage that Mughal-era musicians and writers thought was the most important to remember is, today, not remembered at all.

This is not a criticism of Sharma's or others' meticulous work, nor does it mean that the oral histories are 'wrong' or the progenitors they celebrate unimportant – on the contrary. It simply means that the lineages important to twentieth-century musicians are not the same as those deemed central by Mughal patrons and musicians in their own time. It is also likely that many court musicians were killed in 1857 or left without patrons and disciples, and that their legacies therefore ran into the sand. Regardless, there is an

[101] Amal Das Sharma, *Musicians of India Past and Present: Gharanas of Hindustani Music and Genealogies* (Calcutta: Naya Prokash, 1993), pp. 64–9, 74–7.

irreconcilable mismatch between the late Mughal written records and the pre-1858 remembrances of modern *gharānās*. This means that with very few exceptions – Bade Muhammad Khan and Makhan Khan *qawwāls*,[102] Mir Nasir Ahmad and Basit Khan *kalāwants* – there is an irreparable break in our histories at 1858. We just don't know what happened to most documented late Mughal musicians, though their musical heritage manifestly lived on.

The end of the Persian and Brajbhasha traditions of writing about Hindustani music was even more absolute. I have been unable to find any new writings on music in either language that postdate 1858 (I would love to be proven wrong!). Instead, the Mughal epistemology of writing about music moved abruptly out of the now highly frowned-upon court languages of Persian and Brajbhasha[103] into modern Urdu and Hindi; and out of manuscripts written for individual wealthy patrons into printed publications aimed at a mass middle-class audience. While modern-language authors maintained a continuity with the Mughal past by citing its most hoary, canonical works,[104] the vital move of musicology into print instigated far-reaching – though notably still paracolonial – changes in the ways Hindustani music was described and thought about.[105]

The losses entailed in this shift were great – nearly all memory of the vast, rich ocean of Persian and Brajbhasha writings on music created during the Mughal era; and especially of the remarkable music-theoretical contributions of several generations of literate *ustāds*. Ranj/ Himmat's systematic graphical notation for modern *tālas* was completely overlooked as post-Uprising authors went right back to the obsolete systems of the *Tuhfat* or the *Saṅgīta-darpaṇa*, then leapt straight to their own ideas. Bhatkhande did remember Ghulam Raza's work – but not as he was, a literate, hereditary Delhi-lineage *qawwāl*, but rather as one 'Nawab Raza Khan', a 'nobleman' of 'Patna' writing in '1813' (a set of errors that refuses to die in the secondary literature). As the substantial intellectual

[102] Both these Gwalior *gharānā* founders were named as *qawwāls*, directly descended from Taj Khan *qawwāl* of Delhi; Imam Khan, *Ma*ᶜ*dan*, pp. 30–1, 34–5. The Gwalior *k̲h̲ayāl gharānā* is a rare case in which Sharma's post-1858 oral histories match the pre-1858 written records; cf. A Sharma, *Musicians*, pp. 78–81.

[103] Busch, *Poetry*, pp. 3–17, 202–39.

[104] e.g. the Bengali *Saṅgīta-taraṅga* (1818), Williams, 'Hindustani Music', pp. 257–61; Sadiq ᶜAli, *Sarmāya*, pp. 5–6.

[105] Williams, *Scattered Court*, and 'Music, Lyrics'; Miner, *Sitar*; Walker, *India's Kathak Dance*; Katz, *Lineage*; James Kippen, *Gurudev's Drumming Legacy: Music, Theory and Nationalism in the* Mṛdang aur Tablā Vādanpaddhati *of Gurudev Patwardhan* (Aldershot: Ashgate, 2006); see also forthcoming publications of Gianni Sievers.

contributions of literate *kalāwants* and *qawwāls* to the modernisation of Hindustani music were forgotten, it became possible for Bhatkhande to characterise hereditary *ustāds* unchallenged as 'illiterate, ignorant, and narrow-minded'[106] – a falsehood that has stuck ever since.

Wajid ^{c}Ali Shah knew when he was forced to leave Lucknow that the end was nigh for the rich late Mughal culture of music and dance that was so central to who he and his people were. He was fully aware, when he sang his last *ṭhumrī*, that music can break, as well as make, kings. For the palanquin he sang about so poignantly is understood metaphysically as a funeral bier leaving the house for the last time on the way to the burial ground or pyre. When the British deposed and exiled him, when Captain Jones tore Orpheus from the wall, they metaphorically extinguished the guttering candle of the Mughal *majlis.*[107] Wajid ^{c}Ali Shah may have lit a beautiful new lantern in Calcutta. But ever since 1856, Babul Mora has become a metacommentary on the wrenching human condition of separation – a lament for the irretrievability of all things loved and lost.[108]

Eurydice's Echoes in Music's Modern Histories

Finally they destroyed you, hunted down out of vengeance,
While your timbre abides in lions and cliffs
And in trees and birds. In these you sing still.

So what, then, of Orpheus, and my most fundamental question: can Orpheus ever bring Eurydice back from the dead? If Eurydice is, as I have hinted throughout, the late Mughal still abiding in Hindustani musical life, then this quotation from the post-Uprising *Ma^{c}dan al-Mūsīqī* is crucial. 'A singer', wrote Imam:

> was like a necromancer (*^{c}āmil*) and the *rāga* was like a spirit (*muwakkal*) he conjured up. When a conjurer utters his prescribed prayers and preparations (*ko'ī du^{c}ā bā tarkīb*) and invokes a spirit, we call his formula effective, powerful (*pur asar*). Similarly, if anyone sings a particular *rāga* in its prescribed way and that *rāga* produces its assigned effect we call that *rāga* effective (*bā ta'sīr*).[109]

[106] Bhatkhande, *Short Historical Survey*, p. 40.

[107] cf. Mirza Farhatullah Beg's (1885–1947) *tazkira*, *Delhi's Last Candle*, recalling the last Mughal poetical *majlis*; *Dehlī Kī Ākhirī Sham^{c}* (New Delhi: Dihli Urdu Akademi, 1986).

[108] Rumi, *Masnawī*, p. 4. [109] Imam Khan, *Ma^{c}dan*, pp. 111–16.

Looking back over this book, it is remarkable just how many Orpheuses there were in late Mughal India – how many great singers' voices were praised as magical, as possessing supernatural power over their listeners' sensibilities: Khushhal Khan Gunasamudra, Shaikh Sher Muhammad, Shaikh Moin-ud-din, Sadarang, Anjha Baras, Raushan-ud-daula's *qawwāls*, Shori, Khanum Jan, Mahlaqa Bai, Jaipur's *bhagtans*, Himmat, the last King of Lucknow (even if he did say so himself). In the earliest published Urdu treatise on music, the *Ghuncha-i Rāg* (1862/3), there is even a lithograph of Wajid ^{c}Ali Shah as Shri Rag simultaneously depicted as King Solomon, Orpheus' great Islamicate cognate, pacifier of warring animals and king of the *jinns*, held aloft on his palanquin by *devs* and *parīs* (supernatural beings).[110] The idea that great *rāga* interpreters might have power to call down spirits with their song was no metaphor, either. In the hallowed assembly for spiritual listening, the *majlis-i samā*^{c}, Indian Sufis had long believed that the narrow isthmus (*barzakh*) separating the worlds of the living and the pious dead was momentarily thin – that during the *majlis* it was possible for great figures who had gone before to be supernaturally co-present with the living through the powerful vocal ministrations of singers.[111] This belief, for both the Sufi and the courtly *majlis*, is represented visually in this book in Figures 7.5 and 3.1.

But we who write on music do not possess such extraordinary powers. I am no Orpheus, as Rasikh also knew. The answer to the question 'Can Orpheus bring Eurydice back from the dead?' – can the broken pens of long-dead men and women tell us exactly, in complete fullness, what it felt like to make music and to experience it in the Mughal *majlis*? – is, as it always will be: no. Nor can I, a historian who was once a musician, ever conjure up the ephemeral world of late Mughal India for you, as it was then, with my own impoverished words. In this book, I have tried to keep faith with the musical dead, to bear true witness to Zia-ud-din's 'everliving spirits'. But the result is still a polyphony of broken and scattered fragments harmonised by little more than a flicker of historical imagination and a musician's instinct for resonance.

What this journey into the underworld of the late Mughal past does teach us, though, is how and where to hear Eurydice's many echoes, still

[110] Mardan ^{c}Ali, *Ghuncha*, '[Plate] No. 13. Shri Rag. Portrait of the honoured Sultan of the World, Wajid ^{c}Ali Shah, the Suleiman of Awadh'; see Williams, *Scattered Court*; Koch, 'Mughal Emperor'.

[111] Nile Green, *Sufism: A Global History* (Chichester: Wiley Blackwell, 2012), pp. 8–9, 78–9; Shahab Ahmed, *What is Islam? The Importance of Being Islamic* (Princeton: Princeton University Press, 2015), pp. 423–30; Schimmel, *Pain*, p. 65.

resounding in Hindustani music today. Despite the Uprising, and despite the even more terrible cataclysm of Partition that was to come in 1947, we can still hear the late Mughal in many corners of the Hindustani musical field: in Sadarang's *khayāl* compositions, in Begum Akhtar singing a Sauda^c *ghazal* just as Khanum Jan did, in the way *tabla* players count *tīntāl*, in Ustad Irfan Muhammad Khan's *sarod* playing – in the enduring belief that, if sung correctly at midnight, Rag Malkauns can still raise the *jinns*.

So many stories remain untold in this book. It should be clear by now that it is not because Hindustan's musicians and music lovers left nothing to speak of behind. It is because I do not have the many lifetimes I would need to tell them all. I leave that for you to do. For the very least we historians of the ephemeral can do for Eurydice, and for Orpheus too, is to sing their songs once more – *tāza ba tāza no ba no*.

Glossary

abhinay(a) stylised eye movements and upper-body gestures used by dancers (and in this period singers) to express the meanings of lyrics or plot

abjad traditional system of allocating numbers to each of the letters of the Arabic alphabet

adhyāy(a) chapter of a treatise

akhāṛā arena for dance performance or wrestling competition; gymnasium

akhbārāt official newsletters of daily court (or British residency) business

alankār(a) ornament

ālāp unaccompanied introductory presentation of the rāga in dhrupad performance

ᶜāmil necromancer, conjurer

amīr-al-umarā' 'lord of lords', commander-in-chief of the Mughal empire

andarūn the interior apartments of a palace, usually the women's quarters (see bīrūn)

angiyā bodice, blouse

antarā second verse of a classical bandish (composition), usually higher in tessitura than the first verse

apsarā celestial dancer in Indra's court; courtesan (also abcharā)

arbāb-i nishāṯ bureaucratic department of entertainment

ᶜarẓī petition, legal statement

asāmī people, community

aṡar effect, mark (pl. āṡār)

āshob tumult, disturbance

ᶜaṭā'ī gifted one; self-taught or amateur musician

avartan one whole cycle of a tāla

avatār incarnation of a deity

bād-farosh panegyrist, 'seller of wind'

bhakti devotion, religious worship

baḥr poetical metre, rhythmic flow

bāhurūpiya community of male tricksters, magicians and dancers

bā'ī honorific 'lady', used for high-status courtesans

bairāgī wandering Hindu mendicant

bakhshī-al-mulk paymaster-general of the Mughal empire

bandījān bard, especially of the bhāṭṭ community (spelling is James Skinner's)

bandish fixed musical composition in rāga and tāla

bā'orī community of skilled engineering workers with earth, stone and water

barzakh Sufi concept; isthmus between two worlds, usually the spiritual and mundane

bazār bazaar, marketplace

be'opārī goods dealers and traders

besyā (veśyā) courtesan

bhagat male jugglers, satirists and mimics whose young men performed as trans-feminine dancers (see bhāṅḍ)

bhagtan(iyā) specific class of auspicious courtesan employed in the Rajput courts

bhāṅḍ male jugglers, satirists and mimics whose young men performed as trans-feminine dancers (see bhagat)

bhāṭṭ principal bards, genealogists and scholars for Rajput rulers and landowners

bhūm land, i.e. land rents

bībī honorific 'wife, lady', used for common-law Indian wives of Europeans

bīn (rudra-vīṇa) iconic stick zither with two large gourd resonators exclusive to kalāwants and associated with dhrupad

bīrūn the exterior apartments and open spaces of a palace, associated with men (see andarūn)

brāhmaṇ the highest caste of the four Hindu varṇas; the priestly caste

Brajbhāṣā the dialect of early modern Hindavi associated with the land of Braj, Lord Krishna's birthplace, used for Mughal court poetry and song lyrics

bol syllable; drum/dance mnemonic

ćāl choreographed gliding walk in kathak dance or nāch

ćāraṇ panegyrists for Rajput rulers and landowners; also traders and transporters

ćhand praise genre sung by ćāraṇs

ćūṛī-sāz bangle-maker

daf/dā'ira large circular frame drum, with or without small cymbals in the rim

dargāh 'threshold, portal'; the tomb shrine of a Sufi saint

dev a supernatural being, monster, demon

devanāgarī Indic script used for Sanskrit, Hindavi and modern Hindi

dībācha preface of a book

dīwān 1) collected ghazals of a single poet 2) assembly hall 3) revenue minister; dīwān-i khwāss o ᶜām – Hall of Public Audience

ḍhaḍha small ḍhol-type drum played by the ḍhāḍhīs; possibly an old or regional name for the ḍholak

ḍhāḍhī community of musicians specialising in ḍholak and later tabla and sārangī accompaniment, and panegyric and martial singing

dharma expected religious duty

ḍhol large cylindrical or barrel drum, generally played with one or two sticks

ḍholak medium-sized cylindrical or barrel drum, generally played by hand

dhrupad the oldest song genre currently in the Hindustani repertoire; a four-verse, generally serious genre on a wide range of topics.

dhyāna word-painting in verse of the iconic form of a rāga or rāginī

dohā short couplet of Hindavi poetry

ḍom alternative (earlier and generally derogatory) name for the ḍhāḍhī musician community
duʿā bā tarkīb prayer with (medicinal) preparation, formula
faqīr wandering Sufi mendicant
fatha short diagonal diacritical line above a Perso-Arabic letter, generally the short vowel 'a'
fihrist list or table of contents
firangī 'Frank'; European
firqa sect, distinct class of person
gaṇikā a class of courtesan
gat a fixed composition/choreography in instrumental/dance performance
gat nikās an opening choreography in kathak dance characterised by a ćāl
ghadar 'rebellion, sedition, riot'; the Uprising of 1857
gharānā multigenerational household guild of hereditary musicians and their disciples
ghazal Persian and Urdu genre of lyrical poetry characterised by couplets
gobārī anything made of cow dung, which is auspicious; usually plaster
got family lineage, caste, tribe
grām(a) in early modern music theory, the three octave-registers of the human voice
gunijān-khāna bureaucratic department of virtuosos
ḥakīm sage, medical doctor
ḥāl mystical state in the Sufi assembly that may be attained through listening to music (see wajd)
ḥalāl lawful, positively approved
hangāma turmoil, uproar, disorder
ḥarām forbidden, proscribed; sacrosanct
ḥavelī mansion house
hijrī/al-hijrī the Islamic calendar, which counts lunar years from the ḥijra, the Prophet's migration from Mecca to Medina
Hindūstānī of/from Hindustan (North India)
hoḷī/hoṛī Hindustani song genre sung during the season of the Holi festival in praise of Lord Krishna
ʿīd feast, festival (Muslim)
ʿīd-i ghadīr Shiʿa festival celebrating 18th Zu'l Hijja when the Prophet declared 'whoever calls me master, ʿAli is also their master'
ikhtirāʿ invention, innovation
ʿilm-i mūsīqī musical science
inʿām gift, generally of rent-free land or other property
ʿīsawī Christian calendar (CE)
jadīd new
jāgīr assignment of government land to support the holder
jagīrdār holder of a jāgīr

jaldhārā in this context, holy water container

jaltarang musical instrument; china cups filled with varying levels of water and played with sticks

jashn feast, festival

jashn-i ḥaidarī the festival of the birth of Hazrat ᶜAli, son-in-law of the Prophet and the first Imām of Shiᶜa Islam

jashn-i nabī the festival of the birth of the Prophet of Islam

jāt genus or tribe

jharokā window, arch, baldachin

jinn supernatural figure, djinn, genie

jogī male Hindu ascetic, practitioner of yoga and/or tantra

joginī female Hindu ascetic and magical being with tantric powers

kabit (kavitta) Sanskrit and Brajbhasha poetical and song form

kaiyāl weighmen in the salt industry

kalāwant hereditary community of male musicians who specialise in dhrupad and playing the bīn and Indian rabāb; some lineages took up k̲h̲ayāl in the eighteenth century

kanćan(ī) highest-status class of courtesans at the Mughal court

karma righteous action

kathak 1) The modern name for North Indian classical dance; 2) the hereditary community of male dancers who practise it

kāyasth/khatrī professional scribal and administrative communities

k̲h̲ālī 'empty', the unstruck section(s) of a tāla cycle indicated by a wave of the hand

k̲h̲alīfa chief, head of a lineage

k̲h̲āndān family

k̲h̲ayāl the dominant song genre in the Hindustani repertoire today; a two-verse genre usually on love characterised by virtuosic vocal runs

khilāᶜ/at robe of honour gifted by a ruler to a subordinate

kingara a small vīṇā

kobid a learned man

komal flat; scale degree flattened by a semitone

kos distance of a little over two miles

kṣatriya the second-highest caste of the four Hindu varṇas; the military and ruling caste

kyār(ī) a salt work consisting of a shallow rectangular dam constructed in the bed of a salt lake out of mud and stone

lākh 100,000

madda long horizontal diacritical line above a Perso-Arabic letter, generally the long vowel 'ā'

maḥal place, palace

majlis assembly, gathering for music, poetry, eating, drinking, conversation, friendship; also meḥfil

majlis-k̲h̲āna assembly hall, hall for such gatherings

majlis-i samā^{c} assembly for spiritual listening (Sufi)
makrūḥ disapproved of
mālzādī a class of courtesan ('daughter of the coin')
mandir temple
maṅgalā-mukhī auspicious face, auspicious presence
manṣab official rank in Mughal service, consisting of a nominal hierarchical position (ẕāt) and the number of cavalry (suwār) theoretically under the official's control
manṣabdār holder of a manṣab
mardāna men's quarters, where public business is also pursued; see zanāna
mars̱iya lament in Persian or Urdu verse performed in rāga by Shi^{c}as during the Muharram commemoration period
mat system, school; rāgamālā system
matla^{c} the first couplet of a g͟hazal
mātra beats of a tāla
maund/man measure of weight
mazār tomb, shrine
meḥfil see majlis
mirāṣ̤ī 'hereditary', later name for the ḍhāḍhī community of musicians especially in Punjab and Rajasthan
miẓrāb plectrum for plucking the strings of an instrument
mṛdang see pak͟hāwaj
mubāḥ allowable, permitted
mućalkā a written note of agreement, memorandum of understanding
muftī magistrate, expounder on Islamic law
mujrā salutation: 1) ritual respects; 2) a salutation piece of music/dance
muk͟hammas five-line Persian and Urdu poetical form
muk͟htārnāma written statutory declaration, written power, certificate
munājāt supplication to god
munshī multilingual secretary and/or language tutor
murawwaj current, in current use
mūsīqī music
muta'ak͟hk͟hir modern
muwakkal spirit (one upon whom power is delegated)
nāć/nautch dance, especially the dance of courtesan troupes
nag͟hma music, musical sound, melody; nag͟hma-i Hindūstān(ī) – Hindustani music
namak salt
namak-ḥalālī faithful to the salt, loyal
namak-ḥarāmī faithless to the salt, disloyal
nartakī female dancer or actress
nast^{c}alīq Perso-Arabic script used for Persian, Hindavi and modern Urdu
nāth Shaivite Hindu warrior ascetics

-nawāz 'player'
nāyak honorific term for great musicians before the mid-sixteenth century; the hero in classical Indic poetry
nāyikā the heroine in classical Indic poetry
nāyikā-bheda catalogue of types of nāyikās
naẕr/naẕrānā ritual/spiritual offering to a superior, usually monetary
niyāriyā see ćūṛī-sāz
no new
nuq̤ṭa dot, diacritical marking
nṛti dance
pakhāwaj iconic barrel drum with tuned heads, used to accompany dhrupad
paṇḍit Sanskrit scholar, knowledge authority
parda 'veil', female seclusion; musical note or mode
pargaṇa subdivision of a district (ẕila^{c})
parī a supernatural being, fairy
pātur a class of courtesan
paṭwārī foreman, registrar of a community or village
payas liquid
prastār a layout of all the possible combinations of a fixed set of numbers; in music of the notes of the rāga
pūjā Hindu worship, worship rituals
pūjārī Hindu priest who performs pūjā
purāṇa 'old'; major genre of Sanskrit literature concerning stories of the deities
qāfiya internal rhyme in a g̲h̲azal directly preceding the radīf
qānūn 1) 'canon'; 2) West Asian plucked dulcimer
qānūngo hereditary official of a district who preserved its demographic, land tenure and revenue knowledge
qaum community of people
qawwāl 'singer of qaul'; hereditary musicians attached to Sufi shrines who also sang certain genres at court, notably ṭappa and k̲h̲ayāl
qāẓī Muslim judge
rabāb 1) iconic large plucked lute exclusive to kalāwants and associated with dhrupad; 2) smaller pear-shaped Afghan lute
radīf the end rhyme of a g̲h̲azal wherein the second line of each couplet finishes with the same word or words
rāga melodic system of Hindustani music; melodic mode with a specific pitch set and rules that characterise how those pitches should be deployed
rāgamālā 'garland of rāgās'; system of ordering the rāgas as a set of six male rāgas each with five female rāginīs
rāginī female rāga in the rāgamālā system
rāg-sāgar practice of singing a dhrupad composition sequentially in different rāgas
rājā Rajput king
rānī Rajput queen

rāmjanī a class of courtesan
raqṣ dance
ras powder coloured powder thrown at the Holi festival
ravish mode or manner, here stylistic school
rekhta 'mixed'; earlier term for Urdu
risāla treatise
rudra vīṇā see bīn
rubā^{c}ī Persian or Urdu quatrain
sajjāda-nishīn spiritual leader of a Muslim religious institution, such as a shrine
samā^{c} 'audition', Sufi practice of spiritual listening to music
saṅgīt(a) music and its associated arts of dance and drama
saṅgīta-śāstra theoretical treatises on saṅgīta
saptak 'seven-fold'; the octave
sāqī cup-bearer
sargam oral notation similar to sol-fa used to notate and improvise on rāgas
sarishtadār chief officer or overseer of an institution
satī the Hindu ritual practice of widows burning themselves to death on their husbands' funeral pyre (now a criminal offence)
suwār cavalryman, the number of cavalry theoretically under the control of a manṣabdār
silsila 'chain', genealogical lineage
shāgird disciple; shāgird-i khāṣṣ – special disciple
shahr-āshob 'city-disturber'; a topos of the Persian and Urdu ghazal that poetically catalogued the representative beauties of a city
śāstra body of knowledge, treatise
śruti microtones of the Hindustani scale: 1) theoretical 22 shrutis to the octave; 2) the semitonal accidentals (komal Re, Ga, Dha and Ni, and tīvra Ma)
śuddh natural, the unmodified notes of the Hindustani scale.
ṣuḥbat 'conversation, company'; a synonym for majlis
soma moon
somavaṅśī the Rajput lineages descended from the moon god
sthāyī first verse of a classical bandish (composition), usually emphasising the middle tonic and octave
ṣulḥ-i kull 'universal civility, peace with all', the Mughal ideology of harmonious ecumenism
sur/swara note of the Hindustani scale
sūrya sun
sūryavaṅśī the Rajput lineages descended from the sun god
surod/sarod 1) music; 2) lute with metal fingerboard developed in the nineteenth century from the Afghan rabāb
svabhāv innate personal characteristics
tabarruk ritual/spiritual offering, usually material gifts including food
tafriqa scattering

tāʿifa troupe
tak͟hallus̤ nom de plume
tāla rhythmic system of Hindustani music; single metrical cycle distinguished by unique patterns of claps (tāli) and waves (k͟hālī)
tāli a clapped beat in a tāla
taʿlīm instruction, training
taʿlīm-k͟hāna Jodhpur's bureaucratic department of music
tambūr Persianate lute now obsolete in India with a carved wooden resonating chamber, either plucked with both hands as a melody instrument or with one hand as a drone (see tambūra)
tambūra large lute with a gourd resonating chamber used as a drone instrument
tān virtuosic vocal or instrumental run in rāga performance
ṭappa originally a species of k͟hayāl in the Punjabi language that became a virtuosic song genre in its own right
tarānā/tillānā virtuosic vocal form utilising the non-lexical syllables of dance and drumming to improvise around a Persian or Urdu couplet
t̤arz-i tāza 'fresh style'
ta's̤īr effect
tawā'if meta-category for high-status North Indian courtesans
tāza fresh
tāzagī-i t̤arz freshness of style
taʿziya a ritual model of the shrines of Imams Hasan and Husain carried in Shiʿa Muharram processions
taẕkira memorative collection, collection of biographies of a particular category of person
ṭhagī highway robbery, supposedly involving ritual murder
ṭhākur Rajput hereditary landowner
ṭhāṭh scale, or the fret setting of an instrument like the sitār
ṭhumrī virtuosic and emotive song genre that emphasises the evocation of lyrical meaning
tīvra sharp; scale degree sharpened by a semitone
ʿurs death anniversary of a Sufi saint, celebrated as a wedding
ustād master musician, master teacher
uṣūl the rhythmic cycles of the Persian musical system
uttam the best quality, in this case of musical ensemble
vibhāg a section of a tāla marked at its beginning by a clap or wave
wajd ecstatic state in the Sufi assembly that may be attained through listening to music (see ḥāl)
wakīl lawyer, agent
wāris̤an class of hereditary courtesan
wazīr prime minister, vizier
zanak͟hī endearment for a woman's female lover
ẓarb beat; see tāli

ẕar^{c} unit of length based on an adult male forearm
ẕāt class of person, nominal hierarchical rank of a manṣabdār; ẕāt-i sharīf – the respectable classes
zīr short diagonal diacritical line below a Perso-Arabic letter, generally the short vowel 'i'

Bibliography

Primary Sources

National and Regional Archives

UK National Archives
India Office Records, British Library (IOR)
General Correspondence (E)
Board of Control General Records (F)
Military Records (L/MIL)
National Archives of India (NAI)
Foreign Department Consultations (FDC)
Foreign Department Proceedings (FDP)
Foreign Political (FP)
Foreign Secret (FS)
Andhra Pradesh State Archives
Norfolk Records Office
Fraser of Reelig Archive, Invernesshire

Recordings

Chapman, Jane, harpsichord, with Yu-Wei Hu, flute. *The Oriental Miscellany: Airs of Hindustan, William Hamilton Bird.* Signum Classics, 2015. SIGCD415.

Primary Sources: Manuscripts

ᶜAbd-ul-hamid Lahori. *Pādishāhnāma.* Royal Collection Trust, RCIN 1005025 (1656/7).

ᶜAbd-ul-karim, Shaikh. *Jawāhir al-Mūsīqāt-i Muḥammadī.* British Library, Or. 12,857 (c. 1570/c. 1630).

ᶜAbd-ur-rahman Shahnawaz Khan. *Mir'āt-i Āftāb-numā.* British Library, Add. 16,697 (1803/4).

Ala-ud-din Muhammad Chishti of Barnawa, Shaikh. *Chishtiyya-i Bihishtiyya.* Asiatic Society of Bengal, Curzon Coll. 78 (1655/6).

Anon. Edinburgh 585(4). *Untitled Treatise on Tāla.* University of Edinburgh, Or. MS 585 no.4, ff. 37v–66r (1788).

Ghunyat al-Munya. British Library, I O Islamic 1863 (1375).

Risāla dar ᶜIlm-i Mūsīqī. Salar Jung Museum Library, P Kash 38, ff. 369v–387r (1770–1).

Untitled. British Library, Delhi Persian 1501 (Late 18 C, for Shah ᶜAlam II).

[Anon.] attr. ᶜInayat Khan ᶜAli. *Sangīt Sarāvalī*. British Library, Delhi Persian, 1502d (late 18 C/early 19 C).

attr. Rashik Kalyan. *Sangīt Sarāvatī*. Khuda Bakhsh Oriental Public Library, hl. 2782 (late 18 C/early 19 C).

Anup, Khushhal Khan. *Rāg Darshan*. University of Pennsylvania Library, Lawrence J Schoenberg Collection, LJS 63 (Brajbhasha 1800).

Rāg Darshan. Government Oriental Manuscripts Library, University of Madras, Persian MS D515 (modern copy D1024) (Persian 1808/9).

Rāg-Rāginī Roz o Shab. Salar Jung Museum Library, Urdu Mus 2 (1833–6).

Bahadur Singh. *Yādgār-i Bahādurī*. British Library, Or. 1652 (1834).

Bakhshu, Nayak. *Sahasras*, or *Hāzār Dhurpad-i Nāyak Bakhshū*. Compiled by Islam Khan. British Library, I O Islamic 1116 (1637–46).

British Library, I O Islamic 1808.

Basit Khan. *Collection of Three Treatises: Sangīt Sarāvartī* [*Sarāvalī/Sarāvatī*], *Shams al-Aṣwāt and Uṣūl al-Naghmāt al-Āṣafī*. Private collection of Ustad Irfan Muhammad Khan, Kolkata (1856).

Crotch, William. 'Lecture I: On the Music of the Ancients and National Music.' Lecture at the Royal Institution London. Norfolk Records Office, 11066 (1829).

'Lecture on National Music'. Norfolk Records Office, 11229, pp. 3–16 (1798–1829).

'National Tunes.' Handwritten musical examples. Norfolk Records Office, 11097 (1798–1806).

Damodara/Harivallabha/Jivan Khan. *Saṅgīta-darpaṇa*. British Library, I O San 2399 (late 18 C).

Dinanath son of Basudeo. *Collection of Treatises on Music*. Royal Asiatic Society, London, RAS 2010 (5) (1725).

Diyanat Khan, Shah Qubad. *Collection of Treatises on Music*. British Library, Or. 2361 (1660s).

Ghulam Raza ibn Muhammad Panah. *Uṣūl al-Naghmāt al-Āṣafī*. Salar Jung Museum Library, Hyderabad, Persian Mus 2 (1793/4).

Uṣūl al-Naghmāt al-Āṣafī. Khuda Bakhsh Oriental Public Library, Patna, h.l. 3971 (1792/3).

Uṣūl al-Naghmāt al-Āṣafī. British Library, I O Islamic 2083 (c. 1790).

Harivallabha. *Saṅgīta-darpaṇa*. British Library, Add. 26,540 (1653).

Hasan bin Khwaja Tahir, Qazi. *Miftāḥ al-Surod*. Indur (Nizamabad), 1691. Victorian and Albert Museum, IS–61:1–197 (1663/4).

Miftāḥ al-Surod. Salar Jung Museum Library, Hyderabad, Persian Mus 13.

Miftāḥ al-Surod. Bodleian Library, Ms.Pers.c.38.

Surod al-Baḥr. Salar Jung Museum Library, Persian Mus 8, ff. 1v–14r (1662/3).

Hasan Maududi Chishti, Hakim. *Risāla-i Mūsīqī*. Salar Jung Museum Library, Persian Mus 7 (1761/2).

Imam Khan, Hakim Muhammad Karam. *Maᶜdan al-Mūsīqī*. British Library, MSS Urdu 143 (1855/6–post-1858).

ᶜIwaz Muhammad Kamilkhani. *Risāla dar ᶜAmal-i Bīn*. Bodleian Library, Oxford, Ouseley 158, ff. 123r–32v (1668/9).

Jana Begum. *Risāla-i Mūsīqī*. Bodleian Library, Ouseley 225 (early 17 C).

Johnson, Richard. *Untitled Collection of Songs*. British Library, I O Islamic 1906 (c. 1780–5).

Kalimatullah, Safdar Ali Khan Bahadur. *Rāgsandhav*. British Library, Or. 14,328 (1812).

Kaukab, Asadullah Khan. *Jauhar-i Mūsīqī*. Private collection, Ustad Irfan Muhammad Khan (1915).

Lacchiram, Diwan. *Buddhi-prakāsh-darpaṇa*. British Library, Or. 2765 (late 17 C).

Ludlow, Maj-Gen John. Letters and Papers. British Library, MSS Eur D814 (1773–1880)

Mahlaqa Bai Chanda. *Dīwān-i Chandā*. British Library, I O Islamic 2768 (1799).

Mazhar Khan, Nawab. *K̲h̲ulāsat al-ᶜAish-i ᶜĀlam-Shāhī*. Bodleian Library, Oxford, Elliott 182, ff. 1–288 (1763/4).

   K̲h̲ulāsat al-ᶜAish-i ᶜĀlam-Shāhī. Bodleian Library, Oxford, Ouseley Add. 123 (1798).

   K̲h̲ulāsat al-ᶜAish-i ᶜĀlam-Shāhī. British Library, I O Islamic 3623.

Metcalfe, Sir Thomas. *Reminiscences of Imperial Delhi*. British Library, Add. Or. 5475 (1843).

Mir Salih Qawwal Dehlavi. *Risāla-i Nishāṭ-ārā*. Royal Asiatic Society, RAS Persian 210 (5), ff. 78–89 (c. 1660).

   Risāla-i Nishāṭ-ārā. British Library, Delhi Persian 1502c.

Mirza Khan ibn Fakhr-ud-din. *Tuḥfat al-Hind*. British Library, RSPA 78 (c. 1675/1768).

   Tuḥfat al-Hind. British Library, I O Islamic 1861 (c. 1675).

Najm, Muhammad Riza Tabataba'i. *Nag̲h̲ma-i ᶜAndalīb*. British Library, Or. 1811 (1845).

Nizami Ganjavi (1140/1–1202/3). *K̲h̲amsa*. Imperial Mughal. British Library, Or. 12,208 (1593–5).

Plowden, Sophia. *Album* and *Tunebook*. Fitzwilliam Museum, University of Cambridge, MS380 (1788).

   Diary. British Library, MSS Eur F127/94 (January 1787–January 1789).

   Letter. British Library, Eur MSS B187 (1783).

Ranj, Mir Muhammad Nasir Muhammadi and Miyan Himmat Khan. *Aṣl al-Uṣūl*. Andhra Pradesh Government Oriental Manuscripts Library, Falsafa 326 (c. 1815).

   Aṣl al-Uṣūl. British Library, I O Islamic 3162.

Shah ᶜAlam II, Emperor of Hindustan (r. 1759–1806). Royal *farmān* giving Sophia Plowden the title of Begum. British Library, I O 4439.

Shakir Khan. *Tārīkh-i Shākir Khānī*. British Library, Add. 6568 (1768).

Skinner, James. *Kitāb-i Tashrīḥ al-Aqwām*. Library of Congress, Ms. No. 34/ Rosenwald 2076 (1825).

Tashrīḥ al-Aqwām. British Library, Add. 27,255 (1825).

Tazkirāt al-Umarā'. British Library, Add. 27,254 (before 1830).

Wajid ᶜAli Shah, Nawab of Lucknow (r. 1847–56, d. 1887). *ᶜIshqnāma*. Royal Collection Trust, RCIN 1005035 (1849/50).

Zamir, Mirza Raushan. *Tarjuma-i Kitāb-i Pārījātak*. British Library, Egerton 793 (before 1666/7).

Tarjuma-i Kitāb-i Pārījātak. British Library, RSPA 72 (1688 copy).

Zia-ud-din. *Ḥayy al-Arwāḥ*. John Rylands Library, University of Manchester, Persian 346 (c. 1785–8).

Primary Sources: Published

Abu'l Fazl. *Áín i Akbarí*. Edited by Henry Blochmann. Bibliotheca India Series. Calcutta: Baptist Mission Press, 1869.

The Ain i Akbari. Vol. i. Translated by Henry Blochmann. Bibliotheca Indica Series. Calcutta: Baptist Mission Press and Asiatic Society of Bengal, 1873.

Ain-i-Ākbari. Vol. iii. Translated by Col. Henry S Jarrett, revised by Jadunath Sarkar. Calcutta: Royal Asiatic Society of Bengal, 1948.

Akbarnāma. Vol. i. Translated by Henry Beveridge. Bibliotheca Indica Series. Calcutta: Asiatic Society and Baptist Mission Press, 1897.

Ahobala Pandit. *Saṅgīta-pārijāta*. Hathras: Sangit Karyalaya, 1971.

Alladiya Khan. *My Life: As Told to His Grandson Azizuddin Khan*. Translated by Amlan Das Gupta and Urmila Bhirdikar. Calcutta: Thema, 2000.

Anon. *Ghunyat al-Munya: The Earliest Known Persian Work on Indian Music*. Edited and translated by Shahab Sarmadee. Bombay: Asia, 1978.

Anup, Khushhal Khan. *Rag Darshan and Risala-i-Mosiqi-e Mast Mohammadshahi*. Edited by Chander Shekhar. New Delhi: National Mission for Manuscripts, 2014.

Argyll, Duke of [George John Douglas Campbell]. 'Opening Address, Session 1864–5'. *Proceedings of the Royal Society of Edinburgh* 5 (1866), 263–320.

[ᶜArzani', Muhammad Akbar]. *Tashrīh-ul-Moosiqui: Persian Translation of Tansen's Original Work 'Budh Prakash'*. Edited by Najma Perveen Ahmad. New Delhi: Manohar, 2012.

Babur, Emperor of Hindustan (r. 1526–31). *The Bābur-nāma in English (Memoirs of Bābur)*. Translated by Annette Susannah Beveridge. London: Luzac, 1922.

Bakhshu, Nayak. *Sahasarasa: Nāyaka Bakhśu ke Dhrupadoṃ kā Saṅgraha*. Edited and translated by Prem Lata Sharma. New Delhi: Sangit Natak Akademi, 1972.

Bakhtawar Khan. 'Mir'āt-i ^{c}Ālam'. In Sir Henry Myers Elliott and John Dowson (eds.). *The History of India as Told by its Own Historians*. Vol. vii, 144–64. London: Trübner, 1877.

Beg, Mirza Farhatullah. *Dehlī Kī Ākhirī Sham^{c}*. New Delhi: Dihli Urdu Akademi, 1986.

Bhatkhande, Vishnu Narayan. *A Comparative Study of Some of the Leading Music Systems of the 15th, 16th, 17th and 18th Centuries*. Delhi: Low Price, 1990.

A Short Historical Survey of the Music of Upper India. Baroda: Indian Musicological Society, 1985.

Biggs, Edward Smith. *A Second Set of Hindoo Airs with English Words Adapted to Them by Mrs Opie*. London: Robert Birchall, c. 1805.

Bird, William Hamilton. *The Oriental Miscellany; Being a Collection of the Most Favourite Airs of Hindoostan, Compiled and Adapted for the Harpsichord, andc*. Calcutta: Joseph Cooper, 1789.

The Oriental Miscellany; Being a Collection of the Most Favourite Airs of Hindoostan, Compiled and Adapted for the Harpsichord, andc. Edinburgh: Gow and Shepherd, 1805.

Broughton, Thomas D. *The Costume, Character, Manners, Domestic Habits and Religious Ceremonies of the Mahrattas*. London: John Murray, 1813.

Bushby, Henry Jeffreys. *Widow Burning: A Narrative*. London: Longman, Brown, Green and Longmans, 1855.

Crooke, William. *The Tribes and Castes of the North-Western Provinces and Oudh*. 4 vols. Calcutta: Government of India, 1896.

Crotch, William. *Specimens of Various Styles of Music Referred to in a Course of Lectures Read at Oxford and London and Adapted to Keyed Instruments*. 2 vols. London: Robert Birchall, 1807.

Damodara, Catura. *Saṅgīta-darpaṇa*. Edited by K. Vasudeva Sastri. Madras Government Oriental Series, Saraswathi Mahal Series, no. 34. Tanjore: Saraswathi Mahal, 1952.

Dargah Quli Khan. *Muraqqa'-e Dehli: The Mughal Capital in Muhammad Shah's Time*. Translated by Chander Shekhar and Sharma Mitra Chenoy. Delhi: Deputy, 1989.

Muraqqa^{c}-i Dehlī. Edited by Khaliq Anjum. New Delhi: Anjuman-i Taraqqī-i Urdu, 1993.

Dawwani, Jalaluddin. *Akhlāq-i Jalālī*. Lucknow: Nawal Kishore Press, 1879.

Dodwell, Mr and Mr Miles. *Alphabetical List of the Officers of the Indian Army*. London: Longman, Orme, Brown, 1838.

Doyley, Charles and Thomas Williamson. *The European in India: From a Collection of Drawings*. London: Edward Orme, 1813.

Dyce Sombre, David Ochterlony. 'Exhibit, No. 46: Mr. Dyce Sombre's Journal or Diary [1833–38]'. In Prerogative Court of Canturbury. *Dyce Sombre Against Troup, Solaroli, and Prinsep, and the Hon. East India Company*. Vol. i. London: Henry Hansard, n.d., 220–415.

[East India Company.] *Abstract of State Trials Held, Under Special Commission, at Jyepoor, for the Trial of the Ex-Minister Sunghee Jotha Ram, His Brother and Son, and Other Persons Implicated in a Plot to Subvert the Local Government, Resulting in an Assault upon the Person of Major N Alves, Agent to the Governor General, and the Murder of Mr Martin Blake.* Calcutta: G H Huttman, Military Orphan Press, 1837.

Eden, Emily. *Up the Country: Letters Written to Her Sister from the Upper Provinces of India.* 2 vols. London: Richard Bentley, 1866.

Fanshawe, Herbert C. *A Handbook for Travellers in India, Burma and Ceylon.* 8th ed. London: John Murray, 1911.

Faqirullah, Saif Khan. *Tarjuma-i-Mānakutūhala and Risāla-i-Rāg Darpan.* Edited and translated by Shahab Sarmadee. New Delhi: Indira Gandhi National Centre for the Performing Arts and Delhi: Motilal Banarsidass, 1996.

Fergusson, James. *The History of Indian and Eastern Architecture.* Vol. ii. London: J Murray, 1876.

Forster, George. *A Journey from Bengal to England, through the Northern Part of India, Kashmire, Afghanistan, and Persia.* Calcutta: Cooper and Upjohn, 1790.

Fowke, Francis. 'On the Vina or Indian Lyre'. Reproduced in Sourindro Mohun Tagore (ed.). *Hindu Music from Various Authors.* 2nd ed. Calcutta: I. C. Bose, Stanhope, 1882 [orig. 1788], 193–7.

Fraser, James Baillie. *Military Memoir of Lieut.-Col. James Skinner, C.B.* Vol. ii. London: Smith, Elder, 1851.

Ghalib, Mirza Asadullah Khan. *Dastanbuy.* Translated by Khwaja Ahmad Faruqi. Bombay: Asia Publishing House, 1970.

Ghalib 1797–1869: Life and Letters. Edited and translated by Khurshidul Islam and Ralph Russell. New Delhi: Oxford University Press, 1994.

Gilchrist, John. *The Oriental Linguist.* Calcutta: Ferris, 1798.

Graham, Maria, Lady Callcott. *Journal of a Residence in India.* Edinburgh: Constable, 1812.

Hasan Shah, Sayyid Muhammad, original 1893 translation by Sajjad Hussain Kasmandavi. *Nashtar.* Edited by ᶜIshrat Rahmani. Lahore: Majlis-i Tarqi-i Adab, 1963 [orig. 1893].

The Nautch Girl. Translated by Qurratulain Hyder. New Delhi: Stirling, 1993.

Hill, Geo. 'Gleanings in Family History from the Antrim Coast: The MacNaghtens and MacNeills'. *Ulster Journal of Archaeology* 8 (1860), 127–44.

Hodson, Maj Vernon C P (ed.). *List of the Officers of the Bengal Army, 1758–1834.* Part III. London: Phillimore, 1946.

Ikhwan us-Safa'. *On Music: An Arabic Critical Edition and English Translation of Epistle 5.* Edited and translated by Owen Wright. Epistles of the Brethren of Purity. Oxford: Oxford University Press and the Institute of Ismaili Studies, 2010.

Imam Khan, Hakim Muhammad Karam. *Ma^{c}dan al-Mūsīqī*. Edited by Sayyid Wajid ^{c}Ali. Lucknow: Hindustani Press, 1925.

Islam Khan. '*Dībācha-i Dhurpad-hā-i Nāyak*.' In Iqtidar Hussain Siddiqi (ed.). *Majmū^{c} al-Afkār*. Patna: Khuda Bakhsh Oriental Public Library, 1993.

Jacquemont, Victor. *Etat politique et social de l'Inde du sud en 1832. Extraits de son Journals de Voyage*. Paris: Société de l'histoire des colonies françaises, 1934.

Voyage dans l'Inde. 4 vols. Paris, 1841. Extracts translated by Giles Tillotson. *Jaipur Nama: Tales from the Pink City*. New Delhi: Penguin, 2007, 90–104.

Jones, Sir William. 'On the Musical Modes of the Hindoos: Written in 1784 and since Much Enlarged'. In Lady Anna Maria Jones (ed.). *The Works of Sir William Jones, in Six Volumes*. Vol. I, 413–43. London: G G and J. Robinson, 1799.

'On the Musical Modes of the Hindoos: Written in 1784 and since Much Enlarged'. In Sourindro Mohun Tagore (ed.). *Hindu Music from Various Authors*. 2nd ed. Calcutta: Bose, 1882, 125–60.

Kamwar Khan, Muhammad Hadi. *Tazkirāt al-Salātīn Chaghta*. Edited and translated by Muzaffar Alam. Mumbai: Asia Publishing House, 1980.

Karamatullah Khan. *Isrār-i Karāmat ^{c}Urf Naghmāt-i Ni^{c}mat*. Allahabad: Janaki, 1908.

Khafi Khan. *Muntakhāb al-Lubāb*. Edited and translated by Anees Jahan Syed as *Aurangzeb in Muntakhab-al-lubab*. Bombay: Somaiya, 1977.

Kindersley, Jemima. *Letters from the Island of Teneriffe, Brazil, the Cape of Good Hope, and the East Indies*. London: J. Nourse, 1777.

Lahawri, Abd al-Hamid. *The Badshah Nama [Pādishāhnāma]*. Edited by Kabir al-din Ahmad and Abd al-Rahim. 2 vols. Bibliotheca Indica Series. Calcutta: College Press, 1867–8.

Leaf, Walter. *Versions from Hafiz: An Essay in Persian Metre*. London: Grant Richards, 1898.

Mardan ^{c}Ali Khan. *Ghuncha-i Rāg*. Lucknow: Naval Kishore, 1862–3.

Martin, Claude. *A Man of the Enlightenment in Eighteenth-Century India: The Letters of Claude Martin, 1766–1800*. Edited by Rosie Llewellyn Jones. New Delhi: Permanent Black, 2003.

Mir, Mir Taqi. *Nikāt al-Shu^{c}arā*. Translated into Urdu by Hamida Khatoon. New Delhi: Dihli Urdu Akademi, 1994.

Remembrances. Edited and translated by Choudhri Mohammed Naim. Murty Classical Library of India. Cambridge, MA: Harvard University Press, 2019.

Selected Ghazals and Other Poems. Edited and translated by Shamsur Rahman Faruqi. Murty Classical Library of India. Cambridge, MA: Harvard University Press, 2019.

Zikr-i Mir: The Autobiography of the Eighteenth-Century Mughal Poet Mir Muhammad Taqi Mir. Translated by Choudhri Mohammed Naim. New Delhi: Oxford University Press, 1999.

A Garden of Kashmir: The Ghazals of Mir. Edited and commentary by Frrances W. Pritchett. www.columbia.edu/itc/mealac/pritchett/00garden/index.html.

Mir Yar ᶜAli 'Jan Sahib'. *The Incomparable Festival*. Edited and translated by Shad Naved and Razak Khan. New Delhi: Penguin Classics, 2021.

Musaddas-e Tahniyat-e Jashn-e Benazīr. Edited by Waqarul Hasan Siddiqi and Imtiaz Ali Khandera. Rampur: Rampur Raza Library, 1999.

Mirza Khan ibn Fakhr-ud-din. *Tuḥfat al-Hind*. Edited by NH Ansari. Vol. i. Tehran: Bunyād-i Farhang-i Īrān, 1968.

Mundy, Captain Godfrey. *Pen and Pencil Sketches Being the Journal of a Tour in India*. Vol. i. London: John Murray, 1832.

Mushafi, Ghulam Hamadani. *Tazkīra-i Hindī*. Edited by Moulvi Abdul Haq. Aurangabad: Anjuman-i Taraqqī-i Urdu, 1933.

Pernau, Margrit and Yunus Jaffery (eds. and trans.). *Information and the Public Sphere: Persian Newsletters from Mughal Delhi*. Oxford: Oxford University Press, 2009.

Phipps, Osmond George. *Taza ba Taza, Nao ba Nao: The Famous Song of the Persian Poet Hafiz*. British Library, H.1771.o.(39), 1857.

Polier, Antoine. *A European Experience of the Mughal Orient: The Ijaz-i Arsalani (Persian Letters, 1773–1779) of Antoine-Louis-Henri Polier*. Edited by Seema Alavi and Muzaffar Alam. New Delhi: Oxford University Press, 2007.

Pratap Singh, Maharaja Sawai of Jaipur (r. 1778–1803). *Saṅgīt-sār*. Edited by Balwant T. Sahasrabuddhe. Pune: Poona Gayan Samaj, 1910–12 [1799].

Prinsep, James. *Benares Illustrated in a Series of Drawings*. Calcutta: Baptist Mission Press, 1831.

Useful Tables, Forming an Appendix to the Journal of the Asiatic Society: Part 1, Coins, Weights, and Measures of British India. Calcutta: Bishop's College Press, 1840.

Qutban Suhrawardi, Shaikh. *Mṛgāvatī*. Translated by Aditya Behl as *The Magic Doe*. Edited by Wendy Doniger. Oxford: Oxford University Press, 2012.

Ras Baras Khan. *Shams al-Aṣvāt: The Sun of Songs by Ras Baras*. Edited and translated by Mehrdad Fallahzadeh and Mahmoud Hassanabadi. Uppsala: Acta Universitatis Upsalensis, 2012.

Rasikh, ᶜInayat Khan. *Risāla-i Zikr-i Mughanniyān-i Hindūstān*. Edited by Syed Ali Haider. Patna: Arabic and Persian Research Institute, 1961.

Rumi, Maulana Jalaluddin. *Masnawī Maulawī Maᶜnawī*. Lucknow: Naval Kishore, 1860.

Sadiq ᶜAli Khan. *Sarmāya-i ᶜIshrat, Maᶜrūf Qānūn-i Mūsīqī*. 1st ed. Delhi: Faiz-i ᶜĀm, 1869.

Sama ᶜUmar ibn Yahya Kabuli. *Lehjāt-e-Sikāndershāhi*. Edited by Shahab Sarmadee. New Delhi: Indian Council of Historical Research, 1999.

Samsam-ud-Daula Shah Nawaz Khan and ᶜAbdul Hayy. *Maāthir-ul-Umara*. Edited by Henry Beveridge, revised edition by Baini Prashad. 2 vols. Patna: Janaki Prakashan, 1971.

Saqi Musta'idd Khan. *Ma'āsir-i ᶜĀlamgīrī.* Translated by Jadunath Sarkar. Bibliotheca Indica Series. Calcutta: Baptist Mission Press, 1947.

Sayyid Ahmad Khan. *Āṣār al-Ṣanādīd.* 1st ed. Shahjahanabad: Matbaᶜ-i Sayyid al-Akhbār, 1847.

Asār-us-Sanadīd. Edited and translated by Rana Safvi. New Delhi: Tulika, 2018.

Shah ᶜAlam II, Emperor of Hindustan (r. 1759–1806). *Nādirāt-i Shāhī.* Edited by Imtiaz ᶜAli Arshi. Rampur: Raza Library, 1944 (1797).

Sher ᶜAli Khan Lodi. *Tazkira-i Mir'āt al-Khayāl.* Edited by Hamid Hasani and Bihruz Safarzadeh. Tehran: Rawzaneh, 1998.

Singh, Munshi Hardyal. *Report on the Census of 1891.* Vol. ii: The Castes of Marwar. Jodhpur: Marwar Darbar, 1894.

Sleeman, Lieut. Col. William H. *Diary of a Tour through Oude.* Vol. ii. Lucknow: n. p., 1852.

Solvyns, Balt[hazar]. *A Catalogue of 250 Etchings Descriptive of the Manners, Customs, Character, Dress, and Religious Ceremonies of the Hindoos.* Calcutta: n.p., 1799.

Sprenger, Aloys *A Catalogue of the Arabic, Persian and Hindustany Manuscripts of the Libraries of the King of Oudh.* Calcutta: Baptist Mission Press, 1854.

Sutherland, James CC *Reports of Cases Determined in the Court of Sudder Dewanny Adawlut.* Vol. v. Calcutta: Sreenauth Banerjee, 1871.

Tagore, Sourindro Mohun. *Saṅgīta-sāra-sangraha.* Calcutta: IC Bose, 1875.

Tod, Lieut. Col. James. *Annals and Antiquities of Rajast'han.* 2 vols. London: Smith, Elder, 1829.

Vyasadeva Ragasagara, Krishananda, and Basu (1842–9). *Saṅgīta-rāga-kalpadruma.* Calcutta: Bangiya Sahitya Parishad, 1914.

Wajid ᶜAli Shah, Nawab of Lucknow (r. 1847–56, d. 1887). *Parīkhāna.* Edited by Tehseen Sarwari. Karachi: n.p., 1958.

Ṣaut al-Mubārak. Lucknow: private publication, 1852/3. British Library, 14835. e.1.

Willard, Capt. N Augustus. 'A Treatise on the Music of Hindoostan'. Reproduced in Sourindro Mohun Tagore (ed.). *Hindu Music from Various Authors.* 2nd ed. Calcutta: Bose, 1882 [orig. 1834], 1–124.

Zahir Dehlavi. *Dastān-i Ghadr: Yā Tarāz-i Zahīrī.* Lahore: Academy Punjab Trust, 1955.

Secondary Sources

Ahmad, Najma Perveen. *Hindustani Music: A Study of Its Development in Seventeenth and Eighteenth Centuries.* New Delhi: Manohar, 1984.

Ahmed, Shahab. *What Is Islam? The Importance of Being Islamic.* Princeton: Princeton University Press, 2015.

Aitken, Molly Emma. *The Intelligence of Tradition in Rajput Court Painting*. New Haven: Yale University Press, 2010.

'The Laud Rāgamālā Album, Bikaner, and the Sociability of Subimperial Painting'. *Archives of Asian Art* 63.1 (2013), 27–58.

'Parataxis and the Practice of Reuse, from Mughal Margins to Mīr Kalān Khān'. *Archives of Asian Art* 59 (2009), 81–103.

Aktor, Mikael. 'Social Classes: Varṇa'. In Patrick Olivelle and Donald R. Davis (eds.). *The Oxford History of Hinduism. Hindu Law: A New History of Dharmaśāstra*. Oxford: Oxford University Press, 2017, 60–77.

Alaghband-Zadeh, Chloë. 'Listening to North Indian Classical Music: How Embodied Ways of Listening Perform Imagined Histories and Social Class'. *Ethnomusicology* 61.2 (2017), 207–33.

Alam, Muzaffar. *The Crisis of Empire in Mughal North India: Awadh and the Punjab, 1707–48*. New Delhi: Oxford University Press, 1986.

Alam, Muzaffar and Sanjay Subrahmanyam. 'Envisioning Power: The Political Thought of a Late Eighteenth-Century Mughal Prince'. *Indian Economic and Social History Review* 43.2 (2006), 131–61.

'The Making of a Munshi'. *Comparative Studies of South Asia, Africa and the Middle East* 24.2 (2004), 61–72.

Alavi, Seema. 'Medical Culture in Transition: Mughal Gentleman Physician and the Native Doctor in Early Colonial India'. *Modern Asian Studies* 42.5 (2008), 853–97.

al-Faruqi, Lois. 'Music, Musicians, and Muslim Law'. *Asian Music* 17.1 (1985), 3–36.

Andrews, Walter G and Mehmet Kalpaklı. *The Age of Beloveds: Love and the Beloved in Early-Modern Ottoman and European Culture and Society*. Durham, NC: Duke University Press, 2005.

Archer, Mildred and Toby Falk. *India Revealed: The Life and Adventures of James and William Fraser*. London: Weidenfeld Nicolson, 1989.

Arondekar, Anjali. 'In the Absence of Reliable Ghosts: Sexuality, Historiography, South Asia'. *Differences: A Journal of Feminist Cultural Studies* 25.3 (2015), 98–122.

Asafjahi, Syed Ali Asgar Bilgrami. *Landmarks of the Deccan: A Comprehensive Guide to the Archaeological Remains of the City and Suburbs of Hyderabad*. New Delhi: Asian Educational Services Reprint, 1992 [orig. 1927].

Ashton, F. 'The Salt Industry of Rajputana'. *Journal of Indian Art and Industry* 9 (1902), 23–32, 48–64.

Asif, Manan Ahmed. *The Loss of Hindustan: The Invention of India*. Cambridge, MA: Harvard University Press, 2020.

Avery, Peter. 'Ouseley, Gore'. *Encyclopaedia Iranica*. Online edition, 2004. www.iranicaonline.org/articles/ouseley-sir-gore.

Babayan, Kathryn. *The City as Anthology: Eroticism and Urbanity in Early Modern Isfahan*. Stanford: Stanford University Press, 2021.

Bakhle, Janaki. *Two Men and Music: Nationalism and the Making of an Indian Classical Tradition*. New York: Oxford University Press, 2005.

Banerjee, Sumanta. *Dangerous Outcast: The Prostitute in Nineteenth Century Bengal*. Kolkata: Seagull Books, 1998.

Barley, Nigel. *White Rajah: A Biography of Sir James Brooke*. London: Little, Brown, 2002.

Barlow, Jon and Lakshmi Subramanian. 'Music and Society in North India: From the Mughals to the Mutiny'. *Economic and Political Weekly* 42.19 (2007), 1779–87.

Basu, Analabha, Neeta Sarkar-Roy and Partha P Majumder. 'Genomic Reconstruction of the History of Extant Populations of India Reveals Five Distinct Ancestral Components and a Complex Structure'. *Proceedings of the National Academy of Sciences* 113.6 (2016), 1594–9.

Bates, Crispin. 'Race, Caste and Tribe in Central India: The Early Origins of Indian Anthropometry'. In Peter Robb (ed.). *The Concept of Race in South Asia*. New Delhi: Oxford University Press, 1995, 219–59.

Bayly, Christopher A. *Empire and Information: Intelligence Gathering and Social Communication in India, 1780–1870*. Cambridge: Cambridge University Press, 1996.

Rulers, Townsmen and Bazaars: North Indian Society in the Age of British Expansion, 1770–1870. Oxford: Oxford University Press, 1983.

Bayly, Susan. *Caste, Society and Politics in India from the Eighteenth Century to the Modern Age*. Cambridge: Cambridge University Press, 2001.

Behl, Aditya. 'Pages from the Book of Religions: Encountering Difference in Mughal India'. In Sheldon Pollock (ed.). *Forms of Knowledge in Early Modern Asia: Explorations in the Intellectual History of India and Tibet, 1500–1800*. Durham, NC: Duke University Press, 2011, 210–39.

'Poet of the Bazaars: Naẕīr Akbarābādī, 1735–1830'. In Kathryn Hansen and David Lelyveld (eds.). *A Wilderness of Possibilities: Urdu Studies in Transnational Perspective*. New Delhi: Oxford University Press, 2005, 192–222.

Bor, Joep. 'The Rise of Ethnomusicology: Sources on Indian Music c. 1780–1890'. *Yearbook for Traditional Music* 20 (1988), 51–73.

'The Voice of the Sarangi: An Illustrated History of Bowing in India'. *Quarterly Journal of the National Centre for the Performing Arts* 15.3–4 and 16.1 (1986–7), 1–183.

Bor, Joep, Françoise 'Nalini' Delvoye, Jane Harvey and Emmie te Nijenhuis (eds.) *Hindustani Music: Thirteenth to Twentieth Centuries*. New Delhi: Manohar, 2010.

Bor, Joep, Suvarnalata Rao, Wim van der Meer, and Jane Harvey. *The Raga Guide: A Survey of 74 Hindustani Ragas*. Monmouth: Nimbus, 1999.

Bor, Joep and Philippe Bruguiére (eds.). *Gloire des princes, louange des dieux: patrimoine musical de l'Hindoustan du xive au xxe siècle*. Paris: Musée de la Musique, 2003.

Brittlebank, Kate. *Tiger: The Life of Tipu Sultan*. New Delhi: Juggernaut, 2016.

Brown [Schofield], Katherine Butler. 'Did Aurangzeb Ban Music? Questions for the Historiography of His Reign'. *Modern Asian Studies* 41.1 (2007), 77–120.

'Evidence of Indo-Persian Musical Synthesis? The *Tanbur* and *Rudra Vina* in Seventeenth-Century Indo-Persian Treatises'. *Journal of the Indian Musicological Society* 36–7 (2006), 89–103.

'Hindustani Music in the Time of Aurangzeb'. Unpublished PhD Dissertation. SOAS University of London, 2003.

'If Music Be the Food of Love: Masculinity and Eroticism in the Mughal Mehfil'. In Francesca Orsini (ed.). *Love in South Asia: A Cultural History*. Cambridge: Cambridge University Press, 2006, 61–83.

'The Origins and Early Development of Khayal'. In Joep Bor, Françoise 'Nalini' Delvoye, Jane Harvey and Emmie te Nijenhuis (eds.). *Hindustani Music: Thirteenth to Twentieth Centuries*. New Delhi: Manohar, 2010, 159–91.

'Review of Janaki Bakhle, Two Men and Music: Nationalism and the Making of an Indian Classical Tradition (New York: Oxford University Press, 2005)'. *Journal of Asian Studies* 67.1 (2008), 335–7.

'The Social Liminality of Musicians: Case Studies from Mughal India and Beyond'. *Twentieth-Century Music* 3.1 (2007), 13–49.

'The Ṭhāṭ System of Seventeenth-Century North Indian Rāgas'. *Asian Music* 35.1 (2003–4), 1–13.

Brown, Rebecca M. 'Colonial Polyrhythm: Imaging Action in the Early 19th Century'. *Visual Anthropology* 26.4 (2013), 269–97.

Burgess, James. *The Chronology of Modern India*. Edinburgh: John Grant, 1913.

Busch, Allison. *Poetry of Kings: The Classical Hindi Literature of Mughal India*. Oxford: Oxford University Press, 2011.

Buyers, Christopher. 'India: The Timurid Dynasty'. *The Royal Ark*. 2001–22. www.royalark.net/India4/delhi6.htm.

Bywater, Michael. *Lost Worlds: What Have We Lost and Where Did It Go?* London: Granta, 2004.

Capwell, Charles. 'Marginality and Musicology in Nineteenth-Century Calcutta: The Case of Sourindro Mohun Tagore'. In Philip V. Bohlman and Bruno Nettl (eds.). *Comparative Musicology and Anthropology of Music: Essays on the History of Ethnomusicology*. Chicago: University of Chicago Press, 1991, 228–43.

Chancey, Marla K. 'The Making of the Anglo-Hyderabad Alliance, 1788–1823'. *South Asia: Journal of South Asian Studies* 29.2 (2006), 181–214.

Chatterjee, Indrani. 'Monastic Governmentality, Colonial Misogyny, and Postcolonial Amnesia in South Asia'. *History of the Present* 3.1 (2013), 57–98.

'Women, Monastic Commerce, and Coverture in Eastern India circa 1600–1800 CE'. *Modern Asian Studies* 50.1 (2016), 175–216.

Chatterjee, Kumkum. *The Cultures of History in Early Modern India: Persianization and Mughal Culture in Bengal*. New Delhi: Oxford University Press, 2009.

Merchants, Politics and Society in Early Modern India: Bihar, 1733–1820. Leiden: Brill, 1996.

Cohn, Bernard S. *An Anthropologist Among the Historians*. New Delhi: Oxford University Press, 1987.

Cook, Nicholas. 'Encountering the Other, Redefining the Self: Hindostannie Airs, Haydn's Folksong Settings and the "Common Practice" Style'. In Martin Clayton and Bennett Zon (eds.). *Music and Orientalism in the British Empire, 1780s–1940s*. Aldershot: Ashgate, 2007, 13–37.

Cowgill, Rachel. '"Attitudes with a Shawl": Performance, Femininity, and Spectatorship at the Italian Opera in Early Nineteenth-Century London'. In Rachel Cowgill and Hilary Poriss (eds.). *The Arts of the Prima Donna in the Long Nineteenth Century*. Oxford: Oxford University Press, 2012, 217–51.

Dadlani, Chanchal B. *From Stone to Paper: Architecture as History in the Late Mughal Empire*. New Haven: Yale University Press, 2018.

'Transporting India: The *Gentil Album* and Mughal Manuscript Culture'. *Art History* 38.4 (2015), 748–61.

Dalrymple, William. *The Anarchy: The Relentless Rise of the East India Company*. London: Bloomsbury, 2019.

City of Djinns: A Year in Delhi. London: Penguin, 2003.

(ed.). *Forgotten Masters: Indian Painting for the East India Company* (London: Philip Wilson, 2019).

The Last Mughal: The Fall of a Dynasty, Delhi 1857. London: Bloomsbury, 2006.

Return of a King: The Battle for Afghanistan. London: Bloomsbury, 2013.

White Mughals: Love and Betrayal in Eighteenth-Century India. London: Bloomsbury, 2003.

Dalrymple, William and Anita Anand. *Koh-i-noor: The History of the World's Most Infamous Diamond*. London: Bloomsbury, 2017.

Dalrymple, William and Yuthika Sharma. *Princes and Painters in Mughal Delhi, 1707–1857*. New Haven: Yale University Press and Asia Society Museum, 2012.

Dalton, Dennis. *Mahatma Gandhi: Nonviolent Power in Action*. New York: Columbia University Press, 2012.

Dane, Richard M. 'The Manufacture of Salt in India'. *Journal of the Royal Society of Arts* 72.3729 (1924), 402–18.

Delvoye, Françoise 'Nalini'. 'Collections of Lyrics in Hindustani Music: The Case of Dhrupad'. In Joep Bor, Françoise 'Nalini' Delvoye, Jane Harvey and Emmie te Nijenhuis (eds.). *Hindustani Music: Thirteenth to Twentieth Centuries*. New Delhi: Manohar, 2010, 141–58.

'Indo-Persian Literature on Art-Music: Some Historical and Technical Aspects'. In Françoise Delvoye (ed.). *Confluence of Cultures: French Contributions to Indo-Persian Studies*. New Delhi: Manohar, 1994, 93–130.

Tânsen et la tradition des chants dhrupad en langue braj, du XVIe siècle à nos jours. Paris: Université de la Sorbonne Nouvelle Paris III, 1990.

'The Verbal Content of Dhrupad Songs from the Earliest Collections, I: The Hazar Dhurpad or Sahasras'. *Dhrupad Annual.* (1990), 93–109.

Dirks, Nicholas. *Castes of Mind: Colonialism and the Making of Modern India.* Princeton: Princeton University Press, 2002.

D'Souza, Florence. *Knowledge, Mediation, and Empire: James Tod's Journeys among the Rajputs.* Manchester: Manchester University Press, 2015.

Dudney, Arthur. 'A Desire for Meaning: Khan-i Arzu's Philology and the Place of India in the Eighteenth-Century Persianate World'. Unpublished PhD Dissertation. Columbia University, 2013.

India in the Persian World of Letters: Ḳhān-i Ārzū among the Eighteenth-Century Philologists. Oxford Oriental Monographs. Oxford: Oxford University Press, 2022.

Eaton, Richard M. *India in the Persianate Age: 1000–1765.* London: Allen Lane, 2019.

'The Rise of Written Vernaculars: The Deccan, 1450–1650'. In Francesca Orsini and Samira Sheikh (eds.). *After Timur Left: Culture and Circulation in Fifteenth-Century North India.* New Delhi: Oxford University Press, 2014, 111–29.

A Social History of the Deccan, 1300–1761: Eight Indian Lives. Cambridge: Cambridge University Press, 2005.

Ebeling, Klaus. *Ragamala Painting.* Basel: Ravi Kumar, 1973.

Erdman, Joan L. *Patrons and Performers in Rajasthan: The Subtle Tradition.* Delhi: Chanakya, 1985.

Ernst, Carl and Bruce B Lawrence. *Sufi Martyrs of Love: Chishti Sufism in South Asian and Beyond.* New York: Palgrave Macmillan, 2002.

Ethé, Hermann. *Catalogue of Persian Manuscripts in the Library of the India Office.* Vol. i. Oxford: India Office, 1903.

Ethé, Hermann and Edward Edwards. *Catalogue of Persian Manuscripts in the Library of the India Office.* Vol. ii. Oxford: Clarendon Press, 1937.

Farrell, Gerry. *Indian Music and the West.* Oxford: Oxford University Press, 1997.

Faruqi, Shamsur Rahman. 'A Long History of Urdu Literary Culture, Part I'. In Sheldon Pollock (ed.). *Literary Culture in History: Reconstructions from South Asia.* Berkeley: University of California Press, 2003, 805–63.

The Mirror of Beauty. New Delhi: Penguin, 2013.

Faruqui, Munis D. 'At Empire's End: The Nizam, Hyderabad and Eighteenth-Century India'. *Modern Asian Studies* 43.1 (2009), 5–43.

The Princes of the Mughal Empire, 1504–1719. Cambridge: Cambridge University Press, 2012.

Fischel, Roy S. 'Deccan Sultanates'. In John Mackenzie (ed.). *Encyclopedia of Empire.* Oxford: Wiley–Blackwell, 2016. https://search.credoreference.com/content/entry/wileyempire/deccan_sultanates/

Fuller, Christopher J. 'Ethnographic Inquiry in Colonial India: Herbert Risley, William Crooke, and the Study of Tribes and Castes'. *Journal of the Royal Anthropological Institute* 23 (2017), 603–21.

Gandhi, Supriya. *The Emperor Who Never Was: Dara Shukoh in Mughal India*. Cambridge, MA: Harvard University Press, 2020.

Gaur, Archana. 'Halophiles of Sambhar Salt Lake'. In Joginder Singh and Praveen Gehlot (eds.). *Microbes in Action*. Jodhpur: Agrobios, 2015, 355–68.

Ghosh, Durba. *Sex and the Family in Colonial India: The Making of Empire*. Cambridge: Cambridge University Press, 2006.

Ghuman, Nalini. *Resonances of the Raj: India in the English Musical Imagination, 1897–1947*. New York: Oxford University Press, 2014.

Gold, Daniel. 'The Instability of the King: Magical Insanity and the Yogis' Power in the Politics of Jodhpur, 1803–43'. In David N. Lorenzen (ed.). *Bhakti Religion in North India: Community Identity and Political Action*. Ithaca: State University of New York Press, 1995, 120–32.

Gommans, Jos. 'The Warband in the Making of Eurasian Empires'. In Maaike van Berkel and Jeroen Duindam (eds.). *Prince, Pen, and Sword: Eurasian Perspectives. Rulers and Elites Series*. Leiden: Brill, 2018, 297–383.

Gordon, Stewart. 'Babur: Salt, Social Closeness and Friendship'. *Studies in History* 33.1 (2017), 82–97.

Green, Nile. *Sufism: A Global History*. Chichester: Wiley–Blackwell, 2012.

Guha, Ramachandra. *Gandhi 1914–1948: The Years that Changed the World*. New Delhi: Penguin, 2019.

Guha, Sumit. *Beyond Caste: Identity and Power in South Asia, Past and Present*. Leiden: Brill, 2013.

Hakala, Walter. *Negotiating Languages: Urdu, Hindi, and the Definition of Modern South Asia*. South Asia Across the Disciplines Series. New York: Columbia University Press, 2016.

Hall-Witt, Jennifer. *Fashionable Acts: Opera and Élite Culture in London, 1780–1880*. Hanover: University of New Hampshire Press, 2007.

Hardgrave, Robert L. and Stephen M. Slawek. 'Instruments and Music Culture in Eighteenth Century India: The Solvyns Portraits'. *Asian Music* 20.1 (1988–9), 1–92.

Hermansen, Marcia K. and Bruce B. Lawrence. 'Indo-Persian Tazkiras as Memorative Communications'. In David Gilmartin and Bruce B. Lawrence (eds.). *Beyond Turk and Hindu: Rethinking Religious Identities in Islamicate South Asia*. Gainsville: University Press of Florida, 2000, 149–75.

Hicks, Andrew. *Composing the World: Harmony in the Medieval Platonic Cosmos*. Oxford: Oxford University Press, 2017.

Hofmann, William Rees. 'Singing Sufis in Text: Music, and Sufi Poetics ca. 1250–1600'. Unpublished PhD Dissertation. SOAS University of London, 2022.

Hooja, Rima. 'Tod Manuscript Collection'. Unpublished handlist. London: Royal Asiatic Society, 2002.

Horstmann, Monika. *In Favour of Govinddevjī: Historical Documents Relating to a Deity of Vrindaban and Eastern Rajasthan*. New Delhi: Indira Gandhi National Centre for the Arts and Manohar, 1999.

Husain, Ruquiya K. 'Mirza Zulqarnain: An Armenian Noble'. *Proceedings of the Indian History Congress* 59 (1998), 260–6.

Hyder, Syed Akbar. *Reliving Karbala: Martyrdom in South Asian Memory*. New York: Oxford University Press, 2006.

Inoue, Takako. 'The Reception of Western Music in South India Around 1800'. *Summer International Symposium, Orient on Orient: Images of Asia in Eurasian Countries*. Hokkaido University, July 2010, 69–96.

Irvine, William. 'The Army of the Indian Moghuls: Its Organization and Administration'. *Journal of the Royal Asiatic Society* July (1896), 509–70.

Later Mughals. Edited by Jadunath Sarkar. Delhi: Oriental Books Reprint Corporation, 1971.

Islamuddin, Shaheen. 'Legalising the Plunder in the Aftermath of the Uprising of 1857: The City of Delhi and "Prize Agents"'. *Proceedings of the Indian History Congress* 72.1 (2011), 670–82.

Jasanoff, Maya. *Edge of Empire: Conquest and Collecting in the East, 1750–1850*. London: Harper, 2006.

'The Unknown Women of India'. *New York Review of Books*, 18 December 2008.

Kaicker, Abhishek. *The King and the People: Sovereignty and Popular Politics in Mughal Delhi*. Oxford: Oxford University Press, 2020.

'Unquiet City: Making and Unmaking Politics in Mughal Delhi, 1707–39'. Unpublished PhD Dissertation. Columbia University, 2014.

Kamińska-Jones, Dorota. 'Aesthetics in the Services of Colonialism: The Picturesque in the Indian Context'. *The Polish Journal of the Arts and Culture* 14.2 (2015), 63–82.

Kapuria, Radha. 'Music in Colonial Punjab: A Social History'. Unpublished PhD Dissertation. King's College London, 2018.

Katyal, Manu. *Nemat Khāṅ-Fīroz Khāṅ evam Samkālīn Saṅgītjña*. New Delhi: Chaukhamba Surbharati Prakashan, 2014.

Katz, Jonathan. 'The Musicological Portions of the Saṅgītanarāyāyaṇa: A Critical Edition and Commentary'. Unpublished PhD Dissertation. University of Oxford, 1987.

Katz, Max. *Lineage of Loss: Counternarratives of North Indian Music*. Middletown: Wesleyan University Press, 2017.

Kaufmann, Walter. *The Ragas of North India*. Bloomington: Indiana University Press, 1968.

Keay, Julia. *Farzana: The Tumultous Life and Times of Begum Samru*. New Delhi: Harper Collins, 2013.

Keshavmurthy, Prashant. *Persian Authorship and Canonicity in Late Mughal Delhi: Building an Ark*. New York: Routledge, 2016.

Khan, Gulfishan. 'Sayyid Ahmad Khan's Representations of Sufi Life of Shahjahanabad (Delhi)'. *Indian Historical Review* 36.1 (2009), 81–108.

Khan, Sumbul Halim. *Art and Craft Workshops under the Mughals: A Study of Jaipur Karkhanas*. New Delhi: Primus, 2015.

Khera, Dipti. *The Place of Many Moods: Udaipur's Painted Lands and India's Eighteenth Century*. Princeton: Princeton University Press, 2020.

Kia, Mana. 'Contours of Persianate Community, 1722–1835'. Unpublished PhD Dissertation. Harvard University, 2011.

Persianate Selves: Memories of Place and Origin before Nationalism. Stanford: Stanford University Press, 2020.

Kidwai, Saleem and Ruth Vanita (eds.). *Same-Sex Love in India: Readings from Literature and History*. London: Palgrave, 2001.

Kinra, Rajeev. 'Infantilizing Bābā Dārā: The Cultural Memory of Dārā Shekuh and the Mughal Public Sphere'. *Journal of Persianate Studies* 2 (2009), 165–93.

'Revisiting the History and Historiography of Mughal Pluralism'. *ReOrient* 5.2 (2020), 5137–82.

Writing Self, Writing Empire: Chandar Bhan Brahman and the Cultural World of the Indo-Persian State Secretary. South Asia Across the Disciplines Series. Oakland: University of California Press, 2015.

Kippen, James. *Gurudev's Drumming Legacy: Music, Theory and Nationalism in the Mṛdang aur Tablā Vādanpaddhati of Gurudev Patwardhan*. Aldershot: Ashgate, 2006.

'Les battements du cœur de l'Inde'. In Joep Bor and Philippe Bruguiére (eds.). *Gloire des princes, louange des dieux: patrimoine musical de l'Hindoustan du xive au xxe siècle*. Paris: Musée de la Musique, 2003, 152–73.

'Mapping a Rhythmic Revolution through Eighteenth- and Nineteenth-Century Sources of Rhythm and Drumming in North India'. In Richard K Wolf, Stephen Blum and Christopher Hasty (eds.). *Thought and Play in Musical Rhythm: Asian, African, and Euro-American Perspectives*. Oxford: Oxford University Press, 2019, 253–72.

The Tabla of Lucknow: A Cultural Analysis of a Musical Tradition. Cambridge Studies in Ethnomusicology Series. Cambridge: Cambridge University Press, 1988.

Koch, Ebba. 'The Mughal Emperor as Solomon, Majnun, and Orpheus, or the Album as a Think Tank for Allegory'. *Muqarnas* 27 (2010), 277–312.

Kothiyal, Tanuja. *Nomadic Narratives: A History of Mobility and Identity in the Great Indian Desert*. Cambridge: Cambridge University Press, 2016.

Kugle, Scott. '*Qawwālī* between Written Poem and Sung Lyric, or . . . How a *Ghazal* Lives'. *Muslim World* 97 (2007), 571–610.

When Sun Meets Moon: Gender, Eros, and Ecstasy in Urdu Poetry. Chapel Hill: University of North Carolina Press, 2016.

Kulshreshtha, Seema, BK Sharma and Shailaja Sharma. 'The Ramsar Sites of Rajasthan: Ecology and Conservation of Sambhar Salt Lake, Jaipur and

Keoladeo National Park, Bharatpur'. In BK Sharma, Seema Kulshreshtha and Asad R Rahmani (eds.). *Faunal Heritage of Rajasthan, India: Conservation and Management of Vertebrates.* Vol. ii. Heidelberg: Springer, 2013, 173–219.

Leante, Laura. 'The Lotus and the King: Imagery, Gesture and Meaning in a Hindustani Rāg'. *Ethnomusicology Forum* 18.2 (2009), 185–206.

Lee, Joel. *Deceptive Majority: Dalits, Hinduism, and Underground Religion.* Cambridge: Cambridge University Press, 2021.

Leech-Wilkinson, Daniel. 'The Emotional Power of Musical Performance'. In Tom Cochrane, Bernardino Fantini and Klaus R Scherer (eds.). *The Emotional Power of Music: Multidisciplinary Perspectives on Musical Arousal, Expression, and Social Control.* Oxford: Oxford University Press, 2013, 41–54.

Leonard, Karen B. 'The Hyderabad Political System and Its Participants'. *Journal of Asian Studies* 30.3 (1971), 569–82.

'Palmer and Company: An Indian Banking Firm in Hyderabad State'. *Modern Asian Studies* 47.4 (2013), 1157–84.

'Political Players: Courtesans of Hyderabad'. *Indian Economic and Social History Review* 50.4 (2013), 423–48.

Levesque, Julian. 'Debates on Muslim Caste in North India and Pakistan: From Colonial Ethnography to Pasmanda Mobilization'. *CSH-IFP Working Papers* 15 (2020), hal-02697381.

Llewellyn-Jones, Rosie. *A Fatal Friendship: The Nawabs, the British, and the City of Lucknow.* New Delhi: Oxford University Press, 1985.

The Last King in India: Wajid Ali Shah. London: Hurst, 2014.

Losensky, Paul. 'Vintages of the *Saqi-nama*: Fermenting and Blending the Cupbearer's Song in the Sixteenth Century'. *Iranian Studies* 47 (2014), 131–57.

Welcoming Fighani: Imitation, Influence, and Literary Change in the Persian Ghazal, 1480–1680. Costa Mesa: Mazda, 1993.

Losty, Jeremiah P. *Delhi: Red Fort to Raisina.* New Delhi: Roli, 2012.

'Depicting Delhi: Mazhar Ali Khan, Thomas Metcalfe, and the Topographical School of Delhi Artists'. In William Dalrymple and Yuthika Sharma (eds.). *Princes and Painters in Mughal Delhi, 1707–1857.* New Haven: Yale University Press and Asia Society Museum, 2012, 52–9.

'Sita Ram'. In William Dalrymple (ed.). *Forgotten Masters: Indian Painting for the East India Company.* London: Philip Wilson, 2019, 172–81.

Losty, Jeremiah P, and Malini Roy. *Mughal India: Art, Culture and Empire.* London: British Library, 2013.

Lunn, David and Julia Byl. '"One Story Ends and Another Begins": Reading the *Syair Tabut* of Encik Ali'. *Indonesia and the Malay World* 47.133 (2017), 391–420.

Lunn, David and Katherine Butler Schofield. 'Desire, Devotion, and the Music of the Monsoon at the Court of Emperor Shah ᶜAlam II'. In Imke Rajamani,

Margrit Pernau and Katherine Butler Schofield (eds.). *Monsoon Feelings: A History of Emotions in the Rain*. New Delhi: Niyogi, 2018, 220–54.

Mahmood, Saif. *Beloved Delhi: A Mughal City and Her Greatest Poets*. New Delhi: Speaking Tiger, 2018.

Mallinson, James. 'Yoga in Mughal India'. In Debra Diamond (ed.). *Yoga: The Art of Transformation*. Washington, DC: Smithsonian Institution, 2013, 69–83.

Manuel, Peter. 'The Popularization and Transformation of the Light-Classical Urdu *Ghazal*-Song'. In Arjun Appadurai, Frank J Korom and Margaret A Mills, (eds.). *Gender, Genre and Power in South Asian Expressive Traditions*. Philadelphia: University of Pennsylvania Press, 1991, 347–60.

Ṭhumrī in Historical and Stylistic Perspective. Delhi: Motilal Banarsidass, 1989.

Markel, Stephen and Tushara Bindu Gude (eds.). *India's Fabled City: The Art of Courtly Lucknow*. Munich and New York: Prestel, 2010.

Marshall, Dara N. *Mughals in India: A Bibliographical Survey of Manuscripts*. London: Mansell, 1967.

Masselos, Jim, Jackie Menzies, and Pratapaditya Pal (eds.). *Dancing to the Flute: Music and Dance in Indian Art*. Sydney: Art Gallery of New South Wales, 1997.

McBurney, Nicholas G. *The 1836 Tazkirat al-Umara of Colonel James Skinner: A Catalogue*. London: Bernard Quaritch, 2014.

McClymonds, Marita P. 'Aria (It.: "Air"), 4. 18th Century'. *Oxford Music Online*. Oxford University Press, 2001. https://doi.org/10.1093/gmo/9781561592630.article.43315.

McInerney, Terence. '"Chitarman II (Kalyan Das)" and "Mir Kalan Khan"'. In Milo C Beach, Eberhard Fischer and Brijinder Nath Goswamy (eds.). *Masters of Indian Painting*. Vol. ii, 1650–1900. New Delhi: Niyogi, 2016, 547–62, 607–22.

Miner, Allyn. 'Raga in the Early Sixteenth Century'. In Francesca Orsini and Katherine Butler Schofield (eds.). *Tellings and Texts: Music, Literature, and Performance in North India*. Cambridge: Open Book, 2015, 385–406.

'The Scandalous Ghulam Raza'. Unpublished paper. Annual Conference on South Asia, Madison, 16 October 2013.

Sitar and Sarod in 18th and 19th Centuries. New Delhi: Manohar, 1993.

Miranda, Lin Manuel and Jeremy McCarter. *Hamilton: The Revolution*. New York: Little, Brown, 2016.

Misra, Susheela. *Some Immortals of Hindustani Music*. New Delhi: Harman, 1990.

Moin, A Azfar. *The Millennial Sovereign: Sacred Kingship and Sainthood in Islam*. New York: Columbia University Press, 2012.

Moxham, Roy. *The Great Hedge of India: The Search for the Living Barrier that Divided a People*. London: HarperCollins, 2001.

Murphy, Anne. *The Materiality of the Past: History and Representation in Sikh Tradition*. New Delhi: Oxford University Press, 2013.

Naqvi, Naveena. 'Writing the Inter-Imperial World in Afghan North India ca. 1774–1857'. Unpublished PhD Dissertation. University of California, Los Angeles, 2018.

Natif, Mika. *Mughal Occidentalism: Artistic Encounters between Europe and Asia at the Courts of India, 1580–1630*. Leiden: Brill, 2018.

Nechtman, Tillman W. *Nabobs: Empire and Identity in Eighteenth-Century Britain*. Cambridge: Cambridge University Press, 2010.

Neuman, Daniel M. 'Indian Music as a Cultural System'. *Asian Music* 17.1 (1985), 98–113.

Life of Music in North India: The Social Organization of an Artistic Tradition. Chicago: Chicago University Press, 1990 [orig. 1980].

'A Tale of Two Sensibilities: Hindustani Music and Its Histories'. In Jonathan McCollum and David G Hebert (eds.). *Theory and Method in Historical Ethnomusicology*. Lanham: Lexington, 2014, 279–308.

Neuman, Daniel M, Shubha Chaudhuri and Komal Kothari. *Bards, Ballads and Boundaries: An Ethnographic Atlas of Music Traditions in West Rajasthan*. Calcutta: Seagull, 2006.

Neuman, Dard. 'Pedagogy, Practice, and Embodied Creativity in Hindustani Music'. *Ethnomusicology* 56.3 (2012), 426–49.

Nevile, Pran. *Nautch Girls of India: Dancers, Singers, Playmates*. New Delhi: Ravi Kumar, 1996.

Newell, Stephanie. '"Paracolonial" Networks: Some Speculations on Local Readerships in Colonial West Africa'. *Interventions* 3 (2001), 336–54.

Norton-Wright, Jenny. 'A Mughal Miscellany: The Journey of Or. 2361'. *British Library Asian and African Studies Blog*, 31 July 2020. https://blogs.bl.uk/asian-and-african/2020/07/a-mughal-musical-miscellany-the-journey-of-or-2361-1.html.

Nussbaum, Felicity. *Rival Queens: Actresses, Performance, and the Eighteenth-Century British Theater*. Philadelphia: University of Pennsylvania Press, 2013.

Oesterheld, Christina. 'Entertainment and Reform: Urdu Narrative Genres in the Nineteenth Century'. In Stuart H Blackburn and Vasudha Dalmia (eds.). *India's Literary History: Essays on the Nineteenth Century*. New Delhi: Permanent Black, 2004, 167–212.

O'Hanlon, Rosalind and David Washbrook. 'Histories in Transition: Approaches to the Study of Colonialism and Culture in India'. *History Workshop Journal* 32.1 (1991), 110–27.

Oldenburg, Veena Talwar. 'Lifestyle as Resistance: The Case of the Courtesans of Lucknow'. In Violette Graff (ed.). *Lucknow: Memories of a City*. New Delhi: Oxford University Press, 1997, 136–54.

Orsini, Francesca (ed.). *Before the Divide: Hindi and Urdu Literary Culture*. Hyderabad: Orient Blackswan, 2010.

Orsini, Francesca and Katherine Butler Schofield (eds.). *Tellings and Texts: Music, Literature and Performance in North India*. Cambridge: Open Book, 2015.

Ostrom, Elinor. *Governing the Commons: The Evolution of Institutions for Collective Action*. Cambridge: Cambridge University Press, 1990.

Pauwels, Heidi Rika Maria. *Cultural Exchange in Eighteenth-Century India: Poetry and Paintings from Kishangarh*. Berlin: EB Verlag, 2015.

Mobilizing Krishna's World: The Writings of Prince Sāvant Singh of Kishangarh. Seattle: University of Washington Press, 2017.

Pauwels, Heidi and Anne Murphy (eds.). 'From Outside the Persianate Centre: Vernacular Views on "ᶜAlamgir"'. Special Issue of *Journal of the Royal Asiatic Society* 28.3 (2018).

Peabody, Norbert. 'Cents, Sense, Census: Human Inventories in Late Precolonial and Early Colonial India'. *Comparative Studies in Society and History* 43.4 (2001), 819–50.

Pelló, Stefano. 'Persian as a Passe-Partout: The Case of Mīrzā ᶜAbd al-Qādir Bīdil and His Hindu Disciples'. In Thomas de Bruijn and Allison Busch (eds.). *Culture and Circulation: Literature in Motion in Early Modern India*. Leiden: Brill, 2014, 21–46.

'Persian Poets on the Streets: The Lore of Indo-Persian Poetic Circles in Late Mughal India'. In Francesca Orsini and Katherine Butler Schofield (eds.). *Tellings and Texts: Music, Literature and Performance in North India*. Cambridge: Open Book, 2015, 303–26.

Pernau, Margrit. *Ashraf into Middle Classes: Muslims in Nineteenth-Century Delhi*. New Delhi: Oxford University Press, 2013.

'Celebrating Monsoon Feelings: The Flower-Sellers' Festival of Delhi'. In Imke Rajamani, Margrit Pernau and Katherine Butler Schofield (eds.). *Monsoon Feelings: A History of Emotions in the Rain*. New Delhi: Niyogi, 2018, 379–407.

The Delhi College: Traditional Elites, the Colonial State, and Education before 1857. New Delhi: Oxford University Press, 2006.

'Studying Emotions in South Asia'. *South Asia History and Culture* 12.2–3 (2021), 111–28.

(ed.). *South Asia History and Culture* 12.2–3 (2021), 111–355.

Pinch, William R. 'Prostituting the Mutiny: Sex-Slavery and Crime in the Making of 1857'. In Crispin Bates (ed.). *Mutiny at the Margins: New Perspectives on the Indian Uprising of 1857*. Vol. i. New Delhi: Sage, 2013, 61–79.

Platts, John T. *A Dictionary of Urdū, Classical Hindī, and English*. New Delhi: Munshiram Manoharlal, 1997 [orig. 1884].

Plowden, Walter FC Chicheley. *Records of the Chicheley Plowdens, A.D. 1590–1913*. London: Heath, Cranton and Ouseley, 1914.

Pollock, Sheldon. 'Forms of Knowledge in Early Modern South Asia: Introduction'. *Comparative Studies of South Asia, Africa and the Middle East* 24.2 (2004), 19–21.

Powers, Harold. 'Sargam Notations and *Rāg-Rāgiṇī* Theory'. In Joep Bor, Françoise 'Nalini' Delvoye, Jane Harvey and Emmie te Nijenhuis (eds.). *Hindustani Music: Thirteenth to Twentieth Centuries*. New Delhi: Manohar, 2010, 579–671.

Pradhan, Aneesh. *Hindustani Music in Colonial Bombay*. New Delhi: Three Essays, 2014.

Pritchett, Frances W. 'A Long History of Urdu Literary Culture, Part II'. In Sheldon Pollock (ed.). *Literary Culture in History: Reconstructions from South Asia*. Berkeley: University of California Press, 2003, 864–911.

Pritchett, Frances W. and Khaliq Ahmad Khaliq. *Urdu Meter: A Practical Handbook*. New York: Private printing, 1987. www.columbia.edu/itc/mealac/pritchett/00ghalib/meterbk/00_intro.html.

Qureshi, Regula Burkhardt. 'Other Musicologies: Exploring Issues and Confronting Practice in India'. In Nicholas Cook and Mark Everist (eds.). *Rethinking Music*. Oxford: Oxford University Press, 1999, 311–35.

Rahaim, Matt, Srinivas Reddy and Lars Christensen. 'Authority, Critique, and Revision in the Sanskrit Tradition: Rereading the *Svara-mela-kalānidhi*'. *Asian Music* 46.1 (2015), 39–77.

Raja, Masood Ashraf. 'The Indian Rebellion of 1857 and Mirza Ghalib's Narrative of Survival'. *Prose Studies: History, Theory, Criticism* 31.1 (2009), 40–54.

Rajamani, Imke, Margrit Pernau and Katherine Butler Schofield (eds.). *Monsoon Feelings: A History of Emotions in the Rain*. New Delhi: Niyogi, 2018.

Ramusack, Barbara. *The Indian Princes and Their States*. New Cambridge History of India Series. Cambridge: Cambridge University Press, 2004.

Ranade, Ashok Da. *On Music and Musicians of Hindoostan*. New Delhi: Promilla, 1984.

Richards, John F. *The Mughal Empire*. New Cambridge History of India Series. Cambridge: Cambridge University Press, 1993.

Rieu, Charles. *Catalogue of the Persian Manuscripts in the British Museum*. Vol. iii. London: British Museum, 1883.

Rilke, Rainer Maria. *The Sonnets to Orpheus*. Translated by Robert Temple. London: Eglantyne, 2022.

Robinson, Dylan. *Hungry Listening: Resonant Theory for Indigenous Sound Studies*. Minneapolis: University of Minnesota Press, 2020.

Rocher, Rosane. 'The Creation of Anglo-Hindu Law'. In Timothy Lubin, Donald R. Davis and Jayanth K. Krishnan (eds.). *Hinduism and Law: An Introduction*. Cambridge: Cambridge University Press, 2010, 78–88.

Rogers, John D. 'Introduction: Caste, Power and Region in Colonial South Asia'. *Indian Economic and Social History Review* 41.1 (2004), 1–6.

Roque, Ricardo and Kim A Wagner. 'Introduction: Engaging Colonial Knowledge'. In Ricardo Roque and Kim A Wagner (eds.). *Engaging Colonial Knowledge: Reading European Archives in World History*. London: Palgrave Macmillan, 2012, 1–32.

Rosin, R. Thomas. 'Quarry and Field: Sources of Continuity and Change in a Rajasthani Village'. in Paul Hockings (ed.). *Dimensions of Social Life: Essays in Honor of David G Mandelbaum*. Berlin: De Gruyter Mouton, 1987, 419–38.

Sachau, Eduard, and Hermann Ethé. *Catalogue of the Persian, Turkish, Hindûstânî and Pushtû Manuscripts in the Bodleian Library*. Oxford: Clarendon Press, 1889.

Sachdev, Vibhuti. *Festivals at the Jaipur Court*. New Delhi: Niyogi, 2015.

Sachdeva [Jha], Shweta. 'Eurasian Women as *Tawa'if* Singers and Recording Artists: Entertainment and Identity-Making in Colonial India'. *African and Asian Studies* 8 (2009), 268–87.

'In Search of the Tawa'if in History: Courtesans, Nautch Girls and Celebrity Enterainers in India (1720s–1920s)'. Unpublished PhD Dissertation. SOAS University of London, 2008.

Salam, Abdul. 'Foundation and Early History of Jaipur City'. Unpublished PhD Dissertation. Aligarh Muslim University, 2011.

Sampath, Vikram. *My Name is Gauhar Jaan! The Life and Times of a Musician*. New Delhi: Rupa, 2010.

Sanadhya, Sudhanshu, Ramesh Nagarajappa, Archana Jagat Sharda et al. 'The Oral Health Status and the Treatment Needs of Salt Workers at Sambhar Lake, Jaipur, India'. *Journal of Clinical and Diagnostic Research* 7.8 (2013), 1782–6.

Sanyal, Ritwik and Richard Widdess. *Dhrupad: Tradition and Performance in Indian Music*. SOAS Musicology Series. Aldershot: Ashgate, 2004.

Sarkar, Jadunath. *A History of Jaipur, c. 1503–1938*. Revised edition by Raghubir Sinh. Hyderabad: Orient Longman, 1984.

Scarimbolo, Justin. 'Brahmans Beyond Nationalism, Muslims Beyond Dominance: A Hidden History of North Indian Classical Music's Hinduization'. Unpublished PhD Dissertation. University of California, Santa Barbara, 2014.

Schimmel, Annemarie. *Pain and Grace: A Study of Two Mystical Writers of Eighteenth-century Muslim India*. Leiden: Brill, 1976.

Schofield, Katherine Butler. 'Chief Musicians to the Mughal Emperors: The Delhi *Kalawant Biradari*, 17th to 19th Centuries'. In ITC Sangeet Research Academy (Kolkata) (ed.). *Dhrupad, Its Future: Proceedings of the 2013 ITC-SRA (West) Seminar*. Mumbai: ITC-SRA, 2013.

'The Courtesan Tale: Female Musicians and Dancers in Mughal Historical Chronicles'. *Gender and History* 24.1 (2012), 150–71.

'Emotions in Indian Music History: Anxiety in Late Mughal Hindustan'. *South Asian History and Culture* 12.2–3 (2021), 182–205.

'Indian Music in the Persian Collections: The Javahir al-Musiqat-i Muhammadi'. Parts 1 and 2. *British Library Asian and African Studies Blog*, 7 and 13 October 2014. https://blogs.bl.uk/asian-and-african/2014/10/indian-music-in-the-persian-collections-the-javahir-al-musiqat-i-muhammadi-or12857-part-1.html and https://blogs.bl.uk/asian-and-african/2014/10/indian-music-in-the-persian-collections-the-javahir-al-musiqat-i-muhammadi-or12857-part-2.html.

'Learning to Taste the Emotions: The Mughal *Rasika*'. In Francesca Orsini and Katherine Butler Schofield (eds.). *Tellings and Texts: Music, Literature, and Performance in North India*. Cambridge: Open Book, 2015, 407–21.

'Music, Art and Power in ^{c}Adil Shahi Bijapur, c. 1570–1630'. In Kavita Singh (ed.). *Scent Upon a Southern Breeze: The Synaesthetic Arts of the Deccan*. Mumbai: Marg, 2018, 68–87.

'Musical Culture under Mughal Patronage: The Place of Pleasure'. In Richard Eaton and Ramya Sreenivasan (eds.). *The Oxford Handbook to the Mughal Empire*. Oxford: Oxford University Press, forthcoming.

'Musical Transitions to European Colonialism in the Eastern Indian Ocean: Final Summary Report'. Project ID 263643; Principal Investigator Katherine Butler Schofield. European Research Council, 2016. https://cordis.europa.eu/project/id/263643.

'Musicians and Dancers in the Indian Office Records'. *British Library Asian and African Studies Blog*, 26 March 2019. https://blogs.bl.uk/asian-and-african/2019/03/musicians-and-dancers-in-the-india-office-records.html.

'Review of Kavita Panjabi (ed.). Poetics and Politics of Sufism and Bhakti in South Asia: Love, Loss and Liberation (Hyderabad: Orient Blackswan, 2011)'. *The Indian Economic and Social History Review* 52.1 (2015), 116–19.

'Reviving the Golden Age Again: "Classicization", Hindustani Music, and the Mughals'. *Ethnomusicology* 54.3 (2010), 484–517.

'Sophia Plowden, Khanum Jan, and Hindustani Airs'. *British Library Asian and African Studies Blog*, 28 June 2018. https://blogs.bl.uk/asian-and-african/2018/06/sophia-plowden-khanum-jan-and-hindustani-airs.html.

'"Words without Songs": The Social History of Hindustani Song Collections in India's Muslim Courts c.1770–1830'. In Rachel Harris and Martin Stokes (eds.). *Theory and Practice in the Music of the Islamic World: Essays in Honour of Owen Wright*. London: Routledge, 2017, 171–96.

Schofield, Katherine Butler and David Lunn. 'The SHAMSA Database: Sources for the History and Analysis of Music/Dance in South Asia'. Zenodo, 2018. https://doi.org/10.5281/zenodo.1445775.

Schwartz, Kevin L. 'A Transregional Persianate Library: The Production and Circulation of Tadhkiras of Persian Poets in the 18th and 19th Centuries'. *International Journal of Middle East Studies* 52.1 (2020), 109–35.

Secretary of State for India. *The Imperial Gazeteer of India*. Vols. xiii, xiv and xxii. New Edition. Oxford: Clarendon Press, 1908.

Seyller, John. 'The Inspection and Valuation of Manuscripts in the Imperial Mughal Library'. *Artibus Asiae* 57.3–4 (1997), 243–349.

Shackle, Christopher. 'Persian Poetry and Qadiri Sufism in Late Mughal India: Ghanimat Khanjai and His Mathnawi Nayrang-i ^{c}Ishq'. In Leonard Lewisohn (ed.). *The Heritage of Sufism: III. Late Classical Persianate Sufism (1501–1750)*. Oxford: Oneworld, 1999, 435–63.

Shaffer, Holly M. *Grafted Arts: Art Making and Taking in the Struggle for Western India, 1760–1910*. New Haven: Yale University Press, 2022.

Sharma, Amal Das. *Musicians of India Past and Present: Gharanas of Hindustani Music and Genealogies*. Calcutta: Naya Prokash, 1993.

Sharma, Sunil. 'If There is a Paradise on Earth, it is Here: Urban Ethnography in Indo-Persian Poetic and Historical Texts'. In Sheldon Pollock (ed.). *Forms of Knowledge in Early Modern Asia: Explorations in the Intellectual History of India and Tibet, 1500–1800*. Durham, NC: Duke University Press, 2011, 240–56.

Mughal Arcadia: Persian Literature in an Indian Court. Cambridge, MA: Harvard University Press, 2017.

'Reading the Acts and Lives of Performers in Mughal Persian Texts'. In Francesca Orsini and Katherine Butler Schofield (eds.). *Tellings and Texts: Music, Literature and Performance in North India*. Cambridge: Open Book, 2015, 285–302.

'Representation of Social Groups in Mughal Art and Literature: Ethnography or Trope?' In Alka Patel and Karen Leonard (eds.). *Indo-Muslim Culture in Transition*. Leiden: Brill, 2012, 17–36.

Sharma, Yuthika. 'Art in between Empires: Visual Culture and Artistic Knowledge in Late Mughal Delhi, 1748–1857'. Unpublished PhD Dissertation. Columbia University, 2013.

'Ghulam Ali Khan and the Delhi School of Painting'. In William Dalrymple (ed.). *Forgotten Masters: Indian Painting for the East India Company*. London: Philip Wilson, 2019, 140–70.

'Mughal Delhi on My Lapel: The Charmed Life of the Painted Ivory Miniature in Delhi, 1827–1880'. In Supriya Chaudhuri, Josephine McDonagh, Brian H Murray and Rajeswari Sunder Rajan. (eds.). *Commodities and Culture in the Colonial World*. London: Routledge, 2017, 15–31.

'Village Portraits in William Fraser's Portfolio of Native Drawings'. In Crispin Branfoot (ed.). *Portraiture in South Asia since the Mughals: Art, Representation and History*. London: IB Tauris, 2018, 199–220.

Sheth, Sudev. 'Manuscript Variations of Dabistān-i Maẕāhib and Writing Histories of Religion in Mughal India'. *Manuscript Studies* 4.1 (2019), 19–41.

Sims-Williams, Ursula. 'British Interest in Indian Music in the Late 18th and Early 19th Century'. *India Office Library and Records Newsletter*. No. 22. March 1981.

Singh, Kirit. 'Sikh Patronage of Hindustani Music and Śabad Kīrtan in Colonial Punjab, 1857–1947'. Unpublished PhD Dissertation. SOAS University of London, 2022.

Sobers-Khan, Nur. 'Muslim Scribal Culture in India Around 1800: Towards a Disentangling of the Mughal Library and the Delhi Collection'. In Christopher D Bahl and Stefan Hanß (eds.). *Scribal Practice and the Global Cultures of Colophons, 1400–1800*. London: Palgrave Macmillan, 2022, 197–218.

Soneji, Davesh. 'Exploring Complex Histories of Islamic Musical Production in Colonial South India'. Unpublished Lecture. British Library, 19 April 2021.

'Memory and Recovery of Identity: Living Histories and the Kalavantulu of Coastal Andhra Pradesh'. In Indira Peterson and Davesh Soneji (eds.). *Performing Pasts: Reinventing the Arts in Modern South India*. New Delhi: Oxford University Press, 2008, 283–312.

Unfinished Gestures: Devadasis, Memory, and Modernity in South India. Chicago: University of Chicago Press, 2012.

Steingass, Francis J. *A Comprehensive Persian–English Dictionary*. London: Routledge and Kegan Paul, 1963 [orig. 1892].

Stern, Philip J. *The Company-State: Corporate Sovereignty and the Early Modern Foundations of the British Empire in India*. New York: Oxford, 2012.

Stern, Robert W. *The Cat and the Lion: Jaipur State in the British Raj*. Leiden: Brill, 1988.

Stoler, Ann Laura. 'Colonial Archives and the Arts of Governance'. *Archival Science* 2 (2002), 87–109.

Subramanian, Lakshmi. *From the Tanjore Court to the Madras Music Academy: A Social History of Music in South India*. New Delhi: Oxford University Press, 2006.

'The Reinvention of a Tradition: Nationalism, Carnatic Music and the Madras Music Academy, 1900–1957'. *Indian Economic and Social History Review* 36.2 (1999), 131–63.

Suri, Anju. 'British Relations with Jaipur State under the Company and the Crown: A Critical Appraisal'. Professor G N Sharma Memorial Lecture, *Proceedings of the Rajasthan History Congress* 30 (2014–15), 35–48.

Tabor, Nathan Lee Marsh. 'A Market for Speech: Poetry Recitation in Late Mughal India, 1690–1710'. Unpublished PhD Dissertation. University of Texas, 2014.

Talbot, Cynthia. *The Last Hindu Emperor: Prithviraj Chauhan and the Indian Past, 1200–2000*. Cambridge: Cambridge University Press, 2015.

Te Nijenhuis, Emmie. *Musicological Literature*. A History of Indian Literature Series. Vol. vi. Wiesbaden: Otto Harrassowitz, 1977.

Thackston, Wheeler M. *A Millennium of Classical Persian Poetry*. Bethesda: IBEX, 2000.

Tharoor, Shashi. *Inglorious Empire: What the British Did to India*. London: Hurst, 2017.

Tillotson, Giles. 'Indian Architecture and the English Vision'. *South Asian Studies* 7 (1991), 59–74.

Jaipur Nama: Tales from the Pink City. New Delhi: Penguin, 2007.

Tillotson, Giles and Mrinalini Venkateswaran. *Painting and Photography at the Jaipur Court*. New Delhi: Niyogi, 2016.

Topsfield, Andrew. 'The Kalavants on Their Durrie: Portraits of Udaipur Court Musicians, 1680–1730'. In Rosemary Crill, Susan Stronge and

Andrew Topsfield. (eds.). *Arts of Mughal India: Studies in Honour of Robert Skelton*. London: Victoria and Albert Museum, 2004, 248–63.

Travers, Robert. *Empires of Complaints: Mughal Law and the Making of British India, 1765–1793*. Cambridge: Cambridge University Press, 2022.

Ideology and Empire in Eighteenth-Century India: The British in Bengal. Cambridge: Cambridge University Press, 2007.

Trivedi, Madhu. *The Emergence of the Hindustani Tradition: Music, Dance and Drama in North India, 13th to 19th Centuries*. Gurgaon: Three Essays Collective, 2012.

The Making of the Awadh Culture. New Delhi: Primus, 2010.

Truschke, Audrey. *Aurangzeb: The Life and Legacy of India's Most Controversial King*. Stanford: Stanford University Press, 2017.

Vanita, Ruth. *Dancing with the Nation: Courtesans in Bombay Cinema*. London: Bloomsbury, 2018.

Gender, Sex, and the City: Urdu Rekhti Poetry in India, 1780–1870. New York: Palgrave Macmillan, 2012.

Vashishtha, Vijay Kumar. *Rajputana Agency, 1832–1858*. Jaipur: Aalekh, 1978.

Wade, Bonnie C. *Imaging Sound: An Ethnomusicological Study of Music, Art and Culture in Mughal India*. Chicago: University of Chicago Press, 1998.

Wagner, Kim A. *Thuggee: Banditry and the British in Early Nineteenth-Century India*. Cambridge: Cambridge University Press, 2007.

Walker, Margaret E. *India's Kathak Dance in Historical Perspective*. SOAS Musicology Series. Aldershot: Ashgate, 2014.

'The "Nautch" Reclaimed: Women's Performance Practice in Nineteenth-Century North India'. *South Asia: Journal of South Asian Studies* 37.4 (2014), 551–67.

Wall, Derek and Michael Egan. *The Commons in History: Culture, Conflict, and Ecology*. Boston: MIT Press, 2014.

Weber, Thomas. *On the Salt March: The Historiography of Mahatma Gandhi's March to Dandi*. New Delhi: Rupa, 2009.

Webster, Mary. *Johan Zoffany, 1733–1810*. New Haven: Yale University Press, 2011.

Weidman, Amanda. *Singing the Classical, Voicing the Modern: The Postcolonial Politics of Music in South India*. Durham, NC: Duke University Press, 2006.

Widdess, D Richard. *The Ragas of Early Indian Music*. Oxford: Clarendon, 1995.

Williams, Richard David. 'Hindustani Music between Awadh and Bengal, c. 1758–1905'. Unpublished PhD Dissertation. King's College London, 2015.

'Krishna's Neglected Responsibilities: Religious Devotion and Social Critique in Eighteenth-Century North India'. *Modern Asian Studies* 50.5 (2016), 1403–40.

'Music, Lyrics, and the Bengali Book: Hindustani Musicology in Calcutta, 1818–1905'. *Music and Letters* 97.3 (2016), 465–95.

'Reflecting in the Vernacular: Translation and Transmission in Seventeenth- and Eighteenth-Century North India'. *Comparative Studies of South Asia, Africa and the Middle East* 39.1 (2019), 96–110.

The Scattered Court: Hindustani Music in Colonial Bengal. Chicago: University of Chicago Press, 2023.

'Songs between Cities: Listening to Courtesans in Colonial North India'. *Journal of the Royal Asiatic Society, Series 3* 27.4 (2017), 591–610.

Wilson, Jon. 'Early Colonial India Beyond Empire'. *Historical Journal* 50.4 (2007), 951–70.

India Conquered: Britain's Raj and the Chaos of Empire. London: Simon and Schuster, 2016.

Wolf, Richard. 'Embodiment and Ambivalence: Emotion in South Asian Muharram Drumming'. *Yearbook for Traditional Music* 32 (2000), 81–116.

Woodfield, Ian. 'The Calcutta Piano Trade in the Late Eighteenth Century'. In Christina Bashford and Leanne Langley (eds.). *Music and British Culture, 1785–1914: Essays in Honour of Cyril Ehrlich*. Oxford: Oxford University Press, 2000, 1–22.

'Collecting Indian Songs in Late 18th-Century Lucknow: Problems of Transcription'. *British Journal of Ethnomusicology* 3.1 (1994), 73–88.

'The "Hindostannie Air": English Attempts to Understand Indian Music in the Eighteenth Century'. *Journal of the Royal Musical Association* 119.2 (1994), 189–211.

'The Keyboard Recital in Oriental Diplomacy, 1520–1620'. *Journal of the Royal Musical Association* 115.1 (1990), 33–62.

Music of the Raj: A Social and Economic History of Music in Late Eighteenth-Century Anglo-Indian Society. Cambridge: Cambridge University Press, 2000.

Yang, Anand. 'Bandits and Kings: Moral Authority and Resistance in Early Colonial India'. *Journal of Asian Studies* 66.4 (2007), 881–96.

Zebrowski, Mark. *Deccani Painting*. London: Philip Wilson for Sotheby's, 1983.

Ziad, Homayra. 'I Transcend Myself Like a Melody: Khwaja Mir Dard and Music in Eighteenth-Century Delhi'. *The Muslim World* 97.4 (2007), 548–70.

'Poetry, Music and the Muhammadi Path: How Khvājah Mīr Dard Brought Three Worlds Together in Eighteenth-Century Delhi'. *Journal of Islamic Studies* 21.3 (2010), 345–76.

Zubrzycki, John. *Empire of Enchantment: The Story of Indian Magic*. London: Hurst, 2018.

The Last Nizam: The Rise and Fall of India's Greatest Princely State. New Delhi: Picador India, 2007.

Tazkira: List of Names

Musicians, Performing Artists, Writers on Music

ᶜAbd-ul-karim, Shaikh (fl. 1630s–50s), author of the *Jawāhir al-Mūsīqāt -i Muḥammadī* (Persian, Bijapur, c. 1570/c. 1630).

Abu'l Fazl, see Historians.

Adarang, Firoz Khan (d. 1760s), chief *kalāwant* to Emperor Muhammad Shah, nephew of Sadarang, *k͟hayāl* composer, earliest known *sitār*-player (Chapter 3).

Ahobala *paṇḍit* (fl. early 17C), author of the *Saṅgīta-pārijāta* (Sanskrit, North India, c. 1650).

Alladiya Khan, Ustad (1855–1946), *k͟hayāl* singer and founder of the modern Jaipur *k͟hayāl g͟harānā*.

Allah Banda (d. 1752–3), *qawwāl* of Muhammad Shah's time and a famous male beauty.

Amaman (fl. 1840s–50s), courtesan from Rampur, sister of Aman, introduced *ṭhumrī* to Wajid ᶜAli Shah, Nawab of Lucknow.

Aman (fl. 1840s–50s), courtesan from Rampur, sister of Amaman (above).

Amir Khusrau, see Poets.

Amrit Sen (1813–1893), *kalāwant* to the Nawab of Jhajjhar, the Raja of Alwar and Maharaja Ram Singh II of Jaipur, and son of Rahim Sen (2).

Anand Baras Khan (fl. late 17C), *kalāwant* of Aurangzeb's time, son of Khushhal Khan Gunasamudra and brother of Ras Baras Khan *kalāwant*; possibly maternal great grandfather of Khushhal Khan Anup.

Anjha Baras Khan Muhammad Shahi, Miyan (d. 1760s), chief *kalāwant* to Emperor Muhammad Shah, son of Ras Baras Khan *kalāwant*, son-in-law of Sadarang, *bīn* player, *dhrupad* composer and *ustād* (Chapter 3).

Anonymous author of Edinburgh MS 585(4) (fl. 1780s), *kalāwant* belonging to the Ras Baras Khan branch of the direct Tansen line, the Gorari *bānī*. Author of unnamed treatise on *tāla* (Chapter 4).

Anup, Khushhal Khan (2) (d. c. 1836), *kalāwant* to the Nizams of Hyderabad, son of Karim Khan, *ustād* of courtesan Mahlaqa Bai

Chanda. Author of the *Rāg Darshan* (multiple versions, Brajbhasha and Persian, c. 1800–1815) and compiler of the song collection *Rāg-Rāginī Roz o Shab* (1833–36) (Chapter 5).

^{c}Arzani, Muhammad Akbar (fl. late 17C), medical doctor. Author of the *Tashrīh al-Mūsīqī*, which purports to be a translation of a work by Tansen, *Budh-prakāsh*.

Bade Muhammad Khan, *qawwāl* (d. c. 1840), one founder of the Gwalior *gharānā*, nephew of Makhan Khan and descendant of Miyan Taj Khan (2) (chief *qawwāl* to Emperor Muhammad Shah) via his grandfather Ghulam Rasul and father Shakkar Khan.

Baiju Bawra, see Nayak Baiju.

Bani Thani Rasik Bihari (d. 1760s), courtesan, consort, and muse to prince Savant Singh of Kishangarh.

Baqa, Miyan (fl. 1720s–40s), *ḍholak*-player of Muhammad Shah's time.

Basit Khan, *kalāwant* (d. c. 1887), *rabāb* player to Wajid ^{c}Ali Shah, Nawab of Lucknow, son of Miyan Chajju Khan and brother of Pyar (2) and Jaffar, founder of the Lucknow–Shahjahanpur *sarod gharānā* via his Afghan disciples (Chapter 8).

Baz Bahadur, Sultan of Malwa (r. 1555–62), famous *dhrupad* singer and patron.

Begum Akhtar (1914–74), *ghazal* and *ṭhumrī* virtuoso.

Behram Khan, Ustad (d. c. 1880), founder of the modern Dagar *bānī* of *dhrupad* and scholar of music theory.

Bhatkhande, Vishnu Narayan (1860–1936), musicologist and most important nationalist reformer of Hindustani music. Author of music-technical works in Sanskrit, English, Marathi and Hindi.

Bhavanidas (fl. 1720s–40s), *pakhāwaj*-player of Muhammad Shah's time.

Bhupat (1) *kalāwant* (fl. late 17C), son of Bisram Khan.

Bhupat Khan (2), Miyan, *kalāwant* (fl. early 18C), son of Nirmol Khan, brother of Sadarang, father of Adarang.

Bilas Khan *kalāwant* (fl. late 16C), son of Tansen and chief musician to emperors Akbar and Jahangir, father-in-law of La^{c}l Khan (1) Gunasamudra.

Bisram Khan *kalāwant* (d. 1671), son of La^{c}l Khan (1) Gunasamudra, brother and duet partner of Khushhal Khan (1) Gunasamudra, father of Bhupat (1).

Braganza, John (fl. 1780s), Goan Portuguese musician at the court of Asaf-ud-daula, Nawab of Lucknow, and transcriber and arranger with Sophia Plowden of her Hindustani Airs (European notation, Lucknow, 1788).

Burhan Khan (fl. 1720s–40s), *qawwāl* of Muhammad Shah's time.
Burhani (fl. 1720s–40s), *qawwāl* of Muhammad Shah's time.
Chabbar Khan (fl. mid–late 18C) *pak͟hāwaj*-player from Delhi who migrated to Patna then Murshidabad.
Chajju Khan, Miyan (fl. 1780s–1820s), *kalāwant* of Asaf-ud-daula's reign, reputed son of Adarang, father of Basit, Pyar and Jaffar Khan.
Chandu 'dancing girl' (fl. 1830s), Sambhar Lake.
Chapala Sarup (fl. 1720s–40s), courtesan of Muhammad Shah's time.
Chau Baras Khan (fl. 1720s–40s), *ustād* of Muhammad Shah's time.
Damodara, Catura (fl. early 17C). Author of the *Saṅgīta-darpaṇa* (Sanskrit, North India, c. 1600–25).
Daulat Ram (fl. 1780s), piano repairer for Mistry Instrument Makers, Calcutta.
Dinanath (1) son of Basudeo (fl. early 18C), compiler of the music treatise collection RAS Persian 2010 (5) (Persian, North India, 1725).
Dinanath (2) (fl. 1720s–40s), *pakhāwaj*-player of Muhammad Shah's time.
Diyanat Khan, Shah Qubad (d. 1672), *mansabdār* of emperors Shah Jahan and Aurangzeb, major collector of music treatises (multiple languages, North India, 1660s).
Faqirullah, Saif Khan (d. 1684), *mansabdār* of Aurangzeb. Author of the *Rāg Darpan* (Persian, Kashmir, 1665/6).
Fazil Khan (1) Miyan (fl. 1720s–40s), *qawwāl* of Muhammad Shah's time.
Fazil Khan (2) 'Tan Baras' *kalāwant* (d. c. 1780–3), nephew of Sadarang and *shāgird* of Anjha Baras Khan, migrated to Benares.
Fazlu (fl. 1720s–40s), *qawwāl* of Muhammad Shah's time.
Gangalee 'dancing girl' (fl. 1830s), Sambhar Lake.
Gauhar Jan of Jaipur (fl. 1930s–40s), Jaipur *g͟harānā* singer and courtesan belonging to the Jaipur *gunijān-k͟hāna*.
Ghulami (fl. 1720s–40s), *qawwāl* of Muhammad Shah's time.
Ghulam Rasul *qawwāl* (fl. mid–late 18C), son of Miyan Taj Khan (2) *qawwāl*, brother of Jani and Jivan Khan *qawwāls*, father of Ghulam Nabi Shori, Makhan Khan and Shakkar Khan, grandfather of Bade Muhammad Khan.
Ghulam Raza (1) bin Muhammad Panah (fl. late 18C), Delhi-lineage *qawwāl* and *bīn* player based in Faizabad. Author of the *Usūl al-Nag͟hmāt al-Āsafī* for Nawab of Lucknow Asaf-ud-daula (Persian, Lucknow, c. 1790) (Chapter 7).
Ghulam Raza (2) Razi-ud-daula *ḍom* (fl. 1840s–50s), *sitār*-player to Wajid ᶜAli Shah, Nawab of Lucknow.
Giyan Khan (fl. 1720s–40s), *qawwāl* of Muhammad Shah's time.

Gora Mistri (fl. 1770s–90s), employed by Antoine Polier to tune and play Asaf-ud-daula's organ.

Harivallabha (fl. early 17C), author of the Brajbhasha translation of Damodara's *Saṅgīta-darpaṇa* (Brajbhasha, North India, c. 1653).

Hasan bin Khwaja Tahir, Qazi (fl. mid–late 17C), author of the *Miftāh al-Surod* (Persian, Daulatabad, 1663/4).

Hasan Maududi Chishti, Hakim (fl. early–mid 18C), author of the *Risāla al-Mūsīqī* on *tāla* (Persian, Delhi, 1761/2).

Himmat Khan, Miyan (d. c. 1840) (Chapter 7), *kalāwant* of Shah ^{c}Alam II – Bahadur Shah Zafar, son of La^{c}l Khan Parab Lal, brother of Nur Khan, grandfather of Mir Nasir Ahmad, coauthor of the *Asl al-Usūl* (Persian, Delhi, c. 1815).

Irfan Muhammad Khan, Ustad (b. 1954), *sarod* player and last living *ustād* of the Lucknow-Shajahanpur *gharānā*.

Islam Khan (fl. early 17C), compiler of the *Sahasras* (Persian introduction, Brajbhasha songs, Delhi, 1637–46).

Jaffar Khan, *kalāwant* (fl. early–mid 19C), son of Miyan Chajju Khan and brother of Basit and Pyar Khan.

Jagannath Kabirai (fl. early 17C), *dhrupad* composer and Sanskrit and Brajbhasha poet for emperors Jahangir and Shahjahan.

Jana Begum (fl. early 17C), daughter of Abd-ur-rahim Khan-i-khanan, author of a *Risāla-i Mūsīqī* (Brajbhasha, early 17C).

Jani, Jan Muhammad Khan *qawwāl* (fl. mid–late 18C), son of Miyan Taj Khan *qawwāl*, brother of Ghulam Rasul and Jivan Khan *qawwāl*.

Jivan Khan (1) *qawwāl* (fl. mid–late 18C), son of Miyan Taj Khan *qawwāl*, brother of Jani and Ghulam Rasul *qawwāls*.

Jivan Khan (2) *kalāwant* (fl. 1780s–1820s), brother of Chajju Khan *kalāwant*.

Jivan Shah (Khan?) (3) *kalāwant*, brother of Pyar Khan (or Sen) *kalāwant*, *bīn* player who worked with Francis Fowke and probably Sir William Jones.

Jivan Ram (fl. 1830s), probably a male accompanying musician, Sambhar Lake.

Kabir, Shaikh (fl. mid 17C), *qawwāl* of Shah Jahan's time.

Kallu (fl. 1720s–40s), *qawwāl* of Muhammad Shah's time.

Kamilkhani, ^{c}Iwaz Muhammad (fl. mid–late 17C), author of the *Risāla dar ^{c}Amal-i Bīn* (1668/9).

Kanhri Khan (fl. 1720s–40s), *qawwāl* of Muhammad Shah's time.

Karamatullah Khan (1848–1933), Lucknow–Shahjahanpur *sarod ustād* and brother of Kaukab Khan. Author of the *Isrār-i Karāmat ^{c}Urf Naghmāt-i Ni^{c}mat* (Urdu, Allahabad, 1908).

Karim Khan Ghogha-awaz (d. 1791), *kalāwant*, son of Nanhe Khan, possibly maternal grandson of Anand Baras Khan, special *shāgird* of Adarang, father of Khushhal Khan Anup.

Karim Sen Nad Baras (fl. mid–late 18C), *shāgird* of Anjha Baras Khan, father of Pyar Sen.

Kaukab, Asadullah Khan (1858–1915), Lucknow–Shahjahanpur *sarod ustād* and brother of Karamatullah Khan. Author of the *Jauhar-i Mūsīqī* (Urdu, Calcutta, 1915).

Kesur 'dancing girl' (fl. 1830s), Sambhar Lake.

Khamiya Bai (fl. 1720s–40s), courtesan of Muhammad Shah's time.

Khanum Jan (fl. 1770s–90s), celebrated Kashmiri courtesan at the court of Asaf-ud-daula, Nawab of Lucknow (Chapter 4).

Khushhal Khan (1) Gunasamudra *kalāwant* (fl. 1640s–70s), chief *dhrupad* singer to emperors Shah Jahan and Aurangzeb, son of La^{c}l Khan (1), brother of Bisram, father of Ras Baras and Anand Baras, *ustād* of Mirza Raushan Zamir (Chapter 2).

Kripa Ram *paṇḍit* (fl. 1720s–40s), Sanskrit theorist of Muhammad Shah's time.

Kunhi Khan, Miyan (fl. late 17C), *kalāwant* ancestor of Khushhal Khan Anup.

Lacchiram, Diwan (fl. late 17C), author of *Buddhi-prakāsh-darpaṇa* (Brajbhasha, Lahore, late 17C).

Lakshman *bhāṅḍ* (fl. 1830s), Sambhar Lake.

Lal Kanvar (fl. early 18C), courtesan, apparently daughter of Khasusiyat Khan *kalāwant*, consort to Emperor Jahandar Shah.

La^{c}l Khan (1) Gunasamudra *kalāwant* (d. 1654), *dhrupad* singer, son-in-law of Bilas Khan and disciple of Tansen. Father of Khushhal Khan Gunasamudra.

La^{c}l Khan (2) Parab Lal (fl. mid–late 18C), *kalāwant* of Muhammad Shah – Shah ^{c}Alam II, *bīn* specialist, nephew of Sadarang, brother of Adarang, father of Himmat and Nur Khan.

Lalita Bai (fl. 1720s–40s), courtesan of Muhammad Shah's time.

Lallu (fl. 1720s–40s), *qawwāl* of Muhammad Shah's time.

Mahlaqa Bai Chanda (1768–1824), celebrated courtesan at the court of the Nizams of Hyderabad, and disciple of Khushhal Khan (2) Anup (Chapter 5).

Mahmud Khan Muhammad Shahi *kalāwant* (fl. early–mid 18C), son of Anand Baras Khan, nephew of Ras Baras Khan, brother of Mansur Khan and cousin of Anjha Baras Khan.

Mahtab Kanvar Bai (fl. late 18C), courtesan, Mahlaqa Bai's sister and second wife of Rukn-ud-daula, prime minister to Nizam ^{c}Ali Khan.

Makhan Khan, *qawwāl* (fl. 1770s–1810s), one founder of the Gwalior *gharānā*, uncle of Bade Muhammad Khan, and a direct descendant of Miyan Taj Khan (2), chief *qawwāl* to Emperor Muhammad Shah, via his father Ghulam Rasul.

Malageer *tawā'if* (fl. early 19C), celebrated Delhi courtesan.

malzādī 'dancing girl' (fl. 1830s), Sambhar Lake.

Mamola *dā'ira* player (fl. 1830s), Sambhar Lake.

Mansur Khan Muhammad Shahi *kalāwant* (fl. early–mid 18C), son of Anand Baras Khan, nephew of Ras Baras Khan, brother of Mahmud Khan and cousin of Anjha Baras Khan.

Mardan ^{c}Ali Khan (fl. mid–late 19C), author of *Ghuncha-i Rāg* (Urdu, Lucknow, 1862/3), and disciple of Mir Nasir Ahmad.

Mayalee 'dancing girl' (fl. 1830s), Sambhar Lake (Chapter 6).

Mazhar Khan, Nawab (fl. mid–late 18C), author of the *Khulāsat al-^{c}Aish-i ^{c}Ālam-Shāhī* (Persian, Delhi/Lucknow, 1763/4, 1798).

Mir Nasir Ahmad *kalāwant* (d. 1860s), last *bīn* player to the Mughal emperors, grandson of Miyan Himmat Khan, *ustād* of Urdu musicologists Mardan ^{c}Ali Khan and Sadiq ^{c}Ali Khan (Chapter 7).

Mir Salih *qawwāl* Dehlavi (fl. early–mid 17C), author of *Nishāt-ārā* (Persian, Delhi, mid 17C).

Mirza Khan ibn Fakhruddin (fl. late 17C), author of *Tuhfat al-Hind* (Persian, Delhi, c. 1675).

Mirza Tali^{c} Yar (fl. mid 18C), amateur musician.

Moin-ud-din *qawwāl*, Shaikh (fl. early–mid 18C), important *khayāl*-singer of Muhammad Shah's time, grandson of Shaikh Sher Muhammad.

Muhammad Karam Imam Khan, Hakim (fl. mid–late 19C), author of the *Ma^{c}dan al-Mūsīqī* (Urdu, Lucknow, c. 1856–1860).

Muhammad Panah, *qawwāl* (fl. mid 18C), *bīn* disciple of Anjha Baras Khan and father of Ghulam Raza (1).

Munshiram Mishra (fl. 1830s), probably a male accompanying musician, Sambhar Lake.

Musahib Khan *kalāwant* (fl. late 18C), son of Fazil Khan Kalan *kalāwant*, grandson (? unclear) of Rahim Sen of Muhammad Shah's time.

Muzaffar Khan *kalāwant* (fl. late 18C), son of Taj Khan (3) and grandson of Mansur Khan Muhammad Shahi.

Nagi 'dancing girl' (fl. 1830s), Sambhar Lake.

Nanhe Khan (fl. early 18C), father of Karim Khan *kalāwant* and grandfather of Khushhal Khan (2) Anup.

Nayak Baiju (fl. 16C), *dhrupad* musician associated with Gwalior who has become legendary as Tansen's rival Baiju Bawra.

Nayak Bakhshu (fl. 16C), early *dhrupad* composer attached to the courts of Gujarat and Gwalior. His songs are preserved in the 17C *Sahasras*.

Nayak Gopal (fl. 14C), legendary musician of the Delhi Sultanate who competed with poet and song composer Amir Khusrau.

Ni^{c}matullah Khan (c. 1816–1911), Afghan musician, special disciple of Basit Khan, one of the earliest *sarod* virtuosos, father of Karamatullah and Kaukab Khan.

Nur Bai (fl. early–mid 18C), famous courtesan of Muhammad Shah's time.

Nur Khan Nur Rang (fl. c. 1770s–1820s), *kalāwant* of Shah ^{c}Alam II – Akbar Shah, brother of Himmat Khan, father of Rag Ras Khan.

Nur Muhammad, Miyan (fl. mid–late 18C), *qanūn*-player of Muhammad Shah – Shah ^{c}Alam II.

Oomda 'dancing girl' (fl. 1830s), Sambhar Lake.

Paida Beg (fl. early 17C), author of the *Sabha-vinod* (Brajbhasha, early 17C).

Panna Bai (fl. early–mid 18C), courtesan of Muhammad Shah's time.

Panna *naqqāl* (fl. late 18C), male dancer at the court of Nizam ^{c}Ali Khan of Hyderabad.

Premanand (fl. 1720s–40s), *pakhāwaj*-player of Muhammad Shah's time.

Pyar Khan/Sen (1) *kalāwant* (fl. late 18C), brother of Jivan Shah (3); known to British patrons.

Pyar Khan (2) *kalāwant* (fl. mid 19C), son of Miyan Chajju Khan and brother of Basit and Jaffar.

Pyar Sen (Khan?) (3) *kalāwant*, son of Karim Sen *kalāwant*.

Qutub ^{c}Ali Khan (fl. 1840s–50s), *sitār* teacher to Wajid ^{c}Ali Shah, Nawab of Lucknow.

Radhamohan Sen Das (fl. early 19C), author of *Saṅgīta-taraṅga* (Bengali, Calcutta, 1818).

Rag Ras Khan *kalāwant* (d. c. 1840), son of Nur Khan Nur Rang and nephew and disciple of Miyan Himmat Khan.

Rahim Sen (1) *kalāwant* (fl. early–mid 18C), important *dhrupad* singer of Muhammad Shah's time.

Rahim Sen (2) (fl. early 19C), *kalāwant* and *sitār* player at the court of the Nawab of Jhajjhar and father of Amrit Sen.

Raj Kanvar Mida Bai (fl. mid–late 18C), courtesan and Mahlaqa Bai's mother.

Rang Khan *kalāwant* (fl. early 17C), singer at the court of Shah Jahan.

Ranj, Mir Muhammad Nasir Muhammadi (d.1845), *sajjada-nishīn* of the Khwaja Mir Dard shrine in Delhi. Co-author with Himmat Khan of *Asl al-Usūl* (c. 1815) (Chapter 7).

Ras Baras Khan *kalāwant* (d. after 1700), chief musician to Aurangzeb, son of Khushhal Khan (1) Gunasamudra, father of Anjha Baras and Anand Baras. Author of *Shams al-Aswāt* (Persian, 1697/8).

Ras Bin, Muhammad (fl. early–mid 17C), *bīn* player to Aurangzeb.

Rasikh, ^{c}Inayat Khan (b. 1701/2), author of the *Risāla-i Zikr-i Mug̲h̲an-niyān-i Hindūstān* (Persian, Delhi, 1752–3) (Chapter 2).

Rasiya *tawā'if* (fl. early 19C), courtesan of Kishangarh.

Ras Kaphur (fl. early 19C), courtesan and consort of Maharaja Sawai Jagat Singh II of Jaipur.

Ratni *bhagtan* (fl. early 19C), courtesan of Jaipur.

Raza Khan *kalāwant* (fl. late 18C), son of Karim Khan and brother of Khushhal Khan (2) Anup.

Sadarang, Ni^{c}mat Khan *kalāwant* (d. 1746/7), *bīn* player and the greatest *dhrupad* and *k̲h̲ayāl* composer of the eighteenth century.

Sadiq ^{c}Ali Khan (fl. mid–late 19C), author of *Sarmāya-i ^{c}Ishrat* (Urdu, Delhi, 1869).

Sarafraz Mahal (fl. 1840s–50s), courtesan and *mut^{c}a* wife of Wajid ^{c}Ali Shah, Nawab of Lucknow.

Saras Bin *kalāwant* (fl. early–mid 17C), Aurangzeb's favourite *bīn* player.

Saras Rup (fl. 1720s–40s), courtesan of Muhammad Shah's time.

Sawai Pratap Singh, Maharaja of Jaipur, author of the *Saṅgīt-sār* (Hindi, Jaipur, 1799).

Shah ^{c}Alam II, emperor (r. 1759–1806), author of the *Nādirāt-i Shāhī* (1797).

Sher Muhammad *qawwāl*, Shaikh (fl. early 17C), the earliest known *k̲h̲ayāl* singer at the court of Shah Jahan.

Shori, Ghulam Nabi *qawwāl* (fl. late 18C), grandson of Taj Khan (2) *qawwāl*, son of Ghulam Rasul, renowned innovator of *ṭappa* at the court of Lucknow.

Shuja^{c}at Khan (fl. 1720s–40s), *kalāwant* of Muhammad Shah's time.

Subhan (fl. 1720s–40s), *pakhāwaj*-player of Muhammad Shah's time.

Sughar Sen *kalāwant* (fl. early–mid 17C), leading *rabāb*-player of Aurangzeb's time.

Surat Singh *paṇḍit*, Miyan (fl. 1720s–40s), Sanskrit theorist of Muhammad Shah's time.

Surdas (fl. 26C), Vaishnavite poet and singer of *bhakti* devotional songs in Brajbhasha.

Surjoon Rao *bhāṭṭ* (fl. 1830s), Sambhar Lake.

Tagore, Sourindro Mohun (1840–1914), musicologist and important nationalist reformer of Hindustani music. Author of music-technical works in Sanskrit, English, and Bengali.

Tahna (fl. 1720s–40s), *ḍholak*-player of Muhammad Shah's time.

Taj Khan (1) (fl. 1720s–40s), esteemed *kalāwant* of Muhammad Shah's time.

Taj Khan (2) (fl. early 18C), Miyan, chief *qawwāl* of Muhammad Shah's time.

Taj Khan (3) *kalāwant* (fl. early–mid 18C), son of Mansur Khan Muhammad Shahi; possibly the same as Taj Khan (1).

Tan Parbin (fl. 1720s–40s), *ustād* of Muhammad Shah's time.

Tanka (fl. 1720s–40s), *pakhāwaj*-player of Muhammad Shah's time.

Tansen (d. 1589), *kalāwant, dhrupad* composer and the greatest musician of Emperor Akbar's time.

Taqi *bhagat* (fl. early 18C), famous transfeminine dancer, singer and satirist of Muhammad Shah's time.

Tatar (or Nasr) Khan *qawwāl* (fl. late 17C), *khayāl* teacher of Sadarang.

Udit Khan (fl. 1720s–40s), *ustād* of Muhammad Shah's time.

Udit Sen, Miyan (fl. 1720s–40s), *kalāwant* of Muhammad Shah's time.

Wafati *daf* player (fl. 1830s), Sambhar Lake.

Wajid ᶜAli Shah, Nawab of Lucknow (r. 1847–56, d. 1887), impresario, song writer and author of *Saut al-Mubārak* and the *ᶜIshqnāma*, among many other works.

Willard, Capt N Augustus (fl. early 18C), mixed-race author of 'A Treatise on the Music of Hindoostan' (English, Banda, 1834).

Zamir, Mirza Raushan (d. 1666/7), Mughal nobleman, Brajbhasha poet Nehi, disciple of Khushhal Khan (1) Gunasamudra. Author of *Tarjuma-i Kitāb-i Pārījātak* (Persian, 1658–1666/7).

Zia-ud-din Zia, Miyan (fl. mid–late 18C), Mughal official, disciple of Anjha Baras Khan. Author of *Ḥayy al-Arwāḥ* (Persian, Patna, c. 1785–8).

Poets, Novelists, Biographers, Historians

Abd-ur-rahman Shahnawaz Khan (fl. c. 1800), author of the encyclopedia the *Mir'āt-i Āftāb-numā* (1803), which includes a chapter on music.

Abu'l Fazl (1551–1602), chief ideologue of Emperor Akbar I, author of the *Akbarnāma* and the *Ā'īn-i Akbarī* (1593), which includes the first systematic Mughal writing on Indian music in Persian.

Amin Ahmad Razi (fl. c. 1600), author of the encyclopedia the *Haft Iqlīm*.

Amir Khusrau (1250–1325), nobleman of the Delhi Sultanate, Sufi disciple of Hazrat Nizamuddin Chishti, greatest Indian Persian poet, and song writer.

^{c}Andalib, Mir Muhammad Nasir, father of Khwaja Mir Dard, poet, Sufi and founder of the Tariqa-i Muhammadiyya.

Arzu, Siraj-ud-din ^{c}Ali Khan (c. 1688–1756), great Mughal Persian poet and philologist.

Bahadur Singh (fl. early 18C), courtier of Akbar Shah II and author of the encyclopedia *Yādgār-i Bahādurī* (1834), which includes a chapter on music.

Dagh Dehlavi, Nawab Mirza Khan (1831–1905), Urdu poet and son of Wazir Khanum and Nawab Shams-ud-din of Firozpur.

Dard, Khwaja Mir (1720–85), Sufi theologian, major Urdu poet, and amateur musician and musical writer.

Dargah Quli Khan (b. 1710), courtier of Nizam-ul-mulk of Hyderabad and author of the *Muraqqa*^{c}*-i Dehlī* (c. 1740).

Ghalib, Mirza Asadullah Beg Khan (1797–1869), celebrated Urdu and Persian poet and litterateur, courtier of Akbar Shah II and Bahadur Shah Zafar.

Ghulam Husain Jawhar (fl. early 19C), Hyderabadi historian and biographer of Mahlaqa Bai Chanda.

Hafiz Shirazi, Khwaja Shams-ud-din Muhammad (1315–90), celebrated Persian poet.

Iman, Muhammad Sher Khan (d. 1806), Urdu poet of Hyderabad.

Jan Sahib, Mir Yar ^{c}Ali (1818–86), poet and author of the *Musaddas-e Tahniyat-e Jashn-e Benazīr* (after 1866).

Khaqani Sherwani, Afzal-ud-din Badil (c. 1120–1199), Persian poet.

Lahori, Abd-ul-hamid (d. 1654), author of the official chronicle of Shah Jahan's reign, the *Pādishāhnāma* (1636–47).

Mir, Mir Muhammad Taqi (1723–1810), celebrated Urdu and Persian poet, courtier of Muhammad Shah then the Nawabs of Lucknow.

Mirza Farhatullah Beg (1885–1947), author of *Dehlī Kī Ākhirī Sham*^{c}.

Mirza Muhammad Khan (early 18C), Diyanat Khan's grandson and inheritor of his collection.

Muhammad Hasan Shah, Sayyid (fl. late 18C), author of *Nashtar* (1788/9).

Nagaridas, Savant Singh of Kishangarh (1694–1764), Brajbhasha devotional poet and prince of Kishangarh; his consort was the courtesan Bani Thani.

Najm Tabataba'i, Muhammad Riza (fl. early 19C), author of *Naghma-i* ^{c}*Andalīb* (1845).

Rangin, Sa^{c}adat Yar Khan (1747–1835), Urdu poet of Lucknow who specialised in *rekhtī*.

Rumi, Maulana Jalal-ud-din (1207–1273), celebrated Persian poet and Sufi.

Sauda^{c}, Mirza Muhammad Rafi^{c} (1713–81), celebrated Urdu poet, courtier of Muhammad Shah then the Nawabs of Lucknow.

Sayyid Ahmad Khan, Sir (1817–98), Muslim reformer and author of *Āsār al-Sanādīd* (1847).

Shakir Khan (fl. early–mid 18C), Mughal courtier, historian, author of the *Tārīkh-i Shākir Khānī* (1768).

Sher ^{c}Ali Khan Lodi (fl. late 17C), author of the *Mirāt al-Khayāl* (1691).

Skinner, Col James (1778–1841), mixed-race soldier, famous Delhi resident, author of the *Tashrīh al-Aqwām* (Persian, Hansi, 1825).

Tajalli ^{c}Ali Shah (1731–1800), Persian poet and painter in the service of the Nizams of Hyderabad.

Yati Gyanchandra (fl. early 19C), Jain scholar of Sanskrit and Hindavi who worked with James Tod.

Zulfiqar al-Hussaini (fl. mid 17C), author of the *Dabistān-i Mazāhib*.

For political, religious and other cultural figures, see Index.

Index

1857 Uprising, 3, 58, 77, 87, 159, 186, 189, 193, 216, 217, 223, 224, 226, 227, 240, 241, 242, 243, 247
colonial atrocities, 241
loot, 'prize', 227, 241
post-Uprising, 243, 244, 245

Abdali, Ahmad Shah Durrani, King of the Afghans, 22, 48, 73, 235, 236
ᶜAbdul Qadir Jilani, 143
ᶜAbd-ul-hamid Lahori
Pādishāhnāma, 7, 58, 226, 227
Abd-ul-karim, Shaikh
Jawāhir al-Mūsīqāt, 36
abjad, 80
Abu'l Fazl, 7, 37, 38, 44, 198
Ā'īn-i Akbarī, 37, 58, 197, 198
Adarang, Firoz Khan, 21, 24, 49, 51, 53, 55, 59, 62, 63, 65, 66, 67, 68, 71, 72, 74, 76, 89, 118, 132, 181, 183, 224, 243
songs, 66, 122, 133
Addiscombe College, 172
aesthetic
borrowing and reuse, 10, 36, 126, 199, 205, 225
ephemerality. *See* ephemeral, ephemerality
affinity, 87, 88, 94, 102, 105, 114, 209, 229
Afghans, 130, 215
Agra, 2, 26, 124, 146, 161
Ahmad Shah, Mughal emperor, 20, 22, 24, 70, 73
dethronement, 22, 48, 62
Ahmad, Najma Perveen, 10
Ahmadnagar, 139
Ahmedabad, 131, 134
Aitken, Molly Emma, 12
Ajmer, 135, 149, 155
John Macnaghten, superintendent at, 173
Akbar I, 8, 9, 24, 25, 28, 37, 44, 58, 103, 131, 165
Akbar Shah (Akbar II), 9, 182, 184, 194, 225
akhbārāt, Delhi Residency, 151, 152
al-hijrī, 79
ᶜAlamgir II, 2, 24, 66, 73, 133
dethronement and murder, 22
ᶜAli Mardan Khan, 22, 30, 31, 32, 33
havelī, 180
Aligarh, 161
Allah Banda, *qawwāl*, 89
Allahabad, 69, 73, 79, 81, 89
Treaty of, 73, 89
Alves, Major Nathaniel, 170, 171, 177, 178
Amaman, courtesan, 235
Aman, courtesan, 235
Amber. *See* Jaipur
Amin Ahmad Razi
Haft Iqlīm, 197
Amir Khan, *ᶜumdat al-mulk*, 69, 70
Amir Khusrau, 24, 62, 102
Amrit Sen, *kalāwant sitār* player, 159
Anand Baras Khan, *kalāwant*, 132
animals, 32, 42, 165, 166
ants, 167
birds, 138
bullocks, 139, 158, 223
camels, 165
cheetahs, 139
cows, 167, 187
deer, 41
dogs, 167
dogs, nobody brings Cerberus a biscuit, 42
fish, 167
flamingoes, 155
gazelles, 32
hawks, 139
horses, 138, 165, 171
horses, cavalry, 185
mongooses, 110, 199
mules, 165
pigeons, 110, 138, 167
silverfish, 240
snakes, 41, 108, 110
snakes, cobra-capellas, 108
snakes, cobras, 199
tigers, 138
ᶜAndalib, Mir Muhammad Nasir, father of Dard, 183

Anjha Baras Khan, 24, 49, 53, 55, 59, 62, 63, 66, 67, 68, 69, 70, 71, 74, 75, 76, 77, 79, 88, 132, 183, 206, 224, 246
'Sarāpāras' and 'Chūnpāras', 67
anniversaries. *See also* ᶜ*urs*
regnal, 24, 44, 70
religious, 123
Anon
Oriental MS 585 no. 4, Edinburgh University Library, 59, 63, 76, 77, 79, 104, 105, 106, 116, 120, 131, 207, 211, 229, 232, 236
Anup, Khushhal Khan, 24, 50, 52, 58, 72, 77, 117, 118, 119, 120, 121, 123, 126, 127, 128, 129, 130, 131, 132, 133, 134, 136, 137, 138, 139, 140, 141, 142, 143, 144, 145, 146, 181, 209
Rāg Darshan, 50, 51, 59, 63, 72, 118, 121, 123, 124, 126, 127, 131, 132, 136, 138, 139, 141, 142, 145, 146, 236
Rāg Darshan, dispersed early copy, 127
Rāg-Rāginī Roz o Shab, 121, 122, 123, 128, 133, 142, 143, 144, 145
songs, 122
Arabic language, 38, 42, 215
archives and collections, 15, 19, 151, 204, 227, 229
European, 226
private, 240
the awesomeness of archivists, librarians and curators, 241
Arcot, 7
Aristu Jah, Prime Minister of Hyderabad, 136, 137, 138, 140, 141
arts, general, 2, 6, 8, 9, 16, 23, 37, 117, 139, 146, 162, 187
ᶜArzani, Muhammad Akbar, 37
Arzu, Siraj-ud-din ᶜAli Khan, 70
Asa Ram, foreman of the Burs, 173, 174
Asaf-ud-daula, Nawab of Awadh, 74, 81, 83, 88, 89, 99, 103, 104, 107, 206, 224, 225, 226, 227, 233
assassination
attempted, Major Alves, 158, 170
attempted, Shah ᶜAlam II, 22, 180
Maharaja Jai Singh III of Jaipur, 160, 170
Martin Blake, 171
William Fraser, Delhi Resident, 171, 186
astrology, 24, 41, 42, 43, 44, 53, 233
Atrauli, 161
Auckland, George Eden, The Earl of, 100
audiences
appreciation, reception, 6, 9, 15, 21, 34, 38, 41, 42, 45, 46, 53, 69, 110, 112, 124, 125, 126, 186, 201, 205, 228, 232, 237, 239, 240, 247
colonial listening positionality, 229
hungry listening (Dylan Robinson), 229
listener, listening, 1, 7, 8, 9, 12, 17, 19, 27, 32, 35, 41, 42, 43, 94, 95, 103, 104, 112, 162, 183, 220, 221, 236, 238, 239, 246
auditory picturesque, 91, 228, 231
Aurangabad, 133, 135
Aurangzeb ᶜAlamgir I, 2, 11, 24, 25, 26, 27, 28, 31, 33, 35, 37, 38, 42, 45, 62, 64, 124, 158, 224
auspiciousness, 44, 117, 130, 135, 150, 161, 162, 163, 164, 168
maṅgalā-mukhī, 161, 162
Awadh, 21, 22, 50, 63, 73, 74, 81, 88, 89, 153, 198, 209, 220, 221, 222, 223, 224, 240
Aᶜzam Shah, Muhammad, son of Aurangzeb, 24, 64, 65, 126

Babul Mora, 223, 245
Babur, 57
Bade Muhammad Khan, *qawwāl*, 244
Bahadur Shah I (Shah ᶜAlam I), 158
Bahadur Shah Zafar, 2, 182, 194, 217
dethronement and exile, 45, 223
Bahadur Singh
Yādgār-i Bahādurī, 182
Baiju Bawra. *See* musicians and performers: Nayak Baiju
Baksar (Buxar)
Battle of, 73
Bal Kishen, salt weighman, 177
Bani Thani Rasik Bihari, courtesan and consort of Savant Singh of Kishangarh, 159
Baqa, Miyan, *ḍholak* player, 54
barzakh, 246
fantasy *majlis*, 24, 51, 58, 131, 246
Basant festival, 124, 142
Basit Khan, *kalāwant*, 219, 220, 222, 223, 224, 240, 244
Bayly, C A, 151, 152, 166
Baz Bahadur, 62
songs, 121
Begum Akhtar, 247
Begum Samru, 160, 194
beloveds, 53, 75, 94, 107, 110, 111, 116, 135, 137, 197, 238, 240
Benares, 68, 74, 79, 91, 102, 185
Bengal, 7, 21, 63, 73, 83, 89, 223
Bengal Presidency, 155
Bengali language, 14, 38, 126, 230, 240
Berlin, 100

bhakti, 65
Vaishnavite, 74
Bharatpur, 172
Bhatiani Rani of Jagat Singh II, 160
Bhatkhande, Vishnu Narayan, 13, 14, 206, 207, 244, 245
Bhavanidas, *pakhāwaj* player, 54
Bhonsle dynasty, 138
Bhupat Khan, *kalāwant*, brother of Sadarang, 65
Bhupat son of Bisram Khan, 35
Biggs, Edward, 107
Bihar, 63, 89, 219
Bihzad, painter, 71
Bijapur, 36
Bikaner, 127
Bikramjit Singh of Kapurthala, 217
Bilas Khan, son of Tansen, 28
daughter, 28
biography, 98, 121, 130, 131, 138, 143, 183, 188, 189, 191, 193, 195, 218, *See tazkira*
Bird, William Hamilton, 81, 82, 83, 84, 85, 87, 90, 92, 94, 102, 107, 111, 112, 115, 232
Oriental Miscellany, 81, 83, 84
birth ceremonies, 44
Bisram Khan, *kalāwant*, 27, 29, 32, 34, 35
Blake, Martin. *See* assassination
Bodleian Library, Oxford, 46, 227
body, 42
humours, 42, 43, 233
Bombay, 108, 152, 186
books, 23, 50, 80, 104, 110, 118, 140, 146, 186, 207, 214, 225, 226, 237
Boora, salt weighman, 175
Braganza, John, 84, 85, 91, 112
Brahma-vaivarta-purāṇa, 196
Brajbhasha language, 6, 7, 10, 11, 35, 37, 38, 51, 59, 67, 85, 118, 121, 122, 124, 125, 126, 127, 138, 141, 142, 145, 146, 159, 227, 242, 244, *See also* Hindavi language
bribes, 173, 174
British. *See* East India Company; Raj
British Library, 37, 45, 103, 118, 124, 152, 185, 186, 195, 227
British Resident, 89, 90, 91, 118, 137, 151, 152, 153, 194, 230
British Resident, assistant, 180
Brooke, Sir James, 'White Raja' of Sarawak, 172
Brown, Rebecca, 191
Bundi, 161
Burhan Khan, *qawwāl*, 54
Burhani, *qawwāl*, 54
Burhanpur, 135
Calcutta, 81, 84, 88, 91, 103, 148, 150, 152, 211, 223, 240, 243, 245
cantonment, British, 84, 97, 98
Canning, Charles, Viscount, Viceroy, 241
carpet, 20, 29, 32, 35, 48, 67, 238
caste, 4, 131, 186, 187, 189, 190, 191, 192, 193, 195, 200, 230, 231, *See also* community
not 'invented' by the British, 192
Rajput writings, 203
Catalani, Angelica, 99
census, colonial, 190
ceremonial occasions, 35, 135, 150, 153, 154, 159, 161, 162, 184
Chabbar Khan, *pakhāwaj* player, 74
Chajju Khan, Miyan, *kalāwant*, 89, 224
Chand Bibi of Ahmadnagar, 139
Chand, Mihr, 100
Chanda Bibi. *See* Mahlaqa Bai
Chandu 'dancing girl', courtesan, 167
Chapala Sarup, courtesan, 53
Chapman, Jane, 79
recording of *The Oriental Miscellany*, 5
Chau Baras, *ustād*, 54
children, 22, 91, 135, 160
China, 228
Chitragupta *pūjā*, 167
Christian Era, 79
chronogram, 79
definition, 79
cityscape, 56, 191, 197
shahr-āshob, 197
classicisation, 36, 46
canon, 25, 35, 38
Clive, Robert, 73, 228
collecting, 226, 232, *See also* musical collectibles; gifts
and control, colonial, 231
European, 226, 227, 228, 229, 230
extractive, 228, 229
Mughal, 45, 229, 237
colonialism, 3, 4, 6, 14, 15, 16, 17, 27, 37, 83, 84, 87, 114, 147, 151, 152, 165, 169, 190, 192, 193, 195, 204, 216, 226, 230, 231
colonial discourse, 229
material and superstructural changes to the musical field, 230
Combermere, Viscount, Field Marshal Stapleton Cotton, 188
commemoration. *See* remembering
commons, 169, *See also* salt
rights of, 148, 169, 174, 179
salt, 159, 164, 169, 174, 176, 179

community, 12, 56, 58, 70, 131, 162, 186, 188, 189, 192, 196, 199, 204, 214, 215, 217
banjārā, 153, 175
Burs (*bā'orī*), 157, 173, 174, 175, 178, 179
hierarchical order, 44, 57, 190, 191, 195, 222, 230
Kayasth, 133
Kayasth, Khatri, 45
Khatri, 133, 141
sayyid, 134, 217
social categories, 48, 57, 63, 78, 98, 134, 186, 191, 195, 203, *See* also entries under musicians and performers
control, 42, 44, 48, 87, 151, 177, 204, 220, 221, 226, 236
colonial knowledge projects, 230, 231
loss of, 236
music as a means of, 43
of the passions, 221
Cook, Nicholas, 83
Coronation Durbar, 242
corruption, 158, 173, 175, 177
couplet, 92, 95, 103, 141, *See* music: *ghazal*
Court of Directors, East India Company, 172, 174
crime, 152, 153, 170
congenital criminality, 231
cross-cultural engagement, 87, 118
Crotch, Dr William, 85, 108, 110
Specimens of Various Styles of Music, 108, 110
Crown rule. *See* Raj
cupbearer, 94, 238
Curzon, George Nathaniel, Marquess, Viceroy, 242
Customs Hedge, 155

dā'ira. *See* music: *daf*
Dadlani, Chanchal, 198, 199
Dagh Dihlavi, Nawab Mirza Khan, 171
Dakani language, 36
Dalrymple, William, 137, 188, 228
Damodara, 37, 126
Saṅgīta-darpaṇa, 37, 50, 125, 220, 244
dance, 5, 11, 53, 81, 86, 100, 117, 127, 135, 136, 140, 162, 163, 187, 211, 219, 234, 238
chāl, 82, 83
gat nikās, 82, 83
kahārwa, 188, 215
kathak, 82, 83, 159, 220
kite dance, 161
dancing girls. *See* courtesans, dance
Dara Shukoh, 25, 26, 27, 30, 31, 33
Dard, Khwaja Mir, 65, 182, 183, 184
Dargah Quli Khan, 64, 66, 69, 71, 73, 197, 236
Muraqqa^c-i Dehli, 55, 59, 64, 65, 191
dargāh, shrine, 57, 70, 117, 124, 143, 144, 167, 183, 184, 194, 215
Daulat Ram, piano repairer, 104
Daulat Rao Shinde (Scindia), Maratha ruler, 180
Daulatabad, 36
de Boigne, Benoît, 158, 185
Deccan, 3, 7, 26, 31, 33, 36, 130, 133, 134, 135, 138, 223
decline, 26, 69, 75, 88, 193
Delhi, 2, 3, 9, 17, 20, 21, 22, 23, 24, 27, 44, 46, 51, 55, 58, 62, 63, 64, 65, 66, 69, 70, 71, 73, 74, 76, 82, 88, 100, 118, 120, 121, 123, 124, 131, 132, 133, 134, 138, 146, 151, 152, 154, 158, 161, 162, 169, 173, 180, 181, 184, 185, 186, 187, 188, 189, 191, 194, 196, 197, 199, 200, 205, 206, 209, 211, 214, 215, 217, 224, 225, 227, 235, 236, 239, 241, 242, 243, 244
Darya-i Khun, 69
Delhi Customs House, 156
Kucha Chelan, 184, 241
Shahjahanabad, 3, 21, 25, 49, 55, 62, 69, 73, 74, 180, 182, 194, 217, 236, 239, 241
Shahjahanabad, Exalted Fortress (Red Fort), 17, 32, 241, 242
Delvoye, Françoise 'Nalini', 10
Deoliya, 135
Devis, Arthur William, 100
dharma, 187, 196
Dharmat
Battle of, 33
Dhun Raj, salt weighman, 177
Dinanath son of Basudeo, 45
Dinanath, *pakhāwaj* player, 54
Diwali, 167
Diyanat Khan, Abdul Qadir, 46
Diyanat Khan, Shah Qubad, 45
Mirza Muhammad Khan, grandson of, 45
Mut^camid, son of, 45
drama, 101, 162, 163, 219, 220
dress, costume, 32, 91, 100, 117, 118, 127, 153, 162, 187, 191, 196, 201, 204, 231
ritual *khil^cat*, 33, 187
Dyce Sombre, David Ochterlony, 194

early modernity, 4, 5, 7, 9
East India Company, 2, 3, 6, 16, 37, 63, 73, 81, 83, 87, 88, 89, 98, 99, 100, 112, 117, 130, 137, 138, 140, 141, 147, 148, 149, 151, 152,

154, 155, 158, 160, 165, 166, 169, 170, 171, 173, 174, 175, 177, 179, 180, 185, 188, 191, 194, 195, 196, 200, 204, 207, 217, 219, 221, 223, 225, 226, 228, 229, 230, 235, 241
Europeans generally, 6, 15, 79, 81, 84, 89, 98, 99, 103, 104, 112, 124, 158, 160, 186, 189, 198, 200, 201, 227, 228, 229, 231, 232
echoes, 19, 81, 245, 246
Eden, Emily, 100, 102, 188
Edinburgh, 81, 116, 172, 229
Edinburgh University Library, 79
Egan, Michael, 169
elements, the four, 42, 43, 44
élite, 3, 6, 9, 12, 28, 35, 78, 89, 92, 97, 121, 123, 135, 187, 189, 224
élite classes, 9, 10, 15, 21, 32, 44, 47, 55, 57, 62, 71, 76, 78, 81, 87, 88, 103, 107, 117, 119, 125, 134, 135, 137, 141, 146, 162, 163, 182, 184, 187, 192, 194, 200, 217, 223, 226, 227, 244
taste, 234
Elliott, Henry Myers, 27
emotion, 1, 19, 94, 220
admiration, 180
affection, friendship, 12, 30, 53, 70, 75, 89, 94
anger, 70
anguish, 107
anxiety, 25, 58, 62, 68, 72, 75, 236
approval, 98
bittersweet, 1
bliss, 43, 128, 162
celebration, 94, 117
chagrin, 68
compassion, 178, 179
concupiscible faculty (desire), 42
contempt, 178, 219, 221
contentment, 182
deceived, 110
defensiveness, 68, 179
defiance, 150, 179
delight, 81, 87, 102, 237
desire, 53, 67, 100, 116, 220, 237
devotion, 32, 144, 145, 183
dignity, 180
disappointment, 92
disdain, 71, 222
disgust, 70
disheartened, 70
distaste, 101
distress, 27, 75, 110
distrust, 152
ecstasy, 1, 43
emotional pain, *dard*, 183, 238
emotional spaces, 115
empathy, 183
enraptured, 32, 42, 100, 182, 183, 184, 220, 236, 242
envy, 68
fear, 22, 177
flirtation, 53
grief, 69, 219, 223, 237, 245
heart-stealing, 41
helplessness, 144, 221
honour, 165
honoured, 68
horror, 236
intimacy, 6, 12, 139, 237
intoxication, 94, 113
irascible faculty (anger), 42
jealousy, 108
joy, 32, 53, 97, 127, 144, 162, 221, 237, 238
longing, 110, 116, 128, 183, 238
love, 43, 98, 100, 108, 113, 128, 129, 136, 137, 138, 146, 219, 220, 237
love, tragic, 98
loyalty, 137, 165
nostalgia, 21
obsession, 103
paranoia, 177
passion, 101
peacefulness, 42
pitilessness, 242
pity, 180
poignancy of transience, 237, 238, 245
pride, 68, 241
righteous anger, 174
romance, 97
separation, 223
seriousness, 70
shame, 42
smirking, 70
solace, 227
sorrow, 183
submission, 68
submission to fate, 33
suspicion, 176
sweet sadness, 237
sympathy, 18, 87, 151, 166, 174, 243
tearful, 221
temperament, 43
tenderness, 32, 91
trust, 144
uncompromising, 75
vanity, 30, 69, 222
vengefulness, 241, 245

wisdom, 70
without sorrow, 53
England, 97, 223, 242
English language, 4, 6, 38, 80, 91, 99, 101, 107, 116, 126, 148, 194, 204, 229, 240
Englishwoman, 82, 86
Enlightenment, 199
entangled histories, 114
ephemeral, ephemerality, 1, 6, 12, 17, 18, 19, 48, 49, 63, 75, 83, 86, 87, 114, 120, 121, 146, 216, 217, 219, 226, 229, 237, 238, 240, 246, 247
things that cannot be collected or controlled, 237
equilibrium, 10, 43, 44, 46, 48, 197
Erdman, Joan, 162, 163
ethnicity, 97, 133, 190, 191
ethnographic type, 189, 192, 193, 194, 199, 203, 204, 205, 230
ethnography, 188, 189, 191, 194, 195, 199, 200, *See also* writing on music: ethnography
classical Indic (Rajput), 202, 204
colonial, 190, 193, 231
histories of, 193
modern, 193
Mughal and Rajput, 191, 193, 199
Persianate (Mughal), 197
written catalogues, 191
etiquette, 12, 30, 97, 228
European Research Council, 15
Eurydice, 1, 17, 19, 83, 114, 116, 238, 239, 245, 246, 247
exile, 63, 66, 73, 77, 180, 181, 222, 223, 230, 239, 241, 243, 245
experience, musical, 1, 17, 18, 19, 83, 86, 238

Faizabad, 74
Faizabad, Bengal, 63, 74
Faqirullah, Saif Khan, 18, 34, 58, 236
Rāg Darpan, 38, 58, 125
Farrell, Gerry, 83
Farrukhabad, 74
Faruqi, Shamsur Rahman, 171
Faruqui, Munis, 26, 31, 133
father figure, 118, 136, 145
Fazil Khan, *kalāwant*, nephew of Sadarang, 68, 74, 77
Fazil Khan, *qawwāl*, 54
Fazlu, *qawwāl*, 54
female infanticide, 154, 171
fertility, 156
festivals, 163, 197, 240
annual cycle, 123, 124, 142, 143, 148, 149, 161, 166, 167, 168
annual cycle, Maula ᶜAli *dargāh*, 143
paintings, 201
payment for, 167
fireworks, 117
firqa. *See* community
First All India Music Conference, 14
Fitzwilliam Museum, Cambridge, 84
forgetting, 15, 23, 25, 54, 55, 59, 62, 66, 76, 78, 120, 142, 216, 218, 239, 241, 242, 243, 244, 245
Forster, George, 98
Fort William, Calcutta, 223
Fowke, Francis, 38, 91, 102, 104
'On the Vina or Indian Lyre', 105
Fowke, Joseph, 102
Fowke, Margaret, 91, 102, 104, 110, 111
Fraser, James Baillie, 194, 200, 201, 202
Fraser, William, British Resident of Delhi, 180, 186, 188, 194, 195, 200, 201
French, 158, 198, 199
funeral, 27, 245

Gandhi, Mohandas (the Mahatma), 169
Ganga Ram, Pundit, head overseer at Sambhar, 173, 175, 177
trial, 174, 175
Gangalee 'dancing girl', courtesan, 149, 167
Gangaur, 163, 166, 167
Ganges river, 3, 89, 130, 219
garden, 49, 110, 113, 129, 144, 145, 238
Garden Reach (Matiyaburj), 223
Gauhar Jan of Calcutta, 159
Gauhar Jan of Jaipur, 159
genealogy
Rajput bards, 153
Gentil, Colonel Jean-Bapstiste Joseph, 198
Album, 198
geography, 3, 6
George III, King, 227
George V, King Emperor, 242
Ghadar. *See* 1857 Uprising
Ghalib, Mirza Asadullah Khan, 219, 235, 238
ghazal. See music
Ghazi Khan, disciple (and son?) of Khushhal Khan Anup, 140
Ghulam ᶜAli Khan, painter, 186, 201
Ghulam Husain Jawhar, historian, 134, 135
Māh-nāma, 134
Ghulam Qadir, 180
namak-harām, 165
Ghulam Rasul, *qawwāl*, 54, 74, 88

Ghulam Raza, son of Muhammad Panah, 74, 106, 206, 207, 209, 211, 216, 232, 244
  Usūl al-Naghmāt (al-Āsafī), 205, 207, 208, 209, 211, 219, 220, 224, 225, 233, 240
Ghulami, *qawwāl*, 54
gift, 103, 104, 184, 187, 227
  salt, 165, 166, 173, 178, 179
Gilchrist, John, 85, 92, 115, 116
Giyan Khan, *qawwāl*, 54
Goa, 84, 85
Golconda, 133, 143
golden age, 21, 24, 46, 62, 75, 226, 240
Gora Mistri, organ player/maintainer, 104
got. *See* community
Govardhan *pūjā*, 167
governance, 44
  political order, 44
governmentality, colonial, 190, 230
governor-general, 100, 102
Govinddevji (Lord Krishna), 179, *See* temple
Graham, Maria, 108
Greece, ancient, 4, 42
Gudha, 155, 176
Gujarat, 7, 131, 134
Gulshan, Saᶜdullah, 70, 183
Gunasamudra, Laᶜl Khan, 28, 29, 181, 243
gunijān-khāna. *See* music:bureaucratic department
Gwalior, 9, 58

Hafiz, Khwaja Shams-ud-din Muhammad of Shiraz, 100, 111, 112, 113, 188, 237
Haider Beg, Awadhi nobleman, 89
Haji Mir Ghulam Hasan, painter, 127, 131
turmoil, the, 55, 63, 70, 73, 240
Hansi, 186
Harivallabha, 37
  Saṅgīta-darpaṇa, 37, 125
Hasan Maududi Chishti, Hakim, 211, 216, 235
  Risāla-i Mūsīqī, 211
Hasan Raza, Awadhi nobleman, 89
Hasan Shah, 98
  Nashtar, 98, 99, 100, 115
Hastings, Sir Warren, 102
Hawkins, Francis, British Resident of Delhi, 152, 194
Hazin, Muhammad ᶜAli, 235
Hazrat ᶜAli, 123, 128, 129, 143, 144
Hazrat Hasan, 144
Hazrat Husain, 143, 144
Hazrat Husam-ud-din Chishti
  dargāh, Sambhar town, 167
Hermansen, Marcia K, 58
Himalayas, 3, 199
Himmat Farosh, Panna Farosh, Niyamat Farosh and Naba Farosh, reciters, 167
Himmat Khan, Miyan, *kalāwant*, 54, 73, 77, 120, 180, 181, 182, 183, 184, 185, 186, 187, 188, 194, 196, 202, 204, 205, 211, 215, 216, 217, 218, 243, 246
  portrait of, 182, 185, 201
Hindavi language, 5, 7, 38, 120, 121, 124, 126, 146, 159, 162, 232
Hindi cinema, 120
Hindi language, 6, 7, 14, 37, 38, 84, 102, 172, 174, 235, 240, 244
Hindu, 10, 11, 26, 27, 45, 81, 137, 138, 142, 143, 146, 149, 150, 162, 166, 168, 186, 192, 204, 243
Hindu Rao, 194
Hindustan, 3, 5, 6, 7, 10, 11, 20, 23, 45, 46, 51, 53, 56, 75, 93, 97, 130, 161, 187, 197, 199, 205, 215, 223, 232, 234, 247
Hindustani, 6, 91, 94, 137, 141, 187, 191, 206, 243
  language. *See* Urdu, Hindi
Hindustani Airs, 81, 83, 84, 85, 90, 91, 100, 102, 103, 107, 108, 110
Hindustani music, 6, 7, 8, 9, 10, 11, 12, 15, 16, 17, 18, 19, 23, 24, 25, 28, 34, 35, 36, 38, 39, 42, 45, 50, 54, 55, 56, 65, 69, 71, 78, 81, 84, 87, 89, 92, 94, 97, 102, 105, 112, 119, 120, 121, 123, 124, 126, 159, 184, 186, 194, 197, 205, 208, 216, 217, 224, 225, 226, 228, 229, 233, 237, 238, 239, 242, 243, 245, 247
  definition under the Mughals, 7
  modernity, definition, 214
  present day, 77, 97, 209, 243, 245, 247
histories, oral/aural transmission, 15, 243, 244
historiography, 3, 5, 13, 15, 230
  colonial, 27
Holi, 123, 124, 140, 142, 166, 167
Hooja, Rima, 203
Humayun, 24
hungry listening (Dylan Robinson), 231
hunting, 137, 139
  hawking, 138, 139
Hyderabad, 3, 7, 21, 50, 51, 53, 72, 74, 117, 118, 120, 121, 122, 124, 127, 130, 131, 132, 133, 134, 135, 137, 140, 141, 142, 143, 146, 154, 209, 225, 235, 240

ᶜīd-i ghadīr, 143
Iftikhar-ud-daula Mirza ᶜAli Khan, 62

Ikhwan us-Safa, 1, 18
ᶜImad-ul-mulk, Ghazi-ud-din Firoz Jang III, 22, 48, 62
Imam Khan, Muhammad Karam, Hakim
  Maᶜdan al-Mūsīqī, 126, 224, 245
Iman, Sher Khan Muhammad, 136, 138
immortality, 62, 118, 239
India Office collections, 118, 148, 151, 227
Indian patrons, 107, 198, 200, 231, 232
Indic, 10, 107, 126, 207, 208, 225, 243
  aesthetic sciences, 124
individual agency, 16, 158, 189, 205, 209, 211, 214, 215, 218, 225, 233
innovation, 21, 38, 67, 205, 209, 211, 214, 215, 216, 224, 225, 232, 233, 235, 236
intermediality, 139
Invernesshire, 84
Iranian, 30, 133, 137
Islam, 27, 143, 187
  halāl, 27
Islam, Shiᶜa, 117, 123, 137, 143, 144, 146, 220

Jacquemont, Victor, 160, 161
Jaffar Khan, *kalāwant*, 223
Jagannath Kabirai, 29
  songs, 122
Jahandar Shah, 64
  dethronement and murder, 64
Jahangir, 24, 37
Jain, 166, 167, 168, 203
Jaipur, 3, 146, 147, 149, 150, 153, 154, 155, 158, 159, 160, 161, 162, 163, 164, 165, 166, 167, 169, 170, 171, 174, 177, 178, 179, 187, 195, 206, 209, 225, 232, 240, 243, 246
  City Palace, 170
Jal Jhulani, 167
Jamshed, 19, 49, 238
Jana Begum, daughter of Abd-ur-rahim Khan-i Khanan, music theorist, 79
Jani, Jan Muhammad Khan, *qawwāl*, 54, 74, 88
jāt. *See* community
Jaunpur, 9, 197
Javed Khan, chief eunuch of Muhammad Shah, 22, 48
Jeypore. *See* Jaipur
Jhuta Ram, prime Minister of Jaipur, 160, 170
jinns, 246, 247
Jivan Khan/Shah (*see* Tazkira), 37, 232
  bīnkār, 102, 105
  interlinear gloss on *Saṅgīta-darpaṇa*, 37
  kalāwant, 224, 225
  possible authorship of Edinburgh 585(4), 80
  qawwāl, 54, 74, 88
Jivan Ram, musician, 167
Jodhpoor. *See* Jodhpur
Jodhpur, 147, 150, 153, 154, 155, 158, 161, 165, 166, 169, 170, 171, 174, 176, 177, 178, 179, 187
Jodhpur, Maharaja of, 166
Jogul Kishore Mahajan, merchant, 174
Johnson, Richard, 37, 89, 90, 104, 106, 122, 124, 126, 207, 226, 227, 228, 229
Jones, Captain John, 242, 245
Jones, Sir William, 38, 104, 124, 229, 234
  'On the Musical Modes of the Hindoos', 125, 228, 230, 232
judicial proceedings, 152, 153
justice, 43, 46
Jyepoor. *See* Jaipur

Kabir, Shaikh, 89
Kaicker, Abhishek, 21
Kallu, *qawwāl*, 54
Kalyan Das, painter, 21
Kamilkhani, ᶜIwaz Muhammad, 41, 46
Kanhri Khan, *qawwāl*, 54
Kanpur (Cawnpore), 98
Kapurthala, 217, 243
Karamatullah Khan, 240
Karbala
  Battle of, 143
Karim Khan, *kalāwant*, 51, 72, 74, 118, 131, 132, 133, 134
Karim Sen, *kalāwant*, 68, 71, 74
karma, 187, 196
Karnatak (South Indian classical) music, 8
Karnataka, 7
Kashmir, Kashmiri, 83, 91, 97, 211, 234, 235
Kathmandu, 68, 74
Kaukab, Asadullah Khan, 240
Kesur 'dancing girl', courtesan, 149, 167
Khairabadi, 215
Khairunnissa, 137
Khamiya Bai, courtesan, 53
Khanum Jan, celebrity courtesan, 79, 81, 83, 85, 87, 88, 93, 97, 98, 99, 100, 102, 103, 107, 110, 113, 114, 117, 147, 225, 232, 237, 246, 247
  portrait of, 99, 100
Khaqani Sherwani, Afzal-ud-din Badil, 115
Khera, Dipti, 163
Khushhal Khan Gunasamudra, 20, 24, 25, 27, 28, 29, 30, 31, 32, 33, 35, 36, 42, 44, 48, 50, 55, 67, 132, 224, 242, 246
Kindersley, Jemima, 81, 82

King David, Prophet Daud, 183
King Solomon, Prophet Suleiman, 44, 246
King's Royal Rifles, 242
Kinra, Rajeev, 10, 26, 31
Kippen, James, 77, 112, 209, 234
Kirkpatrick, James, 137
Kishangarh, 46, 76, 152, 159
  Raja of, 152
knowledge systems, 42, 76, 123, 229
  affective knowledge, 151, 152, 166
  colonial, 16, 205, 216, 225
  embodied, 14, 76, 83, 88, 120, 134, 209, 218, 219, 224
  ethnography, 199
  human chains of transmission, 76, 237, 239, 240
  impact of colonialism, 4
  Indian, 4, 5, 6, 39
  Mughal, 233, 244
  paracolonial, 16
kobid. *See* writing on music: *paṇḍits*
Koch, Ebba, 44
Kota, 175
Kripa Ram Pandit, 53
Kugle, Scott, 118, 121, 137, 143
Kunhi Khan, Miyan, *kalāwant*, 132

Lacchiram, Diwan
  Buddhi-prakāsh-darpaṇa, 37
La^cl Khan Parab Lal, *kalāwant*, 54, 73, 181, 243
Lahore, 63
Lakshman *bhāṅḍ*, 167
Lal Kanvar, 64
Lalbarga, Calcutta, 104
Lalita Bai, courtesan, 53
Lallji or Hulas Lal, painters, 201
Lallu, *qawwāl*, 54
Lawrence, Bruce B, 58
Lawrence, Sir Henry Montgomery, 172
Leaf, Walter, 113, 116
lesbian, 103
life histories. *See tazkira*
light-classical, 235
liminality, 51, 57, 87, 189, 205, 246, *See also* *barzakh*
  Lucknow as liminal space, 88
London, 21, 88, 99, 118, 131, 174, 203
loot, 228, *See also* 1857 Uprising; musical collectibles
Lord Brahma, 101, 127
Lord Krishna, 123, 124, 138, 142, 160, 163, 165, 167, 220
Lord Shiva, 167
Lord Vishnu, 101
loss, 22, 76, 171, 180, 237, 239, 243, 244, 245
Lucknow, 3, 13, 50, 51, 63, 67, 74, 79, 81, 83, 84, 85, 86, 87, 88, 89, 90, 91, 97, 98, 99, 103, 104, 106, 107, 110, 114, 117, 126, 130, 146, 153, 161, 205, 207, 216, 219, 221, 223, 225, 230, 235, 240, 241, 245
Ludlow, Colonel John, 154, 157, 170, 171, 173, 174, 175, 179, 230
Ludlow, Lieutenant-Colonel James, 171
Lunn, David, 8, 207, 209

Macnaghten, Lieutenant John Dunkin, Superintendent of Sambhar Lake, 171, 172, 173, 174
Macnaghten, Sir William Hay, 172
Madhu Singh, salt-works clerk, 173, 174
Madhyadeshi (Hindavi) language, 36
magic, 53, 54, 67, 110, 246, *See also* music: supernatural powers
  miracle, 47
Mahabat Khan
  havelī, 69
Mahābhārata, 196
Mahadaji Shinde (Scindia), Maratha ruler, 158
Maharaja Chandu Lal, Prime Minister of Hyderabad, 127, 141, 142, 145
Maharaja Sawai Man Singh II Museum, 163
Maharani Ratan Kunvar, mother of Maharaja Ram Singh II, 170
Mahashivratri, 167
Mahlaqa Bai Chanda, celebrity courtesan, 117, 118, 120, 121, 127, 128, 129, 130, 131, 133, 134, 135, 136, 137, 138, 139, 140, 141, 142, 143, 144, 145, 146, 147, 186, 227, 235, 246
  Dīwān, 118, 143, 227
  grandmother, 135
  portrait of, 129
  songs, 122
  tomb, 145
Mahmoud, Yusuf, 112
Mahmud Khan, *kalāwant*, 67
Mahtab Kanvar Bai, Mahlaqa Bai's sister, 135
majlis, 12, 19, 20, 21, 31, 41, 51, 53, 54, 57, 58, 66, 69, 74, 81, 94, 98, 100, 110, 117, 119, 131, 140, 141, 142, 162, 183, 184, 186, 187, 188, 194, 201, 205, 215, 225, 235, 237, 238, 239, 243, 245, 246
  majālis-i bīn-nawāzī, 182, 184
  majlis-i samā^c, 47, 246
  majlis-khāna, 184
Makar Sankranti, 167

Makhan Khan, *qawwāl*, 244
Malageer, courtesan
 portrait of, 201
Malcolm, Major-General Sir John, 118, 141, 186, 194, 195, 218, 227
Malzadi 'dancing girl', courtesan, 167
Mamola, *dā'ira*-player, 167
mandir. *See* temple
Manning, 98, 100
mansab, 30
mansabdār, 27, 45
Mansur Khan, *kalāwant*, 67
Maratha Nimbalkar dynasty, 138
Marathas, 2, 3, 7, 21, 22, 124, 130, 131, 137, 138, 146, 158, 159, 180, 185
Marathi language, 36
Mardan ᶜAli Khan, 217
 Ghuncha-i Rāg, 217, 246
mardāna, 12, 163
marginalia, 14, 16, 123, 143, 149, 150, 155
marriage, 65, 68, 97, 98, 117, 132, 134, 135, 151, 172, 186, 220, 223, 224
 endogamy, 11, 187, 190, 192
Martin, Major-General Claude, 89, 99
Marwar. *See* Jodhpur
mathematics, 41, 42, 184
Mathura, 74, 124
Maula ᶜAli *dargāh*, 117, 119, 121, 123, 124, 143, 144, 145
Mayalee 'dancing girl', courtesan, 147, 149, 150, 152, 155, 158, 167, 168, 173, 177, 179
Mazhar Khan, Nawab, 49, 51
 Khulāsat al-ᶜAish-i ᶜĀlam-Shāhī, 49, 50, 51, 53, 59, 78, 220, 227
medieval, 9, 24, 115
Meerut, 160
mehfil. See *majlis*
Mehrauli, 194
 Zafar Mahal, 194
memorialisation. *See* remembering
memorialising. *See* remembering
memories. *See* remembering
memsahib, 83, 88, 102
mendicants, 167, 179, 183, 186, 188, 197, 199
metamorphosis, 9, 239, 242
Metcalfe, Sir Charles Theophilus, British Resident of Delhi, 194
Mewar, 9, 158
Meyalee. *See* Mayalee
Mida Bai. *See* Raj Kanvar Bai
middle class, 244
Middle Eastern. *See* Arabic, Persian, West Asian
migrants. *See* scattering, the
migration. *See* scattering, the
mind, 42, 67
 contemplative intellect, 43
 rational intellect, 42, 43
Miner, Allyn, 13, 65, 66, 234
Mir ᶜAlam, Nawab Abul Qasim, Prime Minister of Hyderabad, 117, 126, 136, 137, 141, 142
Mir Kalan Khan, painter, 21
Mir Nasir Ahmad, *kalāwant*, 76, 184, 217, 243, 244
Mir Salih *qawwāl* Dehlavi, 120
Mir, Mir Taqi, 21, 49, 73, 88, 238
 Nikāt al-Shuᶜarā, 23
Mirza Khan
 Tuhfat al-Hind, 51, 58, 124, 125, 126, 127, 141, 194, 207, 209, 229, 232, 233, 244
Mirza Najaf Khan, 74
Mirza Taliᶜ 'Yar', 74
Mishra Surat Singh Pandit, 53
Mistry Instrument Makers, Lalbarga, Calcutta, 104
mixed-race people, Eurasians, 16, 172, 185, 186, 194, 195, 205, 226
Miyan Khidar, *tabla* player, 76
modernity, 12, 77, 185, 205, 206, 207, 209, 214, 216, 220, 223, 225, 233, 235, 240, 245
 colonial, 242
 rāga, 209
 tāla, 214
Moin, Azfar, 44
Moin-ud-din, Shaikh, 71, 74, 75, 89, 144, 246
monsoon, 44, 47, 156, 157, 167
moon, 43, 117, 118, 120, 128, 129, 130, 134, 138, 140, 221
Mordaunt, Colonel John, 89
Morrieson, Lieutenant Robert, Superintendent of Sambhar Lake, 149, 150, 166, 169, 171, 172, 175, 176, 177, 178, 179, 185
mortality, 1, 19, 23, 48, 49, 51, 58, 73, 76, 86, 99, 114, 140, 180, 183, 185, 216, 218, 219, 236, 237, 238, 239, 241, 243, 244, 245, 246
mosque, 117, 180
Moxham, Roy, 149, 155
Mughal court, culture, 7, 10, 28, 57, 64, 75, 76, 78, 118, 120, 121, 124, 125, 131, 133, 134, 135, 136, 138, 146, 150, 152, 234, 237, 239, 243
 authority, 133

Mughal library, 227
Mughal throne, 17, 25, 26, 29, 32, 33, 42, 48, 180, 240, 242
Mughal, great, 10, 11, 24, 36, 158, 165, 199, 206, 239
Mughal, late, 2, 6, 12, 14, 15, 16, 17, 19, 40, 51, 54, 65, 72, 75, 77, 78, 84, 98, 116, 121, 130, 186, 188, 189, 191, 193, 197, 200, 204, 205, 211, 224, 226, 228, 231, 233, 235, 236, 237, 238, 240, 241, 242, 243, 244, 245, 246, 247
Muhammad ᶜAdil Shah II, Sultan of Bijapur, 36
Muhammad Panah, *qawwāl*, 74, 206, 224
Muhammad Shah, 2, 20, 21, 23, 46, 49, 51, 53, 55, 62, 64, 65, 66, 67, 68, 69, 70, 72, 75, 118, 131, 132, 134, 226, 234, 235, 240
Muharram, 143, 167, 215
  ᶜashūr-khāna, 117, 145
mukhammas. *See* poetry
Mundy, Captain Godfrey, 188
munshī, 45, 98
Munshiram Mishra, musician, 167
Murshid Quli Khan Khurasani, 30, 31, 32, 33
Murshidabad, 74, 89, 154, 201, 230
  Nazim of, 154
Musahib Khan, *kalāwant*, 88
Mushafi, Ghulam Hamadani, 184
music
  A–A–B–A form, 94, 97
  abhinaya, 81
  ālāp, 29, 32
  and sovereignty, 17, 35, 42, 44, 48, 98, 153, 220, 234, 245
  antarā, 96, 97
  Arabic and Persian, 106
  arrangements, European, 84, 85, 87, 94
  bīn, 11, 24, 28, 29, 32, 54, 57, 64, 65, 66, 102, 105, 132, 180, 181, 182, 183, 184, 187, 193, 204, 206, 216, 217, 232
  bols, 92
  bureaucratic department, 24, 25, 28, 55, 58, 66, 67, 133, 154, 161, 194, 243
  bureaucratic department, Jaipur *gunijān-khāna*, 154, 159, 161, 162, 163, 164
  bureaucratic department, Jodhpur *taᶜlīm-khāna*, 154
  bureaucratic department, Murshidabad *arbāb-i nishāt*, 154
  centres of musical culture, 75
  change, 13, 15, 50, 75, 225, 232, 233, 236
  chhand, 153
  classicisation, 9, 10, 23, 24
  colonial-era reforms, 9, 13, 206, 230, 242
  composition, 11, 21, 24, 29, 41, 65, 66, 67, 71, 85, 123, 124, 131, 136, 144, 183, 236, 247, 288, 291, 293
composition, Tansen, 28
crescendo, 108, 109
da capo, 94, 96
daf, 11
ḍholak, 11, 54, 57
dhrupad, 11, 24, 28, 29, 37, 46, 54, 57, 64, 66, 67, 70, 71, 75, 77, 104, 123, 132, 136, 142, 144, 159, 180, 182, 197, 215, 219, 220, 223, 235, 236
diminuendo, 108, 109
emotional effects, 8, 18, 41, 54, 64, 67, 71, 84, 97, 127, 201
European, 8, 83, 87, 92, 101, 102, 105, 207, 228
European aria, 94, 97
European instruments, 80
European, common practice period, 83, 91, 104
Firozkhani *sitār* style, 66
frets, 105
ghazal, 11, 92, 93, 94, 95, 97, 100, 111, 112, 113, 115, 116, 121, 136, 143, 162, 188, 220, 225, 235, 237, 238, 247
harpsichord, 79, 81, 87, 89, 91, 102, 103, 104, 105, 116
harpsichord, Indian description of, 104
hoṛī, 11, 102, 123, 136, 142, 215
improvisation, 8, 11, 67, 95, 96, 97, 109, 113, 232, 238
Indian music history, 6
innovation, 65, 68, 75, 92, 120
instrumental genres, 7, 11, 41, 57, 162
instruments, 234
jaltarang, 187
jashn, 123, 136
kabit, 142, 153
keyboard, 83, 94, 103, 104
khayāl, 11, 24, 38, 57, 65, 66, 70, 71, 74, 75, 88, 93, 110, 123, 128, 132, 136, 142, 144, 159, 180, 182, 215, 235, 236, 247
marsiya, 220
melodic structure, 94, 95, 96, 97, 110
mujrā, 70, 100
munājāt, 144
naqqāra-khāna, 145
notation, 15, 76, 79, 80, 81, 83, 84, 87, 91, 104, 113, 206, 207, 208, 211, 215, 217, 226, 232, 236

notation, graphical, 105, 106, 107, 211, 214, 244
notation, non-graphical, 106
octave, *saptak*, 42, 96, 104, 105
old, obsolete, 36, 205, 207, 211, 214, 220, 232, 233, 244
opera, 99
oral/aural transmission, 10, 14, 38, 72, 76, 77, 120, 121, 133, 145, 204, 237, 239
organ, 103, 104
pakhāwaj, 11, 54, 57, 74, 187
patronage, 3, 6, 7, 11, 19, 36, 43, 45, 47, 49, 57, 58, 64, 72, 75, 76, 77, 81, 88, 97, 100, 117, 118, 119, 120, 121, 122, 124, 127, 129, 130, 132, 134, 136, 137, 138, 139, 140, 141, 142, 144, 146, 159, 186, 194, 196, 235, 239, 243
Persian and Central Asian, 7
Perso-Arabic music theory, 80
piano, 103, 104
practice, performance, 1, 6, 7, 8, 11, 14, 44, 54, 71, 81, 83, 87, 91, 93, 95, 96, 105, 123, 137, 146, 161, 183, 187, 196, 209, 211, 214, 215, 220, 225, 232, 233, 234, 238, 239
prestige, 75, 97, 118, 134, 137, 235, 243
pungī, 110
qānūn, 54, 73, 104, 105, 184, 187
qaul, 57
qawwālī, 215
rabāb, 11, 28, 29, 54, 57, 132, 219, 223, 224, 237
rāg-sāgar, 71
raschandī, 71
refrain, 85, 95, 96, 110, 111, 112
rondo, 95
rudra vīṇā. *See* music:bīn
salon, 83
saṅgīta, 8
sārangī, 11, 57
sargam, 104, 113
sarinda, 91
sarod, 12, 66, 240, 247
scale, 8, 32, 42, 43, 102, 104, 105
scale, *ṭhāṭh*, 207
science of, *ᶜilm-i mūsīqī*, 38, 41, 52, 72, 186
semitones, 105
shrutis, accidentals, 104
singing, 11, 28, 29, 32, 34, 41, 44, 48, 53, 57, 64, 65, 67, 71, 72, 74, 75, 77, 85, 88, 91, 92, 93, 95, 96, 97, 99, 101, 102, 107, 109, 110, 112, 114, 118, 119, 122, 123, 132, 135, 136, 139, 140, 141, 142, 159, 161, 162, 163, 182, 183, 184, 186, 205, 208, 217, 221, 225, 235, 246, 247, 249
sitār, 12, 65, 66, 91, 159, 220, 222, 234
song tunes, 8, 84, 85, 92, 93, 94, 102, 106, 107, 108, 111, 112
songs, 7, 11, 29, 37, 38, 53, 66, 72, 81, 84, 85, 88, 90, 91, 92, 97, 99, 101, 107, 110, 113, 115, 117, 118, 121, 123, 124, 134, 136, 142, 143, 144, 145, 162, 184, 216, 220, 232, 235, 237, 240, 247
songs on the *majlis*, 237
songs, devotional, 123
songs, English language, 84
sound recording, 17, 84, 122
sthāyī, 95, 96
sthāyī-sthāyī-antarā-sthāyī form, 97, 234
style, 29, 68, 71, 75, 76, 77, 95, 102, 122, 123, 131, 134, 144, 197, 215
style, new, 236
style, Tansen, 28, 29
stylistic school. *See* musicians and performers: *bānī*
supernatural powers, 25, 32, 33, 35, 40, 41, 42, 45, 46, 48, 51, 110, 220, 221, 234, 245, 246
supernatural powers, Orpheus, 44, 48
sursingār, 224
tabla, 12, 91, 234, 247
tambūr, 11, 29
tambūra, 29, 140
tān, 53
ṭappa, 11, 12, 57, 88, 92, 123, 136, 142, 161, 225, 235, 236
tarānā, 11, 53, 66, 92, 182
ṭhumrī, 13, 215, 216, 220, 223, 235, 245
time signature, 112
tonic, 96
transcription, 16, 84, 85, 86, 87, 91, 95, 96, 97, 102, 110, 112, 113, 114
usūl, 106
vādī and *samvādī*, 43
virtuosity, 10, 11, 29, 57, 67, 71, 92, 146
music of the spheres, 42, 44, *See* astrology
music/dance
gat, 81, 82, 83, 220, 225, 234, 235
musical collectibles, 225, 227, 228, 231, *See also* souvenirs
commissioned, 227
extractive, 229
gifts, 227
loot, 227
purchased, 226

musicians and performers, 2, 3, 6, 7, 9, 12, 13, 19, 21, 23, 24, 27, 28, 35, 37, 41, 42, 43, 44, 48, 51, 53, 54, 55, 57, 58, 62, 64, 66, 69, 70, 72, 73, 74, 75, 77, 84, 85, 87, 88, 91, 101, 102, 103, 104, 105, 106, 111, 117, 123, 130, 132, 136, 143, 144, 147, 149, 150, 151, 152, 159, 166, 167, 168, 169, 182, 188, 189, 194, 197, 198, 199, 200, 201, 204, 219, 221, 222, 226, 228, 229, 230, 231, 232, 233, 234, 235, 237, 239, 240, 241, 242, 243, 246, 247
illiterate *ustāds*, 13, 14, 120, 146, 245
legends, 62, 63, 67, 78, 99
authority, 71, 75, 134, 146, 185, 224, 225, 239, 243
bāhurūpiya, 57, 167, 194, 198
bānī, 70, 71, 77, 121, 131, 236
bānī, Dagari, 77, 159
bānī, Gorari (also Gorhari/Gobahari), 77, 131, 159, 224, 243
bānī, Khandari, 65, 68, 77, 123, 132, 134, 136, 181, 182, 183, 184, 185, 187, 188, 216, 224, 243
bānī, Nohari, 77
bāzīgār, 108, 110, 192, 195, 198, 199, 201
bhagat, 57, 135, 198
bhagtan (courtesans), 135, 162, 163, 168, 246
bhāṅḍ, 57, 135, 163, 194, 198, 215, 234
bhānmatī, 198
bhāṭṭ, 153, 154, 186, 196, 230
British amateurs, 102
chāran, 153, 154, 230
charisma, 77, 99, 234, 236
courtesans, 12, 22, 53, 57, 64, 76, 81, 83, 86, 89, 92, 97, 100, 103, 110, 120, 127, 129, 131, 132, 134, 135, 141, 146, 148, 149, 150, 152, 158, 159, 160, 161, 162, 163, 179, 188, 201, 211, 220, 234, 235
courtesans, term *tawā'if*, 81
dancer, 83
ḍhāḍhī, *ḍom*, 11, 57, 58, 197, 222, 230
East India Company suppression, 153
European, 94
gaṇikā (courtesans), 162
gentlemen-amateurs, 62, 63, 71, 74, 76
grants, non-monetary, 98, 138, 150, 152, 162, 164
Gwalior *gharānā*, 244
hereditary guilds, *gharānā*, 11, 13, 28, 56, 75, 77, 78, 104, 118, 146, 225, 242, 243
Jaipur *gharānā*, 159
kalāwant, 11, 24, 28, 29, 34, 51, 53, 54, 55, 57, 58, 63, 64, 65, 67, 68, 69, 71, 74, 75, 76, 79, 88, 102, 105, 118, 120, 123, 131, 132, 163, 180, 184, 185, 186, 187, 188, 192, 194, 195, 196, 197, 199, 201, 204, 205, 206, 211, 214, 215, 216, 218, 219, 220, 222, 223, 224, 230, 235, 243, 245
kanchanī (courtesans), 162
lineage, 28, 51, 55, 62, 63, 65, 67, 68, 71, 75, 76, 77, 79, 124, 131, 144, 146, 217, 240, 243
lineage, *k͟hāndān* (core family), 77
literate, 15, 98, 120, 123, 146, 225, 233, 240, 244, 245
livelihoods, 153, 154, 155, 163, 231
maimūnwāla, 198
mirāsī, 220
names, 49, 51, 54, 55, 57, 58, 62, 63, 68, 71, 72, 75, 76, 78, 181, 246
nāṭ, 199
Nayak, 41, 59, 182
pensions, 152
qawwāl, 11, 47, 54, 57, 58, 63, 65, 70, 71, 74, 75, 77, 88, 106, 123, 184, 185, 194, 197, 205, 206, 214, 215, 216, 224, 225, 232, 235, 244, 246
rāmjanī (courtesan), 162
reinvention, 75
rights and obligations, 161, 163
rivalry, 49, 55, 59, 63, 67, 68, 69, 72, 76, 78, 222
tawā'if (courtesans), 162
transfeminine, 11, 57, 135, 163
trumpeter, 167
ustād, master-teacher, 12, 14, 18, 29, 53, 71, 75, 76, 118, 120, 133, 136, 145, 161, 183, 223, 240, 244
wārisan (courtesans), 162
women, 83
Muslim, 2, 11, 81, 120, 137, 149, 159, 161, 162, 167, 168, 180, 186, 187, 192, 241, 243
Mutiny. *See* 1857 Uprising
Muzaffar Khan, *kalāwant*, 71, 74, 89
Mysore, 117

nāch, 81, 82, 84, 100, 108, 110, 117, 161, 201, 211, 234, *See* dance
nāch set or troupe, 91, 97, 98, 100, 135, 153, 188, 234
Nadir Shah, 20, 21, 22, 24, 62, 69, 73, 133, 236
Nagaridas, Savant Singh of Kishangarh, 159
Nagi 'dancing girl', courtesan, 167
Najm, Muhammad Riza Tabataba'i, 27, 67, 182, 236
Nag͟hma-i ᶜAndalīb, 27, 66, 224
Nampally, Hyderabad, 136
Nanhe Khan, Anup's grandfather, 132
naqqāl. *See* musicians and performers:*bhāṅḍ*

naqqāra-khāna. *See* naubat ensemble
Naraina, 174
nast^{c}alīq script, 80
National Archives of India, 147, 148, 151, 152
naubat ensemble, 30
Nauroz, 32, 124, 137, 142
nautch. *See nāch*
Navratri, 166, 167
Nawa, 155, 176, 177
Nawab ^{c}Ali Muhammad Rohilla, 66
Nawab Raza Khan. *See* Ghulam Raza, son of Muhammad Panah
Nayak Baiju, 59
Nayak Bakhshu
  Sahasras, 28, 37, 46, 227
  Sahasras, Islam Khan's preface, 37
Nayak Gopal, 62
Nepal, 7, 130
Neuman, Daniel M, 75, 77
Newell, Stephanie, 16
Ni^{c}matullah Khan, *sarod* player, 240
Nizam ^{c}Ali Khan, Nizam of Hyderabad, 117, 118, 133, 137, 138, 140, 143, 146
Nizami Ganjavi
  Khamsa, 103
Nizam-ul-mulk, Chin Qilich Khan, Nizam of Hyderabad, 133, 135, 138
North India. *See* Hindustan
North Indian classical music. *See* Hindustani music
North West, 97, 211
nostalgia, 46, 51, 53, *See also* remembering
Nur Bai, *ḍomnī* (courtesan), 21, 53, 89
Nur Khan Nur Rang, *kalāwant*, 54, 73, 181, 184
Nur Muhammad, Miyan, *qānūn-nawāz*, 54, 73

obeisance. *See mujrā*
occasion piece. *See* music:*jashn*
occupation, 56, 98, 144, 186, 189, 191, 192, 196, 197, 199
  civil offices, 167
  hereditary, 163, 189, 192, 193
  hereditary guilds, 192
  hereditary, painters, 200
Ochterlony, Major-General Sir David, British Resident of Delhi, 194
'of the age'
  master, 71
  Nayak, 59, 182
  perfume, 215, 216, 235
  Tansen, 63, 67
  the exceptional ones, 53
  Zulqarnain (Alexander the Great), 63
official records, 15, 230
  East India Company, 16, 147, 149, 151, 152
old age, 22, 34, 181, 185, 218, 219
  fifty, threshold of, 27, 34
Oldenburg, Veena, 103
Oomda 'dancing girl', courtesan, 149, 167, 168
Opie, Amelia, 107
Orientalism, 4, 50, 195, 204
Orissa, 232
orphans, 242
Orpheus, 17, 20, 32, 42, 44, 48, 83, 224, 242, 245, 246, 247
Ottoman, 12
Ouseley, Sir Gore, 46, 50, 227
Outram, Lieutenant General Sir James, British Resident of Awadh, 223, 230

Paida Beg
  Sabha-vinoda, 125
painters, 37, 55, 127, 186, 195, 198, 199, 231, 232
Palashi (Plassey)
  Battle of, 3, 73, 228
palimpsestic. *See* aesthetic: borrowing and reuse
Panipat, 20, 22, 46, 51
  Battle of, 22, 73
Panna Bai, courtesan, 76
  portraits of, 76
Panna, *naqqāl*, 136
paracolonial, paracoloniality, 4, 5, 16, 87, 151, 191, 205, 216, 225
  knowledge, 193, 195, 204, 244
paradise, 23, 223, 238
Partition 1947, 247
Parvati Devi, 156
Patna, 22, 62, 73, 74, 79, 244
pen and sword, arts of, 26, 138
Persian language, 5, 6, 10, 11, 23, 25, 26, 35, 37, 38, 42, 45, 50, 52, 54, 55, 59, 66, 80, 81, 84, 85, 91, 92, 94, 97, 98, 101, 102, 110, 111, 112, 113, 115, 116, 120, 121, 123, 124, 125, 126, 127, 136, 141, 142, 146, 151, 152, 153, 172, 174, 186, 188, 194, 195, 196, 197, 204, 205, 224, 227, 232, 233, 235, 240, 242, 244
Persianate, 10, 12, 42, 126, 225, 243
petition, 31, 32, 33, 221
picturesque, the, 191, 199, 205
Plato, 42, 103
pleasure, 35, 53, 81, 98, 102, 117, 163, 185, 238
  arts of, 12
  serious place of, 221
Plowden, Geoffrey, 88

Plowden, Richard Chicheley, husband of Sophia, 88
Plowden, Sophia Elizabeth, 79, 82, 83, 84, 85, 87, 88, 89, 91, 92, 94, 96, 97, 99, 100, 103, 104, 107, 108, 110, 111, 112, 113, 114, 115, 117, 122, 207
  Album, 85, 88, 92, 94, 99, 102, 110, 227
  Diary, 89, 91, 97, 99
  Tunebook, 85, 88, 102, 109
poetry, 12, 20, 21, 23, 55, 62, 65, 67, 70, 72, 81, 92, 97, 102, 103, 107, 110, 115, 117, 124, 136, 138, 141, 143, 146, 159, 182, 183, 197, 220, 238
  dīwān, 118
  feminine voice, 103
  ghazal, 118
  majlis, 237
  *matla*ᶜ, 96
  metre, 80, 92, 96, 110, 112, 116
  metre, *rajaz musamman matwī makhbūn*, 112, 113, 116
  mukhammas, 92
  qāfiya, 113
  radīf, 96, 111, 113
  rāgamālā, 38, 41, 124, 126
  rekhtī, 103
  rubā'ī, 92, 94, 96, 97
  song lyrics, 66, 67, 84, 85, 92, 93, 94, 97, 102, 107, 108, 110, 111, 112, 113, 121, 124, 142, 143, 145, 146, 235
  structure, 94
Polier, Colonel Antoine-Louis Henri de, 76, 89, 97, 99, 100, 102, 103, 104, 229
Pollock, Sheldon, 4, 5
Portuguese, 103
postcolonialism, 102
posterity, 15, 62, 66, 75, 146, 194, 216, 240
Powers, Harold, 209
precolonial, 4, 5
Premanand, *pakhāwaj* player, 54
preservation, 72, 78, 146, 216, 224, 236, 239
primogeniture, 25, 26
princely states, 16, 152, 153, 154, 155, 196
  Rajput, 171
Pṛithvīrāj Rāso (*Qissa-i Prithī Rāj*), 196, 202
Prophet, of Islam, 75, 123, 134, 143
prosperity, 155, 158, 161, 169
Pune, 138
Punjab, 7, 97, 130, 234
Punjabi language, 85, 123, 235
Purtab Qanungo, 177
Pyar Khan, *kalāwant*, 102
Pyar Khan, *kalāwant* (Lucknow), 220, 223
Pythagoras, 42, 105

Qandahar, Kandahar, 30
qaum. *See* community
Qazi Hasan, 7, 41
  Miftāh al-Surod, 7, 45
Qur'an, 26
Qutub ᶜAli Khan, *sitār* player, 220

Radha, Lord Krishna's consort, 160, 163, 220
Radhamohan Sen Das
  Saṅgīta-taraṅga, 126
Rag Ras Khan, *kalāwant*, 184, 216
rāga, 7, 8, 9, 10, 11, 13, 27, 29, 32, 36, 37, 40, 41, 42, 43, 45, 46, 50, 65, 67, 71, 75, 76, 92, 93, 97, 104, 107, 118, 123, 126, 129, 134, 136, 186, 205, 206, 207, 208, 209, 214, 220, 225, 232, 233, 234, 235, 245, 246
  Asavari, 143
  Bahar, 123, 142
  Basant, 123
  Bhairav, 41, 186, 208
  Bhairavi, 113, 144, 208, 223
  Bilaskhani, 32
  Desh, 97
  Dipak, 43
  emotion, 8
  Gaund, 123, 209
  Hindol, 123, 142
  Hindol family, 209
  Jhinjhoti, 220
  Kalyan family, 209
  Kedara, 143
  Khamaj, 121, 128, 129
  Khambhavati, 124, 127, 128, 129
  Malhar, 123
  Malkauns, 247
  Megh, 41, 44, 123
  Megh family, 209
  monsoon, 123
  Nat family, 209
  organisation by aesthetic criteria, 123, 206
  organisation by melodic criteria, 123, 206, 207, 209
  organisation schemes, 206
  rāga-based, 8
  rāgamālā, 8, 15, 36, 121, 123, 206
  rāgamālā, Hanuman *mat*, 9, 37, 126, 207, 209
  Sarang, 41
  Sarang family, 123
  Shri, 246

sonic and iconic forms, 234
soundmark, 8, 207, 209
spring, 142
Sur Malhar, 123
time theory, 41, 42, 43
Todi, 32, 35, 42, 43, 48, 242
Todi Darbari, 32
Rahim Sen, *kalāwant*, 54, 88, 159
Rai Venkatchallam, 127, 139
Raj, 2, 45, 120, 148, 159, 191, 226, 240, 242
Raj Kanvar Bai, 131, 135, 136
Raja Bala Pershad, 142
Raja Rao Ranbha Nimbalkar Jayawant Bahadur, 118, 124, 126, 127, 128, 129, 130, 132, 134, 137, 138, 139, 140, 141, 142, 145, 146
Rajasthan, 130, 135, 147, 155, 157, 159, 196, 202, 204
Rajasthani, 196, 202, 203, 204
Rajput, 5, 9, 10, 11, 132, 135, 147, 150, 153, 154, 159, 162, 165, 170, 175, 177, 185, 186, 188, 195, 196, 202, 204, 206, 225, 249
Chauhan, 165
Kachchwaha, 165
Rajputana. *See* Rajasthan
Rajputana, EIC Agency to, 149, 158, 171, 178, 186, 203
Ramji Das, painter, 163
Rampur, 161, 235, 243
Ranade, Ashok Da, 14
Rang Khan, *kalāwant*, 29
Rangin, Sa^c^adat Yar Khan, 103
Rangoon, 223
Ranj, Mir Muhammad Nasir Muhammadi, 77, 183, 184, 185, 211, 215, 216, 217, 233
Ranj, Mir Muhammad Nasir Muhammadi, and Miyan Himmat Khan
Asl al-Usūl, 63, 185, 211, 214, 215, 216, 236, 244
Ras Baras Khan, 28, 36, 44, 67, 120, 132, 224
Shams al-Aswāt, 28, 42, 67, 206, 208, 209, 211, 219, 224, 233, 240
Ras Bin, 35
Ras Kaphur, courtesan and consort of Jagat Singh II of Jaipur, 159, 160
Rasikh, ^c^Inayat Khan, 20, 21, 22, 23, 24, 25, 27, 30, 44, 46, 48, 51, 58, 59, 63, 76, 236, 246
Risāla-i Zikr-i Mughanniyān-i Hindūstān, 23, 24, 30, 35, 48, 49, 51, 55, 58, 59, 63, 64
Rasiya, courtesan, 152
Raslila, 163, 167
Ratni *bhagtan*
portrait of, 163
Raushan-ud-daula Zafar Khan Bahadur Rustam Jang, 47, 49, 53, 246
Raza Khan, brother of Khushhal Khan Anup, 134
Razi-ud-daula, Ghulam Raza, *sitār* player, 222, 230
regency, 160, 170
remembering, 23, 24, 46, 48, 51, 54, 55, 56, 57, 58, 59, 63, 66, 71, 72, 73, 75, 76, 78, 134, 146, 153, 185, 218, 225, 239, 240, 241, 243, 244, 246, 247
renunciation of the world, 70
resistance, 149, 150, 158, 169, 171, 190
reviving, 17, 19, 83, 85, 87, 88, 208, 245, 246
Richmond, Lieutenant-Colonel Archibald Fullerton, British Resident of Awadh, 153, 222, 230
Rilke, Rainer Maria
Sonnets to Orpheus, xxviii, 241, 245
Rohilkhand, 66, 74, 130, 133
Royal Asiatic Society, 45, 203
rubā^c^ī. *See* poetry
Rukn-ud-daula, Prime Minster of Hyderabad, 135
Rumi, Maulana Jalal-ud-din, 183
Masnawī, 70
Rupnagar, 76

Sa^c^adat ^c^Ali Khan, Nawab of Awadh, 50, 74, 206, 227
Sa^c^dullah Khan, 66, 74, 133
Sadarang, Ni^c^mat Khan, 20, 21, 24, 35, 51, 53, 54, 62, 63, 64, 65, 67, 68, 70, 72, 74, 75, 77, 131, 132, 144, 181, 183, 224, 236, 243, 246, 247
daughters, 68
songs, 122
Sadiq ^c^Ali Khan, 217
Sarmāya-i ^c^Ishrat, 217, 224
Safavid, 12, 30
Safdar Jang, Nawab of Awadh, 22, 73
Sahib Ram, painter, 163
Sahibganj, 63, 74, 219, 224
Salar Jung Museum, Hyderabad, 121, 206, 208
salon. *See majlis*
salt, 147, 149, 150, 153, 155, 156, 157, 158, 164, 165, 167, 168, 176, 179, 229
as commodity, 169
as commons. *See* commons:salt
bond, 165, 166, 169, 179
manufacturing, 155, 156, 157, 174, 175, 177, 178
namak-halālī, 150, 165, 179
namak-harāmī, 165

salt (cont.)
revenues, 148, 149, 155, 158, 166, 169
rights and obligations of and to salt-eaters, 165, 166
rights in, 175, 176, 177, 178, 179
sales, 173, 175, 178
salt-eater, 164
stipends, 149, 150, 173, 176, 177
tax, 155, 165
workers. *See* community:Burs
salt maund, 147, 150, 157, 165, 175
Ajmer/East India Company, 149
Sambhar, 149
Sambhar Lake, 147, 148, 149, 150, 153, 155, 156, 157, 158, 161, 165, 166, 168, 170, 173, 174, 179
Affair, 173, 175, 177, 179
British superintendents 1835–42, 171
labour strike, 178
land rents, 173, 174
pensions, 147, 148, 150, 163, 173, 178
region, 169, 175
revenue accounts, 147, 148, 149, 150, 155, 166, 169, 173, 175, 179
sequestration, 147, 170, 171, 176
Sambhar town, 155, 167, 173
Sambhur. *See* Sambhar Lake
Sangīt Sarāvartī, 219
Saṅgīta-nārāyaṇa, 232
Sanskrit language, 8, 10, 11, 13, 14, 28, 35, 36, 38, 42, 106, 120, 125, 126, 195, 202, 203, 204, 217, 224, 227, 229, 232, 240
Sanskrit writings
dharma-shāstra, 196, 204
purāṇa, 153
shāstra, 153, 195, 196, 204
upaniṣad, 26
veda, 153, 195, 196, 204
Saras Bin, 29
Saras Rup, courtesan, 53
Sardhana, 160
sargam, 92
Sarmadee, Shahab, 10
satī, 171
Sauda^c, Mirza Muhammad Rafi, 21, 88, 235, 247
Sawai Jagat Singh II, Maharaja of Jaipur, 159, 160
Sawai Jai Singh II, Maharaja of Jaipur, 158
Sawai Jai Singh III, Maharaja of Jaipur, 160
Sawai Madho Singh I, Maharaja of Jaipur, 165
Sawai Pratap Singh, Maharaja of Jaipur, 158, 159
Saṅgīt-sār, 159, 206, 209
Sawai Ram Singh II, Maharaja of Jaipur, 159, 160, 172
Sayyid Ahmad Khan, Sir, 182, 197, 217
Āsār al-Sanādīd, 55, 182, 191
Sayyid Muhammad Muttaqi, father of Sayyid Ahmad Khan, 182
scandal, 35, 64, 152, 153, 160, 172, 222
scattering, the, 3, 49, 55, 62, 63, 70, 72, 73, 74, 76, 88, 130, 134, 146, 205, 232, 235, 236, 237, 239, 240, 242, 243
scent, 114
Scotland, 180, 199
secretary to the governor general, 150
separation, 183, 238, 245
sex, erotics, 41, 49, 50, 81, 94, 97, 98, 99, 103, 110, 111, 113, 135, 141, 142, 162, 219, 221, 238
poetry, 103
Shah Bhikha of Thaneswar, 47
Shah ^cAlam II, 22, 50, 69, 73, 74, 89, 107, 180, 181, 184, 209
exile, 49, 66, 73
Nādirāt-i Shāhī, 206, 209
Shah Jahan, 7, 24, 25, 26, 28, 29, 30, 31, 32, 33, 35, 37, 44, 48, 58, 62, 71, 226, 241, 242
Shakambhari Mata, 156, 165, 169, 179
Shakambhari Mata Mandir, 156
Shakir Khan, historian, brother of Rasikh, 22, 46
Shams-ud-daula Lutfullah Khan Sadiq, 21, 46
Shams-ud-din, Nawab of Firozpur, 171
Sharad Purnima, 167
Sharma, Amal Das, 243
Sharma, Prem Lata, 10
Sharma, Sunil, 94, 115, 197
Sharma, Yuthika, 188, 200
Sharngadeva
Saṅgīta-ratnākara, 36
Sher ^cAli Khan Lodi, 1, 17
Sher Muhammad, Shaikh, 71, 236, 246
Shivlal Mahajan, 175
Shori, Ghulam Nabi Miyan, 88, 225, 235, 236, 246
Shuja^cat Khan, *kalāwant*, 69, 70
Shuja^c-ud-daula, Nawab of Awadh, 74, 89
Sikandar Jah, Nizam of Hyderabad, 118, 126, 141
Sikh, 243
silence, 15, 17, 32, 221, 237, 238, 239, 242
silsila. *See* musicians and performers: lineage
Singapore, 84
Singh, Kirit, 217
Singhana, Yadava king of Devagiri, 36

Siraj-ud-daula, Nawab Nazim of Bengal, 73, 228
Skinner, Colonel James, 82, 101, 153, 163, 182, 185, 186, 187, 188, 192, 194, 195, 196, 198, 201, 202, 204, 205
Tashrīh al-Aqwām, 153, 162, 182, 185, 186, 191, 194, 195, 198, 201, 204, 218, 227
Skinner's Horse, 185, 186, 204
Sleeman, Major-General Sir William Henry, British Resident of Awadh, 221, 230
snake charming, 108, 110, 116
soirees. *See majlis*
Solvyns, Balthazar
Catalogue of 250 Etchings, 200
Somavanshi *rājas*, 187, 196
Sotheby's, 127
South Kensington Museum, 242
souvenirs, 188, 200, 226, 231
sovereignty, 17, 30, 35, 42, 43, 44, 46, 48, 89, 146, 155, 158, 161, 165, 170, 220, 221, 222, 226, 241
spring, 32, 94, 123, 124, 142
Srirangapatanam
Siege of, 227
stillness, 32, 221
stories, 19, 25, 27, 30, 35, 54, 55, 64, 65, 66, 68, 69, 71, 77, 78, 83, 98, 114, 123, 127, 150, 223, 247
burial of music, 27
cautionary, 48
courtesan tale, 98
Strachey, Sir John, 155
Subhan, *pakhāwaj* player, 54
Sufism, 18, 47, 49, 55, 57, 62, 65, 66, 70, 132, 143, 144, 167, 182, 183, 211, 216, 218, 246
Chishti order, 144
ecstatic state, 47, 215
Naqshbandi Mujaddidiyya, 65, 132, 187
Naqshbandi order, 70, 183
spiritual lineage, 184, 185
Tariqa-i Muhammadiyya, 65, 132, 144, 182, 183, 185, 187
Sughar Sen, 29
sulh-i kull, 10, 197
Surdas
songs, 121
Surjoon Rao *bhāṭṭ*, 167
survival, 68, 69, 73, 75, 76, 165, 169, 217, 239, 240
Suryavanshi *rājas*, 187, 196
Sutherland, Major-General James, 178
svabhāv, 162, 187, 196
tā'ifa. *See* community
Tagore, Sourindro Mohun, 13, 230
Tahna, *ḍholak* player, 54
Taj Khan, *kalāwant*, 53, 54
Taj Khan, *qawwāl*, 54, 244
Taj Mahal, 25
Tajalli ᶜAli Shah, 127, 136
takhallus, 65, 118, 141
tāla, 11, 13, 76, 79, 80, 92, 105, 106, 112, 136, 184, 185, 186, 205, 209, 211, 214, 215, 216, 225, 233, 234, 235, 236, 244
beats (*zarb*), 106, 211
bols, 105
chautāl, 144
dā'ira diagrams, 106
dā'īra diagrams, 240
khālī, 106
mātra, 106, 211
rupak, 112, 215
sam, 215
tāli, 106
tīntāl, 106, 214, 247
vibhāg, 106, 211
West Asian models, 105
Tan Parbin, *ustād*, 54
Tan Tarang Khan, 58
Tanjore, 7, 199
Tanka, *pakhāwaj* player, 54
Tansen, 24, 28, 29, 32, 34, 37, 51, 54, 58, 62, 63, 67, 68, 70, 131, 182, 224, 243
Second Tansen, 67
songs, 121
tantra, 234
Taqi, *bhagat*, 21, 57
Tatar (Tatari or Nasr) Khan, *qawwāl*, 65
Tate Britain, 89
Tāza ba tāza, 84, 110, 111, 112, 113, 115, 236, 237, 247
tazkira, 12, 15, 20, 23, 48, 49, 51, 54, 55, 56, 57, 58, 59, 62, 63, 66, 68, 72, 73, 75, 76, 78, 192, 237, 239, 243
commemorative texts, 56, 73
memorative communication, 58
tea, 228
Telangana, 7
temple, 162, 163, 166, 167, 171
Govinddevji (Lord Krishna), 165, 166
Hanuman, 166
Jain, Sambhar town, 166
Seetaram, 167
Shakambhari Mata, 166
testimonies of historical listeners, 19
ṭhagī (thuggee), 170

Thaneswar, 47
Thoresby, Captain Charles, 195
Tillotson, Giles, 163
Tipu Sultan, 117, 138, 227
Tod, Lieutenant-Colonel James, agent to Rajputana and Orientalist, 160, 161, 186, 194, 195, 202, 204
  Annals and Antiquities, 202
  broken pen, 17, 48, 237, 240, 246
Tonk, 161
topography, 191, 195
transition
  Mughal to British rule, 2, 3, 5, 6, 13, 16, 151, 189, 216, 224, 226, 227, 229, 234, 235, 240
translation, 30, 36, 37, 38, 44, 101, 105, 113, 116, 124, 125, 126, 127, 141, 142, 224, 288
travellers, 16, 63, 98, 188, 230
Treaties, 73, 89, 140, 147, 158, 160, 170, 223
Trevelyan, Sir Charles Edward, British Resident of Delhi, 194
tribute, 147, 160, 166, 170
Trivedi, Madhu, 10, 13
tutelary deity, 165

Udaipur, 158, 161, 187
Udham Bai, queen of Muhammad Shah, 22, 48
Udit Khan, *ustād*, 54
Udit Sen, *kalāwant*, 54
Umrao Khan, *kalāwant*, 75
underworld, 19, 114, 243, 246
union, 183, 218
University of Pennsylvania Special Collections, 127, 128
Uprising. *See* 1857
Urdu language, 6, 7, 14, 20, 21, 23, 38, 55, 81, 84, 85, 88, 91, 92, 94, 95, 97, 98, 103, 107, 110, 112, 117, 126, 136, 141, 143, 172, 174, 186, 188, 216, 217, 235, 238, 240, 244, 246
  rekhta, 7, 23, 92, 103, 107, 110, 122, 235
ᶜurs, death anniversaries, 143, 184
Ustad Alladiya Khan, 159, 161
Ustad Behram Khan Dagar, 159
Ustad Irfan Muhammad Khan-sahib, 240, 247

Venkateswaran, Mrinalini, 163
Victoria and Albert Museum, 198
Victoria, Queen, 223, 240, 241
Vijay Dashami, 167
violence, 3, 16, 22, 77, 87, 170, 216, 230, 237, 239, 241, 242
  epistemic, 87
visual records, 15, 191, 226
  lithograph, 246
  painting, 12, 16, 21, 51, 85, 89, 90, 94, 99, 103, 118, 126, 127, 129, 138, 139, 140, 146, 159, 163, 181, 186, 188, 195, 196, 199, 221, 226, 227, 229, 231, 240
  painting, courtesans, 201
  painting, ethnographic, 110, 189, 192, 198, 199, 201, 204, 231
  painting, late Mughal–Company style, 186, 189, 199, 200, 201
  painting, *majlis*, 237
  painting, *nāch*, 201
  painting, *rāgamālā*, 8, 15, 32, 37, 41, 46, 46, 124, 126, 127, 129, 227, 229, 234
vitality, 23, 51, 53, 75, 111, 113, 165, 194, 225, 237, 238, 239
Vrindaban, 124

Wafati, *daf*-player, 167
Wajid ᶜAli Shah, Nawab of Awadh, 67, 153, 216, 219, 220, 221, 222, 223, 230, 235, 245, 246
  ᶜIshqnāma, 220
  dethronement and exile, 87, 223, 245
  Saut al-Mubārak, 220
Wales, 179
Walker, Margaret, 79, 81, 83, 234
Wall, Derek, 169
War of Succession, 25, 26, 27, 33
Watkins, Captain James, 195
Wazir Khanum, 171
weddings, 33, 92, 142, 153, 154
Willard, Captain N Augustus, 234
  'Treatise on the Music of Hindustan', 126, 194, 229
Williams, Richard David, 223
Wilson, Jon, 4
wine, 31, 49, 53, 94, 111, 113, 238
Wombwell, John, 99
women
  secluded women, 103, 162, *See also zanāna*
Woodfield, Ian, 83, 94, 96, 98, 111
writing on music, 1, 2, 6, 10, 11, 12, 14, 15, 16, 17, 19, 27, 42, 54, 72, 78, 86, 88, 104, 118, 121, 126, 130, 146, 181, 185, 218, 219, 223, 225, 226, 227, 229, 230, 231, 237, 239, 240, 246
  Arabic and Persian, 45
  bilingual, 126
  biographies, 72, *See tazkira*
  Brajbhasha, 37, 118, 124, 125, 244
  canonical, 10, 15, 25, 28, 35, 36, 38, 45, 124, 126, 130, 198, 205, 208, 211, 217, 220, 224, 231, 232, 233, 236, 239, 244

English, 125, 228
ethnography, 15, 56, 180, 189, 195, 198, 204, 205, 218, 230
European, 98
genealogies, 15, 51, 54, 55, 56, 57, 58, 59, 63, 68, 75, 76, 78, 185, 239, 243
Indian regional languages, 36
majlis, 237
new, 13, 15, 45, 50, 105, 189, 205, 211, 214, 232, 233, 236, 237
palimpsestic technique, 36, 39, 38, 51, 58, 125, 126, 206, 229
paṇḍits, 53
Persian, 28, 35, 36, 37, 38, 40, 50, 118, 120, 124, 125, 220, 244
pre-1858, 244
print, 14, 15, 122, 216, 217, 220, 244, 246
saṅgīta-shāstra, 13, 36, 37, 224
Sanskrit, 10, 36, 125, 211
sex, erotics. *See* sex, erotics
song collections, 28, 72, 76, 84, 87, 89, 91, 92, 94, 97, 99, 100, 108, 121, 122, 123, 128, 134, 142, 143, 145, 209, 237, 239, *See* music: songs
song lyrics, 85
tān-prastār, 207
tazkira. See tazkira
theorists, 7, 9, 29, 38, 41, 42, 50, 131, 182, 207, 211, 214, 232
theory, theoretical writing, 6, 8, 14, 15, 16, 18, 25, 38, 49, 79, 105, 120, 121, 123, 124, 142, 145, 159, 183, 184, 185, 188, 205, 215, 220, 224, 228, 229, 232, 239, 240
woman author, 79

Yamuna river, 3
Yati Gyanchandra, 203
youth, 24, 35, 45, 49, 94, 161, 182, 216
Yusuf ᶜAli Muhammadi, 184

Zain-ul-ᶜabidin, Khwaja, maternal uncle of Sayyid Ahmad Khan, 182
Zamir, Mirza Raushan, 28, 29, 36, 41, 44
Tarjuma-i Kitāb-i Pārījātak, 42, 45
zanakhī. See lesbian
zanāna, secluded women's quarters, 135, 162, 163
zāt. See community
Zia-ud-din, 55, 62, 63, 64, 67, 68, 69, 70, 71, 72, 73, 74, 76, 106, 120, 130, 131, 211, 239, 246
Hayy al-Arwāh, 59, 62, 63, 68, 106, 229
Zoffany, Johan (John, Johann), painter, 89, 99, 100
Zulfiqar al-Hussaini
Dabistān-i Mazāhib, 197